PRETTY BOY

ALSO BY MICHAEL WALLIS

Oil Man:
The Story of Frank Phillips
and the Birth of Phillips Petroleum
(1988)

Route 66:
The Mother Road
(1990)

P R E T T Y   B O Y

THE LIFE AND TIMES OF
CHARLES ARTHUR FLOYD

ST. MARTIN'S PRESS   NEW YORK

End Papers: Portrait of the Walter Floyd family. Hanson, Oklahoma, 1915. Front row, left to right: Charley, E. W., Mary. Back row, left to right: Walter, Mamie, Emma, Ruby, Bradley, Ruth.

Grateful acknowledgment is made for permission to reprint the following:
"BALLAD OF PRETTY BOY FLOYD" by Woody Guthrie. © Copyright 1958 (renewed) by FALL RIVER MUSIC INC. All rights reserved. Used by permission.
"BROTHER CAN YOU SPARE A DIME?" by Jay Gorney and E. Y. Harburg. © 1932 WARNER BROS. INC. (Renewed). All rights reserved. Used by permission.

Design by Carol Haralson

Library of Congress Cataloging-in-Publication Data

Wallis, Michael
    Pretty boy : the life and times of Charles Arthur Floyd / Michael Wallis.
        p.   cm.
    ISBN 0-312-07249-X
    1. Floyd, Pretty Boy, 1904–1934.   2. Criminals—United States—Biography.   I. Title.
    HV6248 .F563.W35   1992
    364.1′ 092—dc20
    [B]   91-36513
                                                  CIP

First Edition: April 1992
10 9 8 7 6 5 4 3 2 1

To Suzanne Fitzgerald Wallis,
the woman who knows better than all others
how to dispense magic, love, and inspiration

To Herbert Wallis,
a man who wisely experienced
the sadness and bittersweet glory
of the Depression, a man who encouraged,
aroused, and breathed life into his son
so that the story could, at last, be told

To all lost boys and absent sons,
in hope they may be found

C O N T E N T S

Prologue: The Conkle Farm Near Clarkson, Ohio   ix

PART ONE

1 9 0 4 - 1 9 1 4

CHARLEY

1. Child of Aquarius   3
2. The Floyds   6
3. Georgia Roots   9
4. Baptism by Fire   15
5. Adairsville, Georgia   24
6. Sequoyah County   28
7. Outlaw Ghosts   34
8. King Cotton   42
9. Heroes   46
10. America's Robin Hood   51

PART TWO

1 9 1 4 - 1 9 2 5

CHOC

11. Moonshine   63
12. Akins, Oklahoma   70
13. Over There   78

14. WANDERLUST 88
15. BOOTLEG HARVEST 97
16. ONE STEP OVER THE LINE 108
17. STAR LIGHT, STAR BRIGHT 119
18. RUBY 131
19. THE ST. LOUIS BLUES 137

PART THREE

1925-1934

PRETTY BOY

20. THE PEN 149
21. TOM'S TOWN 161
22. THE WALLS COME TUMBLING DOWN 174
23. WHIRLWIND 186
24. DOG DAYS 201
25. ON THE SCOUT 216
26. THE PHANTOM TERROR 232
27. THE MIDNIGHT RAMBLER 250
28. BROTHER, CAN YOU SPARE A DIME? 268
29. THE SUMMER OF '33 288
30. THE MASSACRE 304
31. TRAIL'S END 318

Epilogue: Sallisaw, Oklahoma 340

Select Bibliography and Source Notes 355
Acknowledgments 363
Photograph Credits 368
Index 371
About the Author 376

"A man has three names—
the name he inherits, the name
his parents give him, and the name
he makes for himself."

—AUTHOR UNKNOWN

THE CONKLE FARM

NEAR CLARKSON, OHIO

OCTOBER 22, 1934

*"Alongside every outlaw who survives beyond brief days
hover this nameless legion whom the law does not know or
may not touch. Call them his protective angels if you
like."*
— When the Daltons Rode (*EMMETT DALTON*)

HARLEY FLOYD RAN for the trees and the freedom
that lay beyond. If he could just get across the
field of corn stubble to the tree line, he would be
safe. The weeds and the wild grapevines, the
honeysuckle and the brambles would grant him
yet another reprieve. He would race into the woods and down the slopes, up
the steep hills and across the crumbling masonry of abandoned canal locks
filled with water from the recent autumn rain.

He was known to some as the Sagebrush Robin Hood, to others as the
Phantom Terror. But he was most commonly called Pretty Boy Floyd—public
enemy number one. He was invincible, and he always got away.

The weather was warm on this October afternoon. Charley's white shirt and
silk underwear were soiled and sweaty, and he needed a shave and bath. His
dark blue suit was stained and covered with hundreds of tiny thistles, Spanish
needles, which ran the length of his sleeves and trousers. He was a country boy
dressed in a city slicker's clothes. A farmer's wife had given him ginger cookies
and apples that morning, and he stuffed them in his suit coat pockets. He
grasped a .45 pistol in one hand, while his other pistol was tucked in the top
of his trousers.

Just moments before, he had chatted with Stewart Dyke and his wife,

Florence. The farm couple had kindly agreed to give him a lift up the road a ways in their automobile, away from the farm owned by Dykes's sister, Ellen Conkle. Charley had passed an hour with Mrs. Conkle. She had just fed him a hot meal. Inside the farmhouse, she still held the dollar bill the stranger had insisted she take in exchange for the plate of spareribs. Ellen Conkle watched him wolf down the dinner she had prepared. He sat in a rocking chair on her porch and ate in silence. Afterward, she saw him pacing around, waiting for Stewart and his wife to finish with their cornhusking. Charley fingered the keys in the car's ignition, deciding not to steal the machine. He waited for the farmer to come along.

Just before the Dykes walked out of the cornfields, Charley pulled out his pocket watch. It was almost four o'clock in the afternoon. Sunset was about an hour and a half away. He stared at the fifty-cent piece attached to the watch fob. Ellen recalled that he smiled when he rubbed some dirt off the cameo ring he wore. No one knows, but perhaps he thought about Ruby, or Dempsey, or the cotton fields of Oklahoma and the times before he went on the scout.

An airplane, an unusual sight in those parts in 1934, droned overhead. Charley turned his face toward the cloudy sky. The rains of the past few days had disappeared, and even though it was deep into autumn, there were smells of new life in the woods where the maples showed their true colors. Soon, killing frosts would give way to snow that would enrich the land.

Ellen Conkle watched as the stranger climbed into the backseat. Her sister-in-law got up front as Ellen's brother started his automobile. They waved goodbye, and she went back to the kitchen chores. Suddenly, she heard machines driving up to the front of her house and the sound of car doors slamming shut. When she looked out the window again, she saw a band of men in suits, carrying guns. They began fanning out over her property. The stranger jumped from her brother's car behind the corncrib and began his run across the field toward the trees.

The run only lasted a few seconds. It must have seemed forever to Charley. Maybe it was like one of those dreams, filled with monsters, that seem to last forever in slow motion. Many years later, a federal agent remembered that Charley ran like an athlete, that he cut and dodged in a broken field sprint. Cookies and apples fell from his pockets and bounced on the ground. Someone yelled for him to halt. Then gunfire erupted and the bullets bounced up puffs of dust around his feet. He ran on toward the trees.

He gulped in mouthfuls of freedom as he ran.

Chester Smith, a policeman from East Liverpool and a sharpshooter who had proudly fought in France and Belgium, knew the man running away was Charley. There was no doubt in his mind.

It was now ten minutes past four. Smith shouldered his .32–20 Winchester rifle. He took aim at the man running in zigzags across the field. When he had Charley in his sights, Smith wrapped his finger around the trigger. He took a breath and held it. He slowly squeezed.

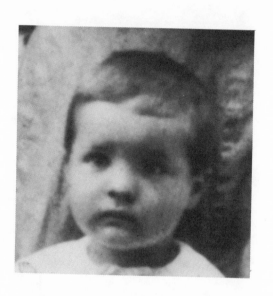

CHARLEY

1 9 0 4
~
1 9 1 4

"Though little, I'll work as hard as a Turk,
  If you'll give me employ,
To plow and sow, and reap and mow,
  And be a farmer's boy"
        —The Farmer's Boy (ANONYMOUS, BEFORE 1689)

PREVIOUS PAGE: *The Walter Floyd family. Sitting, Walter and Emma. Standing, left to right, Ruby, Ruth, Bradley, Mamie, Charley. Adairsville, Georgia, 1907.*

RIGHT: *The Buman Floyd family. Front row, left to right, Buman, W. Gick, Gussie. Back row, left to right, Dossie, Velva, Winston, Walter. Akins, Oklahoma, ca. 1922.* BELOW: *Claude and Undeen Griffith with sons Charles Brooks, left, and Worth. Charles Brooks married Velva Floyd, one of Charley's cousins. Price's Chapel community, ca. early 1900s.*

Charley Floyd's grandparents, Charles Murphy and Mary Elizabeth Floyd, with their son Burley and daughter Susie. Sallisaw, Oklahoma, 1914.

Charley's future wife, Ruby Hardgraves Floyd, on the lap of her grandfather, Perry Commodore Edwards, with other family members. Near Morris, Oklahoma, ca. 1915.

Bradley and Bessie Watson Floyd. Sallisaw, Oklahoma, 1918.

RIGHT, CLOCKWISE FROM UPPER LEFT: *Jesse Woodson James in Confederate guerrilla uniform at age 17. Platte City, Missouri, 1864; Henrietta Younger, Bob Younger, left, Cole Younger, right, and Jim Younger. 1889 photo made while the brothers were serving time in the Stillwater, Minnesota, penitentiary; Henry Starr, Oklahoma's King of Bank Robbers. Tulsa, Oklahoma, 1919; Belle Starr and her lover Blue Duck, ca. 1886.*

BELOW: *First National Bank in Stonewall, Indian Territory, August 16, 1904.* BOTTOM: *Reunion of Deputy U.S. Marshals who served in Indian Territory. Fort Smith, Arkansas, 1908.*

Henrietta Younger, Bob Younger, (left) and
Cole Younger, (right) and Jim Younger, photo.

Photo by J. L. River

Top: *The posse that captured Cherokee outlaw Ned Christie. The Cookson Hills, Indian Territory, 1892.*
Bottom: *Necktie party in a barn. Frontier justice for the slaying of City Marshal A. A. Bobbitt. Ada, Oklahoma, April 19, 1909.*

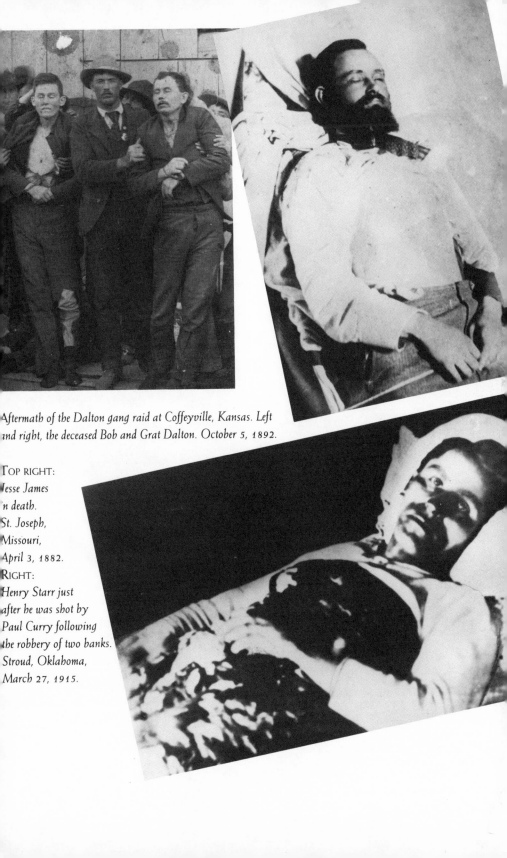

Aftermath of the Dalton gang raid at Coffeyville, Kansas. Left and right, the deceased Bob and Grat Dalton. October 5, 1892.

TOP RIGHT:
Jesse James
in death.
St. Joseph,
Missouri,
April 3, 1882.

RIGHT:
Henry Starr just
after he was shot by
Paul Curry following
the robbery of two banks.
Stroud, Oklahoma,
March 27, 1915.

CHILD OF AQUARIUS

CHARLES ARTHUR FLOYD came squalling into the world on his family's farm at the midpoint of the winter season. It was a fallow time in the northwest corner of Georgia. Cottonseed and other crops would soon be planted, but for now the growing fields were fast asleep. Pink and white dogwood blossoms were months away from erupting on the mountainsides among the stands of hickory, thickets of mountain laurel, and tangles of wild honeysuckle.

The baby arrived just thirty-four days into 1904. It was the third day of February—the month named for Februus, a Roman deity associated with purification who eventually became god of the underworld. This Floyd was a child of Aquarius. The baby was born on a Wednesday, and, according to those who followed astrology, that was a lucky day for Aquarians.

The Floyds were Baptists, Democrats, and hardworking farmers rooted to Georgia's red chocolate clay. They did not pay much heed to the influence of stars and planets on human affairs, except when it came to the planting of crops or a coon hunt under the harvest moon or as a topic of conversation when chores were completed and they searched the night heavens for streaking meteors.

Dr. Richard S. Bradley, who rode in his buggy from the nearby community of Folsom to deliver the baby at the Floyd home, charged a fee of $7.50. The Floyds paid every last cent, but it took five installments—two dollars initially, followed by one dollar in paper currency, a dollar and twenty-five cents worth of corn, two dollars in greenbacks, and a final payment of a dollar and a quarter that was not made until November, nine months after the boy's birth. Many years later in her published memoirs, Ora Lewis Bradley, the attending physician's widow, recalled that the Floyd baby boy "had good, law-abiding parents and grandparents. He was a fine, pretty baby, weighing ten pounds."

The Floyds were known to be solid citizens. They were respected and trusted. It was said that they "were as good as gold." So neighbors were pleased when the word spread across Folsom and the nearby town of Adairsville, seven miles to the east, and through the hollows and over the hills in Bartow County that yet another Floyd had been born.

The latest Floyd baby's birth was not of much consequence to anyone except the immediate family. Business went on as usual, with not a newspaper notice in the small county papers. Naturally, the newspapers in Atlanta and the larger cities were filled with more important events. Old men, who congregated at the square to whittle and spit, and peddlers, who paused at country stores with their wares, had plenty else to gab about.

After all, it had been only a month since the death of James Longstreet, the Confederate general who had been raised in Georgia. Longstreet fought at both battles of Manassas, at Gettysburg, Chancellorsville, Chickamauga, and in the Wilderness Campaign. While the Floyd baby's birth marked the forty-third anniversary of the formation of the Confederate States of America, life for these hardscrabble farmers had scarcely changed since the days following the war.

Less than two months had passed since brothers Orville and Wilbur Wright, self-taught inventors from Dayton, Ohio, had made their first successful flight from a "heavier-than-air machine" at Kitty Hawk, North Carolina. And, of course, there was the big news out of St. Louis. After almost six years of frantic preparation, the Louisiana Purchase Exposition—destined to become the "grandest of all world's fairs"—was only a few months away from opening, complete with John Philip Sousa and his celebrated band.

There was also much talk in Adairsville of the panic in the demoralized cotton market, a run caused by a struggle between southern growers and the domestic and foreign mills. During the previous week, prices had gone through a series of convulsions, fluctuating up and down like never before in the annals of the cotton exchange. Trouble was also brewing abroad. Marines were fighting Columbian troops in Panama, where the United States was attempting to build a canal to connect the Atlantic and Pacific oceans. In Asia, it had become apparent that Russia and Japan were just short days away from a formal declaration of war, their rival ambitions in Korea and Manchuria the chief cause. *The New York Times* reported that there were "crowds of wrinkled, filthy Chinamen assembled at the stations, and among them, like young oaks, towered the stalwart Russian frontier guards, with pale, energetic faces, and wearing sheepskin hats."

On this particular day, February 3, 1904, the birth of another boy baby in rural Georgia didn't seem to matter much. There were too many other considerations.

Off the northwest coast of France, search parties looked for bodies and survivors in the wreckage of capsized ships and shattered cottages after a tidal wave swept the Brittany shore.

In Newark, New Jersey, a fourteen-year-old boy, despondent because he had been discharged from his job delivering packages for a local store, swallowed a dime's worth of carbolic acid and killed himself.

In New York, a mass meeting of coffee and cake saloon waitresses was called to discuss organizing a union because the women were anxious "to be relieved from the tyranny of long gowns," which annoyed them when attending customers. A boy in that same city, named Norman Rockwell, had ten candles to blow out on his birthday cake.

In southeast Washington, D.C., at his family residence of 413 Seward Square, John Edgar Hoover—just a little more than a month into his ninth year and considered an aloof mama's boy by the other lads attending the Brent School—read from his Bible before going to bed.

That evening in the nation's capital, following a banquet attended by veterans of the Grand Army of the Republic, who just forty years earlier had fought in the Civil War, President Theodore Roosevelt spoke for a half hour about the duties of citizenship. Gen. Nelson A. Miles, recently retired after more than four decades spent battling Confederates, Indians, and Spaniards, nodded in agreement as the commander in chief delivered his fiery speech through clouds of cigar smoke. When all the talking and applause stopped, the guests bundled up in overcoats and hats and hurried to their carriages and hacks. The old warriors no longer feared rebel bayonets and minié balls, but the threat of pneumonia hiding in the damp night air gave them pause.

To the north and west of Washington, winter raged in the darkness. Steamships departing New York that morning for European ports faced high winds and frigid weather as far as the Grand Bank, southeast of Newfoundland. Temperatures over most of the nation were far below the seasonal average. There were storm warnings all along the Pacific coast. The wide sweep of a snowstorm isolated northern New York counties and tied up train service across the Midwest. Mail delivery was halted because of snowdrifts as high as the coaches in the railroad cuts. In Indiana, passengers had to abandon stranded trains and seek shelter and food at farmhouses or hire farmers to take them to nearby towns by sled.

Down in Georgia, even in the shadowy mountains, the winter was not as severe. Warmer weather beckoned, and during the night and early-morning hours, fresh winds descended from the west and flushed the chill from the forests and fields. Hounds curled up in straw beds with gnawed hog bones and dreamed of treed bobcats and fox chases through thickets and meadows. From the forest's edge came the resonant voice of an owl, a bird of wisdom and ruler of the night. *Hoo, hoo-oo, hoo, hoo.* Then there was a hush. And soon the owl's call came once more. And again. Finally there was silence.

Inside the Floyd home, it was as quiet as a mouse wetting on a cotton boll. Oak and ash logs burned in the fireplace and shadows from the flames danced on the walls and ceiling. The lingering smells of supper mixed with wood smoke. There was also the slight scent of corn whiskey in the air from an elated father's solitary toast to his newest child. Beneath a goose-down quilt, the baby snuggled against his mother's breast. Charles Arthur Floyd had survived his first day on earth.

2

THE FLOYDS

N SPITE OF THE MUDDY WINTER SKIES, another baby was sweet tonic for the Floyd family. The birth lifted their spirits. The entire household was rejuvenated. The baby made it seem as if spring had reached Georgia early.

Charles Arthur's parents—Walter Lee Floyd and Mamie Helena Echols Floyd—were quietly proud and wasted no time in summoning relatives and friends to see their newborn son. Following church services on the first Sunday after the infant's birth, wagons and buggies surrounded the Floyd's residence. The women fussed around the baby and exchanged stories. Out behind the house where Walter Floyd kept his prized hounds, the men stayed busy with their tobacco, a jug of homemade sipping whiskey, and gossip of their own. Guests brought fruit pies, spice cakes, and pots brimming with venison stew. There were plenty of gifts and hand-me-down clothes for the baby.

Months before he was born, Mamie and Walter, anticipating another boy, had chosen their son's names. Charles was from the Anglo-Saxon *ceorl* and the English *churl,* meaning "manly, strong," or, literally, "full-grown," and Arthur from the Gaelic *art,* meaning "a rock," or from the Celtic *artos,* meaning "a bear." His first name was for his paternal grandfather, Charles Murphy Floyd; his middle name was the same as his mother's oldest brother, Arthur Echols.

From the beginning, almost everyone called the boy Charley.

He was Walter and Mamie's second son and fourth child. Carl Bradley was their eldest. He had been followed by a pair of daughters, Ruth and then Ruby Mae. All the children were born at predictable two-year intervals at the Floyd's home in Bartow County, not far from the town of Adairsville.

This branch of the Floyd family had lived in the Georgia hill country for seventy-five years. Most of their genealogy was preserved through oral history that was passed around the supper table along with the bowls of field peas and collard greens and platters of fried chicken and pork chops. Some of the family's bloodlines, however, were also inked in Bibles or scribbled on paper and handed down to offspring. The Floyds seemed to have a good sense of who they were and who they had been.

They proudly traced their name and lineage back more than three centuries to Wales, the western peninsula of Great Britain, bounded by St. George's Channel on the west, which separates it from Ireland, and Bristol Channel on the south. Among those early inhabitants who roamed that rugged highland country, they claimed kinship to Sir John Floyd, a sixteenth-century writer of note and lecturer with the Society of Jesus who had battled the Spanish Armada as a youth and had been knighted by Queen Elizabeth I. The Floyds also counted a missionary, as well as boat builders and surveyors in their family tree. Most of the Floyds, in fact, had been Welsh farmers, tillers of the soil who left the country that became known not only for its tradition of poetry but also its contrast of coalfields and castles. In the early seventeenth century, they had sailed to America with some of the first waves of colonists.

Family records spoke of Floyds coming in 1619 to Jamestown, the first permanent English settlement in the New World, founded on the James River in 1607. They arrived at the Virginia colony aboard the *Rova*, a ship they had helped build. That same year, ninety single women were sent to the colony from London, while twenty blacks were imported as indentured servants rather than slaves. Presumably, the young women immigrants became wives of stalwart colonists, including some of the Floyds.

Although the family history is at best sketchy, anecdotes of Floyd ancestors include mention of Walter Floyd, the owner of four hundred acres of property in the Virginia colony in the mid-1600s; Nathaniel Floyd, who in 1632 maintained eight hundred acres on the Isle of Wight, the diamond-shaped island off the central southern coast of England; and Richard Floyd, a 1653 visitor to Jamestown before he established himself at Long Island, New York, when the English gained control of the island from the Dutch. There were also family stories, with no specific dates attached to them, concerning four Floyd brothers—William and Frederick, early settlers in Accomack County, Virginia; John, about whom it was said, "he went north, lost to family"; and Charles, who married a wealthy woman and settled in Georgia.

The family also claimed kinship to William Floyd, an American patriot and signer of the Declaration of Independence, who was described as "a practical, firm, unpolished man who enjoyed hard work." He was apparently distantly related to the Floyds of Georgia. What *is* known about this particular Floyd is that he was born December 17, 1734, in Brookhaven, Long Island, New York, the son of Nicoll and Tabitha Floyd. William's parents were wealthy, and as a young man, he led the life of landed gentry on Long Island. He later became a civic and military leader, and by the outbreak of the American Revolution, he was a major general in the Suffolk County Regiment of the New York militia. Floyd fought for the patriots against the British and served competently, but without distinction, as a member of the Continental Congress from 1774 to 1777 and again from 1778 to 1783.

In 1776, Floyd was the first New York delegate to sign the Declaration of Independence. That same year, the British seized Floyd's farm as rebel property. Throughout the rest of the war, he lived solely on his congressional pay while his family sought refuge in Connecticut. After independence from Britain was won, Floyd sat in the first U.S. Congress, ran unsuccessfully for lieutenant governor of New York, and served as a New York state senator and a presidential elector. He died in 1821, and was buried at Westerville, New York.

It is doubtful that any of the Floyds from the Georgia hills ever stood over William Floyd's grave to pay their respects. Nonetheless, they always savored being able to say—without a hint of smugness—that they believed they were related to one of the country's first genuine mavericks. There would be others.

The Floyd family chronicle, largely based on hearsay and lore of Welsh pioneers, left a lasting impression on young Charley Floyd and remained one of his most vivid childhood memories. Listening to his older relatives relay the litany of family stories that retraced the Floyds' movements through Virginia, Tennessee, the Carolinas, and Georgia—including tales of kinfolk who had been killed by Indians and others who had eaten bear steak for breakfast— became the farm boy's favorite evening and Sabbath pastime. He particularly savored the stories about Georgia, his birthplace, a state with a history as rich as the sorghum he poured over his biscuits.

3

GEORGIA ROOTS

OR GENERATIONS, Georgia's northwest mountains had been home to the Floyd clan. They were suited to the land. Every one of them was a die-hard Georgia Cracker.

Centuries before, the same countryside where the Floyds raised crops and hunted wild game had been the dwelling place for the Etowah Indians—prehistoric Mound Builders who wore shell ornaments, carried long flint swords, and buried their nobility in elaborate costumes made of feathers and wild cotton. Europeans first visited the area in 1540 when Spanish explorer Hernando de Soto and his company of iron-suited soldiers prowled the forests and mountains in their quest for gold. Almost two hundred years later, in the early 1730s, Gen. James Oglethorpe came to Georgia, named for England's George II, and established settlements for debtors and religiously oppressed Englishmen. There, he found a loose confederation of Cherokee Indians, living more or less at peace with neighboring Creeks and Chickasaws. Poorest of the New World colonies, Georgia soon became a haven for the persecuted and the downtrodden, and acted as a military and geographic buffer between the thriving Carolinas and Spanish Florida.

Following the American Revolution, more white settlers poured into Georgia from the Carolinas and neighboring states. They established towns and cultivated the land. With the invention of the cotton gin and because of newfound profits reaped by the harvest of King Cotton, the state began to prosper. While Georgia's coastal seaport cities, especially Savannah, grew larger in the early 1800s, however, northern and western Georgia remained home to large tribes of Indians and was sparsely populated by whites. The Cherokees were one of the primary tribes. Like law-abiding whites, they built cabins and lived as farmers or raised cattle and ran trading posts. Some of these Indians owned black slaves and used them to work their fields. The Cherokees founded their capital at New Echota in northwest Georgia, lived as a true independent nation governed by their own constitution and code of laws, published their own newspapers, and taught their children an alphabet developed by Sequoyah, the half-breed Indian scholar.

Northwestern Georgia, the ancestral home of the Cherokees, offered a climate cooler than elsewhere in the state, given its mountains and river valleys covered with pine and oak woodlands. It appeared to be an ideal place to raise children and crops. Among the branches of the Floyd family who settled in the Georgia mountains were those who moved there from the more settled lands in eastern Georgia and South Carolina in the late 1820s. Some of these settlers were latter-day Hernando de Sotos, nineteenth-century explorers in search of gold. At the same time, others fled the coast and moved into the Georgia highlands to escape yellow fever and other diseases that flourished near the ocean.

Included in this vanguard of newcomers was Patience Floyd, born in 1796 in South Carolina to Tennessee parents. Patience was a determined woman, not afraid of man or beast. She was also Charley Floyd's great-great-grandmother.

Widowed, with a pair of sons to raise, Patience, whose name came from the Latin word *pati,* meaning "to suffer," toiled day and night in order to carve out a living from the untamed land. Her sons—Walter Floyd, born in South Carolina in 1822, and Redding Floyd, born in Georgia in 1828—learned how to handle plow, ax, and muzzle-loader rifle when they were still small boys. Although she could not read or write, Patience saw to it that her sons got some schooling, learned their letters and how to cipher. She nourished her family on wild game and corn cakes prepared in an iron skillet over an open fire. There was always plenty of fresh milk, eggs, and vegetables. Her children grew sturdy and tall. They liked their new home.

As law-abiding as Patience was, she raised her boys in an area of Georgia that had long served as a sanctuary for the lawless. During this period, an organized gang of cutthroats and thieves, who called themselves the Pony Club, operated throughout the region. This pack of killers preyed upon frontier settlers and travelers who used the old Federal Road, a trail that ran through the Cherokee country. Fur trappers, farmers going to market, hog and cattle drovers, and unsuspecting pioneers, such as the widow Floyd, were forced to journey back and forth on this crude highway that served as the white newcomer's initiation into the territory. One preacher called the north Georgia countryside along the highway "the darkest and most dangerous place in the old Cherokee Nation." Because of the criminal element that thrived there, the state of Georgia passed legislation that required all settlers on Indian lands to take an oath of allegiance obliging them to obey the laws and uphold the state constitution. Patience gave her promise to walk the straight and narrow, but she and her boys also kept loaded muskets at the ready just in case a mountain brigand came calling.

In 1830, Patience Floyd resided in Hall County. The following year, William Lumpkin, Georgia's newly elected governor, a man who had an eye on white expansion and regarded all Indians as a handicap to the state's progress, ordered Indian territory surveyed. Land west of the Chattahoochee

River and north of the Carroll County line, including parts of Hall, Carroll, and several other counties, were combined to create the large county of Cherokee. Each of the ten counties in the Cherokee purchase was surveyed and divided into four sections. Some areas were designed as forty-acre "gold lots," because it was believed there were rich gold deposits in the soil, but most of the area was measured off into large 160-acre "land lots" for farming.

Later the county was subdivided into ten smaller counties, including Floyd County, named after noted Indian fighter and statesman John Buchanan Floyd. A Virginia native who was educated in South Carolina, Floyd failed at both law and cotton farming in Arkansas before returning to Virginia, where he became governor. Years later, he became an outspoken supporter of states' rights and helped secure the election of James Buchanan as President. For his effort, Floyd was appointed Secretary of War, but he resigned in 1860 and within a short time became a Confederate brigadier general during the War Between the States.

In 1880, more than a half century after she first moved into northwest Georgia, Patience Floyd—by then an old woman surrounded by her grandchildren and memories—contended that she was kin to Gen. John B. Floyd. In the 1830s, however, Patience and her boys were too busy farming and worrying about Pony Club riders to care about relatives with highfalutin pedigrees. During this earlier period of her life, land in the newly formed counties was distributed through a lottery system, open to Georgians who met certain guidelines. Caucasian adult males were at the top of the preferred list. Other persons qualified to draw lots included white widows and orphans under eighteen years of age. Patience Floyd and her boys vied for a parcel of property to call their own, as did thousands of other newcomers.

Before this allotment could occur, the whites had to rid the land of the Indians. The Cherokee Nation—an Indian government patterned after that of the United States—faced imminent destruction. It was increasingly clear that the Native Americans were in the way of the white settlers. Finally, in 1832, when the land lottery was held and after many treaties were drafted and broken, the Cherokee Nation was effectively abolished. President Andrew Jackson's Indian-removal policy took hold, with a warped vision of "progress" that preceded Manifest Destiny by many years. Then, in 1835, a small faction of Cherokees signed yet another treaty, one that ceded the Cherokee lands in Georgia to the United States. However, when the document was presented to the tribal council, the Cherokee leaders declared it illegal. By year's end, the same faction of Cherokees met at New Echota, the Cherokee capital situated at the confluence of the Coosewattee and Conesauga rivers, and signed still another treaty with the federal government. This time, they ceded all Cherokee lands east of the Mississippi River to the United States. In return, the federal government promised to pay the Indians $5 million and grant them 7 million acres of land in the West. Although most tribal leaders and their followers again rejected this document, the government held them to the terms of the treaty and gave them two years to vacate their lands in Georgia.

There was resistance, but the whites prevailed. Betrayed by a combination of government officials, missionaries, and a few of their own unscrupulous people, the Cherokees were rounded up and placed in stockades. Some were evicted at musket point from their homes. During 1838 and 1839, all Indians were expelled from the area and forced to march under the supervision of Gen. Winfield Scott and his seven thousand mounted soldiers along the notorious Trail of Tears to the lands provided west of Arkansas that became known as Indian Territory.

Indian removal was a brutal process, more than a mere dislocation of land, but a policy intentionally designed to inflict degradation and shame. War Department regulations stipulated that no one, except the infirm or infants, could ride in a wagon or on horseback during the twelve-hundred-mile trek from Georgia across the mid-South. Thousands of disenfranchised Indians died of exposure, cholera, hunger, and heartbreak on their long walk west. One Georgia volunteer, who went on to serve as an officer in the Confederate army, said, "I fought in the Civil War and have seen men shot to pieces and slaughtered by the thousand but the Cherokee Removal was the cruelest work I ever knew." Some Cherokees hid in the mountains of North Carolina, and members of other southeastern tribes managed to elude the white soldiers, but most of the Cherokees, along with Creeks, Choctaws, Chickasaws, and Seminoles were placed in the distant Indian Territory, where they eventually became known as the Five Civilized Tribes.

With the Indians removed, white settlers such as the Floyds continued to spread throughout Georgia. By the decade of the 1840s, Patience Floyd and her sons had moved to Carroll County, named for another signer of the Declaration of Independence. Strapping men in their twenties, the Floyd brothers by this time had taken wives, and before 1850, they had moved with their growing families once again. They went farther north to Cass County, named for Lewis Cass, a native of New Hampshire who was Secretary of War in 1831, a candidate for the presidency in 1849, and a senator from Michigan. The land in Cass County was known to be some of the most desirable in the entire Cherokee section. In the late 1840s, this land sold for thirty dollars per acre and produced anywhere from twenty-five to fifty bushels of corn to the acre.

The Floyds quickly cleared off the sassafras, persimmon, papaw, and witch hazel in order to plant such crops as corn, wheat, cotton, rye, barley, and oats. They turned to the thick Appalachian forests and built stout log homes. Water was abundant from the many springs and streams. The Etowah, Oostanaula, Coosewattee, and Conesauga rivers wound through the county's valleys and were fed by many clear creeks, including the Raccoon, Pettis, Euharlee, Pine Log, Two Run, Oothcaloga, and Stamp.

The widest and most fertile of all the valleys were formed by the Etowah River, flowing in a crooked course like a big bow from the eastern side of the county southwestward across the southern part, then turning northwestward into neighboring Floyd County. Frontiersmen on horseback or in wagons drawn by yokes of oxen came out of the hills to barter tobacco for other supplies in the towns scattered throughout the county. New towns sprouted like spring cotton. There was Cassville, Allatoona, Cartersville, Free Bridge, Iron Works, Kingston, Little Prairie, Cold Run, and Wolf Pen. In some of these burgs, such as Cartersville, not only farmers but professional men settled—judges, doctors, teachers, and even a marshal whose main duties were to collect taxes, supervise grave diggers and volunteer firemen, ring the city bell each night from 10:00 P.M. until 4:00 A.M., and deal with the rabid dogs and wild boars that wandered into town.

The Floyd brothers built their homes near Adairsville, a settlement on the Western & Atlantic Railroad located exactly halfway between Atlanta and Chattanooga. Five miles to the north of Adairsville lay a Cherokee village called Oothcaloga—the Cherokee word for beaver. The name was from the stream that ran through the valley known as the "garden spot of the Cherokee country" by the pioneers who settled there. At one time, Oothcaloga had been home to the Adair family, descendants of Scottish adventurers who had settled among the Cherokees, married into the tribe, and, by the time the Cherokee lands were taken by the government, become prominent representatives of the Indians. After the Cherokees left, the town of Adairsville was created and given its name to compliment the Scotch-Cherokee chiefs who had been friendly to the whites. Stores, churches, and schools were built, and in 1854, Adairsville was incorporated. By then, the Floyds had become fixtures in the community.

Walter, Patience's firstborn son, and his wife, Charlotte, had three children—fraternal twins named May and James, born in 1842, and a second boy, Harry, born in 1848. In her old age, Patience Floyd, always the epitome of a pioneer farm woman, lived with Walter and his family. Her youngest son, Redding, and his wife, Catherine, born in 1825 in South Carolina, settled nearby with their eight children: Clark, 1853; Frances (Fanny), 1855; Charles Murphy, 1857; Theresa (Treasy), 1860; their own set of twins, Jefferson and Martha, 1863; Nancy, 1866; and finally, Franklin, 1869.

During the decade of the 1850s, Cass County witnessed a period of great growth and improvement. Cotton was steadily replacing corn as the dominant crop, and had already become the largest cash crop in dollar value. Corn and wheat mills were built near Adairsville, and during this last decade of peace before the Civil War, more than a half dozen iron furnaces went into operation, turning out thousands of tons of pig iron each year. Like cotton, slaves still fetched good prices. By 1860, the county reached the height of its antebellum prosperity. Palatial mansions, belonging to the wealthy planters, appeared grandly around the region, log cabins for the more ordinary folk were remodeled, and schools were constructed.

Nonetheless, discontent and violence appeared like dark clouds on the horizon. War was imminent. One of the saddest chapters in the nation's history was about to unfold. Georgia and the rest of the South would never be the same. Neither would the Floyds.

4

BAPTISM BY FIRE

WAR EXPLODED ACROSS THE UNITED STATES in 1861. In the North, it was called the Civil War. Southerners knew the struggle as the War Between the States or the War of Northern Aggression. No matter which name was used, the results were the same—misery, devastation, and sorrow. This was especially true for the South and the thousands of families such as the Floyds who were caught in the cross fire.

With the outbreak of the war, Cass County's prosperity and growth abruptly ended. Although all three of the county's representatives to Georgia's Secession Convention of 1861 initially voted to remain in the Union, as did most other north Georgia convention delegates, many local men and boys joined the Confederate army when the majority of convention delegates ultimately chose to leave the Union. On January 19, 1861, when Georgia officially seceded from the United States, volunteer companies mustered overnight. Military units, such as Etowah's Infantry and the Cherokee Cavalry, formed and the soldiers left home in handmade uniforms to do battle with the damned Yankees at Manassas and Spotsylvania.

Area residents, bitter that the man for whom their county was named was a Northern sympathizer, voted on December 6, 1861, to change the name from Cass to Bartow, in honor of Francis Stebbins Bartow, a Georgia native and a general in the Confederate army. Bartow died during a gallant charge against a Union battery at the first battle at Manassas at Bull Run, Virginia, in 1861, but lived long enough to encourage his brigade, comprised mostly of Georgia and Kentucky regiments, with the stirring words, "Boys, they have killed me, but never give up the field!" That dying pronouncement inspired countless Bartow County lads, including a good many Floyds, for years to come when they played at war in the woods and pretended they were bold soldiers in gray vanquishing imaginary Yankee invaders.

There were frequent skirmishes in the area throughout the war, but the first significant action to take place in Bartow County occurred on April 12, 1862, and became known as the Great Locomotive Chase. The Floyd family and the other local citizens never forgot the audacity of those involved in this incident.

Union spy James J. Andrews, a mysterious double agent who spent the first year of the war smuggling medicines into the South, only to return with intelligence reports for the Union command, determined one way to defeat the Confederacy was to sabotage its railroad network. Andrews focused most of his spying efforts on the Western & Atlantic Railroad that snaked 138 miles northward from Atlanta through the mountainous terrain of northern Georgia. The W & A then crossed into Tennessee and entered Chattanooga, where it tied into other railroad lines. Financed and owned by the state of Georgia, the W & A was probably the South's best-run railroad. Some of the Floyds and their circle worked for the W & A, which served as a lifeline artery for Bartow County and the rest of northwestern Georgia. A single-track line, with sidings at Adairsville, Calhoun, Tilton, and Dalton, the W & A crossed several major streams on covered wooden bridges and raced through a long tunnel that sliced through towering Chetoogeta Mountain.

Andrews's plan was to steal a Confederate train just north of Atlanta and then chug full steam ahead into Chattanooga, destroying bridges, tunnels, and telegraph lines all along the W & A line. Andrews and twenty-three volunteers dressed in civilian clothes and tucked pistols beneath their coats. All but one of the raiders were Ohio soldiers who had volunteered to leave their Buckeye regiments for this secret mission behind enemy lines. They ranged in age from eighteen to thirty-two, and most of them had seen action during several frays in Kentucky and at Bull Run the year before.

The disguised raiders were careful to minimize their conversation so their northern accents would not give them away. They traveled southeastward from their Union army camps in Tennessee to Chattanooga, where they broke into small parties and boarded trains headed south to Marietta, Georgia, just above Atlanta. They determined that if they were stopped and questioned, they would say that they were Kentuckians on their way to enlist in the Confederate army. On April 12, Andrews and his men assembled in a Marietta hotel room for one final briefing. At the end of the meeting, Andrews vowed to "succeed or leave my bones in Dixie." Then they walked to the station and boarded a train being pulled by the *General,* a powerful wood-burning locomotive built for the Western & Atlantic in 1855.

During the twenty-minute breakfast stop in Big Shanty, they uncoupled all but three of the cars and seized the locomotive. Their action did not go unnoticed. Some startled W & A crewmen led by conductor William Fuller, at first assuming a band of rebel deserters from a nearby training camp had stolen the *General,* borrowed a repair crew's handcar and chased the train thieves. Eventually, the pursuers were able to commandeer another locomotive and pick up additional volunteers for the chase. Because of the close pursuit, Andrews and his raiders were not able to cause much damage to telegraph and rail lines as they thundered through Bartow County, pausing only briefly at the Adairsville station on their northbound adventure. Near the Tennessee border, the *General* literally ran out of steam when the locomotive's boiler water and firewood supply was exhausted. The raiders deserted their locomotive and took to the woods.

News of the train chase spread like scarlet fever across northern Georgia. Within a few hours, Confederate cavalrymen patrolled the countryside and guarded crossroads. Soldiers home on leave and farmers, such as the Floyd brothers and their neighbors, took up squirrel rifles, shotguns, and even butcher knives. They formed posses and scoured fields and forests with their best tracking dogs in hope they would encounter the Yankees. Within a week, most of the raiders were captured. Seven of them, including Andrews, were tried and convicted as spies, and were hanged from an Atlanta gallows. Some of the others managed to escape prison and the rest were exchanged for Confederate prisoners. In 1863, the entire band became the first recipients of a new military award, the Congressional Medal of Honor. The survivors were invited to the White House, where President Abraham Lincoln himself pinned the decorations on their tunics.

Although the Andrews expedition was unsuccessful, the Floyds and other Bartow Countians endured hardships far greater than pesty Yankee raiders bent on tearing up railroad tracks and pulling down telegraph wires. In 1863, the Civil War was long from over, and its travails and sorrows would leave a lasting impression on the farmers and merchants of north Georgia. Early Southern victories soon gave way to defeats. Union blockades forced shortages of food and munitions, and many of the fertile fields grew wild because few men were there to tend them. The saying was that Confederate conscription had "robbed the cradle and the grave." In many instances, only old men and boys were available as home guards to repel the Yankee sorties. Despite the gloom that had settled over these parts, there were a few bright moments.

In the spring of 1863, Union Col. Abel D. Streight led a sixteen-hundred-man mounted infantry regiment in an invasion of western Georgia. His mission was to destroy the Western & Atlantic Railroad and capture Rome, the seat of nearby Floyd County. An important manufacturing center at the head of the Coosa Valley, Rome was built where the Oostanaula and Etowah rivers converge to form the Coosa River, which drains to the Gulf of Mexico. Rome was also the home of the Noble Foundry, a factory that produced cannon for the Confederacy. Despite the size of his regiment, Streight was outmaneuvered by the four hundred rebel soldiers commanded by Gen. Nathan Bedford Forrest, a clever tactician who convinced his foe that the superior Union force was actually outnumbered.

There were also bittersweet triumphs, such as Chickamauga, the greatest Civil War battle fought in the West. The name Chickamauga derived from the Cherokees and meant "river of death." It was a fitting name. This bloodbath took place on September 19 and 20, 1863, in the woodlands north of the

Floyds' stomping grounds along the black waters of Chickamauga Creek on the Tennessee and Georgia border. The battle there was considered a victory for the South—but at the cost of 18,000 Confederate and 16,000 Union soldiers either dead, wounded, or missing. The Pyrrhic nature of the victory may have well sounded the death knell for the Confederacy. After the fighting stopped, Confederate Gen. Daniel H. Hill said, "It seems to me that the élan of the Southern soldier was never seen after Chickamauga; the brilliant dash which had distinguished him was gone forever. He fought stoutly to the last, but after Chickamauga, with the sullenness of despair, and without the enthusiasm of hope. That 'barren victory' sealed the fate of the Confederacy." Nonetheless, the war continued for another nineteen bloody months.

With each passing day in the years between 1863 and 1865, more fresh graves sheltered by magnolias and mimosas appeared in the cemeteries of northern Georgia. Patience Floyd and her daughters-in-law, with their broods of children, and the other wives and mothers of the Confederacy prayed for their men's safe return. They celebrated the victories and mourned the defeats. Sometimes only inspiration from the King James Bible preserved morale. Other times, the sweet strains of "Dixie," a song written by a member of an Ohio minstrel troupe that became the unofficial national anthem of the South, kept the Confederate faithful strong.

> *I wish I was in de land ob cotton,*
> *Old times dar am not forgotten*
>
> *Look away, look away,*
> *Look away, Dixie Land.*

Then, in 1864, along came Gen. William Tecumseh Sherman. Here was a man clearly intent on making his own stand in Dixie. Sinewy, with unkempt hair and a red beard, Sherman was affectionately called "Uncle Billy" by his troops. Northerners viewed him as the Union's avenging angel. To the South and especially the citizens of Georgia, however, Sherman was a "ruthless fiend," an incarnation of Satan himself.

The story of his famous march to the sea is a frequently told one in American history, but it needs to be repeated again here, for the Georgia that the Floyds would face after 1865 bore little resemblance to the land they had known before the war.

Sherman was determined to conquer the South. His plan was to march a massive army down the length of Georgia—one of the largest slave-owning states of the South—to the Atlantic Ocean and split the Confederacy in half. His hope was to destroy further the disintegrating southern economic system and to demoralize the civilian population. Sherman's route followed the Western & Atlantic Railroad to Atlanta, the Macon & Western Railroad from Atlanta toward Macon, and the Central Railroad to Savannah. It passed through Adairsville and the Floyd's property. More than any other warrior, Sherman brought the war home to the women and children of Georgia.

On May 4, 1864, Sherman with the Army of the Cumberland, the Army of the Tennessee, and the Army of the Ohio, together with four cavalry divisions, crossed from Tennessee into Georgia. This combined force of 98,797 seasoned Union soldiers, mostly from Ohio, Illinois, and Minnesota, faced only scant resistance from Gen. Joseph E. Johnston and his smaller Confederate army.

Walter and Redding Floyd and many other Georgia farmers and townsmen had already answered the call to arms when broadsides issued by the governor were posted across the state, urging "all able bodied men between the ages of 20 and 50" to join the Confederates. There were few men left in Georgia to resist Sherman. Most were outside the state, fighting in Tennessee with Hood or with Lee in Virginia. When the call went out, a battalion of cadets from the Georgia Military Institute at Marietta reported for field duty. Many of them died in battle before they had their first shave. Bartow County's landed gentry sent off its sons to serve as cavalry officers or to command companies of conscripts. A few became secret agents and conducted spy missions. These young aristocrats saw themselves as chivalrous protectors of their Greek Revival mansions, their sprawling plantations, and a vanishing way of life. They directed farmers and shop clerks in battle and tormented the Northern invaders every way possible. They set up ambushes, led scouting missions behind enemy lines, and derailed Yankee supply trains. Some of the more daring Confederates ended up with "dead or alive" rewards on their heads. They believed they could stop Sherman and his brutal horde of Yankee rogues.

Sherman's detractors, especially the pro-Southern English press, said the Union strategy of moving through Georgia was pure folly. Some even compared Sherman to Napoleon, and predicted his march to the sea would end up "a second edition of the French retreat from Moscow." Meanwhile, the combined Union armies led by Sherman and his generals moved south from the city of Calhoun into Bartow County.

On May 19, 1864, Union forces took Cassville without a fight, but there was still skirmishing throughout the area, with heavy losses on both sides. A few days earlier, when federal troops were known to be approaching Adairsville, a gun factory was quickly disbanded and moved elsewhere. Bridges, flour and corn mills, cotton gins, and depots were burned to the ground.

The Yankees foraged from the fields and pillaged from smokehouses. The Northerners found ripening fruit, cribs filled with oats, and knee-high green corn. They took all the chickens, hogs, and cattle in sight and gorged on blackberries growing in the river bottoms. Acting on orders from above, the soldiers shot any bloodhounds they encountered—in the belief that most of these dogs had been used to track escaped Union prisoners or runaway slaves. Army teamsters reaped wheat and other grains to feed their horses and mules.

In some instances, the federal troops took desks and benches from local schools and academies and ripped strings and keyboards from plantation pianos, using them as feed troughs for horses.

Hardly a kitchen, cellar, or pantry shelf went untouched as the Yankees plundered farms and towns like packs of famished wolves. They hauled off eggs, pickles, lard, flour, and wine. Bales of cotton, bedding, furniture, and paintings, which could not be carried away, were put to the torch. Delicate china and fine old glassware were smashed. Sofas and ottomans upholstered in black horsehide were ripped open with knives and bayonets. Handsome grandfather clocks that had not missed a tick in a century came crashing down on hardwood floors. Churches, schools, and libraries were destroyed. Manicured shrubs and formal gardens were trampled under the marauders' horses. Civilians were strung up by their thumbs and tortured with bayonets to make them tell where they had hidden their family heirlooms. As in most wars, women and children were terrorized and often raped, especially black women, who the *Northern* soldiers considered to be subhuman. Silk dresses snatched from the armoires in the antebellum mansions were placed under Yankee officers' saddles. The larger residences were used to house officers or set up as military hospitals, and the inside walls were defaced with the writings and drawings of the soldiers. A few homes were left untouched on account of the Masonic emblem attached to doorways.

Every evening for many months during 1864, Patience Floyd and her family saw the distant camp fires stoked by fence rails and planks the soldiers pulled from barns. Union pickets gathered around those flames, broiling hunks of confiscated beef and pork at the end of a ramrod. The Floyd children trembled at the sound of artillery booming in the mountains. Although they managed for the most part to escape harm's way, the terrible horror of war could not be avoided or ignored. Many nights, they went to bed hungry, fearful that Yankee troops would break into their homes.

In June of 1864, General Johnston's 65,000 Confederate troops, still stinging from a series of defeats, including losses at Resaca and points north, managed to hold the high ground at Kennesaw Mountain, just a few miles from Marietta. Johnston was up against a numerically superior Union force, but Sherman made the mistake of abandoning his strategy of flanking movements and instead launched a bloody frontal assault. This maneuver cost Sherman almost three thousand killed and wounded, compared to fewer than five hundred Confederate casualties. Sherman was relentless, however, and a short time later, he outflanked the Confederates and forced them to retreat.

After the battle at Kennesaw Mountain, Sherman wrote his wife, "I begin to regard death and mangling of a couple of thousand men as a small affair, a kind of morning dash."

Jefferson Davis, President of the Confederacy, relieved Johnston of his command. The new Confederate commander, Gen. John Bell Hood, tried his best to stop the onslaught of Union soldiers. It was futile. Rebel troops, many of them boys, were offered shots of liquor to give them courage in combat. Years later, Union veterans recalled how the Southern soldiers pulled their hats down before they charged, as if they did not want to see the certain death awaiting them. Despite brave attempts by the outnumbered Confederates to halt them, the Yankees kept coming.

On September 2, 1864, after four months of fighting across 130 miles of rugged northwestern Georgia, Sherman's troops marched into Atlanta. The next day, Sherman wired Washington, "So Atlanta is ours, and fairly won."

Several days later, Sherman himself rode into the city with a letter of congratulations in his pocket from a grateful Abraham Lincoln. Sherman saw that months of siege had taken a horrendous toll. All roads into Atlanta were lined with the bloated carcasses of horses, cattle, and men. A pall of gunpowder and death hung like poisonous fog in the air. Victorious Union soldiers broke open barrels of whiskey. They shouted and danced and sang while the civilians fled. The actual march to the sea would not begin until November, when the Yankees put the torch to Atlanta. In the twilight of the summer, as Sherman planned his continued drive, the end was clearly in sight for the Confederacy, however.

The war persisted as Northern troops remained in Bartow County for several months. The heaviest fighting in the county took place October 5, 1864, at Allatoona Pass, where more than fifteen hundred men lost their lives. Jenkin Lloyd Jones, a private in the Sixth Wisconsin battery, wrote in his diary after the battle: "I don't think there has been more desperate fighting done this year than yesterday at Allatoona." The grave of an unknown soldier on the edge of the railroad track in Allatoona Pass was left as a memorial to this bloody engagement. For many years, the workmen of the W & A Railroad cared for this grave and left wildflowers and verses to the nameless hero who "died for the cause he thought was right."

On November 5, 1864, a party of about three hundred soldiers from the Fifth Ohio Cavalry occupying Cassville received orders from Sherman to destroy the town. They burned down homes, colleges, hotels, and the courthouse. Only the town's churches and a few residences, used as hospitals, were allowed to stand. Cassville's population dwindled, and the town never regained its prominence. Years later, the county seat was moved to Carters-ville. After he burned Cassville and some other neighboring Georgia towns, Sherman consolidated his positions and brought up fresh reserves. His most famous burning was of Atlanta, and then he continued his march toward Savannah and the ocean, leaving a path of devastation and death in his wake that measured three hundred miles long and sixty miles wide. Sherman's orders were quite clear. The troops were to continue to forage liberally as they destroyed farms, mills, gins, barns, and warehouses.

Destruction rained everywhere in Bartow County. Bands of deserters and robbers from both the Northern and Southern armies hid in limestone caves in the mountains. Many of them claimed to be "scouts" but were in truth renegade guerrillas with jingling spurs and long, dirty hair tucked under broad-brimmed hats. They pillaged and raped, becoming more feared than the Yankees. In Atlanta and the other cities, wild dogs slept in ruined homes and piles of rubble by day, and at night formed packs and roamed the streets. One Southern lady turned refugee later wrote that "the baying of these animals in unison was the only sound to break the profound stillness."

By the time the war ended in April of 1865, abandoned breastworks and rotting horses littered the landscape. Defeated soldiers, some of them with the mud and dust of six states on their tattered clothes, straggled back to their homes on foot. They scrounged parched corn, withered peaches, and raw turnips to eat. According to the terms of the declaration of peace, paroles were given to these sad-looking men with empty eyes who gathered and quietly recited oaths of allegiance to Andrew Johnson, the new federal president. It was said that there were 18,000 men paroled at the Bartow County town of Kingston alone.

Both Redding and Walter Floyd survived the war. They returned home, rolled up their sleeves, and rebuilt their ruined farms. If they could endure the torment of battle in their own backyard, they knew they could survive the indignities of Reconstruction and the exploitation of the carpetbagger. It was a difficult time. Georgia was forced to endure two periods under military rule, and was not readmitted to the Union until July 15, 1870. The older Floyd children, tempered by years of conflict and strife, had become resilient young men and women. By the mid-1870s, fields of cotton returned and Bartow County began to recover. It was during this time that the next generation of Floyds, including Charles Murphy Floyd, Charley Floyd's grandfather, struck out on their own.

Charles Murphy, Redding's third-oldest child, was only nineteen years old when he married Mary Elizabeth Morris just two days after Christmas in 1877. It was the same month that Georgia's new constitution, which increased the strength of rural counties in the legislature, was ratified. Mary was born in Georgia on June 6, 1858, to J. W. Morris, a native Georgian born in 1831, and his wife, Emily Maddox, born in North Carolina that same year. Mary's younger brother, Augustus Morris, born in 1860, came to live with the young couple for a time and worked as a hired hand on his brother-in-law's farm.

Soon after their home and farm were established, Charles and Mary wasted little time in starting a family. They had a total of nine children, seven of whom lived to adulthood: Walter Lee, born November 2, 1878; Pearl, April 18, 1882; twins, Cordia Bunia and her brother Buman, December 20, 1884; Beller Redding, November 9, 1887; Burley, March 25, 1893; and Emma Orgedell, better known as Susie, January 21, 1899.

They named their eldest son, Walter Lee, for his grandfather Redding's big brother. When he was just a new baby, Walter could make his eighty-two-year-old great-grandmother Patience smile, and sometimes even laugh whenever she held him. His name fit. The name Walter came from the Old English *weald,* meaning "woods," and from the start, it was evident Walter was more at home when he was in the forest under a canopy of trees than anywhere else. In time, he would grow into a lean and strong youngster who could hold his own with the other boys. He and his siblings cut wood, hauled water, and worked in the cotton fields alongside their parents. They fished and swam in the ponds, creeks, and rivers and stalked game in the hardwood and pine forests still scarred from the war.

Like his father and the other Floyds before him, young Walter became a crack marksman and had a way with horses and hounds. And his dark good looks did not go unnoticed by the young women of the county. Mamie Helena Echols, a pretty girl from a big Georgia farm family, was one of those attracted to the eldest Floyd boy. She apparently did not escape Walter's gaze, either. He was impressed with her appearance and style and wasted no time before he came calling at the Echols's home, located near the Cedar Creek community. As the country boys would put it, Mamie could make a man plow through a stump.

Born in Bartow County on March 13, 1881, Mamie was the daughter of Elmer Wilton Echols and Emma Elizabeth Gaines Echols. Elmer had been born in Bartow County in 1852, and Emma, the daughter of South Carolina natives, was born in the county the same year. Married in 1877, Elmer and Emma had two other daughters besides Mamie: Eula Vernon, 1879; and Julia, 1886. They also had four sons: Arthur, 1882; Wiley Erwin, 1888; Forest, 1883; and Royal, 1891. Devout Baptists and capable farmers, the Echols were as respected and well liked in their community as the Floyds.

On December 19, 1897, the beguiling Mamie—quite sweet at sixteen—married nineteen-year-old Walter Floyd in a simple ceremony attended by their relatives and some close friends. They were soon able to set up housekeeping and start their own family, and by the time she turned twenty-one, Mamie already had three children. First came Carl Bradley, who was always called by his middle name, born on November 7, 1898, followed by Rossie Ruth, born on September 17, in the first year of the new century. Another daughter, named Ruby Mae, arrived on May 2, 1902.

Mamie treasured her trio of healthy babies. So did Walter. Still, as much as he loved Bradley and the two little girls, he was ready for another son.

Then along came Charley.

5

ADAIRSVILLE, GEORGIA

CHARLEY FLOYD'S BOYHOOD was not particularly remarkable. As a baby, he survived a bout of pneumonia that came close to snuffing out his life. He spent many of his formative years in the Deep South, in a typically rural early-twentieth-century household that was governed by a strict father and religiously devout mother. His parents, blessed with ample and equal amounts of country horse sense, love of family, and stamina, tried to pass these qualities on to their offspring.

Given their own upbringing, Walter and Mamie taught their children to be courageous in the face of adversity, to hoe row crops until their muscles burned, and to respect their elders. Both of them believed in disciplined children. They were staunch advocates of the old adage that good manners were a sure sign of good breeding. It took no time at all for Charley and the others to learn this fact. A sassy tongue was likely to result in a mouth filled with soapsuds. Those caught in mischievous acts were treated to a trip behind the woodpile with Walter or an on-the-spot ass whipping from Mamie. Either way, the punishment meted out was unforgettable.

The Floyds had no time for frivolity. It was true that Walter had a penchant for a nip of moonshine whiskey now and again and enjoyed running his hounds, and that Mamie, like many other rural ladies of her station, partook of a discreet dip of snuff behind her lip. Except for these simple pleasures and a very occasional community dance, however, they kept their noses to the grindstone. There was always plenty of work to be done. Even in the early 1900s, Georgia was still attempting to overcome the deleterious effects of the Civil War as well as the problems brought on by Reconstruction and the panic of 1893, the nation's worst depression of the nineteenth century. The state was slowly becoming more industrial but faced the social, economic, and political woes that accompanied the transformation of a region that had previously been totally agrarian.

Walter Floyd was not the kind of man to sit around wringing his hands and pondering the past. He had mouths to feed. He managed to put plenty of bacon and bread on his family's table by hiring on as a fireman for the Western & Atlantic Railroad on the run between Chattanooga and Atlanta. However, when he was injured in a train accident in the days before workmen's compensation, Walter was forced to quit riding the rails and had to look elsewhere for other employment. He soon went to work in the bauxite mines. Discovered in 1883 in northwest Georgia, bauxite had become a major business as the industrial applications of such minerals and ores became apparent. Bauxite's most important use was for the production of metallic aluminum. Vast deposits of bauxite, varying from a few hundred to many thousands of tons, were discovered near Adairsville and other parts of Bartow County. Mining companies in the area needed men and mules to work their operations.

The attraction of earning wages by taking bauxite from the earth wore thin. Walter Floyd was a farmer at heart. Georgia dirt was caked beneath his nails. He longed to breath air scented by pine trees and manure. Before too long, the lure of making a living by raising cotton—still the staple crop of the South—pulled him out of the mine shafts and open pits and back to his trusty plow and team in the fields. He did not have to look far when it came to finding dependable help. His young sons Bradley and Charley, even as small boys, could handle a hoe with the best of them. When it was time for autumn harvest, the entire Floyd family turned out with their long sacks to pick cotton.

And as they toiled the land, Walter and Mamie continued to augment their family. Four children were not enough. Emma Lucille arrived on August 28, 1905, and on May 13, 1908, a third son blessed the Floyd home. Walter and Mamie named him E.W. The rest of the family was never quite sure what the initials stood for or whether they really were anything more than just letters. Some thought the *E* might be for Elmer, the first name of Mamie's father, and that the *W* was for Walter. No explanation was offered. All of his life, the boy was called E.W. Four-year-old Charley was just delighted no longer to be the youngest boy in the family. He would tease his little brother as Bradley had teased him.

During Charley's early years, Walter moved his family at least once. They left the Folsom community and moved closer to the heart of the town of Adairsville, to a frame house on Hotel Street.

When they were old enough to trudge off to school, the Floyd kids still had to tend to their daily chores at home. That meant rising before sunup for early morning milking and egg gathering. After school, there was wood to cut and the fields to weed. Fortunately for the Floyd boys, the Georgia summers were long and the winters short. They managed to find time to break away from their farm tasks to explore the woods and pick up pieces of Indian pottery from the creek banks and freshly plowed fields. They used their penknives to dig Civil War musket balls and slugs from tree trunks as big around as four men.

They swiped watermelons and peaches, shot squirrels and rabbits, and found the best swimming holes and secret caves. They also listened to the battle stories of the varicose old men whose faded Confederate uniforms of butternut and gray were folded neatly as shrouds in cedar chests.

The town of Adairsville offered other diversions for the Floyds. Charley and his siblings played around the Adairsville depot. Among the chief attractions were the drugstores. There were several to choose from: Scott and Bowdoin, Dykes and Whitworth, and Dr. Gary Bray's Drug Store. An occasional visit to the drugstore was a treat for any farm youngster. It was almost better than swigging a bottle of Coca-Cola, the soda water that had started out in 1886 as a hangover cure brewed up in an iron pot in the backyard of an Atlanta pharmacist.

The smells at the drugstore wafted across the room like a magical tonic or elixir—perfumes with the aroma of honeysuckle and lilac, bay rum, scented tobacco, Sen-Sen, and tar soap. The shelves were lined with apothecary jars filled with herbs, spirits, and other potions. Country physicians toting little black bags came in to chat with townspeople about politics and weather or to whisper about "some darkie" who had been lynched for insulting a white woman. Amid the din of gossip, the pharmacists worked their mortars and pestles, concocting remedies for the doctor to deliver in person to house-bound patients. If there had been time, Charley could have stood there for hours and watched the druggists filling prescriptions and doling out free advice.

Sometimes when Charley and the other Floyd children lingered around one of the drugstores scheming the best way to spend a nickel, they occasionally encountered the socially elite of Adairsville—matronly ladies or elegantly dressed teenaged girls—discussing the latest Symphony Club musicale or perhaps the Happy Hour Society's winter picnic staged at the Masonic Hall, complete with evergreen-bough garnishes. The Floyd girls lacked the satin slippers, brocaded dresses, and ornamental combs of these wealthy folk, but they were never ashamed of the pinafores Mamie sewed for them. They were as presentable as anyone making the rounds of Adairsville on Saturday afternoons.

Adairsville also boasted two well-stocked department stores to serve the public. At the Adairsville Mercantile, there were men's suits, collars, hats, dresses, shoes for the entire family, corsets, bolts of yard goods and lace, as well as fancy foodstuffs, animal feed, and live poultry. The town also supported blacksmith shops, a livery stable, a half dozen grocery stores, a jewelry store, banks, and a millinery shop, where each season a milliner "from the style centers of America" was sent to introduce the latest in hats. Several young local ladies were also chosen to go to Cincinnati in order to learn the millinery business.

For a short time, there was a bakery, but since most of the local women did their own baking, it soon closed its doors. Down the street, the Bailey Meat

Market was more successful. The proprietor, a Confederate veteran with a distinctive voice, thanks to a Yankee bullet that tore through his throat, sold links of spicy sausage, prime steaks, and roasts to townsfolk who didn't butcher their own meat as the Floyds did every autumn.

Adairsville, in the first decade of the century, also provided enough business to support two photograph "galleries." Customers paid from fifteen cents to a quarter for postcard-size photos of themselves and family members posed in front of a landscape backdrop.

In the autumn of 1907, Walter decided to capture his growing family on film. But he wanted something more substantial than a postcard remembrance. He did not hesitate for an instant when he was asked to shell out a hard-earned dollar bill for a full-sized family picture. For the formal portrait, Walter slicked down his dark hair. He was clad in a necktie, dark suit, and a clean shirt with starched collar. His lace-up shoes suggested a recent shine. He sat as stiffly as a spinster, with baby Emma perched on his knee. Standing by their father, with ribbons in their hair and dressed in white frocks, were the girls, Ruby and Ruth. Bradley stood beside his sisters. He wore a bow tie, and, at nine years, was already almost as tall as Mamie. Her long hair was done up, and she wore a fine high-necked blouse and a floor-length skirt. There was no way to tell that she was pregnant with E.W. As the photographer worked the shutter of the big box camera, Mamie's hand barely touched the shoulder of her youngest boy, who was standing in front of her.

There was no intimation that Charley Floyd—a wide-eyed lad of three in short pants—would one day have a price on his head.

6

SEQUOYAH COUNTY

THE FLOYDS MADE A DECISION to leave Georgia early in 1911, about the time of Charley's seventh birthday. It can best be said that itchy feet got the best of them. They wanted a change of place, a chance to start over. The South had been rising again for over four decades, but the resurrection was much too slow for Walter. Half-century-old wounds from the war with the Yankees and others from Reconstruction remained raw. Sometimes it seemed to Walter as if the revival of the Southern economy was stuck in a hopeless bottleneck like a rebel yell caught in the throat of a dead soldier. Although northwest Georgia had been their family's home for generations, Walter and Mamie concluded that there was more opportunity waiting for them and their children beyond the hill country they loved. They looked to the West.

Walter first thought about moving to Texas, where there was plenty of room for cattle and cotton, but, for whatever reason, that notion did not last. He talked to other farmers and got their opinions and he listened to old pals from his railroad days who had traveled around the country. Finally, he settled on Oklahoma, a relatively new state with an abundance of farm and ranch land and thousands of acres of cotton fields. Oklahoma had long attracted Georgians ever since the infamous Trail of Tears. Then, in 1889, tens of thousands of eager claim stakers, including many from Georgia, poured into land that had once been given to the Indians when the federal government opened the unassigned lands to white settlement. Following that great land rush, farmers continued to trickle out of the South and strike out for the land where their grandfathers had long before driven the Indians they displaced.

Despite the promise of fertile land, Walter chiefly picked Oklahoma because several Floyd family members and friends, including his folks, Charles and Mary Floyd and his younger brothers and sisters, had already made the move.

Mamie's parents, Elmer and Emma Echols, had also moved to Oklahoma. They had left Bartow County back in 1904, the year Charley was born. They first settled at Hanson, a small railroad town near the Arkansas River in what was then known as Indian Territory. The Echols subsequently quit cotton farming and moved farther southwest to McCurtain, Oklahoma, where Elmer died and was buried in 1910, three years after Oklahoma gained statehood. His widow remained in McCurtain and her sons worked in the nearby coal mines. Even though Mamie's daddy was gone and her people had moved to another county, Walter's parents, as well as other fellow Georgians, lived at Hanson. There were enough close kin in the small communities scattered in the nearby Cookson Hills to make Walter Floyd and his family feel welcome.

Once they decided to leave, the Floyds sold off their home and livestock. The boys had a final romp in the dense Georgia woods filled with deer, turkey, and the ghosts of old soldiers. Mamie could not resist pulling up weeds sprouting around her beloved roses—roses the color of fire and lightning when they bloomed in the yard all summer and long into fall. She and her girls toured the stores of Adairsville one last time. At the old homestead, Walter took long pulls from a jug of seasoned mash before he ran his hounds down the dark trails and lanes until their thick tongues hung out as long as leather strops.

Then they packed up their things and said their goodbyes to neighbors. Walter, Mamie, and their three daughters and three sons dressed in their Sunday best. They took their few belongings and a basket of food, boarded a northbound train at the Adairsville station, and left Georgia behind in a cloud of vermilion dust. Charley and the other children were as excited as colts. All the way to Oklahoma, they dined on fried chicken and canned fruit. They pressed their faces against the cold windows to watch the passing landscape. They wondered about the new country that awaited them. It was difficult to sleep as the train bounced across the mid-South and the conductor stalked the aisle and sang out the destinations. The trip seemed especially long for Mamie, who was unable to get much rest because she was fearful of losing one of her children on the train. Her worries were for naught. Everyone arrived safely.

When they finally stepped from the train in Hanson, the Floyds were met at the railroad siding by family and friends, who put them up until Walter could find a house and some land to sharecrop. As soon as they pulled off their neckties and good britches and changed into bibbed overalls, the Floyd boys dashed off to see what kind of place they were now going to call home. Bradley and Charley, with little E.W. behind, ran as fast as they could up the dirt roads. They crossed the steel tracks, and raced up a mountain covered with timber and a strawberry patch. They could see for miles in any direction. They liked what they saw.

Situated in Sequoyah County in extreme mideastern Oklahoma not far from the Arkansas border, Hanson was flanked by two small mountains on the south and east. Between the mountains ran Wolf Creek, a tributary of Big Skin Bayou, and Little Sallisaw Creek, on the west side. Old-timers said the town of Hanson took its name from a railroad official and got its start back in 1888, when a store and post office had been opened on the Robert Sutton farm located about one mile to the east. Two years later, the store and post office were moved to be near the tracks of the Iron Mountain Railroad. A new town site was established and the village began to grow. Hanson served as the headquarters for railroad crews and many people came there to live and work. A large public well was dug for a fresh water supply. There was a depot, bunkhouse, section house, and a water tank for the steam engines. Across the track was a long loading platform to ship the bales of cotton to eastern markets, and there was a stockyard with pens and a loading chute for the cattle being sent north to Kansas City slaughterhouses.

By the 1890s, Hanson developed into an active trading center, an entrepôt, with several general merchandise and clothing stores, and drugstores, as well as a two-story hotel, several churches, a schoolhouse, blacksmith shops, a gristmill, and two cotton gins. During this period, Hanson surpassed Sallisaw, the nearby county seat, in population and importance. The town even managed to survive the depression of 1893, when the price of cotton plummeted from twelve to seven cents per pound and some of the stores had to close their doors. The economy gradually improved, however, and when cotton-picking season arrived each autumn, more people came to the area to work the fields. Hanson's gins ran twenty-four hours a day. Trains loaded with bales of cotton departed every few days.

Besides cotton, the town also relied on the booming cattle industry. Ben Garvin, a prominent cattle rancher in Sequoyah County, sold beef to the railroad company so it could feed its crews. The son of a full-blooded Cherokee mother and a father who had been killed by bushwhackers, Garvin grazed a large herd of cattle, with his brand on their hips and jaws, from the Boston Mountains of Arkansas west to the Illinois River and all through the bottomlands of the broad Arkansas River. In some of the meadows, the bluestem grass reached the tops of the stirrups of the horsemen who rode out from the line shacks to guard the herds. Noted ranchers like Frank Faulkner and Jake Wright also ran substantial cattle operations in the area. These men and others held periodic roundups that became major events for the town.

Before the cattle were shipped off to the slaughterhouses of Missouri, the citizens of Hanson got little sleep. Long lines of cattle cars arrived in town around 3:00 A.M. Sunday in order to be ready for the train to make Kansas City in time for the Monday-morning market. The combination of cowboys' curses, screeching train wheels, and the bellowing of stubborn steers could arouse the dead. So could the stench of manure. By dawn, almost every citizen in town as well as quite a few sharecroppers and farmers from out in the sticks turned up to watch them load. It was better than a hanging, a Fourth of July picnic, and a revival service rolled into one.

Disaster struck the town in 1899 when a fire swept through Hanson and destroyed all but one of the businesses. Some merchants rebuilt; others moved to Sallisaw, since the Kansas City Southern Railroad officials had selected the county seat over Hanson as the site of its rail junction with the Missouri Pacific Railroad. In 1910, just a year before the Floyds arrived, another fire roared through the business district and burned nearly all of the mended structures. This time, Hanson never really recovered.

Before he and the family left Georgia, relatives wrote Walter and told him about the fire that had left much of the town in ashes. Still, when he first arrived in Oklahoma and saw Hanson's charred foundations and vacant buildings, he thought that just maybe he had made a mistake. He was not nearly as taken with the place as his curious sons. Looking for a fresh start, Walter had stumbled into a town that appeared as if it had just hosted Sherman and his Yankee raiders. Rather than panicking, Walter took stock of the prospects. In only a few days, he realized there was much more to Sequoyah County than the town of Hanson.

The history of the county was tied to early Indian cultures, and the name Sequoyah, which meant "shut in" or "shut away," honored the inventor of the Cherokee alphabet, who had settled in the area in the late 1820s. Throughout the county were communities and small towns, each with stores, churches, schools, and cotton gins to serve the farmers. The Floyd youngsters soon learned to recite a litany of new town and schoolhouse settlement names. There was Badger Lee, Bethel Chapel, Blunt, Box, Dwight Mission, Evening Shade, Gans, Gore, Maple, Marble City, Miller Ridge, Muldrow, Nicut, Paw Paw, Price's Chapel, Roland, Shiloh, Short, Sloan's Chapel, Vian, and many more. The county seat of Sallisaw, at one time a trading post and camping site, was situated in a picturesque valley through which flowed a tributary of the Arkansas River—Sallisaw Creek, the stream that gave the town its name. The word Sallisaw came from early fur trappers, a corruption of the French word *salaison,* or "salt provisions." To the south of Sallisaw lay Wild Horse Mountain, and to the north was Brushy Mountain and the Cherokee and Cookson Hills. The Cooksons, along with the Boston Mountains, formed the southern part of the Ozark Plateau, while to the south of the Cooksons, the San Bois and Ouachita mountains were formed by a series of curving ridges known as the Kiamichi and Winding Stair mountains. There was no shortage of wood or water, and the soil of the surrounding countryside appeared to be fertile enough for settlers to scratch out a living.

Once he was able to saddle a borrowed roan horse and ride out across the country, Walter quickly saw the promise the growing fields held. He scooped up a handful of the earth and smelled the future in the soil. Within a short time, Walter leased some acreage and went to work as a tenant farmer. He acquired horses, milk cows, and some poultry. The Floyds raised cotton, corn, hay, and sorghum grain. Mamie became a pillar of the Hanson Baptist Church. She canned vegetables and made jelly and jam from the wild fruit that grew along the fence lines. She and her girls kept the family's frame house tidy. All the Floyd children also helped work the land just as they had learned to do back in Georgia.

In little time, the Floyds made many new friends. There were kinfolk galore in the area, as well as other northwest Georgia families. They had surnames such as Wofford, Amos, White, Gilbert, McEver, Randolph, Trotter, Dysart, Pannel, and Maulden. Some of them had known Walter and Mamie and their children back in Bartow County. A few were kissing cousins. There were also plenty of folks from Arkansas and Alabama and other places—the Lessleys, Watsons, Farmers, Hawkins, Matlocks, Fullbrights, Hensleys, Walkers, and Caseys. Like the Floyds, they had made the move by train, or else in wagons pulled by teams. Still more were old Indian families who had lived on their land allotments near town for a long time before the others even thought of coming. They included the Faulkners, Garvins, Lattimores, Fleetwoods, Millers, Riders, Choates, Twists, Seabolts, Baldridges, Ganns, Burrows, McQueens, and many more.

For several years before the new schoolhouse was built, the Indian settlers had sent their children to the Cherokee National School located near the railroad station. Some of the students rode in from surrounding farms on horses or jennies. Later the school was opened to white children, whose parents paid a subscription fee of five cents per day. The school ground was also used for picnics and as the site for Cherokee Green Corn Stomp Dances. Barbecued beef and freshly squeezed lemonade left no one hungry or thirsty on these occasions. Sometimes the feasts lasted three days, and at night, the Indians in their costumes—with bells on their ankles—would dance around the camp fires to the steady beat of drums. By the time the Floyds came to the county, most everyone attended classes in a two-room frame schoolhouse built at the foot of Hanson Mountain just after statehood in 1907. The older Floyd children, along with other youngsters, went to the new school and squirmed on the hard wooden seats. For holiday programs or special events, the folding partition that separated the two rooms was taken down so parents could sit like cigar store Indians and watch their nervous children sing or recite poetry and memory work.

The Floyd children instantly adjusted to their new surroundings. Oklahoma seemed to be an untamed country of cowboys and Indians. It was an exciting place for Charley, his brothers, and his sisters. They enjoyed the town band concerts, picnics on Sallisaw Creek, hayrides, and especially Saturday after-noons in the summer when they cheered themselves hoarse as Hanson's baseball team was matched against one of the other communities. They played hide-and-seek amongst the old gravestones in the nearby Fleetwood Cemetery. And, just a year after they arrived in Oklahoma, the family welcomed yet a new member to the fold.

The children were happy to have someone else who could eventually help with the endless chores. Unlike the others, this Floyd came after four years, breaking the more frequent cycle that Walter and Mamie had maintained for years. The baby was born June 25, 1912, the same day the Democratic convention commenced in Baltimore. A week later, the convention delegates gave Woodrow Wilson, a son of the South, the nod to run for President. The Floyd baby was a girl, however, so Walter and Mamie could not name their child for their candidate. Instead, they named her Mary Delta. She was a true Oklahoma baby, and became in time the consummate little sister for Charley and the rest of the brood. With four girls and three boys in the Floyd household, Walter knew he would never be caught shorthanded when the cotton harvest came due.

That same year, in 1912, disaster struck the family when Mamie's younger brother Forest was killed in a coal-mine explosion at McCurtain, along with seventy-seven other miners. He was only twenty-nine. After Forest was buried next to his father, Emma Echols, Mamie's mother, moved back to Hanson to live with her daughter's family. She stayed with the Walter Floyds until her death in 1916, when her body was taken back to McCurtain for burial alongside her husband and son.

During this busy summer of 1912, with the arrival of the baby girl and Mamie's mother, Walter took the entire family by surprise. After a revival sponsored by the Hanson Baptist Church, Walter—not nearly as active a Christian as his devoted wife—was moved by the spirit. Following the services, Walter, and some others who had similarly been stirred, marched to the banks of the Big Skin Bayou Creek. He pulled off his shoes and stockings, and waded fully clothed into the creek until the coffee-colored water reached his knees. There in the sight of an old-time-religion God, with his family and friends watching, Walter allowed the preacher and some deacons to dip him backward under the murky water. He came up gasping for air, dripping, with his hair slicked back. Walter Floyd now was baptized. All around him, the others stood in the creek, with folded hands, waiting their turn to take the plunge and receive the Holy Ghost.

In the tall grass, Mamie, with tears in her eyes, held her new baby daughter and beamed like an angel. All up and down Big Skin Bayou Creek echoed shouts of hallelujah. Another soul had been saved. Charley observed the ritual and then went home with his family to eat dinner. As the Floyd wagon creaked down the dirt roads, the summer sun climbed into the afternoon sky. By the time the Floyds reached their house, Charley saw that his father's wet clothes and hair had dried.

7

OUTLAW GHOSTS

T
HE FIRST TIME ANYONE ever caught him stealing, Charley Floyd was not even ten years old. A box of fancy iced cookies was his downfall. Although Mamie Floyd regularly baked enough sugar and oatmeal cookies to overflow a big dishpan, there was always something special about getting store-bought treats. Later on, as a grown man, Charley was not able to remember exactly how old he had been at the time he stole those cookies, but he damn sure never forgot getting nailed red-handed.

That first incident took place in Sallisaw at a grocery store owned and operated by J. H. Harkrider, a respectable fox hunter and merchant who came to Indian Territory from Arkansas in 1899. Harkrider was not just another middle-aged shop clerk with an apron tied around his soft belly. He could take care of himself. He had the ability to talk drunken Indians into surrendering their gun belts and sometimes their whiskey. When he was a younger man running a shoe and harness business, Harkrider had repaired a saddle for Henry Starr, one of the territory's most notorious outlaws. He remembered that Starr was "in every way a perfect gentleman." When the storekeeper heard people "talking about how mean and ugly" Starr was, Harkrider "just told them that they didn't know what they were talking about for that was all lies."

In the decade after Oklahoma's statehood, Sallisaw was still as wild and woolly as an unbroken mustang. According to an old account, there were so many gun battles in the streets on a single afternoon that Harkrider had to dive headlong into his bathtub three different times in order to stay clear of stray bullets whistling through the windows. With all the troublesome cowboys and tough farmhands he dealt with through the years, Harkrider did not even think that the Floyd boy he caught snitching sweets from his store would one day be branded as America's public enemy number one.

"I had some little cakes and cookies in boxes and they kept disappearing," Harkrider remembered many years later. "I marked some of the boxes and watched to see where they went."

Soon enough, Charley Floyd rambled into the store. He was all alone. The youngster stood around for a few minutes, perused the neat rows of canned goods and bins of dried beans, ran his fingers over the countertops, and then left. As soon as Charley slipped out the door, Harkrider, who had been watching the lad like a hawk, swooped down on the cookie boxes and found that one was missing from the shelf.

"I got an officer and we went around to the alley and there was Charley Floyd eating some cookies. I asked him where he got the cookies and he admitted getting them out of my store after I showed him the mark. We tried to scare him up some and show him he shouldn't steal, and then we let him go."

As far as Harkrider was concerned, Charley had learned his lesson. The boy never stole anything else from him. At least, he was never caught again stealing in the store.

Charley tried to learn from mistakes and always did his level best to escape parental discipline, especially the wrath of his father. He wanted to keep his nose clean enough to stay on Walter's friendly side. That was no easy task. Walter could be stern and unbending. Even so, when his father was in a good mood, Charley liked to be in his company. The hunting and fishing outings with his father did not happen nearly often enough for the boy, however. Charley soon discovered that there was more to life in Oklahoma than summertime baptism celebrations, berry-picking parties, or pie suppers.

Work always came first. People cherished their share of good times, but the everyday rural experience was not always idyllic—far from it. Charley quickly figured that out, too. There was an abundance of bitterness that mingled with the sweetness. For every teaspoon of honey, there was a tablespoon of castor oil—sometimes a double dose. There were endless prayer meetings and monotonous school lessons for every snowball fight or game of marbles. Charley knew he would have to invest long hours sweating in the fields to make up for his more frivolous moments.

To be properly enjoyed, pleasure had to be earned. Before sitting down to a fine squirrel dinner, there needed to be a hunt. Sweet milk to wash down the slabs of hot gingerbread resulted from a trip to the barn in the early-morning darkness. Thick molasses did not just appear in the can by magic. That took some effort, too. Community events, such as quilting bees, hog slaughters, and barn raisings, were associated with struggle and strain. Dances and play parties came at the end of a strenuous week of work. Oklahomans at this time played hard but had to work even harder.

Out in the country, where the majority of people lived, the hands of the women and children were as callused and rough as the men's. Farm life was harsh and demanding. There was nothing easy about it. Most families had to toil like peasants from sunrise to dusk in order to keep the wolf from the door. Among honest people, nobody was exempt from labor. If a youngster showed any promise or ambition, his elders said it was because the child had grit or spunk. There was no tolerance of sissies or malingerers, and no such thing as being allergic to hard work. Everyone was expected to pull together and do his or her share.

It was certain as sunup that nothing was free. That became clear to Charley when old man Harkrider and the town policeman caught him in the alley with the cookies. Likewise, it was true that a stolen watermelon could be sweet and juicy enough to risk a load of bird shot in the butt and legs, but before a boy slipped beneath a fence with a melon tucked under his arm, at least for an instant, he weighed the consequences of getting caught in the act. Playing hooky from school, skinny-dipping at the creek, or laying up in the woods with cohorts to smoke corn silks usually resulted in extra hours spent cutting kindling, scrubbing chalkboards, and a good country whipping to boot.

Charley and the other rough-and-tumble farm youngsters were raised with an old saying: One had to pay for the piper if one wanted to dance. That single maxim was ingrained in them as much as all four Gospels and the Ten Commandments combined.

However, some of the boys of Charley's generation, like others before them, soon discovered that when it came to earning a living, not everyone chose to go to the cotton field or on cattle roundups—not by a long shot. The promise of slopping hogs was not enough to keep everybody on the farm. There were those who believed that they simply were not suited to honest labor. They stayed alive by operating on the other side of the law. They took up arms in order to steal from people, rob banks, trains, and stores. Cattle and horses were routinely stolen. Sometimes, during the perpetration of a crime, innocents were shot and even killed. Illegal whiskey was made and sold in the same deep woods where these fugitives hid. Some of these lawless people lived on the fringes. A few were able to keep a foot on both sides of the law. It was a difficult balancing act, though, and most of them eventually toppled and fell.

Folks who lived in Oklahoma recognized that it was a land conceived in violence, the last frontier of the outlaw. This was particularly true in eastern Oklahoma, called Indian Territory until statehood came in 1907. Even more than Oklahoma Territory to the west or the narrow panhandle strip known as "no-man's-land," the eastern half of the "twin territories" acted as a true refuge for the lawless and untamed. These seemed to thrive there in great numbers.

When Charley and his family first came to Oklahoma, some of those old-school desperadoes, including that infamous bank robber Henry Starr, were still in business. Stories of hidden loot, gun battles, heroic deputy sheriffs turned outlaws, vigilante justice, and ruthless villains who met their Maker at the business end of a hemp rope fueled the imagination of Charley and his chums.

Most of these outlaw stories had been tampered with over the years. Lots of spice and garnish had been added. What had once been reasonably sound historic accounts were now seasoned with ample portions of hearsay and exaggeration and twisted into tall tales. Some were nothing more than pure country bunk. Bandits and outlaws were mythologized beyond recognition by dime novelists or by grandfathers who embellished their fireside yarns with each telling. Newspapers did little to help. Publishers and their reporters were not as concerned with accuracy as they were with selling papers. One day, the accused could be indicted in headlines, while the next day, the same ordinary thief might be made into an overnight celebrity. The public was confused. Fact and fiction merged uneasily. Reality was often as elusive as smoke.

In truth, outlaws had presented problems in Indian Territory from the very beginning. This was clear even in Georgia prior to the Indians' removal from their ancestral lands in the late 1830s. While still back in Georgia, the Cherokees were forced to employ a band of armed riders called "regulators," whose mission, according to the tribal council, was "to suppress horse stealing and robbery, to protect the widows and orphans, and kill any accused person resisting their authority." Once the Cherokees and the four other Civilized Tribes were forcibly moved to Indian Territory, similar groups called light horse companies were formed to preserve the peace and act as a shield against fugitives from justice who wandered into the lands.

Some of the Indians' light horsemen guarded the territorial borders against the importation of diseased cattle, while others helped put down tribal insurrections. Almost all of them were particularly effective when it came to terrorizing white whiskey peddlers who crept into Indian Territory with their barrels of hooch. Among the Indian tribes, justice was sure and punishment swift. For example, those who were found guilty of stealing a horse or mule knew they would receive one hundred lashes on their bare backs. If they repeated their crime and were found guilty again, they also understood that they would go the way of convicted killers and rapists. That meant taking the long walk to the nearest gallows or a hanging tree.

For the most part, the members of the Five Civilized Tribes became prosperous farmers during the long period between their eviction from Georgia and other Southern states and the outbreak of the Civil War. When the war came, however, it took its toll on the residents of Indian Territory. Although there was a definite division of allegiance among the Indian nations, old blood ties made the Southern influence strong. Many *Indian* slaveholders knew that they faced substantial investment loss if the Yankees won out. As a result, regiments of full and mixed bloods were mustered. They proudly carried the Confederate Stars and Bars into battle. Guerrilla bands also operated in the territory, including Col. William Quantrill's dreaded raiders. Local renegades stole livestock and burned both Union and Confederate Indian villages, and pro-Confederate Cherokees destroyed military targets as well as the homes and barns of civilians who billeted enemy troops and stored their supplies.

After the war, there was not much improvement of conditions for the Indians. Punitive treaties schemed up in Washington during the period of Reconstruction diminished the holdings of the various tribal properties. The federal government transformed much of the land forcibly taken back from the Five Civilized Tribes into a dumping ground for other Indians, who were moved into the twin territories. Former slaves and vagabonds from Arkansas, Texas, and Missouri emigrated to Indian Territory and squatted on tribal lands. Many of these people raided the Indians' smokehouses and corncribs. Vigilante groups were formed to halt the rise in crime.

Besides the addition of more Indian residents and freedmen, white newcomers also entered the Indian nations via a network of cattle trails, stage routes, and railroad tracks that crisscrossed the land. As postwar problems mounted, the Indian governments were left without adequate funds to maintain their law-enforcement efforts. Federal troops were too busy policing the western frontier to help out. Indian courts that had once been so effective were now in utter chaos and had no jurisdiction over the tidal wave of misfits who poured into Indian Territory.

The brush-covered hills, hidden caves etched in the river bluffs, and the chain of secluded towns all acted as meccas for criminals. Along with the droves of drifters, gamblers, and whores came murderers, rapists, and rustlers. If a man or woman was wanted by the authorities in his or her own state, all he or she had to do was mount up and "light out for the nations." No questions were asked of strangers and there were no white man's courts to extradite the outlaws. The authority of the various tribes' light horse forces applied only to Indian citizens. Indian Territory became known as a "robber's roost," and its sinister reputation spread faster than fresh gossip at a church supper. A popular saying sprang up that fit the situation perfectly: "There's no Sunday west of St. Louis—no God west of Fort Smith." Tribal leaders and decent citizens could not agree more. They cried out for help.

Finally, in 1871, the federal government responded to these pleas by moving the Western Arkansas Federal District Court from Van Buren to Fort Smith, just one hundred yards east of the Indian Territory boundary line. A series of federal judges was brought in and charged with protecting the public by cleaning up the nearby breeding grounds of some of the most evil felons ever to pack a six-gun. However, most of the judges were either incompetent, corrupt, or inefficient. The situation did not improve in Indian Territory. A Fort Smith newspaper editorial, published in 1873, came right to the point: "It is sickening to the heart to contemplate the increase of crime in the Indian country . . . if crime continues to increase there so fast, a regiment of deputy marshals cannot arrest all the murderers."

Within two years, however, some changes for the better were made. The major adjustment came in 1875 when Isaac Charles Parker was named presiding judge at the burgeoning river town of Fort Smith. Parker was only thirty-six years old when he arrived at the courtroom, but he had a strong background in law and politics. He had been city attorney, district prosecutor, and district judge in St. Joseph, Missouri, and had put in two terms in Congress, representing a district in western Missouri that knew only too well the guerrilla escapades of Quantrill, Bloody Bill Anderson, and the James-Younger gangs.

A big, broad-shouldered man with piercing blue eyes, a mustache, and a goatee, Parker was the youngest judge on the federal bench when he got the nod from President Ulysses S. Grant to rule the troubled court. Parker was an ardent Republican, a strict Methodist, and a careful student of the Bible. He believed that without exception the wicked should be punished to the letter of the law. On May 10, 1875, only eight days after he and his family arrived by steamboat at Fort Smith, the judge opened his first term of court. Out of eighteen persons brought before him on murder charges during that initial session, fifteen were convicted. Eight of them were given death sentences.

The very first murder trial he presided over ended in a swift conviction. Parker delivered a lengthy condemnation of the prisoner, but instead of telling the man he would be hanged "until dead," the judge emphasized the convict's fate by declaring, "I sentence you to hang by the neck until you are dead, dead, dead!" Parker did not hesitate in doling out death sentences, and more often than not, the condemned also received Scripture lessons, long lectures, and was urged to repent before he met his Maker. Parker's closing words to each sentenced prisoner were the same: "Farewell forever until the court and you and all here today shall meet together in the general resurrection."

Parker's draconian style won him national acclaim. Newspaper reporters came from all over the country to see Parker in action and hear his pronouncements. The law-abiding citizens and outlaws alike soon dubbed him the Hanging Judge, a nickname he despised. Others called him "Bloody" Parker and "Butcher" Parker. Actually, the execution chores were left to George Maledon, a capable hangman with long whiskers and deep-set eyes who took great pride in his work. Maledon became a familiar sight on the streets of Fort Smith, usually carrying a basket that contained the handwoven hemp rope he so deftly used at the gallows. Each rope was handwoven in St. Louis and was soaked with a pitchy oil to prevent the hangman's knot, with its thirteen wraps, from slipping. This ensured a quick death for the black-hooded convicts. Of the seventy-nine criminals who swung limply from the Fort Smith gallows, Maledon's handiwork sent sixty of them to eternity. This number included the first ever six-man hanging, considered his master-piece. When he finally retired as a hangman, Maledon toured country towns and cities with one of his treasured ropes and lectured about the lives and consequent deaths of many of the culprits he had executed in the name of law and order.

"I've never hanged a man who came back to have the job done over,"

Maledon quipped without the hint of a smile. "The ghosts of men hanged at Fort Smith never hang around the old gibbet." Like the judge he served, Maledon earned a sobriquet all his own. The severe Bavarian native was called the Prince of Hangmen. Posted over his well-used scaffold was a sign that read THE GATES OF HELL.

In order to mete out his brand of punishment and to restore peace and tranquillity to Indian Territory, Parker appointed two hundred deputy marshals to ride for him. They were to bring all wrongdoers to the dungeons at Fort Smith, which became known as "Hell on the Border." Certainly not all those who served Parker and the court were angels. Several of them had been either brigands themselves or would later resort to the life of an outlaw. The righteous Parker had to swallow hard and sometimes even turn the other way. As he put it, he was "obliged to take such material for deputies as proved efficient in serving the process of this court." Although Parker had to permit some rascals and questionable characters to represent him in the field, there was one kind of man he could never tolerate. No marshal who was a coward was allowed to venture out into the Indian country.

The tough lawmen who rode west out of Fort Smith had to cover an area of more than 74,000 square miles, an area about the size of New England. It was at best a difficult assignment. Nonetheless, Judge Parker required that his men risk their lives to patrol the nations and serve arrest warrants. "Bring them in alive or dead" was the standing order, but the officers tried their damnedest to return with live prisoners in order to collect all the mileage expenses and fees due them. Deputies were paid no salaries but received six cents a mile travel pay while on official business and a flat fee of two dollars a head for every criminal brought in alive. They depended for the balance of their income on rewards offered for the most sought-after felons.

Courageous deputies such as Paden Tolbert, David Rusk, Willard Ayers, Dave Layman, and many others took an oath to serve Parker and his court. At least one-third of Parker's total force of lawmen died in the line of duty. The best-known of Parker's deputies were Bill Tilghman, a former buffalo hunter and Dodge City marshal; Heck Thomas, a Confederate veteran who was twelve when he fought under Robert E. Lee; and Chris Madsen, a Dane who had served with the French Foreign Legion in Africa and the U.S. Cavalry in the far West. This intrepid trio was called the Three Guardsmen. They were the top guns of all the Men Who Rode for Parker, as the deputies called themselves.

During the late 1880s and early 1890s, new federal laws were passed that stripped away large portions of Parker's jurisdiction. As the Indian Territory's population increased, more courts were needed to meet the demands. The judge's critics, including the eastern press, which called him "harsh, cruel, and tyrannical," also helped bring about the end of his long legal career. Finally, in September 1896, after the balance of his jurisdiction was taken from him,

Parker retired. It had been twenty-one years since he had first come to Fort Smith. His dark hair and beard were now totally white, and although he was only a month shy of turning fifty-eight, he looked like a man of at least seventy. He died two months later on November 17, 1896, from a heart attack, and was buried at the national cemetery at Fort Smith, just a few blocks from his courtroom and gallows.

Like most other country boys of his day, Charley Floyd was well acquainted with the story of "Hanging Judge" Parker and his band of deputy sheriffs. Charley was mesmerized with the old Indian Territory legends of the pursued and those who chased them. Charley especially liked hearing about the ones on the other side of the law.

He knew by heart the escapades of Jesse and Frank James, Belle Starr—the "Bandit Queen"—the Daltons, the Youngers, Bill Doolin, and all the other desperate men and women who had operated for many years in and around the Oklahoma hills where the Floyds grew cotton and corn. Those old desperadoes, shrouded in cobwebs and fantasy, made potent dreams for the young cookie thief. They became Charley's legacy.

8

KING COTTON

OTTON.

Nothing but cotton.

Cotton. Endless acres of puffy bone-white cotton as far as the eye could see.

Visions of cotton mixed with Charley Floyd's fantasies of Jesse James, Belle Starr, Ned Christie, Al Spencer, and other old outlaws who had found comfort in the Oklahoma backwoods. The images of eternal cotton fields did not yield sweet dreams for the boy. They were more like nightmares. These recurrent dreams of chopping and picking cotton kept Charley grounded in reality, a place he wanted to avoid at least while he slumbered.

Besides dominating Charley's thoughts, cotton also acted economically as the primary cash crop for Walter Floyd and many other farmers of Oklahoma. Cotton's seasonal cycles created a way of life for many of them. In spring, money was tight when the crop was planted. After the cotton harvest in the fall, the Floyd children got new shoes and overalls, and Mamie bought cloth, kerosene, and other necessities that the family could not grow or make themselves. The level of the yearly cotton crop was important to the Floyds.

A subtropical plant, cotton was grown both for its soft white fiber and also for the seeds contained in the pods, or bolls. Since earliest recorded history, cotton has provided mankind with one of the basic fibers for clothing. Cotton was grown in the Indus valley in India as early as 3000 B.C. Ancient Egyptians cultivated cotton, and the plant grew in the Sudan and other areas of North Africa. Medieval Arabs gave cotton the name *qutn,* meaning "a plant found in conquered lands." That was appropriate. Marching armies from ancient Rome to antebellum Virginia had fought battles in fields covered with broken cotton plants.

Cotton reigned as king of the cash crops in Oklahoma for more than a century. The cotton culture arrived along with the Five Civilized Tribes when these Indians migrated from the southeastern United States. By the 1830s, Choctaw farmers in Indian Territory shipped five hundred bales of cotton to market each year. The Cherokees presented silver loving cups to their top growers as early as 1845, and a few years later, some large cotton farms appeared along the Red River. Because individual farmers and sharecroppers raised most of the cotton in the territories, there was never a true plantation system with a large slave population as there was in the southern states. Without this leisure class, cotton farming was never romanticized in Oklahoma.

To the west in Oklahoma Territory, cotton farming took off right after the big land run of 1889, when floods of white settlers streamed across the border. By the turn of the century, more than 240,000 acres of Oklahoma Territory were annually planted in cotton. Oklahoma cotton growers gained worldwide attention. At the Paris International Exposition of 1900, Alfred Smith, a black cotton farmer from Oklahoma County, took home both the first- and second-place honors for his superior cotton samples.

Every rural community had at least one, if not several, cotton gins. In the early 1900s, Oklahoma farmers were shipping bales not only to New England but to France, Germany, and Japan. In 1913, cotton went for 11.77 cents per pound, and by all appearances, the price seemed likely to climb even higher. Still, no matter how much money it earned, it required a great deal of hard labor to get the crop planted, grown, and harvested.

Knowing that cotton was familiar to the great prophets of the Bible gave a modicum of comfort to those who worked the fields. Black sharecroppers and poor white tenant farmers from the Carolinas to Texas, and throughout America's Cotton Belt, found solace in the fact that the cotton they picked traced its origins to ancient varieties grown in the Nile valley, where Moses once walked.

When they labored in the cotton fields, the black workers, even in Oklahoma, leaned on spirituals and gospel music to help them get through the long day. In the early 1900s, Huddie (Leadbelly) Ledbetter, a black folk and blues singer and a furious twelve-string guitarist, who ended up serving two terms for murder, popularized an old plantation song that was originally sung by field hands trying to pass the time.

You got to jump down, turn around, pick a bale uh cotton
Got to jump down, turn around, pick a bale uh day.
O Lawdy, pick a bale uh cotton,
O Lawdy, pick a bale uh day.

Music broke up the monotony of picking and helped the workers forget the constant pain in their fingers. It also made them remember that cotton was not just king but a tyrant.

Charley never forgot that. He cursed the fields of cotton all the time he was growing up. The annual crop was the largest source of the Floyd family's income, but it was not any less of a burden to those who toiled in the fields. Year in and year out, there was cotton to tend and pick. Charley and the other

Floyd children could have set their watches, if they had had them, by the cotton cycle.

Every spring, Walter and his mule plowed and harrowed the soil. Between April and May, or just after the last frost, the cotton seeds were sown eight to eighteen inches apart in rows separated by about four feet. Once the plants broke through the top of the earth, the Floyds thinned or "chopped out" with hoes, kept the weeds under control, and cultivated the soil. All the while the crop grew, the farmers worried about weather and fought boll weevils, stinkbugs, leaf worms, and root rot. Within several weeks, the first buds appeared on the young plants and they soon blossomed into flowers with creamy white or yellow petals. After the flowers opened, they turned various colors and shades and eventually withered and dropped off, leaving an egg-shaped cotton boll. Inside the segmented boll, white fibers grew from the newly formed seeds. Gradually, the boll expanded and then burst open. Fluffy white fibers swelled from the split segments like powder puffs ready to be picked. In late summer and early autumn, the real work commenced. The first of as many as three cotton pickings got under way.

Harvesting was unquestionably the most arduous of all the steps in the cotton-farming process. Picking seed cotton from the open bolls kept most of rural Oklahoma busy until early December. Big landowners hired local and migrant harvest hands for wages that were based on the price of cotton at that time. Sharecroppers and the smaller farm operators, such as the Floyds and their neighbors in Sequoyah County, could not afford to hire extra help. Large families were there to do the chores. Grandparents, pregnant women, and even small children turned out and were given harvest assignments. During "cotton time," everyone helped with the picking. There was no alternative. Country schools were dismissed for six weeks in October and November and the children picked up gunnysacks and took to the harvest fields.

Often the workers got to the field so early they had to wait for daybreak to have enough light to pick. A typical day in the cotton patch lasted twelve hours. It was strenuous work, pulling the open bolls of cotton off the stalks and putting them inside the long cotton duck sacks that the adult pickers then dragged behind them. Most of the time, workers were so thirsty, it felt as if they had cotton stuffed in their mouths. Rest stops for a dipper of water or a moment to wring out a sweat-soaked bandanna were few and far between. The continuous act of picking the delicate fibers from the thorny pod was tedious. It also hurt like the dickens. By day's end, the cotton burrs had chewed through the work gloves of those lucky enough to have a pair and slit open their fingers and palms. Knees were raw and bloody, and shoulders and backs were racked with pain that came from bending or from hauling fifty-pound sacks up and down the rows. The first few mornings after harvest began, hardly anyone could move. After a week or so of stooping in the rows and grabbing the cotton tufts, muscles became toned and hands suitably callused, however.

Pickers competed with the other workers and even with themselves. They all tried to pull just a little more cotton every day. Some of the larger boys and young men liked to brag that they could pick more cotton than anyone else. A few wildly claimed they could "pick a bale uh day." That kind of talk brought guffaws, since everyone knew that to pick a full bale a day required a half-dozen seasoned hands working as hard as an oil field whore on payday. But laughter, like the songs echoing across the fields and the pails of cool well water, brought relief during long hours spent in the cotton patch.

In the autumn evenings, Charley climbed on top of the loaded cotton wagon and stretched out long as a cat. The night air was crisp and smelled of clean cotton, dying leaves, and the earth itself. While the wagon rolled on home, Charley lay there under the cold stars and mused about things other than cotton picking. Sometimes a big slice of moon lighted the way.

This was the best time for a boy's imagination to run wild. Visions of the James brothers on the scout, masked men burying their loot, and Billy the Kid making a break for it raced through his mind. After the family ate supper and the evening chores were completed, the lanterns were turned low and the weary household settled down to rest. Charley, snug in bed with his brothers, closed his eyes with the wild West still on his mind. In a heartbeat, he was asleep.

By dawn, the gunfights were finished and the dust had settled. With dawn, all the bandits had disappeared. He was once more dreaming of cotton—bales of that damned old cotton everywhere.

9

HEROES

T HERE WAS NO SHORTAGE of idols for Charley Floyd and his bold mates. Any suntanned boy with the nerve of a cat burglar who grew up picking cotton and shooting agates during the adolescent years of the twentieth century had a glut of champions to choose from and imitate. Most of them were distant images— pictures in a book or newspaper, or popular names that came up during conversations at the cotton gin or after church services. Some were larger-than-life characters—a blustery Teddy Roosevelt ranting from a podium draped in bunting or an aging Buffalo Bill Cody with white hat in hand, riding into the arena's limelight for a final bow. Still others were far less grand or conspicuous.

A few of the young fellows from Sequoyah County doted on Woodrow Wilson, a Princeton-educated historian and the U.S. President who tried in vain to keep the country out of the menacing war that started in Austria-Hungary in 1914 and stormed across the continent. Wilson was a Virginia native and had lived as a boy in Augusta, Georgia, where in the spring of 1865 he peered from his father's Presbyterian parsonage window and saw a dejected Jefferson Davis pass as a captive in a guarded carriage on his way to federal prison. It was a scene Wilson would never forget.

After he completed his education, Wilson briefly practiced law in Atlanta before he became a professor and college president and then entered the political arena. In 1910, Wilson gave up the presidency of Princeton University and became the governor of New Jersey. In 1912, he was the Democrats' choice for President. He won the election with only 41.9 percent of the popular vote. In the 1916 election, he won more handily with 49.3 percent. Although Wilson was certainly not a landslide President, every male member of the Floyd family—from Bartow County, Georgia, to Sequoyah County, Oklahoma—backed the Democrat for President in both elections. Wilson was their man.

Schoolboys from Hanson, Muldrow, Akins, Vian, and the other dirt-road towns that dotted the hills of eastern Oklahoma respected the distinguished

President just as much as their elders. Woodrow Wilson also served as a role model for the bookworms and teacher's pets. Unlike Buffalo Bill, he wore spectacles and dressed in tailored suits and neckties almost every single day of his life. Sometimes he had on soft gloves and top hats when he gave speeches before large audiences. Wilson described himself this way: "I am a vague, conjectural personality, more made up of opinions and academic prepossessions than of human traits and red corpuscles."

Charley thought the President was solemn and scholarly. Along with preachers, judges, and doctors, Wilson was placed in a category of exalted figures beyond reproach. He clearly was not someone an ordinary kid had any desire to emulate. Charley would have just as soon patterned his life after the Sunday school superintendent or the Prince of Wales as pretend to be the President of the United States.

John Joseph "Black Jack" Pershing, a mustachioed Missouri warrior and ultimately America's first six-star general since George Washington, was quite another story, however. Here was a man any lively boy could mimic.

During summertime games in the days before the United States entered the conflict in Europe, the farm boys around Hanson pretended that Pershing and his troops had come to the rescue. Charley's patched overalls became Pershing's immaculate uniform. The imaginative boy pretended a folded Sallisaw newspaper was the general's smart cap with gleaming leather brim. Ribbons, once given out at the county fair for pear preserves or layer cakes, now masqueraded as battle decorations awarded for acts of bravery above and beyond the call of duty. Branches torn from sumac trees turned into make-believe sabers of forged steel, and wooden stakes used for holding up Mamie's tomato plants served as sham Enfield rifles. In the minds of Charley and his friends, dried cornstalks left standing in the field were really advancing enemy regiments, and sun-bleached corn leaves were glistening bayonets. Morning fog in the cotton patch became the Hun's deadly poison gas hovering over the trenches, and, with a bit of imagination, the frame schoolhouse was transformed into the French fortress at Verdun in 1916, the year before the United States went to war.

The general turned the heads of the more adventuresome young people who considered war to be child's play. They had grieved right along with Pershing when his wife and three of his four children burned to death in a fire at San Francisco's Presidio in 1915. They rallied with him when Pershing found just the therapy he needed—a call to arms. He gave his troops a taste of combat and also titillated the little boys back home as he pursued the revolutionary Pancho Villa and his elusive rebels along the Mexican border. Finally, in 1917, when Wilson at last asked Congress to declare war, Pershing got his chance to confront the German peril. The flocks of red-blooded lads who whistled and waved flags for the eager doughboys, who sailed to glory and gore at Belleau Wood and the Somme, had already fought and won thousands of rehearsal battles against the Kaiser in the yards and forests across America.

In the turbulent teenage years of the century, the disparate duo of Wilson and Pershing were but two of the vaulted names youngsters held in high regard. The country had more than enough icons to go around. Military and political leaders abounded. There were global explorers, big business tycoons, and stars from the fledgling motion picture business to choose from. Many of these instant folk heroes grabbed the headlines as well as the hearts and minds of much of America's youth. Sports figures captivated even more.

Major league baseball, having just reached the status of the national pastime, provided the public with the likes of Tris Speaker, Christy Mathewson, Cy Young, Larry Lajoie, Walter Johnson, "Shoeless" Joe Jackson, and Honus Wagner. A left-handed batter and right-handed thrower out of Narrows, Georgia, who played for the Detroit Tigers, was no slouch, either. Named Tyrus Raymond Cobb, his adoring fans knew him as Ty Cobb. He was the Georgia Peach. The Floyd brothers, all adept ball players themselves, approved of Cobb's fiery competitive spirit. They especially liked his daring base running characterized by the way he slashed spikes when he slid hard into the legs of opponents. Cobb was as tough as his last name.

There were other sportsmen worthy of worship. Jim Thorpe, a sturdy Sac and Fox Indian from near Shawnee, Oklahoma, was one of them. Thorpe excelled at several games, including football, and was considered by some to be the greatest athlete in the world. Charley, as well as every other farmer's son, was stunned when Thorpe confessed that he had earned wages playing professional baseball and thus was ruled ineligible to keep the track and field medals he had won for his record performances at the 1912 Olympics in Stockholm. "I was not very wise in the ways of the world and did not realize this was wrong," admitted Thorpe after the honors were stripped away. Lots of Oklahoma boys were sympathetic.

Charley and the other lads who liked a good scrap and wore their black eyes and split lips like badges of courage also admired the big-time prizefighters. Good news for many of those fight fans came in 1915 when Jess Willard, a 250-pound behemoth, gained notoriety as the Great White Hope after he defeated Jack Johnson, the first black to hold the heavyweight championship. Willard decked Johnson in the twenty-sixth round of a match held in Havana, Cuba, because Johnson's legal problems prevented him from fighting in the United States. Johnson had become involved with a white woman and was in trouble with the law for transporting her "across state lines for immoral purposes." While awaiting trial he jumped bail, left the country, and fought in exile. Years before, when he first won the heavyweight crown, the victory of a black man had touched off race riots throughout the nation resulting in the deaths of at least a half-dozen blacks. When Willard knocked out Johnson, there were predictable roars of approval across the land. Someone had finally taught that "uppity nigger" a lesson.

Charley knew the big Kansan could not retain the champ's crown for very long. There was a real battler waiting in the wings who fought under the name Kid Blackey. Charley had his eye on him all along. A savage puncher, the Kid was soon tagged with another nickname that was taken from the tiny Colorado town where he was born. He became known as the Manassa Mauler. His real name was William Harrison Dempsey, but he was better known simply as Jack, and those who climbed into the ring with him soon found out that he was capable of delivering stinging knockout punches when a fight was only a few seconds old.

Jack Dempsey was one of Charley Floyd's true idols. Charley followed his entire boxing career and never lost faith in the big pugilist. The payoff finally came in 1919 when Dempsey dethroned Willard and became the new champion of the world. So thorough and fierce was the thrashing Dempsey gave Willard that soon after the fight began many of the 45,000 spectators jammed into the Toledo Arena were screaming "Stop it! Stop it!" Just thirty seconds after the conclusion of the third round, Willard's seconds tossed two towels into the ring to signify their man's surrender. Down in Oklahoma, when Charley got word of Dempsey's victory, the fifteen-year-old was so pleased, he cheered himself hoarse. The hammering Dempsey, like the fleet-footed Cobb, was among Charley's favorite champions, but he also looked up to other prominent contemporaries.

Although the radio had not reached the Floyd home by World War I, Charley was reasonably aware of current events. He listened to his parents and their friends as they sat on the porch and discussed the fate of the world. Occasionally, he caught a glimpse of front-page headlines, or read the sports pages from a Tulsa newspaper. A thumbed-over copy of the *Kansas City Star,* left lying around a store, was more of a rarity. The big Sunday newspaper editions out of Tulsa were the best. They were filled with feature stories and comic strips, and in the rotogravure section were scads of photographs of the rich and famous. On posters displayed outside moving picture theaters, Charley saw the images of Tom Mix, Douglas Fairbanks, and Charlie Chaplin. He became familiar with the star bronc riders and bulldoggers of the wild West shows from the tour placards tacked on barns and fence posts.

However, some of Charley's best heroes were plucked straight out of the rudimentary literature and history lessons that were taught at the country school he attended. The curriculum was basic, presented by young men and women who had received teaching certificates after they matriculated from the eighth grade. Some teachers were only a few years older than their students. Interspersed with the arithmetic and penmanship exercises were the predictable sugarcoated accounts of the voyages of Christopher Columbus, the Pilgrims at Plymouth Rock, Colonial soldiers at Valley Forge, and the glories of Custer's Last Stand. Tales of Ivanhoe, Robinson Crusoe, Hiawatha, and Huckleberry Finn were also handed down along with stories about Daniel Boone, Kit Carson, George Washington, and Abe Lincoln.

To Charley, they were all impressive figures. But in his eyes, none of them—not the trim infantry officers in their Sam Browne belts nor the characters described in the history books, not the Georgia Peach drawing blood at second base nor Paul Bunyan and his Blue Ox, not even the great Jack Dempsey with his crushing paws of iron—held a candle to Jesse James.

In Jesse James, a prodigiously talented bank and train robber who was shot and killed in Missouri in 1882, Charley Floyd found his favorite hero of all. He worshiped the bloody ground over which the outlaw once rode.

James left his prints everywhere he went. Unknowingly, he spawned a great many legends throughout the countryside. In contrast to the other heroic figures Charley idolized, James was long dead and buried. But there were many presumably accurate accounts of the notorious outlaw that were passed around like a jar of moonshine making the rounds at a wolf hunter's midnight fire.

Charley eavesdropped on the discussions of old men who met at the country stores. When they had finished solving the problems of the world, these timeworn men were usually good for at least a couple of rousing stories about the days past when the James boys regularly visited the territory. No one dared challenge the authenticity of these tales; no one really wanted to. The old men's romanticized descriptions of wild chases, ill-gotten treasure, hangings, robberies, and shootings were sweeter than pecan pie to Charley Floyd. The murderer and robber had become a folk hero for an entire generation of boys, especially those who lived where the bandit once roamed.

No single criminal left so deep an impression on the American culture as Jesse Woodson James. He was Charley Floyd's guiding light.

10

AMERICA'S ROBIN HOOD

THE JESSE JAMES MYTHOLOGY had a lasting effect on Charley Floyd. Although he gobbled up a constant diet of half-baked yarns and distortions about James and his outlaw band, he still could not get enough. Like his elders, Charley was not concerned with authenticity. He was a schoolboy caught up in the glamour and romance of the James folklore. His appetite for such stories of the legendary desperado became voracious.

There was not a breath of doubt in Charley's mind that of all the glorified outlaw figures, Jesse James was irrefutably America's Robin Hood. And just like Robin Hood, the popular outlaw hero whose exploits with his band of Merry Men in Sherwood Forest became the staple of English ballads, James was also depicted as a gallant highwayman who robbed from the rich in order to give to the poor.

The James family, like the Floyds, traced its roots back many years to Wales. Members of the James clan came to America in the mid-1700s, and through the next century, branches of the family settled in Pennsylvania, Virginia, Kentucky, and finally Missouri. Born in 1847 in Clay County, Missouri, Jesse was the son of a devoutly religious mother and a Baptist minister who doubled as a farmer. Jesse's father left his family on their frontier farm near Kearney, Missouri, and headed to the California goldfields with the other forty-niners to strike it rich. Instead, he became ill and died, and was buried in an unmarked grave near a mining camp. Jesse and his older brother, Alexander Franklin James, or Frank, born in 1843, and their sister, Susan, born in 1849 just before their father left, were raised by their mother, who remarried briefly in 1851 and again in 1855.

The James boys grew up in an atmosphere of hate and fury. Missouri was a free state, but many people there, including the James family, sympathized with the South. Jesse and Frank were caught up in those turbulent years before the Civil War when abolitionist forces and proslavery raiders passed back and forth on the Missouri-Kansas border winning converts and convincing citizens to join their respective causes. Oftentimes, the standard method of persuasion was arson, and numerous towns and farms were attacked and burned. Rapes, robberies, beatings, and murders were committed in the name of the avenging God for both sides of the conflict. Innocents were caught in the cross fire.

When the Civil War commenced, the western counties of Missouri were already acquainted with the horrors of unbridled violence. Frank, and later Jesse and their first cousins, the Younger brothers, rode off to war and served as Confederate irregulars, better known as bushwhackers. They ended up in the guerrilla band of Confederate William Quantrill, the psychopath who was remembered by Northerners as "the bloodiest man known to the annals of America."

In August 1863, Frank James and Cole Younger were with Quantrill when he led 450 raiders into Lawrence, Kansas. The town was sacked and 182 of its citizens murdered. Jesse James and Jim Younger rode with Quantrill's lieutenant, Bloody Bill Anderson, just one year later at the Centralia, Missouri, massacre where more than two hundred Union soldiers, many of them prisoners, were shot and killed. During the terrible war, the James brothers learned the tactics of advance scouting and surprise attack. They honed their survival instincts, such as finding refuge at hideouts they had established in advance of their raid. These skills served them well in later years when they went on the prowl.

At the end of the war, most of the surviving Confederate soldiers who were granted amnesty by the federal government willingly laid down their weapons and went home to farm and put their lives back together. Not all of them were able to make the transition to a quiet civilian life, however, especially not the James boys. As they themselves pointed out, there were no guaranteed assurances of pardon for those who had ridden with Quantrill and the other guerrilla bands. It was even rumored that when young Jesse, with a white flag in hand, tried to surrender to federal troops, he was shot and left for dead.

Frank, a bookish man who enjoyed reading William Shakespeare and Francis Bacon, and the energetic Jesse, the natural-born leader of the duo who sang in the church choir whenever he went home, organized a band of former guerrillas. They later claimed they were forced to take to the outlaw trail by the northern establishment, which controlled the banks, railroads, and real estate.

"We were driven to it," Jesse remarked.

Friends and neighbors believed them and rallied to the James brothers' defense. Bankers and big-business interests were considered to be the real villains, not the James boys and their fellow riders who came from humble beginnings and were victims of the Reconstruction Republicans. Jesse and Frank told everyone they knew that they were persecuted and hounded because they had served with the Confederacy; they claimed they were interested in leading productive lives, but if they had to teach some of the Yankees a lesson, then so be it.

On the afternoon of February 14, 1866, the gang dressed in long soldiers' overcoats and armed themselves with Colt pistols. They rode into the town square at Liberty, Missouri, dismounted in front of the Clay County Savings Association, and entered the bank. With guns drawn, they terrorized the tellers and proceeded to "withdraw" $15,000 in gold and silver coins and greenbacks and about $45,000 in bonds. On the way out of town, a nineteen-year-old student from William Jewell College tried to get out of the bandits' path. One of the outlaws pumped four bullets into the boy. He was dead before he hit the street. The crime made headlines across the land. It was the first recorded daylight bank robbery in the nation's history.

There were reports that Jesse did not participate in the Liberty bank robbery, but nonetheless the brazen crime placed the James gang at the forefront of the public's consciousness. Afterward, additional bank robberies took place in Missouri and the surrounding states and were attributed to the James brothers and their followers. In 1869, the bank at Gallatin, Missouri, was robbed and a cashier was shot—some witnesses said executed—by one of the robbers. Jesse and Frank were positively identified as two of the culprits. For the first time, the James boys were not just suspects but were branded as wanted outlaws.

In response to the charges, Jesse and Frank launched a public relations campaign designed to clear their names. Jesse vehemently denied any wrongdoing, and he even penned a letter of protest to the governor of Missouri. The *Liberty Tribune* saw fit to publish the epistle, in which Jesse said, "[I can] prove by some of the best men in Missouri, where I was the day of the robbery and the day previous to it, but I well know if I want to submit to an arrest I would be mobbed and hanged without trial. . . . Governor, when I can get a fair trial, I will surrender myself to the civil authorities of Missouri. But I will never surrender to be mobbed by a set of bloodthirsty poltroons."

Jesse's words did not go unheeded. Soon the James bunch were worshiped as heroes by the economically disenfranchised as well as many of those citizens still loyal to the ways of the Old South. For more than sixteen years, the James brothers operated in several states, and were thought of by many to be caring bandits who were solely motivated by political and social injustice.

Jesse's showmanship reached its pinnacle in 1872 when he and two others swooped down on the Kansas City Fair and made off with the cash box. Although the bold robbery yielded only about one thousand dollars, a young girl was wounded by a stray bullet. The sheer audacity of the crime brought Jesse much attention, especially from the pro-Democratic newspapers. The day after the robbery, John Newman Edwards, a hero of the Confederacy and the editor of the *Kansas City Times,* praised the robbery as "a deed so high-handed, so diabolically daring and so utterly in contempt of fear that we are bound to admire it and revere its perpetrators."

Edwards went on to explain two days later that these men "are bad citizens but bad because they live out of their time." He compared them to those who might have sat with King Arthur at his Round Table and ridden into tournaments with Sir Lancelot. "Such as these are they who awed us on Thursday. . . . It was as though three bandits had come to us from the storied Odenwald, with halo of medieval chivalry upon their garments and shown us how the things were done that poets sing of."

About two weeks after Edwards's glowing editorial appeared, the *Times* published a letter purportedly written by a member of Jesse's band and perhaps even by "Dingus" James himself. Other newspaper editors and the critics of the Missouri outlaws' admiration society guffawed and said the letter undoubtedly came from none other than John Edwards. Whoever the author was, the letter defended the actions of the trio who had struck at the Kansas City Fair. An apology was extended for the accidental shooting of the little girl, and the mysterious writer offered to cover all medical expenses if her parents would send a bill and give their address through the newspaper columns. The letter also talked about the question of who was and who was not a thief.

Some editors call us thieves. We are not thieves—we are bold robbers. It hurts me to be called a thief. It makes me feel like they are trying to put me on par with Grant and his party. We are bold robbers and I am proud of the name, for Alexander the Great was a bold robber, and Julius Caesar, and Napoleon Bonaparte, and Sir William Wallace. . . . Please rank me with these and not with the Grantites. Grant's party has no respect for anyone. They rob the poor and rich, and we rob the rich and give to the poor. As to the author of this letter, the public will never know. I will close by hoping that Horace Greeley will defeat Grant, and then I can make an honest living, and then I will not have to rob, as taxes will not be so heavy.

In the presidential election of 1872, Grant handily defeated Greeley by taking 286 of the electoral votes. James did not get to hang up his guns and "make an honest living." He continued his life as a bank robber.

At least James could take solace in the continued praise and comfort he received from some of the newspapers as well as a large segment of the public. While Edwards of the *Times* served as almost an unofficial press agent for the gang, James proceeded to build the best possible image, especially considering that he was, after all, a career criminal. He gained support for his exploits by writing letters to newspapers and issuing statements and press releases, including one for a train holdup that was headlined THE MOST DARING ROBBERY ON RECORD. But by far his best ploy for winning public approval came from a series of carefully calculated deeds. Stories abounded about how Jesse and his boys shared their bounty with widows and orphans. Adoring fans said that when Jesse plundered a train, he examined the palms of the passengers and took valuables only from the "soft-handed ones," since, as one of Jesse's gang members said, they were "the capitalists, professors, and others that get money easy." One man, however, riding in a stagecoach robbed by Jesse and the boys, was given his money and pocket watch back when they found out about his loyal service in the Confederate army.

In 1874, James made his cousin Zerelda (Zee) Amanda Mimms a June bride. The occasion was treated like a major social event and was extensively covered by the nation's press, although not on the society page. The *St. Louis Dispatch* reported that finally Jesse had been corralled. His captor was a woman described as "young, accomplished, beautiful." As one historian later said, at last Robin Hood had his Maid Marian. But not everything was rosy for James. Trouble loomed ahead.

Desperate midwestern bankers grew weary of Jesse James and his antics. They hired Allan Pinkerton, the detective dubbed The Eye by the criminals he tracked, to take care of the James problem. A Scottish immigrant who had come to the United States as a young man to avoid arrest for his political activities, Pinkerton worked his way up through the police ranks and became a favorite of Abraham Lincoln when he uncovered a plot to assassinate the President. During the Civil War, Pinkerton acted as a sort of police chief for the federal government while he headed the Secret Service and gathered intelligence for the Union. In the years following the war, Pinkerton quickly became regarded as a henchman for big-business interests and helped to break up mining strikes in Pennsylvania. He was a scourge of the labor unions and the methods used by his men were ethically questionable. Pinkerton was as relentless as a terrier, and so were those who served under him and his two sons, Robert and William. The motto of their agency said it all: We Never Sleep. The Pinkertons and their small army of crack detectives, despised by the stalwart former Confederates of the border states, were determined to snare James, break up his gang, and shatter the outlaws' myth of invincibility.

From the very start, the Pinkerton agents assigned to track the James brothers found the going difficult. Residents of Clay County, Missouri, sided with Jesse and Frank, offering them protection from the snooping detectives. Those citizens who did not sympathize with the outlaws remained quiet out of fear. At least three Pinkertons were murdered during the course of the investigation. Finally, in 1875, a group of special agents, together with some local constables, managed to move in under cover of darkness and surround the James's family homestead. They were convinced Jesse was inside. Two illumination devices were tossed through a window of the farmhouse. One of the flares exploded and showered the room with iron shrapnel. Neither Jesse nor Frank was present but other family members were there. Zerelda Samuel, the James boys' mother, had her right arm shattered so badly that it had to be amputated, and Jesse's nine-year-old half brother was killed by the blast. Press coverage was immediate and overwhelmingly in support of the James family. The Pinkertons were denounced and lambasted. There were heated political debates and investigations about the incident. A grand jury indicted several men for murder. More cries for amnesty for the James brothers followed. So did bank and train robberies in Missouri, Kentucky, and Iowa.

On September 7, 1876, about ten weeks after Lt. Col. George Armstrong Custer and his entire command were annihilated by Sioux and Cheyenne warriors on the Little Bighorn River, the James gang ran into troubles of their own at Northfield, Minnesota. Since newspaper accounts had compared James to Napoleon, the gang's raid on the bank at Northfield, a small northern town far from the gang's familiar territory, was Jesse's Waterloo. Within moments of the Missourians' arrival in their fine linen dusters, all hell broke loose. An alarm went out that the bank was being robbed and the citizens responded. Farmers in town for the day along with merchants armed themselves with rifles and shotguns. Some of the locals threw rocks at the outlaws. In the heated battle that followed, three of the gang were killed outright and the three Younger brothers were shot and captured. Only Jesse and Frank managed to escape unscathed. In just twenty minutes, the desperado gang that had kept the nation entranced for more than a decade was decimated—but not forever.

The Younger brothers recovered from their wounds and went to prison. As he entered the Minnesota State Penitentiary, Cole Younger gave a newspaper reporter the standard James-Younger excuse for their lawless ways. "We were victims of circumstance," said Younger. "We were drove to it, sir."

Meanwhile, Jesse and Frank, although wounded by the posse that hounded them for more than a week, managed to make it to the Dakota Territory. Next, they went south to nurse their wounds and regroup. The brothers visited old haunts, including a few in the nations. They camped in the caves located in the San Bois Mountains and found hot meals and soft bunks at a sanctuary not far from the Indian Territory town of Eufaula, where the South Canadian River made a sweeping turn. Called Younger's Bend, this was the domain of Sam Starr and Myra Maebelle Shirley, also known as Belle Starr. A Missouri girl turned horse thief, Belle had been the lover of an array of outlaws, including Cole Younger, Jim Reed, Jack Spaniard, Jim July, and an Indian known as Blue Duck. She enjoyed her role as outlaw hostess as well as her celebrity status, particularly the many references to her as "the female Jesse James."

During the years when Frank and Jesse laid low after the botched Northfield robbery, they lived quietly under assumed names with their families in Tennessee. Proud of his two children born in Nashville, Jesse especially doted on his son, Jesse Edwards James, his own namesake. The boy's middle name honored the Kansas City newspaper editor who had written the heroic accounts of Jesse's life.

By 1879, even though public sentiment had turned against the James brothers, Jesse and Frank came out of retirement and returned to their old outlaw tricks. They emerged with a new gang and rode out in search of prey. However, the men they recruited were not like the former guerrillas—proud ex-Confederates—who had ridden with the James boys in the past. The new gang members were green and unseasoned. They sometimes overcompensated for their inexperience with extreme shows of violence. Not emotionally bound to the James brothers or each other through Civil War bloodshed, many of them drank too much, while others liked to brag and swagger about their exploits. James longed for the old days when every gang member who filled a saddle could be trusted like kinfolk.

Over the next few years, more banks and trains were robbed, but because of the large rewards on the heads of Jesse and Frank, a natural tension was created within the outlaw band. By the early 1880s, Jesse used the name Thomas Howard and had moved his family to a comfortable cottage on a hilltop in St. Joseph, Missouri. Gang members, however, were being picked off one by one. Some were killed, while others, who were apprehended, confessed to their sins and implicated their accomplices. The infamous James gang was crumbling.

On the morning of April 3, 1882, an event occurred that would become part of popular folklore. Two rookie gang members, Robert and Charley Ford, their minds on the staggering ten-thousand-dollar reward offered for James, decided the time had come to strike. During a secret meeting in Kansas City, Missouri Governor Thomas T. Crittenden had already assured the Fords of the substantial bounty. He had dangled full pardons before their eyes if they could deliver the outlaw leader dead or alive. After breakfast with the Ford boys, James, who had just returned from Indian Territory, where he had planned his next bank robbery, walked into the parlor and pulled off his coat and two pistols. When he climbed onto a chair to brush some dust off a picture,

Charley winked at Bob, who then drew his gun and fired a shot directly into James's head. Jesse James tumbled headlong to the floor. He was thirty-four years old and stone dead.

Bob Ford ran from the house screaming, "I have killed Jesse James!" Within hours, the news spread through the rest of the nation. A banner headline in the *St. Joseph Gazette* shrieked, JESSE, BY JEHOVAH! The fact that the desperado had been shot from behind in his own home by someone from his inner circle fueled the Jesse James myth and forever assured him of a niche in the annals of American folklore.

James's body was taken to the family farm near Kearney and he was buried in a field beneath a coffee-bean tree. An epitaph was cut in the marble tombstone:

> Jesse W. James
> Died April 3, 1882
> Aged 34 years, 6 months, 28 days
> Murdered by a traitor and a coward
> whose name is not worthy to
> appear here.

Five months after his brother's death, Frank James, weary of being hunted, strode into Governor Crittenden's office in Jefferson City, handed over his .44 Colt pistol, and surrendered. There was strong public sentiment in support of Frank. He was tried for his crimes and was, predictably, acquitted.

In subsequent years, Frank went on to do some public speaking. He worked at several jobs, including a position as a doorman at a St. Louis theater. For a few years, he operated a small farm near Fletcher, Oklahoma. Just before his mother died in 1911—the year the Floyd family moved from Georgia to Oklahoma—Frank returned to the James farm near Kearney, where he passed away in 1915. The following year, his cousin Cole Younger, who had been paroled from prison in 1901, died at Lee's Summit, Missouri. Both Frank and Cole lived out the rest of their lives as respectable citizens and as heroes. They maintained to the end that they were not outlaws at heart but had been driven to crime through persecution.

"A lot of robberies blamed on us we never did," Frank wrote when he was an old man preparing to meet his Maker. A good many folks agreed and took Frank at his word. Charley Floyd was one of them.

The stories of Jesse and Frank seemed wonderfully delicious to Charley, as rich and luscious as the divinity candy and chocolate fudge that made a boy's teeth ache. And like the confections Mamie Floyd kept squirreled away in hidden tins that her children usually found, Charley always came back for more. He wanted to know every detail about the elusive Jesse James. He was relentless in his pursuit, and he pestered Grandpa Floyd or some other old man with time on his hands to tell the outlaw stories again and again.

Tales of the James brothers and their crowd, forever portrayed as innocent victims of the Yankee authorities, were as addictive as those first few forbidden cigarettes Charley and the boys clumsily hand-rolled out behind the cedar trees. Jesse James's exploits, together with the stories of the old Indian Territory renegades, served as lessons in courage for Charley Floyd. He learned them very well.

P A R T

1 9 1 4
~
1 9 2 5

T W O

*"In the rotation of crops
there was a recognized season for wild oats;
but they were not sown more than once."*
—The Age of Innocence
(EDITH WHARTON, 1920)

K.C.Studio
FT. SMITH, ARK.

Pʀᴇᴠɪᴏᴜs ᴘᴀɢᴇ: *Choc FLoyd. Fort Smith, Arkansas.* Tᴏᴘ: *Walter Floyd and infant Charles Dempsey Floyd surrounded by hounds. Akins, Oklahoma, ca. 1925.* Bᴏᴛᴛᴏᴍ: *The Floyd family while Charley was on the harvest trail. Akins, Oklahoma, ca. 1922.*

Confiscation of bootleg moonshi[r]
McAlester, Oklahoma, 1930.

The Missouri Pacific Railroad
Depot. Sallisaw, Oklahoma.

11

MOONSHINE

IT NEVER CEASED to amaze Charley Floyd how only a swig of moonshine whiskey—clear as a new-born baby's piss—could loosen the tongue of any storyteller. Just a touch of corn liquor did the trick. It generally improved the telling of an outlaw tale, an Indian myth, or the high times of a fox hunt.

A good dose of home-brewed whiskey made the story—whether it was an escape by Jesse James or the flight of a white-tailed deer—much richer. Invariably, the stolen loot hidden in a cave doubled, the hanged man at the end of the rope twitched longer, and the painted whores of Fort Smith and Tulsa were prettier. A few more sips and the fighting cock that killed all the other roosters turned meaner; the catfish that managed to slip off the hook grew larger. And, upon reflection, the last batch of whiskey cooked up in the woods was the smoothest by a country mile.

Making corn whiskey was one of Walter Floyd's favorite pursuits. Drinking it was another. Like his neighbors and friends with ties to the Old South, Walter knew how to turn out decent sipping liquor. So did his brothers and their father before them and both of their grandfathers and their uncles and cousins. So did Walter's sons. He taught them about distilling whiskey just as he showed them how to shoot and fish, read signs in the woods, and track game. It was part of their way of life.

Whiskey resulted from the distillation of fermented grain mash. It originated in twelfth-century Ireland, where it was considered the "water of life." The early Floyds back in Wales discovered not a small amount of pleasure in a dram of whiskey aged in wooden barrels. No doubt they brought the distiller's art with them when they sailed to America. It was in Britain where King Charles II was the first to impose a tax on distilled spirits back in the 1600s. That action eventually resulted in the word *moonshiner* entering the language as a term for those who smuggled liquor past the tax collectors under the cover of darkness. In time, the whiskey smugglers became known as bootleggers, since they literally tucked small bottles of whiskey in their boot tops. Moonshining was then understood to be the act of distilling illicit whiskey.

Many early Scotch-Irish immigrants who came to America and settled in the southern Appalachian Mountains spent hours perfecting the practice of making whiskey. Various grains, including rye, wheat, and barley, could be used to produce whiskey, but in the mountains of Georgia and throughout most of southern Appalachia and the Ozarks, corn was the preferred ingredient. To avoid paying an excise tax on the whiskey, distillers operated on the sly. The timeless secrets for making Georgia Moon—also known as "white lightning," "panther's breath," "old bust head," "tiger's sweat," "woods whiskey," "rotgut," "mountain dew," "blue ruin," "ruckus juice," and "stump likker"—were passed down from father to son. Boys learned the three basic whiskey-making steps—mashing, fermentation, and distillation—just as the girls were taught how to make lye soap or apple butter.

There were significant differences between moonshine and quality bourbon, a type of whiskey perfected by a Baptist minister in eighteenth-century Bourbon County, Kentucky. Fancy bourbon came from a mash containing less corn, and it also had to be aged for two years in charred oak barrels. Most moonshine was, in fact, corn whiskey made from a mash that contained at least 80 percent corn. It had a sharp taste, but because there was little or no aging, there was no taste or color from a barrel. Moonshine was yellowish or white. Most of the Southern moonshiners, including Georgians and their descendants mixing mash in the woods of Oklahoma, made nothing but gallon after gallon of potent corn whiskey. They left the bourbon making to their Kentucky cousins.

In the days before Oklahoma's statehood, a Whiskey Trail was created in Indian Territory complete with hideouts and grazing fields used by bandits and whiskey runners alike to pasture their horses. Whiskey stills were scattered throughout the Cookson Hills of eastern Oklahoma. There were plenty of streams and creeks, and the bluffs and deep hollows were ideal for those who chose to "farm in the woods." Along with statehood in 1907, however, prohibition was one of the so-called reforms that was adopted. Oklahoma—the forty-sixth state—entered the Union as dry as a bone. The law forbade the manufacture, transportation, and possession of intoxicants. Despite the ban on liquor and the strength of such powerful pressure groups as the Oklahoma Anti-Saloon League and the Women's Christian Temperance Union, the dry state of Oklahoma remained moist, and even sopping wet in some quarters, thanks to the diligent efforts of moonshiners and bootleggers.

Making whiskey was not merely illegal as far as the government was concerned; it was a moral crime, as well. The venerable practice of producing and selling corn liquor continued despite protestations from those with temperance on their minds, who claimed strong drink would prove to be the country's downfall. They scowled and thrust accusatory fingers at those who made the prohibited whiskey and beer or patronized the bootleggers. They pitied the wives and prayed for the children who noticed that their father's personality was slightly altered after he paid a visit to the outhouse and stopped along the way to nip at the jar of homemade liquor stashed in the barn. They considered strong drink to be the telltale sign of a malignant society. They suggested that as long as bootleg whiskey was readily available, and those who drank it went to dances, school, and church, there would be trouble. Nothing was better than a whiff of whiskey to get tongues clucking. To the righteous and the zealous, all strong drink—including blackberry brandy, grape wine, and homemade beer—were the devil's brew. Along with dancing and card playing, alcohol was to blame for the corruption of their sons and daughters. It was the very manifestation of evil.

Despite such harsh sentiments, even some of the strictest of Baptists and Methodists found a way to justify the distilling and consumption of spirits. Some of them pointed out that strong drink was mentioned throughout the Bible. Noah carried wine aboard the ark, and according to the Good Book, one of his first acts after the floodwaters subsided was to plant a vineyard, make some wine, and get good and pickled. Psalm 104:15 spoke of essentials such as oil for light, bread for strength, and "wine that maketh glad the heart of man." A little nip now and then never hurt anybody. After all, some reasoned, had not St. Paul prodded Timothy to "drink no longer water, but use a little wine for thy stomach's sake and thine own infirmities"? Jesus himself turned cold water into wine at a wedding party and he also served it at his last meal the evening before he was crucified. A few wet proponents even ventured that the Lord might have offered his disciples some moonshine had the divine beverage been in existence in those days.

Whiskey surely served as a balm that helped restore a working man's spirit after a crop failed or a child died. It was a salve for troubled souls. It was also a hair shirt for the penitent. Getting drunk on Saturday night provided the wayward with a cathartic experience for the Sabbath. Standing there before God and his neighbors in a hot church with the windows raised, a man with a pounding head and a soul riddled with guilt could let the lyrics of the hymn written by a reformed eighteenth-century slave trader wash his sins away.

> *Amazing grace! how sweet the sound,*
> *that saved a wretch like me!*
> *I once was lost but now am found,*
> *was blind but now I see.*

It was a song with no guile, and became the basis for all Southern folk music. It was a song that was at once joyful and melancholy. It was a song that brought smiles and tears. At least twenty minutes were required to get through the entire hymn. By the time all five verses had been sung, the burden of sin and sorrow was lifted from the shoulders of even the most profane.

Through many dangers, toils, and snares,
I have already come;
'tis grace that brought me safe thus far,
and grace will lead me home.

Afterward, the repentant sinner, with wet eyes and the renewed love of Jesus in his heart, could look forward to the Wednesday-evening prayer meeting as well as the Saturday card game, or an evening coon hunt, when he would once again tumble off the wagon.

All religious implications and powers of reconciliation aside, whiskey acted as an economic commodity for many country people. It had a definite practical value. Those farmers who bootlegged and sold or traded corn liquor by the gallon considered their whiskey production to be another cash crop. Selling jars of moonshine helped keep oil in the lamps and food in the pantry. Many rural citizens thought of moonshining and bootlegging as respectable businesses.

A clay jug, or at least a quart-size fruit jar or two brimming with fresh whiskey, was standard fare at many social events such as weddings, political rallies, hog butcherings, or even funerals. For dances held at homes back in the hills, fiddlers in clean overalls, arriving on horseback and with the promise of a free supper on their minds, knew they would also get a few snorts of corn liquor out in the dark. A drink or two enabled them to rasp out one tune after another that kept folks dancing until the wee hours. Whiskey was also doled out as medicine to break fevers. Mixed with honey, hot water, and tea to make a toddy, whiskey brought relief from pesty chest colds. Mothers rubbed it on the gums of teething babies to ease their pain. A dash of the stuff settled nerves, fought off chills, brought relief to aching bones, and allowed a good night's rest for the elderly.

Most of all, whiskey was an essential ingredient at all fall and winter hunts. Corn whiskey was as important as the pack of dogs, as necessary as the guns and the bright hunter's moon lighting the night sky. Moonshine was as comforting as the bonfire the hunters stoked with squaw wood and half-truths while their hounds chased coons and opossums to the tops of sycamores and oaks. When the wild geese passed high in the heavens and the air was cold enough for a hunter to see his own breath, a spot of strong drink went a long way.

Folks said that whiskey "helps to kill the poison in the night air." Some geezers out cutting timbers for railroad ties took drinks from a freshly made batch and explained that the whiskey protected them from snakebites. They would wink and take another long tug, even though they knew that if they were ever bitten by a cottonmouth moccasin or a rattlesnake, the alcohol would cause the venom to surge through their system faster than ever.

There were probably more recipes and techniques for cooking whiskey than there were for making peach pie or cream gravy. Although the basic steps were always the same, each moonshiner had his own special and mostly secret method for producing corn whiskey. No two men distilled white liquor in quite the same way. Each one was proud of his own particular formula. Whenever an especially mellow batch was distilled, even the most discriminating drinkers would not turn up their noses at a jigger of *'shine.* "If it's older than a year, the mellowness will make you breathe deep and happily" is how one master moonshiner explained it. "If it's stilled less than a month, there's a zip that curls around your neck when you sniff it."

When he was still a boy, Charley Floyd became familiar with the smell of cooking mash on the breeze. He knew that only a novice at whiskey sniffing would place his nose closer than two inches from the mouth of a jug or jar when trying to determine the age and quality of some moonshine. Walter taught him to select the best corn and to cull out the rotten and discolored grains. He learned how to turn out the corn malt that came from changing the starch of the corn into sugar and he found out about hurrying the process by burying sacks of unground corn in the manure pile, where it was always good and warm. Once the corn sprouted, it was dried and ground into a coarse meal called corn grits, or "chop." Water and sugar were added, and the mixture was made into a mush called sweet mash. The mash was allowed to stand in a barrel in a warm place for several days and ferment, and then it was thinned out with more water. Again the concoction was covered and ripened some more until the sweet mash soured as the sugar changed to alcohol. Now the time was right to distill.

Out in the Oklahoma hills, it was said that an experienced moonshiner actually listened to the mash. He knew it was ripe and time to cook in the still when it sounded like side pork in a pan. Farmers had no way actually to test the strength or the proof of their whiskey, and so in order to measure the alcoholic content, they relied on their own judgment, years of experience, and a simple procedure. When a moonshiner shook a jar of fresh whiskey and the foam, or the "bead," rose in small bubbles about the size of number-five bird shot, the proof was just right. "This stuff holds a purty good bead," a moonshiner would tell his friends. If instead the bead would not stand up and remained full of big, loose bubbles that looked like bulging frog eyes, the moonshiner knew he had whiskey that was unworthy of putting in a clean fruit jar. "I don't believe this here beads so good," a moonshiner would then say.

While the old Georgia-bred moonshiners religiously went through the time-tested steps for making corn whiskey, some of the younger bucks thought that process was slow and too much trouble. This younger generation born with the new century looked for a shortcut. Some did not even use corn, and few, if any, corn chops. Instead, they made powerful alcohol that had the kick of a mule by using only water, yeast cakes, and plenty of sugar and bran. They could turn out a fresh batch every few days. A handful of oak chips thrown in provided a little odor and gave the liquor an aged look. Some of the country folks called this one-hundred-proof whiskey, made with only a small amount of corn to start fermentation, "sugar liquor" or "sugar jack." It may not have tasted quite like Georgia Moon, but the end result after consumption was the same. The fiddle music whined just as sweetly, the girls appeared just as comely, and the headache was every bit as mean. And, the morning after a jar of that stepped-up moonshine was drained, the poetry of "Amazing Grace" would still make a band of angels weep.

After the first batch of bran or corn whiskey was run off, any respectable moonshiner knew that the "singlings," a cloudy liquid corrupted with pollutants, had to be purified and the still pot thoroughly cleaned before a second run could be made. Spent mash, or the slop, was thrown out in the barnyard and emptied into feed troughs. It often made roosters that imbibed fall down dead drunk. Likewise, it soothed cattle that managed to get a snootful. Once the slop was pitched, the pot was washed out with some of the unstrained sour beer, or the "choc," that was left in the mash barrel. A good many folks were satisfied by just drinking the murky choc. It was considered a neighborly gesture to put some in a jar and offer it to thirsty friends who came calling.

The word *choc* no doubt came from Choctaw beer, originally a synthetic drink made of barley, hops, tobacco, fishberries, and a small amount of alcohol, which had been schemed up in the old days of the Choctaw Nation. For many years, the law had made it illegal to sell or manufacture choc beer, but the prohibition statutes were often ignored. Wives from the mining communities that dotted Oklahoma supplemented their husbands' wages by selling the beer. It seemed miners especially enjoyed sipping choc. They swore by the renegade brew and insisted it was an essential tonic for their good health. In the oil-field camps—frequented by bootleggers, gamblers, and two-bit whores—a basic 120-proof alcoholic drink that was colored with tobacco juice or creosote was a favorite. Choc beer and "Jamaican" gin—nothing but raw alcohol flavored with gingerroot or bitters—were also much sought-after intoxicants. Those who invested their paychecks at the saloons and barrel-houses or with the local bootlegger often were stricken with "jake leg," a paralysis caused by the consumption of too much strong liquor. Men with muscles hard as walnuts shrugged it off as an occupational hazard.

When Charley visited his mother's kinfolk in the mining district around McCurtain, Oklahoma, he watched the men guzzle choc beer after they had scrubbed the coal dust from their hands and faces. They claimed the brew was better for them than the drinking water available in the area. Sometimes they gave the growing boy sips from their jars. Back home in Sequoyah County, out among the post oaks and brush, Charley developed a taste for this cloudy ferment that was found in the bottom of the mash barrel. He dipped out cups of choc and slurped it down every chance he got.

One afternoon when Charley and his big brother, Bradley, were tending their father's still, they noticed that a stud horse was having a difficult time breeding with a young mare in a nearby pasture. Charley watched for a few minutes and came up with a clever solution. He reached into the bottom of the choc barrel, whistled the mare to him, and slapped a handful of the mash on the skittish horse's rear end. In an instant, the frustrated stallion mounted the ripe mare and, with the help of the lubricant, drove it home as smooth as satin. The sight of the big stallion snorting over the filly made Charley grin, and Bradley saw to it that the story of his brother helping the horses get together spread faster than heat lightning.

Charley Floyd's taste for wild beer, along with his ingenuity at playing Cupid with a pair of amorous horses, created a nickname for the farm boy that some people, mostly his running buddies, called him from his early teens until his death.

Choc Floyd is what they would say when they saw him riding lickety-split on a hell-bent horse down a dirt farm road with the wind at his back: "Here comes Choc Floyd."

12

AKINS, OKLAHOMA

B Y THE CLOSE OF 1916, as the United States neared intervention in the war and as German U-boats declared open season on neutral steamships, Choc Floyd and his family prepared to plow fresh fields near their new and larger home. They had moved only a few miles from Hanson to Akins, another Sequoyah County farming community located about eight miles northeast of Sallisaw. Walter's parents, Charles and Mary Floyd, and his younger brothers, Buman and Burley, lived in Akins, and they maintained some productive farmland nearby. Now, with Walter and Mamie's sizable brood residing in Akins, the entire community seemed to be dominated by the Floyd clan.

Akins became Choc Floyd's favorite place to live. Years later, no matter where he roamed, Choc told folks that only one place was his home: Akins, Oklahoma.

Long before any of the Floyds arrived on the scene, Akins had been called Sweet Town, probably because of all the sorghum molasses that was made there. In 1890, a post office was established and the village took the name of Winchester, but that post office lasted only one year and then was discontinued. In 1894, the postal service reestablished another office in one of the general stores, and a short time later, the town became known as Akins, after Robert Akin, a former postman.

The town boasted a few small grocery stores, a barber, blacksmith, and a cotton gin. The Baptists had worshipped at a church in Akins since 1885. They kept a strict watch on their flock and enforced scriptural discipline. Church members who gossiped, used profane language, or were caught picking strawberries, fishing, or dancing on the Sabbath were brought before the elders. Freight wagons hauled supplies out to Akins from Sallisaw, and there were doctors, preachers, a justice of the peace, and a constable to help keep life civil. Over the years, the town's school had grown from a plain cabin with a floor divided by smooth split logs for the girls and a dirt floor for the boys to a two-story log house. Later, a one-room boxed building arose, and, in 1909, the last schoolhouse was built. Here the younger Floyd children attended classes. It was a two-story frame building and the second floor was used as a meeting place for the Woodmen of the World, for the Odd Fellows, and as a rehearsal hall for the town's brass band. Walter Floyd and other Masons in good standing, who belonged to Mt. Moriah Lodge No. 29, also met at the schoolhouse from 1914 until 1920, when they consolidated with a Masonic lodge at Sallisaw.

Akins provided a real feeling of kinship. This was evident back in 1903 when the residents set up the first community Christmas tree, lighted with candles and trimmed with popcorn and wild holly berries and tufts of cotton for snow. There was much food and drink and some of the boys shot clumps of mistletoe out of the treetops. Legend held that mistletoe, a parasite that would one day become the official state flower of Oklahoma, was once a larger tree, but when the wood was used for the Cross on which Christ was crucified, the tree shriveled in shame. The boys in Akins did not put much stock in the old legend. Rather, they cared about finding an excuse to kiss a pretty girl who passed beneath a sprig of mistletoe tacked in a doorjamb. Sam Martin, a local farmer who dressed like Santa Claus in a white robe, walked through town ringing a cowbell. Families exchanged gifts with one another, and years later, everyone still talked about the fancy saddle that Perry Boydston received that Christmas.

Through the years, people continued to meet for dances and on special occasions at someone's dogtrot home, a cabin characterized by an open breezeway between the living quarters. They also pitched horseshoes or watched the local boys, including the Floyd brothers, play baseball in a cleared hayfield.

Some of the best-known families in the region settled in or around Akins. The one-room log cabin built in 1828 by Sequoyah, the lame mixed-blood who developed the eighty-five-character Cherokee syllabary, was still standing just a few miles east of Akins. The cabin was occupied by a family who had purchased the homesite from the celebrated Sequoyah's widow. Besides the Cherokees who lived in the area, there were many other descendants from white families in Georgia and neighboring southern states. Choc Floyd came to know all their surnames, whether they had Indian blood or not. Many of the Akins families followed a pattern similar to the Floyds; they had also first settled at the railroad town of Hanson when they had arrived in Oklahoma. Faulkner, Boydston, Amos, Fullbright, Cheek, Lessley, Humphrey, Fine, Wickett, Green, Lattimore, Masterson, Mills, Gann, and Miller were but some of the family names associated with Akins. Choc's sisters and brothers and the many Floyd cousins married into these families and started families of their own.

They were all hardworking people without much book learning, but they possessed common sense and the ability to fend for themselves. They held to the customs of another time and never considered them to be superstitions but, rather, simply habits and traditions that deserved to be respected and kept.

Many of these customs were taken from the Indians; for example, the Cherokee belief that if a person pointed at a rainbow, the bone would come out of the fingertip; the Creek warning never to step on a grave, especially a child's, or the trespasser's feet would ache for at least a week. Others were sayings, remedies, and cures that their grandparents had been taught when they were children.

There were curious adages, such as the one that contended that when babies smiled in their sleep, they were talking to angels, or that toads brought warts to the hands of those who touched them. Some of the old women swore that they could get rid of rats by writing them a letter and sealing it with butter. Those same crones paid close attention to the exact day of the week when they trimmed their fingernails. They believed that each itch and pain had a secret meaning, as did every dropped spoon and dishrag or the time of year when a frog croaked and the dandelions bloomed.

In the absence of scientific technology, the country folks watched the weather signs. The clouds, sun, and sky were accurate indicators and much of the other forecasting was the result of observing animal behavior. If a hound dog constantly sniffed the air, the weather was about to change. Crickets chirping inside the house were actually discussing the long winter that was ahead. Rain was expected to come soon whenever dogs ate grass, cats licked their fur or sneezed, or owls hooted in the daytime. A crow flying unusually high meant a windstorm was approaching. It was also said that "onion skin mighty thin, mild winter coming in."

Besides the number thirteen, spilled salt on the table, and a black cat running across someone's path, bad luck was sure to come when a hat was laid on a bed, a horse's name was changed, or wood was burned from a tree that had been struck by lightning. Fortunately, there were also many good-luck omens. Eating black-eyed peas and hog jowl on New Year's Day assured good luck for the entire year, and horseshoes, four-leaf clovers, and rabbit feet all had their place.

With the Lord Almighty's guidance and a modicum of good luck, many of the citizens of Akins believed they could make it on their own with little or no help from the outside world. They were from solid pioneer stock and could build a house, shoe a horse, field-dress a deer, make soap, and work a cotton patch or cornfield with the best of them. They mastered the art of building a proper fire in a fireplace, using slow-burning hickory or oak instead of the sticks of apple wood and sassafras that popped and threw sparks or evergreen logs that filled the chimney with oily tar. In the autumn, they made sorghum molasses from the harvested cane and the children ate the skimmings off the syrup pans. The citizens of Akins worked together, and nobody ever even thought about locking the door. In the evenings, they sat on their porches and watched deer come from the creek bottoms to nibble the clover. If there was ever a need to discipline a wayward youngster, parents could cut a huckleberry switch. When someone in the community died, neighbors brought food to the survivors. They washed and dressed the corpse and sat vigil every night until the burial. Afterward, they came back to clean the house and wash the bedclothes. There was a true sense of caring and duty.

Walter Floyd and his bunch took their rightful place in the community just as easy as pie. The Floyds raised almost all of their own food, including sweet and Irish potatoes, tomatoes, peppers, squash, okra, and pumpkins. They picked and canned fruit from apple and peach trees, and kept cows and chickens. They fattened hogs for slaughter after the first hard freeze, cured their own meat, and rendered enough lard to last the whole year. Mamie and her girls washed clothes on rub boards with tubs of water heated in heavy iron kettles. The women also made bars of soap, using meat scraps or melted bacon fat, hot water, and lye. Sometimes the homemade soap contained wood ashes cooked up in a huge pot with the hog lard. One scrubbing with the strong soap each Saturday night was usually enough to keep even the dirtiest farm boy clean for at least a week.

Soon after moving to Akins, the Floyds enjoyed a successful growing season that yielded one bale of cotton per acre. Walter earned some extra income by hiring himself out as a county road worker during the summer and sold moonshine liquor to thirsty big-city Shriners and Masonic brothers. With the additional wages, he saw clear to lease more fertile land for corn and cotton. He also decided to splurge. He purchased the Floyd family's very first automobile. It was a Ford touring car.

The Floyd youngsters were wild with excitement when Walter drove the shiny black automobile out to Akins and right up to the porch of the family's new home. Mamie was not quite sure what to think, but if her husband's extravagance bothered her, she said nothing. Choc and Bradley were far from quiet. They shrieked rebel yells that would have made their ancestors proud. The boys pestered their father until he allowed them supervised turns behind the steering wheel. They drove the Ford down to the creek and washed it so often that Walter was afraid they would wear the paint off. The boys learned how to fine-tune the motor and they fussed over the automobile just as if it were one of their finest horses.

Walter also tried to teach his eldest daughter, Ruth, a seventeen-year-old schoolteacher at the Rocky Point community, how to drive. He felt sorry that she had to walk home every weekend from work. He lost his patience after only one test run, however. She had handled the auto to Walter's satisfaction on the country roads, but when they returned home and he got out in order to open the gate, there was trouble. Instead of waiting for her father, the nervous Ruth unintentionally mashed her foot on the accelerator. The Ford lurched forward and crashed through the wooden gate like an angry bull. Walter jumped out of the way in the nick of time. As far as he was concerned, Ruth could continue to rely on her feet to get around.

One stormy night not long after the Floyds moved to Akins, Ruth and her sister Ruby found themselves on foot after they had attended a party at a friend's house and were trying to make it home in a driving rainstorm. Thunder crashed around them and the roads turned into rivers of mud. The only way the young women could see was when long streaks of lightning tore through the black sky. Ruth and Ruby knew better than to seek refuge under one of the swaying trees, but they also realized their chances of being struck by lightning were just as good as if they stayed out in the open. Although they were as acquainted with the county's back roads as well as anyone, the young women were not as familiar with the shortcuts near their new home. The intensity of the storm only made the situation worse.

Family legend had it that suddenly, out of the night, a figure on horseback appeared. It was Charley. There before them was none other than their little brother riding bareback through the torrential rain. His woolen cap was pulled down over his face and he was grasping the horse's thick mane. Before the girls could cry out, Charley had pulled up the horse next to them.

"Grab hold of the tail," Charley yelled. "Grab hold of it, and don't let go for anything!"

Ruth and Ruby did as they were ordered. Both girls clutched the horse's tail, and Charley led them through the pelting rain down the flooded road. Soon they spied the oil lamps burning in the windows of their home. There on the porch was Mamie in a patched sweater, with a shawl over her head, waiting for her children like a silent angel. It took an hour to clean the mud off the girls' legs and feet, and to dry their hair. They sat wrapped in quilts before the fire and sipped hot toddies. They told the rest of the family about the dance and how the storm had suddenly descended on them and how scared they were until Charley had appeared like an outlaw ghost. They smiled at Charley, who now sat cross-legged in his long underwear across the room. He smiled back, and then he quickly ducked his head before Bradley and the others could tease him.

By the time he reached his teens, Choc's school days were coming to a close. Although he was as bright as the next one, Charley Floyd saw no future in going on beyond grammar school. Like most farm youths of his day, he received little or no encouragement to do so from his parents. Six or maybe even eight years of school was enough for any tenant farmer's child. When a boy reached puberty, the time had come for him to take his place in the world and go to work. Having started his elementary education in Adairsville, Georgia, Choc continued at the Hanson school and finished up with a brief stint at Akins. He believed that high school held no real promise.

Choc's life work seemed clear. Like his father before him, he would raise corn, cotton, and children. He would run his hounds and make a jug or two of corn whiskey out in the woods. He would go to church and prayer meetings, grow old with his brothers and sisters, and tend to his parents' needs in their final years. However, this was not his own game plan. He could not say exactly how he would end up as a grown man, but he was already convinced that there was more to life than a mule and a plow. There was plenty to see beyond the Oklahoma backwoods.

Choc was quite determined by the time he reached his thirteenth birthday. He was confident of himself and his ability to get ahead. Everyone around him also knew that he was not someone with whom to trifle. He would never turn down the opportunity to fight for his rights or for something in which he believed. That was especially true if a fellow he was fighting was considered to be a bully. Anybody dumb enough to back Choc Floyd into a corner soon found out what it was like to tangle with a wildcat. The sturdy youngster with muscular arms and shoulders was a pure competitor. He excelled at both team and individual sports. He could pole vault, run footraces, and did well at football, basketball, and baseball. He also wrestled as well as anyone in the county. He also knew how to use his fists.

Choc showed his true grit just before he ended his schooling when three local boys in their late teens approached the schoolhouse in a wagon. The ringleader of the trio had a bellyfull of moonshine and was intent on calling on the young woman teacher. He was a mean drunk, and his two friends did their best to keep him from causing a disruption. He was big and strong, though, and they finally went along with him. When the three of them burst through the door, the young woman scolded them in the most stern schoolmarm voice she could muster, but she was about their age. They only laughed and kept coming. Several of the bigger boys from the eighth grade got up and came to her rescue. They wrestled the invaders out the door and a fight commenced. Within minutes, the three rowdies had whipped the schoolboys and run them off. Before they could start to gloat, however, from out of nowhere came a compact cyclone with a Jack Dempsey punch.

It was Choc Floyd, and he was as pissed off as anyone had seen him. His arms were in constant motion and he battled with the measured grace of a contender. Just a few well-placed licks and the scowl on his face were enough to cause the two sober boys to back off and watch with the others. Choc then turned his full attention to the drunk. His fists slammed into the big boy's nose, mouth, and jaw. Decades later, old men and women could still recall the ugly sound of bone and cartilage cracking as Choc punched and jabbed. Blood and spittle dripped from the drunk's chin and then Choc drove a fist into his stomach. That ended it. He beat the tough guy senseless in no time flat. When the fellow was lying on his back in the dust, Choc fetched some rope and he bound the big boy like a boar hog for market. With help from the two forlorn accomplices, Choc pitched him headfirst into the back of the wagon. He told the boys to never pull a stunt like that again, and he sent them on their way. It was a classic case of a ruffian getting his comeuppance. From that afternoon on, Choc Floyd was a hero for more than one farm youngster.

Choc's proficiency with his fists allowed him never to leave a challenge unanswered. Even when a large gang of farm toughs attacked him one afternoon in Sallisaw and tried to gouge out one of his eyes, Choc kept fighting despite the stream of blood and the pain. It took an operation to save his eyesight. After one of the town doctors stitched up the boy's wounds and worked on the injured eyeball, Choc only laughed and talked about how many punches and kicks he had been able to land before the others got the best of him. Word got around that Choc Floyd was not someone to pick on.

Choc became in no time a take-charge type, a natural-born leader. The rest of the boys usually went along with whatever he suggested. Frank "Tickey" Green, Cleon Amos, Aud Farmer, Orphus Franks, and James "Soap" Masterson were some of his closest pals. Together, they were a formidable bunch, filled with mischief and fun. Suntanned and hardheaded, they were intrepid young men.

These were also young men smart in the ways of the woods. When they were just lads, they had learned the hard lessons of life. To make extra money, they trapped opossum and mink for their skins. They listened to the calls of song birds to learn whether someone else was approaching in the forest. They knew how to make a camp fire in the rain, and painful experience taught them that if they did not want to get skunked when they went fishing, they had to get the best bait possible. So they filled tin cans with the fat worms that feasted on the big heart-shaped leaves of the catalpa trees and brought home a mess of crappie and perch. Spitting on the baited hook also brought them good luck. They were wary of hand-fishing, or "noodling," as it was called, when they waded along the riverbanks and searched for fish to grab by the gills and mouth. They stayed mindful of snakes and sinkholes, and were always aware that the rocks and logs below the murky water could conceal a muskrat or beaver or a snapping turtle. Or there might even be a lunker catfish—big as a small boy—that was never anxious to get yanked from its resting place.

Choc and his friends had a passion for the hunt. In the winter, they would wrap their feet in toe sacks and chase rabbits through the snow and follow opossum by lantern light. They looked forward to shooting matches that sharpened their marksmanship. The best shooters stepped off a hundred yards or more and fired with deadly accuracy at bottles and tin cans or paper targets pinned to fence posts. Their horseback-riding prowess would have pleased Jeb Stuart. They all seemed to know the value of good hunting dogs. Walter had kept hounds all his life and he taught his sons how to care for their dogs and horses and keep them in shape for those long chases after wolves and foxes.

Walter and his boys at one time even owned twenty-eight fine hounds that resided at the Floyd home at Akins. All of them were deep-chested and of single intent. Choc's favorite hound was named Buck, a streamlined dog with long ears and a sickle-shaped tail. Buck lived for nothing else but hunting and dreamed about stalking wild game and running full tilt through the open fields and river bottoms. Oftentimes the eager hound, as aggressive as his lively master, would get loose and run off with another pack of dogs out on a hunt. Most of the time, the breathless Buck would return to the Floyd place with the fox's severed paw or tail tied around his neck, which showed that he had sniffed out the quarry before all the others.

Choc liked riding his horse through the woods with old Buck and the other hounds baying far ahead. He also knew the pleasure that came from being alone before sundown under a clump of big trees, with his back against an oak that had grown tall before any white men were around. Sometimes Choc slipped away from the other boys. He went across the fields and into the woods. He watched the birds head for cover as the sun sneaked away and the moon rose. He saw the silhouettes of cattle on the hills. It was good to be there with not another soul to talk to, a time just to listen to the last echoes of the dying day.

13

OVER THERE

HOC FLOYD WAS A THIRTEEN-YEAR-OLD field hand laboring alongside his father and older brother the day the United States went to war. The days of imaginary combat for farm boys yielded to the real thing. Prodded by public opinion, angered over the immoral submarine warfare waged by the German navy, Woodrow Wilson went to the Congress on April 2, 1917, with the recommendation that the United States take up arms against Germany and go to war. Wilson spoke of the German menace, which he said was like "a madman that needed restraining." He also called for a new world order, not a renewal of the old.

"The world," commented Wilson in his most-quoted speech, "must be made safe for democracy."

On April 4, the majority of the Senate agreed with the President. Two days later, after seventeen hours of emotional debate, the House followed suit. Congress voted overwhelmingly in favor of sending America to war against the imperial German government and its forces. The news flashed around the world. Afterward, Wilson returned to the White House and wept. In homes and farmhouses around the country, others also cried.

It was Good Friday. Throughout much of the nation, Christian worshippers filed into the rural churches and big-city cathedrals to mark the anniversary of Christ's Crucifixion. Jews, also preparing for the Passover celebration, lifted prayers for peace and for a swift resolution to the struggle. That afternoon in New York, as U.S. government agents seized German-owned vessels and rounded up suspected enemy spies, the popular composer George M. Cohan, inspired by newsboys who screamed out headlines on the streets, sat down and wrote "Over There." It was a catchy tune that both country folks and city slickers would make their anthem during the dark days ahead.

Across the Midwest and southern plains, a hint of spring lay in the air. In Oklahoma, the weather was already balmy. Men and boys waited at the Sallisaw barbershops to get their Easter haircuts, and farmers congregated at the general mercantile store in Akins so they could trade stories and purchase supplies. When they saw the front page of the *Tulsa World,* they realized their lives would be soon upended. They trudged home past the growing fields still waking from a winter's sleep and prepared for the worst. They did not have long to wait.

The following month, Congress passed the Selective Service Act, which authorized the registration and draft of all able-bodied American men between twenty-one and thirty. America must mobilize and turn the tide of the war. Eventually 4 million Americans entered the armed services, with more than half of them going overseas to fight in the bloody trenches in what was considered to be the greatest military conflict the world had ever experienced up to that time.

The First Regiment of Oklahoma's National Guard had been on active duty since 1916, acting as a part of the force mustered under "Black Jack" Pershing to pursue Pancho Villa along the Mexican border. While local draft boards went to work, farmers and ranchers were urged by the government to strive for maximum production. The public learned to live with meatless days and saved peach pits to be used for gas-mask filters. There were Liberty Loan drives. More than 91,000 Oklahomans would see military duty. Many would be killed or maimed. Others would succumb to disease, especially Spanish influenza.

Certainly not every American, including a number of Oklahomans, was anxious to go to battle. Not since the Civil War had the nation been so divided. Oklahoma's Democratic Senator Thomas P. Gore, a masterful orator who had been blind since childhood, was an outspoken opponent of Wilson's intervention. In the first months of war, there were numerous demonstrations against the military draft staged throughout the country and Oklahoma. A caricature of Woodrow Wilson with the caption "The Man Who Sends Your Boys to Die on Foreign Soil" made the rounds, and the President was identified as Kaiser Wilson. Many of the rural residents still backed Wilson, but they were more concerned with problems at home. They were not convinced of the need for the United States to get involved in a war so far away.

A growing number of disgruntled Oklahoma farmers had flirted with socialism in previous years, and when the United States entered the war, the Socialist party, at one time a strong force especially in the cotton-producing counties, made every effort to capitalize on the rural regions' widespread opposition to America's participation. Political-action groups, labor-union organizers, and committed agitators stayed busy on the home front insisting that the conflict in distant Belgium and France was nothing but a "rich man's war and a poor man's fight." Some discontented farmers and sharecroppers, struggling to make a living, resisted the draft as a form of protest against what they perceived to be social and economic inequities.

A schism formed in Oklahoma. Some called it a war between the classes. On one side were the mostly affluent and upper-middle-class business leaders and white-collar workers from Oklahoma City and Tulsa. They made up the urban central section of the state. They were typically Republican, attended the Episcopal church, and had few if any sympathies for a working class they considered to be backward, corrupt, and lazy. On the other side were rural Oklahomans, many with Indian blood or others whose ancestors were European immigrants who had come to the United States to find honest labor. They were tenant farmers, ranchers, or worked in the mines and oil fields. For the most part, they were Methodists and hard-shell Baptists. They adhered to populist Democratic party lines. Some were Roman Catholic with old-world values. They lived in modest homes with no indoor plumbing or electricity, and their children wore overalls and went barefoot until winter arrived. A region of rural southeastern Oklahoma even became known as Little Dixie because of the political and social views of the tenant farmers and coal miners who lived there. Many of the fine folks who built elegant homes in the state's two main cities, Tulsa and Oklahoma City, worked for big-business interests, oil companies, or banks. They had family and business ties to the established cities of the eastern United States. The large majority of the residents in Little Dixie were the offspring of refugees from defeated Indian nations, the Reconstruction South, or Southern Italy.

In the summer of 1917, some of those country people rebelled. As newly inducted American troops trained for combat, a band of hundreds of laborers and tenant farmers—poor whites, blacks, and Native Americans—roamed through several Oklahoma counties. Part of a much larger group that advocated revolutionary tactics to gain the elimination of rent, interest, and government-owned public utilities, they were also displeased with the country's entry into the war. These militants burned bridges, tore down fences, cut telephone lines, and dynamited oil pipelines, sewers, and water mains to show their strong aversion to the draft and the war in Europe. The rebels' ultimate goal was to march all the way to Washington, D.C., in order to compel the government to pull out of the war. They subsisted by foraging ears of green corn from fields along the route and mixing the corn with barbecued beef to make an Indian stew called *tomfuller* for nourishment.

What became known as the Green Corn Rebellion was quickly crushed along the banks of the South Canadian River in south-central Oklahoma by the authorities and posses of patriotic vigilantes and citizen policemen. The guerrilla leaders of the rebellion were arrested, and newspaper editorials demanded that the dissidents be imprisoned for life or, better yet, go straight to the gallows. Ultimately, eighty-six men were tried and sentenced to prison terms ranging from one to five years. There was some disagreement about the goals of the rebellion. Most state leaders maintained the participants were nothing but a mob in search of a cause. Others were kinder and even sympathetic. Many of the participants said it was more than an antidraft revolt; it was a protest against an unjust economic system. Nonetheless, the prevailing message was very clear that there was no room or tolerance for dissent in Oklahoma. Pacifists and critics of the war effort were as welcome as boll weevils.

As was the case elsewhere in the country, a great propaganda machine churned out a constant stream of rhetoric designed to attack socialist ideas and to intimidate anybody not prepared to grab a rifle and go after Kaiser Bill and his fiendish troops. The International Workers of the World, or the Wobblies, who actively recruited new members in Tulsa, were arrested by the police and harassed by right-wing extremists. Groups such as the Knights of Liberty and the American Protective League, who were largely opposed to labor unions and the antiwar crowd, acted as self-imposed watchdogs on the lookout for those identified as subversives and rabble-rousers. The word *slacker* was coined and applied as a badge of public scorn for all those who supposedly shirked their patriotic duty.

When Oklahoma City staged its first bond drive, the *Daily Oklahoman,* traditionally a bastion of conservatism, ran headlines in bold type that warned, BUY BONDS LEST SLACKER WAGON GET YOU and EMPLOYEES MUST BUY OR QUIT THEIR JOBS. Similar scare tactics were used elsewhere in the state. Some counties built "slacker pens" to hold those who were judged to be less than patriotic. Immigrants, especially German Americans and those who belonged to the Mennonite faith, were treated like common criminals. In some instances, they were made to demonstrate their patriotism in public by kissing the flag or reciting the oath of allegiance. A fifty-dollar bounty was offered in the city of Muskogee for anyone who apprehended a slacker. At Elk City, in the western part of the state, an angry mob tarred and feathered a socialist lecturer and chased him out of town. During the dark of night in Oklahoma City, a dentist's office was broken into and ravaged because the doctor had dared to speak his mind about the war.

A gunslinger mentality lingered as strong as dog's breath in much of the state. As elsewhere in the nation, it was definitely more prudent to be a hawk and not a dove in Oklahoma. Gradually, the allure of socialism wore thin and the remaining antiwar sentiment diminished. Military recruiters worked overtime to fill quotas; so did the draft boards. Volunteers and draftees were sent off to training camps to learn how to salute officers, march in step, and strap on gas masks. They spent hours thrusting bayonets into limp dummies, sharpening their shooting eyes on the rifle range, and listening to lectures about field hygiene or stories of the cunning enemy troops they would soon face in combat. If they were lucky, the fledgling soldiers picked up a few phrases of French along with some barracks wisdom from the older sergeants before they departed to fight "the war to end all wars."

Sequoyah County supplied its share of lads for the cause. The local Council of Defense investigated any charges leveled against those accused of evading their military obligation. Buggies loaded with ladies rolled into Sallisaw, where the women knitted and rolled bandages for the soldiers overseas. Recruits for the war came in from the farms and small towns to join up and go off with the city boys to take on the Germans. Many homes displayed in their windows service flags with a star for each soldier fighting in the war. Some families had flags with three- or four-star clusters.

Bradley Floyd, a strapping eighteen-year-old, was no slacker. He answered when called. He left the mule and plow on his father's leased land out at Akins, enlisted in the army, and went to war. The day Bradley boarded the departing train at Sallisaw, Mamie was distraught, while Walter was as proud as a bantam rooster. Choc and the other Floyd youngsters waved their caps and handkerchiefs and shouted at their brother until the train rolled out of sight.

Willis Booth, an army recruit and an acquaintance of the Floyds from Hanson, was one of the first two boys from Sequoyah County to be killed in the war. The other was Carnie Welch from the community of Price's Chapel. In 1920, after all the dead were buried and the living had come home, one of the American Legion posts organized in Sallisaw was named in Welch's honor.

Booth died tragically in battle in April 1918, one year after the United States became involved in the conflict. He was born in Hanson, the son of a Tennessee native and a Cherokee woman who had died in 1914. The young soldier's body was shipped home from France, and he was taken to Akins to be buried near his mother in the cemetery, just a half mile east of town.

Every community in Sequoyah County had a date set aside for Decoration Day, the time when friends and relatives paid their respects to dead loved ones. The Akins cemetery always had its Decoration Day on the fourth Sunday in May. Two or three preachers would speak under an arbor and people brought basket luncheons and spread tablecloths in the open places for what was called "dinner on the ground." Wildflowers were gathered from meadows and roadsides and others were picked out of the yards. Each grave was cleaned and decorated. Children were taught respect for the dead, and the youngsters played among the oaks, cedars, and pines that towered over the rows of graves. That is where Willis Booth came to rest.

The funeral for the slain soldier was simple. Men from town dug a grave in the soft earth, and friends and relatives in a line of old wagons and newfangled automobiles passed beneath the cemetery's white wrought-iron arch. They entered the fenced grounds to say farewell to Booth, and they laid bouquets of daffodils and forsythia on his grave. A preacher muttered prayers, followed by lilting hymns. It was a ritual to be repeated again and again at Akins, Sallisaw, and Tulsa. For a long time, Choc Floyd and the others working the crops would hear the strains of "The Old Rugged Cross" carrying across the fields as the living took care of their slain warriors.

Booth was soon joined by other dead soldiers. Tommy Miller was the first to die from Miller's Ridge, a community not far from Akins. There was Ruben Siffing, a farm boy of German descent who had raised purebred Silver

Wyandotte chickens and taught school before he enlisted in the army. He was killed in action the last day of the war. Other young men from the county also perished. Some of them were buried in foreign earth, while others were brought home by warships and trains and were laid to rest in their family's chosen burial ground. Bullets, shrapnel, poison gas, influenza, and pneumonia took them all. Years later, a monument would be erected near the old train station in Sallisaw and their names would be chiseled in stone because they had made the supreme sacrifice.

Bradley Floyd's first homecoming after he enlisted was joyous. He returned to Akins as healthy as when he had left. After his basic training was completed at Fort Bliss in El Paso, Texas, Bradley was stationed at Fort Douglas near Salt Lake City, Utah, and then he was sent to Kansas and Camp Funston, one of the largest military training sites during the war. By this time, he had earned two stripes and was acting as a drill instructor. When he was granted leave in the late summer of 1918 to go home and visit his loved ones, Bradley caught a train in Kansas City and headed south to Sallisaw. He looked impressive in his army uniform with puttees wrapped around his legs from ankle to knee and a campaign hat with a gold cord encircling the crown and with tassels on the brim. Mamie prepared every dish and dessert he loved and the entire family sat around the table and listened to Bradley's stories of the rigors of training and the monotony of life in an army camp. Of more interest to the soldier than his mother's cooking was a young woman named Bessie Watson.

She had grown up in Hanson around the Floyds, and Bradley was her beau. One of eight children, Bessie's parents, Sam and Ellen Watson, had come to Oklahoma from Arkansas during the territorial days. Her father was a master carpenter and blacksmith, as well as a successful farmer who ran a sorghum mill and sawed firewood for his neighbors. For fourteen years, Sam Watson served on the school board at Hanson. He was always remembered for advising his children never to "take a piece of string unless you ask for it." Like her father, Bessie was accustomed to hard work. She helped feed many a threshing crew, and was a skillful seamstress who could make a dress or a shirt with just a scrap of cloth and needle and thread. Bradley haunted the Watson place most of the time he was home on leave, but he also took Bessie to his own house for evening visits. His parents liked the plainspoken girl and thought their firstborn had made a good selection.

To commemorate Bradley's wartime visit, Walter had everyone in the family get dressed up. He took them to the Wallace Studio in Sallisaw for a photo session, which had become a Floyd tradition. Through the years, the Floyds had posed for other family portraits, such as the photograph taken a decade before in Adairsville, Georgia, when Charley was only three years old. They also had a framed hand-tinted photograph made outdoors before they moved from Hanson to Akins. For this latest photographic effort, Mamie and her daughters, including little Mary, put on their best dresses, and Walter wrapped a tie around his sunburned neck. Bradley was, of course, in his full uniform, complete with hat at a jaunty angle. Choc and little brother E.W. wore clean shirts buttoned at their throats and new caps. Emma and Mary sat with their parents, while Charley, E.W., Ruby, Bradley, and Ruth stood behind them. Everyone looked straight at the camera and dared not breathe while the photographer snapped the shutter. It was a handsome bunch. Choc, fourteen years old, his gray eyes shining, was a full head taller than E.W., and he was fast gaining in height on his two older sisters and even Bradley.

After the family picture was made, Bradley and his sweetheart posed together for a photograph for Bessie to pine over while her doughboy fought in France. Bradley overstayed his furlough but was willing to face the music for being tardy back at camp. When he packed up his rucksack and returned to Kansas, however, he found out that his outfit had already received new orders and had shipped out for the Western Front without him or the others still home on leave. Instead of joining his comrades, Bradley was busted from corporal to private and was ordered to remain stateside for the duration of the war.

By the time most of the cotton was picked and on its way to the gin late that autumn, the fighting was coming to a close. Then at 5:00 A.M. on November 11, 1918, after a month of tense negotiations, the German government signed an armistice treaty inside a dining car in a French forest. World War I was finished. At last it was all over, over there. The price in lives and money was staggering. Globally, there were 10 million military deaths and about the same number of civilians perished. Twenty million were wounded and another 20 million deaths resulted from the epidemics and famine caused by the war. To the United States, the cost alone was more than $41 million, plus 203,460 wounded and 130,174 dead.

There was a celebration in Akins when Bradley Floyd came back to stay, however. He and his friends broke out a fresh jar of moonshine to toast his return. Bradley packed his uniform in mothballs and gave his mother his discharge papers for safekeeping. He returned to the fields, and, in the evenings, went courting and hatched wedding plans with Bessie.

The war had indeed altered the world. This definitely included Oklahoma. The agricultural changes in Oklahoma brought on by the end of the war would be as profound as those experienced by the Deep South in the years following 1865. The state's agricultural system was clearly overextended. Everywhere the veterans looked, they saw nothing but cotton. They soon realized they were doomed by eastern Oklahoma's single-crop mentality. This method of farming depleted the soil and taxed the farmer with little return.

Cotton and coal prices, which had been good for the three-year period during the war, fell after the hostilities ended. There was no prosperity in Little Dixie nor the rest of rural Oklahoma, where in 1919, cotton prices dropped to fifteen cents a pound. Overall cotton production was slashed by almost 20 percent. Tenant farmers were destined to become virtual slaves to their cash crop. Narrow-minded and bitter, they were wary of city dudes or anyone with a college education, and were not at all interested in the employment of scientific farming methods or the warnings issued by the Department of Agriculture concerning the lack of soil conservation. As a result, the crop overproduction proved devastating. Financial panic was felt beyond the farms. Mining strikes and work stoppages, blamed by business leaders on union organizers, became widespread, and in some instances, National Guard regiments were used when martial law was declared. Labor protests quickly spread to the manufacturing plants and railroads. Farmers and blue-collar workers in the cities did whatever they could to supplement their earnings.

To help bring more income into his household, Walter Floyd purchased a truck and started a freight-hauling business between Sallisaw and Akins. He was also gratified when the two oldest Floyd children decided to start families of their own. On January 31, 1919, Bradley wed Bessie Watson. He was twenty and his bride was a few weeks shy of her eighteenth birthday.

"Bradley came after me and we rode into Sallisaw in a buggy and got married down at the courthouse," recalled Bessie. "There was nobody but us."

The newlyweds moved in with Bradley's folks for the first year of their marriage in order for the young couple to come up with a grub stake to start farming on their own. Walter was glad to keep Bradley around a little longer to help Choc with the cotton and corn, and Mamie appreciated getting a hard worker like Bessie under her roof.

"I worked right out in the fields with the Floyd girls, and when we finished with the crops at our place, we went and helped our neighbors," said Bessie.

Later that same year, nineteen-year-old Ruth, the oldest Floyd daughter, consented to a marriage proposal from Thomas B. Wofford, a young Sequoyah County farmer and war veteran. Walter was quick to give his approval to their union. Like the Floyds, Tom's parents—Bud and Fanny Wofford—came from Georgia by train and settled at Hanson in 1893. They had strong Georgia roots. The town of White, Georgia, had been named for Fanny's father, James White, a Civil War soldier who had been held captive for many years in a Yankee prison. Bud, just a year younger than Walter's father, came from a large family and had lost one brother in the Mexican War and two brothers in the war with the Union. One was killed at Fredericksburg, Virginia, and the other died fighting against Sherman's forces at the Battle of Kennesaw Mountain, near Atlanta.

Bud Wofford farmed near Hanson and also used his drill to open many of the county's water wells. He was a kind man, known as the Peacemaker because of his ability to settle disputes in the community. Fanny raised nine children of her own, but she often made clothes for any of the motherless children living in the area. Anytime a neighbor was sick or near death, she and her husband helped see them through.

The Woffords were also strong churchgoers. Bud was one of the three trustees who signed the deed for the plot of land granted by the Cherokee Nation where the Hanson Baptist Church was built. He also helped organize the Sunday school. When revival meetings were held, he and his three sons hauled wagonloads of logs and branches and built brush arbors. The bowers of tree boughs, vines, and foliage twined together provided the faithful with shade from the unmerciful sun that blazed overhead during the dog days of summer. Worshippers flocked to the brush-arbor services from miles around in wagons bearing children, grandmothers, baskets of food, and covered dishes.

Out in the open air, under the sky and stars, they all felt closer to God. Audience participation was encouraged and expected. Everyone sang and those touched by the spirit shouted in unison "Amen!" and "Go it, brother!" and "Praise the Lord!" They listened to the preaching of visiting evangelists, fully prepared to stay until the last soul was saved. In the evenings, after they stopped to catch their breath and enjoy a bite of supper, the preaching and exclaiming started up again and continued until voices gave out. Often the services would last all night long and into the next day. When the babies fell asleep, their mothers would wrap them in quilts and lay them on beds of straw in the back of the wagons.

It was at one of these brush-arbor revivals that Choc Floyd solidified his reputation as a mischief maker. One sweltering summer night after a whole day of raucous preaching and soul saving, Choc and "Soap" Masterson and, more than likely, teenaged boys from the Green, Farmer, and Franks households decided they had had enough religion and would now have some fun. The boys slipped away from the crowd of true believers and went to the ring of wagons, where most of the next generation of Sequoyah County residents slumbered on the hay. As quiet as Indians, Choc and the others gently lifted a baby from one of the wagons and then switched it with a baby sleeping in another wagon. They repeated this process again and again, being careful not to awaken the infants and cause them to cry. Within minutes, Choc and his friends had finished the exchanges and returned with full piety to the revival.

Soon the services broke up. Folks who lived nearby walked home, carrying their lanterns, while the other families rode in their wagons through the darkness to houses scattered across the hills. When they got inside and managed to get a lamp lighted, they immediately discovered the babies they had brought home were not their own. A collective scream erupted from mothers throughout that part of the Cookson Hills when they found they had the wrong children. There were no telephones, so farmers tried to comfort their frantic wives while they coaxed their tired horses down the dirt roads to a neighbor's place in order to get their own baby back. By then, however, the other family had also recognized that a swap had been made, so they were already on the road, as well. Most of the emotional exchanges of infants took place between wagons on a darkened country road. Nobody got much sleep that night.

Choc swore Soap and the others to secrecy. Although most everyone suspected who was responsible, it was not until many years later that any of the participants in the brush-arbor baby swap dared admit to anyone that he had been one of the culprits.

Such shenanigans at revival meetings, not to mention stolen melons, fistfights with rowdy farm boys, and forbidden sips of unripe brew from the choc barrel, were the type of mischievous capers that kept the high-spirited Charley Floyd in hot water most of the time. Walter's hard hand—adept at boxing ears—combined with Mamie's religious training had some effect. A day would soon come when their son would turn to more daring escapades, however.

By the time he reached his mid-teens, Choc Floyd had become as nervy and restless as a penned wolfhound. He was fast approaching that invisible line that separates boyhood pranks from serious crime. Once he stepped over to the other side, there would be little hope for return.

14

WANDERLUST

OR THE ENTIRE COUNTRY, the twenties would become a period of extremes and contradictions. The Ku Klux Klan would gain strength; the bigots and hate-mongers who swelled their ranks would brazenly march down America's main streets hidden beneath hoods and pure white robes. Women, long exploited at the workplace and in their own homes, would at last gain the right to cast votes in political elections. Children would continue to labor for pitiful wages at man-sized jobs. Good citizens as patriotic as any fourth-generation American would be ostracized because of their accents. Automobiles would roll off assembly lines at a record rate, allowing rural America to go to town like never before.

It would become a time for flappers, jazz bands, and vamps. For each sheba, there would be a sheik. Some people insinuated that this period was the grand orgy before the hangover known as the Great Depression crashed over the land. Others said the twenties merely roared. But not everyone would learn the Charleston or sip bathtub gin from a china teacup.

This new decade, one tempered by discontent and the remnants of war, slammed into the public's consciousness with the shock of a sucker punch. Reform and revolution hung ominously in the air; so did fear. The nation turned inward to prohibit, preach, pray, proselytize, as well as lick its internal sores.

As a giddy America emerged from its twentieth-century puberty and tried to act grown up, Choc Floyd found himself ready to wander. Home and hearth were significant enough, but the young man's sap was rising fast. He felt pulls and tugs within him. He had to struggle to keep his mind on chopping cotton, mixing mash, and cutting the piles of wood required to feed the constant home fires. He was weary of grubbing in the cotton patch, of seeing his neckerchief soaked with sweat. He no longer wished to wear mended overalls and boots caked with manure. A lifetime spent working land leased from another man seemed futile. He did not desire to become his father. Tenant farming meant there would be nothing to show but hands callused hard as hickory and a litter of children. Those prospects held no allure for young Choc Floyd.

Neither did occasional Saturday afternoons spent at the Wonderland Theatre in Sallisaw or the rare forays to Muskogee and Fort Smith. Those good times did not come often enough for Choc. He had heard about new and strange places from the boys who had come home from what was now being called the Great World War. For the first time in history, masses of Americans had been exposed to foreign lands through direct contact. They were changed by the experience. Farm boys had looked death in the face. They had bedded down exotic women, tasted cognac, and gazed at the Eiffel Tower. A popular song of the time said it best: "How you gonna keep them down on the farm after they've seen Paree?" Historian Henry May wrote that the conclusion of the war meant "the end of American innocence." Veterans returned to Sequoyah County with bronze buttons in their lapels to show they had helped defeat the Boche, silver buttons if they had been wounded. They also brought back with them new ideas about people, politics, lifestyle, and just about everything else.

Stories about the fast-paced life in big cities like Tulsa, Oklahoma City, Fort Worth, Kansas City, and St. Louis piqued Choc's interest. He understood that city streets and sidewalks were paved, that the city girls were scented and saucy, and that every night was a cakewalk for a fellow with something more than a streetcar token in his pocket. Buildings, a few more than seven stories high, had elevators. Homes had indoor toilets and electricity, and eating places set tables with clean cloth napkins and pitchers of ice water. Choc itched to escape the confines of the crowded family house and the worn-out tenant farms. He longed to see the wide world beyond the Cookson Hills, to escape those interminable fields lined with row after row of corn and cotton.

Choc Floyd's restlessness mirrored that of the entire country. Widespread strikes exploded throughout the land, combined with postwar unemployment and inflation. The economy began to decline just as the war drew to a close. More than half of Oklahoma's farmers alone were of the tenant variety. When the war ended, all their hopes and dreams literally disappeared in the span of one year. In 1919, cotton prices first rose but then suddenly plummeted by almost 20 percent, tumbling to fifteen cents a pound. The cornucopia of plenty in Little Dixie withered like an old woman's teat. Although the oil industry soared during the twenties, agriculture remained depressed and many marginal farmers began losing their land. The chasm between the oil men in Tulsa and the farmers elsewhere widened, only increasing the bitterness that was felt in rural areas. Life in the Oklahoma coal fields was pitiful, as well. Many mines closed or went bankrupt. Thousands of striking miners in eastern Oklahoma caused Governor James B. Robertson to call out two regiments of National Guardsmen. Business leaders in the big cities blamed the economic anguish and unrest on IWW agitators, who they said stirred up the people to protest the poor working conditions and unreasonable hours.

Hours traditionally had always been long for farmers and miners. Now for working stiffs in the cities, the shifts stretched from twelve to often fourteen hours a day and sometimes much longer in the steel industry. Wages, already reduced by the use of over 1 million children in industry, were cut even further and businesses started to fail. Hatred toward foreign immigrants, who were thought to take away jobs from native-born residents, increased, as did the apprehension of the Communist party. That fear of communism turned into a show of senseless action during the very first days of the new decade.

On the evening of Friday, January 2, 1920, mass arrests of thousands of suspected Reds occurred as the government carried out raids in thirty-three different cities. This campaign was orchestrated by U.S. Attorney General Alexander Mitchell Palmer, a Pennsylvania lawyer and politician, and the Justice Department's William J. Flynn, former director of the Secret Service and, at the time of the raids, chief of the Bureau of Investigation, a precursor of the FBI in those years.

The previous year, Palmer had been one of several prominent Americans, including politicians, judges, and big-business magnates, apparently targeted by a ring of political anarchists. On the evening of June 2, 1919, a pair of would-be assassins ignited a homemade bomb on the front doorstep of Palmer's Washington, D.C., residence on fashionable R Street. Palmer was not injured in the explosion, which badly damaged his house and shattered windows throughout the neighborhood, but the bomb did blow up the two revolutionaries who set off the device and sent shivers of fear throughout the land. Bloody chunks of flesh and bone mixed with burning bits of clothing scattered on Palmer's lawn, and a smoldering body part landed on the front stoop of the house directly across the street where Assistant Secretary of the Navy Franklin D. Roosevelt and his family resided. Another piece of flesh, like a grotesque projectile, shattered the window of the Norwegian Minister's residence. Palmer was outraged by the attack, but he was also aware that he had found the cause he needed to establish himself as a visible political candidate for the 1920 presidential race.

Palmer and Flynn had already created the bureau's General Intelligence Division (GID) to focus on what they called domestic radicalism. They appointed a twenty-four-year-old former file clerk from the Library of Congress named John Edgar Hoover to direct the GID and investigate anyone suspected of being a Communist, a subversive, or a part of the radical left. A graduate of George Washington University Law School, Hoover joined the legal staff of the Department of Justice in 1917, and had previously headed up the Enemy Alien Registration section. He tackled his newest assignment with a vengeance that would become characteristic.

Bureau director Flynn ordered Hoover to concentrate his efforts on uncovering "alien agitators," and the young lawyer believed he knew exactly where to look. Hoover read everything about Karl Marx, Friedrich Engels, Vladimir Lenin, and Leon Trotsky, and soon he became known as an authority on communism and the radical left. From his Washington, D.C., office on K Street, Hoover amassed impressive dossiers on suspected anarchists, as well as IWW members, alien radicals, socialists, Marxists, and Communists. In a brief he prepared about the American Communist party, Hoover warned that advocates of communism "threaten the happiness of the community, the safety of the individual, and the continuance of every home and fireside. They would destroy the peace of the country and thrust it into a condition of anarchy and lawlessness and immorality that passes imagination."

Using information gathered by Hoover, Palmer announced that July 4, 1919, would be the date for the launch of a Communist revolution in America. Police chiefs from all major U.S. cities were briefed, state militias went on alert, and law-enforcement officers protected armories and auditoriums around the country. July 4 came and went with no more than the prerequisite displays of fireworks, however. The only notable act of violence took place in Toledo, where Choc Floyd's pugnacious hero Jack Dempsey pulverized Jess Willard to take the world heavyweight crown. Nonetheless, the undaunted Palmer and his tenacious agents, including young John Hoover, were resolved to continue their warfare on suspected radicals and subversives. They even turned up the heat by several notches.

Hoover's intelligence reports pointed to Communist involvement in the steel and coal strikes that plagued the nation. After reviewing the legal briefs prepared by Hoover and studying these meticulous reports, Palmer believed he now knew how to use the fear of the Red Tide to get elected to the White House. He immediately ordered the Red Raids, later known as the Palmer Raids, to commence. Bureau of Investigation agents, armed with copies of Hoover's briefs and some with arrest warrants issued by the Bureau of Immigration, rounded up approximately 2,600 aliens for deportation hearings. Palmer emphatically agreed with Hoover that the problem was part of an international Communist conspiracy. He declared open season on "the IWW's, the most radical socialists, the misguided anarchists . . . the moral perverts and the hysterical neurasthenic women who abound in communism."

Similar raids had previously occurred in Oklahoma after the war. These actions, also associated with the Red Scare, destroyed the last vestiges of radical resistance organized by IWW militants in the oil fields and coal mines. The raids also virtually dismantled the once-powerful Oklahoma Socialist party.

In reality, of course, the mass chaos that resulted all over the nation was little more than a grab for power and position on the part of Palmer. Even though he remained a hero to many people, Palmer never realized his political dream of a presidential nomination. That was mercifully nipped in the bud.

He was never able to achieve national credibility. Few of the government's charges were ever substantiated, although the Communist party was driven underground. As it turned out, many of the thousands of suspects picked up by the Justice Department agents who stormed union halls, billiard parlors, and bakeries were actually innocent citizens arrested without any foundation. The clamor and protests surrounding the injustices of the Palmer Raids, like the Sacco and Vanzetti case a year later, lasted for decades to come. Palmer was never able to justify the severe abuse many of those apprehended suffered as a result of his overzealous actions. Nevertheless, paranoids throughout the nation, including John Edgar Hoover, would spend their lives peering over their shoulders, terrified of the Communists they believed lurked everywhere.

America's moral crusade did not stop with the pursuit and persecution of Communists, however. Later that same month, a new era of self-righteousness and virtue, equally hypocritical, was officially ushered in, encouraging the very criminal behavior it was meant to prohibit. The Women's Christian Temperance Union, the American Anti-Saloon League, and the other sanctimonious groups that had been crusading for more than a half century against what they perceived to be the insidious influence of alcohol on the country, finally won out.

At precisely 12:01 A.M. on January 16, 1920, the great experiment began. On that date, the manufacture or sale of all alcoholic beverages—except those for medicinal purposes—was made strictly illegal throughout the United States. The Eighteenth Amendment to the Constitution, which banned intoxicating liquors, had been proposed by Congress in 1917. Then in 1919, despite the veto of Woodrow Wilson, Congress also passed the Volstead Act. Authored by Congressman Andrew J. Volstead, a Minnesota Republican, this enforcement measure put teeth in the prohibition amendment. In the first month of 1920, Prohibition became the law of the land. Fines and prison terms awaited those who transgressed. Like it or not, all of America was on the wagon.

For the next thirteen years—when lawmakers gradually came to their senses and repealed the amendment—this ludicrous attempt to legislate morality would result in rampant corruption. Prohibition would build a solid foundation for organized crime and spawn major racketeering. From the start, this constitutional amendment was controversial and despised. Robert R. McCormick, owner and editor of the *Chicago Tribune,* called Prohibition "an insult to American intelligence and maturity." Nothing in the history of the nation was as unpopular, as violated, or as debated as this single law.

Prohibition was hardly new to the United States. The country's first prohibition legislation had been enacted in 1851 in Maine, and within a few years, many more states passed similar laws. Most of those early prohibition acts were repealed during the 1860s, but by the end of the century, a renewed offensive against alcohol surfaced. Joining the temperance groups in the fight against liquor were the distinguished leaders of organized religion, especially the Methodists, and also social reformers who linked strong drink with poverty and prostitution. From 1907, the year Oklahoma became a state, until 1915, nine southern states voted in favor of temperance. By 1916, almost half of the nation's population was governed by prohibition statutes, either on a statewide or local-option basis.

Oklahomans were used to being dry, or at least *pretending* to be. Since statehood, Oklahoma was thought to be as arid as the Sahara when it came to liquor. Of course, legions of moonshiners and bootleggers, along with their grateful consuming publics, knew better. Even after the rest of the country fell under the rule of the Volstead Act, it was business as usual in Oklahoma. A wink and a nod and some folding money slipped into the right hands could turn up a jar or bottle of hooch.

Out in the sticks, farmers increased their production of moonshine and choc beer to accommodate thirsty customers, including many who drove out from the larger cities. In Sequoyah County, out around Akins and Miller's Ridge and the other small communities, the larger-volume whiskey makers continued their lively business with locals, but they also noticed a rise in trade with the lodge men, oil company executives, and others who came from Muskogee, Okmulgee, and Tulsa seeking liquid refreshments for their social functions.

The main concern for those enterprising farmers who cooked mash were the agents who snooped through the woods and creek bottoms searching for illegal stills and moonshine operations. Many of the local law-enforcement officers, especially deputy sheriffs and constables, were kinfolk or friends and looked the other way. Some of them even cooked wildcat whiskey themselves or else found ways to help make the bootleggers' lives easier. A few of the "laws" were not to be trusted, however.

One of the most diligent at busting up moonshiners in the Floyd's area of the Cookson Hills was Welborn Woodward. After a few years of Prohibition, Woodward, a local farmer who had worked for a short time as a streetcar conductor in Muskogee, hired on as a deputy under Sequoyah County Sheriff George Cheek. He soon got the name "Bone Dry," due to his rigid attitude about bootleggers. Welborn's coworker was Andy Edwards, who earned a nickname all his own because of the trick he used when he moved through the woods looking for moonshiners. He would ring a big bell like a lead cow from a herd so no suspicious farmer out working his still would be unsettled by the noise of someone approaching. Walter Floyd and the others who turned out illegal liquor hung the name "Cowbell" Edwards on the deputy, and it stuck.

Walter did not suffer intruders into his personal life lightly, nor did he have much tolerance for anyone who bothered him or his family. That included nosy law officers poking through the weeds hoping to uncover a cache of cooked corn liquor or a stash of choc beer. Like his sons, who mimicked him, Walter was not one to back down from conflict or confrontation.

Elmer Steele grew up in the twenties as a tough orphan kid on the streets of Sallisaw. He washed out chile bowls and did whatever he could to stay alive and out of trouble. He first witnessed Walter Floyd show his mettle at a Fourth of July celebration. The summertime shindigs were popular events that featured big tubs of lemonade, fried fish, deviled eggs, fireworks, and baseball games. On this particular day, Walter made the rounds of the picnics and parties on horseback, a much safer mode of transportation than his Ford when he was nipping moonshine.

"Ol' Walter Floyd rode up and took his saddle off his horse and tied the horse up to a tree," recalled Steele. "He laid the blanket on the ground and stretched out to enjoy all the doin's at the picnic. He had a quart of moonshine whiskey under that blanket, and every once in a while he'd take it out and have a drink. He was just layin' there with his head on the saddle, mindin' his business and not botherin' a soul."

James Woll, the chief of police, better known around Sallisaw as J.C., and Bert Cotton, another city policeman, moseyed through the picnic grounds and stopped at Walter's feet.

"They looked down at Walter," recalled Steele, "and J.C. told him, 'Hey, Floyd, get up and come on with us. You're drunk and we're takin' you to jail.' Mister Walter Floyd didn't move an inch. He just kept layin' right there, and he told those laws, 'No. I ain't drunk and I ain't botherin' nobody. Just go on and leave me be.'

"It seemed they just couldn't do that. They gave his foot a nudge and told him again to get on up and come along to the jail house. He didn't get up. He told them again to quit botherin' him. Well, they came back at him a third time and said that he was to come with them, and that's when Walter Floyd got plumb fed up. He reached under the blanket and pulled out a big ol' pistol. He just looked right at those police and he said, 'Now boys, I told you, I'm not drunk, so just keep right on walkin' and let me be.' And, that was just exactly what they did."

Steele's story was vintage Walter Floyd. During the turbulent twenties, Oklahoma dirt farmers might not have had a great deal of spare walking-around cash, flashy automobiles, expensive suits, or palatial homes like the oil barons and bankers in the big cities; but they did have their dignity. None of the Floyds and their Sequoyah County cousins were ever shortchanged when pride was being handed out. They stood their ground with the best of them. Backcountry folk like the Floyds saw their independence as a natural right. Their personal liberty was as important to them as it had been to old Patience Floyd and her sons. These forebears had relied both on the grace of God and their long rifles to survive in the wilds of nineteenth-century Georgia.

In 1920, Ruby Mae, the third oldest of the Floyd's children, left the jam-packed family nest in Akins. Two years Choc's senior, Ruby married Silas M. Spear, a hardworking young war veteran. Ruby and Silas staged a quiet marriage ceremony. The couple settled down in the area to begin their own family. However, Ruby's big brother, Bradley, and her older sister, Ruth, already had a head start on her when it came to producing grandchildren for Walter and Mamie. On October 14, 1920, Bradley and Bessie became the parents of twin boys. A little more than a month later, Ruth and Tom Wofford had the first of their seven children, a daughter they named Frances. She was Walter and Mamie's first granddaughter, and while everyone adored her, the twin baby boys living over at Walter Floyd's place stole much of the thunder.

Bradley's two sons were especially welcome. Twins had occurred throughout the Floyd family line, but these premature babies were a big surprise. Bessie Floyd had no idea she was carrying twins. "Why, the day they were born everybody was out working the cotton fields, and I stayed home and did the wash for the entire Floyd family," recalled Bessie. "I sure wasn't thinkin' about two babies comin'." Bessie's parents got to the Floyd home in time to see the babies arrive. After the first one was delivered, Sam took Walter aside and suggested he fetch one of his nursing bitch hounds to help with the feeding. "There's more on the way," Sam Watson laughed. "We're gonna have a bunch of 'em."

Bessie and Bradley named their sons Bayne and Wayne. The arrival of his first grandsons tickled Walter Floyd. They provided him and his hunting cronies with a good reason to pause during the cotton harvest and break out new jars of ripened moonshine.

Life was generally bleak that autumn for ardent Oklahoma Democrats. On November 2, 1920, the Democrats got a sound whipping at the polls when Warren Gamaliel Harding, an Ohio newspaper publisher observing his fifty-fifth birthday, became twenty-ninth President of the United States.

It was a stunning landslide for the GOP. Harding and his running mate, the stoic Governor Calvin Coolidge of Massachusetts, received the largest percentage of popular votes of any winner since the Civil War. They were victorious even in many traditional Democratic strongholds, including the home precincts of their opponents, Ohio Governor James M. Cox and Assistant Secretary of the Navy Franklin D. Roosevelt. The Republicans won with the slogan "Return to Normalcy," which appealed to both conservatives and isolationists. Considered generally inept and a poor judge of character, Harding, however, enchanted the common folk, who came to believe that he looked like a President. At the same time, his skill at backslapping and cutting deals played well to those who dwelled in the smoke-filled rooms where candidates were created and shaped.

In 1920, the Oklahoma voters were in a revolutionary mood. It seemed that Oklahomans were disenchanted with the Democratic party. In the general elections that year, with women voting for the first time, the state—for the first time in its history—voted overwhelmingly Republican. The electoral vote went to Harding over the Democratic candidate Cox, and Eugene Debs, the

Socialists' presidential choice, who languished in the penitentiary at Atlanta after being convicted in 1918 of violating the Espionage Act, came in a distant third. Incumbent Senator Gore had already been defeated in the Democratic primary by Scott Ferris, who then lost out in the general election to Republican John W. Harreld of Oklahoma City. Five of the state's eight congressional seats were taken over by the GOP. The state senate remained Democratic, but Republicans won several state offices, including some supreme court seats and a majority in the Oklahoma House of Representatives. That body promptly launched investigations of Democratic Governor James B. Robertson and several other Democratic officials. Sacred cows were no longer safe. Like the rest of the nation, Oklahoma was in a state of turmoil.

Winds of change that swirled around the nation rushed across the southern plains. Those restless currents reached sixteen-year-old Charley Floyd, tucked away in the hills of eastern Oklahoma. As the new decade commenced, he stopped biding his time. That powerful impulse to move took control.

He laid down his hoe and picked up a grip packed with clean long johns, darned socks, and folded work shirts. He told his folks, brothers, and sisters so long and kissed their babies' cheeks.

Charley set out for the distant harvest fields. He would hire on for the going wage and make his own way in the world. He hoped this change of scenery would be the route to help set him free from a lifetime spent as a tenant farmer's son. Choc was now ready to see the country he had heard so much about. He headed west toward the great seas of wheat. The journey would change him forever.

15

BOOTLEG HARVEST

CHARLEY FLOYD PROCEEDED, with the quickness of a hungry prairie wolf, toward the broad harvest lands that stretched across Oklahoma and Kansas. He wanted to explore and discover. Choc was willing to live by his wits and brawn. There was just the suggestion of a swagger in his walk and not an ounce of fear in his heart. This youngster of nerve and resolve, with dark chestnut hair and blue-gray eyes, was as brave as a bigamist.

During his westward journey, Choc watched farmers as they marched down the furrows of red earth, sowing handfuls of clover seed that would grow into valuable forage. He passed Hereford cattle feeding in the shelter of cottonwood breaks and he counted the red-tailed hawks, gorged on mice and snakes, that preened from atop telegraph poles flanking both sides of the dirt highways. He slept in haylofts and on cool sandbars, bathed in creeks, and washed at strangers' water pumps, using his shirttail for a towel. He hitched rides with silent men in their flivvers and hay wagons. They took him through prairie groves to one-horse towns where there were only a few shops, a post office, a pool hall, and maybe a bank. He used some of the money hidden inside his boot to buy dinner from the shelves at country stores where folks swapped eggs, butter, and cream for canned goods and staples. Sometimes he chopped kindling or husked corn in exchange for a hot meal or a sandwich and a glass of buttermilk from a farmer's wife.

Just a glance at the stocky boy told any crew boss or ramrod worth a damn that this was someone who would pull his own weight and then some. They saw in a snap that he was useful with a pitchfork and they thought he would not be one to walk off the job after just a day or two of strenuous labor. They would get their money's worth from Floyd. His thick arms and well-muscled shoulders were suited for baling hay, threshing wheat, or shucking corn. Years of labor in his father's fields and experience gained working on a farm south of Muskogee were enough to recommend Choc to be anyone's hired hand. The young man's humor and quick banter were icing on the cake.

Wheat and corn prices that spiraled downward, just like the other cash crops, plunged to even lower depths in the 1920s. Still, there were fields to tend. It meant more toil but at least, Choc figured, he was out on his own and could control his destiny. That counted for a lot. Harvest work would be a means toward a better end.

Choc worked the fields of hay, corn, and wheat. None of the jobs were easy. Haying was the earliest of the harvests. Mowed hay was hand-raked into piles, forked onto wagons, and lifted into barns or else baled by machines that compressed the hay into box shapes. The bales were wrapped with wire or twine and brought in from the fields. Hay baling could be painful. The straw gouged and cut into flesh and made bare hands and arms look like ground meat. Even green city boys needed only a few hours wrestling with hay bales to learn about wearing long-sleeve shirts and gloves.

Then there was the corn. During the growing season, the corn crop was cultivated several times to kill the weeds. Corn likes hot weather and rain. Farmers joked that after a summer thunderstorm, they could hear the corn making noises. That is how fast it grew. When the autumn frosts came, it was time to bring in the ear corn for feed. Corn picking was one of the toughest jobs any farmhand faced. Ears of field corn were pulled from the stalks and heaved into the back of a wagon. When the wagon bed was mounded with corn, it would creak off and an empty wagon would appear. The procession of wagons seemed never to end. Many a day, Choc strapped on his hand a mitten with a sharp metal barb, called a shucking or husking peg, to strip husks from the cobs. It was a difficult and tedious chore.

Feed corn went to storage bins and was eventually devoured by the carloads of cattle and hogs that were shipped by rail to Kansas City and St. Joseph. The stock was driven from holding pens to the railroad loading chutes early in the morning or in the evening when it was cool. Sometimes live coals sparked from the passing train engines that pulled the cattle cars. The embers flew into the skies and could set a dry field ablaze. Harvest crews were rousted in the middle of the night. They left their bunks to battle the grass fires alongside the railroad section hands.

No matter what the task, Choc liked seeing the unfamiliar territory. He ventured farther and he joined up with a wheat-cutting crew in the outback of western Oklahoma. He stayed with them as the men and machines moved through rippling fields of uncut wheat that reached toward Oklahoma's panhandle—called no-man's-land—and spread up into Kansas and beyond. He gave them a day's work for a day's wages and even managed to send some money home to his mama at Akins. Mamie tucked it away in a can hidden in the cupboard near her secret cookies that everyone always found. She was pleased that her boy was helping supply the country with its daily bread. She figured he would come back home as soon as he scratched his wayfaring itch.

The wheat harvest was as demanding as the gathering of corn and hay. Depending on the variety, wheat was planted in the spring or the fall after the earth had been prepared. Teams of draft horses, sometimes four or six abreast, in their heavy leather harnesses and neck yokes, lumbered up and down the fields pulling plows that sliced open the ancient soil. The wheat grew and the grain turned golden. Not much more work was necessary until harvest time. The crop was in God's hands. Farmers went about their business and other chores. They read seed catalogs and almanacs. They offered prayers at mealtime and on Sunday mornings for divine protection from every form of pestilence and blight. They patiently waited for the itinerant workers to appear and bring the harvest home.

Seasoned farmhands, like ancient food-gatherers of old, spent their whole lives as nomads following the harvests. They would curse the threat of hail or the bane of too much rain that could destroy an entire crop in minutes. These men could tell when the grain was aged by wading into a field. They would break off some wheat spikes and crunch into the kernels. Brittleness meant the grain could be reaped, and the boss leading the harvest caravan then barked his orders to the crew. Choc learned from these men. They also taught him that the sound of the prairie wind hissing through the ripe wheat meant it was time for harvest.

Whether it was wheat to be threshed, corn to be shucked, or hay to be cut and baled, there was never any question that the harvest was going to take long hours. Even on cold days, crews were drenched in sweat. For many years, the field-workers relied on a tool known as the cradle, an improvement of the scythe, to harvest the wheat. During that time, even a strong man could cut only four acres or less in a day. When Choc found his temporary niche in the wheat fields, however, there were machines called binders that were pulled by horses or gasoline-powered tractors. They permitted one man in a single day to cut easily thirty acres of matured wheat. Binders moved over the fields like great insects chewing wide paths. They tied the cut grain into bundles and laborers followed behind and placed these sheaves into shocks, or piles, of bound grain set up in a field with the butt ends down. During a wheat harvest, the shocks were arranged so the warm air would dry the grain heads. Sheaves were then forked from the shocks onto wagons and taken to threshing machines. The mechanized beasts banged and roared. They belched out thick smoke and spit steam all the while men tossed wheat down the machines' throats. Inside, the grain was separated from the chaff and straw. A wire-gauze cap over the smokestack prevented sparks from flying.

At noon, women and girls brought baskets of dinner and lard buckets filled with biscuit sandwiches and doughnuts to the fields so the hands would not have to come in and lose time. Basins of water, soap, and towels were set out and the workers hunkered in the shadows of the wagons and ate in shifts. Throughout the afternoon, boys lugged pails brimming with well water to the parched crews. Sweating field-workers spit cuds of tobacco into their hands while they drank their fill. Choc would drink from a dipper and splash some of the water on his face and throat to cool off and wash away the sweat and dust. In the evening, it was time to rest. The threshers lined up at the wash pans under the trees, put on dry shirts, and waited for the dinner bell to clang. As many as two dozen men and boys sat elbow-to-elbow around tables covered with oilcloth. From out of the kitchen came bowls of cooked spuds and gravy, pickles, green beans flavored with chunks of bacon, platters of spareribs, and hot bread that was sweet as pound cake. There would be several kinds of pie and bowls of fresh berries. The big enamel coffeepots were never empty.

After they ate, the older men would go off to smoke and sneak in a few shots of bootleg liquor that might have served as coffin varnish. The younger bucks, like Choc, were full of piss and vinegar. They shot craps, played cards, and sometimes squared off for friendly boxing matches in the evening shade. They were footloose and felt as free as the crows scolding from the tops of scraggly Chinese elms.

The harvest crew moved across state borders during the dark of night, and, without even knowing, were in Kansas. Farmers there liked to brag that "Kansas grows the best wheat in the world." Other states challenged that boast, but no one could dispute the fact that the rich Kansas soil yielded bumper crops of hard red winter wheat. In the western part of the state, they planted wheat in the autumn and harvested it in late spring and early summer. Eastern Kansas was corn country and farther north were more fields of wheat planted in spring that were reaped in the fall.

When Choc and his fellow harvesters came to Kansas, they saw more of the grain elevators and silos the color of pearls that towered like monuments over the wheat fields. Some farmers called the enormous cylinders "prairie cathedrals." They were America's most original architecture and held enough stores of grain to feed a town the size of Sallisaw. During midday, when heat waves were rising, the elevators appeared to be shimmering mirages. Nearby, small farm villages dotted the land. There was Nicodemus, Friend, Shallow Water, Protection, Bloom, Paradise, and Pretty Prairie. People in these towns lived in tidy homes with hardwood floors and upright pianos. There were storm cellars in every yard. Kansans went to white-framed Methodist churches and attended band concerts and made their living from the fields of tamed yellow grass. They were constantly aware of their vulnerability when it came to weather and the vacillations of the marketplace.

There were also larger towns, such as Liberal, Meade, Great Bend, Dodge City, Medicine Lodge, El Dorado, Newton, Salina, and Hutchinson. Traces of the historic Santa Fe Trail and old cattle trails could still be made out in the rangelands. Wild phlox appeared each spring on the prairies and in the tall grass pastures. Rivers like the Arkansas, Republican, Solomon, Cimarron, and Pawnee snaked all through the plains and hills.

Kansas, like Oklahoma, Texas, and large parts of Colorado and Nebraska, was more than a decade away from the advent of the lean years when dust storms would come howling across the Great Plains to wither crops and snuff out lives. The storms were tempests out of Hades, ferocious enough so that many strong men and women lost faith in themselves and their land. However, for now the farmers—and also the harvest workers they hired to bring in the grain and corn—were more concerned with poor market prices, grasshoppers, Hessian flies, chinch bugs, and renegade tornadoes.

Choc savored his time in America's heartland. He made new friends and saw places he had not seen before. Even after the harvest turned bitter for him, Choc was still glad he had come along for the ride up the dusty prairie roads. When the harvests were over and the shockers and binders returned to prepare for a new season and repeat the cycle all over again, Choc turned in another direction.

He had heard about Wichita, the old wide-open cattle town that had turned into a flour-milling and meat-packing center in the south-central part of the state. Some of the older fellows said there were opportunities there, including barber colleges where a young man could pick up an honest trade and make a clean living. That is all Choc needed to hear. When the crews finished their work, he took his leave. He drew his final paycheck, packed up his belongings, and was on his way.

When his family heard from him again sometime in early 1921, their Charley boy had taken up residency at a run-down boardinghouse with iron bedsteads and cracked mirrors in the largest city in Kansas. Choc had briefly visited Tulsa and Oklahoma City, but Wichita was the largest city in which he had ever spent any significant length of time.

The seat of Sedgwick County, Wichita was set in one of the greatest wheat-growing regions of the nation. About two hundred miles southwest of Kansas City at the junction of the Arkansas and Little Arkansas rivers, Wichita arose from lowly beginnings during the Civil War, when it was a trading post clinging to the riverbank. The city took its name from the Indians who had settled there after they fled the nations to avoid conflict with the pro-Southern tribes. It was incorporated shortly before the railroad arrived in 1872, an event that made Wichita a cattle-shipping center at the head of the Chisholm Trail and a frontier town that would attract many colorful figures, including Wyatt Earp, Bill Tilghman, Bat Masterson, and James Butler Hickok. Early law officers posted crudely painted signs on the outskirts of town that bluntly stated: ANYTHING GOES IN WICHITA. LEAVE YOUR REVOLVERS AT POLICE HEADQUARTERS AND GET A CHECK. CARRYING CONCEALED WEAPONS IS STRICTLY FORBIDDEN. Some early citizens thought they would avoid getting in trouble by wearing their guns in plain view instead of hiding them. Many of those folks ended up in pine boxes beneath the prairie sod.

Before the final decade of the century, Wichita had already shed some of its cow-town image and had become a prominent agricultural trade and milling center. During the harvest rush, wagons, bearing mountains of wheat to be weighed and unloaded at the mills, lined up a dozen blocks long on Douglas Avenue. By 1915, major oil deposits were found in the region, and shortly after World War I, the lucrative petroleum and the fledgling aircraft industries brought newfound wealth to the city on the windy prairies.

By 1921, Wichita had grown into a Great Plains metropolis with a population of almost eighty thousand. Choc Floyd saw women with bobbed hair smoking cigarettes in public. He flirted with fresh-talking waitresses at the cafes where he ate blue plate specials and bowls of red-hot chili, and munched boiled eggs out of gallon jars stored on the back counters near the glass-enclosed pie safes. There were electric trolleys and jitney buses, municipal parks with picnic groves and archery grounds, stockyards teeming with cattle, cemeteries larger than some Oklahoma villages, manicured golf courses, and stylish theaters that hosted road shows and concerts. Residential areas with trim brick and stone bungalows were shaded by cottonwoods and elms, and there was a bustling business district. The city's socially elite were still gossiping about the new residence of *Wichita Beacon* publisher Henry J. Allen, a house built at the corner of Roosevelt Avenue and Second Street. Allen, who had been elected governor of Kansas in 1918 while serving with the American Red Cross in France, was reelected in 1920, the same year construction on his house was completed. The two-story buff brick house with a low-pitched tile roof had been designed by Frank Lloyd Wright, and was touted as a "radical departure" from residential architecture of the day.

Despite rumors bandied about by some family members, it is doubtful whether Choc Floyd even enrolled at one of the Wichita barber colleges, much less parted with some of his harvest earnings to purchase the necessary tonsorial tools. If he did start classes at one of the schools, such as the barber college on Douglas Avenue, he lasted but a short time and he never spoke about the experience. But, then, the Floyds were not privy to much information at all concerning Choc's brief stay in Wichita. This was one of the most puzzling periods in a private life that was eventually to become very public.

What is known is that sometime in 1921, Choc Floyd became acquainted with one of Wichita's most notorious characters—a throwback figure from the city's wild old days. He was a corpulent Irishman with white hair named John Callahan. He affected a brogue, smoked a stubby pipe, and could sling blarney as deep as the cow dung at the Wichita Union Stockyards. Born in 1866, Callahan was a familiar figure to many Wichita police officers, both those who were righteous and true and those who were tainted and corrupt. They knew Callahan as a man of cunning and deceit who managed to keep a low public profile, a person who managed to become one of the most successful fences in the Midwest as well as one of the largest bootleggers in Kansas. Every sneak thief, burglar, and bank robber in the region found his way to Callahan's door to sell stolen goods and contraband or launder his loot. Callahan could dispose of anything including jewels, automobiles, bank securities, or whiskey.

The criminal mastermind used a junkyard on the railroad tracks near Wichita's Union Station as a front for his nefarious business dealings. He lived nearby in a run-down two-story frame house. When Choc was summoned by Callahan to his place, he undoubtedly walked right passed the Carry A. Nation Memorial Fountain, on Douglas Avenue, just east of Santa Fe Street on Union Station Plaza. The granite slab with a drinking fountain was dedicated in 1918 by members of the Women's Christian Temperance Union in memory of Carrie Nation (later in her life she changed the spelling of her first name to Carry), the eccentric reformer who was raised by an insane mother and was married to a hopeless alcoholic. Nation was best remembered for storming into saloons in Kansas, Oklahoma, Arkansas, and Missouri to smash windows, mirrors, bottles, and kegs of beer. Just a block east of the Carry Nation Memorial was the Eaton Hotel, formerly named the Carey Hotel, the site of one of Nation's barroom raids on December 27, 1900. Besides breaking up a sideboard with a cane, Nation pelted a large painting with rocks. All the while, she shattered mirrors and chandeliers and attacked the painting, yelling, "Peace on earth, good will to men." The mutilated portrait by John Noble was titled *Cleopatra at the Bath*, a work described by the shocked Mrs. Nation as "the life-sized picture of a naked woman." Carry Nation went to her reward in 1911, but had she lived, she and her temperance ladies would have had a field day with the likes of John Callahan and his pack of rascals.

In his earlier years, Callahan had robbed some rural banks and headed up a sizable burglary ring. In 1900, Callahan was charged with the robbery of the bank at Clearwater, Kansas, and served a term in the state penitentiary. He later was pardoned. In 1908, he was implicated in the robbery of a bank at Milan, Kansas. The first hearing resulted in a mistrial, but he was convicted at a second trial. Callahan later appealed and was cleared of the charge. In 1910, a reporter for the *Kansas City Star* attempted to get photographs of the notorious "dump" Callahan used for a front, but the newsman was attacked by a bulldog and received some severe wounds for his trouble. The reporter complained to Mayor Charles L. Davidson, who ordered an investigation. Officers who raided Callahan's place found five and a half barrels of bottled whiskey.

About this same time, Callahan spent more time behind bars for his part in the theft and subsequent disposal of more than $6,200 worth of postage stamps from nineteen country stores that maintained post offices. Callahan sold the stamps to a corrupt police chief who then turned state's evidence and resigned his post but did not do any jail time. A prominent Wichita banker who purchased the stamps from the police official for seventy-five to eighty cents on the dollar was convicted and handed a one-year prison term, but his influential friends convinced President William Howard Taft to issue a pardon. The banker returned to his position, made a small fortune, and ended up a highly respected member of the community. Callahan, however, went to prison and served a sentence. That experience convinced him to let others do the actual stealing. He would stick with the fencing and behind-the-scenes work.

By 1915, Callahan controlled most of the graft and rackets in Wichita. Big-name bank robbers and bandits from several midwestern states came to him with stolen bonds taken in train and bank robberies. They collected the usual going rate of twenty cents on the dollar. Some of Callahan's clients included Al Spencer and Frank Nash, two of the most infamous from the legion of seasoned robbers operating out of Oklahoma. When a bandit wished to lay low and allow his trail dust to settle, he could go to Callahan for refuge. Sometimes the cagey old Irishman would hide desperadoes with sizable prices on their heads at the Wichita brothel operated by Clyde and Nellie Miles. When the heat was off and the refugees from justice were ready to be on their way, Callahan was there to collect his cut of the harboring fees.

Criminal historians credit Callahan with educating generations of thieves, bootleggers, and even murderers. They said he became a modern-day Fagin, an adult who instructs youth in the ways of crime and lawlessness. Smooth enough to finesse an old maid out of her knickers, Callahan conjured up visions of easy money that attracted any number of local boys who hung around the billiard parlors and dance halls. He also preyed on wayward kids like Choc Floyd who came through town fresh from the harvest fields. Callahan had developed such a convincing line of malarkey that he could have sold the Pope a double bed. Hayseeds and street punks held no challenge for him. Some of his more notorious recruits were the identical twins Major and Minor Poffenberger and Diamond Joe Sullivan. He also apprenticed Dudley, Roy, and Ray Majors—a trio of reckless brothers. But by far and away, Callahan's star pupil was the deadly Eddie Adams.

Born W. J. Wallace on a farm near Hutchinson, Kansas, in 1887, Adams quit school in his teens and went to Wichita to attend barber college. He cut hair and wielded a straight razor for a short time at a shop on East Douglas Avenue before going back to Hutchinson to marry a local girl. When she jilted him for another man, the barber turned mean. Around 1915, he returned to Wichita with a chip on his shoulder and became involved in bootlegging and petty crime. He promptly hooked up with Callahan and then adopted the Eddie Adams alias. During the day, as W. J. Wallace, he trimmed hair. At night, as Eddie Adams, he ran the back roads for Callahan hauling illegal shipments of liquor from neighboring Missouri into Kansas. Bootlegging profits allowed Adams to take his pleasure at Nellie Miles's bordello, not to mention his taste for narcotics.

Callahan gave Adams further clandestine assignments and introduced him to the Majors brothers. Together, this quartet formed a fearsome armed-robbery team that struck at small-town banks in Kansas, Iowa, Nebraska, and Oklahoma. Back in Wichita, they lived like barons. Then in 1919, Adams and the Majors brothers made the mistake of trying to loot a gambling den in Kansas City, Missouri. This was foreign turf and was strictly off-limits to outsiders. In the resulting gun battle, two dice players were wounded and another gambler was shot dead. Roy and Ray Majors were also wounded and captured along with Adams. Only Dudley Majors managed to escape, although he was later arrested for another crime and sentenced to prison. Adams and the Majors boys were tried and convicted. Roy and Ray were handed five-year terms at the Missouri State Penitentiary. Roy never really recovered from his wounds and died in prison. Ray was later released but could not shake a life of crime and ended up spending his final years in the Kansas State Penitentiary at Lansing.

Eddie Adams was convicted of being the actual triggerman who gunned down the gambler. He was given life in prison, but Adams never served one day of that sentence. On January 23, 1920, while en route to the penitentiary at Jefferson City, Missouri, Adams asked his guards on the train to unshackle him so he could use the toilet. Inside the washroom, Adams broke out a window and wiggled outside. He held on to the railing and waited until the train rounded a curve. When the train slowed down, he dropped to the ground and disappeared in the darkness. It was a spectacular and much-publicized escape and did not go unnoticed by Callahan's other young protégés in Wichita. Adams was soon back in Kansas for fresh clothes, a gun, and an automobile. In a heartbeat, he resorted to his outlaw ways.

He robbed the bank in Cullison, Kansas, but in his haste to escape, Adams wrecked the getaway car. A posse of police officers found him hiding beneath a bridge. This time, after he was tried and found guilty, the authorities were able to deliver Adams to the Kansas state pen. In prison, the bandit took up with another trio of convicts—D. C. Brown, George Weisberger, and Frank Foster. Together, they masterminded an escape plan. On the evening of August 13, 1921, they sabotaged the power plant and threw the entire prison into darkness. The four men then escaped by scaling the walls with a sectional ladder they had secretly built in the penitentiary workshop. On the other side of the wall waited a driver in an automobile with its engine running. He was Billy Fintelman, a decorated doughboy who turned criminal. He had been sent from Wichita to Lansing by old man Callahan. Fintelman's orders were to pick up the escapees and bring them home. Once again, Adams was back in business.

Upon his return to Wichita, Adams found that some changes had taken place. During his time spent in a cell at Lansing, the local police department had purged its ranks and cleaned out some of the internal vice that had been prevalent for so long. The new chief of police was S. W. Zickefoose. Word spread around Wichita that he was a tough copper who could not be bought. Zickefoose and his men swooped down on the criminal element like a duck on a June bug. Even Callahan began sweating bullets. Undaunted, Adams proceeded to go on a three-month crime tear. There were gun duels with police officers and savage killings. An eighty-two-year-old man died as a direct result of a pistol whipping during one bank stickup. Several lawmen were slain or wounded in a series of clashes with the bandit. Adams and his accomplices were also responsible for a multitude of auto thefts, a mail-train holdup, and more bank robberies in Kansas, Missouri, and Iowa. His crime spree reached a fever pitch when he was finally gunned down by detectives in a Wichita garage on South Lawrence Street in the wee hours of the morning of November 23, 1921.

Before Adams was buried, hundreds of curiosity seekers viewed his body at the morgue. Someone even swiped the bank robber's overcoat when the rumor spread that some of his loot might have been sewn in the lining. At the funeral, the Salvation Army provided the pallbearers, and a Baptist preacher volunteered to give a short eulogy emphasizing how Adams had wasted his life. There were no mourners, only a few cops and newspaper reporters. John Callahan was there, however. "He was a nice kid before he went wrong," Callahan told some detectives standing near the coffin with their hats in their hands.

It is uncertain whether Charley Floyd ever met Eddie Adams. They might have both been in Wichita at the same time in 1921, and both had connections to Callahan, but that was about all they had in common. The young harvest hand from Oklahoma was still learning the ropes. Still, there were those who believed that Choc was influenced by some of Adams's escapades. Paul Wellman was working on the city desk of the *Wichita Beacon* during that period. He even helped get out the "extra" edition when Adams was shot and killed. Wellman later suggested in his book *A Dynasty of Western Outlaws* that perhaps Choc had become acquainted with Adams in Wichita. Bliss Isely, another newspaper reporter in Wichita during those years, also theorized that if Choc did not cross paths with Adams, at least he had been inspired by the older bandit's tactics, notably his method of escape from law officers while on a speeding train. Less than ten years after Eddie Adams leaped from a train, Choc would have much the same experience in Ohio.

These two veteran police reporters knew for certain that Choc briefly fell under Callahan's tutelage, however. Wellman contended that although "the raw youth was considered too young for important assignments," Floyd ran errands and did odd jobs for the man who was forty years his senior. Callahan's style was to gain the confidence of young men ages fifteen to twenty. He taught them how to drive the lonely dirt roads between Wichita and Joplin, where they would load up on cases of illegal spirits and bring them back for sale at secluded warehouses in Kansas. Choc may have graduated to a driver's job because he could handle an automobile and had been exposed to the bootlegger's life ever since childhood.

Even if he made some runs to Joplin and back, Choc did not remain in

Kansas long enough to get into any serious trouble. There was never a police record to show that he had been arrested in Wichita. Old police officers in Wichita knew him only as a handyman to Callahan, not a real threat to society. Word among the beat cops and plainclothes detectives was to "keep a close watch on him." Police Captain W. O. Lyle was one of those who recalled seeing Choc Floyd on the city streets. "We considered him a no-good kid," said Lyle, "but hardly worth bothering about."

At some point before his eighteenth birthday in 1922, Choc slipped across the state line back into Oklahoma. He headed due south to Sequoyah County and the Floyd farm near the town of Akins. His family was glad to see him again, even Walter, who was mostly stiff when it came to showing that he truly missed his son. Mamie and the girls laid out a nice feed, and a flock of Choc's friends came by to see him. He told a few of them about his exploits and the characters he had met on the harvest trail and in Wichita.

On his trip, Choc had collided with men who knew Henry Starr and Al Spencer, two outlaws almost as famous in some parts as Jesse James. Starr had been shot and killed in a bank-robbery attempt in 1921, while Spencer was still on the rampage. It was as though the farm boy had touched living history. Callahan's tales of old outlaws would not be forgotten. The time spent out on the road and in the cities had a profound impact on Charley Floyd. He had sampled the outside world and he liked what he had experienced. From the moment that long harvest journey ended until the time he left again a few years later, Choc thought of little else.

16

ONE STEP OVER THE LINE

B ACK HOME IN OKLAHOMA, Choc Floyd was roosted on the edge of a storm. A ruckus was in the works. Almost as soon as he reappeared at the family farm, he was filled with anxiety. Nervous electricity, like heat lightning, seemed to raise the hair on his arms and neck. He became fidgety and felt taut, and grew wary of the folks he loved and trusted the most.

Choc told his pals about the swell times he had had in Wichita, and other stories about the shady side of Joplin, a wide-open Missouri city with its share of bawdy houses and watering holes for parched miners and railroaders in a hurry to part with their wages. He recounted some of his escapades and adventures alone on the dirt-road runs in southern Kansas: highballing it by the light of the moon through Galena, Coffeyville, and Independence; ducking the "laws" hidden in the brush in their shiny black Ford cars. Returning to the fields to work the cotton and corn, Choc told these stories to all who listened.

As he made an attempt to readjust to home life, Choc also had to cope with the growing strain between himself and his father. Walter Floyd failed to recall his own jumpy days and stormy nights when he was a young man in Georgia. He was not of a mind to recollect these tricks and capers. Walter had forgotten all the winter hunts and the evenings filled with fury and liquor. He was incapable of understanding a son who seemed unable to settle down and make a life for himself.

Others in the family also noticed some differences in Charley after he returned from the harvest circuit and the whiskey trails in Kansas and the borderlands of Missouri.

"That's when he met the wrong kind of men," Choc's older sister Ruth Wofford said many years later when she reflected on her brother's life. "They changed his ways of thinking and doing."

When Mamie Floyd was asked about Charley, a look of grief spread over her face, but she stayed dry-eyed and nodded her head in agreement with her daughter.

"He changed when he came back from the harvest," said Mamie of her son. "He changed."

Choc was not the only one who had changed. So had a good many other farm boys, war veterans, and others. The social transformation that had helped propel Choc down the dusty harvest roads continued to reshape America's fiber and fabric, as well. The unstable chemistry that resulted caused the frontier to disappear in Oklahoma and in other western states.

Thanks to Henry Ford—America's new folk hero who had fooled around with machines as a kid because he hated working on the farm—and his new assembly-production techniques, people everywhere were able to shell out money for an automobile. That included farmers and ranchers, who could now go to town faster and more often. As more autos rolled off the lines, the federal and state governments started new highway construction programs that linked the cities with towns.

Between 1910 and 1920, the urban population of the country jumped by 29 percent. In Oklahoma, however, the increase spiraled to 69 percent. Huge oil and gas deposits created booms in Tulsa, Oklahoma City, Seminole, Cushing, Okmulgee, and several other cities. Many tenant farmers in search of a living abandoned their land for jobs in the oil patch. Some sectors of the American economy recovered from the collapse that started in 1920, but for farmers in this region, economic depression began in earnest in the early twenties and never really stopped. They looked for other ways to keep themselves and their families going.

City dwellers made fun of the farmers, no longer regarding them as the backbone of the nation. Instead, they were branded as hayseeds and hicks. Rural residents, like the people in Sequoyah County, conversely considered the cities to be everything that was wrong about the country. City denizens were evil, or not worthy of trust. Cities were associated with prostitution and crime, Jews and Roman Catholics, big-time bootleggers, and conniving bankers. In the cities, people could buy Eskimo Pies, Trojan contraceptives, and factory-made cigarettes. Bathtub brandy, flappers, speakeasies, whiskey women, petting parties, bachelor girls in caftans, and jazz babies abounded.

The General Federation of Women's Clubs, worried about the bad influence of popular music on young people, gave their stamp of approval only to old favorites such as "The Long, Long Trail" and "Keep the Home Fires Burning." But the flaming youth of the twenties burned too brightly. They were more interested in singing along to "When My Baby Smiles at Me," "I'm Just Wild About Harry," "Ain't We Got Fun," or "The Sheik of Araby." The lyrics made the proper ladies' skin crawl.

On the silent screen were images of Latin lovers and vamps. In his book *This Side of Paradise,* the twenty-four-year-old novelist F. Scott Fitzgerald wrote of the new generation. He wrote that they were "dedicated more than the last to the fear of poverty and the worship of success; grown up to find all Gods dead, all wars fought, all faiths in man shaken."

The country folk may not have been reading Fitzgerald or watching the performances of Clara Bow and Rudolph Valentino, but they needed no further proof to believe there was nothing of substance in the cities. When boys and girls left the farms for the larger cities, they lost their values and became corrupted. The Floyds were convinced this was what had happened to Charley.

In the cities and country towns alike, there were those who fought the social movements and the shifts in lifestyle and culture around them. Among these people were some who were motivated by feelings of inferiority and ignorance. They reacted by turning to violence. Secret vigilante groups popped up like wild blossoms in a manure pile. In the early 1920s, the Ku Klux Klan, a terrorist organization that had pursued racist goals during the Reconstruction period, rose like a phoenix from the smoldering ashes of hate.

In the years when Choc's grandparents were struggling to make a living in northern Georgia, the Klan had been a powerful force. The KKK had begun in 1866, in Pulaski, Tennessee, as a social organization devoted to countering the worst excesses of the federal Reconstruction. Klansmen were dedicated to restoring what they referred to as the "old order" in the South by intimidating Negro voters and dispensing their own brand of cruel justice. They emerged at night with their faces veiled and they carried skulls and rattling bags of bones. Besides ropes and guns, the grim riders relied on fear and superstition. They would ride up to a black family's home, announcing they were Confederate ghosts returned from hell.

Federal laws and Supreme Court decisions eviscerated the power of the Klan. However, by 1915, after the appearance of D. W. Griffith's *Birth of a Nation,* a popular film that glorified the Klan as the protector of white supremacy and southern ladies' virtue, a strong KKK revival had begun. That same year, an ex-Methodist preacher named William J. Simmons and his followers helped with the Klan rebirth during their meetings at Stone Mountain, Georgia, not far from Atlanta. Simmons and thirty-four others climbed the mountain on a Thanksgiving night and rekindled evil fires. Simmons liked to say their first gathering was held "in the bitter cold," but the record indicated the temperature that night was actually about forty-five degrees. Exaggeration and deceit were the least of his sins.

The KKK took on an anti-Catholic and anti-Semitic thrust besides an inbred hatred of blacks. During the early twenties, Klan membership rose to more than 4 million. They were particularly strong in the Deep South but were also able to influence politics from coast to coast. In Texas, the hooded Klansmen preyed upon Mexicans and those of Hispanic descent; in California, the Japanese Americans were targets; and in New York and the larger eastern cities, the KKK harassed Jewish immigrants. In their continuing fight to resist the country's changing mores and values, the Klan branded liberals as a menace to be feared almost as much as foreigners, socialists, or even the dreaded Pope. Further bolstered because of the newfound morality that resulted from Prohibition, the Klan gained strength in Chicago, Pittsburgh, Dayton, Indianapolis, Detroit, and other large cities.

Klaverns, or chapters, were formed by avowed God-fearing Christians who wanted to impose law and order on as many people as possible. Each klavern meeting was opened and closed with hymns and prayers. Klansmen even visited churches and Baptist temples during services. A whole klavern, sometimes consisting of as many as two hundred hooded men, would march boldly down the center aisle. They would halt before the congregation, give the minister an envelope filled with money, and then quietly do an about-face and leave. One writer of that period noted that these ecclesiastical visitations had the dramatic punch of a "hold-up in broad daylight."

In Oklahoma—a relatively new state permeated with religious zealots who subscribed to a fundamentalist code of conduct—the Klan unquestionably placed blacks, Jews, and Catholics on their enemies list. Too many of these Klan victims ended up lynched, castrated, or branded because of color and creed—or simply for being in the wrong place at the wrong time. The night riders also wished to enforce community morals and standards, however. In the cities and towns where this occurred, the Klansmen were ruthless.

They took it upon themselves to punish gamblers, bootleggers, and whores. They chastised wayward husbands. Physicians accused of performing abortions, suspected wife beaters, or shopkeepers inclined to shortchange customers were likely to be kidnapped and beaten or else tarred and feathered. Klan "whipping squads" from Oklahoma City boasted that they administered more than 2,500 floggings in a single year. Shawnee, Oklahoma, was the home of at least five whipping squads.

During the 1920s, the Klan was particularly active in Tulsa. Besides thousands of adult men and women KKK members, including clergy and teachers, Tulsa even had a Junior Ku Klux Klan, open to certain white boys from twelve to eighteen years of age. Bigotry and malice became a family affair. The Klan was so strong in Tulsa that in the November 1922 elections, both the Democratic and Republican candidates for sheriff and county attorney were Klansmen pledged to the Invisible Empire. A star-kissed city blessed by its proximity to the oil fields, Tulsa was also home for vigilante groups—the black-robed and masked Knights of Liberty, who had terrorized and tortured socialists, IWW members, and union organizers for many years. A switch to white robes proved hardly to be a difficult maneuver. The *Tulsa World* and much of the other local press referred to these vigilantes as true patriots and condoned their actions. For many years, Tulsa lived on the verge of mob rule and necktie justice.

Still, Tulsa's darkest days occurred between May 31 and June 2, 1921, when one of the most disastrous race riots in the nation's history exploded in the city's streets. As hundreds of thousands of blacks fled the Deep South between 1916 and 1920, a series of racial disturbances broke out in several cities. There were lynchings and riots in Charleston, Chicago, Washington, D.C., Knoxville, Omaha, East St. Louis, and Duluth. The mob slaughter in Tulsa was especially brutal, however.

The rioting in Tulsa resulted after a young black man was wrongly accused and then arrested for having attacked a white woman who operated an elevator in a downtown office building. Rumors of a lynching raged throughout the city. These reports were fueled in large part by scurrilous headlines and biased stories in the local newspapers. Ninety-degree-plus temperatures did not help matters. Neither did an ineffectual police department and sheriff's office. Furious mobs of opposing blacks and whites congregated around the jail. Their threats and accusations provoked violent action. Gangs of enraged whites, armed with guns and stones and goaded on by Klansmen, marched on the black neighborhoods and the thriving black business district in north Tulsa.

A nightmare of burning, looting, and gunfire followed. Finally, the National Guard was summoned and thousands of displaced black refugees were rounded up and kept under guard at Convention Hall, McNulty Park, and the county fair grounds. Red Cross workers doled out hot soup, bread, and blankets. Witnesses to the carnage, who had gathered on Standpipe Hill, said they observed total devastation as far as the eye could see. Black homes, businesses, and churches were torched. Black men, women, and children were attacked and brutalized. What white Tulsans disparagingly called "Little Africa" was a smoking ruins.

For the blacks, there was no place to hide. Airplanes scouted from overhead. There were reports that lighted sticks of dynamite were dropped on homes. The sound of machine guns punctuated the smoky night. An elderly black couple was murdered after offering their prayers in church. A prominent black physician was gunned down as he ran from his burning residence. White vigilantes patrolled well-to-do neighborhoods and apprehended terrified black domestic servants. Corpses of black victims were defiled; some bodies were even tied to car bumpers and dragged through the streets. Officials estimated that ninety blacks and ten whites were killed. Others said at least three hundred black citizens perished. Still others maintained the number of black deaths was many times that number. Seventy years later, murmurs still lingered about trucks that had left the city loaded with black bodies. Once-thriving neighborhoods resembled Atlanta after General Sherman's visit. They looked like bombed battlegrounds with only brick shells left standing. The bustling business area off of Archer Street on Greenwood Avenue, formerly known as the "Negro Wall Street," was devastated and would not even be partially restored for almost sixty-five years. At least a thousand blacks spent the winter of 1922 living in tents. A precise loss in property and lives was never determined.

White leaders vowed they would help rebuild black Tulsa. They lied. The stain that tarnished the city's soul was never truly cleansed. Tulsa remained as segregated, and in many ways as racist, as any city in the Deep South.

In Oklahoma, crime prevailed in many of the towns and cities that were dominated by the oil industry. Violence and prosperity seemed to go well together. Although supposedly solid citizens condoned the moral crusade carried out by vigilantes and the Ku Klux Klan, these same "good Christian men and women" also looked the other way when it came to dealing with certain property crimes and acts of violence. This was especially the case in the rural areas.

Many criminal acts were considered to be almost a form of political protest. They served as a means of striking back at the establishment that dominated the lives of rural citizens. Starting as early as 1910, there had been a steady rise of what became known as "social banditry." To the tenant farmers and sharecroppers scrambling to dig a living from the earth, there was little wrong with a man who had the guts to rob a bank. It was the ultimate expression of protest. Bankers, like the big railroad barons who had fenced off grazing land, were the enemy as far as the poor folks were concerned. They believed the banks cheated them every chance they got.

Oklahoma's dirt farmers, descended from sons and daughters of the frontier South, upheld their outlaw heroes who robbed the banks and trains. Civil disobedience, once part of the agrarian southern way of life, was carried westward to former Indian Territory. Southerners, like the Floyds and their neighbors, adopted Confederate generals and wily moonshiners as their models. Those glorified ancestors and cherished rascals helped bind everyone together.

Wilbur Joseph Cash, a Piedmont Southerner and journalist, argued that southern cultural unity was created in part by frontier violence, climate, and clannishness. Cash labeled this flaw in the southern character "social schizophrenia." For every hedonistic tendency, there was bound to be a corresponding puritanical bias. Unbridled force was always countered by the Southerner's chivalrous code of conduct. A need to honor family roots and community ties was opposed by the burning desire to roam. Life became a precarious balancing act. According to Cash, the Southern social bandit especially epitomized this contradictory or split-personality lifestyle. These bandits took on several guises—the rebel guerrillas who became Missouri's most successful outlaws, the Texas and Oklahoma cowboys who turned into vigilantes, and the farmhands of the prairies and southern plains who emerged as brigands.

Social bandits, in the best tradition of Robin Hood, or, better yet, Choc Floyd's preferred idol—Jesse James—were the "good guys" according to a surprisingly large number of Oklahomans. As early as 1912—just a year after Walter Floyd's brood arrived at the Hanson railroad landing—Oklahoma led the nation in bank robberies. The trend continued. A few of the robberies were inside jobs, with bank employees and even officers staging hoax holdups and making off with the loot. But more often than not, the banks were held up by bandits who were cut from the same cloth as the James boys and others who were glamorized by the dime-novel writers.

During the four-month period between September 8, 1914, and January 13, 1915, there were fourteen bank robberies in Oklahoma alone. They occurred in small towns—Carney, Tupelo, Prue, Owasso, Vera, and the like. The average take was about two thousand dollars. The smallest haul was a paltry seven hundred dollars snatched from the state bank in Byars on a crisp October afternoon. The largest amount seized was $6,400 from the Kiefer Central Bank on the final day of September. A January 4, 1915, robbery attempt at the Oklahoma State Bank of Preston in oil-rich Okmulgee County resulted in twelve hundred dollars' worth of damages to the sturdy vault, but the bandits left town empty-handed. This sort of activity alarmed the financial community as insurance companies threatened to cancel bank policies. Enormous rewards were placed on the bandits' heads and additional money was appropriated to hire a team of manhunters to track down the pesky robbers. Little if any reward money was doled out. Most folks did not wish to get involved.

One of the chief "social bandits" of this period was Henry Starr, who had been born in Indian Territory in 1873 and gave up the cowboy's life about 1890 to go on the scout and launch a career of crime. Starr, who was a half-breed Cherokee and claimed kinship to Belle Starr, the old Bandit Queen herself, graduated from horse theft to bank and train robbery during his more than thirty years on the outlaw trail. After he killed Floyd Wilson, a railroad detective toting an arrest warrant near the town of Lenapah in the Cherokee Nation, Starr fled into the sprawling Osage country. Years later, when statehood was granted, this 2,264-square-mile region of lush bluestem grass and rich oil deposits would become the largest county in Oklahoma. Like the Cookson Hills to the south, the Osage was a favorite resting ground for desperadoes. Starr was not only familiar with the territory but he had many friends and acquaintances who were willing to hide him or provide food and cover. Because of pardons, including one from President Theodore Roosevelt, court dismissals, and some lucky breaks, Starr waltzed away from the hangman's noose at Fort Smith and elsewhere. He used his Winchester to shoot his way out of several confrontations with law officers.

Other well-known bandits who emerged during this period included Al Jennings, a bungling train robber and notoriously poor marksman. Jennings learned the art of storytelling while serving a hitch in an Ohio penitentiary. It was in prison where Jennings befriended a Texas bank teller convicted of embezzlement. Named William Sydney Porter, this convict went on to become known as the celebrated author and short-story writer O. Henry.

After Jennings received a Theodore Roosevelt pardon like the one given to Starr, he settled down to do some writing of his own. He also became an adviser to some of the early Western motion-picture producers, and appeared in a few films himself. He briefly toured the state with a "crime does not pay" message and was even a solid contender of the office of governor. During the campaign, Jennings told some potential voters, "If elected I promise to be honest for a year—if I can hold out that long." In the 1914 Democratic primary, Jennings boasted that the people of Oklahoma could trust a train robber far more than the dishonest politicians. That made perfect sense to some Oklahomans. Jennings wound up with a strong third-place finish, gathering more than 24 percent of the vote.

The comical Jennings may have commanded many of the headlines, but there was little doubt that Henry Starr was still the reigning champion when it came to lawlessness. Starr had also served some time in the Ohio penitentiary at Columbus and was later able to obtain paroles from prison after serving stretches in Colorado from 1909 to 1913 and in Oklahoma from 1915 to 1919. On both occasions, he immediately went back to his wicked ways. He used his time in prison to pore through law books and perfect his bandit skills. No one was about to reform him and he had no aspirations for political office. Starr was the undisputed king of bank robbers.

Choc Floyd was very much aware of Starr and his exploits. Anyone living in Oklahoma during the teens and twenties knew about the busy bandit. Starr, whose name was a household word, was an especially recognized figure in Sequoyah County. It was this same Henry Starr who had his saddle repaired by J. H. Harkrider, the Sallisaw merchant who had caught Floyd red-handed with the box of cookies swiped from a store shelf when Charley was just a kid. Choc also heard the stories that Starr had been a prime suspect in the series of bank robberies between late 1914 and 1915 that had the bankers so riled. Some state authorities were convinced that Starr had a hand in every single one of the robberies, including the aborted attempt at Preston, where the vault was badly damaged. For his part, Starr neither admitted nor denied his involvement in those particular holdups.

Despite all the hoopla about the robberies, Starr had many admirers. Most of them were like Choc, and believed Starr was a reincarnation of Jesse James. Rumor had it that when Starr robbed a train or bank, he never bothered the ladies. He refused to take watches and money from any working men. He was the classic social bandit—at least in the minds of his public.

So it was big news on March 27, 1915, when Starr and some others tried to rob two banks in Stroud, Oklahoma, and a seventeen-year-old kid named Paul Curry shot the bandit leader with a 30-30 rifle used to kill hogs. Starr's goal to rob a pair of banks in the same town in a single afternoon—a difficult feat the Daltons had failed to do many years before at Coffeyville, Kansas—ended in miserable failure. The wounded bandit was apprehended, and during his trial several months later, he pled guilty to bank robbery and was sentenced to twenty-five years in the state prison at McAlester. Before Starr left the courtroom, he went over to the boy who had plugged him and congratulated him for his courage and sharpshooting ability.

As always, Starr was an exemplary inmate. He taught composition and spelling to the other prisoners, worked as a librarian, and won sympathy because of his game leg, which had been crippled from the wound he had received at the hands of young Curry. In 1919, after gaining another parole, Starr followed the lead of Al Jennings and Emmett Dalton and dabbled in the motion-picture business. He bought into a Tulsa film company and played himself in a film that was a reenactment of his daring double bank robbery attempt at Stroud. Starr employed Stroud residents, including bank employees, as actors and he even hired his youthful nemesis, Paul Curry, to reenact his role. The film, *Debtor to the Law,* was a success, but when no financial windfall resulted, Starr felt he had been cheated. He married a Sallisaw woman, moved to Claremore, and borrowed money for lawyers to win back the earnings he was swindled out of by his associates in the moving-picture venture. When those efforts failed and with his debts mounting, Starr had just the excuse he needed to return once more to his bandit ways.

On February 18, 1921, Starr and three companions drove into Harrison, Arkansas, in a high-powered automobile. They parked and entered the People's National Bank with their weapons drawn. Customers and employees were held at gunpoint, and the robbers scooped up six thousand dollars in cash and ordered a teller to open the safe. Former bank president W. J. Meyers happened to be present, and he remembered that twelve years before he had hidden a rifle away in the vault. While the bandits were occupied, Meyers grabbed the gun and opened fire. A bullet struck Starr in the side and severed his spinal cord. He crashed to the floor, and the others fled without any money. They were soon captured.

Starr died four days later on a jail cot. At his side were his mother and his new wife. It was February 22—George Washington's birthday and the Starrs' first wedding anniversary. Also at the deathwatch was a son from his first marriage, named for Theodore Roosevelt.

"I have robbed more banks than any man in the United States," Starr said the day before he died to Dr. J. H. Fowler, the attending physician. "It doesn't pay. I was in debt two thousand dollars and had to have money, so I turned bank robber again. I am sorry but the deed is done."

Henry Starr—who during an endless crime spree in the early teens became the first bandit to use an automobile in a robbery—had been a brazen criminal. He had made the transition from the old days when outlaws rode quarter horses and wore rough work clothes to a time when they donned business suits and neckties and came calling on banks in sedans. Starr was a pioneer in the world of desperadoes and his passing was noted with a bit of sadness even on the part of some law-abiding people who remembered when he was just a small-time cattle rustler.

Choc was probably on the road somewhere in Kansas when Starr met his end. He knew that Starr was a direct tie to the old boots and saddle days on the outlaw trail that Choc and his friends loved so much.

As the twenties proceeded, there were reminders, other than the demise of Henry Starr, that the times were, in fact, changing.

Down in the Cookson Hills, eighteen-year-old Choc Floyd was still trying to come to grips with himself. He was having little luck, but he did experience some good fortune when it came to the nightly dice games and poker parties held in the grove of huge shade trees behind one of the stores in the village of Akins. He could hold his own even with seasoned gamblers, especially if they got a little whiskey in them and lost their edge in a game of five-card stud with a respectable pot on the line. Choc had picked up a trick or two from Callahan and the fellows up in Wichita. He knew how to pace himself and how to bluff his way out of a jam.

However, no bold poker player's bluff worked on a fair evening in May of 1922, when Choc and a couple of his friends jimmied a window at one of the local stores that also served as a post office. Once inside, they took several molasses cans filled with pennies collected for postage stamps. The cans were lifted out of the window and within minutes the thieves were gone. They had talked themselves into burglarizing the store. It was meant to be a lark. As if on a dare, the young men scrambled inside to steal some money to fuel their penny-ante card games.

In the darkness, they had no way to really tell just how much money they had stolen. The next day when the storekeeper found he had been victimized, the news quickly traveled around town and out to the farms and fields. More than $350 in pennies was missing. That was a mighty good sum to most folks, even city dwellers. At Renberg's, a clothing store on Main Street in Tulsa, an all-wool boy's suit could have been purchased for $8.95. Housewives headed to the Piggly Wiggly were prepared to shell out fifteen cents for a can of hominy and a dime for a can of Campbell's baked beans.

By the time everyone figured out just how much was taken, however, it did not really matter. The pennies had already been dumped down a hand-dug water well on the property belonging to Choc's grandpa, old Charles Murphy Floyd, situated near the post office store. The boys had reconsidered the situation, and in the light of the next day, when panic and perhaps some remorse set in, they had decided to get rid of any evidence.

It did not take a Pinkerton detective to figure out just who might be responsible for the store theft. Choc and his usual crew of pals were suspected to be prime culprits. This time, though, the boys had gone too far. There was more involved here than some purloined cookies or a mischievous baby swap at a revival meeting. This was a felony, and since the incident involved money taken from a U.S. post office, the local authorities had to summon federal men from Muskogee. They came down to Akins in their pressed suits and fresh straw hats to poke around and see what they could turn up. Fortunately for Choc, the men were also good Masons, and so they listened to Walter Floyd when he stepped forward and gave them an alibi for his son.

"Ol' man Floyd talked to those feds," recalled Marvin Amos, whose brother Cleon was one of Choc's best running partners. "He managed to convince them that Choc was nowhere near that store. Back then the Floyds were living about a quarter mile south, and ol' Walter Floyd told them that Choc was tucked away in bed at the exact time of that store robbery."

Choc counted his blessings. He knew he was lucky. That same night of the post-office burglary, a band of masked men near the Oklahoma town of Kiefer took a twenty-two-year-old man from his home to a remote area where they gave him a severe whipping because they claimed he had been intimate with some of the local young ladies. Choc and his accomplices had no angry vigilantes to face. Walter Floyd was bad enough.

Not long after that incident, Choc and Cleon Amos and some of the other boys went over to Fort Smith and had a serious chat with the navy recruiter. They were all ready to join up on the buddy system and see the world.

"About four of those boys went to Fort Smith to join the navy," recalled Marvin Amos. "But my dad found out about it and he went down there and got my brother Cleon and all the other boys backed out and came on home. Then later on Cleon slipped back all by himself and he joined up. He stayed in the navy and made it a career. He retired from the service. Charley Floyd was there that first time to join. He was ready to go. He would have, too, if they would have just left him alone. Makes a man wonder. Wonder how that would have changed things. Guess we'll never know."

17

STAR LIGHT, STAR BRIGHT

RUBY HARDGRAVES, a tenant farmer's barefooted daughter with a splash of Cherokee blood, was one of the best things that ever happened to Charles Arthur Floyd. He damn well knew it, too, and so did she almost from the very start. Ruby and her kin lived around Akins, and when she started budding, Choc caught her scent and stayed on her trail like one of Walter Floyd's top-drawer hounds shadowing a vixen fox.

Born February 6, 1907, more than nine months before Oklahoma and Indian territories joined together for admission to the Union as the forty-sixth state, Ruby was almost exactly three years younger than Choc. Also like Charley, she was a pure child of Aquarius, and her birth date also fell on a Wednesday, but her folks, like the Floyds, did not practice astrology or follow the stars.

Ruby's father was Ben F. Hardgraves, a sharecropper born in 1883, a man who spent his life walled in by fields of cotton. Hardgraves was a twenty-four-year-old with not much more than a mule and a strong back when his daughter arrived on a cold winter's day. Ruby's mother, a native of Crawford County, Arkansas, had been born Sarah Adel Edwards in 1888, but many of her family and friends as well as her husband preferred to call her by her pet name, "Deller." She was the sixth of fourteen children born to Perry Commodore Edwards and his wife, Mary Elizabeth McKibben Edwards, and the strain of Cherokee heritage of her mother showed up in the cheekbones of the new baby daughter.

Ruby never really got to know her mother very well. Sarah "Deller" Hardgraves died at the age of twenty on September 24, 1908, in southeastern Oklahoma, while giving birth to another infant girl at the family's small cabin. Ben, whose own father was dead, did the best he could to care for Ruby, and he got some help with his little girl from his mother, Lydia, and her husband, Hugh Gay, a second-generation Irishman who had outlived at least two other wives. The Gays kept a tidy cabin near Akins and Ruby's step-grandfather worked as a janitor at the Akins school after he retired from farming.

Ben Hardgraves kept plowing the rented land, and when he found another wife, he was overjoyed. Her name was Maggie and her disposition was sweet and pleasing. Ben's happiness increased even more when his new wife accepted young Ruby as if the little girl were her own daughter. Maggie Hardgraves, an amiable Irish lady who baked buttermilk biscuits that would have made the devil shout praises to the Lord, gave Ruby the love and attention she needed. Eventually, Ben and Maggie would have four children of their own. There were three Hardgraves sons, named J.B., Jess, and Albert, and a daughter they named Pauline. All of them looked up to their older stepsister, Ruby.

Like others in the vast tribe of cotton farmers who made up the tenant system, the Hardgraves were unadorned folk. The boys were clad in faded denim hand-me-downs and the same kind of caps the factory workers in the cities liked to wear. The women went without rouge and lipstick. The Hardgraves family worked other men's fields and lived in a series of frame houses and cabins, mostly unpainted and weathered, or occasionally covered with whitewash and a few morning glory vines. When they met friends or relatives at a reunion, funeral, or holiday gathering, they used the formal one-pump handshake that was common among country people and full-blooded Indians.

The boys paid no attention to hunting seasons. They roamed the fallow fields and meadows with their .22 rifles and single-barrel shotguns, looking for rabbits that would end up simmering in a frying pan with some onions and potatoes. They staved off the winter with ricks of blackjack oak, and when it was dark and cold, they wrapped up in quilts and listened to the raw wind trying to get inside. In the summer when those winds turned hot and dry and the house was stifling, they took the bedding outside and slept beneath the sheltering night sky. Farmers' children laid on their backs and told secrets. They talked themselves to sleep while they watched for the first star to appear. It cost nothing to make a wish, and sometimes they even came true. Ruby sent a thousand wishes into the dark sky with the hope one of them would come to pass.

Sharecroppers had no sedans or trucks like the Floyds, and most of them never dreamed of owning their own home or their own land. "Don't have a pot to piss in" is what people said about the sharecroppers. There was an Old Testament God and a New Testament Jesus to console them, however, and they did grow some fine produce. They had their vegetables and fruit and chickens. They had a little tobacco and they made up their own whiskey. Everything the sharecropping families consumed they grew themselves. Self-reliance was important to folks like Ben Hardgraves and his bunch. This also meant they held on to the few cash dollars they managed to keep, and did not put the money in a bank, where they felt they were likely to lose it.

It was true enough the banks in the state had come a long way since the early days in the 1700s when ingenious French traders stored away in chests valuable fur pelts that were deposited with them by Indian clients for future trading. During territorial times, the banks managed to move out of temporary buildings and makeshift operations in general stores and even started resembling real banks back in the East, at least in terms of details such as tellers' cages, rolltop desks, vaults, and brass spittoons for the patrons.

Between 1903 and 1920, the number of banks in the state increased from 531 to 978. Not many of the rural banks enjoyed good health, however, especially after World War I when the foreign demand for American agricultural goods returned to normal levels and prices for the farm products tumbled. The banking and financial community reverberated with the force of the agricultural depression. Farmers could no longer come up with their loan payments, so bankers throughout the agricultural areas failed to meet their own obligations. The domino effect escalated, and, as a result, many banks closed their doors and ceased operations. During the decade of the twenties, there was an *average* of 550 bank failures in the United States each year, and the majority were located in small farm towns. In just the two years from 1921 to 1923, seventy Oklahoma banks—including the Sallisaw Bank and Trust Company—failed.

The banks in the farming areas had never acted like the banks elsewhere in the nation. Rural banks were involved both in land speculation and horse trading. Even back in the days of World War I in Europe, when the cotton market began its collapse, farmers felt the squeeze from local bankers who increased agricultural interest rates. Instead of taking in deposits, these bankers mostly loaned money at high and often exorbitant rates to small farmers. Such usurious interest charges led, in large part, to much of the tension between urban and rural Oklahomans.

By the 1920s, worried bankers foreclosed on farm notes and repossessed mules, horses, and plows. They formed associations and worked at convincing rural governments to hire county agents to advise local growers about modern farming techniques. They also continued their efforts to motivate farmers to plant a diversity of crops other than the usual wheat in western Oklahoma and cotton in the eastern half of the state. They waged a losing battle.

Regardless of the desperate nostrums bankers tried, rural America failed to reverse the tide. Farmers packed up their new Fords and fled their property. The number of tenancy farms increased to the point that, by the mid-1920s, tenants worked as much as 80 percent of the land in some counties. The itinerant farmers and tenants failed to heed the advice about forsaking cotton, and they planted their crops from fence post to fence post. Like their fathers and grandfathers before them, they lived no better than serfs. Some of them planted cotton right up into their own dirt yards. They even stopped putting in vegetable gardens so they would have more space to devote to the crop that controlled their lives. During the first half of the decade, the value of farm land decreased by 23 percent and the average gross income for farmers fell to record lows. To poor folks, like the Hardgraves, their few precious greenbacks were much safer hidden away in an old molasses can or placed between the pages of the family Bible than in a bank where the risk of failure or theft was as strong as ever.

During this time, robbers continued to prey upon the surviving small banks scattered throughout the countryside. Hostility toward the bankers of eastern Oklahoma, especially from the small farmers and sharecroppers, remained as strong as it had been a few years earlier when Henry Starr pointed out in his defense that bankers were "in the robbery business, too." The Oklahoma Bankers' Association estimated that at least sixty to seventy-five banks were robbed each year during the twenties. Oklahoma's frontier image was safe with the people in Pittsburgh, St. Louis, Chicago, Philadelphia, and New York, who read in their newspapers about the bank robberies and bandits. As the losses mounted, the bank-association officials urged rural bankers to bar their windows, issue tear-gas guns to tellers, hire armed guards, and install alarms and vaults with time locks. Along with the increase in robberies came a steady rise in the banks' annual insurance rates, from two dollars per thousand dollars to twenty dollars per thousand. To stem the tide of robberies, the association formed a crime-prevention team and even hired the Burns Detective Agency, whose undercover agents snuck around and tried to get chummy with those who knew the bandits. The agents wanted to turn up culprits by infiltrating some of the robbery gangs. They had limited success.

Social bandits were still the rage in Oklahoma. They would remain so for many years to come. Some of the bank and train robbers were heroic figures. These were ordinary criminals who were cast as modern-day legends. A few of them hoped they would be only half as lucky as Henry Starr or even Jesse James and become national celebrities before their deaths. They basked in the image of good old country boys who were driven to a life of crime by outside forces and circumstances beyond their control. Just as in the heyday of the James boys, the banks and railroads remained the villains and scoundrels, not the outlaw rogues who robbed them. Folks still believed that county-seat bankers were only worried about getting their usurious interest rates. It was the bankers, the Working Class Union had once warned, who were to blame for forcing law-abiding cotton farmers to adopt outlaw ways. These men who took up the mask and revolver were content to preserve Oklahoma's old image as the last frontier, all the while adopting the latest in modern weaponry and speedy automobiles for their getaways.

Even though the bank robbers and train bandits of the 1920s were switching from cow ponies to autos, many of the old customs lingered. One Oklahoma outlaw who had a difficult time forsaking the old ways was Al Spencer. Nonetheless, he became one of the few bandits who was able to ride over the cusp separating the old outlaw days and the modern criminal era.

Spencer was born in 1893 near the Indian Territory town of Lenapah, located in what would later be named Nowata County, just south of the Kansas line and the town of Coffeyville, where the Dalton gang was shot to bits in 1892. Crawford Goldsby, the outlaw who met his end on the gallows at Fort Smith and called himself Cherokee Bill, and Sam McWilliams, a bandit known as the Verdigris Kid, were familiar characters in these parts. It was in Lenapah where Henry "Bearcat" Starr committed his first robbery and also shot and killed a railroad detective.

Spencer, like the intrepid Starr, began his career of lawlessness as a cattle rustler and horse thief. He soon went on to robbing stores and banks. Henry Starr was said to have robbed more than fifty banks. Some of the editorial writers and pulp authors, known for exaggeration and ballyhoo more than fact checking or accuracy, claimed Spencer eventually robbed almost that many himself. In headlines, Spencer was labeled the Phantom Terror and the Wild Rider of Oklahoma. He was also called the King of the Osage, in reference to his favorite stomping grounds in the Osage Hills, where some of the clannish people considered outlaws to be respectable businessmen.

Many years after Spencer's death, Paul Wellman, the Oklahoma native and former Wichita newspaper reporter who later wrote for the *Kansas City Star,* came up with an interesting theory that some Western historians disputed but could not disprove. According to Wellman and his best sources, Spencer not only knew Henry Starr but was one of the bandit's companions who managed to escape the fracas in Stroud, Oklahoma, in 1915. Based on his contacts with midwestern underworld figures, Wellman also stated that Spencer, as well as Starr, was well acquainted with the cunning John Callahan.

Throughout the country's tumultuous teenage years, Spencer and a few of his sidekicks continued to operate in northern Oklahoma. They managed to avoid capture until 1920, about the time when oil began flowing in earnest from the Osage fields. On March 8 of that year, Spencer was hauled into a district court and was convicted of horse theft. The judge straightaway sent him off to the state penitentiary at McAlester.

Inside the stout prison walls of "Big Mac," Spencer became reacquainted with old friends and made some new ones, including a balding convict with a prominent nose named Frank Nash. An avid reader of the classics, Nash spouted poetry and used his time in the pen to bone up on his favorite author, William Shakespeare.

Nash was born in Indiana in 1887. He came west with his family and was raised in the southwestern Oklahoma town of Hobart, later the county seat of Kiowa County. Named for the vice president under William McKinley, the town sprang to life in 1901 when the Kiowa-Comanche Indian lands were opened for settlement. By 1902, Nash's father, John O. Nash, had established a hotel in Hobart and, from the first day of operation, horses and buggies bringing customers lined up in droves on the street out front. Known simply as the Nash, the hotel became a favorite resting place not only for commercial travelers and railroad men but also for drummers who tried to arrange their schedules to include at least several nights in the comfortable two-story frame building. Nash later gave the hotel to his daughter and son-in-law, Alice and John Long. Under Alice's shrewd management, and with her younger half brother, Frank, acting as cook, the hotel's reputation as a first-rate place to eat spread like prairie fire.

Frank Nash wearied of the steamy kitchen, however. He hated slinging hash for traveling peddlers and Bible salesmen as much as Choc Floyd despised chopping cotton. Nash had no interest in clerking at the front desk. Instead, he turned to burglary and theft as an added means of support. By 1913, he and two accomplices had carried out several successful capers. When Nash and one of his cohorts suspected the other member of their troika of squealing to the authorities, they shot him stone dead. Nash and the other fellow were arrested and jailed at Hobart. While they awaited trial, Nash's strikingly beautiful half sister, Alice—remembered around town for her velvet dresses, ostrich-plume hats, and diamond jewelry—saw to it that Nash and his fellow prisoners dined on fare brought to their cells hot from the hotel kitchen. Years before when Nash had served a term as a youthful offender at the reformatory at Granite, he had also received sumptuous meals from the hotel, compliments of the thoughtful Mrs. Long.

In July 1913, Nash's first trial on the murder charge ended with a hung jury when the members split their decision. A new court date was set, and on September 12, 1913, a news item with a Hobart, Oklahoma, dateline appeared in several newspapers, such as the *Eufaula Democrat:*

> The second trial of Frank Nash for the murdder [*sic*] of "Humpie" Wartman resulted in his conviction of murder in the first degree, with a sentence of life imprisonment.
>
> John Huber has already been convicted of complicity in the same murder and is now serving a life sentence for the crime.

On September 13, Nash was sent to McAlester to spend the rest of his life. As a convicted killer wearing number 4458, he could no longer sup on hotel cuisine. Nash spent less than five years behind bars, though. A personable fellow and a respected prison trusty, Nash was able to convince the warden he had been rehabilitated and was anxious to serve his country by battling in the trenches of France during World War I. On August 16, 1918, Nash was pardoned. Instead of going straight to the local recruiter and enlisting, the twenty-five-year-old returned to Hobart and went into seclusion. In no time at all, he was back to his old tricks.

On October 18, 1919, Nash was arrested by sheriff's deputies in connection with a bank robbery at Cordell, Oklahoma, but the charge did not stick and he was released. Nash and some other bandits turned right around and hit the bank at the farming community of Corn, Oklahoma. He was again arrested, tried, and this time, he was convicted of burglary with explosives. Nash, sometimes known by the alias Charles B. Edgar or by the name "Jelly," was returned to prison on August 4, 1920, to serve a twenty-five-year hitch. Waiting for him at McAlester was a fresh inmate uniform; a new number, 10672; and Al Spencer, the Osage bandit who had been residing there since March. The two men found plenty to talk about, including how to perfect their bank-robbing techniques.

Spencer, who had been granted a mysterious one-month prison furlough in 1921, escaped from the penitentiary on January 27, 1922. The cagey outlaw made a beeline to the Osage Hills, where he had been born, and immediately began hatching plans for the bank robberies he had been plotting in prison. Jelly Nash was fearful of getting shot in a break, so he had opted not to accompany his friend over the wall but to earn another early release and walk out the front gate. His strategy worked.

Following Spencer's lead, Nash made application to the warden for a leave of absence "for business reasons," and in December 1922, he was again pardoned in time to celebrate the holidays. Nash had no intention of ever returning to prison. The enterprise Nash wished to pursue was business of an unorthodox sort, and he promptly slipped into the wild hills and joined Al Spencer as his right-hand man. They assembled a formidable crew. Some of those who rode off and on with Spencer and Nash included such legendary desperadoes as Ike Ogg, Stanley Snyder, Henry Wells, Earl "Dad" Thayer, Ray Terrill, Curtis Kelly, Grover Durrell, Walter Philpott, Barnard Clark, Frank Billingsly, and Bud Jenkins. Goldie Bates was a young woman who became chummy with Spencer while he and the others operated out of the Osage country. It was a forceful and rugged company, and whether they actually pulled the jobs or not, the Spencer gang took the blame for a good many bank robberies.

Rag towns bloomed almost overnight in the oil-rich hills and prairies of the Burbank field in Osage County. They were rank and bawdy places, and the oil companies hired tough cowboys and ex-soldiers to act as special law officers to help keep the peace. Robbers, whores, bootleggers, and thugs flocked to the oil patch camps to prey on workers or else create new identities for themselves. Innocent farm girls interested in bettering their lives came to the instant towns, but they found the best jobs to be had were at dance halls, where they got to keep only a dime out of every quarter charged for a waltz. Many of the girls learned there was even more money to be made on a brothel cot once the dancing stopped.

Life was cheap in these boomtowns. It was not uncommon to see a curious crowd gathered around a corpse lying dead in the streets, or for workers on their way to the pump jacks in the fields to spy a body with its throat cut from ear to ear lying in a ditch. Hijackers went out to the remote oil rigs and took watches, wedding bands, or anything of value they could find on the drilling crews. Rural mail carriers, and those traveling in buggies and Model T's were often mugged and robbed. Some of the outlaws were "coke heads," as they were called then, and had expensive dope habits to finance.

Not all the thieves carried guns; some used fountain pens. Besides the common criminals, there were also con artists who made enormous profits by selling oil-rich Osage Indians ridiculously marked-up merchandise such as clothing, fancy automobiles, and grand pianos. Some unscrupulous white men in business suits amassed fortunes by cheating Osage Indians out of their valuable mineral rights or even murdering them in order to get at the oil deposits beneath the bluegrass prairie.

One of the wildest boomtowns in the Burbank oil field was Denoya, named for a prominent Osage Indian family but better known locally as Whizbang, after Whizbang Red, a notorious Kansas City madam. Shootings, knifings, and no-holds-barred fistfights were common occurrences in Whizbang. It was said that it wasn't safe for a woman to be on the streets of Whizbang after dark, and in the early 1920s, the town bank was robbed on at least two occasions. During 1923, bandits held up several banks in the Osage territory or adjacent counties where they found refuge. Banks in Burbank, Ripley, Barnsdall, Cambridge, Bartlesville, Denoya, Fairfax, and Shidler were all robbed that year. The bank in the tiny Osage trading center of Grainola was hit twice, although during one of the incidents, a storekeeper with a rifle was able at least to wing a fleeing robber and cause the felon to drop one of the sacks of money.

"Those were very wild times," reflected Pat Patterson, a profane and colorful character who lived in the area many years later. "There were bootleggers and people making whiskey. You could give a buck and get back plenty of ol' 'bang head.' Whole tribes of folks lived out in the hills who had always stayed just one step ahead of the law. Their moral sense was different from most everyone else. They had their own code and ways of doing things and they saw nothing wrong with robbing a bank so long as it was insured and nobody got hurt."

Boomtown banks were juicy targets for robbers. Many of the bank jobs pulled in Oklahoma during that period were credited to Spencer and his followers. Some said the Spencer bunch, armed with sawed-off shotguns, raided the Pawhuska Post Office and robbed as many as twenty-two banks in a twenty-month period following his escape from the penitentiary. Others claimed his total number of bank jobs was at least twice that number. Alva McDonald, a U.S. marshal who was tracking the bank robbers at the time, disagreed. He believed that Spencer's participation in the bank robbery epidemic of the twenties was exaggerated. "Spencer was a good publicity man," said McDonald. The law officer contended that Spencer's gang had a hand in only a small number of the offenses that were marked on their criminal ledger.

By far the most notable crime Spencer engineered occurred on August 21, 1923, when he, Nash, and three other bandits carried out one of the nation's last train robberies on horseback.

The brazen holdup of Katy train number 123 took place on a Tuesday afternoon near Okesa, an Osage County town on the Missouri, Kansas & Texas Railroad line. Located southwest of Bartlesville, the prosperous city that served as the headquarters of Phillips Petroleum, Okesa was named shortly after the turn of the century from the Osage word for *halfway* because the tiny settlement was midway between the Cherokee Nation on the east and the Osage capital city of Pawhuska, only a dozen miles away. Several outlaws were known to live in the countryside near Okesa, and the Sunday before the train robbery, Spencer reportedly planned the escapade with members of his gang over breakfast at a local farmhouse. Spencer's heist of twenty thousand dollars in bonds and cash from the Katy Limited passenger train was a spectacular feat. Even though Nash was opposed to this old-style method of obtaining funds, even he had to admit the nineteenth-century robbery approach of chasing a train from galloping cow ponies and firing revolvers to intimidate the passengers smacked of Jesse James and the Youngers.

During the robbery, Nash chatted with the train engineer and crew, and even commiserated with them about the tragic passing of Warren G. Harding. On August 2, less than three weeks before the Okesa train robbery, the fifty-seven-year-old Republican President, whose private life was surrounded by rumor and controversy, had died of an embolism in a suite at San Francisco's Palace Hotel.

It should have come as no surprise to those on the train that Nash, an avid reader and probably a cut above the average bandit of his day, was thoroughly informed when it came to current events. Besides recalling Nash's cordial demeanor and comments of concern about the late President Harding, eyewitnesses later told investigating law officers that the holdup was carried out with exacting precision and that the outlaws actually expressed regrets for the pistol whipping of Byron Tower, the train's fireman, during the initial moments of the robbery when the horsemen overtook the locomotive.

Local lawmen formed a posse and gave chase. By nightfall, some of those known to be disciples of Spencer were either in custody or had been thoroughly grilled. Within a short time, at least eight conspirators, including Spencer's sweetheart, Goldie Bates, were arrested and held on hefty fifty-thousand-dollar bonds as federal marshals closed in on the chief suspects. Rewards totaling more than ten thousand dollars were offered by Oklahoma Governor John Callaway Walton, the railroad, and federal government.

On September 20, 1923, approximately a dozen law officers, acting on a tip received from sources, located the wily bandit leader just below the Kansas border near a schoolhouse on the Osage-Washington county line. U.S. Marshal Alva McDonald, Deputy U.S. Marshal Luther Bishop, Postal Inspector Jack

Adamson, Bartlesville Police Chief L. U. Gaston, and a Pawhuska police officer, Billy Crowe, were part of the posse that set up an ambush on a dirt road leading from the dense woods.

Around sunset, the officers spotted a lone man wearing what appeared to be an old army shirt, overalls, and a cap. He was also carrying a rifle and revolver, and when the automobile headlights flashed on him, the man dashed from the trees and ran for the road. The manhunters opened fire and the lone figure fell when at least three bullets found their mark. It was said that Luther Bishop, who went on a few years later to become one of Oklahoma's first State Crime Bureau agents, fired the fatal shot. The man killed that evening reportedly had thousands of dollars in bonds hidden on his body. He was Al Spencer. The King of the Osage was dead. Some said his death marked the end of the frontier outlaws. Perhaps so, but it was still a long way from the close of the era of the social bandits.

At the time of Spencer's death, Oklahoma was in turmoil and had been since September 15, 1923, when Governor Jack Walton, despite threats on his life, professed war on the Ku Klux Klan and placed the entire state under martial law. The furor over the Tulsa race riot in 1921 and the Tulsa Klan marches in 1922, when one man even lost his ear when he dared register black voters, continued to reverberate. On September 26, less than a week after Spencer was killed, sixty-five state representatives—angry because they believed the governor had overstepped his power—tried to convene at the state capitol in Oklahoma City in order to impeach Walton. They were turned back by armed guards. Walton, who critics said was nothing more than an opportunist, was justifiably concerned because the KKK had continued to build a head of steam not only in his state but around the nation.

In the summer of 1923, Burton Rascoe, then a prominent Oklahoma writer and literary critic, wrote an article for *The Nation* in which he minced no words and pointed out that his home state had sunk into what he could only describe as a "mental, moral, and spiritual torpor." It was not just the bigots of the Ku Klux Klan to whom Rascoe took exception, but also the wealthy business tycoons, land speculators, and unethical bankers, only interested in their own personal gain at the sacrifice of others. Rascoe, the son of a Seminole County farmer, also wrote about the disgraceful conditions of the tenant farmers and sharecroppers, whose lives were dominated by backward agricultural methods and who wallowed in ignorance. He suggested that because of their sorry condition and lack of education, most of the dirt farmers were paranoid about other people, and that they tended to label nonconformists and unconventional thinkers as Reds. In response, he was branded as Comrade Rascoe in a letter to the editor that appeared in the August 22, 1923, issue of *The Nation,* only a couple of days after the Okesa train robbery.

Meanwhile, Governor Walton, a former mayor of Oklahoma City, who was born in Indiana and raised in Nebraska and Fort Smith, Arkansas, where his father operated a small hotel, had already started his own crusade against the Klan that same month by declaring martial law in Tulsa County.

Walton was a civil engineer turned politician and had been loudly criticized for blatant patronage in his political appointments. He had received endorsements from various labor unions as well as the Farmer-Labor Reconstruction League, considered a radical organization by conservatives. After his election, the establishment politicians and big-business interests saw the writing on the wall. Walton's inauguration party had even departed from the traditional elegant affair and turned into a two-day noisy spectacle, complete with farmers in their work clothes, costumed Indians, and liquored-up cowboys all enjoying fiddle serenades, clog dances, and a feast of wild game cooked over a mile-long open pit. The shindig would have put a lasting grin on Andrew Jackson's face, but it made every self-respecting old-line banker and oil-field patrician cringe in disgust.

In turn, Walton's ineptitude and his efforts to please everyone and appease all political factions caused him instantly to lose credibility even with supporters. His popularity faded more with his radical declaration of martial law in Tulsa and Okmulgee counties, establishment of military censorship over the press, and the suspension of the writ of habeas corpus. The final outrage was Walton's use of martial law statewide, an act that resulted in the formation of a movement to impeach him as governor. Public support turned against Walton. Embarrassed Democrats and anti-Klan forces joined with the Klan itself to get rid of the governor.

In a last ditch try to keep his position, Walton called the legislature into special session on October 11, 1923, in order to destroy the KKK in the state. The lawmakers refused to convene and gathered instead on October 17 at the request of Speaker of the House William D. McBee. The representatives drafted twenty-two separate charges against Walton and voted for his impeachment. On October 23, Walton was suspended from office and Lieutenant Governor Martin E. Trapp, a native of Kansas considered to be the epitome of the professional politician, became the acting governor.

The end was in plain sight for Walton. Rumors had spread throughout the domeless capitol building that he was even a Klan member. Eleven of the charges against Walton were upheld, including public payroll padding, suspension of habeas corpus, illegal collection of campaign funds, excessive use of his powers to pardon criminals, and general incompetence. On November 19, the Senate concurred with the House. Jack Walton was impeached and was formally removed from the post of governor. His tenure of office from January 9 to November 19, 1923, was to go down in history as the shortest term for any elected Oklahoma governor.

Although the civil unrest and impeachment proceedings dominated most everyone's attention in Oklahoma during the last months of 1923, the lawmen tracking down the remnants of Al Spencer's gang did not stop their efforts to round up the others involved in the Okesa train robbery. Soon after they shot and killed Spencer, they apprehended the other train thieves, with the notable exception of Frank "Jelly" Nash.

Throughout the autumn months of 1923, they followed Nash's trail. He headed south, first to Alamogordo, New Mexico, where he allegedly went into business with a lady bootlegger, and then on to the Mexican border city of Juárez, just across the Rio Grande from El Paso. His attempt to establish an alibi for the train robbery failed, and Nash rode a burro into the high mountains of the state of Chihuahua to work as a ranch hand. During a visit to a Juárez cantina, Nash was identified by an off-duty El Paso policeman, who remembered the bandit's face from a wanted poster. The rancher who employed Nash refused to turn him over to the U.S. authorities but did agree to send Nash across the border on a bogus errand so law officers could apprehend him. Although the horse he rode spooked at the shallow river crossing, Nash was able to coax the mare across the Rio Grande into Texas. He rode directly into the waiting arms of Alva McDonald, the U.S. marshal who had been after Nash ever since the holdup at Okesa. Known for his sense of humor, Nash reportedly smiled when he saw the proverbial jig was up and told the law officers about his horse balking at the border. "I should have listened to her," said Nash, laughing.

On March 3, 1924, Frank "Jelly" Nash was convicted of the assault of a mail custodian, and was sentenced to twenty-five years at the federal penitentiary at Leavenworth, Kansas.

Down in Sequoyah County that very same month, Choc Floyd and Ruby Hardgraves spent as much time together as possible. She was seventeen years old, tall and slim. He was twenty, stocky and strong. Choc was surely aware of the Okesa train robbery and the death of Al Spencer the year before. He may even have heard about Frank Nash's capture and subsequent trial in Oklahoma City. Choc was also busy making moonshine with his big brother, Bradley, and playing poker with friends. And there was also Ruby. The two of them thought about little else but the other.

No one could have known that smart-aleck farm kid Choc Floyd and thirty-seven-year-old convict Jelly Nash would one day be linked in a bloody episode that would profoundly affect law-enforcement procedures for years to come.

However, that was all years away—almost a decade—and even a single year seemed an eternity for young lovers or men doing hard time. In March of 1924, Jelly Nash was assigned yet another prison identity and became number 20769 at Leavenworth. As Nash grew accustomed to his newest home, Choc and Ruby pursued their romance. They had secret places to go, and they found themselves alone in the thickets or the piles of hay in the barn. They tried to stay out of winter's way. Choc and Ruby went to the secluded country graveyards of dead family and friends; they made love under a river of stars.

18

RUBY

CHARLEY FLOYD NEVER REALLY got over Ruby Hardgraves. They were kindred spirits—addicted to each other's bodies and souls. It was an easy fit. Both were wild kids full of desire. Both wanted to shake off the dirt and soften their rough cotton-picking hands. They were caught up in their fantasies, with no fears except maybe getting stuck in somebody else's cotton patch.

Choc's quick temper and fists caused the sanctimonious churchgoers to think of him as something of a hellion. Ruby did not have a bit of trepidation, however. She had grown up around rugged country people who worked and played hard. Besides, she liked Choc's easy laugh and the way he swaggered just a bit. When she and her girlfriends sashayed into the store down by the Akins cotton gin or went berry picking along the creeks, Ruby did not go unnoticed by the boys. Choc was aroused by this skinny girl. He soon came calling.

Ruby's Cherokee eyes intoxicated Choc. His sister-in-law, Bessie, recalled that Ruby could captivate Choc with her sun-kissed hair and long, limber legs. Charley became as light-headed as when he was sloshed on home brew. Throughout the winter and spring of 1923 and 1924, the couple spent more and more time together. They made love every chance they got. When Choc got Ruby away from everyone else, he was all over her. They were barn cats in heat.

There was a touch of delicious insanity in them that only other lovers could recognize. Folks saw it in their eyes when Choc and Ruby, grass-stained and flushed, walked down the paths that fed into the thickets and weeds out toward the cemetery. They saw it when Choc galloped on a horse down the road through Akins with Ruby perched behind him. They were oblivious to the graver concerns of the world.

The night before Ruby helped Choc celebrate his twentieth birthday, wartime President Woodrow Wilson, whose dreams were shattered, died while he slept in his third-floor bedroom in Washington, D.C. A few days later, an audience heard for the first time George Gershwin's innovative symphonic work *Rhapsody in Blue,* performed by the Paul Whiteman orchestra at Aeolian Hall in New York. The wailing clarinets kept the house spellbound. Elsewhere, jazz and big-band musicians like Fletcher Henderson, Louis Armstrong, Bix Beiderbecke, and Earl Hines were also tuning up. One of the top records of 1924 was Henderson's *Tea Pot Dome Blues.*

In the spring of 1924, an intensely ambitious young man in Washington, D.C.—despite having no Ruby Hardgraves of his own or even the hint of a sweetheart in his life—knew very well what he wanted to be. John Edgar Hoover was devoted to his job, his mother, and the welfare of the nation. He had no time for frivolity as he marched up the ranks at the Justice Department.

Three years earlier, on August 22, 1921, Hoover had been appointed assistant director of the Bureau of Investigation. He had already altered his name to the more formal J. Edgar Hoover. He thought it was more dignified; it also had a certain ring that fit him better. The chief reason he switched to the use of only his first initial, however, was because he found out that the other Washington resident named John Hoover was considered a poor credit risk by Woodward & Lothrop, a prestigious local department store. Hoover wanted to avoid even the hint of scandal. He had his reputation to consider.

Hoover's appointment as second in command of the bureau came during the Harding administration when Attorney General Harry M. Daugherty, a presidential crony who ran Harding's campaign, picked William J. Burns to succeed William Flynn as the bureau's director. Formerly the head of the famous private detective agency known for its strikebreaking efforts and attempts to round up Oklahoma bank robbers, Burns's checkered past reflected the corruption and opportunism of the Harding era.

The bureau under Burns sank to new lows. Agents were selected in a manner reminiscent of county sheriffs handing out special-duty badges to their supporters. Some of the agents even had served time in prison, including one who had been convicted of murder. One reporter called the bureau nothing but a "goon squad for the Attorney General." To earn their keep, many federal agents relied on bribery and blackmail. They snooped into private citizens' lives and burglarized—fifty years before Watergate—the offices of lawmakers who dared stand up to Daugherty or criticize the excesses of the Harding administration.

One of the most flagrant of Burns's operatives was Gaston Bullock Means, a con artist who had been accused of everything from larceny to homicide. Reportedly a German agent during the war, Means was well connected to underworld figures and power brokers in major bootlegging circles. His job in Harding's Washington was to act as an intermediary between cabinet officials and the big-business barons they cut deals with in exchange for payoffs. Means later admitted to a Senate committee that he delved into the private lives of congressmen and even broke into their offices to gain information to use against them.

The rigid J. Edgar Hoover found Gaston Means abominable. He may have been further disgusted by the antics of Burns and Daugherty, but he clearly did not totally disagree with their policies. Like any good bureaucrat on the rise, Hoover was smart enough to maintain his own counsel and not become linked to any misconduct. He kept his nose to the grindstone and diligently prepared a secret enemies list based on the data collected by Burns. Nonetheless, when the power structure underlying the federal bureau began to crumble with Harding's sudden death, Hoover managed to stay clear of the allegations brought against Daugherty and Burns.

By March 28, 1924, with a reelection campaign ahead of him and in the face of the Senate's probe into the Attorney General's office, Calvin Coolidge demanded and received the resignation of Harry Daugherty. On April 2, Coolidge announced that in Daugherty's place, he was appointing Harlan Fiske Stone as the new Attorney General. Stone had been a classmate of the President's at Amherst College and was a prominent New York attorney.

The new Attorney General ousted Burns as director of the Bureau of Investigation on May 9, and the next day Hoover was summoned to Stone's office. Following a famous conversation during which Hoover allegedly asked for Stone's promise that the bureau would remain divorced from politics and that all future appointments would be based solely on merit, the job of acting director was offered to Hoover. He accepted. He was only twenty-nine years old. Eight months later the word *acting* would be dropped from his title.

The reign of J. Edgar Hoover as the nation's "top cop" lasted for forty-eight years. During this time, he would overhaul the dishonored bureau as he built a force of clean-cut crime fighters. These handpicked special agents catered to Hoover's shortcomings and allowed him to become one of the most powerful forces in the nation.

During this period, Choc and Ruby were occupied with their own frantic plans. During the fertile month of May, Ruby became distressed when her suspicions were confirmed: She was three months pregnant and there was no wedding band on her finger. She went straight to Choc Floyd with the news.

For the better part of the last year, Choc had lived at his brother Bradley's place. Bradley, together with his wife, Bessie, and their twin boys had moved out of his father's home at Akins into a small house with some land not far from the village of Hanson. Bessie, pregnant again, had found it increasingly difficult to get along with her mother-in-law, Mamie, and she knew she had to have a house of her own to raise her family. Bradley realized that it was a strain for his kid brother to live under his parents' roof, especially since Choc had poked around the country and was now a grown man. The post-office penny caper had also put an added strain on the relationship between Charley and his father.

Although he loved and respected his parents, Bradley knew how stern they could be. Walter was bad enough, especially when he had a couple of belts of liquor in him, but even their mother could be overly strict. Bradley recalled the time he had been chopping firewood and accidentally brought the ax down on his foot. The blade sliced through his boot and nearly cut off his big toe. When Bradley dashed into the house to get some comfort, Mamie proceeded to give him a whipping for tracking blood all over her clean floor. As far as Bradley was concerned, Choc was more than welcome to sleep and eat at his house. In return, he would help out with the crops. There were no doubt better moonshiners in business, but the Floyd brothers made and sold a little whiskey to bring in some extra income.

"Choc told me that he'd rather live with us," said Bessie Floyd when she was a ninety-year-old woman thinking about old times in Sequoyah County. "He told me that he liked the way I took care of his clothes for him. And I made sure he was cleaned up and fed. He was fun-lovin', and I always thought of him as a good boy. I can still see Choc and Bradley out there farming. I'd be inside the house with my little twin boys and they'd be pesterin' me to teach 'em how to wash dishes. They aggravated me until I put 'em up to the dishes and the pan of water, and let 'em go on and wash all they wanted. They were only three years old but they wanted to work like the men."

When Ruby went to see Choc to tell him she was carrying his child, he did not flinch. He knew he was in love with Ruby, and he reasoned there was a decent chance that by becoming a husband and father, he would settle down. Ruby went with Choc to the Sequoyah County courthouse, built in 1915, at the corner of Oak and Chickasaw streets in Sallisaw. They obtained a marriage license. Ruby would be a June bride and a December mother. The young couple broke the news to their families and friends. They took care of the few preparations required for the simple wedding.

The temperature on June 28, 1924, was expected to reach one hundred degrees in some parts of the state. In the small hours of the morning, several tornadoes had swept across the upper Midwest, causing thousands of dollars in property damage and leaving injured persons in Iowa. A twister took at least eight lives just to the east of Peoria, Illinois, as another funnel cloud cut a swath two miles wide through the coal black farmlands. Searchers were still on the lookout for an entire passenger train that seemed to have vanished during the storm.

The results of an intensive study of criminals just released in New York and published that Saturday in newspapers across the nation stated that "twenty years ago the bolder type of burglar known as a 'Dutch houseman' was often a man 35 or more; today he is almost exclusively a young man." The report also suggested that "youth is eternally reckless and is prone to take chances that a man of 30, experienced in the ways of the world, would deliberate a long time before taking."

Another prominent wire story was developed in sweltering New York City, where the Democrats had taken over Madison Square Garden for their national convention. They needed to come up with a candidate to challenge Coolidge and the GOP. In early July, after a record-setting thirteen days of fistfights between delegates and 103 ballots cast, they would eventually choose as their nominee West Virginia's John W. Davis, a former U.S. Solicitor General and ambassador to Great Britain.

Out of Kansas City, urgent appeals were being issued for ten thousand harvest hands needed after rainy weather caused a sudden ripening of the Kansas wheat crop. Workers from as far as St. Louis were rushed to help out the panicky grain farmers.

In Oklahoma came the report of several hundred Klansmen heckling Jack Walton, the former governor, during a speech he made on June 27 in the town of Heavener. A candidate for the U.S. Senate, Walton had to delay his campaign talk for a half hour while the hooded men marched in circles around the platform, hooting and jeering and carrying a banner that read, WE'LL HAVE NO JACK IN THE SENATE.

A front-page article in the *Tulsa Tribune* that same June 28 revealed that the long-rumored secret wedding of Vol Whittmore, a life-insurance salesman, and Thelma Kennedy, heiress daughter of a multimillionaire Tulsa doctor, had actually occurred two months earlier. The shocked families were not talking to reporters, and the couple had slipped away to Kansas City for a belated honeymoon trip. This tidbit of romantic gossip was the talk of the city, especially among society matrons at afternoon bridge games.

Choc and Ruby's rather ordinary wedding in Sallisaw hardly rated front-page coverage, not even in their own home country. As was the custom with the other Floyd children, the plain civil ceremony proceeded without any pomp. They were dressed in their best suits of clothes. Ruby held a bouquet of fragrant homegrown blossoms. There was a certain air of dignity about them as Choc and Ruby stood together with a couple of friends who served as witnesses.

Like most rural marriages, there was no honeymoon. Some old friends and relatives later remembered that there was at least some sort of shivaree. At these noisy mock serenades, traditionally given to country newlyweds on their wedding night, celebrants rubbed washboards and beat spoons on pots and pans. Sometimes the revelers even captured the groom, and while the girls and women gently teased the blushing bride, the men folk dragged the kicking husband to a creek and gave him a rude bath. The theory was that if a young couple could survive a shivaree on that first night and if they were still speaking the next morning, then surely the marriage would last forever.

In 1923, one year before Choc and Ruby's marriage, the third-oldest of the Floyd's daughters, Emma Lucille, took the matrimonial leap. Her husband was

Samuel Lessley, a local fellow who preferred to go by his middle name, Clarence. He was the son of Samuel James Lessley, a native of Batesville, Arkansas, whose parents had moved there from Missouri during the Civil War. In 1889, Sam Lessley came to Indian Territory, and the next year, he married Sarotha Arbillia Wickett, daughter of pioneer Georgians who came to western Arkansas before settling on a farm northeast of Akins. Clarence, born December 15, 1901, was one of their eight children and spent his entire life in the Akins area. After he and Emma Floyd wed, Clarence took his bride to live at his widowed mother's house about one mile east of town. There on Epiphany—January 6, 1924—Emma gave birth to a son she named Lawton. He was the first of her five children.

On July 4, 1924, less than a week after Choc married Ruby Hardgraves, another baby was born to Bradley and Bessie Floyd out at their place in Hanson. They named their third son Glendon. He was a healthy baby and became an instant playmate for twins Wayne and Bayne.

This bounty of grandbabies gratified Walter Floyd. He joked with his friends that soon there would be enough for a baseball team. Then Mamie surprised him and the rest of the family when she announced that she was also pregnant. It had been more than twelve years since her last child, Mary Delta, was born. Walter could hardly contain himself. He bragged that his children would not outdo him when it came to producing offspring.

By the mid-1920s, Walter had opened a small general-merchandise store in the town of Akins. The little settlement already supported the Wickett and Green Store as well as another store that was operated by the Mills family. Walter figured there was room for his establishment, however. It was a typical frame building like the others in town. Walter sold a few staples and kept a slim inventory of essentials for local customers. For a time, there was a barber chair, but no one could ever recall seeing Walter cut hair or shave any of the farmers.

Walter said he needed the extra money to plug the gaps that his cash crops failed to fill. The store was also a place to hold forth with his hunting buddies and lodge brothers. Once the afternoon sun started its slow plunge in the western sky, Walter rationed out select sipping spirits and his best tales of the hunt. There was another reason he liked having the store: Family would come there. With the possible exception of running his hounds and drinking whiskey, nothing brought Walter more pleasure than offering his children and grandchildren gumdrops and peppermint sticks from the big glass jars he kept on the store counter. Even an unbending pappy with an ill temper had his tender moments.

And, in the final months of 1924, a year when some American farmers cruelly realized that they were already suffering through a depression that the rest of the nation would not have to endure for another five years, those times were special. To a man like Walter Floyd, a handful of penny candy became priceless.

19

THE ST. LOUIS BLUES

R UBY GAVE BIRTH to her baby on a cold winter's day, December 29, 1924. A plump Monday's child "fair of face" with cherry-pulp coloring, the baby had his father's features and Ruby's eyes. He was late for Christmas but just in time for the New Year.

Choc was right there when the baby came. He was delirious with joy. Some of Ruby's kin, as well as a country doctor, were also in attendance. They cleaned up the baby, wrapped him up in a light blanket, and laid him in Ruby's arms.

Relatives recalled that Choc kissed Ruby and gave her a wink. He picked up his son and held him tightly against his chest. Then he danced in circles around the room. Ruby got up on her elbows in the bed and smiled at the sight of her young husband and their newborn turning and swaying in the early sunlight. It was a sight she would remember for the rest of her life. Choc went to a mirror hanging on the wall over a chest of drawers and held up the newborn baby next to his face.

"Well, he looks just like me," Choc told Ruby and the others in the room. "Just look at him!" It was a story Ruby would tell again and again until the day she died.

"Look at that," Choc exclaimed as the baby balled his chubby hands into fists. "Will you look at this boy's hands! He's gonna be a fighter! A real fighter!"

Despite some mild protests from Ruby, there was no question in Choc's mind what they would call their son. His first name was Charles, for his father and paternal grandfather, and his middle name was Dempsey, after the heroic prizefighter who Choc believed hung the moon.

Charles Dempsey Floyd: Any son named for his daddy and the world's heavyweight champ had to be a contender. Most of the Floyds would call the boy Dempsey.

Ruby had decided that her baby would be delivered at the home of her aunt, Tempie Ring. The small house where Tempie and her family lived was located near Bald Hill, an oil field settlement seventeen miles northeast of Okmulgee, not too far from the Muskogee County line.

Ruby's aunt had been born Tempie Laura Edwards on April 1, 1898, just one mile southeast of Sallisaw. She was the younger sister of Ruby's mother, Sarah, who had died during childbirth. Ruby and Tempie became close and acted more like sisters than niece and aunt.

Tempie met her future husband, Jess Lee Ring, when he was working in the farm fields for her father, Perry Commodore Edwards. The young girl brought water and lunches out to the crews. They married on December 14, 1916, in Muskogee. Jess found work in the oil fields and they started their family. Jess Lee, Jr., was born in 1918; Ruth Josephine, 1920; and Frances, 1922. She did not know it at the time of Dempsey Floyd's birth, but Tempie was pregnant herself. The following August, another daughter, named Eileen, was born. In sum, Tempie would have eight children. Betsy Lavona was born in 1928; Charles Dean, namesake of both Charley Floyd and ace Cardinal pitcher Dizzy Dean, was born in 1933; Shirley Anne in 1935; and finally, Barbara Jean in 1937.

Tempie's children adored Ruby Floyd, and although they were actually her younger first cousins, they called her Aunt Ruby. That December morning when Dempsey was born, the little ones pressed around the new mother lying in bed and they peeked at her sleeping baby. Jess Ring kept Choc company, and every now and then, he pulled on a coat over his overalls and brought in more firewood from the stockpile out on the porch.

It was exactly one week after the solstice and the beginning of winter in the northern hemisphere. The new season wasted little time in making its presence felt. Just two days before the baby's birth, the third in a series of cold waves raged southbound out of western Canada like a runaway freight train. The arctic blast slammed into the Rockies and sent fingers of icy air throughout the land.

In Oklahoma, snow covered much of the ground. The roads were slippery and the subzero temperatures caused a run on heating stoves and brought out a rash of warnings for police officers, railroad switchmen, and others who worked outdoors at night. Although there was a warming trend, Tulsans knew they would have to bundle up if they planned to attend the New Year's Eve dances at The Winter Garden in the basement of the New Orpheum Theater or try the Louvre on North Main Street.

People throughout the state especially looked forward to New Year's since Christmas had been soured by tragedy. At Babbs Switch, just a few miles south of Hobart, Oklahoma, a Christmas Eve fire started from a candle on a decorated cedar tree during a party in the schoolhouse. The building burned to the ground. Thirty-six adults and children perished. Most of them died from smoke and flames when they tried to flee the inferno in a stampede through doors that were quickly blocked with bodies. Heavy screens covered the windows and prevented escape. In the aftermath, only the basketball goals, a few outbuildings, and a barren playground remained. Five days later, as a new Floyd baby caused a celebration of life for a handful of people, hundreds of persons were still going to the site of the fire to remember all the deaths. Some stood and gazed at the jagged outline of the building. Souvenir hunters carried off bits of charred furniture, bolts, nails, and pieces of the screens. Ashes scattered in the wind.

It was snug inside the Ring house the morning of Charles Dempsey Floyd's birth, however. A tamed fire burned brightly in the stove and there was plenty of wood. A big enamel pot of hot coffee never seemed empty. Tempie managed to rustle up some breakfast. Jess was not much of a drinking man, except for an occasional hot toddy, but Choc had a jar stashed in his grip and he laced their coffee with liberal slugs of woods whiskey. Outside, a layer of snow blanketed the fields. The cold spell seemed to snap as the temperature gradually climbed into double digits.

Choc picked up his sleeping son and teased Ruby that he was going to take their baby outside and roll him in the snow to see whether he was up to being a rough-and-tumble Floyd. When Ruby fussed and tried to throw a pillow at Choc, he laughed and returned Dempsey to her.

The weather across the state and much of the nation may have been harsh, but it was not bad enough to keep the lawless from their work. That morning, a fire believed to have been started by robbers destroyed nine buildings, including a Masonic temple and post office at Pottsboro, Texas, about eight miles west of Denison. The fire caused more than $150,000 in damages, and authorities found overturned and emptied safes in several of the burned structures. It was the identical modus operandi of bandits who had recently set fires and looted banks and business houses in the Texas towns of Valley View and Paradise.

The day after Dempsey's birth, the news was again dominated by bank bandits. This time, four unmasked men looted the Farmers' National Bank at Chandler, Oklahoma, of four thousand dollars in broad daylight, after the sheriff's force was decoyed to the nearby town of Stroud on a false alarm. The holdup men were all described as being "less than thirty years old" and conducted the robbery in "a businesslike manner" with a minimum of talk. Three of them entered the bank and the fourth remained in the getaway auto with the engine running. Within hours, Governor Trapp had put up a three-hundred-dollar reward for their arrest and conviction. He also advised law officers to try to take the felons alive but if necessary to shoot to kill.

All the hubbub about banks and bandits did not get the attention of Choc and Ruby. Word of Choc becoming a father went over well in Sequoyah County. He proudly made the rounds at the homes of his relatives and friends. He wanted to show all of them that he was capable of producing more than winning poker hands and moonshine.

Choc and Ruby stayed with the Hardgraves at the time, and one day, after Choc had been off drinking, he came home and decided to take his baby son with him when he visited his parents. He managed to swing up on his horse with Dempsey cradled in his arms. He poked the horse in the side and started down the road. Ruby came flying from her folks' house in hot pursuit. She grabbed Choc's leg and begged him not to ride off in his condition with their baby. Choc only laughed and continued on with Ruby following him every step of the way just in case the baby slipped from his arms.

Mamie Floyd was near to the date when she would be delivering her own baby, so she remained close to the house. A little more than two weeks after Dempsey was born, she knew the time had come. When she went into labor, Mamie was just a couple of months short of her forty-fourth birthday. The baby arrived on January 16, 1925. Just as Walter hoped, it was another boy, to go with the three sons he already had and to balance out the four daughters. There were complications, though. The little boy was not strong enough to make it through the day.

They named him Chester Lee Floyd. They bathed and dressed him and laid him in a handmade coffin no larger than a grocery box. He looked like a sleeping angel. The family took him to the Akins cemetery, where in the wintertime fires had to be burned to thaw the ground for the grave diggers. The family later set a marker over the baby's plot. Some words were cut into the stone. There was not much to say.

CHESTER LEE
January 16, 1925
"Budded on earth to bloom in heaven"

Mamie's girls took care of things at the house and let their mother get some rest. Women from around Akins and the other small communities brought the Floyds pots of cooked supper, jars of preserved vegetables, and fruit pies. The preacher paid a call and told Mamie not to fret about her baby dying without being baptized. He promised that her little Chester Lee had gone straight to Jesus in the kingdom of heaven. Walter found his own kind of comfort. He closed his store and stayed drunk, but that lasted only a few days. A man had to eke out a living and go on with his business. Soon he was back at the store, telling lies with his friends and handing out sweets to his grandchildren.

Later that year, someone took a Kodak picture of Walter mounted on his horse with baby Dempsey sitting in front of him on the saddle. Surrounding the horse were Walter's best hound dogs. Walter cherished the photograph and it became one of his prized possessions.

Besides showing off his son and sporting with his friends, Choc worked extra hard to support his family. In the spring, he and his father and older brother prepared their fields for a cotton crop, and when the new oak leaves got to be just about the size of a squirrel's ear, he helped plant the seed corn.

However, Choc would not be around to harvest any of the crops. He would not be home for Christmas. Shortly after Ruby and Choc marked their first wedding anniversary, restlessness struck once again. He loved Ruby and Dempsey with all his heart, but he was dissatisfied with the meager wages he made from farming and peddling an occasional jar of whiskey. He packed up some clothes and told Ruby and his family that he was going out again on the harvest circuit, maybe back to Kansas or even Missouri, to earn some real money. He said that he hoped even to come up with a few luxuries for his wife and son.

Almost nine years later, Ruby—by that time gun-shy of the press and public—granted a rare interview. During the conversation with Kansas City reporter W. R. Draper, she shared some of the details of her life with Choc and discussed his decision to leave Akins in 1925.

"When we married at Sallisaw, Charley was a hardworking farmer," Ruby told Draper. "But we never hardly saw any money, while the neighbor boys all seemed to have plenty. Charley took this for a while, then decided to do something about it. Charley said he had to make some money, so he left home without telling me where he was going. Some of the boys around Sallisaw said he was working in the harvest fields but I knew better, because he sent me money that he never could have earned so quickly."

Ruby's hunch about her young husband's whereabouts was correct. Choc was up to no good.

Marvin Amos, the younger brother of Choc's friend Cleon, remembered that Choc had paid a visit to the Amos home just before he departed. The Amos boys' father, John Amos, was a man of many trades. Like most everyone else, he farmed and raised stock. He also did some barbering around the communities of Akins and Maples, owned a blacksmith shop for many years, and had served as a jailer under the sheriff. Old man Amos proudly claimed he was the first one in those parts to raise melons, and he was known as the Watermelon King.

It was also no secret that John Amos was one of the most successful bootleggers in Sequoyah County. Apparently, Choc had made up what he considered to be a smooth batch of moonshine, because he carried a jug of white lightning when he showed up to do some bartering.

"Choc came over to our place, and he traded five gallons of moonshine whiskey for a pistol my dad had," recalled Marvin Amos. "It was a big ol' pearl-handled pistol. I believe it was an ol' forty-four. I just know it was big and heavy. Choc wanted it, so he gave my dad that whiskey to get it. That was right before Choc left this country. I recall he took the pistol and handed the whiskey over to my dad and said, 'Here, you take this. I'm tired of tryin' to make a livin' with this stuff. Now I'm gonna give this here a try.' Choc was talkin' 'bout that gun when he said that."

In late August of 1925, Choc Floyd left the beloved Cookson Hills behind. Besides a few clothes, he took with him photos of Ruby and Dempsey, and the pearl-handled pistol.

Right off, Choc hooked up with some bad company. His companion on the road was another young rapscallion named Fred Hildebrand. He was also known as the Sheik, the same moniker thousands of adoring movie fans had bestowed on Rudolph Valentino.

The two men had no money to speak of, so they hopped a freight train rolling out of Sallisaw and rode the steel rails into Missouri. Each passing mile brought them deeper into the land that was once home to Jesse James and a swarm of other salty bandits. Along the way, they met tramps who jungled up in makeshift camps near the tracks. Considered to be at the bottom of the working class, the men and boys kept their inconspicuous campsites neat and secure. Stealing from each other was the chief taboo in an unwritten code that governed these migrants as they made their way across the land.

The hoboes cooked batches of slumgullion and hotcakes they called "saddle blankets." Mostly, they were honest men searching for work. They shared their vittles and strong coffee with Choc and his friend. Around the fire after supper, their hosts plied the young men with stories and explained the dangers of their nomadic life. Choc learned that to slip beneath a railroad car and "ride the rods" was tricky, but it was also dangerous to *ride the blinds,* the term used when a hobo stood astride the coupling equipment between the engine and first car. They were also warned to watch out for the railroad detectives, or "bulls," who liked nothing better than to club a man senseless, pitch him from a moving train, or even bludgeon him to death with a length of railroad iron if they caught him hiding inside an empty boxcar.

The young men watched their step. They pushed on in a generally northeastern direction. Somehow along the line, Choc and Fred were able to come up with enough funds to finance their trip and allow Choc to send some money to Ruby in Oklahoma. As they moved across the Ozark highlands, they camped along the banks of the Meramec River, a stream lined with caverns and wooded bluffs.

Choc and Fred Hildebrand had no knowledge that early French and American traders had explored the same river and hiked through the clumps of sycamores and elms. They did not know that in 1774, a pioneer, ironically named John Hildebrand, had cleared a farm and built a cabin on the Meramec. They also did not know that some miles to the southeast in the lead-mining district, on a high bluff overlooking the Big River, was a cave named for Sam Hildebrand. Not a relative of either of the two other Hildebrands, this Civil War desperado used to hide in the cave after he bushwhacked his victims with a rifle he named "Kill-Devil." Choc and Fred only knew that they were tired and hungry. In the evening, while they pulled beggar's-lice from their clothes and washed off road dirt in the shallows of the cool water, cicadas sang in the treetops.

Ahead in a veil of coal smoke loomed St. Louis, spread along a crescent-shaped bend of the Mississippi River just ten miles downstream from its confluence with the Missouri. St. Louis was selected for settlement by French merchants in 1764 and was named for Louis IX of France. The fur-trading center eventually became the crossroads of Western expansion and outgrew its history by surviving hostile Indian attacks, cholera epidemics, the Civil War, and waterfront fires. It was said about this midwestern metropolis that "the world passes through St. Louis."

Famed for its shoe factories as well as its great breweries that were forced to come up with innovative alternatives after being stymied by the Volstead Act, the city had two major league baseball clubs, the second-oldest symphony in the country, excellent daily newspaper coverage, and a provocative past. St. Louis was also the largest city Choc Floyd had ever seen in his twenty-one years.

His visit there was brief but far from uneventful. It was also an experience he would never forget, for what Choc pulled in St. Louis was not just one more youthful caper. Making whiskey, running bootleg hooch, and breaking into a country post office to heist pennies were crimes bad enough. He had some scrapes with the law before, but Choc was about to enter a new realm. The good fortune he had been blessed with in the past was about to vanish.

After a few weeks in St. Louis, Choc headed for home. His sudden reappearance in Sequoyah County after being gone only about fourteen days immediately raised suspicions.

Choc and Fred showed up back in Sallisaw on September 13. It was a Sunday, and the church crowd was out in full force on the streets. The two young men who had left "bumming a freight" in late August came home in style. They had four-bit stogies in their mouths and were decked out in flashy suits and felt hats. They roared into town behind the wheel of a brand new Studebaker. They drove the shiny roadster down Cherokee Avenue past the shops closed for the Sabbath. One of the first persons to spot Choc was Deputy Sheriff Bert Cotton. He was well acquainted with all the Floyds, and had had a few encounters, mostly of a friendly nature, with them over the years.

Cotton was immediately dubious. He knew that when Choc Floyd put his mind to it, there was not a harder worker in the county. However, the law officer also realized there was not a harvest hand in the land who could earn enough wages in just two weeks to buy a new wardrobe and a fancy automobile. Cotton fetched Police Chief J. C. Woll and the two of them waved the Studebaker over to the side of the road, where they questioned Choc and Fred.

Their answers were less than satisfactory. For the most part, Choc was cooperative and neighborly but did little talking. Neither of the young men could reply when Cotton discovered two rolls of money, with one thousand dollars in each roll, hidden on Hildebrand. The money was still in yellow paper wrappers stamped with the name Tower Grove Bank of St. Louis. Within minutes, Choc Floyd and Fred Hildebrand were locked up in the jail house in Sallisaw.

In another of the cells sat Walter Daugherty, a sixteen-year-old who had been arrested the night before after he confessed to the stabbing death of Lonnie Whitney, his seventeen-year-old neighbor. The accused killer said that he and the victim had quarreled after a church meeting several days before, and they had agreed to a Saturday-afternoon duel to settle their differences. Knives were the weapons of choice. The boys walked ten paces apart, whirled about, and rushed at each other. Daugherty struck first and plunged his knife to the handle into Whitney's heart. Death was instantaneous. When Daugherty was arrested, he was in the midst of taking care of his chores. Work had to go on. The recent blessing of more than two inches of welcome rain had broken the drought and benefited vegetable gardens. Some of the early cotton crop was already ripe enough to be picked.

It appeared there would be no cotton picking in store for Choc or Daugherty this season, however. By nightfall, word reached Charley's kinfolk out at Akins that he was back home and in serious trouble.

"The day he was supposed to reach home I dressed in my best and got ready to go to Sallisaw to meet him because I supposed he would be riding in on the train," Ruby Floyd later told W. R. Draper during her interview. "But before I could get ready and get started into town a neighbor came with bad news. He told me that Charley had been arrested the minute he struck Sallisaw because he was driving a brand new motorcar. Bert Cotton, the city marshal, just knew he could not have come by it honestly."

Cotton was dead right. First thing Monday morning, he and Woll called the Tower Grove Bank to inquire about the two rolls of bills they had recovered with the bank's name on them. They were then directed to contact the St. Louis Police Department, and soon the scenario of what had transpired in St. Louis unfolded.

On Friday, September 11, a trio of armed men in St. Louis had robbed couriers of an $11,929 payroll bound for the Kroger Grocery & Baking Company. The payroll taken in the holdup had originated from the Tower Grove Bank, and the bank's name was on the yellow paper wrapped around the money. There were witnesses who thought they could identify the robbers. St. Louis authorities asked Cotton and Woll to keep both Floyd and Hildebrand under lock and key while they sent officers to Sallisaw to interrogate them.

An Associated Press story from Sallisaw on September 15 reported the arrests of Floyd and his friend in connection with the payroll robbery. A front-page headline in the *Tulsa Tribune* hit the nail squarely on the head: AUTO BETRAYS TWO BANDIT SUSPECTS.

In the column below the headline, Charley Floyd was described as "a police character." There was mention of his involvement in the Akins post office theft. "Both men denied participation in the robbery at St. Louis," the AP reported, "but have not been able to give a satisfactory explanation of their sudden prosperity, police officers said."

Curiously, for several days that month, a book entitled *The Rise and Fall of Jesse James,* by Robertus Love, was being serialized in the *Tulsa World.* Love borrowed heavily from the writings of John Newman Edwards, the Kansas City editor who in the 1870s had romanticized James during the fabled Missouri bandit's heyday. The excerpt published on September 11 was highly sympathetic to James. Not a few Cookson Hills readers thought at least one of the sentences about the old James outlaw applied to Choc Floyd's situation as well: "We called him outlaw, and he was, but fate made him so."

On September 16, 1925, Choc Floyd and his alleged accomplice—both charged with highway robbery—were returned to St. Louis for further questioning. It was indeed a sad day for the Floyd family. This time, there would be no way Walter could call in chits with Masonic brothers or make an alibi for his son.

"We came in from the country to Sallisaw that day they took him away," remembered Bradley's wife, Bessie. "There was Choc and they had him in chains. They had big ol' chains on his hands and ankles. They had him chained to a pole at the train depot."

Choc said so long to family and friends who were there to see him off. Despite the chains, he shook hands with his brothers and tried to make a joke. Nobody laughed. They could see the fear in Choc's eyes. Everyone knew there would be a steep price to pay. He kissed Ruby and then he kissed nine-month-old Dempsey in her arms. According to Bessie Floyd, the baby made fists, just as he had the day he was born. For an instant, Choc smiled.

"I won't ever forget seeing Choc standing there in those chains," said Bessie Floyd. "Bradley just couldn't bear to see his little brother all chained up like they had him. He had to turn away and I think he cried."

The train arrived and the policemen with their prisoners boarded. At least this time, Choc would not have to jump a boxcar. He would ride inside in comfort and cover some of the same territory he had moved through only a few weeks before.

He was no longer free. Now he would not be eating in hobo jungles or sleeping next to streams. He would not be cooking up moonshine or playing poker under the stars or chopping cotton. He would not be hearing the call of hounds come autumn or sitting down to a country dinner on Sunday afternoons. He would not be making love to Ruby or playing with his son.

Choc Floyd was now a bandit.

P A R T

PRETTY BOY

1 9 2 5
~
1 9 3 4

T H R E E

If you'll gather 'round me, children,
A story I will tell,
About Pretty Boy Floyd, an outlaw,
Oklahoma knew him well.
—From the "Ballad of Pretty Boy Floyd"
(WOODY GUTHRIE)

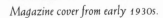

Magazine cover from early 1930s.

LEFT, TOP: *Inmates in the yard at Missouri State Penitentiary. Jefferson City, Missouri, ca. mid-1920s.* BOTTOM: *Missouri State Penitentiary. Jefferson City, Missouri, 1924.*

TOP: *Town council, Boley, Oklahoma, ca. 1908-1910.* INSET: *Farmers & Merchants Bank. Boley, Oklahoma, ca. 1908-1910.* BOTTOM: *Street scene. Earlsboro, Oklahoma, ca. mid-1920s.*

BELOW: *Charley Floyd, left, and Jess Ring. Four miles south of Haskell, Oklahoma, in rural Muskogee County, 1933.* RIGHT: *Bessie Edwards Mayberry (Ruby's aunt), Charley Floyd, and Dempsey Floyd. Fort Smith, Arkansas, 1931.*

ABOVE: *Charles Demps[ey] Floyd. At Jess Ring ho[me] near Morris, Oklahom[a,] 1931.* LEFT: *Downtow[n] Sallisaw, Oklahoma, during the 1936 drough[t.]*

CLOCKWISE FROM UPPER LEFT:
Dempsey Floyd and Ruby Hardgraves Floyd. Fort Smith, Arkansas, 1931; Charley and Ruby Floyd. Fort Smith, Arkansas, 1931; Vintage postcard. Kansas City, Missouri, 1930s; Ruby and Dempsey Floyd. Rural Oklahoma, 1926.

FT, TOP: *Riding the rails,* *early 1930s.* BOTTOM: *A* *r of hangman's nooses serve* *a grim warning to prospec-* *e bidders on a foreclosed* *m. Location unknown. Ca.* *ly 1930s.*

Bonnie Parker.

Clyde Barrow

Geo " Machine Gun" Kelly; Kidnapper of Cha Urschell, wealthy oil man Oklahoma City.

Pub. by Montgomery Foto Service, Kansas City, S. M

OP: *The Great Depression* *its rural Oklahoma, ca.* *rly 1930s.* CENTER, LEFT *RIGHT: Bonnie Parker,* *33; Clyde Barrow, 1933;* *orge "Machine Gun" Kelly,* *33.* BOTTOM: *George* *Aachine Gun" Kelly* *rounded by the law.* *klahoma City, Oklahoma,* *33.*

VERLEAF: *Charley, left,* *uby, and E. W. Floyd. Fort* *ith, Arkansas, 1931;* *ichita* BEACON, *January* *, 1933.*

Pretty Boy' Floyd-Oklahoma's Enemy or Robin Hood?

Desperado With $2,000 Reward on Head Continues to Run at Will Thruout Southwest Beacon Writer in Interviews With Friends and Peace Officers Finds Reason Why

Charles "Pretty Boy" Floyd has almost won the title of the 'hantom," so swiftly, silently and secretly does he move about 'lahoma, eluding capture by the narrowest of margins or shoot-his way to freedom.

A character study of the famous Oklahoma outlaw by Artist Harry Ferman, showing the almost perfect features that early earned him the title of "Pretty Boy."

"Pretty Boy" and Beulah Ash, reputed to be his latest "girl friend" and the girl with whom Floyd is reported to have been seen on numerous recent occasions.

Mrs. Floyd and the son of the famous bandit who were moved by "Pretty Boy" from a house in Tulsa under the very nose of a heavy police guard. Above is Governor Murray who has offered $1,000 reward for Floyd, dead or alive.

he Southwest s Most Daring Bandit Is Credited With Killing Many Persons and Robbing Scores of Banks

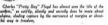

His Friends Are Quite Loyal and Aid in Hiding His Trail, He Showers Much Loot on Them

Editor's note: The following story of Charles "Pretty Boy" Floyd, one he most famous living outlaws in America today, is a result of a per-l trip by H. G. Hotchkiss into the heart of Oklahoma where Floyd is known and from interviews with leading Oklahoma peace officers.

By H. G. HOTCHKISS

KLAHOMA'S Public Enemy No. 1, or—
The Robin Hood of the Southwest.

These are the diametrically opposite pictures ated of the notorious Charles "Pretty Boy" Floyd, aded bank bandit and killer who is still a free man y despite the $2,000 price on his head, "dead or e."

lahoma peace officers rank ty Boy" ahead of many no-us outlaws in the state's ler days, more dangerous Al Jennings, now reformed n evangelist, or Henry Starr, years ago in a raid, or the us Kimes brothers, who g into recent limelight when caped Oklahoma convict who incurred their enmity was and killed as they were re-ng to prison after attending ter's funeral.

oyd's features probably are ibly stamped on the memory ery Oklahoma peace officer. rnor "Alfalfa Bill" Murray posted $1,000 reward from the for the capture of Floyd or alive. The Oklahoma ers' Association doubled the nt on the same terms.

eriffs, policemen and state ers are constantly searching the famous bandit. Sometimes are only minutes behind d but always "Pretty Boy" es capture.

a few instances when the e became too close Floyd shot way out and escaped, appar-bearing a charmed life. In many brushes with officers d's only casualty was a minor wound while many of his nents have been killed or ded.

• • •

FFICERS admit that "Pretty Boy" probably is the most cunning, the most urceful bandit in the history state that has become famous its bad men. Daring, but r reckless, Floyd maps his by carefully laid plans. It been more his own cunning resourcefulness, rather than that keeps "Pretty Boy" a man today.

ficers declare Floyd's pal and st friend, George Birdwell, far more dangerous as a gun-than is Floyd. But Birdwell shot and killed in a recent bank robbery at Boley, Okla., and Floyd still roams the state.

His bank robberies and escapes are carefully planned to the smallest detail, carefully and daringly executed. Knowing that a death penalty almost certainly awaits him, Floyd takes no chances. About him has grown a reputation as a "killer" that undoubtedly is one of "Pretty Boy's" greatest assets.

How many men Floyd has killed probably is not exactly known by anyone but "Pretty Boy" himself. How many banks he has robbed also is in doubt. He has been credited with scores of killings and scores of bank robberies, many of which he knew nothing about.

To peace officers he is Oklahoma's public enemy No. 1, with the price of $2,000 on his head, dead or alive, and the reputation that he will never be captured alive.

BUT to another class that is composed of many law-abiding citizens of Oklahoma he is a far different person, a modern Robin Hood who robs only those who can afford to lose, who helps those in need and distress, who has a happy smile and a cheery word of greeting for his friends, who spends his loot not on himself but on friends, relatives and even strangers if they be in want.

"Pretty Boy" is not a gangster. He avoids large crowds. He rarely has more than one or two accomplices. Since the death of Birdwell, his companion on most of his raids, Floyd has been more inclined to play a lone hand in his fight to the death with Oklahoma officers. With few or no companions the chances for his betrayal are remote.

Down in Seminole County, where both Floyd and Birdwell made their headquarters, are scores of friends ready to defend the reputation of "Pretty Boy."

They make no secret of their admiration for Floyd. Among the oil field shacks of the Seminole field he has found sanctuary scores of times. In one of these now lives the widow and son of Birdwell, a home that "Pretty Boy" has visited many times.

• • •

LOCATED among scores of oil field workers' homes, the house provided almost perfect protection for raiding officers could have proceeded but a short distance toward the Birdwell home before friends would have sounded a warning.

One small boy pointed out the house and told of one night when "Pretty Boy" and Birdwell were warned that strangers were approaching. Floyd rushed to his waiting car, fully armed, and prepared to flee when he learned the strangers were friends.

"Pretty Boy" was mad, the boy said, because he had been wounded in the foot a few days before and it pained him to walk. In the excitement Floyd forgot his injury and ran at his old speed.

Only one man in the neighborhood attempted to "snitch" on Floyd. Neighbors relate that Birdwell called at the home of the "snitch" one night with the intention of terminating his activities permanently. Birdwell kicked in the door but the victim pleaded so hard for his life that he was spared on condition he leave the community.

"These are the squarest people you ever saw," volunteered a neighbor. "If you do them a favor they never forget it and they will try to do two favors for you in return."

Floyd is a popular hero among the children. He never fails to give them a lift to school. And many a child had been clothed and fed thru the generosity of "Pretty Boy."

Friends declare he is generous to a fault. His bank loot is divided, one-half going to his wife and boy, the other half he retains for his own use but most of this is spent to help destitute families and individuals.

Friends tell that Floyd was eating in a restaurant one day. A man came in and begged for a meal, stating it had been days since he had had anything to eat.

"Give that fellow all he wants," spoke up "Pretty Boy." Then addressing the stranger he said, "Here is a twenty. Perhaps that will stake you until you can get on your feet."

• • •

AROUND Seminole "Pretty Boy" is known as the man of many faces and [illegible] cars. They say he carries many changes of clothing with him and that in a few moments he can so change his appearance that his own friends would hardly recognize him.

He has driven all makes of cars. He prefers Fords because they are inconspicuous but changes to other models often to shield his identity.

Peace officers declare Floyd is hard to capture largely because he is almost constantly on the move. Altho he spends most of his time in Oklahoma where he was born and reared and where his wife and boy reside, he is known to have hangouts in other states.

He virtually lives in his auto. He carries his bedding with him. Often he sleeps in pastures and in barns. Many times he has rested for several days in some isolated place with some poor farmer who was well paid for his entertainment.

• • •

TIPPED off one day that Floyd was visiting in a certain home not many miles from Oklahoma City, officers assembled a force of men, surrounded the house and, just as daylight was breaking, two officers went in to arrest him.

Either the tip was wrong or Floyd had been warned for the officers could find no trace of the much sought outlaw.

Officers scoff at the idea that "Pretty Boy" has accumulated a fortune from the many banks he has robbed. They assert that he is nearly broke most of the time. Only six bank robberies can be definitely traced to Floyd and only one of these, at Sallisaw, was a county seat bank.

The aggregate loot of the six robberies, officers claim, could not have totaled more than $15,000 and these robberies were spread over a period of several years. Birdwell participated in almost all six of these robberies and would have reduced Floyd's share.

Floyd exercises the same degree of planning in plotting a bank robbery that a successful business executive displays in carrying out an important business program, officers say.

• • •

HE NOT only knows all about the bank but he is prepared for his escape and seldom goes far. A week or ten days after he had robbed a certain bank it was found that he had gone only a few miles to a ranch house.

He remained there for a couple of days until the excitement of the chase had died down and then left. His hosts stated they did not know of his identity until afterwards. Some officers doubted their statement but there was no proof to the contrary.

Plans for his escape are one of the most important part of "Pretty Boy's" robbery schemes. Many times officers have surrounded places in which they were certain he was located, only to find that he had vanished. On the few occasions when they have found him he has shot his way out.

Peace officers are certain that eventually "Pretty Boy" will be captured but friends say the chase for Floyd has been going on for many months and that police are no nearer the capture of the famous outlaw than they were at the start.

GIVEN IN MARRIAGE - - - By Adele Garrison

SHOULD I show Mary the newspaper column of Paris gossip that I was sure was the real reason for Philip Veritzen's suddenly announced determination to send her to the French capital for a year's study or should I wait until the storm of her humiliated anger at Noel had worn itself out?

The question was taken out of my hands summarily. At Mary's demand to know what Lillian had meant by saying that Philip Veritzen had "advance information," my eyes unconsciously had gone swiftly to the newspaper that Lillian had left upon the table. Mary's perceptions are of rapier-like swiftness, and her pounce upon the paper was as feral as her stride thru the room had seemed to me.

"It's something in this paper," she exclaimed. "Aunt Lillian brought it in, and you stopped her when she said that. What is it? Where is it? Tell me!"

Rushed by a King

"It's that column of Paris gossip," I said, and then watched her as she hastily read it thru. Her foot began to tap angrily after the first few sentences, and I knew that she had found the reference to King Georges. By the time she had finished she was beating a "devil's tattoo," and her eyes were flashing storm signals.

"That's the reason for old Phil's sudden generosity," she said. "Isn't he the wily old ferret, tho? He just figures out that I'm so much of a sap that I couldn't resist being rushed by a king, and that if I gave Noel the go-by for Georges, Olina would be glad to pick little son up and carry him off with her.

"Of course that sounds mighty conceited—the implication that a king would give me a rush—but—"

Her eyes looked at me with unconscious appeal. I answered the hurt in them, which Noel had dealt her.

"Georges is not the man to change," I said, "and from the time he first met you, I never noticed that he had any reluctance to give you a rush. You are keen enough to know, too, Mary, that while Noel heaved a sigh of relief when the betrothal between himself and Olina, entirely engineered by her, was broken off, Georges, despite his renewed happiness with Olina, was distinctly distrait and pensive when he left you. If what you desire is a renewed affair with Georges, I am sure you will get it. But—I do not believe that is what you want."

Noel in on the Scheme?

"Why not?" she flared defiantly. "The boy friend wouldn't turn a hair. He didn't when I told him what his father had proposed.

"Here's a thought! I'll bet he's already seen this paper, or that his father passed on to him the 'advance information' he must have had about this. They're both in this. Noel's seen the light at last, and he thinks it would be sort of pleasant to be married into royalty, just as his silly old father has planned for so long. Maybe he's been yearning for Olina all this time when he's been—"

Her voice trailed off, and if it had not been for the look in her eyes, I should have laughed. But that look spelled misery, absurd jealousy, humiliation; and I put out my arms to her.

"Come here, Mary," I said softly. But she shook her head resolutely.

"Thank you, Auntie Madge, but—but— I can't. I'd be blubbing all over the lot, if I do, and my eyes would get red. I don't mind you knowing I'm shot to pieces over this; but if anybody else did, I'd simply crumple up and die."

"Fixing Things"

"Do you realize how mistaken you are?" I began. But she had begun pacing the room again, and I saw that she did not hear me.

A knock at the door halted her ranging of the room, and brought her eyes to me.

"It sounds like Aunt Lillian," she said.

"Yes, it is her knock," I answered. "Open the door, please."

She crossed the room and flung open the door. Lillian gave her but a cursory nod as she spoke directly to me.

"Did I leave my paper here?" she asked. "Oh, yes; I see I did. May I take it, please?"

"Of course," I answered, and without another look or word at either of us she picked up the paper and went out of the room again. I felt a queer little tingling at my nerve ends, and Mary interpreted it in a burst of hurried words.

"Do you know what she's done? She's pulled Noel into her apartment, and she's trying to fix things up for me! It's mighty kind of her, but I'm here to tell her she can save her breath."

She made a rush for her own door, and I spoke quickly, insistently.

"What are you going to do, Mary?"

(Continued Monday)

(Copyright, 1933)

Joe E. Brown went to Florida from California to recuperate from the flu, and was California's face red! Is Florida laughing?

TOP: *Scene at Union Station following the massacre. The 1932 Chevrolet at right belonged to slain federal agent Ray Caffrey. Kansas City, Missouri, June 17, 1933.* CENTER: *Wanted poster. June, 1933; G-man Melvin H. Purvis.* BOTTOM: *Prison mug shots of Adam Richetti.*

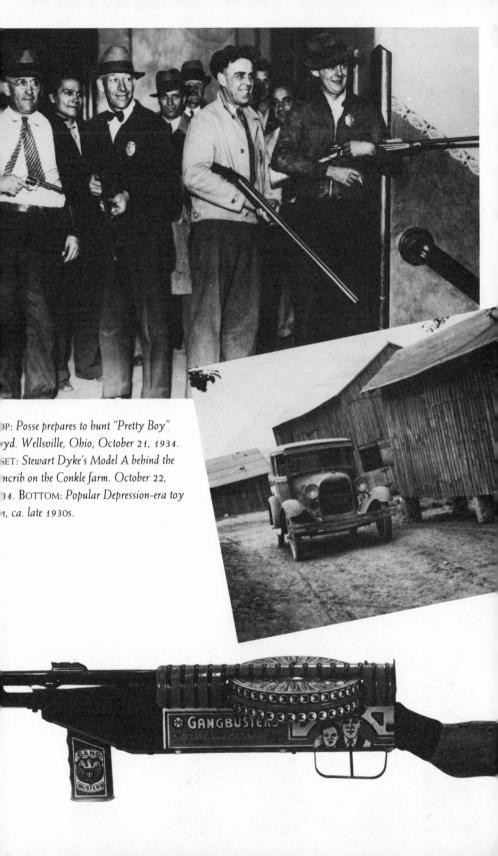

TOP: *Posse prepares to hunt "Pretty Boy" Floyd. Wellsville, Ohio, October 21, 1934. INSET: Stewart Dyke's Model A behind the corncrib on the Conkle farm. October 22, 1934.* BOTTOM: *Popular Depression-era toy gun, ca. late 1930s.*

20

THE PEN

T
HE CHARGE OF HIGHWAY ROBBERY lodged against
Choc Floyd was strong. He would not dare
admit it, but Choc knew as soon as Bert Cotton
pulled him over and found the loot that the law
had him dead to rights. When the St. Louis
authorities arrived and pored over the evidence, Choc became resolved that at
least for a few years he was going to experience life in the home state of Jesse
James. It would not be pleasant.

Seven years after his arrest for the payroll job, Choc would explain to a
tenacious female reporter, "I was just a green country kid that got caught on
a job that I didn't know much about. . . ."

On September 17, 1925, the train out of Sallisaw, which carried "the green
country kid," pulled into St. Louis. It stopped at Union Station, an imposing
four-story landmark made of Bedford stone and part of a twenty-acre complex
on the south side of Market Street. The prisoners were escorted from the
cavernous train shed, the largest in the nation, to an outside entrance where
police squad cars waited to take them five blocks up Market Street to the city
jail at the rear of the Municipal Courts Building.

Inside the jail, Choc was fingerprinted and booked in as number 22318. He
had spent a little time in country jail houses in the past. This was the first
occasion on which he had been given an official identification number. Choc
was also provided with legal counsel, although there was not much a defense
attorney could do but wait for the wheels of justice to grind. That often took
some time.

Intense questioning, which had started back in Sallisaw, continued. Choc,
who did not have any incriminating evidence in his possession at the time of
his arrest, admitted to nothing. Even under pressure in a smoky interrogation
room, he refused to break. Fred Hildebrand, however, spilled the beans. He
not only confessed to his role in the September 11 holdup but also implicated
Choc Floyd and a storekeeper named Joseph Hlavaty as his accomplices. Police
officers went to Hlavaty's Meramec Highland grocery and found a suitcase
containing $2,311 of the stolen payroll money. When he was grilled, Hlavaty

admitted his part in the robbery. He said he had met Hildebrand and Floyd in early September when they were camping on the Meramec River, and they had accosted a couple of local girls. Later, the girls identified Choc as one of their attackers, but the criminal case was weak and no additional charges were filed. The young women's statements, however, did put Choc and Hildebrand together in the state around the time of the robbery.

A Kroger Company paymaster placed Choc at the scene of the crime. The witness picked out Choc as one of the bandits who had confronted him and made off with the payroll. The paymaster reportedly remembered him as "a young fellow, about twenty or twenty-two, with a round, kind of *pretty* face." If the paymaster did indeed call Choc "pretty," that remark undoubtedly hurt the macho Oklahoman's feelings more than the man fingering him as a robber.

Given the state of affairs in the countryside of Oklahoma and elsewhere, the arrest of a young man like Charles Floyd was hardly extraordinary. Many such boys, in fact, came from decent homes much like the Floyds. The day Choc returned as a prisoner to St. Louis, a sixteen-year-old nephew of slain bank robber Henry Starr pleaded guilty to robbery in Newkirk, Oklahoma. He was given a fifteen-year prison sentence. Douglas Starr had been found by lawmen in a cornfield after he was seriously wounded during a gun battle with two men he had tried to rob. Less than a week before, in a separate incident on September 12, as Choc and Hildebrand were driving down from Missouri with their newly purchased Studebaker, another of Henry Starr's nephews—Emmet R. Daugherty—had been fatally wounded by deputy sheriffs. Daugherty, a veteran of World War I, fired three shots from a .45 saddle rifle as the deputies approached him at a midnight drinking party during an Indian stomp dance northeast of Bartlesville. Too much liquor proved his downfall.

The abuse of alcohol was on the rise not only among country boys like Starr's nephew but also with college students and others, according to a national survey that was released that week of 185 representative cities. Prohibition was not working—far from it. As reflected by the arrests for intoxication, drinking had greatly increased in the 1920s at universities across the nation. The survey found that "the college bootlegger is a popular and much sought after person." Prohibition caused other casualties. In Cleveland, Ohio, it was revealed on September 17 that a half dozen federal agents were being treated for partial loss of sight or violent illness after they sampled bootleg liquor they found in a raid, as was required by the government's rules of evidence.

Church officials protested that many Americans were going to the dogs because of alcohol. In Tulsa that September, even a dog was found to have become a hopeless drunk. The bulldog, owned by Police Captain Woodrow Wilson, lost his home because of illegal alcohol. A resident mascot at police headquarters, the dog found an open jar of choc beer and got a taste for the stuff. He became a confirmed rum hound and was given the dubious name Rummy Bull. He could not be stopped from sniffing out other containers of contraband liquor, supposedly evidence in bootlegger raids, and lapping it up until he became too tipsy to patrol the hallways without a noticeable starboard list. When Rummy Bull got tanked up on some corn liquor and battled with Tom, a resurrected alley cat and another revered police mascot, the feline made short work of the drunken dog. Bleeding from scratches, the bulldog went howling for cover. When Rummy sobered up, he found he had been demoted and given to a strict Baptist family. His wild drinking days were over, and no doubt his name was changed.

There were times that boozy autumn when Charley Floyd would have given anything for a swig of Rummy Bull's choc beer to help break the monotony of sitting in a cramped jail cell. However, at least his predicament was not life-threatening, nor was the sentence he finally received as severe as the punishment dealt to the nephews of Henry Starr.

After lingering at the jail and the city workhouse for several months, Choc was finally brought into a district courtroom on December 8, 1925. His appearance in court that Tuesday morning was merely a formality. He had long ago decided to plead guilty and take his medicine. All the paperwork was in order and lawyers from both sides were in their pressed woolen suits with vests.

Choc hardly blinked when he heard the judge say, "I hereby sentence you to five years in the state penitentiary at Jefferson City, Missouri."

Afterward, though, when he was being shuffled back to his cell, the judge's words finally soaked in, and Choc got a lump in his throat the size of one of Maggie Hardgraves's good biscuits. Five years: That was 1,825 days gone right down the hole in the outhouse. That was a mess of living he could never get back.

Hlavaty was also given a five-year prison term, and Hildebrand, the one who had squealed on the rest, was handed an eight-year sentence. So much for being an informer. Ten days after he entered his guilty plea and heard his punishment, Choc was taken back to Union Station to board a train along with forty-eight others, including some female prisoners, bound for the state pen. All of them were dressed in street clothes and were in handcuffs and leg irons linked by a sturdy chain.

If some of the policemen who escorted the prisoners down to Union Station that morning seemed on edge, it was because the night before a pack of bandits had shot and killed a young traffic officer near Grand Boulevard and Olive Street when he surprised the gunmen in the act of holding up a cigar store. The cop killers were at large and none of the men in blue would sleep well until they were nabbed or killed.

Choc's train trip from St. Louis to the state prison was not nearly as exciting as the previous evening's chase. The forty-eight St. Louis prisoners sat quietly on the Missouri Pacific train and looked out the windows as the countryside flashed by their blank faces.

D. L. Thompson, who later traded convict's stripes for a cleric's collar by becoming an ordained minister in Independence, Missouri, was another one of the young prisoners headed for Jefferson City that day. He could always easily recall Charley Floyd and that 129-mile train ride to the penitentiary.

"I remember he bought candy bars for all of us, and the five women on the chain, too," Thompson said almost a half century later. There would be few other pleasant memories for the prisoners once they reached their new home.

The rails ran alongside the Missouri River, and as the train moved west beyond Gray Summit, it took the passengers through villages settled more than a century past by thrifty and industrious Germans. They passed by Washington, with its narrow streets, zither factory, and plants turning out corncob pipes. The towns of New Haven, Berger, Hermann, Gasconade, Morrison, and Chamois came and went. After they reached the Osage River and the land where the Osage Indians had long before maintained their villages, there was a stir among the prisoners who had made this trip before. They knew their final destination was near.

The penitentiary was located in Jefferson City, smack-dab in the center of the state. Named for Thomas Jefferson, Jefferson City, the capital of Missouri, straddled the steep southern bluff of the Missouri River, and was known to its citizens, mostly government employees, as Jeff or Jeff City. Thirty-one miles to the north in Columbia, was the University of Missouri, the state's primary center for higher learning. Railroad lines linked Jeff with Kansas City 148 miles to the west and St. Louis in the east, and had helped draw a few industries to the area. State government was Jeff City's primary business, however. File clerks, stenographers, and an assortment of wearied bureaucrats resided in frame, brick, and stone homes built along the city's hilly avenues.

Jeff had progressed from a rough frontier village with hogs wandering the streets, when it was incorporated in 1839, to a comfortable city of about twenty thousand industrious citizens whose lives depended on the red tape and regulations of civil service. The state's seat of government had been moved to Jeff City from the temporary capital of St. Charles in 1826. Since then, there had been two capitol buildings lost to fires, the first one in 1837 and then again on the night of February 5, 1911, when a bolt of lightning struck the dome. Construction of the new capitol building, located on the site of the former statehouse at High Street between Broadway and Washington streets, had been completed in 1917, only eight years before Charley's arrival. Built of almost eight hundred train carloads of stone and finished with Carthage marble that had been mined out of southwest Missouri, the four stories of the capitol rose above the river into a lanterned dome topped by a bronze statue of Ceres, the Roman goddess of agriculture. The nearby three-story governor's mansion, erected in 1871 when the James gang was gathering a full head of steam, was enclosed with an ornamental iron fence and faced the capitol from the bluff overlooking the river.

Four blocks east of the mansion on Capitol Avenue was the state penitentiary. Authorized in 1832, it was the first state prison built west of the Mississippi River and originally consisted of a few small buildings on a quarter-acre lot surrounded by a wooden stockade. The state legislature set aside $25,000 to build a proper penitentiary in 1833. Construction of the prison was completed in 1836. When Wilson Edison, a twenty-two-year-old Tennessean sentenced from Greene County to two years and forty-five days of solitary confinement for stealing a thirty-nine-dollar watch, was received as the first prisoner on March 8, 1836—just two days after Mexican forces led by General Santa Anna breached the walls of the Alamo and killed all the defenders—the prison property had grown to four acres.

In December 1925, when Charley Floyd and the others attached to the chain of prisoners were delivered at the main gates, the state pen included more than thirty acres within the walls. There were more than three thousand inmates, and the population grew daily. The prisoners lived and worked in red and buff brick cell blocks, dormitories, factories, and other buildings surrounded by turreted limestone walls built by inmate labor. Heavily armed guards kept watch around the clock. Like the nearby capitol building, the penitentiary sprawled over a rocky point above the winding Missouri River, and below the bluffs, near the railroad tracks, were garment and shoe factories and the shops of the Missouri Pacific Railroad. At night, when they were tucked inside their dark cells, inmates lay on their bunks and listened for the passing trains. Above the nightmare cries and the snores, they heard the mournful whistles and they let their imaginations take them far away.

The penitentiary Charley Floyd would know as his home for the next several years was much improved from the old days when prisoners got little nourishing food and wore tattered clothes, but still the pen had many internal problems. Despite the fact that in 1917 there had been some reforms, including abolishment of the punishment known as the "rings," which called for an inmate to be suspended by the wrists for long periods, the penitentiary was a harsh and cruel place. It was practically devoid of any hope or chance that the average inmate would be successfully rehabilitated.

Emma Goldman, the prominent political radical, and Kate Richards O'Hare, a St. Louis socialist organizer, were convicted under the Espionage Act of 1917 for their antiwar activities. They spent time in the women's section of the Jefferson City prison. Both became outspoken critics of the state's explosive prison labor system, which they called "slave labor." Their letters to newspapers, magazines, congressmen, and state legislators brought national attention to this blatant misuse of convict labor.

Twelve-hour workdays remained the standard for both inmates and guards. Flogging was an acceptable method of discipline. Unmanageable prisoners were treated to ice baths, the sweatbox, or locked to a ball and chain. Hard-core recalcitrants ended up in the hole, with only a thin mattress and a steady diet of bread and water. Although it was useless to try to escape, for such flights could easily result in death, some inmates spent every waking moment plotting breakouts from behind the high stone walls. For them, even dying was preferable to life inside the Big House.

On September 13, 1925, the day that Charley and Hildebrand had been picked up by police in Sallisaw, prison officials announced that they had squelched a plot involving twenty-two convicts, most of them members of an inmate musical band, to break out of the Jeff City pen. A tunnel had been dug under the stage in the prison chapel to a sewer that ran below the prison yard and continued beyond the outside walls. The tunnel was discovered after guards found two loaded revolvers and ammunition hidden in some brush near the yard. Prison authorities figured that while most of the inmates were outside taking their exercise, the conspirators from the band rehearsing inside the chapel had loosened floorboards and worked on the tunnel. They used tools stolen from the machine shop, and scattered the dirt under the stage. Two ringleaders were thrown into solitary confinement, and prison officials assured the local citizenry that even if the convicts had been able to reach the sewer line, large steel bars blocked the pipe at the point where it emptied into the river below the penitentiary.

The talk about the foiled prison break was nearly ancient history the afternoon of December 18, when Charley and the other new arrivals were being processed. Christmas was exactly one week away and, even in the pen, there was at least a slight semblance of holiday anticipation. Prison officials had decided to prohibit all gifts of food and other perishables. Even so, the clerks in the outer office at the big institution stayed busy sorting, inspecting, and delivering presents to those unfortunate men and women who had been remembered by the outside world. That following week alone, more than two thousand packages were handled at the prison. The inmate who received the most was Everett Adams, a high school boy from Ohio who was in prison for killing a professor on the road between Jefferson City and Sedalia. Adams was sent more than one hundred Yuletide letters and wrapped presents from family and friends.

Most prisoners would have traded every gift and Christmas card for a chance at freedom. Some of them knew they would never take a breath on the outside again. The day Charley entered the penal system, one of those inmates—Carl Wagman, who had been sent up from St. Louis ten years before for a life sentence—died in the prison hospital after a lengthy illness. He went home in a prison coffin.

Charley was fingerprinted, issued a striped prison uniform, and a few essentials. He was also assigned a new identification number. For the next several years, he would be classified as number 29078. While he was still wearing his civilian necktie and suit, Charley was told to stand up straight and look right at the camera while a clerk took his official penitentiary mug shot. After that he stripped down, showered, and put on his convict clothes. A physical examination showed him to be in good health. Vital statistics listed his height at five foot, seven and one-half inches; weight, 157 pounds; length of foot, ten and one-half inches; hair, black; eyes, blue-gray; complexion, ruddy; religion, Protestant.

He was also given his own copy of an inmate rulebook that had been first issued by the Missouri State Prison Board in 1917. The forty-two rules for prisoners listed inside gave Charley shivers when he read them. A few of the rules were especially noteworthy.

Be gentlemanly everywhere and at all times.

Do not talk or call to men in other cells.

Do not whistle, sing or make any unnecessary noise.

You must not, at any time, have a knife on your person, or in your cell.

When marching in line, keep your head erect, and your face turned toward the front.

Make it your business to keep your cell clean and free from vermin.
Make careful inspection of your bedding every day.
If any bugs are found, report the fact immediately to your guard.

You are not compelled to attend chapel services, but because the moral support of religious instruction is necessary for you, you are admonished to do so.

Cuspidors will be provided and must be used.

Charley was informed that he could receive and keep only certain items, including underwear, sheets, handkerchiefs (white only), shoes (black only), a toothbrush and a hairbrush, tobacco, writing material, family photographs, and "books of proper character." No liquids or factory-made cigarettes were allowed, and all mail and packages coming in and going out were, of course, closely examined. There were also any number of offenses that could get an inmate into trouble, such as profanity, quarreling, mutiny, neglect of work, bed not properly made, crookedness, creating a disturbance, shirt not buttoned at neck, insolence, loafing, laughing and fooling, loud talk, larceny, lying, spitting on the floor, and wasting food.

After he was processed, Charley was assigned to a cell in C Hall, built in 1914 during the years when D. C. McClung served as warden. The cell house was attached by an expansive rotunda with B Hall, and the four-tiered complex was referred to as McClung Hall. Facing it was Q Hall, in later years known as A Hall. Built in 1868 of gray limestone, which had been hand-hewn by inmates and was one of the oldest buildings inside the segregated prison, Q Hall housed hundreds of convicts, including black felons. For many years, even decades after Charley had departed from the penitentiary, there were as many as seven or eight black prisoners jammed into a cell designed for three inmates. Nearby E Hall was built of red bricks before the turn of the century. It also stayed filled to capacity.

Each of the cells on the four levels of Charley's cell house was intended to hold two or more men. On the three upper tiers, the cell doors opened onto suspended walkways. Charley's cell was about nine feet by six feet in size. Inside was a built-in commode, fold-up cots attached to the wall, and the obligatory cuspidors were provided. The cells were icy cold during the winter months, and in the summertime, inmates sweltered at night when they went to their bunks to rest.

It took Charley little time to learn the prison procedures. A bell rang before dawn each morning and he rose promptly and dressed to the sounds of men hacking and coughing and cleaning out their spittoons. Charley and the other inmates made up their bunks and swept and tidied their cells before washing and shaving. At the guards' command, the inmates left their cells, entered the corridor, and marched off in lockstep for breakfast and work assignments.

A whole set of rules existed just for the dining hall. Convicts quickly and quietly took their seats at stools on both sides of long tables in the big room. Only the noise from the exposed steam pipes hissing and rattling overhead could be heard. Inmates remained erect, with their arms folded in front of them and their eyes to the front until a guard gave the signal to commence eating. Strict silence was observed at all times during the meals. Staring at others, any talking or laughter, or gazing around the hall was forbidden.

Meal planning, in the days before nutritionists, showed little imagination. The food served up was basic, bland, and, like everything else in the pen, it was dreary. During the growing season, vegetables abounded from the prison farms, but they were cooked until they were reduced to mush. Choicer cuts of meat were rarely offered, and pie or cake was usually served only on weekends or for special occasions. Many of the standard dishes, such as beans and spuds, were brought to the tables in pans and were passed around family style. Convict waiters served the rest of the food, including meat, bread, and beverages, and the inmates had prescribed signals to use in order to communicate with them. If a man wanted more bread, he held up his right hand; more coffee or water, he held up his cup; more meat, he held up his fork; more soup, he held up his spoon; more vegetables, he held up his knife. If a prisoner at a table wished to speak to a guard about the food or service, he held up his left hand. Wasting food was a sin. Even a small bread crust left on a plate could result in problems for the offender. Water and coffee were served from metal pitchers and the inmates drank from metal cups. After each meal, the eating utensils were carefully counted to make sure no potential weapons had been removed from the premises. A table knife or a spoon that was ground down could make a handy shiv to stick between someone's ribs.

Charley was a survivor. He kept his nose out of other people's business. Whenever he was returning to his block for the evening lock-up, Charley knew better than to stop on the range to look into other inmates' cells, or "cribs." He was careful not to get caught using a hand mirror to watch the comings and goings of officers making their rounds on the range. At 9:00 P.M. when the final bell sounded, signaling lights out and bedtime, Charley placed his shoes at his cell door and laid out his clothes in plain sight. If he approached a guard indoors, he always remembered to doff his cap, and outside he touched the cap before speaking. He learned to use only the officer or guard's last name when addressing him and he put a Mr. in front. If he did not know the person's last name, he called him Sir.

The guards, also known as "bulls" or "screws," were still not part of the state merit system and were hired on the basis of their political affiliation. They did not receive any formal training, were paid poorly, and did not get any overtime, sick leave, insurance, or other legitimate fringe benefits. Prison bulls wore their own clothes and were still years away from donning the blue serge suits that guards were required to buy in the late 1930s. All of the guards carried whistles and small clubs that were made for them by convicts and were used to keep ornery jailbirds in line. The saying around the yard was that "the bulls are just like prison toilet paper—they're rough, always white, and they don't take shit off any prisoner."

Charley Floyd gave the worst of the guards and yard bulls wide berth. That went for certain types of convicts, as well. He stayed away from the rats and stooges, who received favors by informing on other inmates, and the bullies who buggered and gang-raped the "fags" and pretty youngsters and made them into their jail-house punks and penitentiary whores. According to the lingo of the joint, Charley was a stand-up guy trying only to do hard time on a "nickel," or five-year sentence. He made a few friends, including some facing a "dime," or a ten-year hitch, and others who were maximum-security lifers.

The first work detail assigned to Charley was in the kitchen. Later on, he transferred to the machine shop as a plumber's helper and he also worked outside the walls at one of the prison farms. Penitentiary officials remembered Floyd to be a generally good prisoner, and Charles Hargus, assistant deputy warden at the time of Charley's incarceration, pegged him as being smarter than most of the prison population.

"He was intelligent," said Hargus. "That doesn't mean that he was a model prisoner. He would steal things, like most of the convicts, but he didn't go out of his way to hunt trouble. Floyd seemed to have a desire to let alone more than anything else. He kept to himself, went quietly about his tasks, and showed no disposition as a troublemaker."

Charley was not without worries during his tenure in the Jeff City pen. His first year went smoothly enough. Charley kept his head about him and tried not to dwell on his wife and son and the events on the outside that he could not control. Even when Jack Dempsey had his clock cleaned by Gene Tunney, the fighting marine from New York, and lost a ten-round decision on September 23, 1926, Charley remained calm. He wrote off the defeat as a fluke. Dempsey had a good attitude about losing.

"I have no alibis to offer," Dempsey said after the fight. "I lost to a good man, an American—who speaks the English language. I have no alibis." Charley always knew Dempsey was a stand-up gentleman.

But a year later—on September 22, 1927—at Soldiers Field in Chicago, lightning struck once again. In an effort to regain the world heavyweight crown, something that had never occurred before, Dempsey squared off with Tunney in a rematch. It would be one of the most famous fights in the history of twentieth-century boxing. During the seventh round, Dempsey threw a left hook that knocked Tunney to the canvas. Dempsey towered over the dazed Tunney, and even though four critical seconds had ticked off the clock, referee Dave Barry stopped the timekeeper until Dempsey returned to a neutral corner. At nine seconds of the new count, Tunney managed to pull himself up on wobbly legs and square off with his surprised opponent. Somehow he held off Dempsey, not only for the balance of the seventh but the last three rounds of the contest. At the end of the fight, officials said Tunney had won seven of the ten rounds, losing only the third, sixth, and the controversial seventh. Tunney retained the crown. What would be known and argued over in bars, barracks, and jail houses as "the long count" of thirteen seconds had defeated the Manassa Mauler.

"I was robbed," said Dempsey afterward.

Charley, of course, agreed. Jeff City convicts, like inmates at Sing Sing and several other penitentiaries, had been allowed to stay up late to listen to the fight through snarls of static from radios set up on cell block catwalks. Afterward, a well-meaning guard stopped at Charley's cell to chat about the results of the fight and what had transpired in the seventh round. Charley went berserk and kicked a cuspidor into the wall. When he regained his composure, he told his bunk mates and the guard that Tunney and the referee should be in the joint doing ten to twenty for grand theft. In his mind, Dempsey would always be the champ.

Later that year Charley got into a jam of his own. During an unannounced search of the cells, guards found some narcotics in his possession. The offense took place on December 18, 1927, coincidentally the second anniversary of his arrival at the prison. Records listed the infraction only as an inmate "having possession of dope." The ledger did not state the type of drug nor the amount.

Floyd was not a "hop head." He was no doubt bootlegging drugs to make some money. Whatever his reason was for holding drugs, Charley was summarily disciplined. The violation was marked against his "good time" record. This had an adverse impact on Charley's chance for parole at the earliest possible date.

There was only one other official disciplinary action entered on Charley's prison record. This transgression occurred on May 15, 1928. Charley struck a guard—a misdeed that was even more serious than getting caught with contraband dope. It was a Tuesday morning and, like every other day of the week, that meant rising early to face the same routine. Assistant Deputy Warden Hargus handled the matter.

"It happened at morning call," recalled Hargus. "Floyd was a little slow in getting up. One of the guards swore at him and Floyd, who was always hot tempered, knocked the guard down. We put him in solitary for a few days."

Hargus did not remember whether Charley also received a few well-placed lumps for his trouble before being pitched into an isolated cell. There were other breaches involving Charley, but in these instances, a guard or foreman administered discipline on the spot and saw no need to make an entry in Charley's file.

One of his favorite ploys was to steal potatoes from the kitchen. Prisoners brewed up a potato-water concoction that, when fermented and cooked, gave them a dandy alcoholic jolt. A competent Oklahoma moonshiner like Charley Floyd, with all the skills needed, had only to get his hands on the correct ingredients to be back in business.

"Floyd used to come after ice," said Harry Hayes, foreman of the prison cold-storage plant when Charley was in the stir. "He would take advantage of the opportunity to steal potatoes, which the convicts used in making whiskey.

"The potato room was not visible from my office, and while I was sure Floyd was stealing potatoes every time he came after ice, I couldn't catch him at it. I tried to be out in the hall when he came, but he was smart and came at a different time every day."

Finally, Hayes caught on to Charley's tricks. He watched Charley enter the room and saw him pick up a bag of potatoes, carry them outside, and throw them in a wheelbarrow along with a block of ice.

"Floyd saw me coming after him, dropped the wheelbarrow, and started running," said Hayes. "He was rounded up in the yard. He acted insolent and I cuffed his ears a few times."

The exhilaration of stealing and the anticipated comfort of strong drink made the risk of a beating worth it. Charley and other inmates kept their wits by trying to outsmart the screws and the inmate trusties, or hall tenders, at every opportunity. Prison could defeat the strongest men. Some of the best bank robbers and thieves in the business kept their sanity by scheming ways to melt down chocolate bars for forbidden cups of late-night cocoa, or else they cooked up illegal prison coffee, which they called "jamoke." Other tales abounded about crafty cons who dealt in the smuggled cigarette trade. They tied cigarettes with thread around trained cockroaches that delivered their cargo to preferred customers' cells. Nobody questioned how an insect, especially a lowly roach, could be directed to go to a certain cell. It did not matter as far as the inmates were concerned. It was a good story and just telling it gave a convict pleasure. Pulling fast ones somehow made the prisoners feel better about themselves.

Charley found that the penitentiary brought out the worst in men. The population was made up of murderers, cutthroat thieves, rapists, child killers, grave robbers, and degenerates of every kind: men whose skin was gray from fear and loneliness; terrified men; violent men; men who lived with demons; condemned beings with no remorse; men who could not see sunshine or watch the snow fall without someone else's permission.

There were no counselors, no psychiatrists, no psychologists. No one ever heard laughter. Uneducated guards behaved like zookeepers. Some of them could have changed clothes with the inmates and no one would have noticed. That was because no one cared. Plenty of men went stir-crazy. Those who wanted to go home so much that they could not stand it any longer turned to suicide. There was a chaplain and a place to pray, but God was afraid to enter.

Monsters lived there.

21

TOM'S TOWN

I F CHARLEY FLOYD GOT ANYTHING at all from the years at Jeff City, it was a complete and thorough education. He took no courses in grammar, mathematics, or history. Even if he had wanted to, none were offered. The only reading material he was exposed to were newspapers and periodicals, letters from family back in Oklahoma, and the inmate rulebook the warden had given him that first day Charley was ushered through the main gate. A prison, which emphasized convict labor, had no time to fool with book learning for inmates. Charley received his schooling in other ways.

As the years went by, Charley became increasingly aware of the prison hierarchy and his place in it. He had little truck with the sneak thieves and "mission stiffs," who on the outside had subsisted on handouts when they were not pinching old ladies' pocketbooks, boosting shelves in drugstores, and rolling drunks. These men could teach him nothing. He limited his contact with small-time housebreakers and luggage thieves, pimps and pickpockets, grafters and grifters, and shortchangers who had been caught one too many times tricking rubes out of their savings.

Nor did Charley have use for the psychos and sickies, the rippers who mutilated whores, the molesters who preyed on women in parks, or, the most contemptible of all, the monsters who sodomized children. He realized most of them were "bats," the worst kind of crazy. They belonged in the asylum, not in the joint.

His education came from a different type of criminal. The prison slang for the high-grade or more intelligent convicts was "better people," and these were the ones Charley gravitated to for his advanced instruction. They became his teachers. Some of them conducted their nefarious lives with a certain style and pride. A few were even considered to be preeminent in the criminal world. Their problem was, they got caught. Now, they had nothing but time on their hands. They made the most of their situations and passed along some of the tricks of their various trades to youngsters who might make likely recruits. One of those who showed promise was Charley Floyd.

During the twenties, the Missouri State Penitentiary attracted its share of tough guys and hoodlums, ranging from hardheaded farm boys gone bad to big city thugs and racketeers. Some had been sent up the river from Kansas City, a politically corrupt haven for lawbreakers, or from St. Louis, where Prohibition helped nurture a crop of gangsters every bit as mean as the syndicate mobsters of Chicago and New York, or even the feared Purple Gang in Detroit. Across the Mississippi from St. Louis, in southern Illinois, thrived a band of bootleggers led by Charles Birger, who was ultimately hung in 1928 for ordering the murder of the mayor of West City, Illinois, Joe Adams, supposedly a rumrunner and former Birger ally. The dreaded Shelton gang—comprised of brothers Carl, Bernard, and Earl, and more than fifty seasoned torpedoes—fought it out with Birger and other rivals for the control of the illegal liquor business and rackets on the east side.

In St. Louis, many of the criminals emerged from street gangs organized long before in the ethnic neighborhoods. Some hailed from the large Italian section, known lovingly as "Dago Hill." Others showed up amongst the shanty Irish, or in the older neighborhoods of dirty brick tenement houses and vermin-infested flats that surrounded the breweries, factories, and churches. There were the Hogans, the Cuckoos, the Green Ones, the Russos, and the most feared of all—Egan's Rats. A run-of-the-mill street gang organized by Jellyroll Egan in the early 1900s, this bunch was almost inoperative by the outbreak of World War I but revived with the coming of the Volstead Act. By the time Charley was in the pen, Egan's Rats had become the most successful and feared bootlegging gang in St. Louis.

As was the case in most U.S. cities of any size, the criminals were well organized in Kansas City and St. Louis. The pen in Jeff City just happened to be strategically located between these two outlaw meccas on Missouri's east and west borders. Every now and then the police got lucky and picked up a top gun or even a big shot from one of the gangs. If they were able to make the arrest stick and get a conviction, the culprit was sent to the big stone fortress on the river bluffs. Once inside the walls, such criminals became those "better people" who commanded the top position in the convicts' hierarchy and also served as able professors of crime and masters of deceit.

Charley paid close attention to these men. He made careful mental notes. He listened to ace safecrackers explain some of their secrets. He heard seasoned burglars tell how they were able to tunnel like gophers under banks and blow open vaults. He warmed up to strong-arm hooligans who had worked their way up from bouncing at brothels and gambling dens to providing muscle for ward politicians and big-city bosses.

He overheard them argue about whose shyster lawyer was the most unscrupulous and which city had the least corruptible cops. Between innings at convict ball games in the yard, he picked up handy tidbits about various weapons and other helpful hints that he figured he might have to use once he got back on the outside. He learned about the "bootlegger's turn" an evasive driving technique used to escape pursuing lawmen. To make it work, the driver first locked the emergency brake and turned the steering wheel ninety degrees before quickly releasing the brake, mashing the gas pedal, and accelerating the automobile in the opposite direction.

The fellows he listened to were so good at thievery, they could have swiped the tires off a speeding motorcar. He was told about some of the jobs that they had pulled and how the small-town banks were the easiest to hit. They said it was laughable. It was a piece of cake. What they forgot to tell him about were the crimes that went wrong, the botched jobs that got them thrown into the prison.

Charley learned to distinguish between "applesauce" and the truth. He mainly listened. He had figured out very quickly that the only way to get along inside the pen was to "ride your own beef," as the wise old cons put it. He did not bitch and moan about getting a bum rap, even though he felt he really had. He paid close attention to the grapevine chatter and kept his mouth shut.

When he learned from Mamie and others that his father back in Akins had hardened his heart against him, Charley did not fall to pieces. Even his wife's obvious displeasure did not shake him. He had seen it coming. Veteran convicts had warned him early on that "a dame will stick by you for a few months and that's it." Her letters became few and far between. Those that did arrive spoke of the hard times she and Dempsey had to put up with since Charley had become a convicted felon. Gradually, there were only bitter words. By 1928, Charley was lucky if he received any letters at all.

Finally, toward the end of his hitch in the pen, Charley heard only from her lawyer. The attorney's correspondence came right to the point. Ruby wanted a divorce.

On January 4, 1929, Ruby, through her lawyers, Wilson and Searcy, filed the divorce action with the district court clerk at the Tulsa County courthouse. In her petition, she stated that she and Charley had been married in Sequoyah County on June 28, 1924. She charged her husband with neglect and pointed out to the court that he was still serving a five-year robbery sentence in Missouri.

Paperwork had previously been sent to Jefferson City, and Charley had already signed a waiver to the action with a scrawled "Chas. Floyd." He saw no need to fight Ruby's wishes. On January 7, Ruby and her lawyers appeared in the courtroom of District Judge John Ladner. The judge examined the filed documents including the waiver signed by Charley. It was an uncontested divorce action. Ladner issued the decree and gave Ruby full custody of their son, Dempsey, just turned four years old and every day looking more like his father.

Family members recalled receiving sad letters from Charley around the time of the divorce. In the evenings, when the lights were doused in the cell block, Charley lay on his bunk and thought about Ruby. Their marriage had lasted a little more than four years and six months. Of that time, they had actually lived together as husband and wife for less than fifteen months. If she wanted to be free of him, Charley did not blame her. She had every right to break off their relationship. Ruby had been forced to live back and forth between the Floyds and her family and do without. There had been no frills in her life. Charley got angry with himself for putting her in that situation. He still loved and cared about Ruby and their little boy.

Charley was also feeling bitter about his plight. His whole attitude toward life changed during his years in the pen. Over time, he felt he had gotten a bad deal, and even though he had pled guilty to his crime, deep down he believed he had been treated unfairly. As soon as he could get out of prison, he wanted to go find Ruby and Dempsey and make it up somehow.

He did not have very long to wait. Freedom was exactly fifty-nine days away. Charley had not been an exemplary prisoner or else he would have been paroled sooner. One hundred and twenty days had been deducted from the merit time allowed to convicts for good behavior. Sixty days had been taken from his allowance for possession of narcotics and another sixty days for striking a guard.

Charley's big day finally came on March 7, 1929. It was a Thursday; winter was going on a dying rampage.

There was a definite nip in the air, but skies over Missouri, and to the west over Kansas and Oklahoma, were mostly fair and the temperature was slowly rising. As he had done for so many mornings, Charley pulled himself up from his bunk before the early bell stopped ringing. He automatically reached for his faded striped uniform. Then in a split second, he remembered the date. His days as a crack potato thief were done. He would now be set free. There was a plain civilian suit, a clean white shirt, and a pair of new shoes for him to put on. He had almost forgotten how to tie a necktie, but after a few tries, it came out all right.

Charley said so long to his cell mates and the rest of his friends. He gave away most of his personal belongings. He did not want to carry too much. A bull walked him from the cell house to the warden's office, where he signed a few papers and was told to keep his nose clean. Most cons on their way out of the stir promised they would go as straight as a movie star's teeth. Guards remembered that Charley just smiled and did not say anything. They gave him enough money to buy a bus or train ticket, a few meals, and still have some walking-around change.

Before the noon whistles at the shoe factories blew, Charley Floyd was gulping in air on the other side of the penitentiary walls. Charley had been in custody for almost three and a half years. In that instant, when he physically crossed over into freedom, he felt as if he was Choc Floyd once more, not just number 29078.

Right there in front of the entrance to the pen, he swore to himself that he would never again return to prison.

Then he turned his back on all the nightmares, and he walked away. He hiked straight to the train depot and bought a ticket. St. Louis was not in his immediate plans, that was for certain. His last trip to St. Louis still would do him for a while. He was headed due west. He had decided to go to Kansas City, compliments of the state of Missouri.

A couple of days and nights at a K.C. speakeasy was just what Charley needed to wash away all traces of the penitentiary. At least that was the best parting advice he got from some cohorts before he left the prison. After a visit to Kansas City, he would be ready to slip down into Oklahoma and face family and friends and, hopefully, find Ruby and Dempsey and try to make amends.

The train took Charley out of Jeff City and headed west. It gradually entered the prairies of western Missouri and passed towns that still bore battle scars from border wars of a bygone era. Beyond the town of California, the train picked up speed. It raced on toward Tipton, Syracuse, Smithton, Sedalia, past fenced farms with deep black soil that yielded wheat, oats, Irish potatoes, and fed big Missouri mules, handsome hybrids that had long ago proved they were the best of the breed whether in a field of corn or on the field of battle. Charley settled back and enjoyed this ride. It was certainly more relaxing than his last train trip several years ago.

In some ways, the nation was an altogether different place in 1929 than it had been in 1925 when Charley was taken out of circulation. A kaleidoscope of events highlighted what had been a busy five-year period during the last half of the twenties.

Just before Charley went into prison in 1925, Chicago gangland boss John Torrio, seriously wounded in an assassination attempt, had taken early retirement and had surrendered control of his entire crime empire to a former bodyguard, Alfonso Capone, who had served his criminal apprenticeship in Brooklyn; Clarence Darrow and William Jennings Bryan had gone head-to-head at the sensational "monkey trial" of John T. Scopes, a Dayton, Tennessee, high school teacher who had dared to teach Darwin's theory of evolution; and more than forty thousand white-robed Klansmen had marched through the streets of the nation's capital in the largest display of KKK power in history.

In 1926, Aimée Semple McPherson, a flamboyant evangelist, claimed to have been kidnapped, but her mysterious disappearance was actually a secret romantic rendezvous; in Hollywood, a Swedish beauty named Greta Gustafsson became Greta Garbo, while in the same year thousands of sobbing fans paid homage to Rudolph Valentino, dead at age thirty-one of a ruptured appendix and gastric ulcer; Harry Houdini, the master escape artist and magician, could not escape death and succumbed to peritonitis resulting from a fan punching his stomach; and the wraps were taken off a highway named U.S. Route 66, much of it still unpaved, connecting Chicago and Los Angeles.

In 1927, Charles Lindbergh, "Lucky Lindy," made history with his nonstop solo flight from New York to Paris in the *Spirit of St. Louis;* Nicola Sacco and Bartolomeo Vanzetti, a pair of Italian-born anarchists convicted of murder in a highly controversial trial in Massachusetts, died in the electric chair; Lou Gehrig slugged three homers in one day in Boston and Babe Ruth set a record by smashing sixty home runs in a single season; and the first talkie, a film called *The Jazz Singer,* was released and star Al Jolson uttered the memorable line "You ain't seen nothin' yet."

In 1928, Amelia Earhart, a young Kansas daredevil, became the first woman successfully to fly across the Atlantic; Gene Tunney announced his retirement from the ring to study philosophy at the Sorbonne; Republican presidential candidate Herbert Hoover, campaigning with the slogan "A chicken in every pot, a car in every garage," beat Democratic hopeful Alfred E. Smith in a landslide election.

And, in the first few months of 1929, Joseph Stalin was able to expel his most vehement critic, Leon Trotsky, from the Soviet Union; legendary Dodge City and Tombstone character Wyatt Earp died in his sleep in Los Angeles at age eighty; and Charles Lindbergh and his fiancée, Anne Spencer Morrow, escaped serious injury in an airplane crash just ten days after an historic aviation first took place when a commercial airline showed a film to a dozen passengers during a flight from Minneapolis–St. Paul to Chicago.

A convict who had been out of circulation for more than three years found it difficult to adjust to a world that had changed radically in such a short span of time. Choc's rural America had virtually collapsed, yielding a new order that was even more precarious than the one that lay in disarray. A brand-new decade was just around the corner. It had all the markings of more trouble to come. The crime wave that had started in the early twenties was not only continuing but had gained force. From 1924 to 1929, some convincing studies revealed that crime in America had dramatically increased, and no doubt would continue to rise until Prohibition was repealed.

Less than a month before Charley was freed, the St. Valentine's Day Massacre took place in Chicago. About mid-morning on February 14, 1929, six men employed by mob boss George "Bugs" Moran, along with a local optometrist who knew Moran, were lined up against the wall of a North Clark Street garage used as a bootlegger's warehouse. They were quickly frisked, and then all seven were shot to death by archrival Al Capone's heavily armed "gorillas," who had arrived in a Cadillac and posed as policemen conducting a routine bootleg raid.

Publicity generated by this drastic method of settling a gangland dispute stirred the public and created an outcry. Nonetheless, people were fast losing their fascination with the colorful Capone. Like a feudal lord, he ruled the Chicago rackets and ordered hits on rival gangs. Known for his gargantuan appetites for food, women, and drink, the flashy "Scarface" Capone was considered by some folks to be a thoughtful thug. They said he was generous when it came to giving to charities and lavishing enormous tips on bootblacks, hatcheck girls, and waiters.

Several weeks after the massacre, the federal grand jury met in Chicago. Later in the month, Capone would post bail on a contempt-of-court charge following his subpoenaed appearances before the grand jury. And, on May 17, 1929, he and his bodyguard would be arrested again, this time in Philadelphia, for carrying concealed weapons. Within sixteen hours, they would be sentenced to one-year prison terms. Some cynics said that Capone had arranged for his own arrest so he could escape retaliation from the Moran gang. For the next nine months, until he was released for good behavior on St. Patrick's Day 1930, the urban crime czar ruled his vast army and fiefdom of thousands of lucrative speakeasies from the privacy of a comfortable jail suite, with a telephone at his disposal, catered meals, and unrestricted visitation privileges. It would be a far cry from the stark penitentiary cell that Charley Floyd had just left behind.

As a fidgety Charley, trying to get used to being a free man, sat inside the train chugging toward Kansas City the afternoon of March 7, the newspapers lying around the dining car carried a story that told of crime closer to home. Big-city bootleggers and gang wars were in vogue but bank robbery was still a popular occupation, and that trend was destined to proceed. Bandits were continuing what a wire-service reporter called an "orgy of robberies" in Missouri, Kansas, and Oklahoma.

On the national scene, there were fresh reports from Washington, D.C., that Herbert Clark Hoover was doing his part to convince Americans in the mood for some magic that the country was now in good hands. Three days before, on March 4, in a driving rain in Washington, D.C., a resolute Hoover had taken the oath of office as the thirty-first President. In his inaugural speech, he assured the nation he would see to it that prosperity reached everyone and that, at long last, farmers would get some badly needed economic relief. Hoover also mentioned that there were no plans to discontinue Prohibition.

Alcohol remained everywhere despite the President's naïve pronouncements. When Charley stepped off the train that brisk March evening at Union Station, he found a city awash in a sea of bootleg booze. He never forgot his arrival in Kansas City. Years later, he still delighted in telling friends about the occasion.

Charley emerged from the bustling station into the plaza facing the Liberty Memorial, a massive twenty-one-story shaft faced with Indiana limestone sitting on a hill across Pershing Road. At the parking lot's curb, Charley caught a ride in a taxi driven by a uniformed cabbie wearing a rakish cap and gleaming leather puttees. The cab, with running boards and wire-spoked wheels, accelerated below the phalanx of billboards and electric signs advertising Red Crown gasoline, house paint, motorcars, and NuGrape soda pop selling for a nickel a bottle. Turning the corner at Pershing and Main, the taxi crossed the Main Street bridge that spanned the railroad tracks and train sheds, and cruised into the heart of Kansas City.

A young man in a prison-issued suit not interested in flavored soft drinks but with an obvious thirst for wine and women had come to just the right place. Even at the height of the Prohibition years, Kansas City always had a buzz on. And any cabdriver worthy of a two-bit tip knew exactly where to take a fare to get his cravings satisfied and his itch scratched.

Americans in 1929 would be keeping time to new songs such as "Stardust," "You Do Something to Me," "More Than You Know," "Tiptoe Through the Tulips," and "Singin' in the Rain." In Kansas City, there were also brassy melodies from Andy Kirk and other big bands. Soulful jazz poured from clubs, speakeasies, and beer flats. Hit tunes such as "That Old Gang of Mine" seemed to fit the city's lifestyle much better than "Ain't Misbehavin'."

Kansas City was not "behavin'." It was naughty and ill-behaved. The only smell of fear came from nervous beef on the hoof at the stockyard, waiting to enter the slaughterhouses.

The second-largest city in Missouri and the crossroads for the western half of the nation, Kansas City grew like a meat packer's callus at the elbow of the Missouri River, where it joined with the Kaw, also called the Kansas, a stream formed by the confluence of the Smoky Hill and Republican rivers in northeastern Kansas.

However, the Kansas City that Choc discovered for the first time in 1929 had come a long way from its humble origins.

It all began as a frontier river village named Kansas, established in 1821 and not much more than a trading post and cluster of fur trappers' huts. Eventually, the village combined with the nearby town of Westport, platted in 1833 and the jumping-off point for pioneers bound for California, Santa Fe, and Oregon.

Finally, after the citizens settled on the name Kansas City and the bloodbath of border raids and the Civil War ceased, the pack train and steamboat traffic thinned as cattle trails and railroad lines brought droves of cowboys, farmers, and merchants. A major building boom followed while the city became increasingly prosperous from the livestock trade and the farms of the Great Plains.

Kansas City first emerged as a transportation and business hub and the axis of the country's east-west commerce around the turn of the century. Along with the businesses and banks, the meat packers and manufacturing plants, came boulevards, residential neighborhoods, and comfortable apartment houses. Real estate developer Jesse Clyde Nichols built up the south side of the city, including the swank Country Club District and nearby Mission Hills, on the Kansas side of the state line. Nichols wanted his showcase developments to rival other elite suburbs such as Winnetka north of Chicago and Cleveland's Shaker

Heights. They did just that. In the early twenties, Nichols also erected Country Club Plaza, spiffy forerunner of the modern shopping center, on land that had been used as a brickyard and sanitary landfill. The Spanish-style complex built of stucco and cream-colored brick was opened in 1923, and became the city's premier retail district, drawing affluent shoppers from hundreds of miles around.

Early on, Nichols was encouraged by other wealthy civic leaders, especially William Rockhill Nelson, the famed newspaper publisher and editor from Indiana who had founded the *Evening Star,* later called only the *Star,* in 1880. In 1901, Nelson acquired the *Kansas City Times* in order to have a morning edition. His admirers honored him by adding the title Colonel before his name. His enemies called him the Baron or Baron Bill. Before Nelson's death in 1915, the crusader saw his newspapers flourish and dominate public opinion in his adopted city.

While public leaders such as Nelson and Nichols concerned themselves with civilizing Kansas City, however, there were other powerful forces who had a strong grasp on the city's pulse.

The most invincible man in Kansas City was Thomas Joseph Pendergast. He was a take-no-prisoners political chieftain with enormously long and mighty tentacles. There were those who called him the unofficial king of Kansas City. Others simply referred to him as the Boss. From the unadorned offices of the Jackson County Democratic Club housed in three rooms on the top level of a two-story yellow brick building at 1908 Main Street, Thomas Pendergast reigned supreme. For many years, his office was considered to be the true seat of government in Kansas City and Jackson County and, some argued, even the state. What Pendergast wanted, Pendergast got. What he believed was good for the people of Kansas City, they, in turn, received.

"I've never bulldozed anybody and I've never let anybody bulldoze me," the corn-bred Pendergast was once quoted as saying. "Newspapers, churches, reformers, or narrow-minded fellows—they can't bulldoze me. I've never changed my mind when I knew I was right."

The powerful Pendergast machine had begun before the turn of the century. It was started by Thomas's older brother, James, a big, mustachioed alderman out of the West Bottoms area, who joined with other Democratic party leaders and fellow saloon keepers from the working classes of north Kansas City in pitched battles against Baron Bill Nelson's agitating newspapers. After his brother's death in 1910, thirty-eight-year-old Tom Pendergast, already anointed by James, assumed his First Ward aldermanic seat and gradually gained control of the corrupt north side.

By the start of the Roaring Twenties, after years of political infighting with rival factions, Pendergast was close to dominating the entire city. In 1922, his political organization was instrumental in the election of the young Harry S. Truman to the office of judge of Jackson County's eastern district, an administrative rather than judicial position.

Known as a no-nonsense fellow, Truman had been born in Lamar, Missouri, raised in Independence, and had been turned down for West Point because of his poor eyesight. Instead of going to college, he worked for the Santa Fe Railroad and at a Kansas City bank, and also helped run his family's farm. A member of the National Guard, Truman was called to serve as an artillery captain in France during the Great War.

Truman returned to Missouri, married Elizabeth Virginia Wallace, and, along with army buddy Eddie Jacobson, opened a haberdashery business at Twelfth Street and Baltimore Avenue in Kansas City. The business failed during the depression of 1921. Pendergast pulled Truman's fat from the fire the next year when he helped deliver enough votes so that the self-educated Democrat in spectacles beat four other candidates for the county judge's job. In 1924, the same year his daughter, Mary Margaret, was born, Truman lost his reelection bid, partly because he was opposed by the Ku Klux Klan. Despite his defeat, Truman recovered. Two years later, with more help from Tom Pendergast, he was elected presiding judge of the county court, a job he held for the next eight years.

"Keep your word when you give it and when you're after votes, don't wear two-toned shoes, and be sure to wear a coat and pants that match"—these were some of the words of wisdom Pendergast offered when Truman was supervising extensive public building and road projects totaling more than $60 million.

Pendergast happened to own the Ready-Mixed Concrete Company. He was only too pleased to dump his product at construction locations throughout the city, even on the fancier south side of town. A two-mile length of Brush Creek, near Nichols' Country Club Plaza, was even lined with an eight-inch layer of Pendergast cement, making it one of the few paved creekbeds in the nation. And, while he waited for his concrete to harden at hundreds of job sites throughout Jackson County, the wily Pendergast turned Kansas City into a wide-open town.

He advocated the new city charter enacted in 1925, mandating a city manager–council form of government. Pendergast saw to it that his hand-picked puppet, Judge Henry F. McElroy, was given the city manager's job. A majority of the new city-council seats went to other good dues-paying Democrats. The heyday of Boss Pendergast's rule began in 1925 and continued for the next fourteen years. Pendergast owned the city government and the police force. He also relied on a stockpile of sixty thousand ghost voters, whom he summoned to the polls whenever they were needed.

Even those who opposed Pendergast's antics joked that Kansas City was now "Tom's Town."

By 1929, Kansas City bore no resemblance to the more drab cities of the Midwest or even some of the larger cities back east. It had become the crown jewel on a gaudy necklace of lawless havens—a corridor of crime—ranging from St. Paul and Detroit in the North to Joplin, Missouri, and Hot Springs, Arkansas, in the South. A police reporter of that time compared these cities to the imaginary bases used by children playing tag. Once a criminal with local connections made it safely inside one of these cities, he was home free. He was "on base" and could not be "tagged" by the authorities.

Criminals with their mugs on wanted posters bought police protection. They moved about unmolested, showing up at gambling houses open twenty-four hours a day. The menu of choices at the sin palaces was as long as some of the patrons' rap sheets. There were the Cuban Gardens, the Reno Club, the Yellow Front Saloon, and the Spinning Wheel. Customers got drunk as skunks. They dined on platters of succulent barbecue and devoured mounds of boiled crawfish or took in shows at one of the fifty jazz joints operating in the Twelfth Street district. They talked business at the Chesterfield Club. Gorgeous cocktail waitresses wore practically nothing but a smile. For the sporting crowd, Pendergast—a dedicated family man and devout Catholic—operated a racetrack just five miles north of the city limits.

Besides tough guys with silk neckties and tailored suits, any number of accountants, doctors, lawyers, and civil servants enjoyed the pleasures of the flesh that Tom's Town offered. Boogie-woogie sounds from Charlie Parker, Count Basie, Bennie Moten, and many others kept a steady flow of visitors coming to Kansas City. Conventioneers arrived at Union Station en masse. They marched in formation to the Muehlebach, Baltimore, Continental, Aladdin, Phillips, or one of the lesser downtown hotels. Shriners on convention were always anxious to remove their fezzes and settle in at a jazz club, attend the Gayety Burlesque House, or grab a comic's act, such as that of the youthful Red Skelton.

During those tainted times, an especially large group of Shriners, with brass bands blaring, paraded by rows of wooden bleachers erected just to hold crowds of spectators. As they marched along Pershing toward Main, the Shriners chanted a catchy ditty. Newspaper reporters scribbled down every word:

> *There are no wives with us,*
> *There are no wives with us,*
> *There may be wives*
> *With some of you guys,*
> *But there are no wives with us.*

John Lazia provided the muscle that was needed to make sure that Kansas City remained a hospitable refuge for convention delegates. Lazia also ensured that the Pendergast machine functioned with no interruptions. The son of poor Italian immigrants, Lazia rose from the dregs of thieves and petty hoodlums to become a boss of the north side and the premier enforcer for the rackets controlled by the Pendergast organization.

Born in Kansas City's Little Italy district in 1897, Johnny Lazia was eighteen when he was convicted of armed robbery and sent off to the pen at Jeff City. His stay at the pen was cut short by a parole and a promise that he would join the army and use his violent energy to fight the Germans in the trenches. Like certain Oklahoma criminals, such as Frank Nash, who had also earned early releases in this manner, Lazia did not enlist but returned to his hometown and resumed his life of crime. On the surface, he appeared to be a congenial young man, always chewing gum and looking trim and dapper in expensive clothes and rimless eyeglasses. Below this cosmetic veneer lay quite another story.

During the 1920s, Lazia assembled an awesome goon squad that included Solly Weissman, Charley Carollo, Sam Scolla, Gus Fascone, and scores of other triggermen. All of them were capable of protecting the lucrative liquor and gambling rackets and getting out the Democratic vote for key political elections. In 1929, Lazia, who sometimes carried a swagger stick, was at the pinnacle of his power and was flexing his slender muscles.

Modern Kansas City, with its paved boulevards and tall buildings rising over the Missouri River, was in some ways not really that far removed from the Westport Landing that author Francis Parkman had written about in 1846. "Whiskey circulates more freely in Westport than is altogether safe in a place where every man carries a loaded pistol in his pocket." Eighty-three years after Parkman penned those words, not every man in town carried a gun, but there were enough toting pistols to keep alive memories of the frontier times.

That was the Kansas City that Choc Floyd, just turned twenty-five and a one-time loser fresh out of the penitentiary, encountered that March evening as the taxi glided over streetcar tracks into the guts of Tom's Town. Like other newcomers, he rode right by Pendergast's office at 1908 Main Street without giving it a thought. Choc knew it would take some time to learn his way around downtown, extending east from the bluffs above the Kaw and south over the hills from the Missouri. From this downtown area, he could set out farther into the scattered neighborhoods of red-light houses, gambling dens, and gin mills.

A new fellow in town with a jail-house pallor and conspicuously dressed in an ill-fitting suit stuck out like a nun at a crapshoot, however. Choc landed in trouble quickly. On March 9, 1929, just two days following his release from prison, he was picked up by the Kansas City police and held under a charge listed only as "investigation." He was given a number—16950—and placed in a holding tank while the officers checked out his past criminal record. They gave him a hard time but released him with the warning to hit the bricks and go back to Oklahoma where he belonged. There was no room in Tom's Town for another ex-con without the right connections.

Charley beat a hasty retreat out of Kansas City and headed south to

Oklahoma. He was not off to an auspicious start as a man back on the outside. He was not going to go to Akins straightaway. He knew from letters that Bradley had taken his wife and children a little farther west to the big Seminole oil field. Producing wells dotted the land, and Bradley had written to Choc about the feverish boom. His older brother said that there were jobs to be had for the asking. Charley wanted to hook up with a drilling crew and make some money. Then he could go see all the folks at Akins and track down Ruby and the boy.

But try as he might, Charley had a difficult time getting his brief interlude in Kansas City out of his thoughts. He had heard so much about the city all his life, especially from some of the cons at the state pen. They had told him that Kansas City was just the ticket. It was the place to go.

The next day, he got back to Oklahoma. He hitched his way down a Pottawatomie County dirt road to the town of Earlsboro, where Bradley and his family had a small house. Thoughts of Kansas City remained with him, according to later recollections by Bradley's sons. On his head was the cheap straw hat he had bought at a downtown store. Charley still tasted the hunk of strip steak and the whiskey's bite from that one night he went on a splurge. Upon his arrival, the family smelled a trace of bay rum left from the shave Charley had enjoyed in a hotel barbershop.

He was willing to give the oil patch a try, but, by God, he wanted to go back to Kansas City sometime soon to make a name for himself in that town.

22

THE WALLS COME TUMBLING DOWN

AYNE AND WAYNE, Bradley Floyd's twin sons, saw the figure of a man walking toward them. When they first noticed the stranger, the little boys were wrestling in the middle of the oil field road, a few miles east of the boomtown of Earlsboro, that ran in front of their house. The twins stopped playing and watched him come closer to them.

"This guy came down the road carrying a small suitcase, and we saw that he had on a straw hat," recalled Bayne more than sixty years later. "He walked right on by, and then he turned around and looked at us. My brother Wayne, ever since he was a baby, always had this funny eye, an eye that would get all squinty from the sun. It was sort of like his trademark.

"Well, this fella looked right at him. He grinned and said, 'You're Wayne, aren't you?' It was our Uncle Choc. He had remembered that ol' squinty eye of Wayne's, and he knew he'd found where he was lookin' for. We were goin' on nine years old later that year and hadn't seen Choc since we were about five, when we still lived back in Sequoyah County. We had really forgot about him, and now here he was standing right in front of us."

Bradley and Bessie welcomed Charley into their small home, already crowded with the twin boys, five-year-old Glendon, and a fourth son, Cleatus, who had been born in Earlsboro in 1928 when Charley was still in prison. Bessie's parents, Sam and Ellen Watson, and two of her brothers had moved from Sequoyah County to the Seminole oil fields in 1926, and Sam became an engineer in a gasoline plant. They encouraged Bessie and her husband to leave the corn and cotton fields behind, too, and join them.

"My daddy went on out to those oil fields, with one of my cousins, and so Bradley went out to look it over," said Bessie Floyd. "Bradley got himself a job, and I stayed and finished getting in the cotton, sold my cow, and packed up. Then my daddy came and loaded us on his truck and we all moved there."

Bradley took a job as a truck driver. He hauled work crews and equipment back and forth from the rigs that sprouted throughout that country in a Mack Bulldog truck equipped with tire chains and winch. Bessie did her best to make their modest oil patch house into a pleasant home for the family. At one point, Bradley broke down and bought her a trusty Singer sewing machine. With it, Bessie made curtains and sewed for the other folks. She patched, darned, and recycled the boys' shirts and overalls until they wore out. She canned everything edible, from wild berries to garden vegetables. She also canned fresh meat after Bradley and the neighbors killed a hog or calf. On cold winter nights, the Floyd boys licked their lips when their mother retrieved a jar of veal from the cellar across the road and cooked up some biscuits and gravy on her wood-burning stove. Those were usually special meals or at holidays, for even with the wages Bradley made as a truck driver, there were lean spells and some nights the boys went off to bed hungry as boxcar hoboes.

Now and then, Bessie took in a few boarders and put them on mattresses that covered the rough wooden floors. She also sold sandwiches and made up lunches for roustabouts, bored with standing in line for hours at the Oil Flyer Cafe, who stayed down at the Magnolia Oil bunkhouses. Making room for Choc and having one more mouth to feed did not bother a workhorse like Bessie Floyd. She thrived on labor. She did not mind the filthy work shirts and drawers that piled up next to the tub and washboard. There was not enough time to fret about much more than keeping Bradley fed and the men's dinner buckets filled. She felt lucky if she was able to get her boys clean and march them off to prayer meeting and church every week.

An ample dose of good old-time religion was a necessity for a God-fearing woman like Bessie Floyd. The oil fields of Oklahoma during the twenties and thirties were not a place for the faint of will, back, or mind. A spell with the Bible did much to soothe troubled souls.

For the Greater Seminole Oil Field, as it was known, was not just the world's chief producer of petroleum from 1923 until the oil play petered out about 1935, it was also unquestionably one of the most violent and squalid areas in the nation.

Located to the east of Oklahoma City and the city of Shawnee, in an area that included the entire county of Seminole as well as parts of Pottawatomie and three other counties, the oil field covered about thirteen hundred square miles. More than sixty ripe pools were developed over the dozen or so boom years. Before the discovery of oil, it had been one of the poorest sections of the state. Most of the territory was situated in sandstone hills covered with post oaks, blackjacks, and some stands of black walnut. When the oil wells began gushing, tenant farmers and sharecroppers from that area, as well as others like the Floyds and Watsons, deserted their fields to take jobs with oil companies as unskilled workers.

The heart of what was once the Seminole Indian Nation, this area was most proud of six of its largest pools—Earlsboro, Bowlegs, Seminole, Little River, Allen, St. Louis. Each of these pools produced more than a million barrels of oil before they played out. The heavy flow of crude oil predictably brought about both growth of towns and communities and also an explosive increase in criminal activity.

After oil was found, the Seminole County seat of Wewoka doubled in size. With the sudden swell in population came problems caused by poor roads, inadequate telephone service, and a serious shortage of facilities to receive and store freight. Merchandise being shipped to the town was often waylaid or wound up sitting in a boxcar at the Wewoka siding waiting for someone to claim it. Merchants told their customers that they had the item they wanted but it was "in the Wewoka switch." Oil field workers who colored their language with slang coined a catchphrase that fit the situation. To get "caught in a Wewoka switch" meant that a working man found himself in a sudden dilemma. It became one of the most oft-used expressions in the oil patch.

Despite the mayhem and chaos, populations jumped sky-high in towns like Earlsboro, Seminole, Maud, and Bowlegs. In 1926 alone, well over one hundred thousand persons moved into the Greater Seminole area. Overnight they slapped together sheet metal, cardboard, and packing crates and called them houses. Hotels and rooming houses were booked solid, and men slept under the tables in the pool halls or curled up around bonfires at the railroad yards. Groups of shacks and tents became "rag towns." Some even rated names, such as Warmego, Weber City, Wilsonville, Snomac, and there were many others.

There was also Cromwell—called the "meanest town in Oklahoma." Cromwell was founded in 1924. That same year, the town's seventy-one-year-old police chief, who had been the former chief of Oklahoma City's police force, Bill Tilghman, was shot and killed by Wiley Lynn, a drunken Prohibition agent. The evening following Tilghman's murder, every single dance hall and back-alley gin mill in town was locked up in tribute to the legendary Old West law officer who had once ridden for "Hanging Judge" Parker. They all opened the next morning, but oil field history had been made—a law officer finally got a town's dives to shut down, if only for a day.

Another by-product of the Seminole oil boom was Bowlegs, a town created around 1926. Bowlegs was home to scores of dance hall girls, and a large number of bootleggers, gamblers, and automobile thieves. The more high-profile characters in Bowlegs were Wingy McDaniels, operator of a boarding-house that was a favorite location for knife fights and shootings; Spanish Blackey, a Mexican bootlegger skilled at heisting motorcars and throwing daggers with deadly accuracy; and Big Nell, an uncouth oil field gypsy considered the queen of the Bowlegs bootleggers and as good a shot and street fighter as any roughneck in town.

Seminole, one of the largest oil centers in the area, was never the same after that July afternoon in 1926 when the famed well called Fixco No.1 blew in about a mile and a half east of town. By 1929, more than ten thousand people lived there. When the boom hit Seminole, the muddy streets stayed filled with wagon teams, automobiles, trucks, and masses of people after jobs.

Those who did not take legitimate positions set up shop in Bishop's Alley, an unsavory section of town that covered about four square blocks and attracted dope peddlers, pickpockets, whores, bootleggers, and thieves. Field hands just off a twelve-hour shift came to the alley to drink and gamble their woes away. They found all the amusement, as well as trouble, they wanted at dance halls and clubs such as Mule Skinners, Mother Murphy's, Wintergarden, or the Bucket of Blood. To discourage acts of violence, one bellicose Seminole club posted a sign that put it politely: NO FIREARMS OR KNIVES ALOUD [*sic*] HERE. When the *Daily Oklahoman* dared print articles that criticized Seminole for the excesses of Bishop's Alley, the mayor and other city leaders piled all the newspapers they could gather in a prominent downtown intersection and burned them in protest. Nonetheless, undertakers were making top wages and stayed as busy as the harlots on payday.

Although smaller than Seminole and a smidgen less savage, Earlsboro, the nearest town to Bradley Floyd's place, had a mean streak of its own. Founded in the early 1890s, the town was right inside the old Oklahoma Territory, where saloons used to be legal. As a result, residents from nearby Indian Territory went to Earlsboro to buy liquor. Earlsboro became known as a "whiskey town." About twenty-five hundred people, many of them solid citizens and dues-paying Methodists, resided there when Charley Floyd first showed up looking for a job, but the population was already beginning to decline from its peak numbers during the zenith of the boom. By 1930, there were nineteen hundred residents. Still, the downtown main street was sometimes so crowded, it took a half hour to drive two or three blocks. All the streets were lined with drugstores, dry-goods stores, pool and dance halls, and rooming houses. Earlsboro also retained its hurly-burly side, and even federal grand jury investigations into the rampant bootlegging business did not crimp the illegal liquor trade.

Lee Thompson's dance hall was a big contributor to Earlsboro's villainous reputation. Thompson's was one of the town's three principal "evil haunts." It was right up there with the Forty-Niner Club, which was razed in 1929, and the Green Lantern, which was headquarters for some local thugs fondly known as the Earlsboro Mob.

In January 1932, workmen finally ripped down the clapboard walls of Lee Thompson's. Survivors of the vice-infested landmark that had sheltered dope peddlers and white slavers told D. M. Fox, a *Tulsa World* reporter sent to cover the demolition, that they recalled "memories of nights when jazz dance bands moaned out their racous [*sic*] melodies to the accompaniment of the weird throbbing of pumping oil wells."

Bradley's sons remembered just how difficult Earlsboro could be—in those days when men lugged dinner pails in one hand and kept a club at the ready in their other. "Everybody had to be tough just to make it back then," said Glendon Floyd. "You could walk down the streets of oil field towns like Earlsboro, and if you wanted a fight, then you would easily get one. They'd be lined up and ready.

"I recall my father coming home one night, and he damn near had one of his fingers sliced off. He had gotten into a fight, and the fella who jumped him pulled a knife and tried to stab him. My dad had to wrestle that knife away from the guy, and he got cut real bad. But he got the knife and then he picked up a two-by-four and he beat the hell outta that man."

Bradley was happy Choc had come to Earlsboro. He felt sure he could find some sort of job for his kid brother in the oil patch. But first things first. There was still some family to see. After a few days of feasting on Bessie's good home cooking, Choc was ready to visit the other Floyds.

"We had an ol' Model A touring car, and my parents loaded all us kids in it," recalled Bayne. "We took Choc back to Akins to see Grandma Floyd and the others. We went to the house they had then, back off in a field. There was mud hole after mud hole, and we didn't get all the way up there. We had to get out by the gate."

Mamie Floyd saw Bradley's touring car coming. She was out of the house and running toward them before the automobile doors were closed.

"I remember Grandma was so excited to see Choc," said Bayne. "It had been some time back when he had left for prison. I can still hear her words when she got down there to us. She said, 'My boy! My boy! I thought I'd never see ya again!'

"And, of course, then she grabbed him and hugged his neck and knocked off that straw hat he had, and the wind got hold of it and blew it away. We chased it down for him. Then we all went to the house and had a high time, visiting and eating."

Mamie proudly showed Charley the jewelry box he had made her in the prison workshop. The box had a place of honor in the bedroom. It was made to look like a tiny divan, with padded cushions, and there was a mirror inside the lid. His mother cherished the box. Everyone could see that it was special to her.

"Later on, Choc went on down to Grandpa Floyd's store to see him," said Bayne. "I recall Granddad was kind of cold toward him. Some other men were at the store, and one ol' boy asked Choc to come on down after supper and tell them all some stories about what it was like in the pen. My grandpa frowned at that suggestion and wasn't too sold on the idea. We all thought he'd be happy to see Choc, but he just didn't seem too thrilled."

Walter prepared no fatted calf for his prodigal son. He did not even break out any of his good whiskey. Instead, everyone settled for a potluck dinner at Mamie's table. Choc and the Earlsboro band of the Floyd family stayed on in Akins for a few days. Choc caught up on family news and visited with his sisters and brothers. He saw the new nephews and nieces who had been born while he was in Jefferson City. His little brother, E. W., and the youngest Floyd sibling, Mary, were still living at home with their parents. Both of them seemed very grown-up. Mary even had a trophy to show off, which she had won as a member of the girl's high school basketball squad at Sallisaw.

Choc did some asking about the whereabouts of Ruby and his son. He found out that her folks had moved up north to sharecrop some land near Bixby, a small community on the south bank of the Arkansas River just below Tulsa. Folks told him that since divorcing Choc earlier in the year, Ruby had taken up with another man. Perhaps she had even married this other fellow, but no one really knew.

As usual, the big topic of discussion on the front porch and down at Walter's store was politics. Choc heard all about Henry S. Johnston, yet another Oklahoma governor, who had angered the legislature and survived one impeachment attempt, only to end up getting booted out of office following a six-week trial on charges of incompetence. The truth of the matter was, Choc was told, that Johnston, a conservative Democrat, had angered his political enemies, including prohibitionists, Ku Klux Klanners, and members of the Protestant clergy who had supported him.

Besides political hearsay, there was also still some substantial talk about George and Matthew Kimes, the notorious bank-robbing brothers who had plagued Oklahoma in the 1920s. Choc was all ears.

The Kimeses were farm boys who became bootleggers and car thieves, and, just like Choc Floyd, they had become smitten with tales about the James brothers, Henry Starr, and Al Spencer. The authorities believed that it was a former associate of Spencer—a skilled bank burglar named Ray Terrill—who encouraged them to try banditry as a way of life. During the first half of the twenties, and throughout the time Choc was in prison, the Kimes brothers robbed banks and raised hell.

Included in their tally of successful robberies in Oklahoma were stickups at the towns of Depew and Beggs, and, on the afternoon of August 25, 1926, the holdup of two banks in Covington. The Kimes boys managed to elude the posse, and on August 27, they were headed for western Arkansas when they encountered a roadblock about four miles west of Sallisaw. A gun battle commenced and Sequoyah County Deputy Sheriff Perry Chuculate was shot and killed. The Kimeses took Sallisaw Police Chief J. C. Woll, and Will Ross, a civilian member of the posse, as their hostages and fled the scene. Woll and Ross were released unharmed that evening in a wooded area in the north county, and the Kimeses hightailed it to a hideout in the hills near Van Buren, Arkansas. Other law officers pursued them, and although the Kimes boys tried to escape on foot, they were both captured and returned to Sallisaw to be tried for Chuculate's murder.

Matt Kimes was convicted and sentenced to life in prison. George Kimes was also convicted and was handed a twenty-five-year sentence. Neither the prosecution nor the defense was pleased with the results, and Matt was granted a new trial, while George was transported from Sallisaw to the state pen at McAlester. On November 21, 1926, while he was waiting for the next trial to begin, Matt was freed when a band of six men, with guns blazing, overpowered a jailer and broke Matt out of the Sequoyah County jail. During the nationwide manhunt that followed, Matt Kimes, Ray Terrill, and some accomplices struck at banks in Pampa, Texas, and Sapulpa, Oklahoma, where they made off with $41,953. On May 18, 1927, the bandits robbed two banks in one afternoon—Farmer's National and the First National—in Beggs, Oklahoma. As they escaped, they also killed Chief of Police W. J. McAnally.

Always on the run, Kimes was finally captured on June 24, 1927, in Flagstaff, Arizona. He was returned to Oklahoma in manacles. Matt Kimes was convicted of murdering the two law officers, Chuculate and McAnally, and was given two life sentences. He joined his brother George behind the walls at "Big Mac."

Although Choc never ran with the Kimes boys, he was interested in hearing the stories of their exploits, particularly about the shootouts and the jailbreak in Sequoyah County. After listening to such accounts, Choc returned with Bradley and family to Earlsboro. Following his return, Choc went with Bradley to meet some of the men doing the hiring in the oil fields.

Choc was ready to do anything. The oil companies needed tool pushers, mule skinners, and others to work their rigs and wells. He hired on right away as a roustabout, and began to get used to a daily work routine. It seemed like old times—living with Bradley and having Bessie there to take care of his clothes and cook up a storm.

"Dad got him a job but, as I remember hearing about it later, Choc didn't last too long," recalled Glendon Floyd. "I think what happened is the ol' boss found out, or someone told him that Choc had been to prison, and they had to let him go. Back then they were trying to clean things up out in the oil field, and they wanted to keep convicts out. So the rule was that if you'd been to prison, and they found out about it, they fired your ass."

Glendon's mother, Bessie, also had vivid recollections of Charley trying to make a go of it and having little luck. "Choc was out there stayin' with us near Earlsboro, and he went on down and Bradley's boss gave him a job," said Bessie. "It was over soon enough and Choc came on back to the house. He said, 'Well, Bess, don't that just beat all? Here I go and get a good job and they won't let me keep it.' And then right after that he took off and he headed straight back to Kansas City. I felt bad for him. He had an awful lot laid on one soul."

The job he held briefly in Earlsboro was Choc's last attempt at honest labor. He wanted nothing more to do with farming, but he did consider doing something he had actually been taught by experts—bootlegging. If he wanted to make any real money at bootlegging, it meant he would need to establish ties in a larger base of operations. Charley knew just where to go.

Choc's second visit to the Kansas City area did not go much better than the first. He had a difficult time making the right connections. He felt a bit out of his element. On May 6, 1929, he was picked up by the police in Kansas City, Kansas, and was jailed on charges of vagrancy and suspicion of highway robbery. He was booked in as number 3999, and thrown into a jail cell. Whenever the police wanted more time to run down records and grill a suspect in the hopes that he would confess to unsolved crimes, they charged him with vagrancy. In the street parlance, such a sentence was known as a "vag." Charley made no such confessions, but the police did take a mug shot that showed Charley dressed in a dark striped suit, shirt, and tie. His hair was oily and was combed straight back. He looked agitated.

The following day, May 7, Choc was released from custody by the authorities. He immediately headed west. Only two days later, on May 9, 1929, Charley was again arrested. This time, he was all the way out in Pueblo, Colorado. He was charged with vagrancy, and was hustled right off to jail. Just exactly what he was doing out in south-central Colorado was never made clear. He always said he was innocently looking for work when the law decided to roust him once again. There were some jobs to be had in the city. Located on the Arkansas River, Pueblo had become the industrial center of the southern Colorado piedmont and was even called the Pittsburgh of the West.

It would seem more likely, however, that he was running bootleg liquor from Kansas City to the joints in Pueblo that served the drinking needs of the steel plant workers. When he was arrested, booked into the jail as number 887, Charley was not in work clothes but, instead, had on a suit and big bow tie. The Pueblo authorities came down harder on their "vags," and Charley was fined fifty dollars and was sentenced to sixty days in jail. Within two months after his release from the Jeff City pen, Charley had managed to get arrested three times in three states—Missouri, Kansas, Colorado—and also get hired and fired from a respectable oil field job.

After he served his brief hitch in the Pueblo pokey, Choc made a beeline back to Tom's Town. By late August 1929, he had rented a furnished room at 1400 Troost Avenue in Kansas City, a marginal address in a shady part of town. He was intent on continuing serious efforts to penetrate the invisible shell that protected bootleggers and others from police harassment. Without Johnny Lazia's blessing, he had little success.

On September 2, Charley was arrested by the Kansas City police. This time, he decided to use an alias and he identified himself as Joe Scott. He was detained only briefly, and then released. About two weeks later, on September 17, Choc was apprehended yet again by the Kansas City authorities. They took him and some of his friends downtown and questioned them at length concerning the recent robbery of the Sears Roebuck plant. No links could be established, and when Choc's alibi checked out, he was finally set free. That now meant he had been arrested on five separate occasions in only six months. A pattern was clearly developing.

While Charley sought to get rich through bootlegging, get-rich schemes of a different sort had captivated the interests of investors, large and small, throughout the nation. About the only group that seemed unaffected by the dizzying climb of the New York Stock Exchange that September was rural farmers, who already were in terrible shape. The distribution of wealth was appallingly uneven. In 1929, the annual per capita income of an American farmer was only $273 compared to the average for all other Americans of $750. Farmers had no spare money for their kids' shoes, let alone for speculation on the market.

As the widespread practice of buying stocks on credit or margin escalated throughout the nation, many investors found themselves greatly overextended. The Federal Reserve Board raised its rates in an effort to curb some of the stock market activity, but in no time, speculators were back stronger than before. No one paid attention to the danger signs—such as the rapid decline in construction, industrial production, and employment—as a disastrous situation continued to take shape.

Finally, on October 24, the New York Stock Exchange experienced what was undoubtedly the wildest day in its history. The market opened moderately, but the rate of sales gained speed and prices dropped faster than ever before. Some 13 million shares were sold by day's end. This day would go down in history as Black Thursday. The passage of time did not help. A sudden flood of selling created fear and panic and marked the beginning of a five-day cycle of rapid collapse.

The following Tuesday, October 29, was far blacker. It was the most catastrophic day in the 112-year history of the New York Stock Exchange. Well over 16 million shares of stock were sold at declining prices. Most closed at half the value they had showed when trading had started that morning. The Crash of 1929 ushered in a grim period of unemployment and a generation of bad times familiarly known as the Great Depression. For the farmers of Oklahoma, however, economic hard times had begun at least five to six *years* before.

Fortunes that are lost can always be regained. Any shrewd investor subscribes to this maxim. Lives, however, can never be replaced once they are lost. The disaster that traumatized the nation that October 1929 paled in comparison to the personal loss experienced by the Floyds sixteen days later when the world crashed around them.

November 14 was a freezing cold Thursday all over the state, with at least a light snow predicted before the week was out. Filling stations reported brisk sales of radiator alcohol. Home owners in the cities worried about the possibility of frozen water pipes for the first time that season. Out at the village of Akins, business was slow at Walter Floyd's store. He had sold a few items in the morning, a little bit of axle grease and a few sacks of Bull Durham. A couple of ladies came by and bought crackers, salt, and coffee. He gave some boys playing hooky a handful of horehound candy to suck on while they tracked rabbits. A fire burned brightly in the wood stove. By early afternoon, Walter was taking long tugs on his jug of whiskey.

That afternoon, Walter was not a happy man. He had lived with a burr under his saddle blanket ever since he had found out that Jim Mills, a local competitor, had taken the shingles and some lumber from the old Akins cotton gin. When the gin was torn down, Walter had been told by the owners that he could have the material for his own use. Mills had gone and beaten him to the punch. After much deliberation, Walter could not stand it any longer. He took one last swig of moonshine. Then he stalked out of his store, crossed the dirt road, and walked right into the general store the Mills family maintained.

Mills could see from the start that Walter was not paying a social call. The two men squared off. Walter accused Mills of walking away with what was not his to take. Mills thought Floyd was calling him a thief. The confrontation soon deteriorated to a shouting match and was on the verge of turning into a fistfight when Walter stormed out of the Mills store and headed back to his place. Later, Jim Mills said that Walter had not only become abusive but had pulled a knife and threatened him with it. He claimed he was fearful that Walter was going to get a gun. Walter's kinfolk and others who knew him said that Walter would not have pulled a knife and *not* used it.

What later became clear was that Jim Mills picked up his gun—a .410 shotgun cut down to a pistol—from behind the counter and followed Walter outside. Mills shot him point-blank. The slug tore through Walter's body. He got to his feet, staggered into his store, and collapsed over the counter. Then he fell to the floor. Within minutes, he was dead. The sheriff was summoned, and Jim Mills made sure to be right there. He swore up and down that he had no other choice but to use his gun.

"Grandpa was feudin' with Mills about those shingles from the gin, and Mills claimed Grandpa pulled a knife on him and said he was going to kill him," said Bayne Floyd. "Mills claimed it was pure self-defense."

Clayton Burns, the director of the Wheeler-Stephenson Funeral Home in Sallisaw, took care of Walter's body. He saw to the burial, too. He embalmed Walter, dressed him in his only church suit, and combed his dark hair. Walter had marked his fifty-first birthday only twelve days before his death. Mamie and Walter's parents, his brothers, and the Floyd children and grandchildren sat with the body and mourned Walter's passing.

Choc, having been summoned by telephone, slipped down from Kansas City to be there. The family took Walter out to the Akins cemetery. They buried him near his baby boy, Chester Lee, who had been lying under the sod for four years. Some of Walter's old hunting pals showed up. They stood behind the Floyds and chewed tobacco. They listened to the preacher and the wind rattle the branches in the oaks. Over Walter's grave, they put up a tombstone. Cut into the face of it were the words and numbers:

WALTER LEE FLOYD
Nov. 2, 1878
Nov. 14, 1929
Our Loved One

Choc stayed until the last shovelful of earth was patted on his father's grave. Walter had been a hard father to please but he had done the best he could for his kin. After a few days of mourning, Choc helped his mother pack up her belongings. She, E.W., and Mary moved into Sallisaw to live with Mamie's oldest daughter, Ruth, and her husband, Tom Wofford. Walter's beloved hounds went to good homes. Choc saw to that. He knew that every fox in Sequoyah County was breathing a sigh of relief now that Walter Floyd was gone from the woods.

Later, when Jim Mills went to trial down at the old Sequoyah County courthouse, Choc sat quietly in the courtroom. He listened intently to every word of the proceedings. Mamie took the stand and testified about seeing her husband run into his store with blood streaming from the wound. Mills came forward in his own defense and presented his side of the story. When the jury acquitted Mills and ruled he had acted in self-defense, Choc did not have much to say.

Jim Mills stayed around Akins for a short time, but then he left and never came back. The popular story was that Choc Floyd killed Mills to avenge Walter's death. One version had it that Bradley helped his brother get rid of Mills. For years to come, some folks in those parts would even point out the abandoned well where Choc supposedly put the dead body. They said the skeleton of Jim Mills was at the bottom. This was, in fact, all hearsay. Mills was not the victim of a backwoods vendetta. He showed up many years later out in California and Oregon, and he was even seen by friends of the Floyd family. And it was on the West Coast, thousands of miles from Akins, where he died of natural causes when he was an old man.

"That story about Choc killing Mills got around, but that's not what happened," said Glendon Floyd. "Now I'm not saying that Choc or my father may not have wanted to kill Mills, because I think they would have killed him if they would have had the chance. Fact, I think they even looked for him. But the point is that Mills left town, and Choc and my father never touched him. That's just one of the legends that came about, but there's not an ounce of truth to it."

Choc returned soon after his father's killing to Tom's Town. He could not stay away from the lure of the lights and good times, not to mention the promise of bootleg profits. In Kansas City, life was rosy. Pendergast and his boys were doing a pretty fair job of keeping the Depression at an arm's length—at least for a little while.

As he made the rounds of clandestine clubs and warehouses that fronted illegal liquor operations, Choc renewed relationships that had been formed in the penitentiary. He also listened to a hot new song. It first appeared in late 1929, a year already famous for a parade of hits, and it would stay on the top-ten list for several months during 1930. Called "Happy Days Are Here Again," the tune, simply put, offered hope. Those who hummed it while they rode the streetcar believed the melody was good medicine for dealing with the bad times that were yet to come.

It was a sunny tune for a nation that was doomed to spend a long, long time "caught in a Wewoka switch."

23

WHIRLWIND

O NE AFTERNOON IN THE TWILIGHT of the 1920s, just as the decade's bootleg spree was turning into a murderous hangover, Charles Arthur Floyd became known as Pretty Boy.

Beulah Baird, a dark-haired beauty not yet turned twenty, gave Charley his new handle the first time she laid eyes on him.

They met in Kansas City, in a ramshackle boardinghouse at 1410 Holmes, located in an unsavory neighborhood not far from the lively downtown district. It was at that address that Sadie Ash, a strong-jawed former Sunday school teacher, rented furnished rooms to help support the eight children she had brought to the city from a small town in rural Missouri. One of her daughters became a clerk, another girl was a waitress, and one of the Ash boys hired out as an ironworker.

Two of Sadie's other sons—William and Wallace—were swallowed up by the city's wild side. Wallace Ash had once been wrongly accused of murder during a bank robbery in Dadeville, Missouri, but managed to prove his innocence. Since coming to Kansas City, the two Ash boys had become involved with various illegal activities, including gambling and peddling narcotics. When a fellow gambler became belligerent and claimed Wallace was cheating during a high-stakes downtown poker game, young Ash reportedly stabbed his accuser several times. Ash was taken into custody, but he was soon released after paying a fine of a few hundred dollars. He walked out of the courthouse and went straight home to Mama and wife Beulah.

Sadie had come to be known as Mother Ash. She proudly earned a reputation as a naughty landlady who rented furnished rooms to ex-cons, prospective cons, and fugitives evading the law who needed a safe cooling-off place until the heat had subsided. Men in cheap suits, who carried guns and changed their names as often as most people changed their socks, showed up at Mother Ash's place to get some uninterrupted sleep, enjoy the company of a hussy, or wolf down a braunschweiger sandwich.

It was over a friendly card game at Mother Ash's where Charley Floyd encountered Beulah Baird Ash. Flush with cash from a recent run of bootleg booze, Choc was sporting a new necktie and shined shoes. His trousers were creased razor-sharp. He had just been to the barbershop, and his dark chestnut hair was slicked back with fragrant pomade. His suit coat was hung over the back of the chair and his shirt sleeves were rolled up, revealing a fresh tattoo on the inside of his left arm. It was a rose, and inside the bloom was the image of a nurse in a hat. Beulah walked in from the kitchen carrying a tray. She placed a stein of beer before Choc and sat down beside him.

"Hello, *pretty boy,*" she said, "where did you come from?"

Choc looked up from his cards and saw a slim young woman with bobbed hair and brown eyes smiling at him. He smiled right back and told her his name.

"I'm Charley Floyd."

Then he played out his hand—a royal flush. He scooped up the pot. Beulah had brought him luck.

In the years that followed, the legend of how the name Pretty Boy came to be was told more than a dozen different ways, but the Floyd family knew from Charley himself the real story.

Nonetheless, a whole mythology was spawned around his colorful moniker. Some people remembered that back in St. Louis in 1925 when the paymaster from the Kroger payroll heist had identified Charley as one of the holdup men, he had described him as "a mere boy, a *pretty* boy with apple cheeks." Others said that the alias had been acquired in St. Louis all right, but they claimed it was Detective Sergeant John Carroll, later the city's chief of detectives, who looked over the robbery suspects and spoke of Choc as being "a pretty boy."

Others believed that Choc got the name Pretty Boy from friends down in his treasured Cookson Hills. *The New York Times* speculated that "Floyd returned to Sallisaw, where hill folks were impressed by his pocket comb and careful pompadour 'slick as axle grease' and dubbed him 'Pretty Boy.'" But that was not true, either. Relatives and friends always called him Charley or Choc, and only those who did not really know him ever used the name Pretty Boy.

The most popular opinion of all was that an infamous Kansas City madam, Annie Chambers, was the first person who uttered the name Pretty Boy. Choc supposedly ambled into her palace of sin, in its heyday a twenty-four room gilded mansion with a wine parlor and brass beds. He was said to be looking for some female companionship and he met none other than Annie Chambers herself, a lusty, bawdy house madam who had catered to the wealthiest and most influential men of her time. Annie supposedly looked the handsome Choc up and down and smirked, "I want you all to myself, *pretty boy.*" It was a colorful tale but, like the other stories, it was false.

By the time Charley Floyd was trying to establish a foothold in Kansas City, Annie Chambers was pushing ninety years of age, was virtually blind, and was crippled with rheumatism. On top of her age and physical condition, Miss

Chambers had also found religion in her twilight years, and her mansion, a landmark on the city's north side, was transformed into a haven for derelicts and became known as the City Union Mission. Instead of painted ladies pouring bubbly, Salvation Army workers ladled out hot soup and Scripture.

The various myths about how Choc got his famous nickname made good copy, but it was unquestionably the beguiling Beulah who was responsible for coming up with the name. In fact, Choc did not like the name Pretty Boy very much and used it only occasionally himself. He said that it was "all a joke anyway," but nonetheless the name stuck and eventually created a colorful and flamboyant image for the young Oklahoman. It was also an image that would contribute to Choc's inevitable ruin.

Yet every time he showed up at Mother Ash's house on Holmes Street to play cards or visit with one of his friends, Choc was greeted by Beulah with that name.

Choc started spending more time at Mother Ash's, but he was careful to keep some distance between himself and her attractive daughter-in-law. She was, after all, married to Walter Ash, whose brother William was married to Beulah's sister, Rose. Besides being small-time hoodlums, the Ash brothers were generally suspected of acting as informants for the local police. Choc figured it was not worth the risk to mess with the wife of a jealous husband who might also be a stool pigeon. Walter Floyd had not raised a fool. Good old country horse sense prevailed.

At last, Choc was beginning to make a few useful contacts in Kansas City. He hooked up with Red Lovett, another ex-convict he had served time with at the Jeff City penitentiary. Lovett was a proven bank robber and, like Choc, he had also been picked up and questioned about the Sears Roebuck robbery. It was Lovett who had long before told Choc about the opportunities in Tom's Town.

"When you get out," advised Lovett, "head for K.C."

Other familiar faces in Kansas City were James Bradley and Bob Amos, former inmates Choc knew from the pen. Bradley, a career criminal who went by several bogus names including the aliases Bert Walker, Thomas Alexander, Tom Clark, Roy Brown, and Bob Randall, had been sprung from a prison farm near Jefferson City on October 2, 1929. Penitentiary officials always believed the escape had been engineered by Charley Floyd. As 1929 drew to a close, Kansas City was beginning to look like the site for a Jeff City reunion. Charley went back and forth between his bootleg suppliers in the city and the oil patch towns of Oklahoma, where there were plenty of customers ready to drink something more than hastily cooked moonshine.

James Henry Audett, better known in police circles as Blackie, met Choc about the same time as the Oklahoma bootlegger was feeling his way around and acquiring his street wisdom. Audett offered a different perspective than some about Choc's Kansas City experience.

A native of Calgary, Audett had a few years on Charley Floyd and had also started his criminal career at a much earlier age. Audett left Canada when he was a teen, saw action during the Great War, and returned to the United States to become a proficient bootlegger, smuggler, and thief. He escaped from a federal pen where he was serving time for kidnapping, reportedly operated with Jake Fleagle's bank-robbing gang in the twenties, and also shared a cell with Earl Thayer, the old bank and train robber. It was after he did a stretch in Leavenworth, where he met Oklahoma's own Frank Nash, that Blackie Audett came to Kansas City. Because of Nash's recommendation, Audett found a job with Johnny Lazia and the Pendergast machine.

In a colorful book he wrote entitled *Rap Sheet,* published in 1954, Audett talked about the old days in Kansas City when every whore and hustler in the Midwest showed up to grab their share from the trough.

"Quick as these broads would hit town, they would get shook down by crooked cops for a percentage of whatever they made," wrote Audett. "And if they didn't cooperate, they got rousted out of town."

Getting a hard time from the Kansas City police was something Choc knew about. So he became angry when some of the party girls he spoke with at the sporting houses around Thirteenth and Cherry streets were strong-armed by overly zealous policemen.

"He was quite a kid," Audett said of Choc. "Good looking, easygoing and a playboy. He liked the girls a lot. And the girls liked him. He spent his money like a drunken Indian when he had it.

"Well, some of the girls he liked pretty well there in Kansas City was squawking their heads off, around that time, about the payoff they had to make to some of the cops on the vice squad. Charlie [*sic*] Floyd told them girls to hell with it. He told them they didn't have to make no payoff and he would see to it that they didn't."

If what Blackie Audett wrote was true—and there is little reason to doubt his assessment—Charley's behavior, at least in part, accounted for his continuous difficulties with the power structure in Kansas City.

Besides the crooked police officers who were disturbed by Choc giving free financial advice to the local streetwalkers, there were others with their eye on Mr. Floyd. Thomas J. Higgins, at that time the captain of detectives in Kansas City, also became aware of Charley after some of Higgins's boys brought Choc in for questioning on a regular basis.

"I found this youthful ex-convict living among thieves," Higgins later said of Floyd, "and I tried to turn him aside from the ways of crime."

Bert Haycock, another crack Kansas City detective, also tried to follow every move Choc made within the city limits. He combed the underworld dives and pumped his best street informants for any information about Choc's activities. Haycock was stymied at every turn, but he did not give up, even when he found out that Choc had learned of the detective's interest in him.

On December 2, 1929, Haycock was sitting in his automobile on south Sixty-first Street when another vehicle drove alongside. Haycock realized he was "on the spot" and dropped to the floor just as a pair of men in the other car opened fire on him. Bullets shattered the windows and ricocheted off the interior of his auto, but the detective managed to escape unscathed. Angry police officers scoured the streets and checked out every back-alley joint and beer flat looking for the gunmen, one of whom Haycock thought he recognized as maybe being Charley Floyd. No arrests were made, and it was never proved that Choc had any involvement whatsoever with the Haycock ambush. Nevertheless, Charley won no popularity contests with either the legitimate policemen or the corrupt cops in Kansas City. He was considered a renegade, a free-lance bootlegger who ran whiskey, a hood who had more disdain for the dishonest cops, whom he ignored, than the honest ones.

With the Kansas City police turning up the heat, Choc eventually succumbed to the pleas of James Bradley and Bob Amos, his older friends from the penitentiary. They told him that the time was right for them to leave the area, at least for the time being, and try their hand at something a little more lucrative in a new locale. They had put together a list of banks back east that appeared ripe for the taking, and they wanted Choc to join them. Such an invitation appealed to his boyhood fantasies of Jesse James and Henry Starr. It was an offer Choc did not even consider refusing.

In the early weeks of 1930, Choc Floyd and his friends were "on the scout." The Kansas City entourage roamed eastward through several midwestern states and finally set up a base of operations in a rented bungalow in Akron, Ohio, an industrial city on the Cuyahoga River in the northeastern portion of the state. Their new hideout was located in, what was at that time, an isolated part of the city at 731 Lodi Street. Windows at each corner gave the occupants unobstructed views. The frame residence was painted yellow and the occupants dubbed it their "canary cottage."

Choc, James Bradley, and Bob Amos formed a partnership with some other known criminals, including Jack Atkins, a tough guy from Toledo. A Kansas City shoplifter in her mid-forties who went by several names, including Nellie Maxwell, Nellie Denny, and Marie Maxwell, came along for the ride to Ohio. She agreed to keep house and cook for the bandits while they worked their way down the banks on their hit list.

At the very top of the list was the Farmers & Merchants Bank in Sylvania, Ohio. Located in northwest Lucas County, Sylvania adjoined the larger city of Toledo, the county seat situated at the place where the Maumee River flows into Lake Erie.

Shortly before noon on Wednesday, February 5, 1930—the day after Charley Floyd's twenty-sixth birthday—a Studebaker sedan with Michigan license plates cruised into Sylvania and pulled up in front of the Farmers & Merchants Bank at the corner of Monroe and Main. Inside the automobile were Choc and four companions. All five bandits were well dressed and none of them wore masks. The driver remained behind the wheel of the Studebaker, and the others piled out and rushed through the front entrance. Two of them stood just inside the door, Choc ran toward the rear of the bank, and the last robber threatened employees behind a caged railing and shouted, "Stick 'em up! We're not fooling!"

All of the men were armed with revolvers. At least two of them carried a pistol in each hand. Choc's primary weapon of choice was a six-shot double-action Smith & Wesson .32 caliber, a model with a swing-out cylinder. Some witnesses later said he was one of the bandits packing two weapons.

At the back of the bank near the safety-deposit boxes and the vault, Choc confronted cashier John C. Iffland. When the bandits first entered the bank, Iffland saw them and reacted. He instinctively shoved the huge vault door closed and twisted a dial that activated a time lock. That meant the vault, which held tens of thousands of dollars, could not be opened until 5:00 P.M. that evening. Choc was furious.

Many years after the robbery, Martha Iffland, ninety-five years old and the widow of the brave bank cashier, could still recount her late husband's memories. Of course, at the time of the robbery, no one knew who Charley Floyd was. The name Pretty Boy was wholly unknown outside the Sadie Ash boardinghouse in Kansas City. Only later, when his legend spread, would he be identified and linked to the Sylvania bank job.

"Pretty Boy Floyd didn't like the idea that my husband locked the safe on him," recalled Martha Iffland. "He held a gun to John's head."

When Choc ordered the cashier to open the vault, Iffland told him that was impossible because of the time lock. It would have to remain locked for almost five more hours.

"Floyd said, 'I'll give you two minutes to open the safe,' " Martha Iffland recounted.

Iffland responded with the same answer as before. Then Choc lost his temper. According to Mrs. Iffland, Choc swung his pistol and struck her husband on the head with the barrel. Iffland fell to the floor, and Choc gave him a kick and ordered him not to move. (Eyewitness testimony provided shortly after the incident contradicted Mrs. Iffland's belief that Choc was the bandit who had manhandled her husband.)

Meanwhile, another of the bandits had made his way around the back of the cages and forced assistant cashier E. G. Jacobs, tellers Glenn M. Chandler and Lynn Bischoff, and bookkeeper Jeannette Shull to stand along a wall with their arms in the air. Chandler was marched at gunpoint back to the vault area, and was ordered to open the locked door. Like Iffland, who remained lying on the floor, Chandler said there was no possible way he could comply because of the timing device. Charles Pittman, an employee from the Lucas County auditor's office, was in a nearby room checking records and witnessed the robbers threatening Iffland and Chandler.

As the action unfolded behind the cages, the other bandits aimed their revolvers at two customers, Chris Rumpf, Jr., a resident of nearby Adrian, Michigan, and his eighty-two-year-old father, Chris Rumpf, Sr. Both of them were seated in the lobby when the robbery started. The younger Rumpf broke into uncontrollable nervous laughter at the sight of the armed bandits sweeping through the bank.

"Stop that laughing or I'll put a slug in you," one of the gunmen commanded. Rumpf did as he was told.

However, the holdup men made a costly mistake when they lined four of the bank employees against the Monroe Street side of the bank. There were large plate-glass windows, and the foursome with their arms stretched toward the ceiling were in plain sight. Directly across the street, George Carter, Jr., a worker at Howard's filling station, noticed the employees with their hands up. He summoned Ed Howard, the station owner, who also happened to be a vice president of the bank. Howard dashed to the wall telephone and turned in a fire alarm. Bernice Simmons, a Sylvania exchange operator who took Howard's call, set off a shrill fire siren that aroused the entire community. With her fellow operators, she notified the sheriff's office and the Toledo police.

The earsplitting scream of the electric siren mounted on the Council Building across Main Street from the bank caused the bandits to abort their plans.

"Let's get out of here!" Choc Floyd was reported to have yelled to the others.

The four of them raced to the door, pausing only long enough to scoop up some cash from two of the tellers' cages on the way out.

"Floyd backed out to the street with both guns pointed into the bank," recalled Martha Iffland.

By the time the robbers ran toward the black Studebaker, Ed Howard had retrieved and loaded his shotgun. He cut loose with a charge. The blast missed the getaway vehicle and struck the left-front door of a parked automobile. Carter, the filling station employee, ran into the street to jot down the license number of the robbers' car, but he beat a hasty retreat when one of the outlaws threatened to shoot him. Within seconds, all the bandits were in their getaway vehicle, and it roared away down Monroe Street, picking up speed as it headed toward Toledo.

Almost immediately, large numbers of Sylvania residents came running from all directions and flocked to the bank. Ralph Van Glahn, the Sylvania fire chief, drove out of a nearby garage in a bright red fire truck with the siren blowing. Harry Ries, the assistant fire chief, left his job at the Cooper Tire Company to be at the scene. Ries grabbed the shotgun from Ed Howard's hands and leaped onto the fire truck, and away went two of Sylvania's finest in hot pursuit.

The high-speed chase led them down Monroe Street to Dynamite Road, then zigzagged to Central Avenue, and back to Monroe again. Along the way, Van Glahn and Ries somehow managed to jettison five hundred feet of fire hose in order to lighten the load and increase the truck's speed. Despite the firemen's best efforts, the Studebaker outmaneuvered the truck, and the bandits disappeared in heavy traffic in the Auburndale district. However, the pursuers did manage to get the number of the Michigan license plate on the culprits' car and turn it over to the authorities.

As an all-points police bulletin was issued for the Studebaker and its occupants, employees at the Farmers & Merchants Bank sat around the sealed vault. They congratulated each other for surviving the first holdup in the bank's history, and they chatted about Iffland's heroics until 5:00 P.M., when the time lock was released and they could make an accurate check on the amount of money taken in the robbery. They discovered that something under two thousand dollars had been removed from the cashiers' cages—a lot less than had the vault not been locked.

To the robbers, the loot collected at Sylvania was hardly worth the risk when it was divided. The five outlaws stayed out of sight in their canary cottage in Akron. They played cards, ate their female companion's greasy meals, and plotted bigger, and hopefully more lucrative, bank jobs.

Those plans were interrupted on Saturday, March 8, 1930. The previous day, Charley had toasted his first-year anniversary as a free man. Late that evening, a bunch of the canary cottage crowd visited an after-hours joint operated by Bill and Bertha Gannon at 111 Kenmore Boulevard in Akron. The desperadoes had no way of knowing it at the time, but the local authorities had just learned that some of the gunmen from the Sylvania bank robbery had not left the area.

"We got a tip that they were in town," said retired Akron police detective J. Sherman Gandee in 1974 when he was eighty-one years old.

The police were alerted by Bill Denton, pastor of the Furnace Street Mission, in Akron's Little Italy section. During these years, as many as thirty-five bootleggers operated in a two-and-a-half-block stretch of Furnace Street near the mission. Denton told Earl Wilson, later a famous national columnist, then a reporter for the *Akron Beacon Journal,* about the tip that the preacher had received from a man who was a regular at the mission. The informant did not provide the bandits' precise location and Denton would never reveal the exact name of the man who supplied him with the information.

That night, the police got lucky when they conducted a vice raid and found some of the gents from the Sylvania robbery imbibing at the Gannon residence. In the raiding party led by Sergeant Kovach of the vice squad were

Patrolmen Herbert Michaels, Arthur Possehl, both in plainclothes, and Harland F. Manes, dressed in his uniform.

According to Akron police files, two men who were later identified as Bert Walker and Bob Amos, along with Marie Maxwell and Bertha Gannon, left the residence about 1:30 A.M. on March 8 and attempted to drive away. The foursome had been celebrating Mrs. Gannon's birthday and were obviously well lubricated. They attracted the attention of the officers gathered nearby, who were about to raid the place.

"They didn't get very far," said Kovach shortly after the incident. "At the intersection of Old Kenmore Boulevard and New Kenmore Boulevard, they rammed into a westbound auto. Did a good job of it, too. We ran over and I grabbed the man sitting next to the driver and took him to the police car. Manes got the driver. The women crawled out unhurt."

Suddenly, the man who Manes was trying to arrest plunged his hand inside his coat pocket, shoved the policeman away, and opened fire with a pistol. Shot point-blank in the stomach, Manes fell to the ground. Other officers opened fire and apparently struck the suspect in one of his arms, but he managed to escape in the darkness. Manes was rushed to Peoples Hospital for emergency treatment.

Akron's Chief of Detectives Edward J. McDonnell was awakened at 2:00 A.M. by a telephone call from Kovach informing him that a police officer had been badly wounded and the assailant was still on the loose. McDonnell alerted his best men, including Gandee, to go to the scene of the crime. Then McDonnell dressed and drove to the hospital.

"I never had a chance," Manes whispered to McDonnell from his hospital bed. "He pulled the gun before I could do a thing." Manes said he would recognize the gunman if he saw him again.

Gandee prowled around the premises on Kenmore Boulevard and was present when Patrolman Patrick Conley found a revolver stashed in an ash barrel behind the house. Six shots had recently been fired and the caliber matched the gun used to shoot Manes. The Gannons and some of the girls who worked for them were questioned at length, but they were of little help. Officers noticed red clay on the soles of Bertha Gannon's shoes, however. They knew there was an area of town banked with red clay because of a new real estate development. Then police officers further searched the residence and found a telephone number scribbled on the wall in the sitting room. They checked it out and found it was in the area where the red clay was located. These clues led them straight to the canary cottage at 731 Lodi Street.

About 5:45 P.M., a small band of Akron policemen, armed to their teeth, gathered fourteen hours after the shooting near the suspected bandit hideout. Chief of Detectives McDonnell, along with Gandee, led a whole cadre of officers in what was described by the *Cleveland Plain Dealer* as "one of the roughest captures in the history of the police department."

The lawmen slowly crept up on the bungalow with their guns at the ready. Lights were burning inside and they could see movement behind the drawn shades.

"The front door was unlocked," said Gandee. "We stationed some men behind the house and went in. There was a machine gun lying on a couch in the living room. We cleaned fourteen guns out of that place before we were through."

McDonnell and some of his men broke through the door of an upstairs room and found a woman bathing the fresh gunshot wound of Bradley, alias Bert Walker. Covering Walker and the woman, McDonnell ordered one of the detectives to look under the bed, where there had been some commotion. When the officer got down on his knees and took a peek, he saw the form of a man. It was Choc Floyd.

"If he doesn't come out when I count two, blow his damn head off," shouted McDonnell.

Detective Bruce Ward, who had been a close friend of the wounded patrolman, did not wait for the chief to start counting. Ignoring the barrel of the riot gun another officer had trained on the bed, Ward dove underneath and grabbed Choc's leg. He hauled Choc out and administered "one of the most severe cuffings in Akron police annals," according to the *Cleveland Plain Dealer*.

Besides seizing the arsenal of weapons that included a submachine gun, two sawed-off shotguns, a high-powered rifle, five pistols, and some nitroglycerin, the detectives arrested Choc Floyd, Jim Bradley (aka Bert Walker), and the Maxwell woman, who was described by the suspects as their housekeeper. Bob Amos was still in custody.

Choc took the beating he received in the upstairs bedroom without so much as a whimper. He and Bradley were taken in squad cars to Peoples Hospital, and one at a time they were brought before Manes, who had suffered a relapse and was growing weaker by the moment. Choc was brought in first. Manes stared at him for a long time, but finally shook his head and said that he was not the man who had shot him. Manes immediately recognized the wounded Bradley, however, and the officers knew they had their man.

Later under intense grilling, Choc was described as cheerful, but he would still admit nothing to the detectives, including his true name. He told the cops he was from New York and had just arrived in town the night before. Officers noted that on the suspect's inside left forearm was the tattoo of a "Red Cross nurse in rose." They booked him as Frank Mitchell, alias "Pretty Boy" Smith, number 19983, at police headquarters in downtown Akron. Bob Amos, using his Johnny King alias, was also booked. He and Charley were held under $25,000 bond as material witnesses.

On Sunday, Officer Manes rallied for a time but then began to decline. An appeal went out for blood, and within ten minutes, twenty policemen were at the hospital with their sleeves rolled up. It was too late. Manes died at 10:05 A.M.

Jim Bradley was arraigned the following day. He was presented as Bert Walker to the grand jury in Akron. He was eventually charged with first-degree murder in the shooting death of Harland Manes. The suspects were kept under heavy guard at the jail in Akron to prevent any of their accomplices from trying to free them.

Manes was buried on March 13. He was a six-year veteran of the police force, and had a wife but no children. Manes was remembered as a quiet man with a proud war record, having served in most of the major battles in France. Hundreds of police officers and American Legionnaires turned out to escort the coffin. Thousands of citizens lined the streets of Akron in tribute to the fallen officer as his funeral procession moved solemnly through the heart of the city, passing the county jail beneath the window where his slayer was housed. Harland Manes was buried at Rose Hill Cemetery with full military rites.

For a few days following the raid on the Akron hideout, police authorities in Ohio considered Choc and the others as prime suspects in the shooting death of William J. Malone, a watchman for the Standard Oil Company. However, subsequent tests conducted by ballistics experts from Akron and Toledo failed to match the bullet found in the slain watchman with bullets recovered from weapons seized in the Lodi Street raid.

During the continuing investigation, more problems surfaced for Choc and his friends. Toledo detectives John Hovey and Frank DeLora went to Akron and found that one of the three sets of extra license plates uncovered in the suspects' car matched the number of the Michigan plate on the Studebaker used in the Sylvania bank robbery the month before. Charles Pittman, of the county auditor's office, and Lynn Bischoff and John Iffland, two of the employees at the Farmers & Merchants Bank, were also brought to Akron. The trio of witnesses singled out the suspects during a lineup under the spotlights at the city jail.

Contrary to the version given later by Iffland's widow, Pittman told detectives that it was the man called Walker, and not Choc (known then by the alias Frankie Mitchell), who had slugged Iffland when the vault could not be opened. Choc Floyd apparently was not guilty of striking the cashier with a pistol and kicking him while he was down.

After their two-month stint in the Akron jail, Choc and Amos were transferred to Toledo. On May 20, 1930, they were both officially charged with the February 5 bank robbery at Sylvania. Choc's new home for the next six months would remain the Toledo jail, where the bulls knew him as number 21458.

The prosecution had a strong armed-robbery case against Choc. He had little doubt that he was headed back to the penitentiary, and the idea sickened him. The Ohio State Penitentiary at Columbus was as tough and overcrowded as the pen in Jefferson City, Missouri. On April 21, 1930—a month before

Choc was transferred from Akron to Toledo—one of the worst fires in the nation's history swept through Ohio's penitentiary. More than 320 inmates burned to death out of a population of 4,300 housed in a prison designed to hold only 1,500. Choc would spend much of his time in Toledo contemplating his upcoming trial and punishment.

Throughout this early period of the 1930s, crime proliferated greatly. Hard times spelled doom and gloom for farmers and factory workers, but not for those versed in the ways of crime. None of these outlaws would be caught dead peddling apples on a street corner—not when there were still banks in operation.

As wanton crime spread, so did the fame of many Depression-era criminals. They became as well known, although far less venerated, as major league baseball stars, and became household names as familiar as Babe Ruth, Jimmy Foxx, or Dizzy Dean.

Floyd was hardly the only bandit on the verge of "stardom."

John Herbert Dillinger was also poised on the edge of criminal prominence. Born June 22, 1903, in a middle-class residential neighborhood of Indianapolis, he was the son of a hardworking grocer. Dillinger's mother died when he was three. He grew to resent his stepmother, and as a juvenile he got into frequent scrapes for carousing and stealing coal. Dillinger quit school at the age of sixteen, and worked in a machine shop until boredom set in. When his father moved the family to a farm near Mooresville, Indiana, Dillinger quickly tired of rural life, just as Choc Floyd had in Oklahoma.

Shortly after his twentieth birthday, Dillinger got into trouble with the law when he stole an automobile from a church parking lot. Later that year, he joined the navy but immediately regretted the move. The young seaman, assigned to the U.S.S. *Utah* (a battleship that would be destroyed in 1941 at Pearl Harbor), finally jumped ship for good when it docked in Boston. He returned to Indiana, married a sixteen-year-old girl, and began hanging out with Ed Singleton, a pool shark and ex-con who was ten years older than Dillinger.

On the evening of September 6, 1924, approximately a year before Choc Floyd committed his first armed robbery, Dillinger and Singleton got liquored up and robbed sixty-five-year-old Frank Morgan as he walked home with his weekly grocery-store receipts. Dillinger, who had known the old man since childhood, slugged Morgan on the head with a large bolt wrapped in a handkerchief. Morgan fought off his attackers and Dillinger and his accomplice fled empty-handed.

Dillinger was later arrested at the family farm. Singleton pleaded not guilty and was sentenced to two years. Dillinger took his father's advice and confessed to the crime. He was convicted of assault and battery with the intent to rob, and conspiracy to commit a felony, and received joint sentences of two to fourteen years and ten to twenty years in prison. Later that year, Dillinger entered the Pendleton Reformatory. He was stunned by the severity of his sentence and the leniency shown his older partner in crime. As Ruby Floyd would also do, Dillinger's young wife divorced him. When his first attempt at parole was denied, Dillinger became increasingly bitter and hardened.

In the summer of 1929, Dillinger requested and was granted a transfer to the state prison at Michigan City, Indiana. He told authorities he wanted to move to this prison in order to play on the convict baseball team. In reality, the relocation enabled Dillinger to be reunited with Harry Pierpont and Homer Van Meter, incorrigibles he had first met at the reformatory. They introduced Dillinger to convicted bank robber John Hamilton and other seasoned bandits.

While Choc Floyd was awaiting trial in Toledo, Dillinger was being schooled in the art of bank robbery in the Indiana pen. It would be his home until May 10, 1933, when Dillinger would finally gain parole and launch his period of infamy as public enemy number one.

At this time, Lester M. Gillis was also starting his climb toward the limelight. Born in Chicago on December 6, 1908, to immigrant parents from Belgium, Gillis grew up scared but mean around the stockyard district. The slum neighborhood was ruled by a pack of young toughs called the Five Points Gang. His diminutive size—slightly more than five foot four inches tall and only 135 pounds as an adult—was a constant irritation to the cocky street fighter.

In order to survive and compensate for his physical limitations, Gillis became adept with a switchblade and developed a reputation as a bantam rooster who was not afraid to inflict pain. One criminal historian described Gillis as "something out of a bad dream."

In and out of reform school as a youngster, Gillis graduated from stealing cars and muscling whores and bookies to become an enforcer for the racketeers. Some law-enforcement officials even believed that in the late 1920s Gillis went to work for Al Capone's organization but was given the heave-ho when they found him to be unreliable. Instead of intimidating his shake-down targets and, at the most, giving them a good beating, it was rumored Gillis simply shot them to death. A few of his acquaintances from those times even felt Gillis enjoyed killing people.

In 1930, Gillis was roaming the streets, a year away from being convicted in a jewelry-store robbery that would result in a term at the state prison at Joliet, Illinois. By then, he was known by an array of aliases, such as "Big George" Nelson, Alex Gillis, Lester Giles, and Jimmy Williams. However, the name he cared for the least—"Baby Face" Nelson—was beginning to stick. And, during the next few years after Baby Face escaped from prison and went on a bank-robbing spree, it was a name that would go down in criminal history.

Baby Face Nelson, product of the urban slums, had little in common with

Choc Floyd, who had grown up in the country. In the 1930s, though, other farmers' sons, like Floyd and Dillinger, took to the outlaw trail.

One of the most ruthless of these was Clyde Barrow. Born at Teleco, Texas, on March 24, 1909, Barrow was one of eight children from a poor sharecropper family, a family that made the stable Floyds look prosperous by comparison. Some of the folks who knew Barrow recalled that even as a boy he had a sadistic streak. They said he was always into mischief but that he also found pleasure in torturing songbirds and barnyard critters. He dropped out of school after the sixth grade, and along with older brother Melvin Ivan Barrow, fondly known as Buck, eventually became a poultry and car thief and small-time robber.

Tired of rolling drunks, the Barrow boys were responsible for a string of robberies in the late twenties in the West Dallas area, where their tenant farmer father had moved to run a filling station. After a running shootout with police near Denton, Texas, with Clyde at the wheel of their getaway car, a wounded Buck Barrow was taken into custody, tried, and convicted of armed robbery. He was sent off to the Eastham prison farm.

Clyde continued to operate on his own. In January 1930, at the time Choc Floyd and his friends were sizing up their list of banks in Ohio, Barrow met a nineteen-year-old Dallas cafe waitress who would become his accomplice for the balance of his short and angry life.

Her name was Bonnie Parker.

A bricklayer's daughter, Parker was born in Rowena, Texas, on October 1, 1910. When Clyde met the petite Bonnie, she was already married to Roy Thornton, who was serving a ninety-nine-year sentence in the Texas pen. Bonnie was pining away for her convict husband. Most of the entries in her diary from that period are riddled with lines such as "Blue as hell tonight"; or "Have been crying. I wish I could see Roy"; or "Drowning my sorrows in bottled hell."

Clyde was not the kind of man to be put off by the heart and her hubby's name tattooed on Bonnie's thigh. He soon won her over with his array of guns and the promise of relief from a humdrum life that, in Bonnie's own words, left her "bored crapless." At only five foot seven inches tall and 130 pounds, Barrow was no matinee idol. He reeked of cheap thrills and danger, however, and to Bonnie, that was a vast improvement over slinging hash for slim tips in a hamburger joint.

Shortly after they met, Barrow was picked up in connection with the robbery in Denton, but there was insufficient evidence to hold him. Authorities in Waco, however, had an interest in Barrow. He was transported there, and on March 2, 1930, he was charged with several burglaries and car thefts. On March 11, Barrow and two other prisoners escaped from the jail in Waco, using a pistol Bonnie had smuggled inside during one of her visits. Clyde's freedom did not last long. On March 18, he and his friends were recaptured halfway between Cincinnati and Dayton in southwest Ohio, the state that was currently hosting Choc Floyd and his cohorts.

Barrow was returned to Waco, and on April 21, 1930—the day of the deadly Ohio prison fire—he was sent to the penitentiary at Huntsville to begin serving a fourteen-year sentence. He would remain there for only a short time. By February 1932, Barrow would be paroled, back in circulation, and reunited with his girlfriend. The couple would terrorize several states for two years and become known simply as Bonnie and Clyde.

Just as Choc Floyd created his own identity and helped shape an image that would haunt him for the rest of his life, likewise John Dillinger, Baby Face Nelson, and Bonnie and Clyde went through their own metamorphoses. They were wrapped in cocoons of their own making. Before they fell victim to their own devices, however, they would savor the fleeting limelight and honestly believe their own publicity.

Another young man who knew the full value of publicity was J. Edgar Hoover. In Washington, D.C., Hoover spoke of a "criminal army" on the march and suggested that crime was "sapping the spiritual and moral strength of America." Coveys of marauders swarmed throughout the nation. Not all were kindred spirits with the social bandits of the past. Many were driven by pure greed and blood lust. Some, like Baby Face Nelson and Clyde Barrow, were cold-blooded killers. They toted Thompson submachine guns and automatic pistols, and preyed on rural banks, post offices, and businesses struggling to survive.

By mid-decade, there would be so many people operating on the other side of the law that the Justice Department would say that for every doctor there were twenty criminals. By then, however, the cometic rise of this tribe of devils would sputter and die. Dillinger, Nelson, Barrow, and Parker would all be snuffed out.

So would the Oklahoma bandit that Beulah Baird Ash had named Pretty Boy.

24

DOG DAYS

LTHOUGH IT HAD BEEN QUICKLY established by the fatally wounded Akron police officer, Harland Manes, before he expired that Floyd was not the man who had shot him, there was always the erroneous belief that Choc was an accomplice. This myth was perpetuated by newspaper and magazine reports as well as by several historical crime books that directly tied Choc to Manes's death. A few even portrayed Choc as the actual triggerman.

The Akron police knew better. They were satisfied that at the precise time Manes was being gunned down, Floyd was with Bill Gannon, owner of the after-hours joint on Kenmore Boulevard. The two men had left Gannon's residence and were down at the jail house trying to bail out a man and woman Choc knew, friends who had been arrested at Gannon's earlier that evening. Choc, however, had been positively identified as one of the robbers at the Sylvania bank robbery and he was not happy about being back in jail.

While Choc waited for his trial to begin on the bank-robbery charge, the true killer of Harland Manes was slowly making his way through the judicial system in Akron. James Bradley spent the rest of his days known by his favorite handle, Bert Walker, and it was this identity that was used during court proceedings. As Walker, he pleaded not guilty to the charge of first-degree murder, and with court-appointed counsel, he went to trial in May.

Walker was a forty-two-year-old native of Cairo, Illinois, and had a long and varied criminal record, dating back to grand larceny charges in Oklahoma in 1917. After years in and out of state pens, Walker had first met Choc Floyd in the mid-1920s when they were both doing time at Jeff City. Floyd apparently later helped Walker with his escape from a prison farm on October 2, 1929. All that was in the past, however. There was no way Choc could come to his friend's rescue this time.

Walker's trial for the murder of Manes lasted only five days. Defense attorney Robert Azar did his best, but George Hargreaves, the prosecutor, had a solid case, including trump cards such as expert ballistics testimony that pointed straight at the defendant and his .38 pistol. Walker took the stand in his own defense, but his alibi was weak and unconvincing. On May 17, the jury retired to deliberate his fate. Seven ballots were taken. At no time, however, did the question of innocence or guilt enter into the discussions. It was only the defense's recommendation of mercy that kept the jurors in debate for three hours. The last ballot, however, was unanimous. They would show no mercy. Walker was found guilty of first-degree murder and his punishment would be death.

On May 21, Common Pleas Judge E. D. Fritch sentenced Walker in open court to death by electrocution. Material witness Nellie Maxwell, the forty-four-year-old hellcat, whom Akron authorities now knew had previously served time in five institutions and was one of the most notorious shoplifters in the Southwest, was released. She was paid one dollar a day for every day she had been held, and went on to serve more prison time in Texas for grand larceny.

Further defense motions for Walker were filed and overruled. Finally, a stay of execution was exhausted in October when the court of appeals reviewed the case and refused to grant a new trial. By that time, Walker was on death row at the state prison at Columbus and was prepared to die.

On the evening of November 10, 1930, Walker ate a hearty meal in his death-row cell. Reverend Bill Denton from Akron's Furnace Street Mission came to the prison to tend to the condemned man's spiritual needs. Walker's defense lawyers also showed up to witness their client's death.

Walker first had to endure some added torture. Just minutes before his scheduled execution, he listened to the drone of dynamos send the death current through his cell mate, Charles Cramer, a twenty-six-year-old who had also been convicted of first-degree murder. Then Walker talked to Denton and some of the guards. He finally admitted that Walker was not his real name, but he chose to use it in death to spare his family any further embarrassment. He also maintained that he had not killed Harland Manes, but he did not appear overly upset and seemed to accept his fate. When the guards came to his holding cell, Walker looked up and said, "Oh, here they come."

Preacher Denton accompanied Walker down the dimly lit corridor to the death chamber. "He walked to the chair as tough as could be," Denton later said. Walker even cracked a joke.

"I'm due for a shocking this evening," he told Denton and the guards.

At 7:45 P.M., Walker was strapped into the electric chair. A rubber mask was slipped down over his head and face. The signal was given to throw the switch and a lethal wave of electricity poured into his stiffened body. At 7:48 P.M. Walker, now forty-three years old, was pronounced dead.

Denton took the dead man's body back to Akron for burial. A small group, including Walker's lawyers and some other men from the Furnace Street Mission, gathered at the Prentice Funeral Home and followed the funeral car to the graveyard. In keeping with Walker's wishes, there was no formal service. Walker practiced no religion in life and wanted no part of religion in death.

Later Denton admitted that before he died, Walker had given him a message to pass on to Choc Floyd. Denton would never reveal the message, nor would he say whether he had delivered it to Floyd in his jail cell in Toledo. Back in Akron, however, Ed McDonnell, the chief of detectives who had arrested Walker and the others at the canary cottage, was not bashful about discussing some advice Walker had given him.

"He said to me one day while I was talking to him in the county jail, 'You think I'm tough, but you haven't heard the last of that Mitchell boy yet.' "

On May 29, 1930, just nine days after Choc had been taken from Akron to Toledo, J. Edgar Hoover, director of the Bureau of Investigation, sent the Toledo police chief a complete abstract of the criminal record on file of Charles Arthur Floyd. It spelled out Choc's much-checkered resume, including all the arrests in Kansas City. Prosecutors knew they were not dealing with a complete novice.

Like the district attorney in St. Louis in 1925, the prosecution team in Toledo had such an airtight case against Choc in the Sylvania bank job that he decided to plead guilty. That did not mean Choc had any notion of going back to the penitentiary without any resistance.

"I never will be taken alive if I can help it," Choc told fellow prisoners at Toledo. "I'd rather be killed than serve a year in prison."

On November 24, 1930, the day on which he was to be brought before a judge for sentencing, Choc managed to slip away from the barbershop inside the county jail and join some visitors who were exiting the building. He made his way to the front steps. He had almost reached the street when he was nabbed by an officer who recognized him and, by chance, happened to be going to the jail on business. Foiled in his try for freedom, Choc was brought before the judge. He entered his guilty plea, and was sentenced to twelve to fifteen years in the penitentiary. The promise Choc had made to himself when he was released from Jeff City about never going back to a state prison could no longer be kept.

Finally, the date arrived when Choc was to be taken to the Big House at Columbus. It was December 10, 1930, exactly one month to the day since Walker's execution. Deputy Sheriffs Joe Packo and Joe Danielak rode with Choc, who was handcuffed to another prisoner, from the county jail to the station, where they all boarded a train. Unlike his train ride to the pen at Jeff City, Choc had no candy bars to hand out. He knew all too well what life was like behind the walls of a state prison.

It was a Wednesday, with only about a dozen shopping days left until Christmas. Given the state of the economy, however, Christmas gifts were few and far between that December. In the Bronx that day, it would take twelve mounted police officers to drive a milling throng of angry depositors away from a branch of the Bank of the United States at Freeman Street and Southern Boulevard. The crowd formed and refused to leave the bank when word got out that only a few hundred in line inside the bank would be paid. Finally, order was restored when an official appeared and promised that the bank would remain open until all persons in line received their money. Funds were rushed from another bank to take care of the payments and customer demands.

Choc did not speak much to the other prisoner or the guards. As he sat in handcuffs, he looked out the window at the Ohio countryside after the New York Central train departed Toledo. He must have been thinking about Eddie Adams, the Kansas bandit who had worked for old man Callahan in Wichita. Choc knew the story all too well of how Adams had escaped going to prison by leaping from a moving train. When the journey was a little more than halfway over, Choc decided to make his move.

The train was near the town of Kenton on the Scioto River. Two deputies were either dozing or had forgotten about the convicted men. Handcuffed to the other prisoner, Choc rolled over him until the chains twisted and finally broke. Then Choc bolted from his seat and kicked out a window in the bathroom. In an instant, he plunged through the opening and, quicker than an Oklahoma jackrabbit, he was gone. The other prisoner attempted to follow, but the guards came to their senses. They grabbed him and pulled him back inside the train car before he, too, could make his escape.

Choc hit the ground hard and rolled down a steep embankment covered with rocks and winter stubble. He came to rest in a thicket of tall dried grass. Down the track, he heard the train screeching to a halt. Then he heard men shouting. He knew the search was on. Scratched and bruised, Choc felt his heart beating at a rapid pace. He fought to catch his breath. It was cold outside that December, but the temperature was the least of his worries. Less than two years later, in his exclusive interview with Oklahoma reporter Vivian Brown, he gave his only public statements about the escape.

"Instead of jumping up and running," said Charley, "I lay as still as I ever did in my life and tried to keep from breathing. At times they almost walked over me. I could have reached out and grabbed one of them. But luck was with me and it was a dark night. They went up the track a ways and I crawled over into a cane patch and sat there watching them."

After what seemed an eternity, Choc could no longer see nor hear the deputies and train crewmen poking through the weeds. Even after the train started up again and continued on down the tracks, Choc stayed hidden.

"After daylight, I walked to a farmer's house," Choc told Vivian Brown, "got his gun and made him drive me down the highway."

Charles Arthur Floyd would never be in custody again. For the next three years and ten months, he would remain "on the scout," as the old Oklahoma bandits always put it when describing their time on the outlaw trail. As quickly as he shed the handcuffs, Choc was raring to get back in business as soon as possible.

He made his way mostly by night, hitching rides with truckers and farmers and, once in a while, with salesmen who stopped at hamburger stands or cafes for coffee and blue plate specials. He did most of his traveling on back roads that took him through small towns in Ohio, Indiana, Illinois, and Missouri. In those places, night drivers would slow down when they motored past the town square, where the constables or deputies dozed in worn-out Fords. Inside the frame houses that dotted the terrain, residents listened to their radios that played "Embraceable You," the nation's latest number-one tune. They read, in this harshest of Christmas seasons, from their family Bibles and prayed that the Lord would stave off the bad times that had brought ruin to the fields and factories.

As much as he might have wanted to see the family around the Christmas tree in Oklahoma, Choc went straight back to Kansas City to take stock of his situation and consider his options. They were slim.

His latest partner that winter was Willis Miller. Unlike Bert Walker and some of the others Choc had run with in Toledo and Akron, Miller was slightly younger than Charley. He had spent his youth as a "bad boy" around Ironton, Ohio, just across the Ohio River from Ashland, Kentucky. Although he was young, Miller was every bit as dangerous as the more seasoned bandits.

Known as Billy the Killer, a dark nickname earned six years before he met Choc, he had killed his own brother, Joseph ("Alabama Joe") Miller, in a gun battle. The brothers had dueled over a woman in one of the joints at Hell's Half-Acre, a notorious bootlegger hideout on the Ohio and Pennsylvania border near the town of East Liverpool, Ohio.

Miller was tried in Midland, Pennsylvania, for murder, but was acquitted when he successfully pleaded self-defense. Nonetheless, Judge William A. McConnell ordered the defendant held under bond and, because of an old English law that was still in effect, put Miller in prison for more than a year in the Beaver County jail. Since then, Miller had spent his time slipping over penitentiary walls and out of handcuffs. He was wanted by authorities in several midwestern states who wanted to talk to him about some unsolved murders, robberies, and prison escapes.

There was always loose talk among both criminal and police circles that Choc and Miller had actually hooked up with one another in Toledo soon after Charley Floyd's sensational escape. Rumor was that they had bumped off a few small banks in Michigan before they had gone to Kansas City.

However, it is unlikely Choc would have immediately returned to Toledo, the city where he had been convicted of the Sylvania bank job. He undoubtedly still would have had a bad taste in his mouth for that particular city. Also, no official records indicated the two bandits worked together until early 1931 when Choc and Miller were seen in each other's company, both in

Kansas City as well as in such oil patch towns as Earlsboro, Seminole, and Shawnee. Bradley Floyd's oldest sons recalled that their Uncle Charley and his friend Bill Miller visited their home near Earlsboro that winter.

"Miller always had his pistol out and was rubbing it," said Glendon Floyd. "I remember he had his gun fixed up so it wasn't like a regular revolver that you just put the bullets in the cylinder and you could hear them rattle around. Miller had these inserts in each chamber so you couldn't hear a thing."

Both men spent a great deal of time at Mother Ash's place on Holmes Street in Kansas City. They liked the Ash residence not just because it provided cover and was the scene of some ripsnorting poker parties but because of the two young women still affiliated with the Ash brothers who resided there. Choc was still drawn to Beulah, while Miller was attracted to her sister, Rose. It quickly became obvious to others who frequented Mother Ash's that the attractive sisters were also smitten with the two flashy bandits.

Just a couple of minor details—a pair of jealous brothers—stood in the way of Charley and his friend in their pursuit of Beulah and Rose on a more permanent basis. Even after the sisters called a halt to their relationships with Walter and William and moved into their own apartment, there was still a great deal of tension. Choc realized that the sticky situation concerning the Baird sisters was fast coming to an ugly climax.

Then in March of 1931, Choc and Miller began hearing street rumors that the Ash boys had gotten themselves in deep trouble over some narcotics transactions. In order to stay out of the pokey or, worse yet, get themselves in dutch with federal agents, the Ash brothers were trying to cut deals at others' expense.

Later in the month when police began cracking down on bootleg and gambling operations, there were some folks left scratching their heads, wondering just who was providing location tips and other inside information to the law.

Near the end of that month, on March 22, police swept through several downtown Kansas City gambling halls. They arrested more than one hundred patrons and a score of game keepers. They seized dice, cards, and cash. With five halls already raided, the raiders announced they were seeking "loose ends" to complete their operation.

One of the places that was raided, located at 1117 McGee, was described by visitors as "open to all who entered, without questioning." Craps, poker, and blackjack games were the most popular. Several patrol wagons were used to transport prisoners to police headquarters. One wagon's load was so great, it broke down en route.

Choc was almost picked up that night when officers raided a speakeasy on Linwood Boulevard, but he managed, as was becoming his custom, to slip away. It was a close call, too close for a man wanted by the law in Ohio for bank robbery and escape. There had been no love lost between Choc and Miller and the Ash brothers in the first place. However, if the scuttlebutt was true about them going back to their stool-pigeon ways, then the time had come to take action.

Wallace and William Ash left their mother's residence on Holmes in their blue Chevrolet sedan about 8:00 P.M. on the evening of March 25. It was just three days after the gambling raids. They told relatives that they were going down to a spot on Eighth Street and Grand Avenue to take in the "Amos 'n' Andy" radio show. Sadie Ash did not believe this. She later told police officers that her sons had been lured away from home. Sadie explained that earlier the same evening, her sons had taken off in their Chevy after William had received a telephone call. It was a feminine voice. Sadie thought it was Rose calling her estranged husband, suggesting that a reconciliation was in the works. Three hours after the Ash boys left, one of their sisters, Freida Ash, recalled seeing their blue auto tearing back up Holmes. Both of her brothers looked grim, she recalled later, and as they passed, she yelled out to them, "You better be careful."

Babe Walker, another neighborhood resident, was also out on the street at that time. She also saw the Ash brothers as they drove up Holmes. Speeding close behind the Ash automobile was another car, as Babe later told the police, and inside this second vehicle were Charley Floyd and Bill Miller. That was the last time anyone saw either William or Wallace Ash alive.

In a ditch in the rural Rosedale area across the state border in Kansas, their bodies were found March 27. Their snitching days were over. They had been shot execution-style. Each had bullet wounds in the back of the head. The shootings were at close range, and after they were struck, the brothers pitched facedown in a ditch filled with mud and water from late-winter rains. Their blue Chevrolet was parked nearby. The car had been set on fire, and was burned beyond recognition.

Police officers immediately considered Choc Floyd and Bill Miller as the most likely suspects in these ruthless killings. There was a clear motive. Even though the accounts of Freida Ash and Babe Walker were somewhat prejudicial, their statements about seeing the two vehicles racing up Holmes the night of the twin killings provided evidence.

The style of the homicides was out of character for Choc. When it came to Billy the Killer, though, none of the investigating officers hesitated about fingering him as a murderer. Any man who could shoot down his own brother over a woman would have little trouble doing in a resentful husband with a tendency to run his mouth with the cops. It was reasonable to guess that if Miller was involved, so was Choc Floyd. If Choc and Miller were indeed the killers, as most police officials and even some of the Floyd family assumed, then these slayings on a country road marked the first time that Charley Floyd was ever placed at a murder scene.

Police made a feeble stab at finding the men, but given the dubious backgrounds of the brothers, their murders were never a top priority. Mother Ash grieved and screamed for retribution, and furnished authorities with many tips about the whereabouts of Floyd and Miller. She claimed she had received a warning to stop. The anonymous note read, "Quit stooling or we'll give you what the boys got. We're watching and we know what you're doing all the time." No charges were ever filed, however, and the murder of the Ash brothers remained an unsolved mystery.

There was little mystery, however, about who was now keeping steady company with the "bereaved" women. Rose was on the muscled arm of none other than Billy the Killer, while Beulah was with her own Pretty Boy. The amorous quartet beat a quick retreat out of Kansas City. They spent some time down in Oklahoma, in the Shawnee area, and then, in early April of 1930, they went east through Arkansas and Kentucky to pick up where they had left off in the past. Some authorities in Kentucky theorized that Floyd and Miller financed their spring trek by knocking off the Mount Zion Deposit Bank for two thousand dollars.

The honeymoon proved short and violent. Just a few weeks after the Ash brothers' bodies were found, Choc and Miller showed up back in northwestern Ohio and southern Michigan with their two lady friends. They were suspected of renting a cottage near Algonac, Michigan, on the Canadian border. A police raid yielded nothing. Officers followed a trail that led them from Toledo all the way to Hanging Rock, a small Ohio town near the Kentucky line. The nomadic bandits were believed to have robbed a bank at Whitehouse, Ohio, of sixteen hundred dollars but, once again, they vanished without a trace.

Then in mid-April, Choc Floyd, Miller, and their lady friends were spotted in Bowling Green, the seat of Wood County and the home of a state university named for the town.

The foursome were driving a sedan with Missouri license plates. They soon aroused suspicion in downtown Bowling Green, where merchants and police officers watched the strangers for a week or so. Some thought at first they might be shoplifters, while other shopkeepers expressed incredulity about all the money the two couples were spending. For a few days, the newcomers vanished; then suddenly they reappeared on Thursday afternoon, April 16, 1931. Alerted police officers figured them to be robbers casing a bank on South Main Street.

Bowling Green Police Chief Carl "Shorty" Galliher and Officer Ralph "Zibe" Castner answered the call. They cruised downtown in a squad car to check out the scene and make an assessment. Galliher had the reputation of "being afraid of nothing," according to Grant Pansel, a fellow police officer. "He was proud of the fact that no one had robbed a bank in Bowling Green," Pansel recalled.

The two officers slowly drove down Main Street and spied the two women window-shopping. In a few minutes, Beulah and Rose were joined by Choc

Floyd and Bill Miller. They were just about to enter a store and buy some dresses for their ladies.

"Miller and Floyd were all duded up because they had just come out of a barbershop," said Don Wilcox, another former city policeman. "Zibe [Castner] got out of the car on the driver's side, and was unprotected. Shorty [Galliher] got out on the passenger side and was protected by the car."

Tommy Vail, who eventually became chief of police, later reconstructed the confrontation between the bandit suspects and the two officers. Vail had been up in Toledo that morning and returned to Bowling Green on the streetcar just after the lawmen made their move on the outsiders.

"They [Miller and Floyd] cased a bank on South Main Street, and then were walking over to Clough Street when Galliher and Castner pulled up in their car to investigate," said Vail. "The 'gangsters' were accompanied by their girl friends, Rose Ash, 23, and Beulah Baird, 21, sisters from Kansas City. When the police got out of their car, that is when the shooting started. It was quite a thing."

As soon as he saw the two cops climb out of the squad car with their guns already drawn, Choc yelled, "Bill! Duck!"

Miller whipped out his .45, the "quiet" gun that did not make any rattling noise. He pointed it toward the policemen and fired. Miller managed to get off only a single round. Galliher and Floyd drew their guns and also opened fire. Two of Choc's bullets found their mark. Castner fell to the pavement, seriously wounded in the abdomen and right thigh, but he continued to fire his service revolver at the suspects. After falling to the pavement, Castner kept firing from a prone position. Bullets ricocheted off buildings and the curbs. Pedestrians ran screaming for cover. Miller was hit once in the stomach and collapsed dead on the street. During the brief gun battle, the two sisters ran screaming. A stray bullet struck Beulah in her skull and she fell, seriously wounded, not far from Miller's lifeless body. Rose ducked for cover.

When he saw the crumpled bodies of Miller and Beulah lying on the ground, Choc's survival instincts took over. He kept firing until his pistol was out of ammunition, and then he dashed down a nearby alley and sprinted to East Wooster Street, where their automobile was parked. Galliher saw Choc take off, and he decided to pursue him. The chief grabbed Rose and reportedly shoved her into the arms of a startled city councilman who was at the scene and trying to stay out of the line of fire. "Hold this girl for me," ordered Galliher. A former star tackle on the high school football team, Galliher ran as hard as he could, but Choc was too speedy. He raced like a broken field runner with the goal post in view. Galliher, panting for breath, pulled up just as Choc drove off. The policeman jotted down the license number but, like a phantom, Choc Floyd was gone.

Police officers, reporters, and curious citizens converged at the scene of the shooting. Chief Galliher was not harmed during the brief gunfight, but Castner, the wounded lawman, was rushed to a hospital and was not expected to live. Lying in a pool of blood—his dead eyes blank and vacant—Miller was covered with a sheet and taken to a local funeral parlor. A large sum of money, presumed loot from a bank robbery, was removed from Miller's pockets. The two Baird sisters were taken into custody, and Beulah received emergency treatment for her head wound. Physicians said she would recover.

Initial news reports out of Bowling Green that evening were largely unsubstantiated. They were filled with erroneous information about what exactly had transpired. An Associated Press dispatch dated April 16 identified the slain gunman as Charles or Clarence Saunders, a twenty-year-old St. Louisan. Beulah Baird was called Wonetta Ross, a twenty-year-old resident of St. Joseph, Missouri. Beulah's captured sister, Rose, was named as Ruth Saunders of Kansas City, and Choc Floyd was believed to be Ted Shea of St. Louis. Early reports also contradicted the statements later given by Bowling Green police officers. The first wire story erroneously claimed that the two policemen were in their squad car following the four suspects in their sedan.

"After traveling a block," stated the Associated Press, "the car stopped and the occupants opened fire on the police car. The policemen returned the fire, killing Saunders and wounding the Ross girl. After Castner fell, seriously wounded, the man said to be Shea jumped into the car and left the Saunders girl standing in the street. She refused to answer any questions at the county jail except give the names of her companions, officials said."

Authorities in the various Missouri cities given as hometowns for the culprits were busily trying to verify criminal records, but with few results. St. Louis police had no files on the man called Shea, and they discovered the address given for the dead suspect did not exist. E. M. Mathews, chief of police in St. Joseph, investigated the possibility that the foursome from Bowling Green might have been responsible for a series of recent robberies in his city, but Mathews did verify that no one named Wonetta Ross was known to his department.

Later that night, investigators got a break when they found the automobile in which Choc Floyd had escaped. It had been abandoned on the Chicago road near Crissey. The numbers on the Missouri license plates on the sedan were 385 884, and when this information was relayed to the State License Bureau at Kansas City, a check of records showed that the license had been issued to a Ruth Saunders. Police files in Kansas City revealed that a woman using the name Ruth Saunders was twenty-three years old and had been arrested twice in 1929 during raids on beer flats where liquor supplies were seized. Police said that there was no record of any prosecutions.

By the following day, the truth began to surface as persistent questioning of the Baird sisters grew more intense. A fresh wire service dispatch carried by newspapers across the nation told the story of the shootout and gave most of the culprits' true names.

BOWLING GREEN, O., April 17.—Willis (Billy the Killer) Miller, known to police of several Middle Western cities as a desperado, is dead, two of his girl companions are under arrest and a second gunman is hunted today in the aftermath of a fight with police.

Miller was identified by fingerprints after he lived up to his boast that he would never be captured alive and shot it out with Police Chief Carl Galliher and Patrolman Ralph Castner yesterday. His companion escaped after seriously wounding Castner.

One of the two girls, who gave her name as Beulah Baird, 20 years old, Kansas City, divorced wife of Walter Ash, slain in Kansas City a month ago, was picked up near Miller's body with a bullet in her skull. She is in serious condition.

The other girl, thought to be her sister, said she was Ruth Saunders, 23, Kansas City, but gave different names for the other and police were uncertain of their identities.

The second gunman, listed here as Clarence Saunders, Kansas City, was suspected by police of that city as being Charles Arthur Floyd, a pal of Miller wanted in connection with the slaying of Wallace and William Ash. The Ash brothers were thought to have been killed because of their rivalry with Floyd over two Baird sisters.

At the time of his death, Miller was a prime suspect in several robberies, including an Oklahoma City bank job as well as the robbery of the National Bank and Trust Company of North Kansas City that past September. He and Choc were also thought to have robbed the bank in Kentucky and at least two other banks in Ohio that spring. Police in the Kansas City area said they had also linked Miller with the murder of the Ash brothers.

Mother Ash was ecstatic when Kansas City reporters showed up at her house on Holmes Street and told her about the wild shootout in Bowling Green involving the Baird girls and the two main suspects in her sons' murder. The first question out of her mouth was, "Did they get Pretty Boy?" After she heard he was still on the loose, her smile was said to have vanished.

Some of the reporters had never heard the name Pretty Boy used before. They saw to it that the colorful moniker was used in future news stories about Charley Floyd. Several news hounds rushed to telephones and called in their scoops. The next morning, newspaper headlines throughout the nation, especially the big midwestern dailies, for the first time carried the name PRETTY BOY, in bold headline type, and until his death, this nickname contributed as much as any actual feats to Choc's notoriety.

Castner could not rally from his gunshot wound and died. He was twenty-eight years old. On April 25, as the dead officer's funeral was held, and the entire city of Bowling Green mourned his loss, Wood County Prosecutor Raymond W. Ladd prepared a charge of first-degree murder against Charles Arthur Floyd, also known as Frank Mitchell or Pretty Boy.

Local police continued to hold and question the two Baird sisters, and they were also interrogated about recent bank robberies believed to have been staged by Miller and Floyd at the small towns of Whitehouse, located northwest of Bowling Green, and at Elliston, northeast of Bowling Green. The young women were then turned over to authorities in Kentucky interested in asking them about a bank robbery at Mount Zion. Eventually, they were released when nothing could be proved against them. Beulah, or Juanita as she was also known by that time, went down to Earlsboro and stayed with Bradley and Bessie Floyd to recover from her head wound.

"We always called her Juanita," said Glendon Floyd. "She came and stayed at my folks' house after that big shootout up in Ohio. She had been shot in her head and needed to rest up. She helped my mother some around the place. Juanita was a pretty fair cook and she made Italian food. She'd take hamburger and tomatoes and onions and crackers and mix all sorts of stuff up. We thought it was pretty good, cause we never got much Italian food.

"But I do recall that the wound really messed her up for a time. Her equilibrium was all off, and she was kind of shaky. But she got better and went on back to Kansas City I reckon."

Glendon's older brother Bayne also had memories of Choc's girlfriend recuperating at their home. "We all knew that Juanita was the one who gave Choc his Pretty Boy name," said Bayne. "She was sure nice, though, and we all loved her."

In Ohio, a manhunt was under way for Choc Floyd. He was not only charged with the first-degree murder of a police officer; Wood County Sheriff Bruce C. Pratt of Bowling Green also announced that the county commissioners were offering a one-thousand-dollar reward for Floyd's apprehension. The wanted circular that was sent out contained a menacing footnote: "Extreme caution should be used when approaching Floyd as he will not hesitate to shoot."

Some officers believed he would attempt to reach the former hangout of Miller, his slain partner. Prohibition agents and policemen were on the lookout for Pretty Boy in several Ohio cities. In the smaller towns along the Ohio River, from East Liverpool all the way to Ironton, deputy sheriffs checked out numerous leads. The consensus, however, was that Floyd had already found sanctuary for several months with the Licavoli mob in Toledo. A well-known criminal clan, the Licavolis for many years were a major force in bootlegging circles and the rackets in Detroit and several Ohio cities, including Toledo, Akron, and Youngstown. The police conjectured that Pretty Boy had paid the Ohio racketeers for protection with some of the money that he and Miller had gleaned from their past bank robberies at Whitehouse and Elliston.

With the name Pretty Boy emblazoned in newspaper headlines, an intense national search was under way. Sweetened by an offer of a cash reward at a time when money was especially scarce, rumors and alleged sightings of the desperado popped up quicker than sunflowers in a manure pile. On April 18 in Toledo, it was thought Pretty Boy Floyd was the one who had held a pistol to the head of taxi driver Robert Robinson and had stolen his cash and cab. The following day, Robinson's hack was found abandoned near Monroe, Michigan, where that same afternoon another cab driver was victimized by a lone gunman identified as Floyd. The nervy bandit was seen at restaurants, movie theaters, and even church services. Witnesses swore on a stack of Bibles that it was Pretty Boy himself who had attended a marathon dance contest. He reportedly surfaced here and there throughout the Midwest. All of a sudden, Pretty Boy was everywhere at the same time, a media creation of these bleakest Depression years.

Charley Floyd was definitely back in familiar territory by early summer of 1931. He was seen in Oklahoma and in Kansas City, generating income from bootlegging and tending to the needs of Beulah Baird during her continued convalescence.

On the evening of July 20, Kansas City police officers and federal Prohibition agents came close to capturing Choc during a raid on a suspected north-side liquor warehouse. There were a few officers who later stated that the raid was actually a well-laid trap for Floyd, while others felt that he only happened to be there when the raiding party arrived and poured into the two-story brick building at 1039 Independence Avenue. The first level was occupied by the Lusco-Noto Flower Shop, which officers said was a front for the liquor syndicate that operated on the top floor.

Included in the team of law enforcement officers were Lieutenant E. L. Nelson, a police detective, and dry agents Glenn Havens, Joe Anderson, and Curtis Burks. Listed in the 1930 Kansas City directory as a salesman living with his wife, Gladys, on Dunham Avenue, Burks was called a government operative by some of the other officers. Once inside the building, the raiders, led by Havens, quickly made their way to the second floor and paused outside a door at the top of the stairway. They listened for a few seconds and then two agents kicked down the door and Havens yelled, "It's a raid, boys! Put 'em up!"

There were at least nine men seated around a table in the dimly lighted room. They were taken completely by surprise as the agents barged through the door with their guns drawn. Most of the men at the table raised their arms in surrender. One started to protest the intrusion, but he was struck on the head by an officer and said no more. Among those who were confronted was one who was later identified as Charley Floyd. He remained calm and collected during the first couple of minutes of the melee. The smell of whiskey in the room was overpowering. As the officers started searching through the boxes in hopes of finding contraband and alcohol, Choc slowly rose from the table. An agent watched him get up and peered closer at his face.

"Hey, you fellas know who this is?" shouted the agent. "It's that Pretty Boy Floyd character."

Feigning drunkenness, Choc weaved around, mumbling to himself, as if he was about to pass out. What happened next differed from witness to witness. Some said it was a whiskey bottle from the table, while most claimed it was a hat, but no matter what it was, Choc suddenly tossed an object across the room. It landed on a nearby bed and diverted everyone's attention. In that split second, Choc pulled one of his .45 pistols and made for the door.

"Look out, he's got a gun!" shouted Havens.

A gun battle instantly commenced while Choc, firing his pistol all the while, grappled with a couple of the agents. Explosions of police revolvers and automatic pistols were deafening and gun smoke clouded the room. Bullets ignited some combustible material and a fire broke out, but it was soon extinguished. The fracas was over in a few minutes. Choc was gone. He had broken away from the officers. He bolted through the splintered doorway and bounded down the stairs. Witnesses from the crowd forming on the street said that he escaped in a Plymouth that was parked nearby.

Five men were shot in the fight. Joe Careo, a twenty-three-year-old suspect who tried to escape, was cut down by a shotgun blast fired by Lieutenant Nelson. He died instantly. Joseph Lusco, thirty-seven, was arrested and taken to a local hospital to see about his fractured skull. Curtis Burks was wounded in the abdomen, causing paralysis from the waist down. He was listed in critical condition. Joe Anderson suffered a less serious wound from a glancing bullet that struck him in the stomach. Clarence Reedy, a detective, was wounded in the neck. M. P. Wilson, a twenty-three-year-old from Bessemer, Alabama, who had nothing at all to do with the raid, was found lying in the street with a wound in his stomach. Officers believed he was struck by one of Floyd's stray bullets.

Four of the wounded men recovered, but two days after the shootout on Independence Street, Curtis Burks died. Now, besides Ohio authorities, the Kansas City police had a good reason to visit with the elusive Pretty Boy Floyd. Shooting down a couple of snitches like the Ash boys on a muddy Kansas road was frowned upon, but starting a gun battle in Tom's Town that caused several people to be wounded and left an agent dead was going too far.

Like the old bandits and outlaws of the past who rode out of Missouri and found asylum in the Indian nations, Choc made a run for the Oklahoma hills, where he felt as if he still belonged. He received a warm reception.

That summer no rains fell in Oklahoma; only wind as hot as the devil's breath came off the prairies. The Southern plains were on fire. Since the Fourth of July, the sun had seared grasses and crops. The blistering heat had dried up everyone's will to do much more than complain about the weather and being poor. Come nightfall, folks in town had run out of shaved ice and lemonade, and they crept out on their porches to catch a little sleep. Country people, soaked in sweat, lay outside on their quilts and wished that God, who seemed to be in hiding, would send them a cloudburst to break the earth's fever.

The summer was especially brutal that year. Folks had a name for the hot days and nights. The name came from ancient Roman times, when the people believed that Sirius, the Dog Star, coupled its heat with that of the sun, from July 3 to August 11. The Romans called this period *dies caniculares,* or "days of the dog." Down in the country where Choc came from, this time of high temperatures lasted a bit longer, even until September. Most folks just said it was the dog days of summer.

Choc spent those dog days in 1931 laid up in the shade like a smart old hound. He was through with pissing in the wind, and wanted to get back to chasing rainbows. Still, the best rainbows appear only after a storm. Choc knew, sure as shooting, he would have to get through more squalls ahead before he would ever lay his hands on a pot of gold.

But a young man with a bandit's heart was not too fretful. He figured he had all the time in the world.

25

ON THE SCOUT

URING THOSE SULTRY DAYS of July and August and on into September of 1931, Charley Floyd lay low. He kept his pistols oiled and loaded and at the ready at all times. He also continued to rob banks. Choc realized even then that as far as the law was concerned, he had gone beyond the point of no return. If he had wanted to call a halt to his bandit ways and settle down to a regular job, it would have been a tough challenge. He knew that he would have died just trying.

Even though a malevolent dark side had emerged in Charley's personality, he could still be the sensitive country boy capable of demonstrating love and tenderness. He was never completely certain just whose bullets caused the deaths in the gunfights with police officers in Ohio and Kansas City, and he never really discussed with anyone the circumstances of the Ash brothers' murder. He did own up to the biblical maxim that anyone who killed another man, killed a little bit of himself. In his late twenties, Choc told others he sometimes felt like an old man, always on guard and on the run, a man dying with each tick of the clock.

This was hardly surprising, since authorities in several states, including Ohio, Missouri, Kansas, Michigan, and Kentucky, were ready to tack the hide of *the* Pretty Boy, as many now commonly called him, to the barn door. Even if Charley had wanted to work at an honest job, which was not the case, the job market made this impossible. He had no education and had not touched the blister end of a hoe or shovel in years.

Choc had other skills, though. He was adept at swiping cars to use for bank job getaways. He could get an engine going and drive off while the owner ate dinner in a cafe or snored over a newspaper in his front room. Charley handled a revolver and a .45 pistol as well as anyone, and he learned to use a Thompson submachine gun with deadly accuracy.

His inclination was to stay on the scout and hope that his luck held. He kept in mind the old gambler's saying that a faint heart never filled a flush.

Charley stayed mostly with Bradley and his family down at Earlsboro.

Sometimes he slipped over to Sequoyah County to see his mother and kid brother, E.W., and his sisters and their families. He always paid his respects at the Akins graveyard. He also visited with his former in-laws, Jess and Maggie Hardgraves, and their three sons and daughter. The Hardgraves were living as sharecroppers in a small house that was not much more than a railroad car on the Cecil Bennett farm outside of Bixby, just south of Tulsa. They always liked Choc, even after Ruby divorced him and he became a full-fledged outlaw. Choc brought Maggie handfuls of wildflowers and praised her biscuits and gravy until she turned red. He persuaded the Hardgraves to tell him where Ruby and their son were living, and he finally got Jess to take him there.

They drove up to Coffeyville, just north of the Oklahoma line. A trade center of southeastern Kansas, on the west bank of the Verdigris River and bounded by a low range of hills, Coffeyville was the cattle and railroad town where the Dalton gang had been shot to pieces in 1892. The facades of some of the buildings on the downtown Plaza, at Ninth and Walnut streets, even in 1931 still bore the scars and bullets fired during the gun battle between the outlaws and citizens.

Jess took Charley directly to Ruby. When she opened the door and found her ex-husband standing there, she almost fainted. Charley Floyd was as unexpected as a fifth ace. Before her was the man she had committed herself to when she was a fresh farm girl. Now he was all dressed up in a suit and necktie. He smelled sweet. Ruby had kept up with his exploits through the newspapers and family friends. It was hard not to. She knew he was thought to be dangerous as lightning by the lawmen who dogged his tracks. But Ruby was not afraid of Choc. To her, he would always be Charley, and not the mad-dog killer the cops and headline writers wanted the public to believe.

As soon as they saw each other, Charley and Ruby realized they were still in love. Behind Ruby, in the shadows of the cramped apartment, stood Choc's son—Charles Dempsey Floyd. The boy was six years old, and when Choc saw him, it was as though he were looking at himself in a mirror twenty years past. Charley broke out into a grin and swept the little boy up in his arms. The last time he had seen his son, Ruby had been holding Dempsey in her arms. They had been waving goodbye to Choc at the Sallisaw train depot as the St. Louis policemen took him off in chains to stand trial for highway robbery.

"That day when he and my grandpa came to our apartment in Coffeyville was the very first time I can ever remember really seeing my father," recalled Dempsey Floyd. "That's my first real memory of him. I liked him right off."

It was as if the three of them had never been apart. Ruby instantly forgave her wayward husband. She seemed to put aside the years she had spent waiting for him to show up again at her doorstep. Charley did not hold a grudge against Ruby, even though she had divorced him just weeks before he got out of prison. Dempsey took to his father immediately. In fact, he would not leave his side.

But there was a small hitch. Ruby had remarried.

Her new husband was Leroy Leonard, a twenty-two-year-old hardworking man she had met in Oklahoma. He was very much in love with Ruby, and he was kind to her little boy. Friends remembered that he treated Dempsey as if he were his own son. He had brought Ruby and Dempsey to Coffeyville, where Leonard worked long hours in a local bakery. They moved into a second-floor apartment over a store, and Leonard bought little Dempsey a tricycle to ride on the sidewalk out front. Every day around noon, Ruby packed a meal for her husband and gave it to her son to take to Leroy, who worked just a few blocks away.

"Leroy was always very good to me and my mother," said Dempsey. "I'd bring him his lunch and he'd take a hot roll or bun and butter it all up and give it to me."

That evening when Leroy Leonard came home from the bakery, he found that there was company at his apartment. Besides Ruby's father, there was another guest. It was the man who Leonard had long dreaded would one day appear. Tension was thick in the little apartment, and the conversation soon became heated.

"Things got real bad when Leroy found out that my dad had come to Coffeyville to take my mother and me away with him," said Dempsey. "They had quite an argument. It got real loud and there were some sharp words that were said that night. It didn't come to blows but it still scared me to death. Finally my mother got them both to settle down."

By nightfall, Ruby and Dempsey were packed. They left behind a saddened Leroy Leonard and drove south with Charley out of the town of Coffeyville.

Leonard's heart was broken by the callous way Ruby treated him after he had been so kind to her and the little boy he loved. Although she had left him, he and Ruby remained married for a few years. Finally, in 1935, Leonard married a loving woman and they raised a family. Even then, however, problems sometimes arose because of people who became confused and believed his second wife, Bernice, had once been married to Pretty Boy Floyd.

There was always a strong rumor that Charley only wanted to throw a scare into Ruby by going to Coffeyville. A few said that he had even kidnapped Ruby and had stolen her and Dempsey away from the Kansas baker. That was not true; nor was it true that Choc was distrustful of Ruby, despite what some of his friends from Sequoyah County told nosy reporters.

"He never got over the fact that Ruby married another fellow while he was in the Missouri prison, although he did take her away from that fellow and live with her again," one of Choc's schoolmates told a Kansas City reporter two years after Charley and Ruby's reconciliation. "But he never did have much confidence in her."

Choc had enough trust in his former wife to take her and their son to a rented home he found in Fort Smith, the second-largest city in Arkansas. Although Choc continued to maintain a relationship with Juanita Beulah Baird, he also tried to pick up with Ruby where they had left off in 1925. They never remarried, but for periods of time, they lived together as if they were once more husband and wife.

Choc and Ruby's home in Fort Smith—a city at the junction of the Arkansas and Poteau rivers where "Hanging Judge" Parker used to deliver his stern brand of frontier justice—was in a quiet residential neighborhood not far off Garrison Avenue, the main downtown artery. Sallisaw, where Choc's widowed mother and several members of his family resided, and small communities such as Akins, Hanson, and Price's Chapel were within easy driving distance.

Ruby and Charley, living under the alias of Mr. and Mrs. Jack Hamilton, and their little boy, were settled in their neat residence by the late summer of 1931, just in time for Dempsey to begin the first grade in the public school system. Fort Smith would be their home for almost six months. It was unquestionably the happiest period of their lives together.

"My dad stayed with us almost the entire time we lived in Fort Smith," recalled Dempsey. "It was a wonderful time. My folks took me to the local school, but since my dad was using the name Jack Hamilton at the time and was acting as if he was a traveling salesman, they enrolled me as Jackie Hamilton. A lot of people always thought they called me Jack or Jackie because of my name Dempsey, but that really wasn't the case. It was just to go along with my dad's alias. The folks really drilled me about using that name, and they had me say it over and over again so I wouldn't slip up and use the name Floyd in front of strangers. They got me accustomed to the name, and that's what many people called me."

To the Floyd side of the family, the little boy was still Dempsey whenever he came to Oklahoma for visits, but Ruby's relatives and many of her friends always referred to him as Jack or Jackie even after he was a grown man.

"I really have nothing but fond memories of my father, especially when we were in Fort Smith," said Dempsey. "He was a great father to me. He was gentle, and he would make me and my mother laugh all the time. His sense of humor was terrific. He was always telling jokes and teasing my mother."

One afternoon, soon after he started school, Dempsey came home and showed Charley some crayon pictures he had drawn. Choc told his boy how much he liked the artwork, and then he got a devilish look.

"He told me, 'I want you to go out in the kitchen and tell your mother something.' He whispered in my ear and sent me to her," recalled Dempsey. "So I did as he told me. My mom was at the stove cooking supper and I said, 'Mother, guess what I did at school today.' Well, I guess she expected me to say that I made this picture or I learned this or that. She smiled and said,

'What did you do today, son?' And I repeated what my dad had told me to tell her. 'Oh, I got into a little girl's pants today,' I answered—without even knowing what I was saying.

"Mom ran right into the front room and jumped on my dad. She pounded on him with a pillow and scolded him, and they wrestled around and laughed and laughed. Of course, I had no earthly idea what was going on. At that age I couldn't imagine what I would be doing with some little girl's pants."

Charley and his son pulled other fast ones on Ruby.

Dempsey was walking home from school one rainy afternoon and got sidetracked by some little boys who were hauling each other up and down a tree in a bucket attached to a rope and pulley. It was great fun and Dempsey lost all track of time. When he came through the back door and was confronted by a worried Ruby, it was after dusk.

"My mother was in tears," said Dempsey. "She was deathly afraid that someone had kidnapped me, so she marched in and told my father, 'Charley, you are going to give this boy a whipping. You've never whipped him in his life but the time has come for you to do your duty.'

"My father looked up at her and said, 'All right, Ruby,' and he told me in a serious voice to go into the bathroom. I was standing there with my raincoat on, and he walked in with his belt in his hand and closed the door. Then he bent down and whispered, 'You take that coat off and put it over the toilet stool. Every time I smack that coat, you holler and scream your head off like you're really getting a good beating.' So he started pounding away on that raincoat with his belt and I yelled bloody murder, and before too long, my mother was trying to break the door down to get him to stop. We never told her the truth."

Charley spent a lot of time around the house at Fort Smith, getting reacquainted with Ruby and becoming a father to Dempsey. Both baking and cooking relaxed Charley, and he did his share. He donned one of Ruby's aprons and especially enjoyed sliding a hot apple pie out of the oven. He hummed "When the Moon Comes Over the Mountain," "Love Letters in the Sand," or "Where the Blue of the Night Meets the Gold of the Day" as he prepared spicy Italian dishes he had sampled during his days in Kansas City and Akron. Spaghetti and meatballs were his specialty.

"Dad used to take me fishing, too," said Dempsey. "This one day we were way out in the country at some lake, and we just couldn't seem to catch anything. So after a while he turned to me and said, 'You know what we ought to do? Let's teach these damn fish a lesson and shoot 'em!' I was thrilled! He went to the car and brought back his submachine gun and he sort of held it for me and let me fire it into the lake. Of course, we didn't hit anything, but we had a good time. 'That'll show those fish,' Dad told me. 'If we can't catch 'em, we'll at least scare 'em to death.' "

Like other families who tried to keep their minds off the Depression, Choc also looked forward to taking the family to the movies. One of Charley's favorites was the horror classic *Frankenstein*, which premiered in 1931. It was directed by James Whale and starred Colin Clive, Mae Clarke, and Boris Karloff in the title role. Karloff gave a strong, sensitive performance as the synthetic brute who discovers his own humanity yet is compelled to kill and terrorize. Dempsey scrunched down in his seat and hid his eyes when the monster came on the screen, but Charley sat spellbound for seventy-one minutes.

"I remember I was so scared of Frankenstein," said Dempsey Floyd. "But my dad sat down with me and explained it was just a movie and that I shouldn't be afraid."

To all those who knew the young couple and their son, it was an idyllic period. Ruby went shopping in Fort Smith and drove up to Muskogee and Tulsa. She bought all of Charley's sporty clothes, including silk underwear, neckties, fine socks and shoes, scarves, caps, and the black leather gloves he loved to wear. On sunny afternoons, they went outside in the yard and took family photographs and had picnic lunches. All the neighbors admired the Hamiltons. They seemed to be getting along "just swell" on a salesman's commissions, in spite of the bleak times.

"My folks were so good-looking," recalled Dempsey. "My dad was handsome and had that thick hair. He was well built and had such strong arms and shoulders. My mother was tall and beautiful. She was affectionate and loving.

"I used to get up out of my bed there at our place at Fort Smith real early in the morning when it was still dark and quiet, and I'd go to their bedroom and peek inside. I can still see them together asleep in their bed. My mother would be in his arms and their heads would be together like sweethearts do. Their faces were so young and innocent. They looked like sleeping kids. She adored my father and I believe she would have gone anywhere with him."

Charley clearly would have taken Ruby anywhere he went except when he visited his other love interest, Juanita, or when he ventured forth to pull a bank robbery. He felt that being on the scout was no place for a woman. Robbing banks was a man's job.

By the late summer of 1931, Charley had lined up yet another partner as a running mate. His name was George Birdwell and he indeed was all man.

Born in the Cherokee Nation in 1894, Birdwell had Irish, Cherokee, and Choctaw blood, and even as a kid he was prideful and stubborn as a pack mule. His father, James Joseph Birdwell, moved to Texas and farmed, while young George learned to cowboy. With his family, he moved back and forth between Texas and Oklahoma and received his first real notoriety in July 1913 when a farmer named T. W. Jennings, from the Mellette community not far from Eufaula, Oklahoma, shot Birdwell because he suspected the farm boy of fooling around with his wife.

The story was that Jennings's wife had seduced young George, and the jealous husband had filed suit for divorce. In the petition, he named Birdwell as correspondent. When Jennings later encountered Birdwell working in a cornfield, the farmer yanked out a gun and opened fire, striking the young man in the leg, just above his knee. George managed to mount a team of plow horses and escape further damage. He rode to his brother Robert, who put a tourniquet on the wounded leg and then took George on horseback to a doctor thirty miles away. The ride was fast and furious and the horse that carried the two Birdwell boys dropped dead in its tracks. The doctor patched up the wound and George soon recovered. Jennings turned himself in that same evening at Eufaula, was placed under five-hundred-dollar bond, and was released. He was never punished for gunning down George, and the two men stayed clear of one another in the future.

Birdwell never lost his way with the ladies, and he developed a taste for strong drink, as well. He kept at least part of his wild streak even after he married. His wife, Flora Mae Birdwell, was born in the Cherokee Nation in 1898, and from the time she was a girl, she was called Bob by all those who knew her. Bob Birdwell worked hard to make a home and helped midwife her share of babies when she and George lived on a cattle ranch in Texas. She also had two boys and two girls of her own. The Birdwells also raised two of Bob's nephews.

Their oldest son, Jack, was born on the Texas panhandle ranch where George served as the foreman. Located in Hall County, not far from the towns of Esteline and Parnell, the ranch was near the Prairie Dog Town Fork of the Red River. The largest town for miles around was Childress to the east.

George Birdwell was six feet tall. He weighed in at an even 150 pounds, and would not have been caught dead without his Stetson hat and high-heeled cowboy boots. His high cheekbones and dark complexion gave away his Indian heritage. He was lean, bowlegged, and could ride and rope as if he were born in a saddle. Through the years, Birdwell competed in many rodeos. He rode bucking broncs and roped goats four-legged at ranch roundups in West Texas and at rodeos in Shamrock, Drumright, and several other spots in Oklahoma. At a rodeo in Oklahoma City, he once roped a goat in the remarkable time of nine seconds flat.

Shortly after the birth of his first child, Birdwell quit ranching to work in the oil fields. He labored for an outfit outside of Shamrock, Texas, and later took his family to live in several small oil patch towns in Creek County and other boom areas in Oklahoma. Birdwell was an able roustabout and also worked at various refinery tasks. It was said that he could "dig a ditch like a gopher." By the latter part of the decade, George found a job with Magnolia Oil and the Birdwells moved near Earlsboro, close to the home of Bradley Floyd.

Birdwell first met Bradley's younger brother in 1929, right after Charley was released from the penitentiary in Missouri and returned to Oklahoma to find a job with Magnolia. The Floyd brothers and Birdwell became friends and the three of them made a little bit of money by bootlegging in the area.

"Charley Floyd came down there to work, and had hardly got started when the foreman came by and grabbed him off the job," recalled Jack Birdwell. "My father said that the foreman told Charley, 'I don't want no thugs around here.' That's when Charley decided he was gonna show 'em."

By early 1930, as the Depression reached the oil patch, George Birdwell was laid off from his job with Magnolia. He knew peddling whiskey and shuffling poker cards were not going to bring enough money to keep his wife, four kids, and two nephews in food and clothing. That was about the same time that Charley Floyd returned to the area and rented a house in Shawnee with the two Baird sisters and another young man named Bill Miller. Charley and Miller got together with Birdwell and Bradley and discussed some options.

"That's when they went to robbin' banks," said Jack Birdwell. "Charley wouldn't let his brother go with them. Bradley wanted to, but Charley told him no way. My dad was with Charley and Miller that first time they robbed the bank at Earlsboro. Dad was wearing his sheepskin coat and had his cowboy hat pulled down over his eyes and face. It was the first time he ever robbed a bank."

That robbery of the Bank of Earlsboro took place on March 9, 1931, and the three bandits—Choc Floyd, Bill Miller, and George Birdwell—got a total of about three thousand dollars. The holdup at Earlsboro occurred just before Charley and Miller returned to Kansas City, only a couple of weeks prior to the slayings of the Ash brothers across the state line in Kansas. The money they took from Earlsboro provided them with an infusion of cash. It helped finance Choc and Miller when they left, accompanied by the Baird sisters, for Kentucky and Ohio, where Miller met his bloody end on the streets of Bowling Green. Birdwell, who had no intention of joining the four lovebirds on their odyssey, used his share of the take to help pay a pile of bills and keep a roof over his family's head. He also came to the financial assistance of some down-and-out friends.

"Whenever he made a haul from a bank, Dad always helped out others," said Jack Birdwell. "He'd give each of our neighbors a twenty-dollar bill. That went a long way back then."

By late summer of 1931, however, Birdwell was in need of more money. He still had no job. He was ready to sally forth again with Choc Floyd and hit more rural Oklahoma banks.

"My father was a proud man, and he would not take help from anyone," said Jack Birdwell. "He didn't want any relief. I can still hear him when I was just a little kid sitting on his knee in an old Model T Ford working the gas for him and he'd tell me about what to expect from life. He said way back then that there were two kinds of people who robbed—some who did it with a gun and some with an ink pen. He told me to be my own person and not ever to have a price. 'Don't let anybody ever buy you,' is what he told me."

Beginning with the robbery of the Bank of Earlsboro in March of 1931, George Birdwell's bandit career lasted only twenty-one months. During that period, he robbed thirteen banks with Pretty Boy Floyd. In most cases, they recruited one other person, usually one of several younger men they knew, to drive the getaway car. All of the robberies were in Oklahoma and none of them ever netted more than four thousand dollars. The average sum taken was usually a little more than half of that amount.

Accused of holding up more banks than they actually robbed, Choc and Birdwell, in fact, struck at six banks in Oklahoma during the five-month period between August and December 1931.

On August 4, they entered the Citizens Bank of Shamrock, a Creek County oil boomtown that had been in a decline since the mid-1920s. They left with four hundred dollars. The following month, after Dempsey was enrolled in school at Fort Smith, they pulled off two more robberies. On September 8, they took $1,743 from the Morris State Bank, and on September 29, they robbed the First National in Maud of $3,850.

The Maud holdup was one of their most successful. Choc and Birdwell, armed with a submachine gun and revolvers, got in and out of town with relative ease. Local police were fairly certain George Birdwell was one of the armed bandits, and bank employees identified the other when they were shown a photograph of Charley Floyd. The following day, Sequoyah County Sheriff George Cheek and some other law officers near Sallisaw confronted Choc and Birdwell when the bandits visited some of the Floyd relatives. There was a brief exchange of gunfire but both suspects were able to speed away. The frustrated law officers swore up and down that they had shot point-blank at Charley, and yet somehow he got away untouched. This led to the conjecture that Pretty Boy must have taken to wearing a bulletproof vest or body armor.

Despite the narrow escape, the same pair again robbed the Bank of Earlsboro for the second time on October 14. This time, they took $2,498. Talk began to circulate about the Pretty Boy Floyd gang, but most people knew that small-town bank bandits like Floyd and Birdwell had a backwoods style that in no way resembled the operations of gangsters such as Arthur "Dutch Schultz" Flegenheimer, Jack "Legs" Diamond, and Al "Scarface" Capone. The absolute lord of vice, Capone spent more money in a single hour than Choc and Birdwell took in a dozen bank jobs. Charley Floyd and his accomplices never created multileveled criminal organizations such as those managed by mobsters, racketeers, Mafia families, and beer barons in the cities. Choc simply had a style that reflected the nineteenth-century criminal traditions of the Old West.

As the economic collapse of the nation intensified, Charley and Birdwell continued their spree. On November 5, they held up the First National Bank of Conowa of $2,500, and six weeks later, they went back to Okmulgee County and took $1,162 in another robbery of the Morris State Bank. Choc joked with some of Ruby's relatives that the Morris Bank had once turned him down for a loan when he was trying to get enough money together to buy Ruby a ring. Because of the bank's rejection, he took great pleasure in making "withdrawals" from that particular financial institution.

Choc and Birdwell's method of operation in these holdups was the same. They arrived in a small town during broad daylight and drove right up to the bank. While the getaway driver kept the motor purring, Choc and Birdwell entered the bank and announced their intentions. They never wore masks or disguises. Choc was always well dressed in a suit and tie, with his shoes shined and hair slicked back, perhaps feeling that he had now a true public image to maintain. Sometimes he had on a cap, and he often wore gloves. Birdwell's trademarks were his cowboy hat and boots. They went about their work in a businesslike manner, and after they had the money in hand, they left with two or three bank employees. These hostages were ordered to ride on the getaway car's running boards, so no local cop would get any notions about becoming a hero and take potshots at the bandits.

"Hold on tight, and don'tcha worry," were Choc's cavalier words of advice to the terrified tellers or bank officers as the automobile tore out of town.

A few miles down the road, the car eased to a stop and the bank employees hopped off. They watched Choc and his pals disappear in the proverbial cloud of dust. Sometimes Choc stuck his head out of the window. He would bid the hostages farewell and gallantly tip his cap. Most witnesses reported that the bandits minimized gunplay and appeared to go out of their way to avoid violence.

One of Choc's favorite locales for hiding his portion of the booty was at his brother Bradley's in Earlsboro.

"Course, ol' Choc was always welcome around our house," recalled Bessie Floyd. "He had to kind of hide out, ya know. One time he stayed shut up in our place for 'bout a week. Nobody knew he was there and then one morning just after he took off, the biggest string of cars came out there, and we just couldn't imagine what they were doin'. But when they pulled up, we saw that they were laws and were huntin' their Pretty Boy. They 'bout scared my little son Cleatus half to death. He was cryin' and carryin' on so much that Wayne or Bayne—one of those twin boys—jumped up and yelled at those laws, 'Hey, why don't you fellas take those guns, and get off in a field and kill a rabbit and get off our land.' Bradley made the boys hush up."

Despite the constant fear of such visits, Bessie and Bradley's sons enjoyed having their Uncle Charley visit them. Their father would hide Choc's guns and automobile, and their mother helped Choc divide up his loot on the kitchen table and bury it in gallon syrup cans out in the yard. Much of the money would be in the form of coins. No matter how large or small the take, Choc always gave his family and often some of his friends a share of the money to help with groceries.

"I always liked it when Choc came to our house," said Bayne Floyd. "He'd take me places with him, and when we were driving down those country roads, he'd let me drive that old Model T car. Sometimes Ruby would be with him, and we liked her. She was a jovial person."

Glendon Floyd also had pleasant memories of Ruby Floyd. "Even though she divorced our uncle, we never gave up on Ruby," said Glendon. "She was a Floyd, and once you're a Floyd, you are family. That is just the way it is and always will be. She may have fallen out of favor with some, and a few of the other kinfolk may have rebuffed her, but not our part of the family. We accepted her just like we did his girlfriend, Juanita."

Between bank jobs and after the money was divided, Choc headed for Fort Smith to be with Ruby and Dempsey. Each homecoming was a grand event. He would stop to buy gifts, and there would also be a box filled with jars of sorghum and jelly or fresh produce from relatives and friends.

"It was always like Christmas when my dad came home," said Dempsey Floyd. "He'd wait and come in at night so people wouldn't see him, and he and my mother would wake me up, and he would have presents for me. He brought me puppies on two different occasions, and there were always candy bars and all sorts of toys. One time, just after he made a pretty fair haul at a bank, he had me go into his bedroom and fetch a sack of money he had hidden there. 'If you're big enough to bring it to me, it's all yours,' he told me.

"Sure enough, there was a big sack under there and it was mostly coins. It was real heavy, and I had to strain and really work hard to drag it to him. He kept his word and gave it to me, but he told me to keep it hidden and use it if I ever wanted to treat my friends or buy myself something. The sack was filled with nickels, dimes, quarters, and half-dollars, and I dragged it into my room and hid it in the closet. I got pretty popular with the other kids. I'd take everybody to the show to see the latest movies, and we'd go to the ice cream stand for cones, and I'd also buy candy and pop for everyone. But all good things come to an end, and one day my mom figured out I was up to no good, and she looked around and found that stash of money I had. She took it down to the bank, had it converted into folding money, and went to a department store and bought me a bunch of new clothes, including a fancy suit with short pants. I hated short pants and didn't want to be called a sissy, but by golly I wore them."

After a whole host of days that might have seemed like Christmas, the real holiday arrived joyfully in Fort Smith at the end of 1931. Charley and Ruby gave each other rings. Charley cherished the cameo ring he received, and he wore it everywhere. Ruby's gift was as prized as the pocket watch Choc always carried. The fine timepiece had been a gift from Bill Miller, his old running mate who had been shot and killed in Ohio. Attached to the watch fob was a fifty-cent piece dated 1929, to commemorate the year Choc got his freedom from the penitentiary at Jefferson City.

"Every day about that time when we lived in Fort Smith, my dad would get the newspapers, and there would be all these stories claiming that he had just robbed some bank in Ohio or in Kentucky or in New Orleans or up in Kansas," said Dempsey Floyd.

"Sometimes it was actually humorous, because at the same time Dad was supposed to be in a bank hundreds of miles away, he was right there at home with us. We all knew that he had absolutely nothing to do with many of those bank jobs. What was happening was that other fellas were using his method of operation. Some even said that they were Pretty Boy Floyd when they robbed the bank. Then there were also bankers who probably robbed their own banks. We realized that Dad was taking the blame for a lot of bank robberies that he didn't commit."

Although he did not use the name himself, the Pretty Boy epithet was becoming well known in households across the nation. Americans had become conditioned to the use of colorful nicknames for their outlaws.

Back in the twenties, the public had rediscovered Billy the Kid, another classic Robin Hood figure. Billy was depicted as a young man out to avenge an insult to his mother and the death of his employer. Written by Walter Noble Burns, *The Saga of Billy the Kid* was published by Doubleday in 1926, and its selection by the Book-of-the-Month Club confirmed the romanticized youth's status as a mainstay of popular culture in the 1920s and 1930s. In the 1930 movie *Billy the Kid*, the skinny boy from New York City who became an icon of the Old West was lovingly portrayed as a frontier superhero by Johnny Mack Brown. It was a far cry from the dime novels published between the 1880s and the early 1900s in which Billy the Kid was described as a bloodthirsty killer.

During the Great Depression, a new generation of wanted men and women emerged. Some were like Choc Floyd, a young man who was rooted to the lawless history of the country he knew best. He paid close attention to the past and recalled with marked reverence the old sayings of desperadoes such as Emmett Dalton, the outlaw who survived the Coffeyville fiasco and years spent on the scout. Dalton married a Bartlesville, Oklahoma, lady named Julia Johnson and moved to California. He ended up in the real estate and movie business in the early 1920s.

Absolved of his high crimes and completely reformed in his old age, Dalton penned, with some collaborative assistance from Jack Jungmeyer, a colorful and folksy book entitled *When the Daltons Rode*. It was published by Doubleday in 1931, and, according to Floyd kin, served as a source of inspiration to Choc while he lolled around Fort Smith and plotted future bank robberies. The book told of many of Dalton's earlier exploits and some of the descriptive passages fit the new breed of criminal, like Choc Floyd, who was trying to take his place.

An outlaw's got to be cagey as a coyote to live even a short time in the land of his father. The alert outlaw acts a good deal by intuition. His wits and sense become acute as a wild animal's. The ordinary pitch of the faculties is not sufficient. His life constantly depends upon the accuracy with which he judges men. After this has to be snap judgment. He may never have time to rectify it. He must be able to read unconsciously tell-tale signals in the flicker of an eye, the tone of a voice, the movement of a hand. The uppermost thought in the mind of every half-sane outlaw is that some day he will make a big haul and retire to the "Big Rock Candy Mountain." An outlaw's dying command, "Don't surrender! Die game!"

In days past, the outlaw's horse was his most treasured possession. As Dalton put it, "He [the horse] was fed before the man ate. His feet were zealously shod. He suffered no saddle sores, and the slightest ailment was immediately treated." Modern desperadoes put their love and attention into the care of their automobiles. The engines had to be well tuned, and the tires in good shape so the cops and deputies could be outdistanced on the open dirt highways and gravel roads. Dalton also prized his guns—the tools of his trade—and he kept them immaculate as a child going to Sunday school. The weapons of the thirties had improved, but the love and care had not diminished.

Dalton and the other old-timers lived by an unwritten code of survival. It was also a code with taboos, such as not giving the other fellow away. The idea was "to protect a comrade even at the cost of death." Dalton said the unspoken silence in a lawless clan was a social bond. "It is as imperative among the machine-gunning gangster of the skyscraper frontiers as it was among the spurred brigands of the open. It becomes a boasted virtue, and sometimes the cost of maintaining the code is heavy."

Although, as his relatives pointed out, Choc was not exactly an ardent reader, he did stick it out with the Dalton book and read as far as the final chapters. Choc undoubtedly got a chuckle over some of the elderly man's comments about the younger outlaw prototype, whom he called "the kid-glove bandit, a courtly figment of popular fancy."

Generally, the crusty old Dalton believed the 1930s-vintage bandit had an easier time of it than the men who had ridden horseback and carried Colt six-shooters.

To-day [sic] the country-bred outlaw is practically extinct. Crowded places, city canyons, night clubs, and public amusement places are his cradle and his habitat. Naturally he clings to his environment. He takes his spoil close to where he spends it. And amid the millions of jostling but incurious strangers in a Chicago, New York, or Detroit he is as safe or safer than was the plains outlaw in his remote bush camp.

Charley Floyd was none too certain of his safety as he quietly ushered in 1932, however. The new year got off to a violent beginning, and, as usual, the authorities placed Pretty Boy smack in the middle of the mess. Late on the cold and gloomy afternoon of Saturday, January 2, 1932, six peace officers were slain and three others were wounded at a farmhouse near Brookline, about seven miles west of Springfield, Missouri, when they attempted to arrest two local brothers and ex-convicts, Jennings and Harry Young, for auto theft. Harry was also a fugitive murder suspect implicated in the slaying two years before of Mark Noe, the marshal of Republic, Missouri. What came to be known as the Young Brothers' Massacre lasted only a few minutes and established a record for the greatest number of law officers then killed in a single incident in the history of the United States. Armed only with pistols, the deputies and detectives expected little resistance, but instead they stumbled into a hail of shotgun and rifle fire.

The Young brothers vanished in the surrounding countryside as reinforcements and a mob of angry citizens descended on the farm. Former newspaper reporter and publicity man Lon Scott, one of the movers and shakers behind the promotion of U.S. Route 66 in the twenties, was one of the first on the scene. As the moon was coming up, Scott stumbled over some of the dead bodies and jotted down notes. He was able to provide some of the more graphic and accurate reports of the carnage and pandemonium as the rabble broke into the Youngs' vacated farmhouse. Frank Rhoades, a reporter for the *Springfield Leader,* was also with the first posse that swept through the darkened fields. Other news hounds with ink-stained fingers soon appeared like a horde of locusts.

The scene of the crime brought back memories of the gun battle fought on a chicken farm a few miles from the nearby Ozark town of Branson, Missouri, a little more than a year before. In that engagement, officers had shot notorious bank bandit Jake Fleagle—the "Wolf of the West"—during his attempt to avoid arrest. He was taken to a Springfield hospital, where he died. Unlike the Fleagle skirmish, the fight with the Young brothers ended in favor of the outlaws.

News bulletins about the appalling slayings of the law officers in the Missouri Ozarks were first broadcast by KMOX radio from St. Louis. They made the early editions of the January 3 newspapers across the nation. The story of the besieged bad men killing a half dozen lawmen upstaged all other news. Acts of violence involving guns and outlaws always sold newspapers, especially if editors could figure out a way to insert a colorful and recognizable name in the headline or copy. In this instance, Pretty Boy would do just fine.

Based almost solely on the fact that Charley Floyd had served his hitch in the Missouri penitentiary at the same time as Harry Young, the name of Pretty Boy Floyd was almost immediately placed high on the list of murder suspects in the bloody slaughter. Early news reports from Missouri and a wire story out of Oklahoma City quickly implicated Choc.

OKLAHOMA CITY, Jan. 2, (AP)—Oklahoma authorities, notified of the killing of six Missouri officers near Springfield, Mo., tonight, pondered the possibility that one or more of a gang of Oklahoma desperadoes, known to have been active for more than a year in the eastern part of the state, may be among the slayers.

Charles ("Pretty Boy") Floyd, leader of the gang, is wanted on murder and bank robbery charges in several middle western states. A series of bank robberies in Oklahoma and nearby states in recent months is generally believed to have been the work of Floyd and his aids.

Officers have been informed time and again that Floyd carries two machine guns in his automobile, one of them demountable, and that he wears a steel jacket for protection.

Headlines screamed with conjecture and speculation.

SIX OFFICERS SLAIN,
THREE WOUNDED IN
SANGUINARY BATTLE

OKLAHOMA DESPERADOES
MAY BE AMONG SLAYERS

ONE OF THE KILLERS
REARED AT SALLISAW

Another wire story spoke of Oklahoma peace officers with pistols at the ready spreading the search for Choc Floyd. "The steel-vested desperado is noted for the breakneck speed at which he drives and the machine guns which are always with him," reported the Associated Press.

Missouri Governor Henry S. Caulfield put up rewards for the apprehension and conviction of the killers and ordered out National Guard troops, including an artillery battery from Springfield, to help bring down the Youngs and any of their accomplices. Texas Rangers, acting on instructions from Texas Adj. Gen. William W. Sterling, scoured the Mexican border crossings and federal agents looked for the suspects in Tulsa, Oklahoma City, and Kansas City. Rumors spread about the whereabouts of the killers, fueled by the tabloids; the hunted men supposedly popped up in the northeastern Oklahoma towns of

Quapaw and Picher, where Mickey Mantle's father worked the lead and zinc mines. The proprietor of a Kansas City tire shop told officers that a man he identified as Pretty Boy Floyd drove a mud-splattered car carrying a wounded passenger that stopped at his place of business.

Even Chief of Police Carl Galliher from Bowling Green, Ohio, got into the act. Still angry because of Floyd's involvement in the Bowling Green gun battle that ended with the deaths of Bill Miller and one of his police officers, Galliher told Springfield authorities he definitely believed Floyd was one of the killers they sought.

Witness accounts emerged from Texas that the two Youngs had been seen there. The spotlight turned south of the Red River. Finally, on January 5, the Young brothers, tired of running and hiding, and not wanting to return to prison, decided to end it all. They shot each other to death in a small cottage on Walker Street in Houston, Texas, in order to avoid capture.

"We are dead; come on get us," Houston police officers heard one of the brothers yell above the din of gunfire and through the tear-gas fumes. Seconds later, there were more shots from within the cottage. Later that day, the Springfield police announced that they now believed the Young brothers had acted alone in the massacre and were the only two at the farmhouse the afternoon of the raid and shootout.

"I am very positive that only the two were at the farmhouse," said Springfield Chief of Police Ed Waddle.

Fifty-one years after the massacre, the Young boys' sister, Vinita, told newspaper reporters that Choc Floyd had visited the family on two different occasions after her brothers were hunted down and died in Houston. She and her mother had always contended that Harry and Jennings had no help with their slaughter of the lawmen.

"He [Choc Floyd] came by to see us, and stayed a few minutes," Vinita told the reporter. "He said he wanted to know what happened. He probably just read about it and wanted to see the place."

Although he was clear of any involvement in the slayings of the Springfield law officers, the news stories that contained official denials of Floyd as a participant were not nearly as prominent as earlier stories. They contributed to his celebrity, which was fast becoming mythical.

In another seventeen months, Charley Floyd would be named in yet another massacre of lawmen. By 1933, federal agents of the Bureau of Investigation would be involved. J. Edgar Hoover, the diligent and ambitious bureau director, had already become Depression-era bank bandits' nemesis. He would not rest until Pretty Boy Floyd was hunted down.

The Young Brothers' Massacre was a portent of things to come.

26

THE PHANTOM TERROR

B Y EARLY 1932, the "cruelest year of all," the legend of Pretty Boy Floyd was being chiseled into stone. The notoriety made Charley as happy as a dog with two tails, but there was also a definite down side to being the center of atten-
tion. He remembered that out in the barnyard, the rooster that crowed the loudest and shook his tail feathers one too many times often ended up in the fox's mouth or in the stew pot. The best way for a bandit to ensure that he died in bed of old age was to keep a low profile and stay in the shadows.

There were no shadows that year for Charley, however, save for the dust storms that gathered in the prairies and stirred the bowels of hell. As far as the tabloids were concerned, Choc Floyd was the cock of the walk. It was his twenty-eighth year, and he was fair game for every cop and bounty hunter; even his false sightings made juicy fodder for any aggressive reporter interested in page-one by-lines on top of the fold.

Choc and Birdwell did not disappoint their doting public, nor did they eschew controversy.

On January 14, only eight days after Charley's name was at least partially cleared in connection with the Young Brothers' Massacre, the pair of bandits were back in the headlines. This time they were accused of robbing banks in two small Okfuskee County towns in east central Oklahoma in less than twenty minutes during a single afternoon. Again the news stories that resulted were greatly exaggerated.

Pretty Boy Floyd was identified from photographs as one of the trio who had looted $2,600 from the First State Bank in Castle, a small community located only seven miles northwest of Okemah, the county seat where folksinger Woody Guthrie was born in July of 1912.

Witnesses to the Castle robbery said that after Floyd and his companions took the money, they forced two bank officials and two customers to accompany them on the running boards of their getaway car to the outskirts of town.

While local law officers were trailing the Castle robbers, ten miles away in

Paden—a town named for old-time U.S. Marshal Paden Tolbert—three unmasked men looted the First National Bank of $2,500. Two of the bandits forced five bank customers and a lone employee to lie on the floor while the third outlaw grabbed up the money. The customers were then locked in a vault and the robbers made an assistant cashier jump up on the running board of their auto as they raced out of town. The banker was released unharmed at Boley, an all-black town six miles away, and he hitchhiked back to the scene of the crime. First reports pinned the Paden crime as well as the Castle robbery on the Floyd bunch.

By that evening, the Oklahoma Bankers' Association made formal requests to the governor's office to call out the National Guard. The bankers were anxious for the Guardsmen "to hunt down Charles (Pretty Boy) Floyd, steel-jacketed desperado believed to have *directed* two bank robberies in Okfuskee County today," according to an initial wire service story filed from Castle. "Although the banks at Paden and Castle, ten miles apart, were robbed by different gangs, officers believed Floyd, identified as one of the machine-gun robbers here [Castle], was the power behind both raids. . . ."

Eugene Gum, the secretary of the state bankers' association, issued a public statement that insisted that the state call out the troops and "offer a big reward for the capture of Floyd and his pals, who enforce their edicts with machine guns." Gum attributed "a dozen bank raids" to Floyd, whose activities he said supposedly included "so-called 'Robin Hood' acts of charity. In return, the persons to whom he gives financial aid, shield him from the law.

"As long as he stays down there [eastern Oklahoma] and is protected as he is now, he will continue to attack banks," said Gum, who pointed out that the Oklahoma bank holdup insurance rate had doubled effective January 11 and that the mark of fifty-one banks robbed in the state the previous year was likely to be broken in the new year. Towns of fewer than five thousand people, where most of the robberies occurred, would now be paying ten dollars per every thousand dollars in insurance, while rates would be lower for banks in the larger cities.

Choc did not mind being credited with the Castle holdup, but he denied any involvement with the robbery at Paden. He was concerned that now folks were even saying if he did not participate in a bank stickup, that he had "directed" or orchestrated the crime. This helped conjure up more erroneous perceptions of an organized gang or a criminal network that was masterminded in Capone-style by Charley Floyd. Even at the criminal level, rural folks wished to distance themselves from the vulgarity and wanton cruelty of the city.

"That day the banks at Castle and Paden were robbed was really something," remembered Choc's nephew Glendon Floyd. "Down at Earlsboro we heard about the two banks getting hit at the same time, and how they blamed both of the robberies on Charley. The fact was, he and Birdwell didn't know a thing about the Paden robbery. They held up the bank at Castle and were going like hell west down the highway when they passed the guys who had robbed the Paden bank; they were headed east with a bunch of law on their trail. It was all just a coincidence.

The Floyd family began to accept the fact that Choc was now catching much of the blame for the continued rash of bank robberies during the thirties. "People would be claiming that their bank was robbed and that Pretty Boy and his friends did it, and he'd be sitting in our house," said Bayne Floyd, laughing. "We always felt a lot of those banks were never even robbed, or if they were robbed, that the facts and the amount taken was often blown out of proportion."

Many people always believed otherwise, but later reports from Okfuskee County officials actually helped clear Choc and Birdwell of any direct involvement in the Paden robbery. "Although three men were involved in each robbery," the officials told reporters, "their descriptions differed, the method of robbery was different, and the automobiles used were not of the same make." County officials also met with agents from the Oklahoma Bureau of Criminal Identification and Investigation. Created in 1925 to help lawmen combat the increasingly mobile criminals, the agency was commonly known as the State Crime Bureau. State agents sent to the crime scenes were told that witnesses at the Paden stickup had tentatively identified two of the robbers as residents of Seminole and Bristow.

"It is nothing unusual," said O. P. Ray, assistant superintendent of the state bureau. "They have been robbing in Oklahoma at the rate of two or three banks a week. Our information is that the two robberies were by two gangs."

On January 15, a man identified as Troy Self, of Carnegie, Oklahoma, was arrested at the settlement of Boley. He was armed with a pistol and shotgun and was taken to Paden, where he was held as a prime suspect in the First National robbery, but bank officials failed to identify him as one of the robbers. Lawmen across the state were also on the lookout for Luther Goodall, thirty-six, and Arthur Fraley, thirty-three, convicted bank robbers who had escaped the Johnson County jail at Tishomingo the day of the robberies. Goodall and Fraley literally smashed their way out of jail by knocking bricks from around one of the jail windows with a sash weight while the guards were at lunch. The fugitives had just been sentenced to two-year prison terms after pleading guilty to the September 4 robbery of the First State Bank in Mill Creek. They were also implicated in other bank robberies.

Meanwhile, there were reported sightings of Pretty Boy Floyd coming from every direction. The son of a McAlester police officer told authorities that he had met Pretty Boy Floyd face-to-face at a tourist camp near McAlester the night of the twin bank robberies. The young man said Floyd had searched him for weapons and told him to keep quiet. He said he knew it was Floyd from seeing his pictures in newspapers, and that the outlaw was heavily armed and wore at least two or three revolvers. Spiro Barker, a cafe owner in Henryetta, Oklahoma, his cook, H. K. Noel, and two waitresses swore that Pretty Boy had dined at their establishment the night of January 15. They said they also recognized him from his photographs in the newspapers. Tulsa County deputies received information that Choc may also have been spotted in Bixby, the closest town to the farm where the Hardgraves resided as tenants. A news story about the Bixby sighting called Charley "the will-o'-the-wisp Oklahoma bank robber and gunman."

It was apparent that the Oklahoma Bankers' Association was not going to rest or stop hollering for relief until the elusive Choc Floyd was taken out of circulation. The bankers turned up the pressure several notches with the governor's office in Oklahoma City.

Since 1931, Oklahoma had been governed by a colorful and crusty character named William Henry Murray. Born in Texas in 1869, Murray taught at a country school, practiced law, flirted with journalism, and was an unsuccessful candidate for the state senate before he moved north to Indian Territory in 1898, and settled at Tishomingo, then the capital of the Chickasaw Nation. The hard-core Democrat married into the tribe and became a citizen of the Chickasaw Nation and tribal lawyer, an expert at constitutional law, and active in politics. His experiments with growing alfalfa also earned him a nickname he kept for the rest of his life, Alfalfa Bill.

Elected a representative to the first legislature in Oklahoma after statehood, "Alfalfa Bill" Murray served as speaker of the house, was defeated in a bid for governor in 1910, and went on to win a seat in the U.S. House of Representatives. Following his defeat for reelection to Congress and another loss in a second try for a gubernatorial nomination in 1918, Murray grew weary and bitter. He disappeared from the political scene for many years and traveled extensively, especially in South America, where from 1924 until 1929, he attempted to create a utopian agrarian colony of Oklahomans in Bolivia. The experiment was risky and demanding and doomed to fail. Murray finally gave up and returned home.

Despite his five-year absence, the people of Oklahoma had not forgotten Alfalfa Bill. The sixty-year-old maverick, also called the Sage of Tishomingo, tested the political waters and found them to his liking. In January 1930, he announced his candidacy for governor and hit the campaign trail. The third try was a charm. In the Democratic primary, he faced off against Frank Buttram, an Oklahoma City oil millionaire who shelled out big bucks for radio and newspaper advertising and billboards. Murray, careful to avoid becoming the pawn of special interests, circulated throughout the state, eating lunches of crackers and cheese and stumping as a champion on behalf of what he called "the little people"—the poor and struggling tenant farmers and sharecroppers, and the growing numbers of unemployed city workers.

Murray, a gifted orator and showman, appeared to many observers to be cut from the same cloth as Louisiana's Huey P. Long, the colorful political power broker who also had an unusual sense of destiny.

Murray did well in the primary, won a runoff election with Buttram, and survived E. K. Gaylord's lambasting front-page editorials in the *Daily Oklahoman* and the *Oklahoma City Times*. Gaylord also published a series of articles criticizing Murray as a slovenly bumpkin who never bathed, lived in a crude house with a privy, sopped his biscuits in syrup, and wore long underwear beneath his rumpled suits. What Gaylord had not considered was that many of the voters in the state, where farm values had greatly declined and many farms had been sold because of foreclosures or bankruptcy, identified with the down-home candidate.

In the general election, Alfalfa Bill was swept to a record majority victory and the governor's mansion. Thousands had braved the brisk January temperatures in 1931 to watch ninety-one-year-old Uriah Dow Murray, acting in his role as notary public, swear in his son as governor. In his inaugural address, the unvarnished Murray vowed that "this is one time when Oklahoma Indians, niggers and po' white folks are going to have a fair-minded governor."

Aware that the Great Depression was much more than a passing economic downturn, Murray was greeted with a range of endemic problems, including mind-boggling unemployment, a multimillion-dollar deficit in the state treasury, and widespread mortgage foreclosures and bank failures. Like a sharecropper facing boll weevils and dust devils, Murray—the embodiment of a frontier politician with a touch of unwashed Will Rogers—enacted emergency relief measures, including the appropriation of hundreds of thousands of dollars to provide staples and free seed for vegetable gardens the state created on half-acre plots between the executive mansion and the state capitol building. Anticipating the Hundred Days Reforms and the New Deal legislation of Franklin Roosevelt by more than a year, Murray collected money for hungry citizens from state employees, business executives, and even donated six thousand dollars from his own salary for the cause. As the Depression intensified, Murray, a passionate proponent of states' rights, even joined with other governors in calling for a national relief program backed by federal funds—as long as he controlled the purse strings. Little by little, Murray hacked away at his long list of challenges.

In only the first two weeks of 1932, he had emerged as a national political figure and, with the exception of New York's Franklin D. Roosevelt, had become the country's best-known governor. Because of his populist methods, Murray was under bombardment from Oklahoma's frustrated bankers. Alfalfa Bill had yet another thorn in his toe, a pest as annoying and elusive as a chigger in the Osage brush.

The evening of January 14, just hours after the bank robberies at Paden and Castle and following the formal request for a manhunt from the Oklahoma Bankers' Association, the governor was collared by reporters as he journeyed out of the state. They caught up with Murray in Kansas City, where he spent a few hours while en route to Marshalltown, Iowa, to address a Democratic rally.

"Who are these Floyds, anyhow?" Murray blustered when reporters told him about the bankers' plea for help. He did not appear overly upset over the situation, and he expressed his confidence in Lieutenant Governor Robert Burns, the acting chief executive of the state while Murray was gone.

Back in Oklahoma, Burns stopped short of calling out the National Guard, but he did pledge "money and the arms of wartime" when he and Adj. Gen. Charles Barrett hosted in Oklahoma City "a council of war in banditry," attended by twenty Oklahoma sheriffs and peace officers. As the state officials and lawmen convened, and sheriff's officers from a dozen counties joined with state and private investigators in an attempt to capture Charley Floyd, more Pretty Boy sightings occurred. Oklahoma City police alone answered eighteen to twenty telephone calls from persons who thought they had seen Floyd. One of them was Myrtle Dunn, a State Crime Bureau secretary, who told agents that on the evening of January 16 she had seen a sedan with a license tag that had been issued to Floyd two years earlier. She said there were five men inside the mysterious automobile. C. M. Reber, a bureau operative, speculated that Charley might have painted the tag to make it appear a later model, since no similar number had been issued. That same evening, another Oklahoma City man also came forward and told officers that he had spotted Pretty Boy Floyd driving another vehicle and that there was a machine gun inside the car.

"This is a desperate case," said Lieutenant Governor Burns. "Floyd has terrorized the entire east central section of Oklahoma with his outlawry. Already six killings and ten bank robberies have been charged to his gang. He must be stopped."

Burns and Barrett promised to make machine guns, automatic rifles, and ammunition available to civilian officers, and said they would put up substantial rewards in hopes of bringing down the will-o'-the-wisp bandit. No one really questioned Burns about just how he had arrived at the "six killings" he had mentioned, unless he was counting the Ohio shootouts, the Ash brothers, the Kansas City agent and bystander, and Jim Mills, the Akins man who had killed Walter Floyd and then disappeared.

"Rewards will be offered by the state and the Oklahoma Bankers' Association," said the adjutant general. "The national guard will not be called out but the equipment will be at the disposal of the officers. If Floyd is found and resists, the guard will aid the local officers in his capture if necessary."

In one of the published accounts of the "council of war" meeting, Charley was described as an "elusive machine-gun raider, who has sworn he will never be taken alive, and was characterized as a bandit who imagines himself an Al Capone who has never come to a real test of the law." The conferees vowed that they would keep on his trail until "he is killed or captured."

An editorial published January 16 in the *Tulsa World* asked the intelligent question in the headline, CAN SOLDIERS CATCH BANDITS? It was pointed out in the editorial that "bank robbers travel in pairs, or in small groups, and they move fast, without known schedules or any advertising. If a sheriff or marshal or posse in the vicinity cannot get into action immediately, they have rather poor chances of catching the robbers. The case would be the same with soldiers. It is obviously impossible that soldiers shall constantly guard every bank; that would simply transfer bandit activities to property in other places."

Regardless of the debate over the use of armed soldiers, the use of a reward was generally thought to be the best way to stop Charley Floyd. The Oklahoma Bankers' Association matched the state's thousand-dollar reward, and by the evening of January 17, the price on Pretty Boy's head in Oklahoma alone was two thousand dollars. Rewards of one thousand dollars for Charley in connection with the slaying of the police officer in Bowling Green, Ohio, and a one-thousand-dollar reward from the state of Ohio because of Floyd's escape from the train while on his way to the state penitentiary also remained valid, bringing the total to four thousand dollars.

While huge posses of heavily armed deputies and state agents hunted Charley Floyd, he defied them by driving into the town of Wewoka. Witnesses said he had stopped at a local hotel, rounded up the proprietor and the employees, and had them join him as he sat at a table and drank an entire bottle of whiskey. They claimed he had announced that he was Pretty Boy Floyd, and had shown them his bulletproof vest before driving away.

Then on January 20, Lieutenant Governor Burns, still acting as governor, received a personal threat, allegedly from the state's most sought-after bandit. The letter, written by hand in blue ink and unsigned, was postmarked at Altus, Oklahoma, at 3:00 P.M. Tuesday, January 19. The message was brief and to the point.

> Robert Burns, Acting Governor—
> You will either withdraw that $1,000 at once or
> suffer the consequences; no kidding.
> I have robbed no one but the monied men.

Some criminal experts said it was certain that Pretty Boy was the author of the terse warning. Others doubted the authenticity of the threatening note. A couple of days later, Charley allegedly punctuated his threat against Burns with one more daring act: He supposedly visited another bank. The claim was that he was responsible for the robbery of the bank in Dover, a small farm town located near where the Rock Island Railroad crossed the Cimarron River in Kingfisher County. The main force of law officers after Charley had centered their search many miles to the east of Dover in Muskogee County, where there were also stories of Floyd appearances.

PRETTY BOY LOOTS STATE BANK, blared the headline in the *Muskogee Phoenix* on January 22. Immediately, the deputies and others in the posse who had used Muskogee for a headquarters left for Dover.

"The determined search for Charles Arthur 'Pretty Boy' Floyd centered tonight near Dover, where Oklahoma's outlaw is believed to have defied the law once more by robbing a country bank there," said the *Phoenix* story. "Floyd was identified partially by the bank's cashier, A. L. Lash, as bandits entered the bank, a state institution, locked four customers in the vault, kidnapped Lash and escaped with about $700 in currency."

Lash was released unharmed a mile and a half north of Dover. "The man driving the car resembled Floyd," Lash said. "I've seen the outlaw's picture enough to know him by sight."

Although the constant stream of rumors helped keep the authorities running in circles, Charley did not welcome all the attention. He was not totally ego-driven. In a strange way, he only wanted to rob banks quietly, and with as little fuss as possible, and then go home to Ruby and his boy or spend an occasional lost weekend with his girlfriend.

On Saturday, January 23, the day that New York Governor Franklin Roosevelt made clear his intention to enter the presidential race, C. M. Reber, of the State Crime Bureau, appeared in Oklahoma City with what he considered to be valid information picked up on the criminal grapevine: Charles Floyd was willing to surrender to Oklahoma officers. According to Reber, there was one stipulation: Floyd did not want to be turned over to the authorities in Ohio and face the murder charge in the death of Officer Castner at Bowling Green. Floyd wanted to stay in Oklahoma. Governor Murray's office refused to bargain with the bandit and the offer was rejected. The search continued. Much of the time Charley was sitting in his new home.

During the first week of January 1932, about the time of the massacre near Springfield and while state agents and deputy sheriffs turned the countryside upside down looking for Pretty Boy and his confederates, Charley had calmly moved his wife and son out of Fort Smith and relocated in Tulsa. He rented a frame bungalow with a front porch supported by two stone columns, a double-pitched roof, and a garage at 513 East Young Street in a pleasant residential neighborhood a few miles north of downtown.

The house was just a short distance off North Frankfort Avenue, and only three and a half blocks east of Cincinnati Avenue, one of the major streets that connected the neighborhood with the business district. The surrounding brick and frame homes were well kept, and the streets were lined with sycamores, elms, and catalpa trees. Most of the yards had rose trellises and beds of iris, buttercups, and sweet peas. There was a small neighborhood market a half block away and it was fewer than six blocks to the John Burroughs Elementary School, a one-story brick building located on a spacious plot of ground between North Cincinnati and North Boston avenues. Nearby loomed Reservoir Hill, a more exclusive residential area.

Charley rented the house on East Young using his Jack Hamilton alias. Ironically, the last tenant, who had moved out just two days prior to the arrival of the Floyds from Arkansas, was a Tulsa police captain. After they unpacked, Ruby enrolled Dempsey, by then seven years old, at John Burroughs under the name of Jackie Hamilton. He quickly made new friends at the public school and was careful never to use his true name. During recess, he played on the sprawling grounds where in early spring the carpets of white clover blossoms could be tied into necklaces that brightened the heart of any schoolboy's mother.

Ruby frequented the small grocery story operated by Mr. and Mrs. J. J. Smith at 502 East Young Street. She also used the Hamilton name, and other people who lived in the neighborhood during that time remembered her as being attractive and cordial but not very talkative.

"She [Ruby Floyd] was a real nice woman who was very lovely-looking," said Mrs. Smith. "But like many Indian women, she didn't smile very much. The little boy was just as sweet as he could be. I never met Floyd myself, but he and my husband used to talk often when Floyd would drop by the store. My husband said Floyd seemed to be a pretty nice fellow. We actually didn't see too much of Floyd, though. It was usually his wife who came to the store. She told us her husband worked in the oil fields and only came home on weekends."

Often Ruby would stop by the grocery and borrow a little bit of money from the Smiths to get her through until payday, which actually meant when Choc robbed a bank. When her husband returned home, the money was promptly repaid.

"Mrs. Hamilton always paid her bills on time, even if she did pay in slightly corroded silver and hardly ever used paper money," said Mrs. Smith. "The silver looked like it had been buried for a long time. We thought maybe they'd found some old money that was buried. We had no idea where they got the money."

The family kept to themselves and did not bother any of their neighbors. Albert Hardgraves, one of Ruby's three stepbrothers, moved up from Bixby and stayed with the Hamiltons for a while, and also attended classes at John Burroughs.

Thomas Pinson, a native of Carthage, Missouri, whose family came to Tulsa in 1922 so his father could pursue the wholesale grocery business, recalled the Hardgraves youth and the younger boy, from their fleeting school days at John Burroughs.

"My family had lived at 538 East Xyler since 1931, not far from where the Floyds had their rented house," said Pinson when he was a seventy-two-year-old retired podiatrist living in Miami, Oklahoma. "The Hardgraves boy wasn't there with them very long, but when he was, he talked to some of us at school about his sister and brother-in-law, and we all knew that he was talking about Pretty Boy Floyd. It got to be common knowledge that Pretty Boy was around there, and had a good-lookin' wife.

"But nobody was afraid or lived in terror or anything like that. In fact, he helped my dad change a flat tire down on the corner of Garrison Avenue one day. We all knew that Pretty Boy wasn't such a bad guy. We always heard that he was good to most folks, and that he'd steal from the rich and give to the poor. He was no crazed killer."

While some folks, such as the people at the local grocery, believed Jack Hamilton worked in the oil business, others knew him as some sort of vendor. One of Charley's best tricks was to act as if he was a traveling salesman and pile lots of grips and bags in the back end of his car. Then he would drive about as he pleased, posing as a drummer.

When he was home for a few days in Tulsa, he would take his family downtown to window-shop. Once, while the Floyd's car was pausing at an intersection, Dempsey recalled that his father saw a policeman standing on the corner looking at him. Charley tipped his hat, smiled, and wished the officer well. The cop returned the courtesy and Charley was on his way. It was all a picture of civility.

During the brief period he lived in Tulsa, Charley often took the North Cincinnati bus downtown with Ruby and Dempsey to see a movie or go shopping. "Choc, Jackie, and I used to go to town every day," admitted Ruby Floyd a few years after her Tulsa experience. "We often rode on the bus. No officer ever recognized him."

On one occasion, the three of them went to one of the larger movie theaters to see *Dracula*, the horror film made in 1931 that starred Bela Lugosi as the bloodthirsty Transylvanian vampire. Because of the nature of the picture, the management advised parents not to bring small children to the theater. The cashier in the ticket booth took a look at the couple and the small boy and advised Charley that this particular film would be much too frightening for the youngster. If Dempsey had handled *Frankenstein*, Charley knew his boy could take *Dracula*. Ruby was uncomfortable. There was a line of customers behind them. She knew that after the long wait, Charley's temper could reach the boiling point. Charley glared at the cashier for a few seconds and then handed her the money to cover three tickets.

"Choc just shoved Jackie ahead of him and we went in," said Ruby.

Besides the movies, there was other entertainment. Each evening, the magic of radio brought into everyone's home Tom Mix, Ed Wynn, George Burns, Gracie Allen, and a Jack Benny who had not yet reached his perpetual thirty-ninth year. There was the distinctive voice of Walter Winchell, that nasty sultan of gossip and a good friend of J. Edgar Hoover. "Good evening, Mr. and Mrs. America and all the ships at sea."

Americans that year were more despondent than ever. There were almost seven hundred thousand people out of work in Chicago alone, and many more in New York. In Ohio—one of Charley's preferred hunting grounds—the situation was grim. In 1932, at least half of the work force was jobless in Cleveland, 60 percent were unemployed in Akron, and 80 percent of the workers in Toledo were idle.

In Tulsa, even with the promise of spring around the corner, the working class was desperate. By February of 1932, the central file of unemployed persons in the city contained almost twelve thousand names. It was growing daily. Charley was gainfully "employed" as the state's premier bandit, but, like many of his fellow Tulsans, he also found February to be a stormy time. If schoolboys had figured out that Pretty Boy Floyd had taken up residence in their neighborhood, then it was certain that the authorities would eventually make the same discovery.

Police officers began receiving the information that Floyd and Birdwell had been spotted in the city. Detectives and uniformed officers relentlessly traversed the streets in the districts where Pretty Boy had last been seen. Then during the second week of February 1932, right after Charley's twenty-eighth birthday, all hell broke loose.

Late on the evening of February 7, several city policemen, acting on one of many tips, honed in on a suspicious sedan parked on a side street near North Peoria Avenue and Apache Street. Inside the automobile were two men whom the officers believed to be Floyd and Birdwell. The unmarked police car approached the suspects' vehicle at an angle, with the headlamps shining directly inside. The cops leaped out with their guns drawn and called out for the two men to surrender. Their answer was the bark of a tommy gun.

A fusillade of bullets splintered the police car's windshield and tore apart the steering wheel. In the exchange of gunfire, Officer W. E. Wilson received a flesh wound from a submachine gun's bullet. The pair of men the officers were after sped away from the scene. More than fifty rounds were exchanged, and one of the policemen later said that he fired at least six shots point-blank at the man he believed was Floyd. The bullets had no apparent effect. The entire police department went on a Pretty Boy Floyd–George Birdwell alert.

A few minutes after midnight on February 10, another running gun battle transpired between Tulsa police and two men, again identified as Pretty Boy and Birdwell. As they made their way in an automobile near Fifth Street and Utica Avenue, the two men were spotted by Detectives Roy Moran and Homer Myers of the auto recovery squad. The detectives opened fire with a sawed-off shotgun. Much to the policemen's chagrin, they were unable to continue spraying buckshot at the suspects' car when they found out that the extra shells for their twelve-gauge shotgun were intended for a twenty-gauge weapon. Once more, the two suspects were able to make their escape.

An hour after the gun battle, the alleged offenders' car was found abandoned at Thirteenth Place and the Katy railroad tracks. Bullet holes in the car from previous shootouts had been filled with putty and painted. Officers found an extra license plate in the automobile with the same number as the plate on a car used by thieves who robbed the bank in Konawa, Oklahoma, down in the oil patch south of Seminole, three weeks earlier. Floyd and Birdwell were the chief suspects in that robbery.

According to one account, a tag attached to the car battery of the abandoned vehicle led investigators to a garage, and from there to the Floyd residence on East Young. Another version had Detectives R. B. "Blackie" Jones and Earl Gardner following two men on foot to the Floyd house after the officers saw the pair emerge from the Midland Valley right-of-way near Apache Street. The lawmen kept their distance and then reported back to headquarters. A plan of action for a raid was developed. An informant in the neighborhood also reported to the police that he believed Pretty Boy and a companion were living on East Young. According to police, the informant told them that "they [Floyd and Birdwell] have been going into and out of the house at all hours of the night and early morning. They always drove a block or so before they turned on their lights. They came in early Monday morning after the battle with police on North Peoria Avenue."

No matter which version was true, what is known is that about 5:00 A.M. on February 11 as many as twenty armed police officers led by Det. Sgt. Lon Elliot crept into the neighborhood and surrounded Charley's rented house. Fearful of Floyd and Birdwell's shooting prowess, the raiders were supposedly armed to the teeth with shotguns and rifles. They brought a plentiful supply of tear gas, as well as an armored transport truck.

Valuable time was lost, however. The one and only machine gun owned by the police department was carried in Sgt. George Stewart's scout cruiser. Stewart had only two clips, each holding twelve shells. That meant just two bursts of fire and the machine gun would be useless. More than an hour was spent hunting additional ammo at the police station. It was learned that the key for the department's locked arsenal was with Milton L. Lairmore, the captain of the department's pistol team. A squad car hurried to Lairmore's home. He was awakened, and he handed over the key. Then the squad car rushed back to the station, the ammunition was obtained, and the operation proceeded.

As the squad of armed detectives, trailed by the armored truck, came in sight of the house, Ruby and her young son went out the front door, walked down the street, and disappeared into the neighborhood. The officers spread out, with their guns aimed at the dark house. Muffled orders were given and a tear-gas bomb crashed through one of the windows. There was not a sound from inside. Lon Elliot, who had concentrated most of his forces at the front of the residence, was puzzled by the lack of reaction. A few minutes later, he understood why there was no response. Bill Woods, an operative for the American Bankers' Association, walked around to the street and informed

Elliot that Floyd and Birdwell had already made a calm and cool exit out the back door. Woods had spotted them as they escaped.

"Two men dressed in dark suits, wearing topcoats and gray hats, fled out the rear door just after the tear gas was fired into the house," Woods told reporters.

Later, it was revealed by a *Tulsa Tribune* composing-room foreman, who happened to live next door and witnessed the entire episode, that Floyd and Birdwell escaped by walking from the house between bed sheets hanging on a clothesline in the backyard. Both men were armed but managed to slip away without a shot being fired.

The headline in the February 12 *Tulsa World* was an embarrassment to the local police: OFFICERS FOILED BY "PRETTY BOY" IN GAS-BOMB RAID.

Tulsa and northeastern Oklahoma was the center of one of the most intensive man hunts since the days of the Terrill-Kimes gangs yesterday as city, county and state peace officers concentrated here to take the trail of Charles Arthur (Pretty Boy) Floyd, accused bank robber and murderer who has escaped capture after two running gun battles and a gas-bomb raid.

Still smarting from the easy escapes of Floyd and an accomplice, believed to have been George Birdwell, whose name has been linked with the Sequoyah County phantom in many of his daring escapades, Tulsa police officials last night had taken precautionary measures to prevent the recurrence of the "mistakes" on the part of officers which are believed to have contributed to Floyd's repeated escapes.

Thomas I. Munroe, fire and police commissioner, was mortified. February was turning out to be an unforgettable month for him. A federal grand jury had just indicted Munroe on allegations that he was part of a protection ring for seven black bootleggers. By April, when the alleged payoff contact, a former police detective named R. G. Kennedy, developed pneumonia and influenza while in jail and died, the case weakened. Eventually, a jury would exonerate Munroe. For now, however, the commissioner had the federal charges on his mind and there was still the worrisome Pretty Boy, a constant irritation to Munroe and his department.

The commissioner was reluctant to discuss the mistakes made by his detectives, but he publicly promised that an additional six machine guns would soon be purchased for the department. "That will not happen again," said Munroe. "The new gun we are ordering will use drums of fifty shells instead of clips of twelve. We are going to fight fire with fire and next time be prepared for any type machine gunner. We have the men on the force to operate the guns and they will be here within a few days."

The newspaper also spoke of the apprehension of Floyd's ex-wife and their young son. They had been stopped along with Clyde Chuculate, a thirty-two-year-old Floyd family friend, at the downtown bus station just a few hours after the botched raid. All three were arrested and taken to police headquarters for further questioning.

Chuculate, a member of one of eastern Oklahoma's most respected Cherokee families, was the brother of Perry Chuculate, the Sequoyah County deputy who had been shot and killed by George Kimes during a 1926 gun battle that took place on the road between Vian and Sallisaw. W. E. Wilson, the policeman who had been slightly wounded earlier in the week, interviewed Chuculate in a jail cell and tentatively identified him as one of the men in the car who had shot at him. Wilson said that the suspect would not take his eyes off the floor throughout the interrogation. Chuculate admitted he recognized Wilson, but said he could not remember where he had seen him. Wilson's memory was clearer.

"I am sure Chuculate was in the car," said Wilson. "In my mind, there is no doubt about him."

At first, Ruby remained tight-lipped and even refused to tell officers her true name. "My name is Hamilton," she told her interrogators. "Ruby Hamilton. I came here from Oklahoma City January 5 and rented the house on Young. My husband joined me three days later and remained here about two weeks. I have not seen him since. If I was married to Floyd, do you think for a minute I would admit it? Will you please get me the papers? All of them—Tulsa, Oklahoma City, Kansas City, and St. Louis papers. I want to see if they are filled with a bunch of lies."

During their search of the Floyd house, detectives found many newspaper clippings from Seminole, Shawnee, Oklahoma City, Holdenville, and Muskogee that detailed the crimes of Pretty Boy Floyd. There were also recent Tulsa newspaper stories that discussed the two gun battles with police on the city streets. When the officers showed Jackie an enlarged picture of Pretty Boy that had been used to illustrate a story in a detective magazine, the little boy's face brightened and he forgot to stick to his well-drilled story.

"That's my daddy. That's Daddy's picture," shrieked Dempsey as he stopped playing around the matron's quarters of the jail and ran to look at the magazine cover.

The boy's words were important documentation for investigators. Dempsey's identification was the first conclusive evidence to prove it was really Floyd who had eluded the police three times in less than a week.

"I go to school," said Dempsey, who was described by officers as "smart as a whip" and sweet-natured. "I don't know what Daddy does. He always reads the newspapers when he comes home with George Birdwell. He always has plenty of money and we have lots to eat and a radio. I'm going to be an engineer or a doctor when I grow up. Daddy wants me to go to school. That's why we moved to Tulsa."

After Dempsey opened up, Ruby finally admitted her real identity but gave very little additional information. "She denied that there had been another man there," said Chief of Detectives Jack Bonham, "and declared that Birdwell was always with him [Floyd] and that he was the only man he could trust."

Ruby refused to discuss her current marital status with Floyd. She denied that her father lived in Bixby, and would not give officers her maiden name. "It's no concern of yours or the newspapers," she shouted when asked whether she knew Charley Floyd was a robber. "Go away! Take that photographer out of here and don't bother me."

Later she calmed down and finally allowed W. H. Morgan, superintendent of the Bureau of Identification, to take her and Dempsey's photograph. A newspaper photographer managed to grab a couple of quick shots, as well. Ruby and her son spent the night in jail as extra officers assigned to guard all the entrances stayed on alert for Pretty Boy in case he tried to come to the rescue.

On Saturday afternoon, February 13, after being held for more than thirty-six hours, Ruby and Dempsey were released from police custody. A squad car drove them to their residence. The officers helped Ruby set her home in order and pick up the family belongings that had been turned topsy-turvy by investigators looking for clues that might lead them to Floyd. The police guards who staked out the East Young residence were removed. Back at the jail, Clyde Chuculate, who had also remained under lock and key for a day and a half, was cleared. He was also set free and no charges were filed.

Police were still on the lookout for Pretty Boy. That same day, a terrified black laborer named Tom Montgomery burst into the Tulsa County sheriff's office to report that he had been approached by some men, including one who he believed was Pretty Boy, one mile west of the Kennedy golf course on Edison Street. Trembling with fear, Montgomery related his story in gasps to the anxious deputies. He told them that he had been walking along Edison when a light-blue Buick sedan pulled up alongside of him.

"They told me they had a flat tire and wanted me to change it," said Montgomery. " 'No sir,' I said, 'I'm too busy and am going places.' Then two fellows open the back door and shoved awful long cannons at me. 'Nigger,' they told me, 'you change that tire fast.'

"I told them I wasn't going anyplace in particular and that I certainly would be glad to change the tire. I changed it in no time. Then one of them gives me a cigar and off they drive."

Montgomery had been too frightened to notice the license number of the automobile, but he did see at least three "choppers," or submachine guns, in the backseat. From the stack of criminal photos the deputies showed him, Montgomery selected those of Floyd and Fred Barker, a fugitive killer of a Missouri sheriff and one of four brothers raised as criminals by the mean-spirited Arizona Donnie Clark Barker, a Missouri native who ruled her lawless clan with an iron hand and came to be known as the notorious Ma Barker. A second tip also linked Floyd with Barker, but officers who went to Freddie Barker's West Tulsa home found nothing, and Pretty Boy's association with Barker was discredited.

Detectives also drove out Route 66 to Chelsea, Oklahoma, in neighboring Rogers County, after they obtained information that Floyd and two companions were there having their automobile serviced by a local mechanic. When they reached Chelsea and located the garage, however, they found that the three men had actually been tourists en route to St. Louis.

Officers were posted on the road leading in and out of Tulsa, especially on the highway leading to Sand Springs, where there were several reports that Pretty Boy Floyd had been seen driving through the countryside. In Tulsa, a youth identified as R. G. Nathan was arrested at an East First Street boardinghouse when officers got word that he was a suspicious character. A search of his room turned up a suitcase filled with newspaper clippings about Floyd and his exploits. After intense questioning, the officers concluded that the young man was just another one of Pretty Boy's growing number of fans.

Evidence connecting Pretty Boy with recent robberies and killings in Kansas City also surfaced. Ballistics experts said that a bullet that had killed O. P. Carpenter, a Kansas City detective, at dawn on February 8 during the attempted holdup of the Mercantile Trust Company in Kansas City had been fired from the same submachine gun that had wounded Officer Wilson during the February 10 gun battle on North Peoria in Tulsa.

Victor Maddi, of Kansas City, had been arrested in Houston on February 11 and held as one of the participants in the Mercantile Trust robbery. The ballistics report and the arrest of Maddi strengthened the belief of Kansas City investigators that the brush with Tulsa police had occurred during the suspect's flight from Missouri to Texas. Shortly after the Kansas City robbery, dispatches stated Floyd was part of the robbery team. However, despite the ballistics data and Floyd's alleged relationship with Italian criminals in Ohio, most Kansas City officers concluded that because of the timing discrepancies and because he had no history of ever operating with the Italian gangsters in Kansas City, Floyd was not involved. Nonetheless, there were press reports with headlines such as MISSOURI KILLING INVOLVES FLOYD.

On Sunday, February 14, hundreds of curious motorists celebrated Valentine's Day by slowly driving past the frame house on East Young. Since the address had appeared in the newspapers, everyone was interested in seeing the current home of Pretty Boy Floyd. Ruby and Dempsey retreated to her father's home for a few days to avoid the unwanted attention.

The press had a field day with young Dempsey. A mawkish front-page editorial appeared in the *Oklahoma City Times*. Illustrated with an inset photograph of Dempsey Floyd (". . . his head finely shaped, his eyes frank and finely set, his chin square and full of character"), the editorial, written by Walter M. Harrison, was addressed to Charles Floyd, and was to serve as an appeal to the phantom bandit and Oklahoma's public enemy number one. Harrison wrote:

Desperate killer though you may be, you remain a hero to one human being in this world. When Jackie, your 7-year-old son, identified your picture as 'my daddy,' he spoke with pride of possession. He knows your strong arms, your rough play. He tingles with happiness when he sees you coming and he wonders why you go away so unceremoniously and stay so long.

He is innocently proud of you who have treated him so badly. With the blind devotion of every lad for his pater, Jackie now tries to walk like you, to talk like you. He has his hair combed like you comb yours and he is dreaming of the day when he can be a big man like you and go out into the big world after breakfast in the morning and never come back until suppertime.

This picture of your kid gave me a jolt. He is the stuff from which the future is made. He may have the making of a great merchant prince. But you have just about pitched his chances away.

Today you flee from the law. At the end of the trail for you, there is probably a little run in the open for the shelter of a thicket, the bark of a posseman's rifle and a lifeless fall. A pitiful end for the father of a fine son.

Walter Biscup, a top writer for the *Tulsa World* and later the editorial page's editor, had a valentine all his own for the readers. In a big Sunday feature article filled with factual errors and innuendo, Biscup presented an entertaining profile of Charley Floyd beneath a banner headline: 'PRETTY BOY' LEARNED HIS DEADLY TRADE FROM EASTERN GANGSTER. Biscup did say that "in fairness to Floyd," he was not present when six law-enforcement officers were killed near Springfield, Missouri. "That was one opportunity he missed," said Biscup.

A physical description was included, down to the Red Cross nurse and rose tattooed on Charley's left forearm and the four gold caps in the upper front teeth. The article also contained the tally of Charley's crimes to date, and there were more quotes from Eugene Gum, secretary of the Oklahoma Bankers' Association.

"He is the sort of criminal who must be killed before he is captured," warned Gum.

The spokesman for the enraged bankers did not say why there was a need to "capture" a bandit once he was dead. Biscup's own words, especially the lead paragraphs, were the most melodramatic of all the indictments against Floyd, however.

Crime has selected him as the headman in it's [*sic*] carnival!

With a submachine gun nestling in the crook of his left arm and purring an uncontrollable message of sudden death to its objectives, he is acting his part with a macabre flair of seriousness.

Thus pictured in the minds of hundreds of detectives and policemen, Charles (Pretty Boy) Floyd, worth $5,000 dead or alive, struts arrogantly to the forefront of the southwest's present day battle with lawlessness.

From an insignificant start as a small-town bad boy Floyd has suddenly emerged into full bloom as a homicidal bandit who gives promise of making the legendary tales of the exploits of Al Spencer, Henry Starr and Matt Kimes sound like bed-time stories.

Biscup's closing sentences sounded much like the funereal warning contained in the Harrison editorial. "Here today, there tomorrow, 'Pretty Boy' continues on his rampage unmindful of the fact that every officer's gun is trained on him. He is half way down the road and cannot turn back."

Wherever he was that Sabbath morning—safe for the moment cleaning his weapons and planning future escapades at one of his invulnerable refuges— Charley Floyd probably would have agreed. Biscup was correct. Choc could not turn back. All possible exits from a life of crime appeared blocked. The rest of his ride down the road that lay ahead looked to be very bumpy. Only a miracle could save him. And, in 1932, all the miracles had shriveled up with the crops.

27

THE MIDNIGHT RAMBLER

O NCE AGAIN, MARCH lived up to its tempestuous reputation in 1932. An epidemic of violence exploded across the nation with a great ferocity, like a sleeping junkyard dog someone poked with a stick. It was as though a late-winter storm, bringing with it thunder and rage, would not stop.

The most preeminent crime of this period was the Lindbergh kidnapping. During the first evening of March, Charles Augustus, the twenty-month-old firstborn son of Charles and Anne Morrow Lindbergh, six months pregnant with another child, was kidnapped from his crib in a second-story nursery of the family's newly built stone residence near Hopewell, New Jersey. Police found a muddy trail that led from beneath the open window to the edge of the woods, where a makeshift ladder was discovered.

Ever since his solo flight across the Atlantic in 1927, Lindbergh had become a national treasure, an adored icon. In the intervening five years, he had come to epitomize the American dream. At a picnic in St. Louis, for example, a horde of society ladies had practically come to blows while fighting over a discarded corncob from his luncheon plate. It was downright inconceivable for the public to grasp that anyone was capable of stealing a child, much less his. The reaction was as though a baby who belonged to everyone in the nation had been taken away.

The search for America's collective infant was led by Col. H. Norman Schwarzkopf, the superintendent of the New Jersey State Police, a man whose yet-unborn son would become an American hero to another generation. Lindbergh himself also joined in the effort. The prayers of millions from around the globe were offered in hope that the kidnapper would be placated by the fifty-thousand-dollar ransom demanded in a note pinned to the windowsill. President Herbert Hoover promised that a veritable battalion of federal agents would be employed to help solve the case. From his Cook County jail cell, even Al Capone, who was thought to have no scruples, pledged his organization's assistance in the search. The Lindbergh kidnapping dominated the news like no other story for the next several months and stayed in people's minds for years to come.

Despite the country's absorption with the fate of the Lindbergh boy, bank robberies not only continued to occur in the late winter and early spring of 1932 but actually increased at an alarming rate. From Los Angeles to Iowa and Kentucky, a spree of high-wire bank robberies set depositors, already fearful for their savings, on edge and sent tremors through the besieged banking industry. No doubt, the state of the economy drove many of these robbers to despair.

As prominent as the stories about Charley Floyd was that of a bank robbery conducted in Oklahoma on the ninth of March. On that day, two men walked into the First National Bank of Mill Creek in south-central Oklahoma, while two others waited in an automobile. After filling a handbag with cash, the robbers ordered three employees to accompany them outside. Instead of going with the outlaws, the employees, confident that a newly installed alarm system they had triggered would work, dashed into the vault. One of the enraged robbers fired at the vault door, but the bullets only ricocheted off.

As the bandits ran from the bank, they were met by withering gunfire from a pack of local vigilantes. The two holdup men fell to the ground along with the satchel containing only eight hundred dollars. The getaway car sped off in a hail of bullets. One bandit was killed instantly. He was identified as Fred Hamner of Wewoka, a former deputy sheriff and at one time a successful farmer in Seminole County. For the vigilante killing of Hamner, the Oklahoma Bankers' Association would send the bank a reward check for five hundred dollars. The other desperado, who witnesses said appeared to be fatally wounded, was W. A. Smalley of Seminole, and the two accomplices who got away were said to be his brother, L. C. Smalley, and an ex-convict named Adam Richetti.

A few hours after the robbery, Smalley, suffering from bullet wounds, was captured without a fight in a pasture near Mill Creek. Later that day, authorities in Sulphur, Oklahoma, arrested Richetti. Less than a month after the holdup, he was sentenced on a bank-robbery conviction to the state pen at McAlester. No one knew it at the time, but by the end of the year, Richetti would be out of prison and soon after that he would be on the scout with Charles Arthur Floyd.

Two weeks after the robbery at Mill Creek, Charley and Birdwell returned to center stage. On March 23, they were picked as the most likely suspects to have blown into a bank at Meeker, Oklahoma, the hometown of onetime New York Giant pitching ace Carl Hubbell. Witnesses said the men who struck there fit the famous outlaws' descriptions. The doors to the money cages were locked, so the bandit thought to be Floyd scooped up five hundred dollars in loose currency and, while climbing over a partition, accidentally set off the burglar alarm. A posse quickly formed outside, but the bandits marched four employees out in front of them and made them ride the running boards of the car as they drove away.

"If it wasn't Pretty Boy and Birdwell, what difference did it make?" said an old-time Oklahoma deputy. "What was another robbery to their record? And, shoot, those poor ol' bankers would rather say they was robbed by Pretty Boy than just some run-of-the-mill outlaw who didn't have a famous name."

Within weeks, however, the well-known, romanticized legend of Pretty Boy Floyd would turn sour. Even among some of his beloved country folk, the Robin Hood of the prairies would come to be known as a notorious killer.

Less than three hours into April 9, 1932, Charley Floyd indisputably shot and killed forty-six-year-old Erv A. Kelley, a former Oklahoma sheriff and an operative for the State Crime Bureau. The shooting occurred when Kelley and a posse of law officers set a trap for Floyd on the farm where the Hardgraves family lived near Bixby. For at least a few days, the murder of Kelley replaced the unsolved Lindbergh kidnapping as the most talked-about crime in Oklahoma.

Kelley was a lawman's lawman and one of the most diligent peace officers ever to strap on a gun. "He is always on his toes," said John Wolsey, a former Muskogee police chief, "but above all he is always a perfect gentleman."

By 1932, he had retired from law enforcement and was operating a service station when he read about the sizable reward offered for the capture, dead or alive, of Pretty Boy Floyd. Kelley had a wife, three sons, and two daughters to care for, and since the income of a retired sheriff was hardly that large, the lure of thousands of dollars in bounty could not be ignored. Also, although he no longer wore a badge, Kelley found it was difficult to forsake the excitement and satisfaction he had found in law-enforcement work. He was considered one of the bravest peace officers in the state and, during his active years, Kelley was credited with the arrests of no fewer than fourteen bank robbers and six killers.

"He was one of the most fearless and successful law enforcers in Oklahoma," said V. S. Cannon, the former Muskogee County sheriff who had spent time tracking outlaws with Kelley. "He could follow a man across the country almost by instinct."

Kelley left his filling station and went to Oklahoma to offer his services to the State Crime Bureau. "Let me go after him," Kelley reportedly told them. "I want your cooperation, but not one cent of your salary." It was a gamble, but the amount of money on Floyd's head was plenty of enticement. Kelley's friends said that the state authorities were eager to have him join in the campaign to capture Pretty Boy and George Birdwell, as well as Fred Barker, one of Ma Barker's sons.

On Friday afternoon, April 8, Kelley and William Counts, one of his former deputies from Eufaula, staked out the Floyd residence at 513 East Young in Tulsa. They watched as Dempsey came home from John Burroughs School, and about four o'clock, the two men shadowed Ruby and her son as they drove off in a green Ford sedan. Ruby headed south out of town, crossed the Arkansas River, and went to the town of Bixby, a small town surrounded by rich river bottomlands ideal for truck farms and pecan groves.

Careful to keep some distance so Ruby would not see them, Kelley and Counts followed her to the farm of Cecil and Gladys Bennett, three miles west and about three-fourths of a mile south of Bixby. Ruby parked the sedan. She and the boy walked about fifteen feet through a corral gate, crossed a small gully and bald field, and walked to the nearby house of her family. Kelley had recently received information from a pair of local men that Charley Floyd and Ruby used the farm as a trysting place.

Once they had established Ruby's presence at the Bennett farm, the two ex–law officers left to bring in reinforcements. Kelley knew from the two local farmers that Pretty Boy had regularly visited his former in-laws in the past. The word was Floyd was due to make another appearance to enjoy an undisturbed weekend rendezvous with Ruby and his son.

Kelley contacted Crockett Long, a crack agent with the State Crime Bureau in Oklahoma City, to help with the stakeout. He also secured the services of A. B. Cooper, a private detective in Oklahoma City who represented the American Bankers' Association. To fill out the ranks, Kelley recruited his old friend Sheriff Jim Stormont from Okmulgee and Tulsa police detectives M. L. Lairmore and J. A. Smith. The two men who had provided the tips about Floyd visiting the Hardgraves home also agreed to help and were duly deputized. With Kelley designated as the leader of the surveillance team, the nine men met in Bixby at 8:30 P.M. and made plans for a sortie on the suspected Floyd hideout.

They drove out to the Bennett farm and concealed their automobiles. Kelley stationed the men so that every conceivable avenue of approach was covered to the Hardgraves small frame home tucked away behind the Bennett's farmhouse. Kelley, armed with a submachine gun equipped with a silencer and a .38 pistol, took what he thought was the most dangerous position—behind a chicken house approximately fifteen feet away from the corral gate. The two farmers hid nearby. Counts was about five hundred yards away, the closest post to the farmers and Kelley.

The long wait for Pretty Boy began. Midnight came and went uneventfully. There was no sign of any visitors except for some owls who cruised the skies in the wee hours of the morning. Kelley and the others knew there was still a chance the man they were after could appear.

About 2:15 A.M., the situation remained unchanged. The only sounds were the frogs peeping from the ditches. "Looks like a washout," whispered one of the posse. His voice carried through the darkness. Four of the men on the stakeout—Cooper, Stormont, Lairmore, and Smith—decided to take a break. They drove into Bixby to get coffee and sandwiches at an all-night cafe. About five minutes later, a green Chevrolet drove down the road leading to the

Bennett farm. The car turned off on the narrow lane and slowly made its way to the corral gate and stopped. At his hiding place, Counts glanced at his watch and saw it was 2:25 A.M.

Suddenly, the sound of gunfire rang out, shattering the eerie still of the night.

Later, Bill Counts and the pair of deputized farmers recalled hearing distinct pistol shots. Because of the silencer, the burst fired by Kelley's submachine gun had been muffled and made whistling noises. Counts jumped into his car and sped toward the Bennett house, but before he could travel one hundred yards, he saw the taillights of an automobile flash. The Chevy had turned around in the narrow dirt lane, dragging down part of a barbed-wire fence. The getaway car traveled at a high rate of speed into the darkness.

Counts found Kelley's lifeless form doubled over his submachine gun. He was lying on the ground near the gate in a large pool of blood. A semicircular design of rosettes, blasted in the ground by the bullets, silhouetted the body.

"When I got to the Chief, he was dead," said Counts. "He gave them a break, and Floyd got him. I'm sure of that. Kelley had been an officer for years, and had never shot a man. He wanted to catch them alive."

The two farmers who had been deputized to help trap Floyd came out from their hiding places. They told Counts and Crockett Long that they were unfamiliar with the weapons they had and were not able to get off a shot. Obviously shaken from the experience, the farmers also told law officers at the scene that there were two men in the car that stopped at the gate. They said that one of the suspects was Floyd and the other was likely to be Birdwell. Following the shootout, numerous law officers converged on Bixby. A dozen or more shiny black police cars barreled up and down the dirt roads. Spotlights flashed across the fields and danced in the weeds. All-points bulletins were dispatched to police departments and sheriffs' offices throughout the region.

"We trailed the man we think was Floyd two miles south and a mile east of the scene of the shooting, and from that point we have gotten nowhere," said Jack Bonham, the chief of Tulsa detectives. "We know the automobile the killer used turned south, but that is all."

Officers found only seven rounds were left in the twenty-one-bullet clip they removed from Kelley's submachine gun. A few miles from the crime scene, they also located a scarred area where a car, presumed to be the suspect's vehicle, had careened into a ditch but managed to stay upright and returned to the road. While most lawmen searched for the suspects, other officers questioned members of the Hardgraves and Bennett families.

"I was in bed asleep when I heard those shots," Cecil Bennett told the investigators. "I thought maybe there was something wrong outside and then again I thought maybe it wasn't any of my business to see what was wrong, so I just naturally stayed in bed and didn't bother to put my head out the door."

When the lawmen told Bennett that one of the prime suspects was Pretty Boy, the farmer acted surprised and said he did not know him.

"Pretty Boy Floyd? No, I never saw him in my life," replied Bennett without a trace of expression. "I wouldn't know him if he walked in now. Yes, a woman drove in here yesterday, and asked if she could park her car in here. I saw no reason why she couldn't. I don't know her.

"Over yonder? Sure that's Hardgraves's place. He works for me. A good farmer, too. You say he is Floyd's father-in-law? Well, that's something I never knew. Well, well!"

The *Tulsa World* sent its ace reporter, Walter Biscup, and staff photographer Lee Krupnick to the Bennett farm Saturday afternoon in hopes they would get a scoop and enough pictures to sell out the Sunday edition. The editors were not disappointed.

After spending a few minutes with Cecil Bennett and visiting with the law officers, who were still looking for evidence, Biscup and Krupnick trudged across the field to the Hardgraves house. What they found there made peppery copy, even though it was mostly a series of questions and smart-aleck answers. Their depiction of Ruby left the readers with a less-than-flattering portrait of Charley's former wife. She came across in the piece as a hard, uncaring person—a woman who was clearly beginning to have difficulty dealing with the pressure and whose tolerance for snooping city reporters was plainly growing quite thin. The article in the Sunday paper read as follows:

A shepherd dog barks his warning and leaps over the wire fence. A pat on the back and he wags his tail. "Come here, Bob," shouts Floyd's young son, Jackie. The dog meekly runs to him. The two begin to wrestle on the ground. Ruby Floyd, attractive despite house dress and uncombed hair, comes to the door.

"What do you want here?" she asks.

"Just a social visit," she hears.

"What happened here last night?" she asks.

"Your husband knocked off Irv Kelly [sic]."

"Well, that's fine," she smiles.

The dog barks. "Did anyone else get killed?" she asks.

"No, no; no one else," we reply.

"Too bad," she sighs.

"Did you know Kelly [sic] trailed Pretty Boy for three months before he caught up with him this morning?"

"Well, the so-and-so won't trail him any longer, will he?" she laughs.

Mrs. Floyd refused to pose for photographs but the photographer, ever careless of criticism, blithely continues with his snapshooting. She is asked where her husband is.

"How do I know where he is? If I did, I wouldn't tell you. I don't, though. I didn't come here to meet him. I was asleep all night. I never heard any shots. I saw people there this morning so was kinda curious about what happened.

"Sure, my home is Tulsa. I like it here and Jackie goes to school. I don't know how long I'm going to stay here. You might call it a weekend visit," said Mrs. Floyd.

"Your old man certainly is a faithful cuss to take a chance on being knocked off trying to see you."

"Is he?" she questions. "Who told you he tried to see me?"

"All right then, maybe I'm wrong."

"You're a newspaper reporter. Did you see that story they gave my husband in *Startling Detective Magazine*? That burned me up. They weren't even fair to him."

"What do you mean, fair to him?"

"They weren't honest about his life," she said.

"Well, maybe I could do better if you would arrange the interview with him."

"If you want to see him, go look for him," she offered.

"We're too busy looking for anyone—least of all your husband."

"What's it to you?"

"It's nothing to me. What do you intend for Jackie to be when he grows up?"

"That's some more of your business, isn't it?"

"Was it a case of love at first sight between you and Pretty Boy?"

"What do you think?"

"How does it feel to be a gunman's moll?"

"Are you leaving soon?"

Between threatening the photographer and evading to answer questions Floyd's wife said she was tired enough. She laughed a goodbye and entered the house.

In the meantime Floyd continues on the scout with the net tightening around him.

That afternoon, an autopsy performed at the Leonard Funeral Home in Bixby revealed that Kelley had been struck by five .45 caliber bullets, once in each knee, one below his right arm, and two rounds that entered his left side. Kelley's body was then returned to his home in Eufaula. Thousands paid their respects when a funeral was held on April 11 followed by burial at the cemetery in Checotah. The state's peace officers' association presented his widow with their sympathy and a check for fifty dollars, a far cry from the thousands of dollars in reward money Kelley would have received had he captured Charley Floyd.

"The state lost a real man when it lost Kelley," eulogized Muskogee Sheriff V. S. Cannon.

While posses, fueled by rumors and gallons of black coffee, checked out all leads, Charley and Birdwell moved from hideout to hideout. It was a difficult maneuver, since unbeknownst to the authorities at the time, Charley Floyd was badly wounded. Before falling dead, Erv Kelley had managed to strike the desperado with four rounds from the burst of submachine gunfire.

Less than seven months after the Bixby shootout, when Charley granted his famous interview to Muskogee writer Vivian Brown, the outlaw spoke about the skirmish and his close call with death.

Charley told the young woman that he and Birdwell had been prepared for trouble. They had had their guns ready when they drove out to Bixby in the early-morning hours of April 9 to see Ruby. He recalled that when they drove up to the gate, he saw Kelley step in front of the car lights. He heard him shout, "Stick 'em up!" The chances of Charley Floyd giving up were slim to none.

"Erv Kelley nearly got me," Charley told Brown. "There was only one thing to do. It was either him or me, so I let him have it. He had the same idea, I guess. We fired at the same time. I never saw Kelley until he was falling. I fired five shots . . . and four of his shots hit me, one hitting me on the right hip and luckily striking a gun. The handle made quite a sore place on my hip and the bullet bent the gun but it did not hit me."

A second shot nipped Charley's scrotum and entered his right leg between his knee and thigh. Another of the rounds also struck his right leg, just above the ankle, and the fourth bullet lodged in his left ankle.

Charley further explained to Brown that after Kelley had been shot and was crumpling to the ground, the former sheriff kept his finger squeezed on the trigger of the submachine gun. He sprayed more rounds into the earth around his feet. Birdwell leaped from the Chevrolet and picked up Charley. He carried his comrade to the car, and then raced away like a madman for the safety of the oil-patch country to the southwest. They paused at Earlsboro to get Bradley, who took them to Seminole. He knew a friendly doctor there who asked no questions. Charley's wounds were not life-threatening, but he was in tremendous pain and lost a fair amount of blood. The doctor sewed up his scrotum, cleaned and treated his wounds, and decided to leave the bullet in his ankle. He also gave him a healthy dose of painkiller and some fresh dressings.

With all the law officers and detectives descending upon Earlsboro in the wake of the Bixby shooting, however, Choc and Birdwell took their leave and moved to safer hiding places in Muskogee County and points east. They read the newspapers that spoke of the gun battle, their escape, and how a group of law officers heard the gunfire and rushed to the scene. The account about the posse amused Charley, and it became one of his favorite stories.

"Was there really a posse?" Charley would ask his friends with a look of mock bewilderment. "Where were they, and which way did they run when they heard the shots? We never saw one of them."

The Kelley killing was one of the few murders actually pinned on Charley Floyd. It was the lone homicide on his rap sheet that he ever publicly discussed, although he always maintained that Kelley had been foolish to attempt the ambush. Charley said it was a case of survival, and that he had no other choice but to shoot the former law officer. For the next several months, Charley and Birdwell tried to lie as low as possible, but that was tough to do. After all, these bandits were just like everyone else—they had groceries to buy and families to clothe. Choc also had some doctors' bills to pay.

Shortly before noon on April 21, just twelve days after the killing of Erv Kelley and only a day after detectives had received a tip that Pretty Boy had been in Houston, two daring robbers, identified by several witnesses as Floyd and Birdwell, stole eight hundred dollars from the First State Bank in Stonewall, Oklahoma, the Pontotoc County town named in honor of Stonewall Jackson.

The pair, armed with pistols and submachine guns, took as hostages Furman Gibson, a cashier, and Ed Salee, an assistant cashier, and used the frightened bank employees for a human shield to protect themselves from the crowd of heavily armed citizens who had gathered outside the bank. With a captive on each running board, the bandits' green sedan raced out of town. Once past the city limits, Gibson and Salee were released. About half a mile farther north on the highway leading to the larger town of Ada, the robbers stopped a motorcycle ridden by eighteen-year-old Estel Henson. They forced the young man to accompany them in their flight.

Deputies, state agents, and large civilian posses moved through the countryside and reacted to every sighting of Floyd and Birdwell. One report had them at Calvin, on the banks of the South Canadian River, east of Holdenville before they vanished into the wooded hills.

To aid in the hunt for Pretty Boy, the internationally famous aviator and round-the-world record flier Wiley Post offered his services. Post, a popular figure with his eyepatch, who would perish in a plane crash with Will Rogers in 1935, consented to lead what was called an "aerial posse" in hopes of spying Pretty Boy and Birdwell from the skies. Assisted by Lt. Robert Houston of the Oklahoma City police force, Post directed both of the airplanes that departed Oklahoma City and Pauls Valley and circled the hills where the bandits had last been seen. The other plane was piloted by Clint Johnson and carried several Oklahoma County deputies. As the two planes droned overhead, a huge posse on the ground was deployed toward the dark river bottoms. By nightfall, the trail was cold.

Henson, the young hostage, spent the night with Charley and Birdwell in a thicket where the bandits concealed their automobile with brush and tree limbs. He was released unharmed the next morning. He said they treated him "kindly" and were "jovial" during the thirteen hours he had remained their prisoner. Henson said at no time was he afraid of his captors, but he knew "they meant business." The young man also told investigators that one of the bandits told him, "I guess those guys will learn it's no use trying to catch us."

Floyd and his partner vanished without a further trace. With the heat on, Birdwell went off to his own hiding places, and Choc stayed with friends and relatives, such as the Jess Ring family in rural Muskogee County, or others in the Okmulgee area. Never one to be without the company of a lady for long, Charley also went to see Juanita (Beulah Baird) in Kansas City, and crept into Tulsa, usually at the witching hour, to be with Ruby and Dempsey. Bystanders said they saw Floyd doffing his hat to the curb-service girl at the White House Cafe at Admiral Boulevard and Lewis Avenue. The girl said she recognized him, and when she brought a tray with the two sandwiches and mug of coffee, she asked whether he was Pretty Boy Floyd.

"Well, sister," he answered with a sheepish smile, "I'm not so pretty but they call me Pretty Boy." The carhop said he was cordial and made no attempt to hide the several guns in the backseat. "He gave me a thirty-five-cent tip, too."

A little while later, Charley was also seen attending a dance with Ruby at Dustin, a rural town between the North and the South Canadian rivers. After the dance, Charley drove Ruby to the town of Henryetta so she could catch a bus to their home in Tulsa.

Charley's way of survival was to stay on the move. He counted on the clannishness of the country people to protect him from the law. He depended on strong family ties for comfort. Besides keeping tabs on his former wife and child, he shuttled back and forth between the oil-patch area around Earlsboro and the growing fields of Sequoyah County to see his kinfolk.

With the various marriages of Charley's six brothers and sisters, there were now enough nieces, nephews, and cousins to start a Floyd family posse. His two older sisters—Ruth Wofford and Ruby Spear—had a slew of kids between them, and down at Earlsboro, Bradley and Bessie Floyd added a fifth son to their family. Born February 20, 1932, his parents named him Charles Floyd, after his bandit uncle. Decades later, when the namesake nephew was a grown man running a successful oil-field equipment business, he was still proud of his name. He also still had tucked away the crocheted white knit suit that Choc had given him as a baby present.

Family tragedies served to bring the Floyds even closer together. Choc's sister Emma and her husband, Clarence Lessley, had lost their five-year-old son, Bernie, in 1931 when his appendix ruptured. They never forgot that Charley came to the hospital in Fort Smith in their time of grief and slipped them one hundred dollars to cover the doctor's bill. Despite the pain of their loss, the Lessleys still had their oldest son, Lawton, and daughters Dorthene and Charlene.

By 1932, even Choc's younger brother, E.W., and youngest sister, Mary, had started their own households. In 1930, when she was eighteen years old, Mary Delta married Perry Lee Lattimore, a local boy born at Miller Ridge. He was a superb athlete before becoming a farmer and bootlegger. During the early years of her marriage, Mary gave birth to a son, Perry Floyd Lattimore, and a daughter, Pat.

E.W., who always looked up to his older brothers, wed Beulah Wickett in 1932. One of six daughters from a pioneer Sequoyah County family, Beulah had played with Mary Floyd on the championship girls' basketball teams at Sallisaw High School in the late twenties. Like most young men in 1932, E.W. was happy to have any job he could get, be it laboring in the oil patch fixing cars, digging ditches, or working in a cafe. When he suggested to his older brother that he "go out on the scout" with him, Charley took him outside and gave him a sound whipping. There was no way Choc Floyd was going to allow his brother to take the outlaw trail. Years later, E.W. was the first to admit that the beating he got from his big brother was the best thing that had ever happened to him.

Although law officers realized Floyd was constantly in flight and stayed with a host of family and friends, most of his family denied ever seeing him.

"It's been quite a while since we've see him," Charley's sister Ruth told reporters in mid-April right after one of his visits.

Besides stopovers with his siblings and their broods, Charley also made risky midnight runs to Sallisaw to check on his widowed mother. There was even a popular tale that Charley sent the sheriff's office in Sallisaw a note saying, "I'm coming to see my mother. If you're smart, you won't try to stop me." But the story seems spurious. Most law officers in the Cookson Hills of eastern Oklahoma did not require or expect a written warning from Choc. His openhanded generosity won him a host of friends who considered him a modern version of Robin Hood. He was like a sports hero who had come home for a quick visit, to be idolized briefly. Those who disliked him dared not risk his rancor by tipping off the law when they saw him appear at his sister's home for a visit with his mother and other relatives.

"When Charley was a baby, he had pneumonia and nearly died," related Mamie Floyd to a Tulsa reporter after one of her son's visits. "If he had, I wouldn't have to lie awake at night wondering where he is and jumping up after dreaming that he had been shot to pieces.

"Certainly I'm worried. What mother wouldn't worry over her boy. The newspapers have been unfair to him. They've accused him of everything that's happened in the state. I never want him to get caught because he wouldn't get a fair break. I've got faith in him."

In the early spring of 1932, Mamie also spoke about Charley when a *Kansas City Times* reporter paid a call. "I have seen him, off and on," said Mamie as she folded and smoothed a piece of lace. "Every so often he must see his old mother, and he dares them all, and risks his life to come and see me.

"But he can't stay long. We have a little visit together, time for him to hug and kiss me, and time for me to cry over him, and then he has to go. I never know whether I will ever see him again."

Although he had to keep moving in order to remain free, Charley tried his best to live like a normal person whenever he could. That meant attending weddings, baptisms, and funerals.

In the spring of 1932 when George Birdwell's father passed away near Earlsboro, law officers expected his outlaw son to show up to bid farewell at the funeral parlor. When Birdwell arrived, it was not known whether the local authorities were *not* present at the undertaking establishment out of respect for the family or simply because they were afraid of confrontation. With red eyes, George finally pulled up in front of the funeral home, accompanied by Pretty Boy Floyd. The two men walked in the front door, and Birdwell told the undertaker's assistant his name. Charley still moved with some difficulty because of the recent wounds he had received at the Bixby shootout. The wound to his scrotum, however, had not prevented him from contracting a "social disease." Floyd kinfolk remembered he spent a good deal of time seeing a country doctor he trusted for treatment and relief.

While George viewed his father's body in an adjoining room, Choc stood guard near the entrance with a submachine gun cradled in his arms. Word quickly got around town about the illustrious visitors down at the mortuary, and soon a crowd of inquisitive townspeople was bunched around the front of the building. After he finished his prayers at his father's casket, a tearful Birdwell put on his western-style hat. He and Charley emerged from the funeral home. Choc gave a wave of the weapon and flashed a grin, and the crowd pulled back. He and Birdwell got into their car and drove out of town. Not a single shot had been fired.

Family connections in Earlsboro usually worked to Choc's advantage. Even women and children from the rough oil-field town showed no fear when they saw Charley Floyd on the street. One of those who came away with fond memories after a brush with Pretty Boy was Pauline Alfrey. She and her twin brother, Paul, better known as "Buck," had been born in Earlsboro in 1915. The children of Bud Alfrey, a postal-delivery worker, the twins had two uncles—Duke Strain and Harry Alfrey—who ran stores in town.

"We were just young teenagers trying to get through the Depression, and after school Buck and I would head for the old drugstore and each of us would get a nickel ice cream cone," recalled Pauline. "One afternoon we were sitting there with our cones and in walks Pretty Boy Floyd. Everybody was buzzing about him. He was so handsome! His clothes were neat and he wore gloves. He ordered himself a Coca-Cola and drank it down, and as he turned to leave, he gave us a wink. Well, we were ready to leave, too, and when we went to pay for our ice cream, we found out he had already taken care of it for us. Were we ever happy! We had enough money to get a slice of pie!"

On another occasion during 1932, Charley and Birdwell were led to believe that a man who was a town marshal and worked at a local lumberyard was actually one of the many private detectives out to snare the bandits in their own lair. When the man was driving to work, Choc and Birdwell appeared in their sedan. They stopped him, pulled him from his vehicle, and took him for a ride into the country. While he was getting beaten and kicked about, the man managed to whisper that he was the town marshal and not another bounty-hunting detective. Charley and Birdwell stopped their cuffing of the man at once. They apologized for their mistake, and took him back to town. Before the man struggled out of their car, Charley pressed a roll of bills into his hand.

"To pay the doctor," Choc told him.

Even if it meant an innocent party got a good licking he did not deserve, Choc and his lieutenant could take no chances. Like the many rumormongers and gossips who abounded, the bounty hunters and hotshot private dicks were multiplying like mice in a hay barn. All of them had a notion about how best to rid the earth of Pretty Boy Floyd and collect the reward money on his head.

In early May of 1932, the Oklahoma Attorney General's office received a letter written by Thomas E. Haines from Quebec. "Is there any truth about a young gentleman named Charles Arthur Floyd, a two-gun bandit, who already has to his credit 11 victims, and when he was cornered not long ago, those who were after him were afraid to shoot him down just because he had a steel vest on?" wrote Haines.

"Had I been there, he would have been in his grave long ago. If there is any substantial reward, dead or alive, I will do my best to come down to Tulsa to get him."

Closer to Charley's home territory, there were others who had all sorts of free recommendations for those interested in bagging Pretty Boy. S. F. Lindsay, a seventy-eight-year-old pioneer U.S. Marshal from Ardmore, who had spent half of his life tracking outlaws and had survived one hundred gun battles with the likes of the Daltons, had sage advice for the law officers who played hide-and-seek with Floyd.

"You wouldn't have caught an old-time officer lugging around a machine gun even if we had them then," said Lindsay. "Machine guns are dangerous right up against one, but move back twenty feet and the average officer can't hit the side of a barn with one."

As the month of May progressed, there were many reports that Pretty Boy Floyd was again on the prowl. Several more bankers claimed Floyd and Birdwell had robbed them, and each incident brought a predictable onslaught of news coverage. "The most intensive manhunt Oklahoma has seen since the days of Al Jennings and the Dalton Brothers is on in the hills for Charles ('Pretty Boy') Floyd, will-o'-the-wisp desperado, and his tall lieutenant, George Birdwell, wanted for murders, kidnappings, and bank robberies," reported the *St. Louis Post-Dispatch* that May.

"When Floyd visited friends at Earlsboro . . . the Chief of Police confiscated the outlaw's car and placed it in his garage. When the outlaw discovered it he forced a Negro to accompany him to the Chief's home, where, using the Negro as a shield, he forced the Chief to put the car on the street. Disarming the officer, Floyd emptied his pistol, handed it back and fled."

Law officers left no stone unturned. For instance, at a state banking convention that was held in Tulsa in early May, attended by hundreds of bankers from around Oklahoma and "distinguished guests," the Tulsa police received a tip that Charley Floyd might show up to cause trouble. As unlikely as that sounded, the lead was checked out. Detective M. L. Lairmore, one of the law officers who had been out at Bixby when Kelley was gunned down, went to the convention headquarters at the fashionable Mayo Hotel. Lairmore chatted with a young man who worked there as a bellboy.

"Call for Mr. Charley Floyd!" the bellboy yelled in his loud bass voice. "Call for Mr. Charley Floyd!"

A hundred persons, most of them conventioneers, milled around the lobby, but ironically none of them seemed to recognize the name of the bandit who had caused them no end of trouble.

"I can't find him, boss," the bellboy reported back to Lairmore. "Does he live in Oklahoma City?"

Lairmore smiled. "Well, he did live in Tulsa, but I don't know where he is stopping now."

While the bankers met behind closed hotel doors to brood about their aches and pains over tumblers of bootlegged whiskey, the seventy-two-day search conducted by more than one hundred thousand police officers and civilians for the stolen baby son of Charles Lindbergh came to a halt.

On May 12, the decomposed body of the Lindbergh infant was found lying facedown in a depression, partly covered by leaves and windblown debris, in the stubbly Sourland hills of New Jersey, less than five miles from the Lindbergh residence. An autopsy showed that fatal blows to the head had probably been inflicted shortly after the baby was kidnapped.

A crime like the Lindbergh infant's murder disgusted Charley, who told friends he could not sanction such a wanton act. Taking a bank teller or two for a brief joyride as temporary hostages on a getaway car's running board may have been technically kidnapping, according to Floyd's logic, but it was a long way off from stealing a baby in the middle of the night and beating his brains out. Kidnapping anyone for ransom, be the victim an adult or a child, was never part of Charley Floyd's criminal repertoire. That was just one of the reasons why in September 1933 it was doubtful, despite witnesses who claimed the opposite, that Floyd had any connection with the futile attempt to kidnap Frank Phillips or a member of his family at the oil tycoon's Osage ranch retreat named Woolaroc.

By the close of May 1932, as the mimosas broke into feathery blossoms, thousands of disgruntled veterans, including Bradley Floyd, formed the Bonus Army. They began their march to Washington, D.C., to demand payment of the bonuses promised to them by Congress for their service in the Great War. On June 7, thousands of veterans left their makeshift shanties near the nation's capitol at Anacostia Flats and paraded through Washington to get what they felt was owed them.

While the veterans continued their assault on government in Washington, Pretty Boy moved like quicksilver through the Oklahoma countryside, stopping at farmhouses to eat a plate of supper. He always left behind some crumpled money and a lasting impression that his hosts would long treasure and pass along as part of their family's folklore.

That June, Charley Floyd and George Birdwell met at a farmhouse near Stonewall. The clandestine meeting was at a farm owned by E. W. Echols, a farmer who knew both men and had worked with Birdwell in the Earlsboro oil fields. When word reached Pontotoc County Sheriff L. E. Franklin that the bandits were in his territory planning to rob the bank in Stonewall the following day, he formed a sizable posse and summoned the State Crime Bureau. O. P. Ray, of the state bureau, arrived with some of his best agents, including Crockett Long and C. M. Reber. A local man who knew the lay of the land around the Echols farm was enlisted and a plan of attack was mapped out.

That evening, the posse went to the farm one mile north of Stonewall. Echols was in a field with his team of horses. As soon as the law officers appeared on the prairie, the rest of the Echols family took shelter in a storm cellar, and Choc and Birdwell ran from the yard to a barn and took up positions in the loft.

Estel Henson, the young motorcyclist whom Choc and Birdwell had kept overnight after the Stonewall bank job in April, followed the posse to the Echols place. Other townspeople also drove out, and soon there were more spectators than officers at the scene, which had taken on all the elements of a carnival before a summer thunderstorm. Henson stood on a slightly elevated spot not far from the farmhouse and watched the proceedings. He waved to the bandits as they raced for cover, but he had to dive behind a large rock when Birdwell sprayed a burst of gunfire in his direction. Most of the officers found trees behind which to hide.

"Birdwell, carrying a machine gun, led the way, firing as he ran," said Henson. "Floyd followed with a revolver in each hand. Officers continued to blaze away at them, but the bullets apparently failed to reach their marks."

A furious gunfight continued for several minutes. Smoke and noise filled the air. Suddenly, an automobile backed out of the barn. Inside were Charley and George. Bullets shattered the rear glass and windshield, riddled the doors, slammed into the radiator, and blew out a tire as the car turned down a narrow lane, smashed through a gate, and headed north down the farm road. More than one hundred shots were fired but surprisingly not a person was wounded. Yet again, Pretty Boy and Birdwell had confounded the law and escaped untouched, disappearing in the countryside.

Employees at the First State Bank of Stonewall breathed sighs of relief. "They'd have had to borrow money to get out of town," said one of the bank officials. Aware that their establishment had been again marked for robbery, the employees had placed a sign in the front window just in case Pretty Boy showed up.

NOTICE TO BANK ROBBERS
THERE IS NOT ENOUGH CASH IN THIS BANK TO BE WORTH THE RISK OF ROBBING IT.

Following this escape, there were the normal number of Pretty Boy sightings from throughout the region. Floyd was seen camped in the Canadian River bottoms; in Earlsboro; at a filling station in Tulsa; at Leonard, a small community near Bixby; and at several other locations. Police officers in Tulsa checked out the Floyd residence on East Young and found that Ruby and her son had been gone ever since school was dismissed the week before.

Two days after the gun battle, E. W. Wood, principal of the Booker T. Washington High School in Tulsa, was driving with his wife and four children down Highway 64 near the Muskogee County town of Warner. The family was en route to Mississippi for a vacation when three men in a car drove up behind Wood's 1931 black and tan Buick sedan and signaled for him to pull over. Thinking the men were law officers, Woods did just that, only to find he was looking at Pretty Boy Floyd, easily recognizable because his photographs frequently appeared in the Tulsa newspapers.

After driving Woods and his family to an isolated area, the trio of bandits transferred a large cache of weapons, several wooden boxes of ammunition, and cases of machine-gun cartridges from their blue Nash sedan to Wood's automobile. They had already disposed of the bullet-scarred auto they had used to escape from the law at the Echols farm, but now they needed a "faster machine" to continue their flight. Floyd and his accomplices were described as "cheerful and courteous," and ultimately decided to allow the school principal to keep his one hundred dollars in traveler's checks. The outlaws wished the family well, and took their leave in the sleek Buick.

Police and sheriff's departments throughout Oklahoma and Arkansas were put on alert. At Fort Smith, officers were stationed at three downtown banks and guards were posted on the Garrison Avenue bridge leading from

Oklahoma. Some of them had rifles, and others manned mounted machine guns. The wait seemed interminable, but Pretty Boy never came over the bridge.

A week later, at Fort Scott, Kansas, there were eyewitnesses ready to swear that Pretty Boy Floyd had been one of the five armed men who had looted the Citizens National Bank of $32,000, then an unbelievably large amount of money. Officers from Kansas, Missouri, and Oklahoma joined in the investigation, and police watched the major highways in the tri-state area for the bandits. By evening, three of the culprits had been arrested near Nevada, Missouri. None of them was Charley, and his participation in the robbery was considered doubtful.

By the summer of 1932, the hysteria about Charley Floyd's doings reached a national level. While the Fort Scott bank heist took place, Pretty Boy was also supposed to have been in Kansas City. Eighteen policemen—carrying machine guns, revolvers, shotguns, high-powered rifles, and tear-gas guns—responded to a "solid lead" from one of their best street sources and searched a neighborhood where Floyd and Birdwell were reported to have rented a room. The law came up empty-handed.

Charley's continued success at escape and evasion had lawmen throughout the Midwest pulling out their hair. They were stymied whenever they got on Pretty Boy's trail. Most of the hot tips they received were exaggerated or just plain bogus. It was almost a laughing matter. Perhaps that is why in late June of 1932, when a farm boy from Watonga, in northwestern Oklahoma, wrote the State Crime Bureau asking for a chance to go after Floyd, Superintendent C. A. Burns made the youth's letter public.

> All that I ask is that I am furnished a car, two revolvers, a machine gun, a 30-30 rifle, ammunition and a steel jacket. . . . I have read every detective book and magazine and outlaw books that I could get ahold of. I know their ways and how they work.
>
> P.S. If by any chance you cannot furnish me with all of this artillery, just give me the car and the steel jacket. I might be able to manage for the others.

Burns did not take the boy up on his bold offer, but he may have been tempted. It was a summer without pity.

On July 17, while Franklin D. Roosevelt, nominated as the Democratic presidential candidate at the convention in Chicago earlier in the month, gave his first campaign speech, one of the top State Crime Bureau agents was gunned down in a drugstore out in the drowsy town of Madill, between the Washita and Red rivers in Oklahoma's Little Dixie. Crockett Long, the veteran law officer who had been involved in Pretty Boy's Bixby shootout and also the scrap between Floyd and officers at Stonewall, was shot four times by

Wiley Lynn, a former dry agent who had been acquitted in 1924 of killing Bill Tilghman, the U.S. Marshal who had ridden for "Hanging Judge" Parker. As he fell, mortally wounded, Long was able to pull his pistol and shoot Lynn, who died twelve hours later.

"We are almost persuaded that holding a commission as a peace officer is the worst thing that could occur to many men," said the *Tulsa World* in an editorial about the death of Agent Long and the former lawman who shot him. "A great many wind up as Linn [*sic*] wound up. There are too many men carrying guns and not anywhere near all these men should be entrusted with guns or with law enforcement."

When he heard about Crockett Long dying in a gun duel, Choc told some of his friends that he was surprised that he had not been accused of at least some sort of role in the state agent's murder. It would not have been that farfetched. Accusations were flying through the July skies as fast and furiously as the home-run hits of sluggers Babe Ruth, Lou Gehrig, and Jimmy Foxx.

In Washington, D.C., President Hoover, renominated by the Republicans in June for a second term, was fed up with critics attacking his performance. For weeks, he had watched the vagrant army of war veterans who walked, hitchhiked, and rode the rails into the city to tell Congress that the bonus promised to veterans in 1924 and scheduled to be paid off in 1945 was needed now if their hungry families were to survive. Hoover was less than sympathetic. He accused members of the Bonus Army, squatting in their shacks and tents along the Anacostia River, of being nothing but a mob of "Red agitators."

In late July, acting on orders from Hoover, federal troops commanded by Gen. Douglas MacArthur, assisted by two of his up-and-coming young officers, Maj. Dwight D. Eisenhower and Maj. George Patton, used tear gas, fixed bayonets, swords, and tanks to evict the protesting veterans from the nation's capital. The ragged marchers were stunned to see soldiers in the same uniforms they had once worn charging their ranks and torching their makeshift camp.

That summer, as the disillusioned veterans returned to their homes, Choc spent much of his time in Muskogee County, not far from the town of Boynton, at the plain and simple house of the Ring family, part of Ruby's kin, who always had a bed and food for Choc. The tired bandit rested his limbs and massaged his bad ankle, still aching from the bullet put there months before by Erv Kelley. He was also still troubled with a nasty case of the clap, and he felt older than twenty-eight—much older, in fact.

At night, when all the Ring kids were asleep, Charley sat outside beneath the Milky Way. The only sounds were the crickets chirping from the shadows or some wild critter moving through the nearby fields. He would sit out there for a long time, alone in his thoughts, maybe wishing he had stayed a farmer and wondering how everything had gotten to be so goddamn crazy.

28

BROTHER, CAN YOU SPARE A DIME?

T HE OUTLAWS HAD RISEN with the sun and devoured a home-cooked breakfast. Plenty of fire stirred in their bellies. It was Tuesday, November 1, 1932, one week before the historical election day that would usher in Franklin Roosevelt and the New Deal. It was also All Saint's Day in the wild Cookson Hills of Oklahoma, and not a single saint was in sight—only three fallen angels with tommy guns and pistols. They were crammed inside a shiny black sedan that looked like a pissed-on bug as it scooted down the two-lane country road.

Inside the car were Choc Floyd, George Birdwell, and the latest kid they had recruited as a driver. Out at the rural home of his sister Mary and her bootlegger husband, where the three bandits had spent Halloween night, Charley had managed to get Birdwell to lay off the moonshine. It proved to be a wise move. As they drove through the Sequoyah County countryside, their heads were as clear as the morning air.

It was going to be an important day for Choc and his two accomplices. They were off to rob the Sallisaw State Bank. Charley Floyd was indeed coming home.

After looting Birdwell's hometown bank in Earlsboro on two earlier occasions, George and Charley determined it was time they paid a call on a banking establishment in Floyd's neck of the woods. State Bank, a redbrick edifice located in downtown Sallisaw at the corner of Cherokee and Oak Street, was selected.

The men were mostly silent as the automobile passed the clumps of sumac and sassafras standing along the fence rows. The mitten-shaped leaves had already turned orange and red, and the vines and weeds poking through the strands of barbed wire were the color of aged tobacco.

Behind the wheel of the car was Aussie Elliott, an eighteen-year-old from Sapulpa whom Choc had enlisted to drive getaway on this bank job. Elliott was a sparkling minor league shortstop, but had given up a chance at a professional baseball career to go on the scout as a bandit. He was still a little green but had already done some hard time behind bars. Ten weeks before, on August 14, as a crowd of close to 95,000 at the Los Angeles Coliseum watched the closing ceremonies of the 1932 Olympics, he was busily escaping from the reformatory at Granite, Oklahoma. Immediately after he got loose, Elliott took off in search of Choc Floyd. He wished to join up with the one desperado whom law officers and the bank detectives could not kill or capture.

Like so many others in the nation, Elliott was well versed on Floyd's exploits. That past summer, Floyd's name had been on the lips of gossipy housewives counting their pennies at the market. Children at play had vied to take the role of Pretty Boy during games of cops and robbers. Frazzled men killing time in relief lines had discussed Floyd's most recent caper. It was said by reporters that even when Mother Sadie Ash died a bitter old woman at her home in Kansas City that summer, her final thoughts were about Pretty Boy, whom she continued to loathe with a vengeance for his suspected role in the killing of her two sons. She had had a vested interest in seeing Choc Floyd brought to justice. Most people, however, including middle-class churchgoers who dared not publicly admit it, quietly cheered him on.

The nation had grown hungry for exciting characters to take their minds off their troubles. That is why during the decade of the thirties, the public showed a strong preference for gangster films, which linked vice and disobedience with the ordinary lives of the audiences. Newspapermen who had covered crime for years were imported to Hollywood to churn out scripts punctuated with the chatter of machine guns and sinister tough-guy dialogue. Films such as *Little Caesar* and *Public Enemy* became enormously successful, and *I Am a Fugitive from a Chain Gang* and *Scarface* were two of the biggest box-office attractions in 1932.

As had been the case during early economic depressions in the late 1800s, the country's condition in the early years of the 1930s was conducive to the emergence of social bandits. To some, mostly the disenfranchised, this breed of outlaw symbolized justice in a nation perceived by many as being quite unjust. During this period of social ferment and discontent, when, in an attempt to scare off bidders, symbolic hangmen's nooses decorated farms being foreclosed, Choc Floyd was a logical antihero.

Except for bankers, detectives, and the next of kin of Choc's victims, many citizens harbored no ill will against Charles Arthur Floyd. Among his many romantic nicknames was the Sagebrush Robin Hood. It was frequently used to describe Choc because of his generous nature when it came to paying farmers for meals and giving small portions of his stolen loot to the poor. Some folks even suggested that when Charley robbed banks, he sometimes ripped up mortgages in shreds before the banker had an opportunity to get the papers recorded.

Elmer Steele, who had known the Floyds since he was a boy in Sallisaw, emphatically stated that many of the stories were true. Like Aussie Elliott and some other tough youngsters, Steele sometimes acted as a driver for Choc on bank jobs.

"It was no joke. Choc would destroy mortgages and, more than once, I saw him give money to people who needed a boost," reminisced Steele five decades after his own outlaw days were over.

Pretty Boy was the stuff of legends. More than one reporter knew it. Finding a nation enamored of bank bandits, many hack writers and journalists responded with sensational coverage of the criminals and their activities.

Hubert Dail, a writer for the pulp magazine *True Detective,* visited Oklahoma during the summer of 1932 and rode with some of the frustrated posses who tracked Pretty Boy and Birdwell. Dail described how the country people clammed up whenever law-enforcement officers came snooping around.

"In each case, the inhabitants of the hillbilly country didn't know where the famous bandit was at that particular moment," wrote Dail. "At one house, in a hollow, about two miles off the road, a posse advanced in a semicircle to confront a woman chopping wood. She paused, stared at the officers with hostile eyes. 'Whatdya want?' she demanded.

"The deputies said they were looking for 'Pretty Boy.' A crafty glint came into the woman's eyes. 'I reckon he's been here a hundred times,' she said, 'but I ain't seen him recently.' She brought her ax down with a crash."

Floyd's reputation by the summer of 1932 had become so legendary that hoaxes became frequent. One of the most celebrated stories occurred on August 3. Choc had reportedly kidnapped H. W. Nave, an out-of-work salesman from Blackwell, Oklahoma. Nave, who had also served as a private policeman in Tulsa, told investigators that he was driving near Edmond, not far from Oklahoma City, when three men in a Chrysler sedan forced him to stop along the highway. According to Nave, a man he recognized as Pretty Boy Floyd pushed him into the backseat of their car while another bandit drove off in the victim's vehicle. He said the other two captors drove to a secluded area near a creek southwest of Tulsa. They forced him to drink a pint of whiskey and stripped off all his clothing. To add insult to injury, Floyd stole thirty-four dollars from Nave's wallet.

Nave told sheriff deputies that he passed out from the liquor. When he regained consciousness several hours later, he ran nude as a jaybird to the highway but was unable to flag down any passing cars. Finally, a laborer took pity on him and pulled over. The Good Samaritan gave Nave a raincoat to wear and took him to a telephone to contact the sheriff's office.

Nave's story was one of the more acclaimed frauds, however. The day after his highly publicized brush with Choc, police officers in Oklahoma City discovered that instead of being stolen by Pretty Boy Floyd and his friends, Nave's auto had been sold to a used-car dealer in Oklahoma City for $250. The seller was described by the salesman at the car lot as scarred and wrapped in bandages. Officers deduced that Nave and a confederate perpetrated the fraud in order to cover the disposal of his mortgaged automobile. A warrant was issued for Nave's arrest, charging him with obtaining money under false pretenses.

Nevertheless, for years to come the incident involving the unemployed salesman who had tried to scam the mortgage company was continually listed in newspapers and books as yet another one of the high crimes of Pretty Boy Floyd. This episode was magnified even more because the "kidnap victim" was said to have been an active-duty Tulsa police officer, which was yet another falsehood.

Floyd relatives recalled that Choc had a good laugh about the Nave story. He and Aussie Elliott pictured the motorists coming upon a naked man flailing his arms on the side of the road. Money was as scarce as Herbert Hoover campaign buttons in most parts of the land, but there were better ways of getting through the tough times than resorting to preposterous tricks.

Straightforward bank robbery was Charley's preferred line of work, even if he was constantly being credited with far more bank jobs than he actually pulled, such as the October 28 theft of one thousand dollars from a bank in the oil-patch town of Maud, where a robber in overalls tried to convince his victims that he was Pretty Boy Floyd.

Most folks knew better. Pretty Boy didn't wear rough clothes, and he was better mannered. Charley took the crimes being blamed on him in stride, but after a hiatus of several months, he also decided it was time to emerge from hiding and grab some more loot.

That is precisely when the bank in Sallisaw became a prime candidate for the bandits. On that first day of November, Choc and his two colleagues saw no naked men on the road leading to Sallisaw, only some crows, and an occasional hawk eying the fields from atop a fence post. A few farmers in their tired-out Fords automatically waved at the sedan as they passed. Aussie Elliott and Charley cheerfully waved back.

Elliott handled the automobile well. He had seen to it that the gas tank was topped off, the radiator was filled with well water, and the tires were sound. Next to him sat Charley, dressed to the nines in a clean shirt, necktie, and pressed suit, and wearing a cap his brother-in-law, Perry Lattimore, had given him as a gift the night before.

In the backseat, Birdwell was in good spirits. Sometimes George, who toted around a well-used Bible, read Scripture out loud to Charley as they traveled together on the dirt back roads. A few of the folks who knew that about Birdwell even thought he had been a preacher or a brush-arbor revivalist at one time and had lost the call over liquor or women, but that wasn't true.

On this day, as they drove toward their objective, Birdwell stroked a rag up and down the barrel of a Thompson submachine gun. The odor of pomade and bay rum blended with the smell of Cosmoline and gun oil.

It was not as if their planned holdup of the bank at Sallisaw was a well-guarded secret. Several of Choc's friends, and practically the entire Floyd clan, including various in-laws and cousins, knew it was going to take place on November 1. Choc's grandfather, Charles Murphy Floyd, who had just turned seventy-five the past September, got duded up in fresh overalls. He came into town from Akins that morning just to watch the proceedings. The old man took up a place of honor near the train station, directly across the street from the bank. Several of his cronies also gathered there. While they waited for Charley and his two friends to arrive, the men chewed tobacco and talked drought, the Depression, and politics—especially politics. These ancient Democrats were confident that their chosen candidate—Franklin Delano Roosevelt—was going to give Herbert Hoover a proper ass kicking at the polls in just seven days.

"Just need to count them votes, that's all," said one of the grizzled men to some Floyd relatives who recalled coming by to shake hands. "Maybe ol' FDR will get the country out of the mess it's in." The others nodded in agreement and spit long streams of tobacco juice into the dust.

The boy driver and Choc later told friends that, as the car carrying them sailed down the dirt road across patches of sunshine sifted out of clouds that looked like mountains of mashed potatoes, they heard Birdwell softly humming. They could not quite make out the song but it sounded sweet. They said it may have been an old Sunday school favorite.

Shortly before noon, the car entered Sallisaw with the hometown celebrity in the front passenger seat. The car drove directly to the two-story bank. Aussie Elliott parked right in front, on the wrong side of the street, only a few steps from the bank's door. Charley and George quickly got out of the car, leaving Elliott behind with the engine running. As usual, they wore no masks or disguises. Choc held a submachine gun in the crook of his left arm. He rubbed his shoes on the backs of his trousers as he looked up and down the streets. Choc wanted to look his very best.

Since it was close to the noon hour, there were several people, including some students from the Liberty School, hurrying to their homes or a cafe. The many eyewitnesses would later recollect snatches of conversation for newspaper reporters. One of those present, Bob Fitzsimmons, leaned against the bank door, minding his own business. He recognized Charley as soon as the bandits got out of the car. Birdwell growled at Fitzsimmons and ordered him into the bank.

"He's a friend of mine; he's all right," Charley told his partner.

Choc then walked into the barbershop next door to the bank. Otis Shipman was waiting to get a haircut, and Tom Trotter sat in the chair, getting his weekly trim.

"Hello, Tom, we're going into this bank here and you lay off that telephone," Charley said, smiling, casually holding his weapon as if he was walking through the woods on a squirrel hunt.

"You bet we will," assured Trotter. Shipment nodded his head in agreement.

"Good to see you fellas," said Choc. He touched two fingers to his cap in a quick salute and left. Out on the street, he greeted other friends.

"Howdy, what you doin' in town, Choc?" asked a farmer in overalls.

"How you, Newt?" answered Charley, "We're gonna rob the bank."

"Give 'em hell!" cried the man.

Charley and Birdwell entered the bank and found that Bob Riggs, an assistant cashier, was the only person there. Everyone else was still on their lunch break.

"You can keep your hands down but keep quiet," Charley calmly told Riggs. "We don't want to kill anybody."

The two bandits went to work. They stuffed handfuls of currency and coins into money sacks. While they gathered the money, several customers entered the bank. Charley greeted each of them with a big smile and shook their hands. He politely asked everyone to keep quiet and to do as they were told. Within five minutes, nine persons were herded together behind the tellers' cages.

"It's a holdup, all right," Charley told the customers. "Don't hurt 'em, Bird, they're friends of mine."

After they had scooped up $2,530, Choc and Birdwell were ready to leave. As was the normal procedure, they took a hostage. This time, it was the lone employee.

"You're comin' with us, banker," Birdwell told Riggs as he gave him a nudge toward the door.

Outside the bank, Charley explained to Riggs that he would have to go with them so no one would try to block their escape from town. "We won't hurt you, Bob," said Charley. "This is the way we always do it. Just hop up on the runnin' board and hold on tight."

Without another word, Riggs took his place on the left running board. Aussie Elliott gave the bank cashier a grin and a wink from inside the car. He gunned the idling engine. As Choc and Birdwell got into the automobile, the car door jammed and they dropped part of their take. A half-dozen packages of nickels and half-dollars broke open and scattered over the sidewalk.

"Forget it," said Charley, "some kids will come along and get that spilled change. Let's get goin'."

As soon as he and Birdwell were safely inside, Choc yelled out, "All right, hike out!" Elliott screeched from the curb. He headed west down Cherokee for one block, then turned the wheel hard to the left in a U-turn and circled back to the east and pressed the gas pedal. The car sped due east as if they were going to Arkansas and then came to a halt at the edge of town, only five blocks from the bank, so Riggs could jump off the running board.

"Goodbye, old man, take care of yourself," Charley shouted to Riggs as they drove away.

All the time Choc and Birdwell were looting the bank, Chief of Police Bert Cotton was only seventy-five feet from the bank's front door. Cotton, who knew Choc Floyd as well as anyone and had been one of the officers who had arrested him in Sallisaw in 1925 for the St. Louis highway robbery, sat in his parked police car just around the corner. Cotton later said that he did not become aware that anything was amiss until the robbers were long gone and he heard some of the commotion on the street.

Grandpa Floyd also missed seeing his grandson rob the bank. He was so busy chewing the fat with his friends outside the train depot that the bandits were speeding away down the road before the old man looked up and realized that everything was over.

Sheriff George Cheek rushed to the scene and then took off in hot pursuit. He said that he lost them only about five miles east of Sallisaw. Some of the people on the street told Cheek and Cotton that they thought the driver of the car was Fred Barker, the fugitive killer. The most dependable witnesses, however, identified him as Aussie Elliott. There was no doubt about the identity of the other two, especially Charley Floyd.

Fred Green, described by the press as a "militant young Sequoyah County attorney," was a graduate of the University of Oklahoma and was set to begin his second term as prosecutor in January. Green vowed that even though he had grown up at Akins and was Charley's former schoolmate, he would prosecute Choc to the full extent of the law, that is, *if* Charley Floyd was ever captured.

It may not have been the largest amount ever taken in a robbery, but there were few who could deny that it was one of the most audacious bank jobs anyone ever pulled. One of the many reporters who came to Sallisaw afterward put it this way: "It was like the hometown performance of a great actor who has made it good on Broadway."

There were no encores, but Charley later confided to friends that he almost heard the applause ringing in his ears as he and his two sidekicks divided up the stolen money at the rural home of one of his relatives. Around Sallisaw, the townspeople believed the widely spread story that Charley robbed the bank in order to help pay the doctor bills of two of his friends who had been wounded in a fight with law officers. Through intermediaries, Charley got a portion of his share to Ruby. She and Dempsey were now living with her family near Bixby, where the boy attended the Central School and helped his Grandpa Hardgraves and his young uncles with the farm chores.

Once again, Pretty Boy had taken the public's mind off farm foreclosures and bank failures. His life was a continuous gangster movie for the disenfranchised to relish. The little people of the land fed vicariously from his exploits. Through Floyd, they were able to punch back.

Just two days after the Sallisaw bank robbery, Charley met with Vivian Brown, the purposeful newspaper reporter and the only journalist ever to interview Pretty Boy Floyd. As Brown explained it:

"The papers were full of Floyd. The depression was having its demoralizing effect upon society and many of the destitute admired the boy who could go out and take money from the bankers. When banks in our territory began failing, when industry slowed down and farm prices dropped near nothing, public temper was ripe for Floyd to catch the public fancy."

Brown was having dinner with some friends at the Sugar Bowl tearoom in Muskogee in the early spring of 1932 when she had first made up her mind that she wanted to write a book about Pretty Boy Floyd. She decided that the best way to tell Floyd's story was to meet face-to-face with the outlaw.

"The waiter brought the evening paper and we read in it of Floyd's miraculous escape from the Tulsa residence. All of us at the table had been hit by the depression. We had a natural sympathy for the underdog, although we didn't condone crime, and we fell to discussing the chances of Floyd's capture and what he had actually done."

The meeting with Choc was a long time in the making. After many weeks of talking to various parties who knew Charley Floyd, the young woman was finally taken to the "shotgun" home of Jess Ring near Boynton. Jess's wife, Tempie, was Ruby's aunt, and Choc spent much of his time on the lam hiding at their home. Brown sat down for a meal with the Ring family and explained her reasons for wanting to interview Choc.

The Rings politely listened to the persuasive reporter, but they offered little comment and made no promises. Finally, several months later, Brown was again contacted and told to put her request for an interview in writing. In early October, she wrote a letter in which she explained that she believed Choc's life would make a provocative book.

"I told him I was interested in him, not as a hunted criminal, but as an individual, and that he had many friends . . . who were interested in finding out his own version of his life," said Brown. "His exploits were on every tongue, and in the eastern Oklahoma hill country, he was something of a hero-villain. I told him I would not ask him anything or publish anything then that would incriminate him at the time."

A few days before the Sallisaw bank robbery, a response from Charley, scrawled in pencil, was delivered to Brown.

Dear Madam:
I have been informed that you wanted an interview with me or had some questions you would like to ask me. I am sorry that I can't meet you in person. I will send this through a friend and you can publish it if you like but I would ask you not to publish my picture cause as you know I have too much publicity now. In fact, I can't be hurt much or I wouldn't be doing this but I haven't much to say as it is only a few words for Mr. Burns (C. A. Burns of the State Crime Bureau), the man that seems to know me so well and say so much. I can't say anything about him as I

don't know him but I do know him better than he knows me and I would like him better if he'd never abused my little boy (Jackie). As low down as he says I am (maybe I am) but I would have been different with a child of his or any other child because they are all innocent regardless of who their father may be.

In his well-written letter, Charley denied any association with George Birdwell, but Brown knew that was a bald-faced lie and that he was only protecting his friend. Charley also apologized for his penmanship and signed it with his usual, "Yours Truly, Chas Floyd." Then, about 4:00 P.M. on November 3, the young woman returned to her home in Muskogee from a nearby business school where she took shorthand lessons. She found a stranger sitting in a car in front of her house.

"Are you Vivian Brown?" he asked.

"Yes."

"I'm from Jess," he said without introducing himself. "Are you ready to go?"

Brown was elated and apprehensive at the same time. She realized she was going to get her exclusive interview with Floyd himself.

"Hurriedly, I dropped my books, grabbed my pencil and paper, and climbed in the car with him," said Brown.

They drove in complete silence westward out of Muskogee. They snaked down more than thirty miles of back country roads through cotton and cornfields and pastures. Finally, they stopped where some thick underbrush and a grove of large pecan trees rimmed a deep gully. Parked under the shade of the trees was a tan Ford V-8. A bareheaded young man with slicked-back hair stepped out of the car. He was smartly dressed in a tailored suit, white shirt, and tie. Vivian Brown recognized him the instant she saw him walking toward her. His photograph had been published hundreds of times in newspapers and magazines. It was Pretty Boy. There was not a doubt.

"I'm Charley Floyd." He was grinning and seemed nonchalant. Behind him was Jess Ring, in his overalls as always, and he also had a smile on his face.

"I'm Vivian Brown."

The young woman and her subject started out much like strange dogs act when they first meet. They sniffed around each other until both of them were comfortable.

"There oughta be some good quail huntin' over there," said Charley as he pointed to an adjoining cornfield. When all conversation about the weather and crops was exhausted, Ring and the stranger, who had delivered Brown to the rendezvous, slipped away and gave the writer and Charley some privacy.

"I think I made it clear in my letter just what I want," said Brown, "and no doubt these good friends of yours have told you. I am really quite glad to meet you, for your name will live in the history of these country folk for generations."

Charley ducked his head as if embarrassed.

"I guess that's true," he replied. "I do have a lot of friends and have tried to help them like they helped me. I always tried to treat them square and they treated me that way."

Putting her newfound skill at shorthand to use, Brown wrote down every word Charley uttered. He looked her square in the eye and did not duck any of her queries.

"Suppose you tell me just how and when you decided that a life of crime was the only thing you could do?" asked Brown.

"Well, that's a fair question, but now listen, you ain't gonna print anything that will lay a job on me as long as it's gonna hurt me," responded Charley. "There may be a time when it won't do me no hurt to have my friends tell some of the things I have done—they've been aplenty—but not near as many as they say I done."

Charley proceeded to open his heart to the young lady in her prim dress and heels. He told her of his early years, and how he first got into real trouble because of the theft of pennies from the Akins post office. He talked of the payroll robbery in St. Louis and getting sent to the penitentiary at Jefferson City.

"Nothing much happened to me while I was there, but I was thrown together with several fellows who knew a lot more about doing things than I had ever heard of," explained Charley. "I was just a green country kid that got caught on a job that I didn't know much about but I guess that was the job that put its mark on me and I could never shake it off. I tried."

Charley provided details about his criminal career after he was released from prison, including his escapades with Bill Miller and others in Ohio. He also opened up about other adventures that had not made the newspapers, such as the time when he, Birdwell, and Ruby were driving from Tulsa to Sallisaw and a tire blew out on their automobile. The car turned over, caught on fire, and was destroyed. Charley managed to grab his weapons from the backseat, and he and Ruby pulled an unconscious Birdwell from the flaming wreckage. The Floyds hailed a passing car and went to Muskogee, where a taxi was hired to take them to Boynton and on to the Rings' home.

"There we were getting into that taxi," Charley laughed. "Me, with a machine gun under my right arm, and Ruby with luggage and George's gun, and both of us holding George between us."

As time passed, Choc became even more comfortable with the young woman. He hitched his foot up on the car bumper and watched in obvious amusement while she wrote as fast as he spoke.

"What about your life here?" asked Brown. "You have been accused of so many things, I don't see how you do half those things and get by with them."

Choc's smile broadened.

"I guess I've been accused of everything that has happened except the kidnapping of the Lindbergh child last spring." He sighed. "It ain't the names that they call me that makes me sore. I may be an alley rat or a skunk or even worse, but that didn't give them a right to tell that kid [Dempsey] that he could never amount to anything as long as he had a father like me. That kid can't help who his father is or what he does, but he does think the world of me and I sure think he's all right, too.

"Another thing, that talk of me giving up is all baloney. I know what would happen if I did. They would frame me and I'm not getting caught like that. I guess I've done more bank holdups than anything else. It was all bonded money and no one ever lost anything except the big boys. I never shot at a fellow in my life unless I was forced into it by some trap being thrown to catch me and then it was that or else."

Throughout the lengthy interview, Choc was courteous and never contradicted himself except when Brown pressed him about the exact number of banks he had robbed during his busy career. First, he admitted to thirty-two, but later he told her it was more like sixty, a figure she disputed.

"What did you do with all the money?" she questioned.

"It wasn't all mine," said Charley. "I split it, and in this game it ain't the money that counts but it's the safety that money can help you get."

After what seemed to her like several hours, Brown knew the interview had to end. It was now as dark as the inside of a wolf's mouth. She thanked Choc for allowing her to meet with him and told him that she hoped his life story would be published someday.

"Goodbye," said Choc.

He walked back to his car and disappeared in the darkness. In the shadows near the gully, Brown made out the silhouette of another man, and she guessed it was George Birdwell. Then Jess Ring and the stranger reappeared and they took her back to Muskogee.

Vivian Brown carefully transcribed her notes and added them to her burgeoning Pretty Boy file. Although she would never develop the Floyd book she fully intended to write, Brown would one day prepare a detailed newspaper series about the desperado. In those articles published in the *Oklahoma News* in 1934, it became evident that her encounter with Charley under the pecan trees that autumn afternoon left an indelible impression on the journalist.

"There is much to support the picture of Floyd as a modern Robin Hood," Brown wrote. "Like the famed marauder of the English forests, he took money from those who had it—the banks—and divided the proceeds of his raids with the poor. The penniless tenant farmers kept their mouths shut; they had no scruples about taking contraband wrested from bankers."

On November 7, only a few days after Brown's meeting with Floyd, two more Oklahoma bank robberies occurred. At Marlow, in the south-central part of the state, not far from where Texas cowboys once herded cattle up the historic Chisholm Trail, four men toting machine guns burst into the State

National Bank. After scooping up about $5,500 from the tills, the bandits locked the two bank officers and five customers in the vault and fled town.

On the other side of the state in Okmulgee County, two robbers strode into the American State Bank and took $11,352 while a third man stayed at the wheel in their car. Immediately, the blame for this crime was laid on Pretty Boy. The bank bandits were tentatively identified as Floyd, George Birdwell, and young Aussie Elliott. In a huge spread, the *Kansas City Star* implicated the three Oklahomans in the Henryetta holdup and wrote of the desperation of the bankers.

"Floyd could not have robbed both of those banks [Marlow and Henryetta], for the robberies were only five minutes apart, while the towns were more than 100 miles apart," wrote A. B. McDonald in the *Star.* "But the robbery in Henryetta was done in such true 'Pretty Boy' style that the authorities *believed* it was done by Floyd and Birdwell and their new recruit, Aussie Elliott.

"Once inside they sprang into action. They drew revolvers and one, *supposed* to be Birdwell, using the muzzle of his revolver as a prod, lined up the three persons in the bank face in against the wall, while the other, *thought* to be Floyd, handed a sack to A. D. Diamond, Jr., the bookkeeper, and said: 'If any of you give an alarm I'll kill you. Put all the money into that sack.' "

Twelve days after the bank robbery, six alleged accomplices in the Henryetta heist were behind bars in Okmulgee. Two of them had confessed to the crime, naming Ford Bradshaw, Newton Clayton, and Jim Benge, all wanted murderers, as the actual robbers. Subsequent news stories concerning the arrest of those accused with harboring the desperadoes and the manhunt in the Cookson Hills for the three wanted bandits made no further mention of Floyd or his colleagues. Still, the Henryetta robbery was consistently listed in detective magazines as one of Pretty Boy's major crimes.

However, Floyd relatives recounted that on November 7, Charley Floyd was out of the state. More than likely, he was in Kansas City, they had guessed, in the arms of his girlfriend, Beulah. That same day, at the Hardgraves's small home near Bixby, Ruby suffered severe abdominal pains. At first, she thought it was a recurrence of an intestinal disorder that had first struck when Dempsey was born. Ruby's father rushed her to a Tulsa doctor. Late that afternoon, she underwent an appendectomy and was ordered by her physician to remain hospitalized for more than two weeks.

The next day, Roosevelt thrashed the incumbent Herbert Hoover in a stunning landslide victory. The Democratic candidate was committed "to restore this country to prosperity." The 1929 hit tune "Happy Days Are Here Again" was revived and became the anthem for voters desperate for a jolt of optimism. Roosevelt easily carried all but six of the forty-eight states.

Hoover had set himself up for defeat. There were a myriad of reasons. During his term of office, the nation's industrial production was sliced in half. Breadlines and soup kitchens became common sights. Farm foreclosures and bank failures were everyday occurrences. Hoover served as the focus for a nation already weary of an economic depression that had run its course. Prohibition, called by Hoover the "experiment noble in purpose," was clearly a failure, and the brutal treatment of the Bonus Expeditionary Force did not win the President any favor with veterans. Many of them were out of work. By 1932, the total number of unemployed in the country was well over 13 million.

Untold numbers of the jobless were forced to take to the streets. It was impossible even to estimate how many Depression migrants roamed the country in search of work. In 1932 alone, the Southern Pacific Railroad reported that *more than* seven hundred thousand vagrants were booted out of its boxcars. Hoover, who had been known as the "great humanitarian" because of his sterling record as a relief administrator for postwar Europe, paradoxically was reluctant to provide direct federal aid to America's hungry masses.

From along the banks of the Hudson River, below posh Riverside Drive in Manhattan, to a North Canadian River bottom section of Oklahoma City sprang up hundreds of shantytowns. They became familiarly known as Hoovervilles. In the cities, some sad parents rummaged through garbage cans to feed their children. The critic Edmund Wilson wrote of families gathering rancid meat scraps out of refuse dumps in Chicago. Country folk in Oklahoma and Texas served roasted armadillos, derisively called Hoover Hogs.

In contrast to Hoover, Roosevelt represented change. He spoke of a "new deal" for Americans. He pledged to revive farms, revitalize railroads, and regulate banks. He promised that no American would starve.

Wealthy and well-educated, Roosevelt belonged to an aristocratic family. Nonetheless, Floyd relatives recalled that Choc always expressed his respect for the new President. They said Charley openly supported Roosevelt—long crippled from a bout with poliomyelitis—as a champion of the underdog. Charley was understandably never able to vote, but every Floyd who could, cast their ballot for Roosevelt.

As Americans began to adjust to the promise of a new leader who they hoped would lead them out of the wilderness, the homespun "Alfalfa Bill" Murray still reigned supreme in Oklahoma. In many ways, Murray and Roosevelt's philosophies were similar, especially in their championing of the rights of the poor.

Some believed, however, that the state's bankers were being victimized far more than anyone else. The Oklahoma Bankers' Association beseeched Murray to help them, especially in rural counties, where 92 percent of all the robberies took place. Alfalfa Bill thought about the problem and came up with a remedy. Murray called for public punishment of the culprits.

"I am in favor of establishing the whipping post and the stocks for bandits in this state," drawled Murray only a few days after the presidential election.

"Criminals fear the whip worse than any other punishment. I would lay it on. I would whip a criminal in public before he goes into the penitentiary and whip him again when he comes out. That will cure it.

"For the first offense of any kind of banditry I would sentence the man to the penitentiary for a long term and also fifty lashes on the bare back in public. For the second offense, I would give him a longer term and sentence him to stand in the stocks, in a public place, for several hours. For the third offense I would send him to the electric chair."

Bankers were not very interested in the first two of Murray's imaginative solutions to the bandit problem. They wanted faster action. Across the country, the number of bank robberies had steadily increased since 1922. In Oklahoma alone by mid-November, there had been forty-seven bank robberies since January. Small-town merchants were trained to serve as vigilantes when the robbery alarms sounded. At the Bank of Commerce in Jenks, a town on the west bank of the Arkansas River near Tulsa, officials were weary of coughing up funds for armed desperadoes, so they fortified the bank with brick walls, sheets of steel, and bulletproof glass cashier windows. It served as a model for other small-town banks.

Reward posters appeared everywhere for the capture or, better yet, death of Pretty Boy and other thieves. Even the bounty on ordinary bank robbers was a lot of money for that time. The apprehension of a living bandit brought one hundred dollars, and the amount increased to five times that amount for a dead bandit. By November 1932, the OBA had paid rewards on 216 robbers convicted or killed. The larger rewards on Pretty Boy's head remained unclaimed, however.

" 'Pretty Boy' and his partner, Birdwell, have been able to go so long uncaught chiefly because they are protected and tipped off by officers of the law in the hilly country in which they operate," theorized Charles Burns, superintendent of the State Crime Bureau and a former U.S. Marshal. "They have a host of relatives and friends and sympathizers all through there who shelter, protect, and warn them. This fellow Floyd is a shrewd fellow and slippery as an eel."

In November, Governor Murray admitted to reporters: "Floyd has sent me word twice, by his near relatives, that if I would save him from the electric chair he would come in and surrender. . . . I sent word back to him that I would not do it, but that I had instructed Burns to get him." And, when Murray chose the words *get him,* law officers and bankers interpreted that to mean annihilation.

"We are urging the bankers everywhere in the state to tell the people of their towns that we do not want bandits captured alive," said Eugene Gum, the OBA secretary. "We want them dead. We want it known by anyone who is aiming to start into bank robbing as a business that we will pay $500 for him dead. The remedy is to kill them. Don't ask them to surrender. We want no live bandits to go through that farce of trials before weak juries. Let's exterminate them.

"Floyd has been the luckiest bandit that ever lived. It is marvelous how he got out of close corners when surrounded. He has had the 'breaks' for a long time, but he is just about due for a fall. So do not be surprised if you read, almost any day now, that Floyd and Birdwell have been slain. We are after them. More and more people are sending us tips about where they are, and they are bound to walk into a trap before long."

Charles Burns's forecast proved only partially accurate. Just three days after his warning became public, part of the prediction actually happened.

George Birdwell met his end.

For some time, Birdwell had expressed his displeasure with all the attention Charley showered on Beulah Ash, the Kansas City woman who police labeled as Floyd's moll. Although Birdwell had been known to conduct some skirt chases of his own, he largely believed Charley's first obligation was to his former wife and their young son. Also, Birdwell never forgot that Beulah and her sister, Rose, had accompanied the late Billy Miller and Charley when Miller died in a gun battle in Bowling Green, Ohio. He felt the sisters brought bad luck.

"Trouble hangs on to a woman's skirt," Birdwell often told friends around Earlsboro. They knew he was referring to the bewitching Beulah.

On November 21, the Tulsa police learned that Ruby Floyd had recovered from her recent operation and was due to be released from the hospital. Officers staked out her room around the clock, just in case her former husband showed up to visit. News about Ruby's recuperation also trickled down to Earlsboro and reached Birdwell.

"My dad heard that Ruby needed to pay the medical bills before she could get released from the hospital," related Jack Birdwell. "Choc was in Kansas City, so Dad went out to rob a bank and get some money for Ruby."

Birdwell selected the Farmers and Merchants Bank in Boley, a small town just above the North Canadian River in Okfuskee County. It was a poor choice. Boley's population was entirely black. Founded shortly after the turn of the century, Boley was one of twenty-nine all-black communities established in what was then Indian Territory. Situated in the heart of what was once a rich cotton-producing area, Boley was the most successful of the black towns, which had been established by southern blacks, including many freed slaves.

Even though Birdwell engaged a black bandit to help him and another white outlaw rob the bank, the strange trio was conspicuous. They stuck out like whores at a church picnic.

"We were always told that Uncle Charley had already looked into robbing that bank at Boley long before and decided it was too risky," explained Choc's nephew Lawton Lessley. "He told Birdwell that he didn't want anything to do with it."

Birdwell, however, always faithful to Charley, was committed to the goal of getting Ruby Floyd out of the hospital and home to her family at Bixby in time for Thanksgiving. His loyalty to his friend Choc Floyd proved his downfall.

Birdwell's chosen accomplices for the Boley job were C. C. Patterson, an outlaw from Kiowa who was due to go to trial in December in connection with the shooting of a Shawnee policeman, and Charles "Pete" Glass, a young black man from Earlsboro who was familiar with Boley from visits there to meet women and gamble. After spending the afternoon of November 22 lurking around town, mostly in a pool hall across the street from the bank, the three bandits went to the home of one of Glass's sisters near Earlsboro to drink and finalize their robbery plans. They figured the holdup would be a snap. Later it was disclosed that Glass, an outlaw novice, openly bragged to his sister how he was "going to show the gang how to rob a colored bank."

Early the following morning, November 23, Birdwell and his two accomplices ate breakfast at the house of Dock Hearn, a black farmer who lived not far from Birdwell's own home. Then they took off for Boley in a brown sedan. En route to Boley, "Champ" Patterson stopped the car and Glass took over as the wheelman. Patterson later recalled that the three men were silent throughout the journey to Boley. This would be Birdwell's first bank robbery without Choc Floyd. It would also be his last.

By 10:30 A.M., the bandit's car turned off Highway 62, bumped over the railroad tracks, and cruised into Boley. It was Thanksgiving Eve. KVOO radio in Tulsa reported the coldest temperatures on record for that date. There was also a story about four former officials from the Farmers' National Bank of Wewoka. The bank had shut its door months before. The bankers were to be indicted that day by a grand jury on a variety of charges, including embezzlement and misapplication of funds.

Because of the bitter north winds, the streets of Boley were empty except for some farmers in town shopping for Thanksgiving dinner extras and shotgun shells. Quail season would open the next day. Talk in the stores centered on the high school basketball game scheduled that evening between the Boley Bears and their rivals at Wewoka.

Glass parked on the opposite side of Main Street just south of the Farmers and Merchants Bank. He waited in the automobile as Birdwell and Patterson, a sawed-off shotgun under his overcoat, walked inside and went directly to a teller's cage.

"We're robbin' this bank!" shouted Birdwell. "Hand over the dough! Don't pull no alarm!"

D. J. Turner, the bank president, calmly began pushing paper money beneath the steel bars of the window. He also triggered the alarm.

"Did you pull that alarm?" screamed Birdwell.

"Please don't hurt nobody! Please!" pleaded W. W. Riley, the bank treasurer.

"You bet I pulled it!" spat out a defiant Turner.

"I'll kill you for that," growled Birdwell as he squeezed the trigger of his .45 pistol. Shot at point-blank range, Turner was thrown backward, and he slumped to the floor. Birdwell continued to blaze away with his pistol.

Meanwhile, H. C. McCormick, the bookkeeper, whose suspicions were aroused as soon as he spied the two white men enter the bank, had slipped into the vault, where a Winchester rifle was stashed for just such emergencies. He had rehearsed this procedure many times. Seeing that Birdwell had mortally wounded the bank president, McCormick took aim from a crack in the vault door and cut loose with a shot that struck its target. Birdwell, shot in the back, staggered as blood spurted from his mouth and dripped off his chin.

"I'm shot," gurgled Birdwell. He crashed on the hardwood floor at Riley's feet.

Bedlam followed. Patterson, panicky when he saw Birdwell collapse, screamed at bank employees and customers to drag his body out to the car. Patterson grabbed up as much money as possible. Glass, who had heard the alarm and the shots, dashed into the bank with his pistol drawn. By that time, townspeople and city officers led by Sheriff Langston McCormick had gathered outside. Most of them carried rifles and shotguns. Bullets crashed through the bank windows.

"There was a regular war," Riley related afterward to state agents.

The terrified men carrying Birdwell dropped his body on the sidewalk near the bank entrance and bolted for cover. Patterson bent over to pick up the wounded ringleader, but he was hit from behind by a blast of buckshot. Struggling to drag the unconscious Birdwell to safety, Patterson was struck several more times by shotgun pellets and bullets. Witnesses said he yelped like a dog.

Glass bolted for the car and managed to drive off, but he quickly saw that vigilantes blocked his escape. Angry farmers poured withering gunfire into the car. Glass crashed into the curb. He slumped dead over the wheel, riddled with bullets.

At first, the stunned citizens thought they had brought down Pretty Boy Floyd himself, but State Crime Bureau operatives definitely identified the gravely wounded bandit as Patterson. They said the two men "greatly resemble one another," and that Patterson had been mistaken for Floyd in recent robberies. Some officers changed their minds and said perhaps it had been Champ Patterson, and not Floyd, who had fought it out with a posse earlier that year at Stonewall. Critically wounded in the legs, knees, and hip, and tattooed with buckshot, Patterson was rushed to nearby Okemah for treatment. He survived. The wounded bank president, Turner, shot four times through the chest, died before reaching Okemah, however.

Birdwell also died en route.

"My dad was shot in the back, and the bullet passed through his lung and he bled to death," recalled Jack Birdwell. "The day he died, I was just a teenaged kid, but I became a man. I knew all along he was going to die. We had talked about it. He told me that he never would go to the pen and just be a bird in a cage.

"That evening one of my cousins and me cried and cried. We got a hold of one of Dad's friends there in Earlsboro and we begged him to take us to Boley. We were gonna take a bunch of guns and just tear that damn town apart. But the fella calmed us down and talked us out of it. He said enough had been done and to let it rest."

Thousands of mourners and spectators turned out to honor Turner, the slain banker who had left behind a wife and five children. Governor Murray sent his condolences as well as a letter of congratulations to McCormick, the quick-thinking cashier who had gunned down Birdwell. Murray made McCormick an honorary major on his staff. The hero of the hour also received a five-hundred-dollar reward for slaying Birdwell. Another five hundred dollars in bounty was divided among the citizens who shot and killed Glass. Eugene Gum warned Boley officials to be on the alert in case Pretty Boy came to town seeking revenge. That never happened, although McCormick did receive dozens of hate letters, including one that read: "The man who killed my buddy, Birdwell, won't live to see Christmas." It was signed Charles "Pretty Boy" Floyd, but law officers said it was a fake. Nonetheless, McCormick strapped on the .45 pistol that Birdwell had left behind and wore it everywhere he went. Many years after the robbery, the pistol that McCormick kept as a souvenir accidentally discharged and the bullet tore into the old man's leg. The wound never properly healed, and his family contended that it contributed directly to his death.

Bob Birdwell, the dead outlaw's widow, went to Okemah and identified her husband from old scars on his head and the one on his leg that he had received many years before when an irate husband shot him. Officers gave Bob her husband's ring. They sent his body home.

Shortly before the services, a representative of the Oklahoma Bankers' Association asked the funeral home's director to allow the presidents of the banks supposed to have been robbed by Birdwell and Floyd to view the body. He would not allow it. Then O. P. Ray of the State Crime Bureau asked that some agents be admitted to the mortuary in case Floyd came to pay his last respects. The request was referred to Bob Birdwell.

"I bear you no malice," she told Ray. "You have hunted my husband while he was alive; in death he belongs to his loved ones."

Ray disregarded her wishes. Recalling that Floyd and Birdwell had once dared law officers and had shown up at an Earlsboro funeral home when Birdwell's father died, Ray decided not to take any chances. Six carloads of armed agents and local law officers appeared at the funeral conducted in Seminole on November 25. George Birdwell was buried beside his father and brother.

"As ye sow, so shall ye reap" was the text for Birdwell's service, preached by Reverend Robert Hedrick of the Earlsboro Methodist Church. Six old friends of the dead outlaw, including Blackie Smalley, dug a grave. Still wearing overalls, they also acted as pallbearers and carried the plain gray casket to Birdwell's final resting place. Ruby Floyd, just released from the hospital, stood at the grave next to Bob Birdwell and her children, and fifty other mourners. Ruby's father had scrounged up the money to pay her medical bills, and she hurried down to be with Bob when she buried her husband.

A rumor rumbled through the countryside that Choc Floyd appeared in disguise at the graveyard. Perfectly sober men said they saw Pretty Boy in women's clothing, with a veiled hat on his head. They said he was crying over Birdwell's coffin. Several people even claimed he changed into his costume at their home. One woman from Morris, Oklahoma, later told her friends that Pretty Boy often stopped at her family's place and always paid for his food and shelter. She said he borrowed some of her mother's clothes to wear to the Birdwell funeral. The woman swore that she had a photograph of him dressed in drag but it had disappeared.

Talk of Choc in drag added to the Floyd mythology. Choc was saddened by Birdwell's death, but he realized it would be foolhardy to go anywhere near the funeral. Floyd kinfolk knew Charley stayed in Tom's Town, far from the crowd of lawmen who eyed the burial like vultures.

His relatives were confident that Choc would remember Birdwell in his own way. He told them he toasted his old pal with straight shots of first-rate bootleg whiskey in a smoky Kansas City den filled with small talk and music.

A mournful lament, written by Gorney and Harburg, that would remain a hit well into 1933 symbolized the leanest days of the Great Depression. It served as a fitting dirge for George Birdwell, the goat-roping bandit who remained ever loyal to Charley, and as a memorial to courageous men like D. J. Turner, the Boley banker who had not been afraid to pull the alarm. The song was a tribute to all sorts of men and women, of all ages and backgrounds, who waited all across the land for the good times to return.

> *They used to tell me I was building a dream,*
> *And so I followed the mob—*
> *When there was earth to plow or guns to bear*
> *I was always there—right on the job,*
> *They used to tell me I was building a dream*
> *With peace and glory ahead—*
> *Why should I be standing on line*
> *Just waiting for bread?*

Once I built a railroad, made it run,
Made it race against time.
Once I built a railroad,
Now it's done—
Brother, can you spare a dime?

29

THE SUMMER OF '33

J. EDGAR HOOVER AND HIS Bureau of Investigation agents marked Pretty Boy Floyd for annihilation in 1933. Although his demise was not a fait accompli until October 1934, his death warrant was signed and irreversibly sealed sixteen months earlier. Ironically, the single event that ultimately proved his downfall occurred in Kansas City, where Floyd had maintained a tenuous relationship with fellow criminals ever since his release from prison in 1929.

Shortly after 7:00 A.M. on the morning of June 17, 1933, just outside the front entrance of Kansas City's mammoth Union Station, the crackle of submachine guns diminished any hope Choc Floyd may have held for survival. In the span of only a few minutes, two men were wounded and five others were shot and killed, including a federal prisoner. Also among the dead was an agent of the Bureau of Investigation.

No other act of violence, except the kidnapping of the Lindbergh baby, so stunned the nation and galvanized authorities in their persistent warfare against the outlaws spawned by the Great Depression. Neither the St. Valentine's Day Massacre in 1929 nor even the slaying of six lawmen by the Young brothers near Springfield in 1932 affected the way the public looked at the brutality of the criminal world.

Based on slim evidence and marginal eyewitness accounts, Hoover and the authorities in Kansas City eventually placed a large share of the blame for the mass murder at Union Station squarely on the shoulders of Pretty Boy Floyd. Allegations rained like a series of Sunday punches, each one more devastating than the one before. Charley Floyd did not even see them coming.

The sequence of events that transpired that June morning at Union Station remain forever shrouded in controversy. Much of the rancor centers on the identity of the actual triggermen and their motive. Whether Floyd was present or not remains a mystery. He was never tried, so the federal government never proved its case against him. Decades after the bloody incident, several jurists and legal scholars contend that a halfway bright criminal attorney fresh out of law school probably would have won an acquittal for Floyd had he ever been brought to trial. However, even if he was a scapegoat, as some criminal historians and underworld figures have suggested, the Kansas City Massacre was Charley Floyd's proverbial kiss of death. Just the mere association of his well-known name with the crime proved fatal.

Choc had spent most of the first six months of 1933 in the Cookson Hills and the oil patch area around Earlsboro. Following the death of his bandit lieutenant George Birdwell at Boley in November 1932, Floyd had taken up with yet another partner, Adam C. Richetti. He would be the last of many companions to ride with Charley Floyd.

Richetti had grown up in a large family, one generation removed from Italy. His parents had left the old country for the United States in order to earn enough money to start a new life. They settled in Coal County near the town of Lehigh in the coal-mining district of south-central Oklahoma. The Richettis raised several children. Among them was Adam, born in Lehigh in 1909, and a year later, a daughter named Eva, who was always called Eve by the other kids because of her brother's biblical name.

In the 1800s, Choctaw Indians, facing bitter winter storms, had been the first people to discover the value of the coal outcroppings found in the area where the Richetti family lived. The Indians gave the place a name that meant "where the black rocks burned." Mining companies had torn coal from the extensive fields in the old Choctaw Nation starting in the 1880s. The bonanza of the shallow coal beds began to decline following a 1912 mine disaster, however. Continuous labor unrest further snarled the mining operations. Richetti's father spent most of his productive years as a coal miner out on strike. The country folks who came to know the family gave their surname an Oklahoma pronunciation, *Rich-ity,* and made them feel welcome. Despite the congenial neighbors and the names of their last two children, Adam and Eve, the Richettis found Oklahoma to be less than a paradise on earth.

Just to keep some pasta, beans, and a little garlic in the cupboard, Adam's parents hawked bottles of hearty choc beer, the miners' preferred beverage. They also picked up odd bits of coal and sold them to other poor families for winter fuel. Both Adam and his older brother, Joseph, used their talent for tinkering with engines to earn a little money. Like many tenant farmers and out-of-work miners, the entire Richetti clan gathered each year at Hudson's Big Country Store in the nearby county seat of Coalgate. Starting in the early 1920s, Hudson's annually attracted large crowds by tossing five hundred dollars in dimes from the roof of the emporium. Shiny coins fell like manna from heaven. The gimmick was finally suspended because the crush of men scrambling for the free money injured too many women and children. Young Adam Richetti always came away with a bloody nose but pocketfuls of dimes.

"Adam was one tough cookie," recalled Dick Holland, a former resident of Coalgate who was five years Richetti's junior. "He was already a drinker and a fighter when he was only about thirteen or fourteen. Richetti had this reputation, even as a boy, of being mean. He wasn't a very big fellow and he was dark-skinned and had straight black hair. If he put a cap on, he looked like he just got off the boat."

Not everyone took Adam Richetti for a hooligan. He was also thought of as a ladies' man. He was especially popular with the girls from around Lehigh, Coalgate, Tupelo, and the small farm communities near the Muddy Boggy Creek bottoms, where fingers of smoke persistently spiraled from hidden moonshine stills. Adam's swarthy looks got him noticed at the big theatrical shows staged at the Lehigh Grand Opera, or at the downhome parties where guitars, mandolins, and accordions made swell dance music.

"Adam was just an ordinary kid but he was charming and handsome," recalled Ruby Dobson Branom, a classmate of Richetti. "He was popular with the girls. He loved to dance. Those were hard times when we were all growing up and even though we didn't have much, my dirt farmer daddy always said that we were 'rich in everything but money.' Adam got himself a motorcycle and he gave everyone rides. I've never forgotten that the only time in my life that I ever rode a motorcycle, I was behind Adam Richetti and he was tearing down a country road."

Ruby Branom also recollected seeing Adam just after he was caught committing his first serious criminal offense. He and some pals had broken into the high school and carried off all the typewriters. Another boy snitched and the sheriff confronted young Adam. "Poor ol' Mrs. Richetti was standing there by the school flagpole," recalled Ruby Branom. "She was talking to the sheriff and Adam was nearby with his head down and his eyes on the ground. She was plump and had a thick Italian accent. She was crying her eyes out and had her apron pulled up over her head and she was wailing, 'Oh, me Adam! Oh, me Adam! Why? Why?' She said it over and over again."

After a good scolding, the law released the contrite typewriter thief. Neither that act of mercy nor the many candles Mrs. Richetti burned in prayer at Our Lady of Good Council church kept Adam out of hot water, however.

Richetti ventured forth as a professional criminal in his late teens. His first serious brush with the law came at Hammond, Indiana, where he was arrested on August 7, 1928, on a bank robbery charge from Crown Point, Indiana. Sentenced to a term of one to ten years in the State Reformatory at Pendleton, he was paroled on September 22, 1931. Richetti's next arrest took place on March 9, 1932, at Sulphur, Oklahoma, for his role in the robbery of the First National Bank at Mill Creek earlier that same day. Tried and convicted, he served only a little over four months at "Big Mac"—from April 5 until August 25, 1932. He was released and placed on a fifteen-thousand-dollar bond, which he ultimately forfeited when he was implicated in yet another robbery, this time at Tishomingo, Governor "Alfalfa Bill" Murray's hometown.

By his twenty-third birthday, Richetti, an immigrant's son seasoned and savvy in bandit ways, was on the scout with Pretty Boy.

Friends of Richetti said he was honored to be tapped as Pretty Boy's sidekick. They had first met a few years earlier when Richetti was between bank robberies, working as an oil-field hand near Seminole. Hooking up with Floyd was, however, an unwise decision on Richetti's part. Every law officer in Oklahoma, much less the Midwest, was gunning for Floyd. The wiry young Richetti, who spent much of his life battling alcohol addiction, could not have made a poorer choice for a partner. From their first job together—the stickup of a dance hall at Wewoka in late 1932—and throughout their frenetic twenty-three months as allies on the outlaw trail, the duo faced only the wrath of the nation's law-enforcement agencies.

The name Pretty Boy Floyd continually surfaced as the prime suspect in bank robberies across the country. Less than a week after the death of Birdwell at Boley, the November 28, 1932, theft of fifty thousand dollars from the Citizens State Bank of Tupelo, Mississippi, was credited to Floyd. No charges were ever filed and no case against Floyd was ever proved. Although some authorities doubted its authenticity, a letter sent from Hot Springs, Arkansas, allegedly written by Floyd, repudiated his complicity in that incident. Scrawled in pencil and stuffed into an envelope taken from an Ottawa, Kansas, hotel, the letter was sent to the *Memphis Commercial Appeal*. Besides denying any role in the Tupelo robbery, the letter also referred to the bungled Boley bank job.

"The man who killed my pal Birdwell will never live to see Christmas," read the letter. In the postscript, the author referred to his own holiday plans. "I have five men with me and will be over in Oklahoma, my own home state, to spend Christmas with my folks." Law officers could not figure out whether that meant Charley's folks at Sallisaw, Earlsboro, Bixby, or Ruby's kinfolk in Muskogee County. The return address simply stated, "Address me Sallisaw, Okla."

Throughout the early thirties, as the bank-robbery rate continued to mount, so did the number of presumably reliable eyewitnesses who argued that Pretty Boy Floyd most frequently was a perpetrator. For the few crimes in which his name was cleared, such as the Henyretta bank job that resulted in the arrest of Ford Bradshaw in December 1932, another half-dozen new accusations materialized. The cycle could not be broken, as the media perpetuated the legend of Floyd, who had by this time acquired still another sobriquet—the "hoodoo hoodlum."

Even the *Literary Digest* added to the Pretty Boy mythology. In the December 10, 1932, issue, the publication grandly described Choc's felonious deeds. "His name is Charles Arthur Floyd and they call him 'Pretty Boy.' But he's the 'bandit king' of Oklahoma, the latest of that state's long line of outlaw chiefs.

"He robs and laughs. Jeering the polico [*sic*], and even the Governor, he swoops down on a town, holds up a bank, and dashes away again by motor. In two years he has held up at least a score of banks. . . . But nobody has been able to bring him down. And this despite the tremendous risks he takes. That he is one of the luckiest bandits in criminal history is obvious from a reading of his exploits. And that he loves to ride his luck is proved by his noon-day robbery of a bank in his home town of Sallisaw, Oklahoma."

It became increasingly difficult to separate fact from fiction when it came to tracking the lawless movements of Pretty Boy. Oftentimes, there was not much to go on but hearsay and sketchy witness accounts.

On January 22, 1933, a major feature story about Choc written by H. G. Hotchkiss appeared in the *Wichita Beacon,* complete with a photograph of Charley and his girlfriend, Beulah, as well as portraits of Ruby, Dempsey, and Governor Bill Murray. A large illustration depicted a shadowy Charley with his hat brim snapped down, holding a tommy gun. Across the top of the page was the headline "PRETTY BOY" FLOYD—OKLAHOMA'S ENEMY OR ROBIN HOOD? An editor's note explained that the story, considered by the Floyd family to be one of the more balanced reports about Choc, resulted from Hotchkiss traveling deep into the heart of Oklahoma's Pretty Boy country. Hotchkiss did his homework well. Based on interviews with Charley's friends, he discussed such tidbits as Floyd's preference for Ford automobiles (". . . because they are inconspicuous"), and his chameleonlike ability to avoid capture. Almost sixty years after it was first published, Dempsey Floyd was still diligently sending full-size photocopies of the feature story about his father to interested history researchers, authors, and criminal buffs. Hotchkiss wrote:

Officers admit that "Pretty Boy" probably is the most cunning, the most resourceful bandit in the history of a state that has become famous for its bad men. Daring, but never reckless, Floyd maps his life by carefully laid plans. It has been more his own cunning and resourcefulness, rather than luck, that keeps "Pretty Boy" a free man today. How many men Floyd has killed probably is not exactly known by anyone but "Pretty Boy" himself. How many banks he has robbed is also in doubt. He has been credited with scores of killings and scores of bank robberies, many of which he knew nothing about.

Floyd is a popular hero among the children. He never fails to give them a lift to school. And many a child had been clothed and fed thru [*sic*] the generosity of "Pretty Boy." Friends declare he is generous to a fault. His bank loot is divided, one-half going to his wife, the other half he retains for his own use but most of this is spent to help destitute families and individuals. Friends tell that Floyd was eating in a restaurant one day. A man came in and begged for a meal, stating it had been days since he had had anything to eat. "Give that fellow all he wants," spoke up "Pretty Boy." Then addressing the stranger, he said, "Here is a twenty. Perhaps that will stake you until you can get on your feet."

During the winter of 1933, the nation was in a holding pattern, anxiously waiting for Franklin Roosevelt to take the helm after his March 4 inauguration with Texan John "Cactus Jack" Garner as his vice president. In his first hundred days, Roosevelt would move swiftly to combat the Great Depression by creating a remarkable series of New Deal "alphabet agencies." In the meantime, the country's collective stomach—shrunken by 1933—impatiently growled. Proud men and women did whatever they could to keep their families alive.

While money was in short supply, ingenuity was not. For instance, the publisher of the *Sallisaw Democrat-American* renewed yearly subscriptions by accepting either a bushel of sweet potatoes, three dozen eggs, two chickens, two pounds of butter, one gallon of sorghum, one and one-half gallons of honey, or seven pounds of hog meat.

Common fare at the supper tables throughout rural Oklahoma, along with the main course of biscuits and gravy, were the latest yarns about Pretty Boy. Everyone had their own personal theory about where the twenty-nine-year-old bandit was hiding or how the authorities could capture him.

In the spring of 1933, Bradley Floyd walked into an Earlsboro joint to quench his thirst. Jack Birdwell, the teenaged son of the late outlaw, tagged behind. He never forgot what he witnessed there that day.

Bradley was nursing a drink when he heard a liquored-up roustabout bragging about what he would do if he ever got his hands on Pretty Boy Floyd. After quietly listening to the loudmouth run down his younger brother and the entire Floyd family for several minutes, Bradley approached the man. He asked him whether he knew Choc Floyd. The fellow said he did not. Bradley asked whether he had ever met any of Floyd's brothers. Again, the man said he had not, but he allowed that if they ever came around, he would make "short work of them," as well.

"Bradley drained the last of his drink and set the glass down," recounted Jack Birdwell. "Then he turned and he hit that guy just about as hard as I ever saw a man get hit. He knocked that fella plumb through the air and he crashed into the wall and slid down to the floor. Bradley got himself another drink and sat down next to the man and waited for him to come to. When the guy opened his eyes, ol' Bradley looked over at him and said, 'Well, partner, now you can say you've met one of Choc Floyd's brothers.'"

Charley Floyd continued to be everywhere at once. In Bartlesville, a town that oil made prosperous, Russell Davis remembered the morning when one of his sisters and several other local young ladies were having coffee at the Rightway Cafe. Some men they did not know walked in and looked around. "A nice-looking man from the group went over to the girls sitting at a table out in the open and he politely suggested they move to another table concealed beneath a stairway," recalled Davis. "The girls thought it was an odd request but they didn't want to make a fuss, so they complied. The men took their original table and sat drinking coffee and talking in muffled tones. Later on the girls discovered that the nice young man was none other than Pretty Boy. They were told he asked them to move so they'd be out of harm's way in case some law officers came in and there was a confrontation. He was just being thoughtful."

That same spring, George Cheatham was a young cowboy on horseback driving cattle to market. He was about sixty miles west of Kansas City when he came upon a farmer who ran from his house waving his hands and hollering at the top of his lungs. "The old-timer said he had put up a couple of men the night before," recalled Cheatham. "One of them slept in the car and the other one stayed inside. They took turns eating supper at the farmer's table. When they left that morning, they slipped the farmer some money and one of the men said, 'Tell 'em that Pretty Boy slept in your bed.' I was the first person that old farmer saw and he couldn't wait to tell me the news."

Sightings and stories about Charley continued. About mid-spring of 1933, Jesse Berryhill, a young Oklahoma teacher in Choctaw County, ended up, much to his surprise, spending a night with Pretty Boy Floyd. Berryhill, who had just finished the term at his rural school, drove north to Pushmataha County to do some night fishing along the Kiamichi River. His old Chevrolet coupe was loaded with camping gear. A bundle of twelve-foot-long cane poles was strapped on the side of the car. He crossed the Kiamichi ten miles east of the town of Antlers and turned down a little-used trail to a favorite hole he had often fished as a boy. After setting up a camp deep in the brush, Berryhill followed some car tracks until he stumbled across another coupe, half-hidden in a thicket. That is when the schoolteacher met Mr. Floyd. Many years later, Berryhill published his remembrances of the meeting in an Oklahoma newspaper.

"I spun around to stare squarely into the barrel of a machine gun backed by a square-featured, handsome face that I recognized all too well from the dozens of pictures I had seen," wrote Berryhill more than forty years later. After several tense minutes of interrogation, Floyd seemed satisfied that the intruder was not a "law" but only a harmless angler. They returned to Berryhill's camp. They shared a pot of coffee and passed the night snagging catfish by lantern light. Over plates of panfried fish and tin mugs of coffee, Berryhill asked Floyd why he stayed on the scout. Charley glanced up at him through the flames of the camp fire with a look of surprise.

"Man, I can't give myself up," Charley told Berryhill. "I'd never live to face a judge. These lawmen aren't carrying a warrant of arrest, they are carrying a license to kill me. I'm big game. The man who gets 'Pretty Boy' Floyd will be a celebrity, a public hero. And, they will get me, I know that. I can't last much longer. A man gets too tired to be careful. They'll close in on me and shoot me to death without warning and in the back, if possible. Oh, the papers will report that I was shot running away, but it will be a lie."

Shortly after dawn, Floyd let the air out of Berryhill's tires. He took the teacher's shotgun and car keys. "You'll find your keys on the gatepost, and the other things close by," Choc told him. He asked Berryhill to wait at least an hour and not to spread the story of their chance meeting too soon.

"I spent another day and night alone there by the old Kiamichi," wrote Berryhill, "and never even mentioned the incidents described here for almost five years."

Seemingly always on the move, Choc actually spent a great deal of time throughout 1932 and 1933 with the Rings, Ruby's aunt and uncle, who had a house filled with growing children not far from Boynton in Muskogee County. Jess Ring worked around the oil patch, and also served ironically as a special deputy for Muskogee County Sheriff V. S. Cannon, one of Erv Kelley's old friends. Although he was sworn to uphold the law, Ring admired Choc and considered him to be a good friend. Sheriff Cannon respected Ring's dilemma.

"My dad and Sheriff Cannon often talked about Charley," recalled Ruth Ring Morgan, one of the Ring daughters. "The sheriff said that although he knew Dad would never turn in Charley, he would still be coming out to our house to try to catch him. And the sheriff did come, too. He made repeated visits. Sometimes Charley had to hide in a nearby cotton patch but there was never any gunplay.

"One time the sheriff knocked on the front door and stepped inside because it was so cold outside. As he did, Charley slipped out the back door. I looked outside and saw the taillights of his car going down the road. Another time, a bunch of us were home making popcorn. Charley was sitting in a big chair right in front of the fireplace with one of my cousins on his lap and Sheriff Cannon comes in again and asked my dad if he'd seen Charley. 'Well, not in the last few minutes,' my dad told him. After the sheriff left, they all laughed about it because that was the truth—my dad hadn't actually looked at Charley in several minutes. There were some close calls, but Charley promised my mother that he'd never fire a shot around our house. She knew that he'd not endanger our family."

In truth, the Rings always welcomed Choc. A visit from Charley and one of his friends brightened a dull afternoon, especially during the bad times of the thirties when rain was as scarce as cash money. The family got to know George Birdwell, and after Floyd formed his association with Adam Richetti, the Rings also hosted the swarthy bandit at their residence. Adam, an accomplished freehand artist, entertained the children with his pencil sketches drawn at the kitchen table. In the mornings, there were always Milky Way bars under every child's pillow. The candy bars were left by Charley, and were as good as gold bars to a youngster of the Great Depression. On Sunday mornings, he gathered up all the kids and read them the funny papers. Sometimes he would take the older children out to a field and allow them to fire a short burst from his submachine gun while he held the weapon for them.

Although Floyd's ex-wife was actually a first cousin to the Ring children, she and Charley seemed more like an aunt and uncle.

"One of my best memories of Charley Floyd was the time my mother gave him a list of groceries to buy at the store for a needy family," remembered Ruth Morgan. "I went along with Charley and we drove to a little country store in Boynton and he filled up a bushel basket with all kinds of food and put it in the car. Then I showed Charley where the people lived. My mother had also told him that these folks were so poor that their kids had no shoes and had to lay out of school.

"So, we got to their place and Charley carried that basket of groceries to their porch and set it down. He got back in the car and sat there for a minute. Then he took out some money, rolled it up, and put it in my hand. He said, 'Go give this to the man and tell him to buy his kids some shoes.' I went up and knocked and the man came out and I did just what Charley said to do and the man thanked me. Years later I heard that one of the boys in that family not only finished school but went on to become the superintendent of all the schools in the state of Kansas."

Sixty years later, then grandmothers, Ruth and her younger sister Lavona could still clearly recall Charley Floyd baking pies in their mother's kitchen. It was his favorite way to relax.

"He loved to bake, especially those good fruit pies," recalled Lavona. "In 1933, my sisters wanted to take one to a pie supper and Charley made them a great big apple pie. Well, that pie was the hit of the supper. Sheriff Cannon ate a big slice and declared it the best pie he'd ever put in his mouth. Little did he know that it was baked by Pretty Boy Floyd!"

Sometimes Ruby and young Dempsey drove down from the Hardgraves place near Bixby to spend a weekend with Choc at the Ring home. Both Ruth and Lavona remembered several emotional reunions. "Charley would be so happy to see his son that tears flowed down his cheeks," said Lavona.

In May of 1933, just a couple of months following Roosevelt's inauguration, Charley visited his mother in Sallisaw. He took her out to Akins to decorate the graves of Walter, baby Chester Lee, and other family and friends who were buried there. As if he knew his own end was near, Charley took the opportunity to point out a spot not far from his father's resting place where he wished to be buried. The following year, Mamie Floyd recounted her son's instructions.

"Right here is where you can put me," Choc had told his mother, who later related his words to reporters. "I expect to go down soon with lead in me—perhaps the sooner the better."

Although Mamie never disclosed the precise date when her son picked out his grave site, more than likely it was the fourth Sunday in May. This was always the traditional decoration day for the community of Akins, when residents and kinfolk from near and far returned to honor the dead.

If that was indeed the correct date, then there is no question that the May 29 bank robbery and murder in New York state that many criminal historians have blamed on Pretty Boy Floyd was yet another case of mistaken identity. The crime occurred that Monday during the noon hour. Six masked bandits, armed with submachine guns, raided the Rensselaer County Bank in Rensselaer, New York. While in the act of rifling the case drawers, the holdup men were surprised by two detectives answering the bank alarm. A gun battle commenced. One officer, Frederick Rabe, was badly wounded, and the other, James A. Stevens, was shot and killed. The bandits dashed away in a blue sedan, eluding armed pursuit cars that chased them through Albany and then south toward New York City.

Thirty-five miles southeast of Rensselaer, at Lee, Massachusetts, police had flashed word at 4:00 A.M. on that same date that Pretty Boy Floyd was supposedly seen in the area driving in an automobile with Nebraska license plates. When he was shown a photograph of Floyd, the wounded detective *tentatively* identified him as one of the bandits.

In the years before commercial airplanes were common, it would have been physically impossible for Choc to get all the way from Oklahoma to far eastern New York state in less than twenty-four hours. But even if his visit to the Akins graveyard had been earlier that month, there is still a great deal of doubt that one of the gunmen was Floyd. This robbery took place far away from his territory and was completely out of character with his method of operation.

Charley would soon be plagued with far greater difficulties than the Rensselaer robbery allegations, however. A seven-week period of unmitigated criminal violence, from late May until mid-July of 1933, ripped through Oklahoma, Kansas, and Missouri. Although it would not be evident for some time to come, this series of gun battles, prison breaks, kidnappings, and murders—highlighted by the well-publicized Kansas City Massacre on June 17—were all indirectly related.

The corrupt power structure that presided in Kansas City suddenly had been plagued by internal dissension since May 27, just two days prior to the Rensselaer robbery. On that Saturday, Mary McElroy, the twenty-five-year-old daughter of Judge H. F. McElroy, the city manager under the thumb of Tom Pendergast, was kidnapped from the family's South Side residence in broad daylight. The kidnapping of Mary McElroy helped to set events in motion that would unfold throughout the turbulent summer.

The day started innocently enough. Miss McElroy had plans to attend the gala opening of the fourth season at the Riverside racetrack. About 11:00 A.M., she was upstairs taking a bath when there was a knock at the front door. A maid admitted a young man, later identified as Walter McGee, posing as a cosmetic salesman delivering samples. Once inside, McGee brandished a gun and announced his intention to kidnap Mary McElroy. After calmly finishing her bath, she dressed in a summer frock, powdered her nose, and left with her captor. McGee covered the young woman with a lap robe, and he and several accomplices whisked her away to a stucco house on the county line road north of Shawnee, Kansas.

Soon, Judge McElroy received notes in his daughter's own handwriting, demanding sixty thousand dollars in ransom. He bargained the kidnappers down to thirty thousand dollars, and Johnny Lazia was given the assignment of collecting that sum from his loyal following. Reporters, detectives, and politicians crowded into the McElroy home. Boss Pendergast himself stopped by to offer sympathy to his distraught stooge. The situation was particularly frustrating because the kidnappers were strictly amateurs and were virtually unknown in the underworld channels of Kansas City.

Following more negotiations, the ransom was delivered by McElroy and his son to a lonely spot off Muncie Bluff Road. There the masked kidnappers, wearing overalls and carrying shotguns, took the money and told the McElroys to return home. Finally, more than thirty hours after she had first been kidnapped, Mary McElroy was released unharmed near the entrance to the Milburn Country Club.

McGee, his brother, and another man and woman were among those linked to the crime. Five days later, McGee and two of the suspects were arrested. Justice was swift. Stiff jail terms were given for the kidnapping and McGee was sentenced to be executed. However, because of pleas for mercy from Miss McElroy and her father, that punishment was later commuted to life imprisonment.

Even after the safe release of Mary McElroy, tension continued to run high in Kansas City. The McElroy kidnapping was an insult to the pride of the suave Johnny Lazia. The incident undermined the confidence many corrupt Kansas Citians had placed in the chief enforcer of Judge McElroy's Home Rule policy, which tolerated petty violations of the law. Rival gangs, already angered by the concessions shown the Lazia organization by local authorities, screamed that the out-of-town punks and neophyte hoodlums were a growing threat. Tension was building in Tom's Town.

Three days after the McElory kidnapping, while detectives and Lazia's henchmen still searched for the abductors, there was still another shock to Kansas City's already-queasy system. The surprise came on May 30— Memorial Day. Eleven big-time convicts, eight of them convicted murderers and bank robbers, escaped from the Kansas state prison at Lansing, less than forty miles outside Kansas City.

Some of these escaped convicts, especially ringleaders Wilbur Underhill and Harvey Bailey, were soon to be considered prime suspects in the Kansas City Massacre. Given their violent backgrounds, it was easy to see why.

Underhill, a thirty-three-year-old cop killer known in the Oklahoma, Kansas, and Missouri region as the Tri-State Terror, was no choirboy. A convicted bootlegger and hijacker as a youth, he later served time for burglary and armed robbery and had previously escaped from the Oklahoma state penitentiary, where he had been incarcerated for killing a drugstore clerk and an oil field worker. He had been serving a life term at Lansing for murdering a Wichita policeman. Three out of his four years in the Kansas prison he had spent in solitary confinement.

Bailey, at one time a hardworking family man, had prospered as a bootlegger after World War I, before turning to bank burglary and armed robbery in the early 1920s. He was part of the team that struck at the U.S. Mint in Denver on December 18, 1922, escaping with two hundred thousand dollars in five-dollar bills. The undisputed king of bank robbers, Bailey operated at various times with several old pros, including Thomas Holden, Francis Keating, Verne Miller, Frank "Jelly" Nash, and a young bootlegger named George Kelly Barnes, who would later become known as Machine Gun Kelly.

Bailey had been implicated for a time in the Chicago gang massacre on St. Valentine's Day of 1929 and had also been identified as one of the robbers who looted the Lincoln Bank and Trust in Nebraska of a staggering $2.6 million in cash and negotiable securities in 1930. Following his conviction in the June 17, 1932, raid of a bank in Fort Scott, Kansas, Bailey was serving twenty to one hundred years for murder and bank robbery. His accomplices included Freddie Barker and Alvin "Creepy" Karpis. Called Old Harve because of his prematurely gray hair, Bailey was well into his forties at the time of the prison break.

Of the others who escaped from Lansing, convicts James Clark, Frank Sawyer, Alvin Payton, and Edward Davis were serving twenty- to one-hundred-year terms for murder and robbery. Kenneth Coon faced a life term for murder and Robert Brady was a lifer convicted of being an habitual criminal. Lewis Bechtel, Clifford Dapson, and Billy Woods were doing time on five- to twenty-year sentences for robbery and automobile theft.

The gang of hard-core cons, armed with pistols that had been smuggled into the penitentiary, made their break while the rest of the 1,861 inmates watched a Memorial Day baseball game between American Legion teams from Topeka and Leavenworth. Underhill and his cohorts took the warden and two guards hostage. Using grappling hooks and a rope ladder made in the prison twine shop, they slipped over the penitentiary walls and returned to the outside world. Several of the convicts were recaptured in the massive manhunt that followed, but the worst of the lot managed to find refuge in Oklahoma.

The Lansing incident put the authorities in mind of the sensational escape of seven federal prisoners from the nearby Leavenworth Penitentiary on December 11, 1931. Included among that group of grizzled outlaws were Earl Thayer and several former members of the old Al Spencer gang dating back to the wild six-shooter days in Oklahoma. The runaway convicts were soon shot or apprehended.

A prime suspect as the mastermind behind both of the big Kansas prison breaks was none other than Frank "Jelly" Nash, the notorious Oklahoma bandit who had been sent to Leavenworth in 1924 to serve a twenty-five-year term after his conviction in the Okesa train robbery led by Al Spencer. Nash had been on the loose ever since October 19, 1930, when he escaped from the big federal penitentiary. A prison trustee because of his exemplary behavior, Nash was working in the warden's residence and had just prepared a sumptuous dinner for the warden's family when he simply walked out the back door with a three-volume set of Shakespeare under his arm and never returned. Law officers conjectured that Nash had fled the grounds in an automobile driven by some of Johnny Lazia's henchmen.

Warden Thomas White, embarrassed by Nash's departure, told reporters: "We let Nash put it over on us. Anyone who could talk his way out of two life sentences, well, we should have known better."

In 1931, Nash had also been instrumental in the escape of two other Leavenworth convicts, the bank robbers Thomas Holden and Francis Keating. They fled to Kansas City and teamed up with the violent Barker-Karpis gang, robbing several banks over the following year.

For rest and recuperation between bank heists, these men and other criminal cronies enjoyed rounds of golf at the Old Mission Country Club, a Kansas City resort that was popular with underworld figures. On July 8, 1932, Holden and Keating joined Bailey and Nash for a leisurely eighteen holes. Federal agents, including some who would be involved in the Kansas City Massacre less than a year later, and a few local detectives had been shadowing the outlaws. They swooped down on the bandit golfers just as they finished the last hole and were headed to the clubhouse to join their wives and sweethearts. Bailey, Holden, and Keating were taken into custody. The other member of the foursome, Jelly Nash, was still out on the eighteenth green. When he witnessed the arrest of his three friends, Nash quickly ducked into some brush and made his escape. In no time, Nash hooked up with the Barkers and continued his bank-robbing ways. Bailey soon found himself in the Kansas state prison, where he remained until he and Underhill and the rest of their cutthroat crew made their Memorial Day departure over the high prison walls.

In the aftermath of the eleven desperadoes escaping from Lansing, Charley Floyd's continued capers were reduced to minor mentions buried deep in newspapers. On June 3, however, while the search continued for the Mary McElroy kidnappers as well as the prison escapees from Lansing, a dispatch out of Oklahoma caught everyone up on Choc's latest escapade. "The 'Pretty Boy' listed in a thousand rogues galleries as Charles Arthur Floyd, and sought for more than three years by peace officers in a dozen states, again tonight was the object of a search concentrated in one of his favorite hiding places near Seminole."

Floyd and several companions were out for a Saturday afternoon drive on a country road when their stolen automobile had a flat tire. A trio of Seminole County deputies happened along and stopped to make a routine check. One of the officers was suspicious and asked Floyd to identify himself. He did—with his submachine gun. Choc whipped the weapon out from beneath a blanket and stuck it in the deputy's face. "It's none of your business," snarled Choc. "Go to hell!"

The frightened deputies jumped into their car and dashed back to Wewoka for reinforcements. When they returned, the lawmen took into custody Ruby Floyd and Marie Smalley, wife of Blackie Smalley, just as the women poured gasoline over the stolen vehicle. The women were charged with harboring criminals and theft. Officers drove out to Bradley Floyd's home near Earlsboro and also arrested Bradley, Blackie Smalley, and Troy Keesee, the brother-in-law of State Representative C. L. Hill of Seminole County, who owned the stolen automobile. Young Dempsey Floyd, neatly dressed in overalls, was found at the Smalley residence. All of them were taken in for questioning and also charged with car theft.

"No son ever had a more affectionate father and no wife a more dutiful husband than Charley Floyd," spouted Ruby from her jail cell. She and the others were thoroughly grilled and were then released after making bond. The charges were dropped. Choc and Adam Richetti escaped capture and were nowhere to be found.

At the time of this incident, a rumor also circulated that Ruby was preparing her memoirs. Most folks outside the tight circle of Floyd friends and family were not aware that Ruby had divorced Charley back in 1929, much less that she had married a banker from Coffeyville, Kansas. If she actually put down on paper some of her impressions of life with a hunted bank robber, that project was soon put aside, however. There were other distractions, such as show business.

Ruby and her eight-year-old son went on the road with a stage show ironically called *Crime Doesn't Pay.* In June of 1933, the mother-and-son act appeared before sizable audiences at both Seminole and Wewoka. The crowd was so large at Seminole that a special late show was held just to accommodate the overflow of people anxious to see Pretty Boy's son and wife and hear about their tribulations.

"Oftentimes my mother and I would appear on stage between movies at theaters in different cities," remembered Dempsey Floyd. "We went all over Oklahoma, Kansas, Texas, wherever they could book us a show. I'd get all dressed up in a nice white suit, and I'd walk right out on the stage and tell the people who I was and then I'd introduce my mother. We would stand out there together and she'd talk about crime and how it had ruined our lives and kept us separated from my father. I guess people wanted to know what we looked like."

The idea of Ruby and Dempsey appearing in public to talk about Choc did not go over well with all the Floyds. Mamie Floyd was especially upset and made her feelings known, but her feelings about Ruby, especially after she married the Coffeyville baker, were not terribly fond, anyway. Charley, however, apparently was not bothered at all by Ruby's attempt to earn a little money.

"I can recall one time when Ruby and Jackie had a big show to do in Muskogee," reminisced Ruth Ring Morgan. "This particular time, Charley himself took me to see the show. He drove me over to Muskogee and dropped me off right in front of the theater. There were big ol' posters about their talk up everywhere. As I was getting out of the car, he smiled and said, 'I hope you enjoy the show.' He wasn't put out one bit."

On June 14, a series of violent acts transpired in the Show Me State that gave Charley Floyd little to smile about. At 2:15 P.M., a trio of men held up the Farmers and Merchants Bank of Mexico, Missouri. The bandits entered the bank with drawn revolvers and confronted C. F. Merrifield, the bank cashier, and two customers. After looting the vault, cash drawer, and money changer, the robbers even took sixty-five dollars from Robert Lyons, who had stopped to make a deposit. A total of $1,750 was gathered in only a few minutes and then the desperadoes drove south down Highway 54 in a Buick sedan.

Within minutes of the robbery, a statewide alarm went out. Jefferson City police officers stationed guards at the Missouri River bridge to watch for the bandits. Lawmen throughout the central part of the state jumped into their automobiles and scoured the back roads and highways.

Only forty-five minutes after the bank robbery, Boone County Sheriff Roger Wilson and Sgt. Ben Booth, a highway patrolman, pulled over a suspect vehicle on the outskirts of the city of Columbia. As the lawmen began to question the occupants, gunshots erupted from inside the car and both officers fell dead.

By late that afternoon, one of the largest manhunts in Missouri history had commenced. Great posses made up of University of Missouri students, farmers, and businessmen joined with peace officers in search of the killers. Weapons ranged from shotguns to pearl-handled pistols. One old man carried an antique blunderbuss with a flared muzzle. From the university campus at Columbia, the colonel in charge of the Reserve Officers Training Program ordered rapid-fire army rifles to be issued to the possemen. Supply sergeants handed out arms and ammunition to long lines of ex-soldiers who had been deputized. In downtown Columbia and in the nearby city of Fulton, large crowds of incensed citizens milled about while waiting for any word about the progress of the manhunt. Maj. Phil Love, buddy of Col. Charles Lindbergh during their mail-flying days in the twenties, flew in from St. Louis to lead an aerial search. Riverboats were pressed into service to patrol the banks of the broad Missouri. Rewards for the slayers, dead or alive, mounted.

The following morning, a hemp hangman's noose was seen dangling from a signpost near the scene of the double murder. It symbolized the temperament of the grim-faced men on the hunt. Col. Marvin Casteel, head of the state highway patrol, ordered barricades to be maintained on almost every road and bridge in Boone and Callaway counties. In Columbia, swarms of mourners paid tribute to the fallen officers whose bodies lay in state in the rotunda of the Boone County courthouse. Badge number thirteen was pinned on Booth's dress uniform.

A few days after the murders, no suspects had been located, but the United Press found a Columbia woman who came forward with new information. She claimed that she was an eyewitness to the double slaying of Wilson and Booth. Lucy Clark provided reporters and law officers with a detailed account of the crime. She said that she had been walking across the lawn of a tourist camp at the intersection of Highways 63 and 40 and was only about twenty-five feet from the scene of the shooting.

"I saw an auto come over the top of the hill driving slowly," recalled Mrs. Clark. "They seemed to move around a bit and put something up on the ledge behind them in the car."

She watched as Sergeant Booth flagged the car down, and the highway patrolman walked to the right side of the vehicle and leaned on the door. Mrs. Clark heard the officer speak. "Hello, gentlemen, which way are you headed?" questioned Booth. She could not make out the response, but only an instant later Booth jerked open the car door and pulled out the man sitting on the right side. Sheriff Wilson ran up at this point, and the driver of the car fired through the windshield. Two of the bullets struck Wilson and he plunged forward. The suspect turned the gun on the patrolman and shot him once. Booth fell and pulled down the man he was grappling with on the roadside. He also managed to shout for help. The driver raced around the car and both men pushed Booth back down and shot him twice more. Then the two men jumped back in their car and fled.

Mrs. Clark described the driver of the car in detail—down to the cap he wrote at a jaunty angle and the snarl on his face. When police officers showed her a photograph of a known criminal they thought might be involved, she quickly agreed it was a portrait of the killer.

"I'm sure that is one of the men," said Mrs. Clark. "He drove that car."

She was staring at a mug shot of Charles Arthur Floyd.

As a result, law officers from throughout rural America to Washington, D.C., considered Choc to be nothing but a wanton killer. Within only a few days, even the double murder of the Missourians was overshadowed by a crime in Kansas City that stirred the nation to give more power to J. Edgar Hoover. It also guaranteed Choc's life would soon be ended.

30

THE MASSACRE

SHORTLY AFTER A SPREE OF VIOLENCE broke out in central Missouri, Choc Floyd and Adam Richetti entered the state. Sticking to the country roads, they arrived either on June 15 or 16, driving a Pontiac that had been stolen on June 8 in Castle, Oklahoma. The coupe's Oklahoma license plate—number 154 027—had been swiped off a Chevrolet coach in the town of Maud. Hidden inside the vehicle was an extra set of stolen license plates. In the trunk, the outlaws stashed an army-style footlocker filled with a cache of spare guns and ammunition adjacent to the car owner's new golf bag and clubs.

Unbeknownst to Floyd and Richetti, their names were tied to the murders of the peace officers near Columbia and the bank robbery at Mexico just as they slipped across the Missouri border. Their troubles had escalated when the Missouri woman told authorities that she had seen Floyd kill the Boone County sheriff and a state partrolman on June 14.

Despite the eyewitness's claim, it can be safely ascertained that Charley Floyd and Adam Richetti had absolutely no role in either the slayings of the two lawmen or the bank robbery earlier that same day. When those crimes were being committed, Floyd's relatives verified that Choc and Adam were hundreds of miles to the southwest, having a high time in their Oklahoma stomping grounds. Unfortunately, the true culprits, one of whom turned out to be another of the many Pretty Boy look-alikes, did not confess for almost a year and a half. Floyd and Richetti were ultimately cleared of those misdeeds.

Several criminologists and historians who closely examined the case pointed out that Floyd inadvertently brought trouble upon himself when he left his sanctuary of Oklahoma in mid-June to visit Kansas City. It was all a matter of timing, they said. And in Floyd's instance, his timing could not have been worse.

Some of Floyd's kinfolk later explained that Charley and his friend merely intended to visit Kansas City for a tryst with Beulah and her sister, Rose, who by then was enamored with Richetti. Their plan was to have a few laughs, to let down their hair in Tom's Town.

Choc and Adam either drove straight through from Oklahoma during the early-morning hours or else spent the night in a farmer's barn in the Springfield area. Just after dawn on Friday, June 16, Floyd and Richetti traveled north out of Springfield on Highway 13, then a partially paved two-lane road with long stretches of gravel and oil mat. They had not yet heard that they were considered suspects in the recent bank heist and slayings of the lawmen. If they had, they unquestionably would have canceled their visit.

According to Floyd family members, the two bandits anticipated a leisurely drive into Kansas City and a few nights of pleasure with their girlfriends. Not satisfied with a mug of stout coffee from an all-night greasy spoon, Adam swigged a bottle of bootleg whiskey for a morning jolt. His partner's increased drinking bothered Choc, especially so early in the day. He had often asked Richetti to pace himself and not allow his taste for strong drink to get out of hand. Those warnings fell on deaf ears.

Not far from Our Way, a small community a few miles north of Springfield, the stolen Pontiac broke down. Charley was forced to enlist the services of an old man who agreed to fetch his truck and tow the disabled automobile into the town of Bolivar, about twenty miles up the highway. Adam's older brother, Joe Richetti, lived there and worked as an automobile mechanic.

Downtown streets were quiet that morning. The latest issue of the weekly *Bolivar Free Press* was loaded with local news, including a juicy item about a man living north of town who was jailed for being drunk and disturbing the peace. There were reports of folks catching exceptionally big catfish in the area rivers and a notice that blackberries would soon be ready for early harvest. The aroma of fresh bread poured from the bakery, where a large piping hot loaf sold for just a nickel.

The old farmer, pulling the crippled Pontiac with his truck, arrived in Bolivar with Choc and Adam about 7:00 A.M. Most shops were still closed and the streets mostly empty. Adam, frustrated because of the car problems, took to his bottle of hooch as a trusty ally. He directed the old man to drive first to J. E. Smith and Sons Garage, but some men there said Joe Richetti had taken a job with the Bitzer Chevrolet Company. They left and slowly drove past the imposing Polk County Courthouse, where rows of stores and businesses faced the town square. Atop the stately stone building, a statue of the blindfolded Lady Justice held her scales and sword. She stood perpetual guard, ruling a small army of pigeons cloistered in the clock tower.

At about ten minutes past seven, the old man, with the Pontiac in tow, arrived at Bitzer Chevrolet on the corner of West Broadway and Missouri Avenue, just a short distance off the square. Charley paid the old man for his services, and some of the mechanics pushed the Pontiac into the garage.

Joe Richetti greeted his brother and Choc, and then he set to work to fix their automobile. Although he had a wooden leg as the result of an accident, Joe overcame his disability and was adept at solving most mechanical problems. He put in long hours at the garage and became a respected member of the community. Like Charley Floyd, he was distressed to see his brother drinking alcohol so early in the day.

While Joe worked on the car, some of the salesmen, wearing saddle oxfords and summer suits, wandered from the showroom into the shop to check out the visitors and eyeball the big Pontiac. Besides Chevrolets, Bitzer had only recently added Oldsmobiles to his line. The sales force was anxious to peruse the competition.

"I arrived at the garage after the repairs had started upon Floyd's coupe, and talked to him for several minutes," related Ernest V. Bitzer, the proprietor, several days later. Bitzer asked Choc whether he enjoyed the Pontiac. He answered that he liked it just fine. "I recognized Floyd from newspaper pictures. I said, 'That car looks as if it could travel pretty fast.' Floyd said it would do eighty-five."

A man who had just entered the garage suggested that the coupe appeared to have already gone eighty-five miles per hour one too many times. "It looks as if it had been traveling pretty fast," said the newcomer. Choc and Bitzer turned to see Jack Killingsworth, the sheriff of Polk County, standing behind them in his new panama hat. Killingsworth scrutinized the Pontiac's freshly dented fender.

Decades later, Killingsworth clearly remembered his encounter that warm June morning with Floyd. The former car salesman for Bitzer Chevrolet was only in his sixth month as the county sheriff, and he enjoyed returning to his former place of employment for early-morning talk and coffee with Bitzer and the boys. On this particular morning, as was his custom when not on official business, Killingsworth was not even carrying a gun.

"I saw this man and Ernest Bitzer sitting on a bench talking," recollected Killingsworth, twenty-nine years after his chance meeting with Floyd and Richetti. He said he recognized Floyd from the criminal mug shots of the Oklahoma bandit filed away at the nearby sheriff's office. "I knew from the look on his face that something was wrong. It took a second and I knew who it was."

Adam Richetti, familiar with the sheriff from previous visits to Bolivar, became alarmed when he spotted Killingsworth giving Floyd the once-over. Adam reached into the Pontiac and brought out a handy submachine gun hidden beneath a blanket on the backseat.

"That's the law," he shouted to Floyd. Adam waved the weapon at the sheriff and the others. "Line up against that wall. If you try to get away, we will kill you." Adam herded the three mechanics and three salesmen into a corner. Then he turned the gun toward the sheriff, but Joe Richetti jumped in front of Killingsworth.

"If you're going to shoot the sheriff, you'll have to shoot me first," Joe told his brother.

"All right, get him out of here then," said Adam. The drinking appeared to have muddled Richetti's mind. The sheriff started for the door. Richetti urged him to move faster by poking his back with the muzzle of the submachine gun. Killingsworth had just opened the door and was stepping outside when he felt a hard object against the side of his head. It was the barrel of an automatic pistol.

"Take one more step and I'll kill you," Floyd told him.

"There I was with one of them in the back with a machine gun telling me to get out of the door, and the other one with a forty-five telling me to stop," said Killingsworth, recalling the dilemma. However, Charley had no intention of allowing the sheriff to walk away and to alert his deputies that a pair of nationally prominent desperadoes were holed up at Bitzer's garage. Angry and confused, Adam cursed and threatened the terrified men until Choc quieted him down.

"That liquor is getting the best of you," Choc snapped at Adam. Floyd also apologized to Ernest Bitzer for the display of force.

"This is life and death for us," Choc told him. "We had to do it. They would kill us if they could."

The two outlaws stood around for several minutes, undecided what to do next. Then while Floyd stood guard, Richetti, eager to make a quick getaway, left the garage and climbed into Killingsworth's car, which was parked outside. Then he noticed his brother Joe's 1933 Chevrolet sedan just across the street. Adam decided the newer car would make a better escape vehicle. He drove to the dealership's gasoline pump, where a man from the front office, thinking Adam was picking up the car for his brother, innocently filled the tank. Adam then drove around to the garage and retrieved his submachine gun while Choc ordered Killingsworth to get into the car.

"I asked him, 'Why take me?' recalled Killingsworth. "He said, 'You know all the roads and you can keep me off the highways.' "

After the weapons were loaded in the car, Killingsworth got into the backseat with Charley, and Adam slid behind the steering wheel. "You can have my car, Joe!" Charley yelled to Adam's brother as they roared out of Bolivar.

Meanwhile, the alarm spread across the square that Pretty Boy Floyd and Adam Richetti were in town. Claude R. Blue had taken his car to the garage to have it greased. When he discovered the situation in the repair shop, Blue dashed up the street to the City Drug Store. He phoned Roe Newsum, a deputy sheriff, who summoned other deputies and alerted law officers in Springfield and surrounding towns. Newsum arrived at the garage right after the departure of the two gunmen with their hostage. The deputy directed the pursuit from his car. State officers hurried out of Springfield. Other law-enforcement agencies from around the region joined in the chase. Many were already on patrol looking for the alleged killers of the Boone County sheriff and highway patrolman.

"I was in the backseat with Floyd," recalled Killingsworth of the harrowing ride through the Missouri countryside. "Richetti drove for about thirty-five miles, and I was afraid because he was drinking. Then Floyd took the wheel. He sure was a good driver.

"I wasn't so much worried about what Richetti would do to me, but I knew that if someone caught up with us, there was going to be a desperate fight and someone was going to get killed. I figured there was a good chance I would be the first one. What worried me from the start was that the boys [other officers] would try to help me out. Floyd, I saw right away, would kill a man, but not unless he had to. They told me I would be safe if I would direct them to safety. We wandered over roads I knew would be hard to follow."

The chase led north through Polk County, first up Highway 83 and then back and forth on farm-to-market roads into Hickory County. They raced by two-story frame farmhouses with lightning rods spiking each steep roof and a sleeping mutt on every porch. In some yards, manicured vegetable gardens were trimmed with showy zinnias and a border of pungent marigolds to ward off insects. In the shallow ponds, wading cattle stood motionless except for their jaws ruminating wads of cud. The hell-bent car left clouds of dust in country crossroads like Elkton, where farmers took breaks from their row crops to trade at a store that made lunch meat and cheese sandwiches. Passing travelers bought bushels of garden produce. Ripe melons lying in the shade looked like dark green cannonballs.

"Floyd talked a lot at first," recounted Killingsworth. "He asked about the roads and talked about many things. Then sometimes I would ask him a question and he wouldn't let on like he heard me. He was very polite and always called me 'Sheriff.' He never told me to shut up, but sometimes he would go a half hour without saying a word."

At one point, when they reached a stretch of lakefront, Floyd suggested they stop and go fishing. "Don't try it," Killingsworth advised Charley. "There are posses after you now. I don't want them to catch up with you while I'm in this car."

By mid-morning the light tan four-door Chevy sedan was spotted near the towns of Wheatland, Quincy, and Harper as the desperadoes worked their way in a generally northwesterly direction toward Kansas City. They crossed into St. Clair County and scooted up Highway 13 northward by Osceola. Built on the Osage River and settled by Southerners, the town had been looted and burned by Kansas troops in 1861 but rallied to become a trade center and seat of justice for the surrounding farm county. Beyond Osceola and Lowry City, not far from the town of Brownington, the fleeing outlaws were overtaken by a lone state patrol vehicle.

Richetti grasped the submachine gun and Choc took the safety off his automatic pistol. "Wave them back," Floyd told the sheriff.

"I stuck my panama hat out the window and waved as hard as I could," recalled Killingsworth. "Pretty soon the patrolman began to get the idea and dropped back. I'm sure I saved his life. Another time we were hemmed in by possemen. I sure hoped they wouldn't surround us completely because there would sure have been bloodshed."

Again, the outlaws were able to outdistance their pursuers. Once inside Henry County, it was decided to avoid the larger county seat town of Clinton. Charley turned the car toward the Kansas border to the west. During the long journey, they stopped twice to get gasoline and candy bars. At one filling station, Floyd asked the woman attendant whether she had heard any news about the kidnapping of the sheriff. She reported that law officers, who had paused for fuel and drinks of water from the hose, had told her that they figured the desperadoes were headed for Oklahoma. This caused Charley and Adam to chuckle, but they decided they still had to be cautious. They could not let down their guard.

"I told Floyd he'd better get another car, because the one we had wasn't so very fast," related Killingsworth. "He thought it was a good idea and he pulled off to the side of the road."

They were now on Highway 52, about two and a half miles west of the town of Deepwater. Charley and Adam, with weapons at the ready, watched for a probable candidate to motor by them. They did not have long to wait. "After a few minutes, a Pontiac came up the road," remembered Killingsworth. "Floyd said, 'That looks like a likely car,' and chased it. Richetti held a machine gun against me and made me wave the driver down."

Leaving Joe Richetti's Chevrolet behind, the gunmen took their few possessions, including the guns in the trunk. They ordered Killingsworth into the Pontiac. "Move over!" Choc growled at the driver, a fifty-one-year-old Sunday school superintendent from Clinton named Walter L. Griffith. A widower since 1930, he had lately served as a farm supervisor for a life insurance company.

On this day, Griffith was making a business call. He was en route to the Annie McCoy farm near Appleton City when he was flagged down by Killingsworth. The two men who jumped out of their car waving pistols and a submachine gun startled the mild-mannered Griffith, whose greatest source of pleasure was the temperance prayer meetings he led at the First Baptist Church. As the big Pontiac roared down the dusty road, Floyd assured Griffith that they meant him no harm. They had only appropriated his speedy automobile to complete the journey to Kansas City.

"He [Floyd] took the wheel, and Sheriff Killingsworth and Richetti sat in the rear," Griffith told the *Kansas City Star* the following day. "Floyd had one automatic pistol between his knees and another by his left side. Whenever anyone in another car looked at us, Floyd would release the safety catch on the automatic between his knees." Gradually everyone settled back.

"You seem like pretty good fellas. I believe I'll let you get out of this," Floyd told the two captives.

"After a while, I began to think that if we kept our heads, we might get out of it all right," Killingsworth later told reporters. "He's a desperate man, this Floyd. But he was pretty pleasant to me all the time we were together. Floyd made no more threats. He told me to do what he asked and we would get along all right. But I don't think any ten men can capture him alive."

As the curious foursome—the sheriff, the deacon, and the two bandits—continued on toward Kansas City, the shiny new Pontiac rumbled across creeks on narrow bridges and sped past suntanned farmers who waved from their tractors.

"Sometime during the afternoon, an airplane flew down the road, about one hundred feet above us," recollected Killingsworth. "That worried Floyd and it worried me, too, but apparently the pilot didn't notice us, because he went on."

They crossed into Kansas without fanfare. Griffith's Pontiac took the curves gracefully, spraying loose gravel into the weeds. A fog of ashen dust billowed in its wake. The insurance agent was more worried about his new automobile and the paint being scratched than about his life. Griffith complained that Floyd was driving much too fast. Charley did not sass the older man, but Richetti became infuriated and wanted to dump the impudent Griffith from his own car. While Killingsworth smoothed Griffith's ruffled feathers, Charley calmed Richetti down. There were no further outbursts.

In fact, by early evening, a mutual respect developed between Floyd and Killingsworth. Charley pulled the car off the road into a hidden ravine in a wooded area somewhere to the east of Ottawa, Kansas, so they could rest and wait for the cover of darkness before entering Kansas City. Griffith sat in silence in his beloved Pontiac while the others stretched out on the ground. Richetti consoled himself with more than a few snootfuls of liquor. Choc took a few nips to wash down the road dust he had inhaled all day. He quietly shared a few of his personal thoughts with the sheriff.

"We got to be plumb good friends," Killingsworth later said of Floyd. "He got to talking a lot about himself. He told me, 'It's a hell of a life being dogged around, and having to hide all the time. There's no turning back for me now. Too many policemen want me. I haven't got a chance except to fight it out. I don't aim to let anybody take me alive.' " Killingsworth rested his head on a rock and listened to every word. Propped on his elbow, Choc kept his .45 holstered and the submachine gun lay nearby.

"They'll get me," continued Floyd. "Sooner or later, I'll go down full of lead. That's the way it will end. I might not have to been this way, you know, but for the damned police. I might be going straight, be living with a family and working for a living. I finally decided, you're determined I'm a tough guy, a bank robber—that's what I'll be. They [the law] have themselves to thank."

Killingsworth talked about his wife, but when he said that he missed his little boy, Floyd bristled. The sheriff remembered every word.

"You shouldn't kick about one day," Choc told him. "How would you like to be hunted night and day, day and night? How would you like to sleep every night with this thing [Charley touched the barrel of the submachine gun] across your knees? I have a son, too. Maybe you think I wouldn't like to see him. When you get home, you can have your son with you every day and sit and talk with him. All I ever get to do is see mine once in a long while. Then all I can do is to stand off and look at him for a minute."

After a few hours, they climbed back into the car. They drove north through the darkness. At Bonner Springs, they swung east, slowly circling Kansas City. They arrived shortly after 10:00 P.M. Splattered bugs caked the windshield as Griffith's sacred Pontiac crept into the packinghouse district in the West Bottoms.

Floyd stopped the car on a darkened street and left for a few moments to make a telephone call. More than likely, Floyd family members later conjectured, he contacted Beulah. When Choc returned, he drove the hostages to an area near Ninth and Hickory streets. A black Chevrolet sedan drove up beside the Pontiac. Floyd and Richetti transferred the footlocker to the other car, presumably driven by Beulah or her sister. After the transfer was made, Floyd moved the Pontiac a short distance down the road and stopped. He ordered the captives out of the car.

"He told us to wait five minutes and then walk down and get the car," recalled Killingsworth. "He said to drive on home and not to call anyone, because we would be watched." Floyd also recommended that on their way home, Killingsworth and Griffith stop in Lee's Summit for a bite to eat.

Then just before he and Richetti took their leave, Charley turned to the weary sheriff. "Floyd told me to take the golf bag he left in the car they abandoned at the garage to remember him by. But I told him I wouldn't need anything to remember him by."

Charley and Adam drove the Pontiac about one hundred yards down the road to where the Chevy waited. The last Killingsworth saw of them, they were speeding toward downtown Kansas City. He guessed that Richetti, in an alcoholic stupor, would soon pass out.

Killingsworth and Griffith walked to where Floyd had left the dust-covered Pontiac. The keys hung in the ignition. Only the stench of Richetti's whiskey remained to remind the men of their captors. They followed Choc's instructions and did not rush to notify the local authorities. Instead, they drove to nearby Lee's Summit, where the sheriff called his home in Bolivar to let his wife know that he was safe. Griffith then drove south with Killingsworth and reached his hometown of Clinton about 2:30 A.M. The sheriff telephoned Ernest Bitzer, and the car dealer drove up from Bolivar to retrieve him. Killingsworth's anxious wife and their two-year-old son waited at the family home. After he related the details of his fourteen-hour adventure with Pretty Boy through more than five hundred miles of Missouri and Kansas back country, Killingsworth collapsed in bed.

"For the business he's in," the sheriff said of Choc, "Floyd's a perfect gentleman."

The same afternoon that Floyd and Richetti zigzagged toward Kansas City, another group of law officers, reinforced by two companies of National Guardsmen, pressed their pursuit of Floyd and Richetti, certain that they were the bandits who had killed the two peace officers near Columbia. As three thousand mourners walked past the bodies of Booth and Wilson at their memorial service, Boone County's prosecuting attorney vowed to seek capital punishment for the killers. Besides the Columbia woman who had already identified Pretty Boy as the triggerman, a farmer and his wife from Cairo, Missouri, just north of Moberly, came forward to say that Floyd and a companion had spent the night in the Grand Prairie Church near their place about a week before the lawmen's murders. The couple knew it had to be Pretty Boy because of pictures of him they had seen in the newspapers.

The Mexico bank robbery and the slayings of the sheriff and state patrolman near Columbia, coupled with the capricious kidnapping of another county sheriff and a businessman, made Pretty Boy and Richetti as famous as members of the Gas House Gang playing ball in St. Louis.

While one drama was unfolding in Missouri, another was occurring at the same time in Arkansas. In the wide-open resort town of Hot Springs, a popular "safe city" for men on the run, federal agents were closing in on the elusive fugitive Frank Nash. Little did Floyd or Nash—who never even met each other—know it at the time, but they were destined to be linked in one of the most infamous displays of violence of the Great Depression.

Only nine hours after Charley and Richetti parted company with their two hostages, the bloodbath that shattered the calm in Kansas City emblazoned the names of Frank Nash and Pretty Boy Floyd in the annals of American criminal history. Smooth-talking Jelly Nash, the seasoned survivor from the six-shooter and cow pony days of Wild West banditry, never knew what hit him.

The Bureau of Investigation had been on Nash's trail for three years, ever since he had slipped away from the warden's home at Leavenworth and returned to a checkered career as a bootlegger and robber. Federal agents learned that Nash had since married Frances Luce, a divorcée with a small daughter. They received word that the couple had been seen in the company of other questionable characters and their spouses at known criminal hangouts throughout the Midwest. Further information provided by Holden and Keating, two of the bank robbers nabbed in 1932 at the end of a golf game in Kansas City, indicated that Nash was currently receiving protection from underworld contacts in Hot Springs, where he sometimes used the name Doc Williams.

In June 1933, two federal agents from the Bureau of Investigation's Oklahoma City office, Frank C. Smith and F. Joseph Lackey, made plans to capture Nash.

Scuttlebutt on the snitches' grapevine had it that Nash had taken extreme measures to alter his appearance. To make sure they captured their man, Smith and Lackey recruited McAlester Police Chief Otto Reed, a veteran peace officer familiar with Nash from the old days in Oklahoma, to accompany them to Hot Springs. Reed agreed to go along for the ride. He said it would be worth the trip just to see the look on Nash's face when they nailed him.

The trio of lawmen set out for Hot Springs, the venerable spa with a thermal river under its main street. Located fifty-five miles southwest of Little Rock in the oak- and hickory-covered hills, Hot Springs had been for many years a haven for the rich, famous, and infamous, all interested in a soak at one of the luxurious establishments on lavish Bathhouse Row along Central Avenue.

Visitors as improbably grouped as Babe Ruth, Will Rogers, Helen Keller, and Andrew Carnegie took therapeutic baths to unknit muscles. Others came to cure ailments ranging from syphilis to rheumatism. Some gambled for high stakes between dips in the healing waters. Occasionally, such prizefighters as John L. Sullivan, Jess Willard, and Choc's idol Jack Dempsey used Hot Springs as a conditioning site. Several baseball teams came for spring training, most notably the Pittsburgh Pirates, who opened their seasons in Hot Springs from 1901 to 1933. Huey Long, Herbert Hoover, and Al Capone were among the highly disparate guests.

Despite the lure of the waters that beckoned nearby, Special Agents Smith and Lackey and Chief Reed had no time for bathing. They arrived in Hot Springs on the evening of June 15 and checked into the Como Hotel. The agents were careful not to make their presence known to the local authorities, as was the custom whenever they moved into another jurisdiction to apprehend a federal fugitive. They firmly believed that the local police force were thoroughly corrupt. Hot Springs was indeed hostile territory.

The next morning, Friday, June 16, they ate breakfast and went looking for Nash. An informant had given the lawmen a description of Nash's automobile as well as the license number. At five minutes before high noon, they located the vehicle parked in front of the White Front Cigar Store, one of Nash's favorite spots. Inside, the fugitive was drinking a bottle of 3.2 beer. Despite his altered appearance, Otto Reed recognized Nash immediately.

"Nash was bald as an eagle, but he had on a wig and was wearing a mustache," related Lackey many years later. "He was holding a beer bottle behind his back. I walked up behind him and said, 'Get on out there and get in that automobile.' Reed covered the bartender with a rifle." A Bureau of Investigation report from 1934 noted that in apprehending Nash, "the agents took him in an unceremonious manner due to the fact that the escaped prisoner was strongly entrenched with the local police department at Hot Springs."

The legendary bandit offered no resistance, doing exacty as he was told. During the seizure, however, Nash obviously did not go unnoticed. As the three armed men whisked Nash into their waiting car and sped out of town, Richard Galatas, owner and operator of the White Front, dashed to the telephone and, through a series of calls, notified several of Nash's outlaw friends about his capture in Hot Springs. When Nash's wife, Frances, found out about her husband's unscheduled departure, she also helped spread the word via the criminal network that extended from Hot Springs to Joplin and Kansas City.

"It was a wonder that we weren't killed when we took Nash," Smith recalled years later. "He had been there for some time, and was surrounded by his own gang of outlaws and criminals."

Because of these clandestine phone calls, the car carrying Nash and his captors, traveling up to seventy miles per hour, was stopped at roadblocks manned by police officers with riot guns at the town of Benton and later at Little Rock. The officers said they had been notified that a man had been kidnapped at Hot Springs. In both instances, the federal agents displayed their badges and were allowed to continue on their way.

Late that afternoon, they reached the salty border town of Fort Smith, just across the Arkansas River from Choc Floyd's home territory. The three lawmen, with Nash in manacles, planned to depart Fort Smith that evening on a Missouri Pacific train bound for Kansas City. They expected to be met at Union Station the following morning by fellow agents and local detectives who would provide backup for the short trip from Kansas City to the federal prison at Leavenworth. Although the special agents had kept their route secret, word apparently leaked out. A newspaper reporter nosed around the Fort Smith depot just moments before the train pulled away from the platform. Meanwhile, Nash and the other three men passed a quiet night in a stateroom as the train chugged due north through the darkness.

On Saturday morning, the train ground to a halt beside the august Union Station, a Kansas City landmark since it had first opened in 1914. The Harvey House restaurant inside the depot was busy with breakfast diners. Smartly uniformed porters trudged through the great lobby with piles of luggage. Outside, it was a pleasant seventy-one degrees.

Upon arrival at the station, Special Agent Lackey left Smith and Reed to watch Nash while he went out on the platform. Reed E. Vetterli, who had been recruited by Hoover in 1924 and was now in charge of the bureau's Kansas City office, and Raymond J. Caffrey, a thirty-one-year-old Nebraska-bred lawyer who became an agent in 1928, greeted Joe Lackey. Also on hand to add some help if trouble arose were W. J. Grooms and Frank Hermanson, two Kansas City police officers who were trusted by the bureau. The agents surveyed the area and saw nothing to arouse their suspicion. The seven officers and Nash went inside the station. They proceeded through the lobby to the plaza area outside the east entrance, where Agent Caffrey's personal 1932 Chevrolet and a police car were parked. Both Reed and Lackey were armed with shotguns. The others carried pistols. They walked directly to the Chevy sedan. Caffrey unlocked the door and Nash, still in handcuffs, started to get in the back, but Lackey stopped him. He wanted the prisoner to sit up front. Nash slipped behind the steering wheel while Lackey, Smith, and Reed climbed into the rear. At this point, Caffrey walked around to get in the driver's seat, and Vetterli stood with Hermanson and Grooms at the right side near the front of the car. Before Nash could move over so Caffrey could take the wheel, however, two armed men suddenly emerged from behind a nearby car.

Then the officers heard a command: "Put 'em up, up, up!" Vetterli later said he saw another man crouch down with a machine gun trained on himself and the two Kansas City detectives. At that very instant, another voice yelled, "Let 'em have it!" Machine-gun fire commenced. Smith later recalled hearing Nash scream, "For God's sake, don't kill me!"

Nash was one of the first to die. Otto Reed, the old Oklahoma police chief, was also shot to death. Lackey had three bullets lodged in his spine but survived. Smith was unscathed, but the two local officers, Grooms and Hermanson, were killed instantly. Caffrey, shot through the head, died en route to a hospital. Vetterli received only a slight wound in the arm.

"Warm blood still trickled from the five bodies as I arrived," wrote Margaret Richards, a United Press cub reporter at the time of the massacre. "Two men lay sprawled beside the car. Rivulets of blood ran along the pavement, lengthening in a slow ooze.

"In a moment, the area in front of the station was filled with running people. Crowds flowed around the parked cars. Men in overalls, in the uniforms of station porters and in business suits rushed up in wild confusion and ran off again, shouting questions at each other. There were no answers in those first moments. Something had happened that couldn't happen—not on a bustling railroad station plaza in the heart of a big city on a busy morning."

Before the blood had dried, curiosity seekers, like a flock of vultures, swarmed the plaza. They ran their palms across the pockmarked columns near the station doors.

Within days of this widely publicized slaughter, Kansas City authorities had suspects in mind. They included a few Midwestern tough guys and some of the Memorial Day escapees from the Lansing prison break. Several of the suspects, such as Wilbur Underhill, were known associates of Frank Nash or had direct ties to him.

Then key witnesses, whose impressions of the crime had been blurred, regained their memory. Over the course of time, still others changed their stories. Even a questionable underworld figure later came forward with a detailed scenario of the crime, which he swore was the whole truth.

Within months, Hoover fingered Pretty Boy Floyd, Adam Richetti, and Vernon Miller, a former South Dakota sheriff who had gone bad, as the killers. An array of secondary accomplices, including Nash's wife, were also implicated on lesser charges. Bureau agents theorized that the hired gunmen either wanted to free Nash before he was returned to Leavenworth or else, as Hoover himself came to believe, were out to silence the talkative outlaw forever.

Many books and countless feature articles chronicling every known detail of the massacre have been published since that fateful morning in Kansas City. Almost without exception, Floyd, Richetti, and Miller are depicted as the crazed killers. In reality, probably only Miller had any involvement. Likewise, numerous motion pictures present only Hoover's flawed version of the Union Station story.

The same is true of newspaper pieces published every few years on the anniversary of the massacre. A majority of the stories dramatically describe Pretty Boy Floyd and his pals making criminal history with blazing guns at Kansas City. In most case, the writers simply recycle yellowed clippings filed by their predecessors or else rehash the old Bureau of Investigation reports. Myths and half-truths are regurgitated ad nauseam.

Through the years, however, there have also been a few journalists and historians who have taken exception to the notion that "beyond a shadow of a doubt" Choc Floyd wielded one of the death weapons at Union Station.

"Floyd's known presence in Kansas City accounts for the theory that he was a participant in the infamous Union Station Massacre," wrote California State College history professor Kent Ladd Steckmesser in a 1970 magazine article published in *The American West.* "The FBI charged Floyd with being one of the gunmen, but they never proved their case. It now appears unlikely that he was guilty of this particular crime. The job is too much at variance with the usual Floyd pattern. The actual machine gunners were killed by the mob for having botched their assignment."

Former associates of Charley Floyd also believe that Choc's hands were free of the massacre victims' blood. "It was just Choc's bad luck that he happened to be in Kansas City when that shooting at the train station went down," lamented Elmer Steele, one of Floyd's former getaway drivers, almost six decades later. "All of us on the scout back then knew at once that he didn't have anything to do with that mess. Others did it and he took the fall. Choc was never a hired gun."

To his own dying day, Floyd swore on his father's grave that he had no hand in the massacre. Soon after the mass murder, he even sent a postcard with a message to that effect to the Kansas City police. Surviving family members assert that not a soul who knew Choc ever believed he was involved.

In 1978, some of the Floyd siblings gave statements disputing their brother's alleged role in the massacre to James Lea Lessley, grandson of Choc's sister, Emma Lessley. James Lessley used their comments in a research report on the Kansas City Massacre that he prepared for a university graduate course. Never ones to make excuses for their brother or deny that he was indeed a bank robber and killer, the Floyd family members stressed that Choc always owned up to the crimes he committed. But, they added, he would also vehemently repudiate anything that he did not do.

"He wasn't there, I know he wasn't in Kansas City when that happened," stated Bradley Floyd.

"I just don't think he did it," said Emma Lessley.

"He told us he wasn't in on it," reported Charley's younger sister, Mary.

Ruby Floyd never believed her former husband was one of the Kansas City hit men, and she often said so to close friends and relatives. "I talked to my mother many times about the Kansas City Massacre and she always said that my father *definitely* had nothing to do with it," related Dempsey Floyd in 1991.

Even at the time of the massacre, many law-enforcement officers and underworld figures agreed that Floyd was not the type to be drawn into such a deadly caper. Choc was never a "torpedo," the name given to a professional assassin. Except for the execution-style slayings of the Ash brothers—if, in fact, Floyd was one of the executioners—he was a bank robber who never engaged in gunplay unless he was trapped, such as the incidents of violence in Ohio or when he shot and killed Erv Kelley near Bixby. The Union Station slayings did not fit his modus operandi.

Nonetheless, one of the bloodiest mass slayings of the gangster era remains on Charles Arthur Floyd's official record.

Six decades later, when the grand old station stood empty and abandoned, a few old men returned to the scene of the massacre. They came to whisper the stories, to remember. They came to lift up their grandchildren so they could touch the scars in the smooth granite. Even with the passage of time, however, the questions that rang out on that June morning so long before still went unanswered.

31

TRAIL'S END

CTOBER WINDS SWEPT ACROSS the Canadian border into Buffalo, lying below the thundering falls of the Niagara River in far western New York State. Choc Floyd already felt winter's approach deep in his bones, especially in the ankle where Erv Kelley's slug remained lodged. He wrote to his family in the autumn of 1934 that he enjoyed watching the sun make its nightly descent beyond Lake Erie. Perhaps the fiery sunsets reminded him of twilights in Oklahoma's Cookson Hills.

The skeins of Canada geese were already winging their way south in the night skies. The Fall Classic had come and gone, with the Dean brothers, Dizzy and Daffy, having pitched the St. Louis Cardinals to victory, four games to three, against the Detroit Tigers in the 1934 World Series. The odor of burning leaves and factory smoke crept through Buffalo's streets and alleys. It oozed beneath the doors of homes where supper pots simmered. The smell seeped into corner taverns packed with shift workers. Steelworkers and grimy steamfitters leaned against the scarred wooden bars. They drank shots of whiskey, legal since Prohibition had finally been repealed in December of 1933. The feel of a schnapps chased down with cold ale somehow softened the pain caused by the depressed economy.

Over a year of hiding in a bleak Buffalo neighborhood had made Floyd stir-crazy. He was not alone. Life in a cramped apartment had taken its toll on the three others with him, Adam Richetti, Juanita Beulah Baird, and Rose Baird. All four of them felt like climbing the dingy walls. Charley said so in the infrequent letters he wrote to his brother Bradley and other kinfolk. He told them it was as though he had gone back a decade and was locked away, once again behind the stone walls of the penitentiary at Jeff City.

Living on the lam was worse than doing hard time, Choc explained in his letters. His heart jumped at each knock at the apartment door. Every stranger who paused to light a cigarette by the streetlamp below the window caused him to reach for his pistol. On rare nights, when he emerged for some fresh air, he saw ghosts in the eyes of the tramps stumbling toward the railroad tracks. It seemed less threatening to stay put in the confines of the flat.

At the wobbly kitchen table, he played card games of pitch and double solitaire with the girls while Richetti, his mind thick with drink, sulked over his pencil drawings. Choc cooked pots of spaghetti and baked apple pies. He listened to the radio and read detective magazines, many of them containing purportedly true stories about Pretty Boy that read to him only like pure fiction. Mostly, he paced, however. Neighbors later recalled hearing him tramp back and forth at all hours of the day and night. He stalked about the tiny apartment like one of his father's penned-up Oklahoma wolfhounds—anxious for the start of another hunt.

Charley and Adam had gone into self-imposed exile in Buffalo with their girlfriends in the fall of 1933 after they realized the authorities were determined to charge Floyd and Richetti with murder—for helping mow down the four officers and their prisoner at Union Station.

Floyd vehemently denied any complicity in the Kansas City Massacre. Just three days after the murders, he even dashed off a note disavowing any knowledge of the crime. Floyd's message, addressed simply to the Kansas City Police, was printed in pencil on the back of a plain business postcard. Dated June 20, 1933, and stamped with a Springfield, Missouri, postmark, the card read:

> Dear Sirs:
> I—Charles Floyd want it made known
> that I did not participate in the massacre
> of officers at Kansas City.
> Charles Floyd

Police experts compared the writing on the card with samples of Floyd's handwriting in their files. They declared the note to be genuine. Some investigators scoffed. They said Floyd might have written the disclaimer but that he probably had a confederate mail it to throw the authorities off his trail. Immediately after Floyd's note was made public, however, three persons told law officers that they were positive they had seen Pretty Boy and two other men eating supper in a Springfield restaurant the evening the correspondence was mailed.

Thomas J. Higgins, the chief of detectives in Kansas City, believed Floyd not only sent the note but that his denial was sincere. Higgins had followed the bandit's movements since 1929. He told the *Kansas City Star* that he unequivocally did not consider Charley to be a suspect. Like several others who knew Floyd's criminal habits, Higgins was cocksure the mass murder was not his type of job. So was Harry Chaney, a close friend of Otto Reed, the McAlester chief of police who had died in the plaza. "Floyd is just a country boy," explained Chaney. "It is unlikely that he has had the big time connections with gang members who probably were responsible for Saturday's slayings."

Jackson County Sheriff Thomas B. Bash, considered one of the top law-enforcement officers in the Kansas City area, disagreed, however. So did a phalanx of Bureau of Investigation agents, who poured into Kansas City in the wake of the murders. They were convinced otherwise largely because of the testimony of one Lottie West, a Traveler's Aid worker at Union Station, who claimed she had witnessed the shooting. Mrs. West, who no doubt had seen countless shots of Floyd in the newspapers, selected a photograph of Floyd as that of one of the machine gunners. "That's the man!" she exclaimed when Bash spread some mug shots before her. However, her physical description of the suspect she believed to be Floyd was flawed.

According to Mrs. West, the Pretty Boy she had talked to inside the station just prior to the shooting and later saw again during the turmoil in the plaza weighed "nearly two hundred pounds." Several Kansas City law officers knew that Charley weighed, at the very most, 160 pounds. They realized the woman was way off the mark.

Other witnesses to the massacre were more reliable. However, their statements do not appear to have carried as much weight with federal agents as the West testimony. Critics of the investigation later suggested the statements of Lottie West were given more credence because of her race. She was Caucasian, while several of the other witnesses were, in the words of one bureau report, "colored." Many of the other accounts appear in a bureau file dated July 29, 1933, a little more than a month after the murders. They do not show up in subsequent reports that were periodically updated over the years, however.

One of those witnesses, Kansas City businessman Samuel Link, stated that about 7:15 A.M. on June 17, he was driving near the east end of Union Station when he saw a man with a submachine gun emerge from a green 1932 Reo sedan. Link said he parked his own car, and a moment later, he watched as another armed man got out of a black Chevrolet sedan. Link said both of these men lifted their guns as if to fire just as the peace officers and Frank Nash walked out of the depot into the parking lot. At that moment, Link ducked. He heard the firing but did not see the shooting. Afterward, he watched the Reo and Chevrolet flee the scene.

When shown police photos, Link identified the subject in the Reo as Harvey Bailey. He said there could be no mistake, since he had once worked as a deputy constable in Kansas City and had met Bailey while serving some legal papers. Link recognized the driver of the car as Wilbur Underhill. He then spied a photograph of Verne Miller and told the agents that Miller was also the one who had given the signal to start shooting.

Another witness, Margaret Turner of Olathe, Kansas, arrived at the station about 2:30 A.M. to meet a cousin arriving on a 3:30 A.M. train that had been delayed for several hours. She provided federal agents with a detailed statement about activities in the parking lot, where she waited prior to the massacre. Mrs. Turner stated that at about 3:00 A.M. she spotted a Reo automobile and a black Chevrolet parked in front of the depot. She said parties in the two cars conversed and, at one point, a woman left the Chevrolet and went into the depot for about ten minutes. Then the woman returned to the car and it drove off. The mystery woman was not seen again, but the Chevy periodically returned to cruise the parking lot. Each time, the men inside exchanged greetings with those in the other car.

According to Mrs. Turner, she got a good look at two of the men in the Reo. She positively identified them as Bailey and Underhill. When the shooting started, Mrs. Turner was already inside the depot. She dived for cover. Until her death many years later, Mrs. Turner never deviated from her original statement. Agents noted in their file that she "appears to be a very reliable colored woman," yet her comments were eventually purged from official reports.

J. D. Jameson, employed as a Union Station redcap, could not positively place either Underhill or Miller at the scene. However, Jameson told the agents that early during the morning of the slayings, a man, whom he later identified from police photos as Harvey Bailey, accosted him. Bailey inquired about the arrival of a Missouri Pacific train from Arkansas. Jameson learned it was the same train that carried Nash. None of these witnesses identified Richetti or Floyd.

Neither did the actual survivors of the massacre—at least not at first. In the original bureau reports filed by the surviving trio of agents, two of them, Lackey and Smith, stated that they positively could *not* identify any of the individuals who had opened fire on them. Vetterli, the third agent, wrote that he was "convinced" one of the assassins was Bob "Big Boy" Brady, one of the eleven convicts who had escaped the Lansing prison on Memorial Day. More than a year later, however, these same agents had changed their minds and were to say unequivocally that Charles Floyd was one of the culprits.

James "Blackie" Audett, a member of John Lazia's organization and at one time Mary McElroy's bodyguard, insisted the true killers at the train station included Verne Miller and the brothers Homer and Maurice Denning. He also implicated William Weissman but refused to name a fourth culprit. "Floyd was nowhere near the station that day," wrote Audett in his book *Rap Sheet,* published in 1954. "The FBI had to solve the case fast because one of their own men got killed so they pinned it on two guys [Floyd and Richetti] who were already wanted and widely known." Audett somewhat dampened the veracity of his story by claiming he and Miss McElroy had actually observed the massacre from a vantage point in the parking lot.

Another staunch advocate of the theory that Pretty Boy and Richetti were not involved in the Union Station murders was Jack Killingsworth, the Missouri sheriff abducted by the pair of Oklahomans on June 16, 1933. "I don't believe they had anything to do with the Kansas City killing this morning," Killingsworth told reporters only hours after the massacre. "I think they are figuring on 'holing in' somewhere for awhile." Killingsworth also took exception to Lottie West's description of the man she had identified as Floyd. "I think they got it wrong. Floyd don't weigh two hundred pounds, he's nearer to one hundred sixty." Killingsworth added that he had asked Floyd point-blank about the slayings of the Boone County sheriff and the state patrolman. The bandit replied he had had nothing to do with those prior murders of law enforcement officers.

Killingsworth was attacked for his remarks, especially by Republican foes, who said the sheriff placed Floyd "in the role of dramatic hero." They called for his removal from office, as did several newspaper editors. When Killingsworth's term expired, he did not seek public office again until 1958, when he was elected by a three-to-one margin as mayor of Bolivar, Missouri, a job the Democrat proudly held for many years to come.

While Killingsworth, the unassuming country sheriff, was humiliated for speaking honestly, the career of the nation's top law enforcement officer, J. Edgar Hoover, was enhanced as a result of the mass killings at Union Station. Hoover became the man of the hour. On June 20, he sent a letter to Joe Lackey, one of his wounded agents, which read, "It is needless for me to say to you that no time, money or labor will be spared toward bringing about the apprehension of the individuals responsible for the cowardly and despicable act of last Saturday morning. *They must be exterminated and must be exterminated by us, and to this end we are dedicating ourselves.*"

Although Hoover personally grieved over the loss of life, the massacre was exactly the cause célèbre he knew how to exploit. Many suspected that Hoover was on the verge of losing his job as bureau director after Roosevelt came into office in 1933. The murder of a young federal agent and three other lawmen may indeed have spared him that indignity.

The outrageous act of shooting down law officers in broad daylight enraged Americans who had been sympathetic to crooks they previously believed only robbed from the rich to give to the poor. It did not take a genius to figure out that had the Kansas City of 1933 been free of political and underworld corruption, a spectacle like the one at the train station would probably not have been possible. The public outcry for reform and retribution, not to mention all the sensational headlines, played right into Hoover's hand. As Fred J. Cook so aptly pointed out in his 1964 book, *The FBI Nobody Knows,* when Hoover learned of the killings at Kansas City, he was able to become "the knight on the white charger riding down the forces of evil." Hoover called the massacre a "turning point in the nation's fight against crime."

U.S. Attorney General Homer Cummings also jumped on the bandwagon and became Hoover's ally. "So far as lies within my power, no criminal, either high or low estate, shall go unscathed," pontificated Cummings. "Moreover, it is my hope that in the field of law enforcement and in the detection and prosecution of crime, I may be able to bring about a better coordination of federal and state activities. We've got to win this war."

Over the next year, a host of legislative measures was passed by Congress to increase the bureau's jurisdiction and broaden its authority. At last, agents would be permitted to carry firearms. They were granted the power of arrest anywhere in the country. They were also allowed to investigate certain cases of stolen property, bank robbery, racketeering, or flight to avoid prosecution. This momentous legislation, signed into law by Roosevelt in the late spring of 1934, sounded the death knell for Depression-era outlaws and gave rise to the modern Federal Bureau of Investigation, as the agency became known in 1935.

Besides the FBI becoming the most potent police force in the world, the often-ruthless Hoover would gain almost as much power as the eight U.S. Presidents elected during his forty-eight year reign. However, on July 29, 1933, when he was asked by Cummings to continue as director, the full impact of Hoover's influence on the nation was still unknown.

During the balance of 1933 and well into the following year, several underworld figures who had past associations with Nash—Underhill, Bailey, Brady, Ed Davis, Jim Clark, Verne Miller, Maurice and Homer Denning, and William Weissman, a brother of slain Kansas City gangster Solly Weissman—remained on the active suspect list. And the names of Pretty Boy Floyd and Adam Richetti stayed right at the top.

A flurry of Floyd and Richetti sightings popped up throughout the Midwest, especially in Oklahoma shortly after the massacre. On June 22, in Bristow, the hometown of several of Ruby Floyd's relatives, including the police chief, a cobbler admitted to authorities that Choc had visited his shop to get some shoes resoled. He claimed that Pretty Boy gave him a large bill and told him to keep the change. That evening, Floyd and Richetti supposedly kidnapped a Tulsa couple and held them captive until dawn, when the outlaws fled with their victim's automobile. A few days later, a tourist-camp proprietor in Wichita reported that, following a domestic argument, his wife hired Pretty Boy to beat him up. The man checked into a hospital with a broken rib. Later that week, Floyd was suspected of a bank robbery at Seneca, Missouri, while at just about the same time, witnesses swore they saw Pretty Boy in downtown Tulsa delivering bootleg liquor to the host of a party.

As more Floyd accusations came to light, an assortment of mistaken-identity reports surfaced. A Kansas City cosmetics salesman who bore an uncanny resemblance to Pretty Boy became so nervous after the massacre at

Union Station that he finally obtained credentials from the police department to prove he was a respectable citizen. Near Webb City, Missouri, a force of deputies, assisted by policemen from nearby Joplin, swooped down on an old ambulance parked on a country lane after an excited farmer reported seeing Pretty Boy napping in the vehicle. When the posse yelled for Floyd to come out with his hands up, they were surprised to find a groggy black man emerge, rubbing the sleep from his eyes. Almost as comical was the incident in Tulsa involving William Martin, a Floyd look-alike from Honey Grove, Texas. Martin was en route to Chicago in a chauffeur-driven car when he was stopped no fewer than three times by officers toting sawed-off shotguns. Each time, they were convinced they had caught Pretty Boy.

Floyd found none of the stories very amusing, however. Caught in the midst of the propaganda war being waged in the newspapers by Cummings and Hoover, the bandit grew weary of seeing his name in print. As Jay Robert Nash observed in his narrative encyclopedia of American criminals, *Bloodletters and Badmen,* "where Dillinger was romanticized in the newspapers of the day, 'Pretty Boy' got the worst press of any outlaw in the 1930s, and for a crime—the Kansas City Massacre—many believe he never committed."

Floyd's problems were further exacerbated as many other massacre suspects were arrested for other crimes, or else were slain by fellow hoodlums or lawmen.

One of the first of the prime suspects to fall was the bank-robbing fugitive Harvey Bailey. A little more than a month after the massacre, he was implicated in the July 22 kidnapping of millionaire oil tycoon Charles F. Urschel during a bridge game at the victim's Oklahoma City residence. It was a poorly planned scheme hatched by George Kelly and his wife, Kathryn, who pumped up her husband's reputation by giving him the nickname "Machine Gun." After nine days of captivity, Urschel was released unharmed when a two-hundred-thousand-dollar ransom was negotiated. A trail of clues helped the authorities track down the offenders. Bailey was apprehended August 12 on the Texas farm where Urschel had been held. The next month, Kelly was captured in Memphis. This was a well-publicized incident in which Kelly reportedly threw up his hands and screamed, "Don't shoot, G-men, don't shoot!" Years later, it was revealed that *G-men,* a term that became synonymous for the bureau's hard-charging agents, was actually a public-relations gimmick invented by Hoover.

The Kellys, Bailey, and two other accomplices were given life sentences. Kelly and "Old Harve" Bailey were shipped to Alcatraz, the island in San Francisco Bay where, in 1933, Attorney General Cummings established the premier maximum-security prison designed to hold hordes of gangsters. Bailey was never charged in the Union Station murders.

The mutilated corpse of Verne Miller, the two-time South Dakota sheriff trained as a machine gunner during the Great War, was found November 29, 1933, in a roadside ditch on the outskirts of Detroit. Federal agents maintained that they had found Adam Richetti's latent fingerprints on a beer bottle in the basement of Miller's former Kansas City residence on Edgevale Road. They believed Miller, based on a recommendation from John Lazia, had hastily engaged Richetti and Floyd to help free Frank Nash.

Miller would not be of any help to the agents in solving the great mystery killings in Kansas City, however. He had been beaten and strangled. His head was crushed. His nude body was trussed up with clothesline in a jackknife fashion. Kansas City agents were not surprised by the rubout. They realized that Miller, in their own words, had "turned the heat on the whole underworld." Revenge-minded gangsters were known to be stalking him. Hoover checked another name off his list.

Then, on December 30, the number of Union Station murder suspects shrunk even further when Oklahoma laws officers shot down Wilbur Underhill in downtown Shawnee. The "mad dog of the underworld" succumbed to his wounds a week later in the state prison hospital. At the moment of death, he supposedly uttered this cryptic sentence: "Tell the boys I'm coming home." Officers were left to puzzle over Underhill's final words, as well as his exact role in the Kansas City slayings.

In February of 1934, the month Choc Floyd celebrated his thirtieth birthday, a massive force of more than one thousand peace officers and mobilized National Guardsmen swept through the rain-soaked Cookson Hills of eastern Oklahoma. Crack *Tulsa Tribune* reporter Joe Howell termed the operation "the biggest single manhunt in the nation's history." For all their troubles, the huge army turned up only a handful of wrongdoers. Not one of those captured was of the caliber of Pretty Boy, Clyde Barrow, or other high-profile fugitives sought by the expeditionary force. Only later did the nation learn that Floyd had been nowhere near Sequoyah County or any of his other choice hiding places.

In fact, Choc and Richetti had bid farewell to friends and relatives in September of 1934. With Beulah and Rose Baird, they drove east, pausing briefly at a few familiar spots in Ohio. Newspaper editorials from that period suggested that Pretty Boy was the ghost of Jesse James, risen from the grave. Floyd was flattered. During a brief stop in Canfield, Ohio, he even sent a thank-you note to a staff artist at an Ohio newspaper that had published a series of sketch strips comparing Floyd's career to that of James.

> Thanks for the compliments and the pictures
> of me in your paper.
> I'll be gone when you get this.

Jesse James was no punk himself.

I'm not as bad as they say I am.
They just wouldn't leave me alone
after I got out.

Yours truly

Chas. A. Floyd

The two couples snaked their way northeast through Pennsylvania, finally stopping in Buffalo. Federal agents later discovered that on September 21, using phony names, they rented an apartment in a middle-class neighborhood. Charley and Juanita were known as Mr. and Mrs. George Sanders. Adam and Rose took the alias Mr. and Mrs. Ed Brennan. The apartment was their home for the next thirteen months.

Choc doled out money for living expenses from a stash accumulated from past bank robberies. Except for a few quick excursions, they did not leave the city. In fact, other than trips to the grocery or to a beauty salon, where the women overindulged themselves for a rare moment, the foursome hardly left the apartment.

Life in Buffalo was monotonous. There were no friends, no parties, no callers. Little mail came except for rare letters from family or responses to advertisements the women received under their aliases. Neighbors thought it odd that neither of the men went off to jobs. All they heard were muffled voices and Choc's incessant pacing. There were few exchanges between the mysterious couples and outsiders. Juanita and Rose occasionally threw coins and candy from the window to children playing in the streets. Sometimes Choc slipped youngsters, who lived in the building, a slice of pie or cake. He scanned the *Buffalo Courier-Express* to stay abreast of the outside world.

In March 1934, Choc read that Ed Davis, a Memorial Day prison escapee suspected in the Kansas City killings, had been captured by officers in an apartment-house raid in Los Angeles. Davis, charged with other crimes, was soon dropped from the massacre suspect list, however. Just prior to the arrest of Davis, another escaped Lansing convict and alleged massacre culprit, Bobby Brady, was slain near Paola, Kansas: more checkmarks for J. Edgar Hoover's list.

The papers were filled throughout the spring of 1934 with the obituaries of tough killers, bank robbers, and kidnappers. Some Floyd knew. Aussie Elliott, one of Choc's early getaway drivers, was killed by Creek County officers in a raid near Sapulpa, Oklahoma. Ford Bradshaw, a Sequoyah County graduate of the bootleg school who became a bandit chieftain himself, was also shot and laid in a fresh grave.

Stories about Floyd competed with those about John Dillinger, Ma Barker and her sons, and Clyde Barrow and Bonnie Parker. Although Choc never met the psychotic pair, familiarly known as Bonnie and Clyde, he had been sent word that they admired his style. They indicated a desire to join Choc on some bank jobs. Floyd's family later said Choc did not give the proposal a second thought. He admonished them to ignore Barrow and Parker if they ever came looking for him. "Those two give us all a bad name," Choc reportedly told several of his kinfolk. Yet, despite Choc's warning, both E. W. and Bradley fed the outlaw duo and gave them comfort on one their jaunts through Oklahoma. "We just couldn't turn anyone away in those bad years, even the likes of them," explained Bessie Floyd.

When news broke on May 23, 1934, that Bonnie and Clyde's bloody career had finally been terminated, Charley Floyd most likely did not go into mourning. The couple's nemesis, former Texas Ranger Frank Hamer, led the possemen who shot the ruthless lovers in an ambush along a road near Arcadia, Louisiana.

Hidden in the cramped Buffalo apartment, Choc was undoubtedly surprised to see that Pretty Boy stories still made the papers. Some reporters had him dead from old gunshot wounds or dying from blood poisoning and disease. According to some reports, he was supposedly dickering with a Hollywood film company to sell his life story. Other published tales circulated that Pretty Boy was living in Mexico, Virginia, or the mountains of Arkansas and had dyed his hair red and grown a long beard. Almost at the same time, he was reported to have joined the Chinese army and robbed a bank in New York City. Pretty Boy was seen on both coasts on the same morning. He was figuratively behind every bush and billboard.

During the summer of 1934, the spate of news stories about other criminals still on the scout dominated the headlines. The month of July was especially action-packed. In Kansas City, where rival gangs continued to battle for position, two hoods wielding a shotgun and submachine gun murdered John Lazia, the North Side crime boss and ranking lieutenant of Tom Pendergast's political machine. Lazia, whose underworld activities were chiefly characterized by his attempts to prevent major crimes and keep outside gunmen from Kansas City, was shot in the early hours of July 10 as he alighted from his sedan in front of a hotel. It was discovered only later that the fatal bullets came from a Thompson submachine gun used in the Union Station killings.

Twelve days later, on the evening of July 22, the nation's most celebrated felon, John Dillinger, was killed. Dillinger was shot in front of Chicago's Biograph Theater, where he and two lady friends, one of them the infamous Woman in Red, had just watched *Manhattan Melodrama,* starring Clark Cable. Dillinger's killers were not rival outlaws but a team of Department of Justice agents led by Hoover's crackerjack crime fighter, Melvin H. Purvis, Jr., the agent in charge of the bureau's Chicago office.

Choc was not surprised to hear of the bank robber's death, but he indicated to his family that he was dismayed to learn that with Dillinger gone, Hoover had determined the nation's new public enemy number one was indeed Charles Arthur Floyd.

Over the course of the next few months of 1934, Floyd grew even more cautious. He dashed off notes to Ruby and Dempsey, who continued their *Crime Does Not Pay* stage shows. In July, Dempsey had been baptized by a crusading Fort Worth preacher. The boy even had an official business guardian appointed to oversee the vaudeville engagements, which included a brief film showing his baptismal ceremony. At the close of each performance, Ruby never failed to mention that "we know positively that Charles had nothing to do with the Kansas City Massacre." Apparently the public grew tired of listening to the canned lecture of the former wife and nine-year-old son of Pretty Boy, for Ruby and Dempsey gave their final show on September 11, 1934. Fittingly, it was staged in Kansas City—Tom's Town.

About a month later, Choc Floyd decided it was time to go home. His decision was prompted in part by dwindling financial resources but also by a startling announcement made public on October 11. On that date, it was disclosed that government witness James LaCapra had provided information that John Lazia had arranged a meeting of Floyd, Richetti, and Verne Miller the night before the trio committed the massacre at Union Station. A Kansas City hoodlum with illusions of taking over the local rackets, LaCapra swore that when Lazia heard of the plot to free Nash, he told Miller not to use any "local muscle." Instead, Lazia hooked up Miller with Floyd and Richetti. After the attack, LaCapra stated that the killers, including Floyd with a bullet wound to his shoulder, remained in Kansas City for twenty-four hours before local gangsters escorted them out of town.

Friends of the dead Lazia labeled LaCapra's confession as the ramblings of a desperate man out to cut a deal. Hoover and his agents felt otherwise. The headline in the October 11 *Buffalo Courier-Express* read:

U.S. MEN SOLVE MASSACRE
OF 5 IN KANSAS CITY

PRETTY BOY FLOYD, TWO OTHERS
NAMED BY FEDERAL AGENTS IN
RAILWAY STATION TRAGEDY

The story read like a death notice to Charley Floyd. He knew that Hoover's G-men would be relentless.

Less than a day after LaCapra's damning statements appeared in newspapers, sightings of Floyd and Richetti were reported throughout Iowa, Minnesota, Missouri, Arkansas, and Oklahoma. A National Guard airplane was used in the manhunt in Missouri. Near Cresco, Iowa, officers claimed they had engaged

Floyd in a gun battle when they flushed Pretty Boy and his companions from a farm hideout near the Minnesota border. On October 13, a front-page story in the *Buffalo Courier-Express* told of heavily armed posses on the "trail of the West's notorious killers." Six weeks later, officers figured out that they were not chasing Floyd and Richetti but some other wanted men, including the killer of the two law officers near Columbia. Nerves grew taut in the Buffalo apartment. Charley felt compelled to make a move. Oklahoma's familiar hills and prairies beckoned.

"The last letter my Uncle Bradley got from Uncle Charley came that October from Buffalo," recalled Choc's nephew Lawton Lessley. "The letter said, 'We're comin' home.'"

Federal agents subsequently learned that on October 18, Floyd, down to the last of his cash reserve, gave Rose Baird six hundred dollars. He instructed her to buy a Ford tudor coach. Around 3:00 A.M. on October 19, with Choc behind the wheel of the two-door sedan, the couples bid farewell to Buffalo. Several days later, investigators were told that a fresh-baked apple pie was left on the kitchen table.

Choc and his friends drove through the early-morning darkness, only stopping for gasoline and meals. They kept the Ford on a southerly course. Charley wanted to return to a refuge he knew of on the banks of the Ohio River. For many years, bootleggers and bank robbers found comfort there, if only for a few hours. It was situated near East Liverpool, Ohio, on the Pennsylvania-Ohio border, just above the northern tip of an intruding finger of West Virginia. Only a wide spot in the road, Hell's Half-Acre is what the locals called it. Choc's old partner, Willis "Billy the Killer" Miller, had frequented the area in the twenties. In the early 1930s, he took Floyd to one of the saloons run by a crusty lady who asked no questions about her patrons' private lives.

Richetti was also not unaware of the pleasure at Hell's Half-Acre. He and Charley figured on wetting their whistles at the joint operated by State Line Jenny, before moving on to visit with some of Adam's relatives. One of Richetti's sisters and her husband, Minnie and Henry Sustic, resided near the small Ohio burg of Dillonvale, downriver between Steubenville and Wheeling, West Virginia. After a brief stopover, the foursome planned to head out on the back roads and drive like fury all the way to Oklahoma.

On Saturday, October 20, folks in the small Ohio and West Virginia towns dotting the river awoke to learn that the previous day the bank had been robbed in Tiltonsville, Ohio, not far from Dillonvale. Two men with heavy beards had entered the bank brandishing shotguns and made off with five hundred dollars in cash. One of the bandits reportedly comforted a four-year-old girl who was terrified by the commotion. "There, there now, don't cry, little girl," the robber was overheard to say. "Why, we ain't goin' to hurt you. No, sir." When the child's worried mother extended three dollar bills clutched in her hand, the robber ignored the money and added, "Nor you, either, ma'am."

To the north, in the Columbiana County towns of East Liverpool, Wellsville, Calcutta, and Lisbon, no one really thought too much about the bank heist. After all, Tiltonsville was more than forty miles downstream. Some of the sheriff's deputies and local police departments took notice, however. There was always the chance that the bank robbers were still in the area and could strike again. Some citizens with lively imaginations even wondered out loud whether the outlaws might be Pretty Boy Floyd and his Italian pal who had family living close by.

Early that Saturday morning, clouds of thick fog wafted over the banks of the Ohio River and shrouded the steep Columbiana County hills. The Ford sedan, carrying Choc, Adam, and the two Baird sisters, sped along at a rapid clip down Route 7, along the Wellsville–East Liverpool Road. They were just shy of the Wellsville city limits, near a closed brickyard in an area the natives called the Silver Switch, when a combination of poor visual conditions and the rain-slick road caused Choc to lose control of the automobile. In an instant, the car skidded into a telephone pole. No one was injured but the new Ford was damaged. Choc was able to get it back on the road but he did not feel the car was in any shape to continue without some repairs.

Not wanting to risk detection, and remembering the sticky situation that had arisen the year before at the gargage in Bolivar, Choc told Beulah and Rose to take the vehicle to a mechanic in Wellsville. After getting the car fixed, they were to return for Floyd and Richetti. Before the women drove off, the men grabbed firearms and blankets from the backseat.

Charley and Adam walked a short distance into a hollow next to the road. They climbed a hillside covered with scrub brush and maples until they reached some large rocks. It appeared to be a good place to wait without attracting the attention of passersby on Route 7. Within minutes, they gathered enough dry tinder and twigs for a small fire to ward off the morning chill. From their resting place, Choc and Adam had a commanding view of the Ohio River, the railroad tracks, and the deserted brickyard.

Overnight, there had been a hard frost. Joseph Fryman, who lived in one of the small houses on top of the hill, and his son-in-law, David O'Hanlon, went out early that morning to salvage vegetables from their garden. Fryman was disabled and had a wife and eight children to feed. His garden was planted not far from the river, on a strip of ground between the railroad tracks and the road. As Fryman and O'Hanlon started for home, they looked up and saw Floyd and Richetti sitting on the side of Elizabeth Hill.

At first, Fryman thought the men were tramps. When he got closer, however, he saw they did not look like the kind who rode the rails. As Fryman and his son-in-law, carrying baskets of tomatoes and squash, walked by the strangers, the larger of the men by the rocks spoke. "Say, where are you fellas goin'?" Fryman replied that they were on their way home. "We live up here," he told them. Still wary of the men, Fryman went to one of his neighbors, a retiree named Lon Israel. "There are some guys camped out down below your house," Fryman told him. Israel was immediately suspicious.

He and Fryman walked to the nearest telephone, located at a small store that sold essentials to area residents. Israel phoned Wellsville Chief of Police John H. Fultz to report a pair of "shady characters" lurking near his place. Fultz promised that he would be out to investigate. A ten-year police veteran, Fultz did not have an inkling that he was about to come face-to-face with public enemy number one.

Fultz later said that after receiving Israel's telephone call, he theorized the strangers might have been the Tiltonsville bank bandits. To be on the safe side, Fultz took along Homer Potts and William Erwin, some local men he deputized as special patrolmen. All three were in plainclothes but, for unknown reasons, only Fultz carried a weapon. They drove out Route 7 to the Silver Switch, near the Kountz Avenue hollow, and parked the car on Elizabeth Hill next to Israel's home.

The police chief, with his helpers bringing up the rear, worked his way toward the rocks where the strangers were located. Choc was on lookout. He bristled when he saw Fultz and demanded to know where he was going. "I told him I was a working man on my way to the brickyard," recounted Fultz.

Floyd, a .45 pistol in his hand, did not buy the story. He realized the brickyard was no longer in operation. "You ain't no workin' man," Choc told Fultz. A heated discussion ensued as they walked farther down the hill.

"He [Floyd] stepped to one side of the path, stuck his gun in my ribs, and told me to go on down the hill, warning me not to run," Fultz wrote the next day in a first-person newspaper story that was syndicated across the nation. "I kept trying to get further ahead of him and when I gained a little distance, tried to pull my gun.

" 'Keep your hands in the air,' " said Floyd. "He walked us down the hill about one hundred feet and there I saw a fellow sitting on some blankets.

"I said, 'Hello, buddy, how are you?' "

Adam smiled at Fultz, but just then Floyd yelled out, "Stop him, shoot him! Don't let him kid you, he's an officer!" Richetti whipped out a .45 automatic and opened fire. Fultz pulled his .32 revolver and returned the shots. He fired away at Floyd, then he wheeled and started shooting at Richetti. The unarmed Erwin and Potts were helpless. "All they could do was stand off and watch," explained Fultz.

Richetti's gun misfired. He dumped it in a clump of briars and raced toward a nearby house. Although he was slightly wounded in an ankle from a grazing bullet, Fultz followed in hot pursuit. He found Richetti trying to get inside the house, but the door was locked. Seeing that he was trapped, Richetti had no other choice. He raised his arms and surrendered. Fultz handcuffed Adam and took him to the city jail at Wellsville.

Meanwhile, Floyd moved to the blanket and uncovered his Thompson submachine gun. He let loose a spray of bullets, then turned and ran up the hill. Potts and Erwin had already reached the hilltop. They borrowed shotguns from Israel and took up positions. When Floyd dashed by, the two men blasted away but missed. Floyd fired back at them on the run. One of his bullets struck Potts in the left shoulder. Another round tore through the front wall of Israel's house and lodged in a sewing machine. Then the tommy gun jammed. Choc threw it on the ground.

Unaware that his partner had been captured, Choc kept running. He stopped at the house of thirty-year-old Theodore Peterson and his widowed mother. A friend of the family, George McMullin, was having a late breakfast with the Petersons before calling on his girlfriend in Wellsville. "This fella, who we later found out was Floyd, told us that his car had broken down by the brickyard and he needed to get to Youngstown," Peterson recounted fifty-six years later. "He was willing to pay ten dollars for a lift. That was a lot of cash during the Depression." Peterson was not able to break away from apple-picking chores, but McMullin decided his girlfriend could wait. He jumped at the chance to earn some easy money and told Floyd to hop in his 1925 Model T Ford.

Once on the road, Choc pulled out his two .45 automatics and showed them to the surprised McMullin. "I don't mean you no harm, but I've got to get away," McMullin recalled Choc saying. "Just stay on the back roads to Youngstown and don't stop for anything." The farmhand did what Floyd asked. McMullin did not stray from the dirt farm roads. The two men had not gone very far when the Ford sputtered and stopped; it was out of gas.

With the hapless McMullin in tow, Floyd walked to a brick bungalow where James Baum, a sixty-five-year-old florist, was busily loading flowers into his Nash automobile. "I was in the greenhouse," Baum told reporters. "This man came in and said, 'Get your car, Dad.' We got in and then he said, 'Now, Dad, I want you to do what I tell you and when I want you to.' "

Choc and his two hostages took off, with Baum at the wheel. "When we started away," recalled Baum, "he said, 'I want you to turn onto the first dirt road you find. There are too many cars around.' He wasn't very nervous. Occasionally, he would duck down, but most of the time he just sat up straight. I wasn't scared."

The Nash roared up Route 45 onto Route 30 in a northwesterly direction toward the village of Lisbon. Law officers back in Wellsville had already figured out that the stranger whom Fultz had arrested earlier that day was not just some camper packing a gun. Although Richetti said very little, Fultz had his suspicions concerning the true identity of the other gunman. He called law-enforcement offices throughout the area and told them to be on the alert for an armed man believed to be Floyd.

By the time Baum's automobile approached the outskirts of Lisbon, officers there had moved a railroad boxcar across the highway. Choc spotted the movable roadblock in the distance. He quickly ordered Baum to turn his car around and backtrack. He then told Baum to cut off the main highway. The florist veered onto a side route with plenty of dips and curves, known to the locals as Roller Coaster Road.

Back at the roadblock, Deputy Sheriff George E. Hayes and Lisbon police officer George Patterson watched Baum's car beat a hasty retreat. The lawmen were on the lookout for a Ford, but the sudden movement of the Nash demanded further investigation. Hayes and Patterson jumped in their car and followed. They caught up with the Nash in just a few minutes.

From the backseat, Floyd kept watch. He spotted the other car gaining on Baum's automobile. Choc told the old man to pull over and let them pass. When Baum maneuvered his vehicle to the side of the road, the officers also pulled over and screeched to a halt. Witnesses offered conflicting versions of what happened next. According to Hayes, Floyd fired through the back window of Baum's car at the pursuit vehicle. One of the bullets shattered the windshield, narrowly missing the deputy's head. Hayes related that during the mayhem that followed, McMullin and Baum leapt from the front seat and ran to the front of the car, seeking protection. Floyd also fled the Nash. "In all the excitement," as Hayes put it, the lawmen opened fire and accidentally shot Baum in a leg when he was mistaken for a fugitive.

When the smoke cleared, Choc Floyd was gone. Armed with his pair of .45 army Colt automatics, he rolled under a fence and vanished in a thick forest known as Spence's Woods. The Phantom Terror was back in his natural habitat.

That Saturday afternoon, law officers in Wellsville pressed their interrogation of Richetti. He told them his name was Richard Zamboni. He said the ninety-eight dollars they had found in his pockets was part of his winnings from a recent card game at Medina, Ohio, south of Cleveland. When confronted with his own fingerprints, Adam finally admitted his true identity, but he insisted his elusive companion was a Toledo gambler named James Warren. Richetti divulged that he knew Floyd, but he maintained he had not seen him in over a year. Fultz was not swayed. Too many photographs of Floyd had crossed the chief's desk over the years. He was completely convinced the other man running amok in the woods was indeed Pretty Boy. Despite the steady rain that fell throughout the night, huge posses spread across Columbiana County searching for the fugitive.

Not a trace of Pretty Boy was uncovered in the dense woods by Sunday morning, October 21. There were only a few rumors that did not pan out. That afternoon, however, two employees from the Tiltonsville bank tentatively identified from photos Floyd and Richetti as the bandits who had robbed them. Fultz became worried that Floyd might try to free his partner. He placed riflemen outside the city hall and in the corridors to the basement jail where Richetti was being held.

When the Bureau of Investigation learned that Richetti had been positively identified, they knew Floyd had to be close by. Late Sunday evening, Melvin Purvis, the top G-man for J. Edgar Hoover, flew into the small airstrip near Wellsville. If Purvis could take out John Dillinger, Hoover was confident he would do the same with Floyd. A dozen handpicked federal agents from the Cincinnati, Cleveland, and Pittsburgh bureaus arrived on the scene to assist Purvis. More were on their way from other locations. Jackson County Sheriff Tom Bash, who had mistakenly placed Floyd at the massacre, came from Kansas City to lend his support.

Purvis decided not to say in Wellsville. Instead, he drove a few miles north to East Liverpool, an historic river town settled by English potters in the 1840s, many years after George Washington camped on Babb's Island in the Ohio River in 1770 during a survey mission. Through the years, East Liverpool had become known as the Pottery Center of America, but in 1934, the town of hills and idle kilns was no longer booming. The city was floundering on the edge of decline. Once in town, Purvis set up a command post at the Traveler's Hotel. A reporter from the *Pittsburgh Press* who visited the agent's headquarters described it as resembling "a miniature arsenal, for the room is lined with rifles, sawed-off shotguns and submachine guns."

That night, Purvis and his men returned to Wellsville and interrogated Richetti. They conducted raids on the homes of Adam's relatives, and made sure guards were posted on the bridge across the Ohio River. The ace federal agent, however, ran into problems with Chief Fultz, who had grown somewhat cocky after surviving his duel with Pretty Boy Floyd. Enjoying the limelight, Fultz decided to keep Richetti in Wellsville to face Ohio charges and not to release him to the bureau. Purvis fussed and fumed. Fultz told him to get a federal warrant.

Late Sunday, Purvis issued a statement to the *East Liverpool Review.* "We have had information for some months that Richetti was one of the participants in the Kansas City massacre," Purvis told reporters. "Two weeks ago we received definite proof of that fact. We have, of course, been searching for him for many months. Tonight I made a formal demand upon the chief of police of Wellsville for custody of Richetti and he refused to turn over the prisoner. Meantime, we shall continue our concentrated effort to find 'Pretty Boy' Floyd."

About 2:00 A.M., a band of two hundred searchers was called in from the rugged countryside where Floyd had last been seen. Purvis feared the trigger-happy possemen would fire upon their own men in the darkness or expose themselves to potshots Floyd might take at them from ambush. He ordered the manhunt resumed after sunrise. Hot baths and a few hours of sleep were needed.

Lights burned in farmhouses throughout the night. Men leaned shotguns or rifles on the walls next to their beds. Some folks locked their front doors for the first time in memory. There had not been so much excitement in Columbiana County since the summer of 1863, seventy-one years earlier, when John Hunt Morgan, a daring cavalry officer, had surrendered his exhausted raiders there after making the Confederacy's deepest thrust into Union territory.

Monday, October 22, dawned with no fresh news about Floyd. He had not been spotted since Saturday afternoon when he fled the skirmish on Roller Coaster Road. Unconfirmed sightings of the bandit flooded overworked police dispatchers and switchboards. All of them proved to be dead ends. Some of the deputies and policemen believed Fultz had managed to pump a bullet into Floyd's stomach during the scrap on Elizabeth Hill. A few of them speculated that the outlaw was either dead or dying out in the hilly terrain north of Wellsville and East Liverpool.

This was not so. Choc was tired, dirty, and hungry, but he was very much alive. His wounds proved real only in the minds of pursuing officers. No bullets had found their mark. Choc spent two days and nights roaming the backwoods, living off the land, not realizing the irony of his situation. A son of the South, who flourished in the hills of Oklahoma with taproots reaching back to Georgia, Charley Floyd found himself tromping through fields worked by farmers whose fathers or grandfathers had donned Union blue to do battle on land that was home to generations of Floyds. Choc had no way of knowing that men from these parts had once trudged across his own family's land and fought against Floyd kith and kin at Allatoona Pass in 1864.

Now, just as Morgan, the Thunderbolt of the Confederacy, had done with his guerrillalike raids in 1863, Charley Floyd, armed with a pair of Colt automatics, penetrated enemy territory. Choc's true foes, however, were not the struggling farmers or the unemployed pottery workers in the towns along the broad river. Choc's chief adversary here was Melvin H. Purvis, Jr., a product of Timmonsville, South Carolina. On October 22, 1934, Purvis, just two days shy of his thirty-first birthday, was primed and ready for combat.

Charley Floyd, however, was not looking for a fight. He was interested only in finding a way to get home. The terrain he covered was mostly steep hills blanketed with trees and vines. There were some springs, and Little Beaver Creek and Long's Run wound through the landscape. At night, he may have slept on the bank of a stream, under a canopy of stars and sycamores. He no doubt found hickory nuts and was able to forage from frost-withered gardens. By that Monday, though, hunger drove Choc from the sanctuary of the brambles.

Several people from the area, especially those about ten miles north of East

Liverpool, near the St. Clair Townships towns of Calcutta and Clarkson, reported seeing a man that day that they believed was Charley Floyd. Some looked up from their work and saw a solitary figure walking over the fields. Others offered him water or directions.

Around high noon that Monday, Charley approached the farmhouse of Robert Robinson. The farmer's daughter, Mabel Wilson, allowed the man to wash his face, and she made him a sandwich. She gave him some ginger cookies and apples. Choc had not been gone long when Constable Clyde Birch came to the farm and heard about the man. From the description, Birch knew it was Pretty Boy. At once, he drove to a telephone and relayed the information to a Department of Justice agent and the East Liverpool police.

Purvis swiftly responded. He chose three of his best agents, W. E. "Bud" Hopton, Sam McKee, and Dave Hall, to accompany him to the area where Floyd had last been seen. East Liverpool Police Chief Hugh J. McDermott was asked to provide backup assistance. McDermott, fifty-three years old at the time, had become a policeman just after the turn of the century, when he walked a beat on the rough riverfront with an Airedale terrier named Turk. He selected three of his officers to go along. They were Herman Roth, a feisty cop whose trademark was a gun belt with two pearl-handled pistols he carried butts aimed forward; Glenn "Curly" Montgomery, a barrel-chested man built like a fireplug; and Chester C. Smith, a crack shot and decorated veteran of the Great War who had encountered Choc Floyd and even talked to him years before at Hell's Half-Acre. The four local policemen led the way in McDermott's 1934 Chevy, followed by the four G-men, who had piled into Hopton's 1933 government-issue Chevrolet.

At approximately three o'clock that afternoon, Choc appeared at Ellen Conkle's fifty-acre farm on Sprucevale road between the towns of Clarkson and Calcutta. Mrs. Conkle, a widow, was cleaning out a smokehouse when she heard someone knocking on the back door. She always remembered the events of the next hour, especially the words exchanged between herself and the young man who paid an unexpected visit. The following day, their conversation appeared in newspapers throughout the land.

"Lady, I'm lost and I want something to eat," Charley told her. "Can you help me out with some food? I'll pay you."

Like most country people, Ellen Conkle had always been taught to be kind to strangers, even tramps, because they might be angels in disguise. The polite young man before her was dirty and bedraggled. He wore no hat and his blue suit was covered with Spanish needles, the pesty thistles that thrived in the fields. The tip of a blue necktie extended from a suit-coat pocket crammed with apples. The man's silver belt buckle was initialed with a large *C*. His black oxfords were scuffed. He needed a shave.

"I look like a wild man, don't I?" Floyd laughed. "But I've been drinking.

I was hunting squirrels with my brother last night and I got lost. The more directions I got, the more confused I became. I don't where I am now.'

Mrs. Conkle, suspicious because she knew no one hunted squirrels at night or even went near the woods in business suits, nonetheless told Choc to wash up in the kitchen while she fixed him a dinner. "He had a sort of a wild look about him," recalled Mrs. Conkle, "but I couldn't refuse him food." She asked Choc what he wanted to eat.

"Meat," he replied. "All I've been eating is apples, and some ginger cookies. I'm hungry for meat."

There was no bacon or ham, so the farm woman fetched some cold-packed spareribs from her smokehouse. As she fixed a meal of spareribs, potatoes, and rice pudding, Choc sat in a rocker on the back porch and studied the Sunday edition of the *East Liverpool Review,* which Mrs. Conkle had not read. It was the most recent paper on hand, since the Monday edition would not reach the Conkle farm until the following day. As he read the front page, dominated by news of the massive manhunt and the promise from Melvin Purvis to bring down Pretty Boy Floyd, Choc devoured slices of freshly baked bread. He ate everything on the pottery plate, except for the pudding, and finished his meal with coffee and a slice of pumpkin pie. It would be a superb last supper.

Afterward, Choc declared that the dinner was "fit for a king." He pulled out a roll of money to pay for the food. Mrs. Conkle refused, but he insisted she at least take a dollar bill.

Floyd then asked the woman whether she could assist him in getting to a bus station so he could go to Youngstown. She said she could not help, but she had a suggestion. Her brother, Stewart Dyke, and his wife, Florence, were out in her fields husking corn. Perhaps when the Dykes finished their work, they would be willing to give the young man a lift in their Model A Ford. Choc climbed in the car parked out back and waited. It was almost 4:00 P.M. when the Dykes walked up to the Conkle house. They spied Choc sitting in their car. He was toying with the keys while he studied a road map. Choc asked whether, for a fee, they would drive him to Youngstown. Dyke refused. That was too far, he said, and they were tired. "I'll not take you there tonight," Dyke remembered telling Charley. "I'm going home. I'll take you to Clarkson, though."

Choc accepted the offer. He opened the car door and got in the backseat of the Ford. Florence Dyke sat up front with her husband. Choc borrowed the woman's powder puff to pat his cheeks, apparently to cover the heavy beard. As they drove off, they waved goodbye to Ellen Conkle. The Model A had barely moved when two Chevrolet cars appeared on the Sprucevale Road. It was Melvin Purvis and his men, and they happened just to be driving by, alerted by the constable that Floyd was in the general vicinity.

"I saw the two automobile loads of officers before Floyd saw them and wondered who they were," recounted Dyke. "When Floyd saw them, his face paled and he ordered me to drive to the back of the corncrib. After I backed up he said, 'Get going!' and called me a nasty name. He pulled out his gun and jumped out of the car and crawled under the corncrib. An instant later, he darted out and came toward the car. Then he started across a pasture."

In the meantime, the eight armed agents and policemen scrambled from their cars in the front yard. They had seen the Ford and saw the man in the blue suit leap out. There was little doubt in their minds who he was. Their mission was clear.

"As we were passing the Conkle farm, I spied a hatless man dodging back behind the corner of a corncrib," Chester Smith, an East Liverpool policeman, related to reporters that evening. "We stopped and I jumped out with my rifle and ran toward the shed. I saw the man running up a hill in the rear, and shouted to him to halt. He kept going, darting to the left and right, trying to make the crest of the hill. I'd had a good look at him, and was sure it was Floyd. I called again, but he wouldn't stop. Then I knelt down and took aim at him."

The other law officers spread out behind the farmhouse.

"Halt!" yelled Purvis. Choc kept going.

"Fire!" commanded Purvis. A blaze of gunfire commenced. Their target was five hundred feet away, running like a hunted wolf.

"My first shot hit him in the arm above the elbow and knocked the .45 out of his right hand," Smith remembered decades later in the *East Liverpool Review*. "I didn't want to kill him, just bring him down." Choc staggered from the shock of the bullet and went to his knees, but he righted himself and kept moving toward the distant tree line. "My second shot hit him in the side above the shoulder blade and brought him down."

Smith and the others ran to the fallen man. "Why didn't you halt when I yelled?" Smith asked Choc. "If I'd gotten in them woods, you'd never got me," Choc replied. The officers picked up the Colt pistol Floyd had dropped. Another .45 automatic was tucked in the top of his trousers. "You might as well take it," Choc said with a slight smile. "I have no more use for it." He managed to prop himself up on an elbow. Some of the officers lifted Floyd and carried him over to an apple tree and laid him in the shade. "Who the hell tipped you?" asked Choc. They did not answer him.

Purvis questioned the wounded man about the Kansas City Massacre. Choc glared and spat out, "I ain't telling you sons of bitches anything." Then Choc thought of his partner and asked, still using Richetti's last alias, "Where's Eddie?"

It was apparent that death was near. "You got me twice," Choc said, his voice choking.

"You're Pretty Boy Floyd," stated Purvis, as if to convince himself that he had brought down yet another public enemy. The eyes of the two Southerners locked, one a lawman, the other a bandit, both the same age.

"I'm Charles Arthur Floyd," Choc told him.

"You are Floyd, though, aren't you?" asked Purvis.

"I am Floyd," said Choc. That was the last he had to say.

Charley Floyd died at 4:25 P.M. His end came where his life had begun, on a hardscrabble farm. He took his final breath just as the last rays of the sun fell on the hills.

He would be thirty years old forever.

SALLISAW, OKLAHOMA

"Men at some times are masters of their fate."
—Julius Caesar (WILLIAM SHAKESPEARE)

HARLEY FLOYD WAS STONE DEAD but lawmen put handcuffs on him, anyway. Then they bound his legs with rope. It was as if they feared the Phantom Terror might come back to life and attempt yet another escape. Seconds after Choc died, Melvin Purvis hurried to the nearest telephone in the village of Clarkson. The other officers assumed he was summoning an ambulance to retrieve the corpse. However, when he returned, Purvis told them the only call he had made was to J. Edgar Hoover in Washington, D.C., dutifully to report that another public enemy had been felled.

By the time they removed Charley's manacled body from the Conkle farm, a veil of evening fog shrouded the darkened field. Officers toted his body through the corn stubble and Choc rode silently into East Liverpool in a police car. It had been determined that he had fled without firing a single shot from either of his two fully loaded pistols. They carried the slain bandit to police chief McDermott's Chevrolet. Choc was propped up in the backseat between Glenn Montgomery and Chester Smith, the marksman whose .32-20 Winchester rifle bullets had hit Floyd as he raced for the protection of the distant trees. Someone closed Choc's eyelids. His head slumped forward on his chest. The drive from the farm to East Liverpool was less than ten miles, but the officers later said that it seemed to take an eternity. They drove in awkward silence down Sprucevale Road toward the town of Calcutta. Lamps burned in the windows of homes along the way. It was suppertime.

The police cars went directly to the Sturgis Funeral Home at 122 West Fifth Street, operated by E. G. Sturgis and his son Ernie, who also moonlighted as the county coroner. Frank A. Dawson, twenty-eight years old at the time, did much of the embalming at the funeral home. He had just returned from the barbershop when the officers carried Floyd from the garage entrance through a back door into a preparation room. "Give me a good haircut because I'll probably be in the newspapers," Dawson later recalled instructing the barber. He knew that if the G-men found their quarry, he would be called upon to prepare Floyd's body.

"They had also just brought in a transient laborer they'd found dead in a field where they were building the airstrip," recalled Dawson in 1979. "I took the clothes off both of them and threw them in a corner and began working on Floyd." Later someone pitched the dead drifter's clothing outside in the alley. Morbid citizens quickly pounced on the trash can and passed off the tattered clothing as Pretty Boy souvenirs. "Somebody, somewhere has a pair of shoes he thinks were Floyd's," remembered Dawson.

Police officers then cut Choc's blue suit into scores of small swatches to give away as mementos. They removed $122 in cash from his pockets—twelve tens and two ones. The money would help defray the cost of preparing Floyd for burial. The ring that Ruby had given him and the watch with "Billy the Killer" Miller's lucky fifty-cent piece attached were set aside for next of kin. Chester Smith and some of the others in on the chase took the spare .45 bullets from Floyd's pockets for keepsakes. They found photos of Dempsey and Ruby tucked away inside Choc's suit-coat pocket.

That evening, curiosity seekers and scoop-hungry reporters flocked to the Conkle farm, where forty-one-year-old Ellen Conkle announced she intended to keep the dollar bill Choc had given her for his last meal. "I have that dollar and I'm going to frame it," she told them. "He [Floyd] seemed to know, as I appreciate now, that he was being hunted. He yelled to my brother when he saw the machines: 'They're after me!' "

For several days, the smiling widow obliged photographers who snapped pictures of her house and Stewart Dyke's automobile still parked beside the corncrib. She posed with the tray bearing the plate of gnawed bones and a desert dish filled with rice pudding. Some people offered her as much as one hundred dollars just for the dinner plate. She refused. For two days, Mrs. Conkle even left the dishes unwashed. Then she packed them away along with the newspaper Floyd had read during his meal, as if they were treasured heirlooms. She also preserved the rocking chair that Charley had sat in while he ate.

In February 1935, nearly four months after Floyd died on her farm, Ellen Conkle received two letters from Ruby Floyd, thanking her for the hospitality she had showed Ruby's former husband. "Charles was one of the nicest men you ever met if you only knew him," wrote Ruby in her first letter. "If he had lived he would have repaid you a thousand times." In her next letter, Ruby confided that one day she hoped to visit the farm where Charley had died. "I loved him so much and do hope that some day I am able to visit you and even come by the place where he died. He was not bad but he didn't have a chance. I can't tell you how much I appreciate you feeding him because he really liked to eat. I am sending you my love and praying that God will reward you for your kindness." Mrs. Conkle carefully packed away the letters. Ruby never came to the farm.

"I never dreamed our place would be the scene of anything like that," Ellen

Conkle explained to the reporters the same night Floyd died. Her sister-in-law, Florence Dyke, rejected a proposition from a stranger who coveted the powder puff Charley had used to camouflage his beard. Within hours of Floyd's death, possemen and sightseers scooped up the ginger cookies and apples that had dropped from Choc's pocket when he bolted across the field. By the time newsreel crews arrived on the scene from New York, rags fluttered from three stakes, marking the spot where Pretty Boy Floyd had fallen in his last attempt to elude the law.

In East Liverpool, large crowds gathered outside the Sturgis Funeral Home. "The hunt is over! Floyd is dead!" Purvis announced to the crush of reporters. Asked who had actually killed Choc, Purvis replied, "We all did." Chief McDermott admitted that "it was just luck" that they even got Floyd. "He died like a rat," the seasoned cop muttered. Then Purvis issued a formal press statement:

> The killing of Charles Arthur (Pretty Boy) Floyd brings to a close the relentless search and effort on the part of the department of investigation of the United States department of justice.
>
> The search was directed by J. Edgar Hoover, director of the department, from Washington and I have been in constant contact with him by telephone and telegraph. Mr. Hoover has been particularly anxious as have we all to bring about the apprehension of this and other similar hoodlums.
>
> Mr. Hoover and all the special agents were particularly interested in Floyd because he killed one of our men in the Kansas City massacre of June 17, 1933.

From his office in Washington, Hoover revealed for the first time that on four separate instances, Floyd had offered to turn himself in if the government promised not to seek the death penalty against him. Hoover divulged that Floyd's last plea for immunity from a death sentence came just two weeks before he was killed. However, word was sent back to Buffalo by family members that no promises would be made and that Floyd had to face the consequences for what he had done. With Floyd out of the way, Hoover quickly let it be known that the title of public enemy number one now belonged to Lester Gillis, better known as Baby Face Nelson.

Little more than a month later, on November 28, Nelson's bullet-riddled body was found in a roadside ditch outside Chicago after he engaged federal agents in a gunfight. And in January 1935, two more of Hoover's targets, Ma Barker and her outlaw son Fred, long sought as killers and kidnappers, would die during a six-hour machine-gun battle at their Florida hideout. In 1936, Hoover—embarrassed by criticism for having never made an arrest himself—went to New Orleans, where he and some agents captured Alvin Karpis, a former Barker associate. These actions led to an avalanche of publicity favorable for Hoover. An era clearly was drawing to a close.

The outlaw of the hour in October of 1934, however, was still Pretty Boy Floyd. Inside the funeral home, Choc's body was photographed. Several policemen stood behind the metal embalming table for the picture session. He was also fingerprinted, despite the fact Charley had sanded down his fingertips in an attempt to obliterate his prints. A pair of local physicians, Drs. Ed Miskall and Roy Costello, performed the postmortem examination. Their official findings contained in the coroner's report certified by Ernie Sturgis six weeks later, on December 1, 1934, listed the cause of death as internal hemorrhage. Newspaper extras hawked on the streets the evening of October 22, and the following day, mentioned at least fourteen or fifteen bullet wounds. The autopsy report mentioned only three gunshot wounds—"two through the chest and abdomen and one through the forearm." There was never any doubt that the number of wounds reported in some newspapers was greatly inflated.

Little was made of the fact that an examination of Floyd's body showed no sign of a bullet wound to his left shoulder, as was claimed by the government's star witness in the Kansas City Massacre case. It was a missing link that definitely weakened the case against Floyd. The only noticeable bullet scars, other than the fresh death wounds, were in the foot, sustained during the shootout with Erv Kelley. To add to the confusion, a mysterious notation, reportedly in Ernie Sturgis's handwriting, was casually penciled on the funeral record dated October 22. It stated:

4 wounds
shot in stomach

Many years later, Dawson told veteran *East Liverpool Review* reporter Bob Popp that "probably" two rifle bullets had entered Floyd's body from the side, then crisscrossed and went into his abdomen. The wound on his right forearm may have been made by one of those bullets, according to Dawson. But no matter whether three or four bullets found their mark, for decades questions remained about who had actually shot Floyd and how the bandit had died.

Almost forty-five years after the autopsy, a controversial version of Floyd's death that had been long discussed in East Liverpool emerged in the nation's press. In 1979, Chester Smith, by then an eighty-four-year-old retired police captain, broke decades of silence concerning what he contended to be the true circumstances of the Floyd slaying. Smith claimed that after Pretty Boy lay wounded in the field, Melvin Purvis had actually ordered another of the federal agents at the scene to execute Floyd.

"Back away from that man. I want to talk to him," Smith recalled Purvis yelling as the agent ran up to the fallen bandit. Smith remembered that Floyd, although wounded, was sitting upright while Purvis questioned him. "Were you in on the Kansas City Massacre?" demanded Purvis. Floyd spat back, "I wouldn't tell you son of a bitch anything." According to Smith, Purvis at that point turned to Agent Herman Hollis and barked the command "Fire into him!" Smith said Hollis obeyed. He leveled his service revolver and blasted Floyd once in the breastbone. Some of the subsequent news stories quoted Smith as saying that the agent used a tommy gun to dispatch Floyd.

"It all happened very quickly," Smith told reporters. Shocked by the swiftness of the execution, Smith said he asked Purvis why he had ordered Floyd shot. "Mr. Hoover, my boss, told me to bring him in dead!" Smith recalled was the cavalier reply.

"It was a cover-up," Smith told the *Lisbon Morning Journal* in October of 1979. "They [the FBI] wanted the credit," Smith related during other interviews. "Purvis reported to Hoover that they had killed him so nobody could collect the reward." A story headlined BLASTING A G-MAN MYTH, in the September 24, 1979, issue of *Time* magazine, quoted Smith as saying that "they didn't want it to get out that he'd been killed that way." Smith explained that he felt compelled to clear the air since he was the last of the eight lawmen involved in the celebrated deed.

Unbeknownst to Chester Smith, who passed away on October 23, 1984— just one day after the fiftieth anniversary of Floyd's slaying—he was *not* the sole survivor from the Pretty Boy death squad. W. E. "Bud" Hopton, one of four special agents at the Conkle farm when Floyd went down under fire, was still alive in Tennessee.

A twenty-one-year FBI veteran, Hopton was livid when he saw the news stories branding Purvis as Floyd's chief executioner. A letter of protest was quickly fired off to the editors of *Time,* taking issue with Smith's claims. "Nothing could be further from the truth," wrote Hopton, who was twenty-eight at the time of Choc's demise. "The allegation that Purvis ordered an Agent to 'Fire into Floyd' as described . . . is absolutely false. The truth is that when the several members of the East Liverpool Police Department came up to where Floyd was lying on the ground, he had already been mortally wounded." The retired agent also pointed out that Herman Hollis, who was slain in the gun battle with Baby Face Nelson just a month after Floyd was killed, was "not even present" during the Floyd manhunt. "I knew Herman Hollis, and he wasn't there."

In 1991, when the eighty-six-year-old Hopton was again asked about Chester Smith's allegations, he remained just as vehement in his denial. "That's baloney," Hopton commented. "That's a bunch of crap!" Hopton recalled that federal agents' bullets, and not those fired by Smith, actually brought down Choc Floyd. "When he ran across the field, Sam [Agent McKee] and I just cut down on him with a submachine gun. We dropped him and then the police came running down there. We told them not to get too close to him, because as he came down, he rolled on his side. He was still trying to take aim at us, but Sam McKee was a wonderful shot. He sawed him off with a single shot. It was a single shot that hit the arm he had raised with a gun in his hand. Sam was a hell of a good shot."

In East Liverpool, many people who sided with Chester Smith, including his daughters, stood by Smith's version of the Floyd story. "Our father just wanted to set things straight," explained Naomi Nortrup, Smith's eldest daughter. "He was tired of reading and hearing those things that weren't true. He wanted it all said to get it over with. He wanted some peace of mind."

Like the Kansas City Massacre, the true facts surrounding Floyd's final moments on Ellen Conkle's farm remain forever clouded by disputed tales of his death. Unlike Chester Smith, however, not all of those who were present when Choc Floyd passed into the ranks of the departed were able to find peace of mind. One of those was Melvin Purvis.

The famous FBI agent who tracked down Dillinger and Pretty Boy lasted in Hoover's service for only ten more months after Floyd was killed. On August 5, 1935, Purvis retired from the FBI and headed west. The rumor out of Washington at the time was that Hoover had become jealous of Purvis grabbing all the headlines. The boss believed there was no excuse for anyone stealing limelight that he felt belonged on himself. Sources out of the capital reported that Hoover not only harassed his former golden boy but even assigned other agents to spy on Purvis. Many years later, Purvis family members publicly admitted that he and Hoover had become bitter enemies when the director attempted to push him into obscurity.

Purvis practiced law in San Francisco for three years. He also became involved in promotional campaigns of a variety of products, ranging from razor blades to cars. On a radio show he narrated for Post Toasties, he commanded the "Melvin Purvis Law and Order Patrol." He invited youngsters to send in cereal box tops for Junior G-Man badges, whistles, and pistols. Purvis also wrote his autobiography, *American Agent,* published by Doubleday in 1936. During World War II, he became active in military intelligence work, gathering evidence to use against captured Nazis. After his discharge, Purvis went home to his law practice and ownership of a radio station and newspaper.

On February 29, 1960, at his residence in Timmonsville, South Carolina, the fifty-six-year-old Purvis, despondent because of poor health, picked up the same automatic pistol he carried when tracking down Dillinger and Floyd. His wife, Rosanne, was in the garden outside their home. She heard the shot ring out. In East Liverpool, when he was told that Purvis had committed suicide, Chester Smith frowned and shook his head. "I wonder if that was on his mind all these years," Smith said to his daughter.

However, on the evening of October 22, 1934, twenty-five years before Purvis took his own life, he was still consumed with a sense of triumph. No ghosts had yet materialized. As he packed his bags at the Traveler's Hotel and prepared to take on the next assignment, he basked in the glory. Outside, on the crowded downtown streets, newsboys screamed out, "Pretty Boy Floyd Killed by Police!"

A few blocks away at the funeral home, Frank Dawson completed embalming the body. The mortician shaved Choc and combed back his hair. He took note of Floyd's manicured nails and neatly plucked eyebrows. Then Dawson summoned a local pottery worker who made a death-mask mold of Choc's face. A number of cream-colored plaster casts were later distributed, like macabre hunting trophies, among some of the officers and Dawson's friends.

In a telegram sent to Chief McDermott, filed at Sallisaw at 8:05 P.M. that evening, Mamie Floyd, Choc's widowed mother, instructed the funeral home how to handle her boy's body. McDermott gave the telegram to news reporters.

I am the mother of Charles Floyd. If he has been killed, turn body over to reliable undertaker and forbid any pictures being taken of him and bar the public. Pass this request to the United States department of justice. Hold body until I arrive.

Mrs. Walter Floyd

But Mamie's wire arrived too late, and her wishes would not have been honored in any case. The photographs had been taken. Already curious crowds were jamming the Sturgis Funeral Home to see the man who had helped take their minds off the Depression, if only for a short time. Charley, with freshly rouged cheeks, was laid out on a small cot in the front room. A blanket of crushed velvet was pulled up to his chin. He looked in repose as though he were asleep. An estimated twenty thousand people, in all likelihood a greatly exaggerated number, filed through the parlor in double lines from 8:30 P.M. to 11:30 P.M., according to Dawson's best guesses. Others said the crowd was only half that number. Men in overalls and business suits, women carrying babies, and students shuffled past for a quick glimpse of the desperado. Police officers and firemen tried to keep order. At times, the crowd got out of hand. "They tore down the hedges and ruined the carpet," recalled Dawson. "They even came in through the coal chute."

During the night, Mamie Floyd decided she could not afford to go to East Liverpool to claim Choc's body. She and the rest of the family would wait for Charley at Sallisaw. "The prince of the underworld," as one newspaper called him, would come home alone. A hat was passed around town and money was wired to Ohio. Even the Sallisaw bank that Charley and Birdwell had robbed two years before chipped in to bring the outlaw home. Along with the cash found on Choc, there was enough to cover rail shipment of the body and the other expenses. The bill for embalming and a shipping coffin came to $175.

On the Sturgis record book Choc's occupation was listed as "bandit." The cost to transport the corpse was $71.18, two times the regular first-class fare.

On Tuesday, October 23, Frank Dawson and Ernie Sturgis prepared Charley Floyd for his final trip. They placed him in a cloth-lined shipping box, encased with unfinished pine. On one end was penciled the word *Head.* Tacked to the side of the box was an envelope containing documents signed by the city registrar, attesting to the fact that inside the pine coffin were the remains of Charles Arthur Floyd. The undertakers drove the body to the East Liverpool station, near the river. They watched as the crate was shoved inside a Pennsylvania Railroad baggage car. In Wellsville, just a short distance down the track, Adam Richetti wept when jailers showed him the newspapers and finally convinced him that his partner was dead. "I don't see why he stuck around so long," Richetti wondered out loud. Later that day, schools were dismissed early so the children could watch Richetti as he was transferred to the ancient county jail at Lisbon. Eventually, he would be returned to Kansas City to stand trial for murder for his alleged role in the Kansas City Massacre.

At 11:30 A.M. the train pulled away. By 2:00 P.M. a crowd of porters saw Floyd off in Pittsburgh as the coffin was shifted to the St. Louis Flyer. The train chugged westward, through the afternoon and evening, across Ohio, Indiana, and Illinois. The next day, it crossed the Mississippi River at St. Louis, stopping at Union Station. The box was moved to another train, which continued through the Missouri countryside, virtually following the same route Choc had taken a decade before when he was sentenced to prison. As the train passed below the bluffs at Jefferson City, thousands of convicts heard the whistle sound. It was high noon.

Arriving at Kansas City, the train pulled into the sheds just a few hundred yards from the scene of the massacre. Coincidentally, a federal grand jury was meeting at that same time to consider indictments against conspirators in the attempt to free Frank Nash. After a fifty-minute stop, only a few workmen were on hand when Choc's coffin was loaded once more, this time on a Kansas City Southern train, for the last leg of the trip. The train lurched forward and built up speed, heading due south.

Not everyone in Oklahoma lamented Floyd's passing. Most law officers, editorial writers, and city folks rejoiced at the news. So did the bankers. The government's aggressive war on bank robbers and bandits would produce swift results. In 1935, only nine banks in the state were robbed. And, in the four-year-period from 1936 to 1940, bandits were able to loot only ten more banks. Many of those who had been victimized or harassed by Pretty Boy were delighted with the news of his death. "I would much rather done it myself," said a somber Howard Kelley, brother of Erv Kelley, the former lawman who Choc had gunned down near Bixby in 1932. "I approve of it one hundred percent. I am glad he is gone."

Charley Floyd's admirers outnumbered his detractors, however. In country villages scattered over the Oklahoma hills and in oil patch towns, people who had followed the bandit's exploits for years had a difficult time accepting his death. They said they would not truly believe Charley was dead until they saw his body. His death seemed to symbolize for many folks, particularly the poor, something in themselves that was now gone.

Ruby Floyd remained outwardly calm the evening of October 22 when the first news stories broke. Reporters, armed with the fresh wire reports from Ohio, began showing up at her father's home near Bixby, where she and Dempsey lived. "I haven't a statement to make at this time," Ruby said, sobbing. "When the information was phoned me at Okmulgee, where I was visiting, I didn't believe it. They have been wrong so many times. Now I don't know what to say."

Several reporters turned to Dempsey, Choc's nine-year-old son, who was busy with a jigsaw puzzle on the floor. "Who told you your daddy was dead?" a reporter asked Dempsey. "He can't answer your questions," interrupted Maggie Hardgraves, Ruby's stepmother. "The boy feels bad, of course, and there is no statement he could make."

When she regained her composure, Ruby managed a few words. "It is as I expected," she whispered. "It is as I have told him countless times." Then she had some friends drive her into Bixby so she could telephone Mamie Floyd at Sallisaw. After placing the call, Ruby broke into tears again. Her friends whisked her away in their truck, telling reporters their questions would have to keep.

"I guess it's better as it is," Bradley Floyd said when another reporter came to his Earlsboro home to tell him that his brother had been killed. Bradley and Bessie prepared their boys for the trip to Sallisaw to comfort Mamie and bury Choc.

Sequoyah County was in a state of mourning. "The pall of death fell over Sallisaw as a sorrowing hill country people heard the news that they had expected from day to day for a long time," reported the *Muskogee Phoenix*. "It was a matter of speculation for street corner gossipers and hillfolk in and about Sallisaw today whether they would ever again see the sleek features of Charles A. 'Pretty Boy' Floyd. It was hard for them to realize that at last the unswerving forces of justice had laid him cold and lifeless."

Earlier that week, when Mamie first heard that her son had been killed, she tried to remain stoic. "It can't be true," she told a reporter. "Charles was not a bad boy at heart and he has always warned all boys to steer clear of violations of the law." Friends and family gathered around Mamie at the small frame house where she lived with her youngest child, Mary. "They shot my brother down like a dog," cried Mary, whose husband, Perry Lattimore, had died at age twenty-five of a heart attack only two months before, leaving her with their small son and daughter to raise on her waitress wages. "Charley never had a chance like other boys. He worked in the sand hills for a cornbread living.

We have always been poor. Charley craved a few luxuries. That was his downfall."

Shortly after 2:00 A.M. on Friday, October 26, the train arrived at Sallisaw. Folks were waiting for its arrival. The sound of the whistle carried over the hills and through the hollows.

"I've never forgotten those last days at Sallisaw when we buried my dad," recalled Dempsey Floyd almost six decades later. "One thing that really stands out in my mind was that everybody got up in the middle of the night and went down to the station to meet him. I can remember that train coming and it kept blowing its whistle. Over and over again, that damn ol' whistle blew. We were all standing there by the tracks. The whole family was there. I looked around us and there was a throng of people. Friends, neighbors, it seemed like everyone came to show their respect. It was very emotional. And, to this very day, whenever I hear a train whistle, that whole scene comes to my mind and I'm taken back to that time."

Bradley and E. W. Floyd, with tears streaming down their faces, stepped forward to help the undertaker from the Moore Funeral Home unload the coffin. They grabbed the metal handles on the crate and gently lifted it from the baggage car.

The mourners returned to their homes in silence as the mortician took Choc to the funeral parlor to prepare him for burial. More than one thousand people walked by the coffin at the mortuary that day before the undertaker brought Choc's body to Mary's home. They laid his coffin in the front room. All of Charley's brothers and sisters, his grandparents, an array of other relatives, and the closest family friends came. Ruby and Dempsey arrived from Bixby. Pies, cakes, and covered dishes filled the tiny kitchen. Bradley went to the open casket and gently undressed Choc from the waist up to see for himself exactly what had been done. The family sat with the body all through the night.

On Saturday, Jess Ring brought his family to the house and Bradley opened up Choc's shirt again to show him the wounds. Dempsey, in the suit he had worn when he and his mother performed their stage show, took each of the young Ring girls by their hand and led them to the coffin to view his father's remains. "Little Jackie gave us girls a red rose and our father lifted all of us up so we could see Charley's bullet wounds," remembered Ruth Morgan, one of the Ring daughters.

A huge crowd congregated outside. The city police chief hired extra men to help control all the people. Two signs were tacked on the front of the house: NO VISITORS ALLOWED. George Cheek, a nominee for county sheriff, sat in his car with a shotgun in his lap. He warned the curious to leave the family alone. Ironically, a petition opposing clemency for outlaw Matt Kimes was circulated throughout the crowd. Friends of the family took up another collection to buy flowers for the funeral. Others went out in the country and picked wild autumn blooms to take to Choc's grave. That Saturday afternoon in nearby

Fort Smith, Arkansas, a sedan pulled up in front of Lee's Flowers and Seeds. Two men in suits walked into the shop and bought every blossom and stem in stock. They put their cash on the counter. "Send it all to Sallisaw," one of the strangers told the clerk. "Send it to Pretty Boy."

Charley Floyd's funeral was the largest in Oklahoma history. It took place on Sunday, October 28. It was an Indian summer day, unusually hot for mid-fall. A crowd estimated at over twenty thousand showed up. Other estimates placed the number at closer to forty thousand people.

A grave site waited for Charley out in Akins, at the cemetery where the year before he had shown his mother the exact spot he wished to be buried. He would rest next to his father and baby brother. Sallisaw was preparing to host an American Legion convention, so the streets were fittingly draped in bunting. At 1:15 P.M., the casket was placed in a hearse for its last ride. Family members followed in their cars. A five-mile-long cortege of automobiles, trucks, and buggies followed the hearse down the country roads leading to Akins. Five cars were packed with floral displays. People came, according to newspaper accounts, from twenty states, some in taxis, others in buses carrying Sunday school classes. Many left their cars parked along the road and walked to the graveyard. One farmer claimed he actually walked thirty miles just to see them lower Choc's coffin into the ground. It took the hearse an hour to make the seven-mile drive.

"You could look out from Sallisaw and see great clouds of dust rising up from around Akins," recalled William Burns, at the time a teenaged neighbor of Mamie Floyd. "The sun was actually blocked by all the dust."

The unruly crush of sightseers turned the funeral into a spectacle. People fainted in the October heat. There were fistfights. Officers labored to keep the traffic moving. The Floyds became so enraged, they cursed at the gawking strangers whose cars blocked the way. One of the Floyds even threw a rock through the window of an obnoxious driver who tried to cut in front of the procession. Another show-off driver received a bloody nose from one of Choc's uncles.

Two dozen special guards waited at the cemetery. One of them had a .30–.30 rifle hidden in the brush, "just in case one of them newspaper fellas thinks he's smart and tries to fly over here in an airplane," he told the others. Some of the mob had camped overnight in the graveyard. Many brought picnic baskets. They sat on tombstones eating their lunches. Jugs of corn liquor were seen being passed around. The swarm of people overflowed into nearby pastures. Fences were torn down to make room for parked cars. "There ain't nothin' better than a good funeral to draw out folks in these parts," one grizzled old man told an *Oklahoma News* reporter. "That Floyd, he was a great fella, he was."

When they finally arrived at the Akins Cemetery, family members had to battle their way through the crowd to reach the log arbor where the service was held. Choc's sister Mary yanked a news photographer out of a tree. Deputies chased outsiders from the cane-bottomed chairs reserved for the Floyds. An armed lawman stood at the head of the casket in a futile attempt to keep order. The pallbearers, all men who had grown up with Choc, removed the coffin, covered with a blanket of carnations, from the hearse. They carried it to the arbor. A quartet sang "God Will Take Care of You," and the men's choir from the Akins Baptist Church offered the standard hymns, "Old Rugged Cross," "Rock of Ages," and "Abide with Me." The sobs of the family could be heard over the singers' voices.

Reverend W. E. Rockett, pastor of the First Baptist Church of Sallisaw, where twenty-seven members of the Floyd family worshipped every Sabbath, rose to admonish the thousands of people jammed around the arbor. He told them to show some respect to the family and the deceased. Then he delivered the eulogy, taking his text from John 19:30. "When Jesus therefore had received the vinegar, he said, 'It is finished,' and he bowed his head and gave up the ghost," Rockett sermonized. "When he said, 'It is finished,' it meant that his life's work in the form of man was ended," explained Rockett. "It meant that he would walk the shores of Galilee and the hills no more. So it was with Charles Arthur Floyd when he was called upon to finish his work here on earth. It meant that never again would he return in this fleshly body to those loved ones who are some of the finest people it is my privilege to know."

When the preacher concluded his remarks, long lines of people continued to pass by the coffin, until Mamie Floyd asked the undertaker to stop them. A young Indian girl tried to throw herself on the casket, but a law officer grabbed her and led her away. The casket was moved from the shelter to the Floyd plot, which had been dug through the hard shale. Choc's body was slowly lowered into the earth. There were more prayers. "You can't tell when a lost soul is saved, and Charles did try to change his life," Reverend Rockett advised the family.

"My boy never hurt nobody," screamed Mamie. Then she was quiet.

Ruby, draped in widow's weeds, collapsed in the arms of Bob Birdwell, the wife of the late bandit. Wearing black dresses and veiled hats, Beulah Baird stood discreetly nearby with her sister, Rose. The two women drove down to Akins in the same Ford they had been in with Choc and Adam Richetti when the mishap occurred in Ohio. After they heard that Adam had been captured and Choc was on the run, they fled Ohio and returned to Kansas City. Beulah, the young woman who had given Choc his infamous nickname, had come to say goodbye. Ruby glared with swollen eyes across the grave at Beulah. After the funeral, the Baird sisters visited with some of the other Floyd family members. But within a few years, they disappeared in the mists of time and even the Floyds lost contact with them.

Long after the services were over, a swarm of people remained in the cemetery. Many looked for remembrances. They stripped leaves and bark off the cemetery trees. Some grabbed up handfuls of dirt from the mound of earth over Choc's grave. Curtains were torn from the hearse. By nightfall, all the flowers had been taken to be pressed in family Bibles.

For several months after the funeral, local men armed with shotguns patrolled the graveyard to make sure no outsiders tampered with Charley's burial place. A cedar tree, the Cherokee's symbol of immortality, was planted near the grave. A grass fire later damaged the tree, and it was chopped down. A headstone was put in place, inscribed with Charley's full name and the dates of his birth and death. Souvenir hunters attacked it. Through the years, several stones were chipped away. Once the entire headstone was stolen and had to be replaced. For many years on Decoration Day, a single .45 caliber bullet would always be found on Choc's tombstone. None of the family ever knew who left the bullet.

One year from the day that Charley Floyd died, an advertisement, a poem, ran in the *Kansas City Star*. It was a memorial to Choc, placed by Beulah and Rose, and Adam Richetti.

> *We never knew what pain he had,*
> *We did not see him die;*
> *We only knew he passed away,*
> *And did not say goodbye.*
> *We are thinking of you Daddy dear,*
> *Thinking of the past.*
> *You left behind some broken hearts*
> *That loved you to the last;*
> *That never did, nor never will*
> *Forget you, Daddy dear,*
> *And while you rest in peaceful sleep*
> *Your memory we shall always keep.*

By that time, Adam Richetti had been brought back from Ohio and was jailed in Kansas City to be tried on a first-degree murder charge stemming from the Kansas City Massacre. On June 17, 1935—exactly two years after the massacre—the jury, despite contradictory testimony, returned a guilty verdict. Richetti was sentenced to be hanged. He appealed his conviction, but it was affirmed by the Missouri Supreme Court on May 3, 1938. Several months later, he was again sentenced to death, this time in the gas chamber at the Missouri State Penitentiary at Jefferson City.

The last day of his life, Richetti listened to the World Series and conversed briefly with a priest. He asked no favors and was served the same dinner as the rest of the inmate population—eggs, steak, potatoes, corn, pineapple, and a cookie. Shortly before midnight, he was taken from his cell to a small stone building that housed the gas chamber. He was to be the sixth man executed by lethal gas in Missouri. Stripped to his shorts, Richetti was blindfolded with goggles and led to the chamber as the lips of two priests in attendance moved in prayer. In an adjoining room waited thirty-five witnesses, including the son of the Kansas City cop Richetti was convicted of killing. As he was being strapped into the chair, Richetti murmured, "What have I done to deserve this?" A guard told Richetti to breathe deeply when the fumes reached his face.

The prison warden read the death warrant at 12:02 A.M. It was October 7, 1938. Richetti was twenty-eight years old. The lever was pulled to release the gas. Richetti tried to hold his breath, then he gasped and screamed. He was pronounced dead at 12:14 A.M. His body was sent to his brother in Bolivar, Missouri, for burial.

To the very end, Richetti denied that he and Choc had had any role in the massacre. So did the Floyd family. Until the day she died, June 16, 1978, at the age of ninety-seven, Mamie Floyd maintained her son had been unjustly accused of many crimes, including the massacre at Kansas City. So did Choc's siblings.

E. W. Floyd, the kid brother who at one time had to endure a whipping when he wanted to go on the scout with Charley, was one of his staunchest defenders. In a twist of fate, the mild-mannered E.W. decided to pursue a career quite the opposite of his notorious brother. In 1948, he was elected to serve as Sequoyah County Sheriff. "He ain't perfect, but he's honest" was his catchy campaign slogan.

Remembered for seldom even carrying a gun, E.W. became one of the finest law-enforcement officers ever to wear a badge in the state of Oklahoma. Sequoyah County citizens liked to boast that the culprits their sheriff chased seldom resisted arrest, because of E.W.'s persuasive powers. In his later years, Bradley Floyd returned to Sallisaw and worked as his younger brother's radio dispatcher. For twenty-two years and nine terms, E.W. served with distinction. He died on August 20, 1970, while still in office.

On July 29, 1970, just three weeks after E.W. passed away, Ruby Floyd died in a Broken Arrow, Oklahoma, nursing home of cancer at the age of sixty-three. Her life had been marked by turmoil. She suffered through several unhappy marriages and relationships. "My mother had to cope with so much throughout her life," recalled Dempsey Floyd. "I know there were some very rough times, but she always told me that she loved my father and I have to believe those few good times they had together had to count for something." Ruby was laid to rest at Bixby.

Dempsey graduated from high school in 1942 and served in the navy. Following his discharge in 1945, he resettled in California, where he started his own family and worked as a dealer in a casino. He has kept alive the memories of his parents, especially his father, who was immortalized in John Steinbeck's Pulitzer Prize–winning novel, *The Grapes of Wrath,* and in a song by Woody Guthrie, the "Ballad of Pretty Boy Floyd."

Published in 1939, *The Grapes of Wrath* tells the story of the Joad family's Dust Bowl journey from Sallisaw to California. In essence, the Joads could have been a fictionalized version of the Floyds, except that the Floyds were more prosperous and did not leave Oklahoma. Steinbeck had heard the tales of Pretty Boy from Oklahoma migrants in California during the late thirties. In the novel, the Joads talked favorably of Floyd. They discussed how he was driven to a life of crime by unbearable conditions. Likewise in 1939, Guthrie, in his famous ballad, mythicized Charley Floyd as a sympathetic folk hero. "There's many a starving farmer the same old story told / How the outlaw paid their mortgage and saved their little home."

Down in Sequoyah County, almost six decades after Pretty Boy's burial, old-timers still stew over past lives. Many of them actually knew Choc Floyd or his kinfolk. They gather most mornings in Sallisaw at Lessley's Cafe, a popular haunt operated by Choc's nephews Lawton and Jim Lessley, located just down the street from the bank their uncle robbed. The bank building now houses a beauty salon and the nearby train station has been transformed into a public library. Over coffee and pie at Lessley's where Floyd family photos adorn the cafe walls, the man and not the legend is remembered.

Among the press clippings and correspondence the family has received over the years about Charley is a copy of a letter sent to newspaper editors in 1960 by Mamie and Choc's brothers and sisters. The letter challenges the misinformation that had been perpetuated about Floyd through the years. "We know he did some things that were wrong, but not nearly all he was blamed for," the family wrote. "But in the final analysis, we also know, as he did, that crime does not pay. Yet, even the worst of us deserve justice, especially after the supreme penalty has been paid as Charley did."

Hardly a soul in Sallisaw who knew the man ever calls him Pretty Boy. To them, he will always be Charley or Choc.

"There aren't many of us left who really knew him," Dempsey related in 1991 from his home in California as he held Choc's ring and watch. "We still talk about my father, but we remember his good points. I think that must be the way many other people remember him. Maybe that's the way it should be."

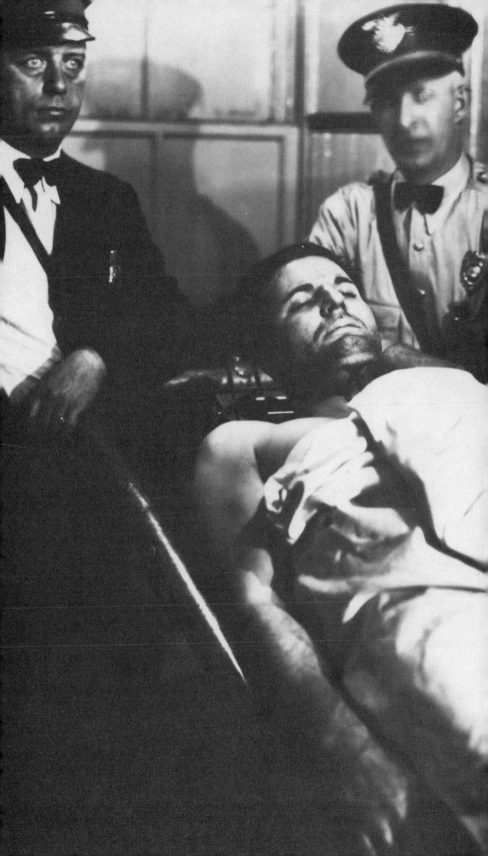

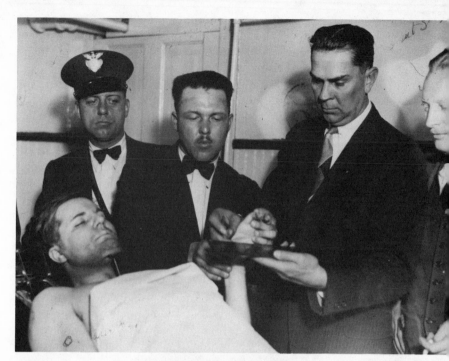

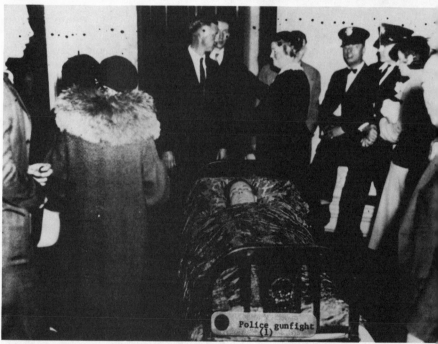

PREVIOUS PAGE: *Charley Floyd's corpse at the Sturgis Funeral Home. East Liverpool, Ohio, October 22, 1934.* TOP: *Chester Smith, the police officer who downed Charley Floyd, takes the deceased Floyd's fingerprints. East Liverpool, Ohio, October 22, 1934.* BOTTOM: *Curious citizens file through the Sturgis Funeral Home to view Floyd's body. East Liverpool, Ohio, October 22, 1934.*

Ellen Conkle poses in her kitchen with the dishes and utensils used by Charley Floyd for his final meal. October 22, 1934.

LEFT: *Special officer Grover C. Potts after he was wounded by Charley Floyd near Wellsville, Ohio. October 20, 1934.* RIGHT: *Stewart and Florence Dyke pose for a portrait after Floyd's death. October 1934.*

Adam Richetti, left, and Wellsville Police Chief John Fultz, following Richetti's capture. Wellsville, Ohio, October 1934.

OVERLEAF: *Charley Floyd's funeral record. East Liverpool, Ohio, October 22, 1934; Charles Dempsey, Ruby, center, and Mamie Floyd at Charley's grave. October 28, 1934.*

RECORD OF FUNERAL

Date... Oct. 22 1934

Total No...............
Name of Deceased... Chas A. Floyd (Single—Married—Divorced) Husband—Wife—Widow of } Ruby   White   Adamsville Ga (What Race) (When Born)

Residence of Deceased... Sallisaw Okla.

Occupation of Deceased... Bandit
Name of Employer... Charles Arthur Floyd

Charge to...............
Address...............
Connection...............
Order given by...............
How Secured...............
Date of Funeral... Oct 24 1934 (Day of Week) (Hour) M.
Services at... Akins Okla
Clergyman...............
His Address...............
Certifying Physician... E. R. Sturgis, coroner (or Coroner)
His Address...............
Cause of Death... Killed on Mrs. Ellens
Contributory Cause... 320 by Police (Autopsy) bandits from 7 miles north
Remarks...............
Date of Death... New Burdale
Place of Death... Oct 22 1934
Religion...............
Resided in the State... (Years) (Months)
Date of Birth... Feb. 3, 1904
Age... 30 Years   19 Days (Months)
Name of Father... Lifford Walter Floyd
His Birthplace... Sallisaw Okla Ga
Maiden Name of Mother... Oct 24 1934
Her Birthplace... Ga
Motor Ship } Remains to...............
Size and Style of Casket... (State Color)
Manufactured by...............
Interment at... Akins Okla (Cemetery—Crematory)

Complete Funeral	$ 175 00
Casket	
Metallic Lining (State Kind)	
Outside Box (State Kind)	
Burial Vault (State Kind)	
Embalming Body with Fluid	
Barber $ Hair Dressing $	
Dressing Body	
Suit or Dress, $ (State Color) Hose, $	
Underwear, $ Slippers, $	
Folding Chairs, $ Tarpaulin, $	
Candelabrum, $ Candles, $	
Door Badge, $ Gloves, $	
Hearse, $ Ambulance, $	
Limousines to Cemetery @ $	
Autos to R. R. Station @ $	
Getting Remains from	
Taking Remains to	
Delivering Box to	
Flowers to	
Removal Charges	
Getting Burial Permit (State Number and District)	
Certified Copies of Death Certificate (State Physician's or Coroner's)	
Professional Charges	
Pall Bearer Service	
Personal Service	

Diagram of Lot or Vault

Lot No.	
Grave No.	
Section No.	
Owner	

Outlay for Lot in Newspapers	
Death Notices in	
Flowers, $ Rental of Palms, $	
Rental of Tent, $ of Temporary Tomb, $	
Lowering Device, $ Cremation, $	
Opening of Grave or Tomb	
Lining Grave, $ Matting, $	
Outlay for Shipping Charges.	
Minister, $ Singers, $ Organist, $	
Railroad Tickets, $ Aeroplane Service, $	
Telegr., Phone, Cable or Radio Charges	
Cash Advanced	$ 175 00
Total Footing of Bill	$
Less Balance	$
Entered into Ledger, page or below.	
By Cash	$

Funeral Charges... Total, $

Oct 11 61

SELECT BIBLIOGRAPHY AND SOURCE NOTES

Much of this book is based on original research gleaned from hundreds of field and telephonic interviews conducted in several states, including Oklahoma, Missouri, Kansas, Arkansas, Georgia, Ohio, Pennsylvania, New York, Texas, and California. The majority of the interviews involved relatives of Charles Arthur Floyd, surviving Floyd associates and friends, former criminals, retired state and federal law enforcement officers, prison officials, historians, journalists, and others who had direct contact with Floyd.

Several historical societies, university and public libraries, book, newspaper, and magazine publishers, chambers of commerce, and law enforcement agencies, including the Federal Bureau of Investigation and the Oklahoma State Bureau of Investigation, provided critical records, documentation, photographs, correspondence, and other pertinent material. Many of the individuals, institutions, and agencies contacted by the author during the book's development are further discussed in the acknowledgment section, photographic credits, or are directly credited within the text.

The Floyd and Lessley families were especially helpful in providing family history and background as well as remarkably candid firsthand accounts of Charles Floyd's life in Georgia and Oklahoma. Interviews with various family members were conducted in Sallisaw, Oklahoma City, and Moore, Oklahoma, throughout the summer and autumn of 1990. This marks the first time that so many members of the Floyd family have lent their full cooperation to any author. From the beginning, it was understood that every aspect of Floyd's brief life would be thoroughly explored with no restrictions.

A principal source for material used in the preparation of this work has been the daily and periodical press of the twenties and thirties, with major reliance on the microfilm files of the *Tulsa World, Tulsa Tribune, The New York Times,* and significant input from the files of several other key newspapers such as the *Oklahoma Times, Kansas City Times, Kansas City Star, St. Louis Post-Dispatch,* and *Buffalo Courier-Express.* Walter Biscup's feature and news articles from 1932 and 1933 published in the *Tulsa World,* although not always the most reliable as far as factual material, were helpful because of his first-person interviews with Ruby Hardgraves Floyd and others.

A wide variety of books, monographs, correspondence, academic papers, photographs, newsreels, and films were thoroughly examined during the research phase. It is impossible in this space to list separately the hundreds of books, booklets, brochures, pamphlets, newspaper microfilm files, and other source material consulted.

Especially helpful sources included a series of newspaper articles written by Vivian Brown, the only journalist who was ever able to conduct a formal interview with Charles Floyd. Brown's series was published in October of 1934 in the *Oklahoma Times,* following Floyd's death in Ohio. Several passages from Brown's interview are directly quoted in this book.

A twelve-part newspaper series written by Robert Unger, national correspondent for the *Kansas City Times,* published in June of 1983, was also of value to the author in the preparation of this book. Unger's articles focusing on the events leading up to and including the massacre at Union Station on June 17, 1933, were written after the newspaper, under the Freedom of Information Act, obtained five volumes of previously unexamined files from the Federal Bureau of Investigation.

Nonfiction Books

Adams, Vernon R. *Tom White, The Life of a Lawman.* Texas Western Press, 1972.

Allen, Eric. *Crossfire in the Cooksons.* Hoffman Printing Company, 1974.

Allen, Frederick Lewis. *Since Yesterday: The 1930s in America.* Harper & Row Publishers, Inc., 1939.

———. *Only Yesterday.* Harper & Row Publishers, Inc., 1964.

Andrew, Geoff. *Hollywood Gangsters.* Gallery Books, an imprint of W. H. Smith Publishers, Inc., 1985.

Audett, James Henry. *Rap Sheet.* William Sloane Associates, Inc., 1954.

Badger, Anthony J. *The New Deal: The Depression Years, 1933–40.* Farrar, Straus & Giroux, Inc., 1989.

Barrett, Paul W., and Barrett, Mary H. *Young Brothers Massacre.* University of Missouri Press, 1988.

Bernstein, Irving. *The Lean Years: A History of the American Worker, 1933–1941.* Houghton Mifflin Company, 1960.

Bernstein, Michael A. *The Great Depression.* Cambridge University Press, 1987.

Bird, Caroline. *The Invisible Scar.* David McKay Co., 1966.

Bonnifield, Paul. *The Dust Bowl: Men, Dirt, and Depression.* Univesity of New Mexico Press, 1979.

Botkin, B. A., ed. *A Treasury of Western Folklore.* Crown Publishers, Inc., 1951.

Bowman, John S. General Editor. *The World Almanac of the American West.* World Almanac, an imprint of Pharos Books, 1986.

Brooks, Elston. *I've Heard Those Songs Before, Volume II.* The Summit Group, 1991.

Brown, A. Theodore. *Frontier Community: A History of Kansas City to 1870.* University of Missouri Press, 1963.

Bryant, Keith L., Jr. *Alfalfa Bill Murray.* University of Oklahoma Press, 1968.

Burbank, Garin. *When Farmers Voted Red: The Gospel of Socialism in the Oklahoma Countryside, 1910–1924.* Greenwood Press, 1976.

Burns, Walter Noble. *The Saga of Billy the Kid.* Doubleday, 1926.

Butler, William J. *Fort Smith, Past and Present; A Historical Summary.* The First National Bank of Fort Smith, Arkansas, 1972.

Callahan, Clyde C., and Jones, Byron B. *Heritage of an Outlaw: The Story of Frank Nash.* Schoonmaker Publishers, 1979.

Chandler, Lester. *America's Greatest Depression, 1929–1939.* Harper and Row, 1970.

Clarens, Carlos. *Horror Films.* G. P. Putnam's Sons, 1967.

Clayton, Merle. *Union Station Massacre, The Shootout That Started the FBI's War on Crime.* The Bobbs-Merrill Company, 1975.

Cook, F. P. *The American Struggle.* Doubleday & Company, Inc., 1974.

Cook, Frederick J. *The FBI Nobody Knows.* Macmillan, 1964.

Cooper, Courtney Riley. *Ten Thousand Public Enemies.* Blue Ribbon Books, 1935.

Cunyus, Lucy Josephine. *History of Bartow County.* Tribune Publishing Co., Inc., 1933.

Dalton, Emmett (in collaboration with Jack Jungmeyer). *When the Daltons Rode.* Doubleday, Doran & Company, Inc., 1931.

Daniels, Jonathan. *The Time Between Wars.* Doubleday & Co., 1966.

Davis, Burke. *The Civil War: Strange & Fascinating Facts.* The Fairfax Press, 1982.

Debo, Angie. *And Still the Waters Run.* Princeton University Press, 1940.

————, and Oskison, John M., eds. *The WPA Guide to 1930s Oklahoma.* Originally published by the University of Oklahoma Press in 1941 under the title *Oklahoma: A Guide to the Sooner State.* Published by the University Press of Kansas, 1986.

deFord, Miriam Allen. *The Real Ma Barker.* Ace Publishing Corp., 1970.

Demaris, Ovid. *The Director: An Oral Biography of J. Edgar Hoover.* Harper's Magazine Press, 1975.

Dorsett, Lyle W. *The Pendergast Machine.* Oxford University Press, 1968.

Draper, W. R. *On the Trail of "Pretty Boy" Floyd, A Reporter's Thrilling Pursuit of an Outlaw's Story.* Haldeman-Julius Publications, 1946.

Edge, L. L. *Run the Cat Roads: A True Story of Bank Robbers in the '30s.* Dembner Books, 1981.

Ellsworth, Scott. *Death in a Promised Land.* Louisiana State University Press, 1975.

Elman, Robert. *Fired in Anger, The Personal Handguns of American Heroes and Villains.* Doubleday & Company, Inc., 1968.

Evans, Harold C., ed. *The WPA Guide to 1930s Kansas.* Originally published by Viking Press in 1939 under the title *Kansas: A Guide to the Sunflower State.* Published by the University Press of Kansas, 1984.

Faherty, William Barnaby. *The St. Louis Portrait.* Continental Heritage Press, Inc., 1978.

Fischer, LeRoy H., ed. *Oklahoma's Governors 1929–1955.* Oklahoma Historical Society, 1983.

Foreman, Grant. *A History of Oklahoma.* University of Oklahoma Press, 1942.

————. *Sequoyah.* University of Oklahoma Press, 1938.

Fugate, Francis L., and Fugate, Roberta B. *Roadside History of Oklahoma.* Mountain Press Publishing Company, 1991.

Galbraith, John K. *The Great Crash: 1929.* Houghton Mifflin, 1955.

Gentry, Curt. *J. Edgar Hoover: The Man and the Secrets.* W. W. Norton, 1991.

Gibson, Arnell Morgan. *Oklahoma: A History of Five Centuries.* University of Oklahoma Press, 1980.

————. *The Oklahoma Story.* University of Oklahoma Press, 1978.

Gilmore, Robert K. *Ozark Baptizings, Hangings, and Other Diversions.* University of Oklahoma Press, 1984.

Gish, Anthony. *American Bandits.* Haldeman-Julius Publications, 1938.

Glassman, Bruce. *The Crash of '29 and the New Deal.* Silver Burdett Company, 1986.

Gordon, Lois, and Gordon, Alan. *American Chronicle, Seven Decades in American Life 1920–1989.* Crown Publishers, Inc., 1987.

Graves, Richard. *Oklahoma Outlaws.* Oklahoma Publishing Co., 1909.

Green, Donald E., ed. *Rural Oklahoma.* Oklahoma Historical Society, 1977.

Gregory, James N. *American Exodus.* Oxford University Press, 1989.

Haley, J. Evetts. *Robbing Banks Was My Business.* Palo Duro Press, 1973.

Harrington, Michael. *The Other America: Poverty in the United States.* Macmillan, 1962.

Hartman, Mary, and Ingenthron, Elmo. *Bald Knobbers: Vigilantes on the Ozark Frontier.* Pelican Publishing Company, 1989.

Hendrickson, Kenneth D., Jr., ed. *Hard Times in Oklahoma.* Oklahoma Historical Society, 1983.

Hicks, Roger W., and Schultz, Frances E. *Battlefields of the Civil War.* Salem House Publishers, 1989.

Hill, Lois, ed. *Poems and Songs of the Civil War.* The Fairfax Press, 1990.

Hinton, Ted, and Grove, Larry. *Ambush—The Real Story of Bonnie and Clyde.* Shoal Creek Publishers, Inc., 1979.

Horan, James D. *The Authentic Wild West: The Outlaws.* Crown Publishers, Inc., 1976.

Jenkins, John H., and Frost, H. Gordon. *"I'm Frank Hamer."* Pemberton Press, 1980.

Karpis, Alvin, with Trent, Bill. *The Alvin Karpis Story.* McCann & Geoghegan, Inc., 1971.

Kelley, Robert Lloyd. *The Shaping of the American Past, Volume 2, 1865 to Present.* Prentice-Hall, 1986.

Kelly, Charles. *The Outlaw Trail.* Bonanza Books, 1938.

Kellner, Esther. *Moonshine.* The Bobbs-Merrill Company, 1971.

Keylin, Arleen, and Bent, Christine, eds. *The New York Times at the Movies.* Arno Press, 1979.

Kirkpatrick, E. E. *Voices from Alcatraz.* The Naylor Company, 1947.

Kirschten, Ernest. *Catfish and Crystal.* Doubleday, 1960, and The Patrice Press, 1989.

Kohn, George C. *Dictionary of Culprits and Criminals.* The Scarecrow Press, Inc., 1986.

Kooistra, Paul. *Criminals as Heroes: Structure, Power & Identity.* Bowling Green State University Popular Press, 1989.

Lamb, Arthur H. *Tragedies of the Osage Hills.* Red Corn Publishing, 1964.

Lane, Mills, ed. *Marching Through Georgia.* Arno Press, 1978.

Leuchtenburg, William E. *Franklin D. Roosevelt and the New Deal, 1932–1940.* Harper & Row, 1963.

Logan, William Bryant, and Muse, Vance. *The Smithsonian Guide to Historic America: The Deep South.* Stewart, Tabori & Chang, 1989.

Lomax, Alan, compiler; Guthrie, Woody, notes on songs; Seeger, Pete, ed. *Hard-Hitting Songs for Hard-Hit People.* Oak Publications, Inc., 1967.

Long, R. M. *Wichita Century.* The Wichita Historical Museum Association, Inc., 1969.

Long, E. B., *The Civil War Day by Day.* Doubleday & Co., 1971.

Louderback, Lew. *The Bad Ones: Gangsters of the '30s and Their Molls.* Fawcett, 1968.

Love, Robertus. *The Rise and Fall of Jesse James.* G. P. Putnam's Sons, 1926.

Lurie, Nancy Oestreich. *North American Indian Lives.* Milwaukee Public Museum, 1985.

Marriott, Alice, and Rachlin, Carol K. *Oklahoma, The Forty-sixth Star.* Doubleday & Company, 1973.

Marsh, Dave, and Leventhal, Harold, eds. *Pastures of Plenty.* HarperCollins Publishers, 1990.

McBee, William D. *The Oklahoma Revolution.* Modern Publishers, Inc., 1956.

McElvaine, Robert S. *The Great Depression.* Times Books, 1984.

Meltzer, Milton. *Brother, Can You Spare a Dime?* Alfred A. Knopf, 1969.

Merz, Charles. *The Dry Decade.* Doubleday, Doran & Company, 1931.

Miller, Merle. *Plain Speaking.* Berkley Publishing Corporation, 1973.

Milligan, Maurice M. *Missouri Waltz.* Charles Scribner's Sons, 1948.

Morgan, H. Wayne, and Morgan, Anne Hodges. *Oklahoma.* W. W. Norton & Company, 1984, 1977.

Morris, John W. *Cities of Oklahoma.* Oklahoma Historical Society, 1979.

———. *Ghost Towns of Oklahoma.* University of Oklahoma Press, 1977.

———; Goins, Charles R.; and McReynolds, Edwin C. *Historical Atlas of Oklahoma.* University of Oklahoma Press, 1976.

Nash, Jay Robert. *Bloodletters and Bad Men: A Narrative Encyclopedia of American Criminals from the Pilgrims to the Present.* M. Evans and Company, Inc., 1973; and Warner Books, 1975.

Nevin, David. *Sherman's March: Atlanta to the Sea.* Time-Life Books, 1986.

Nix, Evett Dumas. *Oklahombres.* Eden Publishing House, 1929.

Parrish, William Earl. *Turbulent Partnership, Missouri and the Union, 1861–65.* University of Missouri Press, 1963.

Patterson, Richard. *Historical Atlas of the Outlaw West.* Johnson Publishing Company, 1985.

Perkerson, Medora Field. *White Columns in Georgia.* Bonanza Books, a division of Crown Publishers, Inc., by arrangement with Holt, Rinehart and Winston, Inc., 1952.

Perrett, Geoffrey. *America in the Twenties.* Simon & Schuster, 1982.

Phillips, Cabell. *From the Crash to the Blitz, 1929–1939.* The New York Times Company, 1969.

Poling-Kempes, Lesley. *The Harvey Girls, Women Who Opened the West.* Paragon House, 1989.

Polley, Jane, ed. *American Folklore and Legend.* The Reader's Digest Association, Inc., 1978.

Powers, Richard Gid. *G-Men: Hoover's FBI in American Popular Culture.* Southern Illinois University Press, 1983.

————. *Secrecy and Power: The Life of J. Edgar Hoover.* The Free Press, 1987.

Purvis, Melvin H. *American Agent.* Doubleday, Doran & Company, 1936.

Quinby, Myron J. *Devil's Emissaries.* A. S. Barnes and Company, Inc., 1969.

Reddig, William M. *Tom's Town: Kansas City and the Pendergast Machine.* Harper & Row, 1953; University of Missouri Press, 1986.

Russell, Francis. *The Shadow of Blooming Grove: Warren G. Harding in His Times.* McGraw-Hill Book Co., 1968.

Ruth, Kent. *Oklahoma Travel Handbook.* University of Oklahoma Press, 1977.

———— and Argo, Jim. *Here We Rest: Historic Cemeteries of Oklahoma.* Oklahoma Historical Society, 1986.

Sabljak, Mark, and Greenberg, Martin H. *Most Wanted: A History of the FBI's Most Wanted List.* Bonanza Books, 1990.

Sann, Paul. *Fads, Follies and Delusions of the American People.* Crown Publishers, Inc., 1967.

————. *The Lawless Decade.* Crown Publishers, Inc., 1957.

Scales, James Ralph, and Goble, Danney. *Oklahoma Politics: A History.* University of Oklahoma Press, 1982.

Schlesinger, Arthur M., Jr., ed. *The Almanac of American History.* G. P. Putnam's Sons, 1983.

Sellin, Thorsten. *Research Memorandum on Crime in the Depression.* Reprint edition by Arno Press, Inc., 1972.

Sequoyah County Historical Society. *The History of Sequoyah County 1828–1975.* The Sequoyah County Historical Society, 1976.

Settle, William. *Jesse James Was His Name.* University of Missouri Press, 1966.

Shirley, Glenn. *Henry Starr: Last of the Real Badmen.* David McKay Company, 1965.

————. *Law West of Fort Smith: A History of Frontier Justice in the Indian Territory, 1834–1896.* University of Nebraska Press, 1968.

————. *West of Hell's Fringe: Crime, Criminals, and the Federal Peace Officer in Oklahoma Territory.* University of Oklahoma Press, 1978.

Sinclair, Andrew. *Prohibition, The Era of Excess.* Little, Brown and Company, 1962.

Smallwood, James M. *An Oklahoma Adventure of Banks and Bankers.* University of Oklahoma Press, 1979.

Smith, Leon E. *High Noon at the Boley Corral.* Detroit: Leon E. Smith, 1980.

Steele, Philip W. *Jesse and Frank James: The Family History.* Pelican Publishing Company, 1989.

————. *Ozark Tales and Superstitions.* Pelican Publishing Company, 1988.

Stradler, Francis Hurd. *St. Louis Day by Day.* The Patrice Press, 1989.

Steckmesser, Kent. *The Western Hero in History and Legend.* University of Oklahoma Press, 1965.

Taylor, Deems. *A Pictorial History of the Movies.* Simon & Schuster, 1949.

Terry, Dickson. *There's a Town in Missouri.* New Sunrise Publishing, 1979.

Theoharis, Athan G., ed. *From the Secret Files of J. Edgar Hoover.* Chicago: Ivan R. Dee, 1991.

————, and Cox, John S. *The Boss: J. Edgar Hoover and the Great American Inquisition.* Temple University Press, 1988.

Thompson, John. *Closing the Frontier: Radical Response in Oklahoma, 1889–1923.* University of Oklahoma Press, 1986.

Time-Life Books. *The Old West.* Prentice Hall Press, 1990.

Toland, John. *The Dillinger Days.* Random House, 1963.

Treherne, John. *The Strange History of Bonnie and Clyde.* Stein and Day, 1985.

Trekell, Ronald L. *History of the Tulsa Police Department 1882–1990.* Tulsa: Ronald L. Trekell, 1991.

Tully, Andrew. *The FBI's Most Famous Cases.* William Morrow, 1965.

Ungar, Sanford J. *FBI.* Atlantic Monthly Press Book, Little Brown and Company, 1975.

Vaughn-Roberson, Ann and Glen, *City in the Osage Hills.* Pruett Publishing Company, 1984.

Wamsley, Burkett. *Ad Libs to Bixby History.* Citizens Security Bank and Trust, 1974.

Watters, Pat, and Gillers, Stephen, eds. *Investigating the FBI.* Doubleday & Company, Inc., 1973.

Wecter, Dixon. *The Age of the Great Depression.* The Macmillan Company, 1948.

Wellman, Paul I. *A Dynasty of Western Outlaws.* Doubleday & Company, 1961.

Welsh, Louise; Townes, Willa Mae; and Morris, John W. *A History of the Greater Seminole Oil Field.* Western Heritage Books, Inc., 1981.

West, C. W. "Dub." *Muskogee: From Statehood to Pearl Harbor.* Muscogee Publishing Company, 1976.

————. *Only in Oklahoma.* Muscogee Publishing Company, 1982.

————. *Outlaws and Peace Officers of Indian Territory.* Muscogee Publishing Company, 1987.

Whitehead, Don. *The FBI Story: A Report to the People.* Random House, Inc., 1956.

Wilson, Charles Reagan, and Ferris, William, eds. *Encyclopedia of Southern Culture.* The University of North Carolina Press, 1989.

Wilson, Steve. *Oklahoma Treasures and Treasure Tales.* University of Oklahoma Press, 1976.

Witt, Margaret A., ed. *Pause in Missouri.* American Association of University Women, Missouri State Division, 1979.

Worster, Donald. *Dustbowl: The Southern Plains in the 1930's.* Oxford University Press, 1979.

Fiction Books

Carroll, Lenore. *Annie Chambers.* Watermark Press, Inc., 1989.

Cunningham, William. *The Green Corn Rebellion.* The Vanguard Press, 1935.

Cunningham, Walter. *Pretty Boy.* The Vanguard Press, 1936.

Steinbeck, John. *The Grapes of Wrath.* Viking Press, Inc., 1939.

Magazines and Journals

A host of magazines and periodicals provided helpful information for this book. Some of the publications include: *Americana; American Heritage; American History Illustrated; American Magazine; American West; America's Civil War; Chronicles of Oklahoma; Civil War, The Magazine of the Civil War Society; Colliers; Current Opinion; Fortune; Georgia Historical Quarterly; Harper's Weekly; Journal of American Folklore; Journal of Negro History; Kansas City Business Journal; Life; Literary Digest; Memories; Missouri Historical Review; The Nation; National Geographic; New Republic; North American Review; Ohio Magazine; Oklahoma Monthly; Oklahoma Today; Reader's Digest; Saturday Evening Post; Scribner's Magazine; Smithsonian; The Independent; The Investigator; The Outlook; The Peace Officer; Time; Timeline; True Detective; Western Historical Quarterly.*

Newspapers

The more significant newspapers (including some no longer in existence) used for researching this book include: *Akron Beacon Journal; Boliver* (Mo.) *Free Press; Blackwell* (Okla.) *Morning Tribune; Bolivar Herald-Free Press; Buffalo Courier-Express; Chicago Tribune; Cleveland News; Cleveland Plain Dealer; Columbus Citizen-Journal; Columbus Dispatch; Daily Oklahoman; Dallas Morning-News; Denver Post; East Liverpool Review; Eufaula* (Okla.) *Democrat; Florence* (S.C.) *Morning News; Fort Worth Star-Telegram; Jefferson City* (Mo.) *Post-Tribune; Joplin Globe; Kansas City Journal-Post; Kansas City Star; Kansas City Times; Liberty* (Mo.) *Tribune; Los Angeles Times; McAlester* (Okla.) *News-Capital; Memphis Commercial Appeal; Muskogee Daily Phoenix; New York Daily News; The New York Times; Norman* (Okla.) *Transcript; North Bartow News; Oklahoma News; Oklahoma City Times; Pittsburgh Post-Gazette; Pittsburgh Press; Pittsburgh Sun-Telegraph; St. Joseph Gazette; St. Louis Globe-Democrat; St. Louis Post-Dispatch; Sallisaw Democrat-American; Seminole* (Okla.) *Producer; Sequoyah County Times; Springfield* (Mo.) *Daily News; Springfield* (Mo.) *News-Leader; Stillwater News-Press; Sylvania Herald; Toledo Blade; Topeka Capital; Tulsa Tribune; Tulsa World; Youngstown Vindicator; Washington Evening Star; Wichita Beacon; Wichita Eagle.*

ACKNOWLEDGMENTS

The seeds for this book were sown more than forty years ago when I was a boy growing up in Missouri. I feasted on tales of Jesse and Frank James and the other outlaws my home state had yielded during the period following the Civil War. My love of American history was nurtured by family stories of life in early-day St. Louis, Kansas City, and Texas. I was also provided with a comprehensive education concerning the social history of the twenties and thirties, especially the years of the Great Depression, through the poignant stories of my parents, Herbert and Ann Wallis. It became obvious to me that there were direct ties linking the incarnations of "social bandits" that have appeared through the various decades.

Many years later, as a journalist and author, I grew more aware of the outlaw gangs and individual desperadoes who surfaced whenever the nation experienced depressed economic times. During the writing of my earlier works, *Oil Man: The Story of Frank Phillips and the Birth of Phillips Petroleum* and *Route 66: The Mother Road*, I learned more about these bandits, especially those who operated during the bittersweet years of the 1930s.

In July of 1989, those seeds planted so long past took root during a visit to New York. My wife and I, and our friend, Joyce Gideon, spent a Sunday afternoon in the Greenwich Village apartment of my brother-in-law James W. Fitzgerald, Jr., Executive Editor at St. Martin's Press. Jim served us icy drinks and the latest war stories from the world of publishing. He put on a music cassette tape entitled *Folkways: A Vision Shared,* a tribute to the great Oklahoma balladeer Woody Guthrie and Huddie Ledbetter, a Louisiana-born musician nicknamed Leadbelly.

Discussion turned to new book projects for me to consider. In the background Doc Watson, Pete Seeger, Taj Mahal, Emmylou Harris, John Mellencamp, and others sang the music of the Great Depression and Dust Bowl. My ears perked when I heard the acoustic guitar and distinctive voice of Bob Dylan as he began singing Guthrie's ballad *Pretty Boy Floyd.* There was a lull in the conversation. Only the rumbling air conditioner competed with the haunting song. I looked at the others.

"What about a book about Floyd?" I asked. "Yes, a big 'Pretty Boy' book," responded Jim. "Not a bad idea." Suzanne and Joyce agreed. The rest of the day and well into the night we dicussed the notion of a Floyd biography. I could hardly wait to return to Oklahoma and draft a proposal to submit to Robert Weil, my editor at St. Martin's.

Weil, a New Yorker who realizes that intelligent life exists beyond Manhattan, proved to me as he has in the past that the relationship between editor and author is key to the success of any book. Bob is a valued friend. Thanks to his understanding of the subject matter, based on a passion of history as well as an interest in the geography and culture of the Middle West and Southwest, Bob acted as a guide for me as I looked for clues and evidence about the real Charles Arthur Floyd. Bob accompanied me on several interview sessions including visits to some of Floyd's family members and former criminal associates. His editorial hand added nuance to my words.

Others at St. Martin's Press were also supportive of me throughout the development of this book. My gratitude to Michael Accordino, Barbara Andrews, Andy Carpenter, Erin Collin, Glen Edelstein, Christine Foye, Roy Gainsburg, Geoff Kloske, Mark Kohut, Amelie Littell, Josh Marwell, Thomas McCormack, John Murphy, Michael Pratt, Claudia Riemer, Richard Romano, and Jeanette Zwart. Also a salute to the diligent St. Martin's sales representatives across the nation.

The handsome book design by Carol Haralson would make any author proud. My thanks to you, Carol, for your care and forbearance. Your excellent efforts are much appreciated by me and I am sure by all readers.

My wife, Suzanne, was the major source of inspiration and encouragement. She was especially supportive during the demanding process of separating fact from fiction. She gave up many evenings and weekends in order to help me trail the elusive Pretty Boy. Suzanne also convinced our steadfast cats, Beatrice and Molly, to serve as my muses.

Allen Strider, a stalwart Oklahoman and my friend, stood by me throughout the development of this book. Allen accompanied Bob Weil and me on some of the initial research trips to Sequoyah County—the heart and soul of "Pretty Boy country" in Oklahoma. To sit with Bob and Allen in an old bootlegger's camp in rural Oklahoma and listen to the stories of an eighty-nine-year-old former bandit or drink coffee at the kitchen table of a man who once drove getaway cars for Floyd was nothing short of pure pleasure. Allen also helped me locate surviving Floyd relatives and friends and generally encouraged me at every opportunity. His tenacity and spirit did not go unnoticed.

A tip of my author's hat to Carol Mann. A tip of the hat and an extra bow to Michael V. Carlisle, my resourceful literary agent and a vice president of the William Morris Agency.

The partners and staff of Wallis Gideon Wallis, Inc., earned my undying appreciation. Their expertise when it comes to research, publicity, and promotion cannot be equaled. Thanks to Joyce Gideon, Deborah Bendler, Myna Bourk, Nancy Edwards, David Reid, and Kathryn Sanford. Donna Lee Cross, the capable administrative assistant for Wallis Gideon Wallis, put in many long hours transcribing tapes, ferreting out important research contacts across the country, and typing correspondence. Her help was invaluable. So were the contributions of Norma Brewer. A team of others also assisted with typing chores and general research. They include: LaVeta Alwine, Georgiana Cathey, Sue Clemens, Sylvia Clevland, Julia Cox, Betty Dawson, Linda Ledbetter, Gretchen Manhart, Mark Owens, and Kari Woodson. Thanks to Ann Childers for her fine assistance.

I am most obliged to the family of Charles Arthur Floyd. Many members of the immediate Floyd family as well as other relatives of Charles Floyd provided their full cooperation. They offered family records, correspondence, and photographs. I am especially indebted to Charles Dempsey Floyd, the only child of Charles Arthur Floyd. His candor was very much valued. Thanks to Geraldyn Wofford for helping connect me with Dempsey Floyd. Other family members who deserve to be singled out for their help include Mary Floyd Lattimore Carleton; Beulah Floyd; Dale Floyd; Bessie Watson Floyd; Bayne Rois Floyd; Glendon Leroy Floyd; Charles Bradley Floyd; Barbara Ellen Floyd Moore; Lawton Lessley; James Lea Lessley; Jim Lessley; Terry Griffith.

Ruth Ring Morgan and Lavona Stark Webb, two of Ruby Hardgraves's cousins, called up a storehouse of memories for me during intensive interview sessions. They were also kind to locate and offer rare photographs of Charles Floyd and other family members, including his former wife and their son.

In Sequoyah County, Echo and Tom "Spide" Rider were my salvation when it came to honing in on specifics concerning life-style and customs in Sequoyah County. They introduced me to several other persons who also provided interesting points of local history.

At the Oklahoma Historical Society (OHS) in Oklahoma City I received invaluable assistance from a variety of sources. Mary Katherine Huffman, Supervisor of Public Services/Library Resources Division, spent many hours helping me gather up important documents including the Georgia Federal Census records from 1830 through 1900 for Hall, Carroll, Cass, and Bartow counties. Others from the OHS who made significant contributions to the book were Chester R. Cowen, Photo Archivist; Fred Smith Standley, Archivist; Keith Toman, Director of Central Services Division; Judith L. Michener, Archives/Manuscript Division; R. Ann Ogle, Director of Museum Sales.

Timothy R. Brookes, President of the East Liverpool Historical Society, was particularly helpful in providing information and assistance in reconstructing the final days of Floyd's life in eastern Ohio. Brookes wrote a Floyd profile published in the August-September 1990 issue of *Timeline,* a publication of the Ohio Historical Society. He took time from his hectic law practice to shepherd me around East Liverpool and Columbiana County during August of 1990. He also helped pinpoint several important sources and served as an initial editor for chapters of the book dealing with Floyd's Ohio experience.

Many local, state, and federal law enforcement officers and agencies willingly opened their records to me. Key information, including U.S. Department of Justice memorandums, files, photographs, and other source information, was offered by the Federal Bureau of Investigation's Research Unit in Washington, D.C., as requested under the Freedom of Information Act. Thanks to J. Kevin O'Brien, of the FBI's Chief Freedom of Information Privacy Acts Section; Bob A. Ricks, FBI Special Agent in Charge, Oklahoma City Office; and Henry C. Gibbons, Principal Legal Advisor, Oklahoma City Office. Special thanks to W. E. "Bud" Hopton, retired FBI agent and the last survivor from the team of police officers and federal agents who confronted Charley Floyd on the Conkle farm on October 22, 1934.

Dee Cordry, Special Agent, Oklahoma State Bureau of Investigation, deserves extra praise for coming up with critical reports not provided by the FBI. In Ohio, James C. Buie, a retired Akron police officer, made available files and records, including some from the Ohio State Bureau of Criminal Identification and Investigation.

Officials and staff with the Missouri State Penitentiary at Jefferson City were hospitable, cordial, and extremely helpful. My gratitude to Bill M. Armontrout, Warden, Missouri State Penitentiary; William L. Rutledge, Assistant Warden; Donald R. Schroeger, Administrative Assistant/Public Information–Legislative Liaison, Department of Corrections and Human Resources; Mark S. Schreiber, Executive Assistant/Adult Institutions, Department of Corrections and Human Resources; Laurie Stout, Public Information Specialist, Department of Corrections and Human Resources; and Bernard J. Poiry, retired Department of Corrections officer.

Besides these very special people, this book is the result of the effort and love of many others. It could never have been completed without the assistance of countless individuals and institutions. The majority of newspapers and magazines I relied upon are listed in the bibliography. Others who must be acknowledged for all their assistance and contributions include the following:

Arkansas Parks and Tourist Commission; Associated Press; Buffalo Public Library; Crown Point (Indiana) Chamber of Commerce; Community Development Foundation, Tupelo, Mississippi; Scott Fitzgerald; Fort Smith Chamber of Commerce; Fort Smith National Historic Site; Eleanor M. Gehres, Manager, Western History Department, Denver Public Library; Jim Harris; Hot Springs National Park; The Library of Congress; Rick Mattix; National Association and Center for Outlaw and Lawman History; New York Public Library; Joe Pinkston, Director, The John Dillinger Historical Wax Museum.

In Georgia: Etowah Historical Museum; Vara Gaddis; Gordon County Chamber of Commerce, Calhoun; Greater Rome Convention and Visitors Bureau; Richard Hicks; Michele Rodgers, Executive Director, Etowah Historical Foundation; Rome–Floyd County Library.

In Kansas: Thomas P. Barr, Research Analyst, Kansas State Historical Society; Bernice Leonard; Christie Stanley, Center for Historical Research, Kansas State Historical Society, Topeka; Wichita Public Library.

In Missouri: Bolivar Area Chamber of Commerce; Chamber of Commerce of Greater Kansas City; Doran L. Cart, Director/Curator, Liberty Memorial Museum and Archives; Charles and Carolyn Dunlap; Keith and Jan Fitzgerald; Joplin Area Chamber of Commerce; Marjorie Kinny, Kansas City Public Library, Missouri Valley Special Collections; Richard and Marilynn Krenning; Joel and Nancy Knickmeyer; Patricia M. Luebbert, Archivist, Missouri State Archives; Jan McCoy; Kay White Miles, *Clinton Daily Democrat;* Missouri Historical Society; Denise Morrison, Archivist, Kansas City Museum; James R. Powell; Pulitzer Publishing Company; St. Louis Public Library; James A. Schaid; Shifra Stein; Thomas Jefferson Library, Jefferson City; Chris N. Vedos; Eleanor Wallis.

In Ohio: Akron Police Department; Akron Public Library; Mary K. Berger; Bowling Green State University; Glenn Clark, *East Liverpool Review* staff writer; Cleveland Public Library; Frank C. Dawson, Dawson Funeral Home, Inc.; Christopher S. Duckworth, Editor, *Timeline,* Ohio Historical Society; East Liverpool Area Chamber of Commerce; Harold Fryman; John W. Graham, Public Library of Cincinnati and Hamilton County; Tauni Graham, Archives Associate, Ohio Historical Society; Lenora Hopper, Wellsville Historical Society; Nancy Johnson, Sylvania Area Chamber of Commerce; Nell Toland Lyons; James C.

Marshall, Manager, Local History & Genealogy Department, Toledo–Lucas County Public Library; Theodore and Edith Peterson; Naomi Smith Nortrup; *Ohio Magazine;* Robert F. Popp; Janice Smith Twyford; Margueritte Shingler, East Liverpool Museum of Ceramics; Tessa Unwin, Public Information Officer, State of Ohio Department of Corrections.

In Oklahoma: Mary E. Alexander; Pauline Alfrey; D. C. Anderson; Marvin Amos; Deldee Anderson; Ruth Sigler Avery; Bea Barrett; Jerry Barett; Lee Barrett; Jack Birdwell; Ruby Dobson Branom, Lehigh Historical Society; Suzette Brewer; Carmen Buchanan; Bea Davenport Buffington; William Burns; George M. Cheatham; Peter A. Childs; Russell Davis; Jeanne M. Devlin, Editor, *Oklahoma Today;* Dave Dobie; Brandon T. Dutcher; Eastern Oklahoma District Library System; Paul Endacott; Robert Ernst; Lee Gideon; Martha Gregory, Tulsa City–County Library/Info II; Jim and Dorothy Hamilton; Herbert P. Haschke, Jr.; T. R. "Dick" Holland; Joe Holmes; Jim Hubbard, Sapulpa Historical Society; Irene Hughes; Dr. Joe Humphrey; Mabel Humphrey; Mitchie Hunt; Carl Janaway; Cindy Killion; Denise Kindy; Jack Leonard; John R. Lovett, Photographic Archivist, Western History Collections, The University of Oklahoma; Richard Manus; Robert Medley; Muskogee Public Library; Hettie Miller; Oklahoma Christian College; Martha Overton; PhotoSmith of Tulsa; Thomas B. Pinson; Sallisaw Chamber of Commerce; Elmer and Dixie Steele; Oklahombres, An Association for the Preservation of Lawman and Outlaw History for the Indian Territory; Jim Roberts; Pauline Sampson; Vinnie Scott; Bonnie Speer; Lu Tehee; David Tilghman; Dr. James Turrentine; Tulsa County Historical Society; Washington County Historical Society, Inc.; Shirley Webster.

PHOTOGRAPH CREDITS

End Papers. Photograph courtesy Glendon Leroy Floyd.

The Walter Floyd family. Photograph courtesy Jim Lessley.

The Buman Floyd family. Photograph courtesy Brooks and Velva Floyd Griffith Collection.

Claude and Undeen Griffith . . . Photograph courtesy Brooks and Velva Floyd Griffith Collection.

Charley Floyd's grandparents . . . Photograph courtesy Beulah Floyd.

Charley's future wife . . . Photograph courtesy Ruth Ring Morgan.

Bradley and Bessie Watson Floyd. Photograph courtesy Charles Bradley Floyd.

First National Bank . . . Photograph courtesy Archives & Manuscripts Division of the Oklahoma Historical Society.

Reunion of Deputy U.S. Marshals . . . Photograph courtesy Archives & Manuscripts Division of the Oklahoma Historical Society.

Jesse Woodson James . . . Photograph courtesy N. H. Rose Collection in the Western History Collections, University of Oklahoma.

Henrietta Younger, Bob Younger . . . Photograph courtesy N. H. Rose Collection in the Western History Collections, University of Oklahoma.

Henry Star . . . Photograph courtesy N. H. Rose Collection in the Western History Collections, University of Oklahoma Library.

Belle Starr . . . Photograph courtesy Archives & Manuscripts Division of the Oklahoma Historical Society.

The posse . . . Photograph courtesy Archives & Manuscripts Division of the Oklahoma Historical Society.

Necktie party . . . Photograph courtesy Archives & Manuscripts Division of the Oklahoma Historical Society.

Aftermath . . . Photograph courtesy Archives & Manuscripts Division of the Oklahoma Historical Society.

Jesse James in death. Photograph courtesy N. H. Rose Collection in the Western History Collections, University of Oklahoma Library.

Henry Starr just after he was shot . . . Photograph courtesy N. H. Rose Collection in the Western History Collections, University of Oklahoma Library.

Choc Floyd. Photograph courtesy Charles Bradley Floyd.

Walter Floyd . . . Photograph courtesy Dale Floyd.

The Floyd family . . . Photograph courtesy Bayne Rois Floyd.

Confiscation of bootleg moonshine. Photograph courtesy Mrs. Ottie Lee Collection in the Western History Collections, University of Oklahoma Library.

The Missouri Pacific Railroad . . . Photograph courtesy John B. Fink Collection from the Archives & Manuscripts Division of the Oklahoma Historical Society.

Magazine cover . . . Photograph courtesy Ruth Ring Morgan.

Inmates in the yard . . . Photograph courtesy Mark S. Schreiber, Missouri Department of Corrections.

Missouri State Penitentiary. Photograph courtesy Donald R. Schroeger, Missouri Department of Corrections.

Town council. Photograph courtesy Archives & Manuscripts Division of the Oklahoma Historical Society.

Farmers & Merchants Bank. Photograph courtesy Archives & Manuscripts Division of the Oklahoma Historical Society.

Street scene. Photograph courtesy Archives & Manuscripts Division of the Oklahoma Historical Society.

Charley Floyd, left, and Jess Ring. Photograph courtesy Ruth Ring Morgan.

Bessie Edwards Mayberry . . . Photograph courtesy Ruth Ring Morgan.

Charles Dempsey Floyd . . . Photograph courtesy Ruth Ring Morgan.

Downtown Sallisaw . . . Photograph courtesy Farm Security Administration Collection in the Western History Collections, University of Oklahoma Library.

Dempsey Floyd . . . Photograph courtesy Ruth Ring Morgan.

Charley and Ruby Floyd. Photograph courtesy Ruth Ring Morgan.

Vintage postcard. From author's collection.

Ruby and Dempsey Floyd. Photograph courtesy Ruth Ring Morgan.

Riding the rails. Photograph courtesy Farm Security Administration Collection in the Western History Collections, University of Oklahoma Library.

A pair of hangman's nooses . . . Photograph courtesy Farm Security Administration Collection in the Western History Collections, University of Oklahoma Library.

The Great Depression . . . Photograph courtesy Farm Security Administration Collection in the Western History Collections, University of Oklahoma Library.

Bonnie Parker. Photograph courtesy N. H. Rose Collection in the Western History Collections, University of Oklahoma Library.

Clyde Barrow. Photograph courtesy N. H. Rose Collection in the Western History Collections, University of Oklahoma Library.

George "Machine Gun" Kelly. From author's collection.

"Machine Gun" Kelly surrounded . . . Photograph courtesy N. H. Rose Collection in the Western History Collections, University of Oklahoma Library.

Charley, left, Ruby, and E. W. Floyd. Photograph courtesy Bayne Rois Floyd.

The *Wichita Beacon.* Photograph courtesy Charles Dempsey Floyd.

Scene at Union Station . . . Photograph courtesy Federal Bureau of Investigation/Rick Mattix.

Wanted poster. Photograph courtesy Federal Bureau of Investigation.

G-man Melvin H. Purvis. Photograph courtesy Federal Bureau of Investigation.

Prison mug shots . . . Photograph courtesy Missouri Department of Corrections.

Posse prepares . . . Photograph courtesy Wellsville Historical Society/Ohio Historical Society.

Stewart Dyke's Model A . . . Photograph courtesy East Liverpool Historical Society/Ohio Historical Society.

Popular Depression-era toy gun. Photograph courtesy Robert Heide/John Gilman Collection.

Charley Floyd's corpse . . . Photograph courtesy Naomi Smith Nortrup/Ohio Historical Society.

Chester Smith . . . Photograph courtesy Naomi Smith Nortrup/Ohio Historical Society.

Curious citizens . . . Photograph courtesy Naomi Smith Nortrup/Ohio Historical Society.

Ellen Conkle . . . Photograph courtesy East Liverpool Historical Society/Ohio Historical Society.

Special officer Grover C. Potts . . . Photograph courtesy East Liverpool Historical Society/Ohio Historical Society.

Stewart and Florence Dyke . . . Photograph courtesy East Liverpool Historical Society/Ohio Historical Society.

Adam Richetti . . . Photograph courtesy East Liverpool Historical Society/Ohio Historical Society.

Charles Floyd's funeral record. Photograph courtesy Frank Dawson Funeral Home.

Charlie Dempsey, Ruby, and Mamie Floyd . . .Photograph courtesy Jim Lessley.

Adam, Joe, 162
Adams, Eddie, 104–6, 204
Adams, Everett, 152
Adamson, Jack, 127–8
Alexander, Thomas, *see* Bradley, James
Alfrey, Pauline, 261–2
Allen, Henry J., 102
American Bankers' Association, 243, 253
American Protective League, 81
Amos, Bob, 188, 190–6
Amos, Cleon, 76, 118
Amos, John, 141
Amos, Marvin, 118, 141
Anderson, Joe, 213–4
Ash, Beulah Baird (Juanita), 186–8, 206, 208–12, 226, 239, 259, 279, 282, 304, 311, 318–9, 325–6, 329–30, 351–2
Ash, Freida, 207
Ash, Rose Baird, 206–12, 282, 304, 318–9, 325–6, 330, 351–2
Ash, Sadie (Mother), 186, 188, 206–8, 211, 269
Ash, Wallace, 186, 206–7
Ash, Walter, 188
Ash, William, 186, 188, 206–7
Atkins, Jack, 190–3
Audett, James (Blackie), 188–9, 321
Azar, Robert, 201

Bailey, Harvey, 298–300, 320–1, 323–4
Baird, Beulah, *see* Ash, Beulah Baird
Barker, Donnie Clark (Ma), 247, 326, 342
Barker, Fred, 246–7, 342
Barrett, Charles, 237
Barrow, Clyde, 199–200, 325, 327
Barrow, Melvin Ivan, 199
Bash, Thomas B., 320, 334
Bates, Goldie, 125, 127
Baum, James, 332–3
Bennett, Cecil, 217, 254–5
Berryhill, Jesse, 294
Billingsly, Frank, 125
Billy the Kid, 227
Birch, Clyde, 336
Birdwell, Flora Mae (Bob), 222, 285–6, 351
Birdwell, George, 221–5, 232–4, 243–5, 251, 254, 257–9, 261–2, 264–5, 268, 271–4, 276, 278–9, 283–6, 295
Birdwell, Jack, 222–4, 282, 285, 293
Birdwell, Robert, 222
Birger, Charles, 162
Bischoff, Lynn, 191, 196
Biscup, Walter, 248–9, 255
Bishop, Luther, 127–8
Bitzer, Ernest V., 306–7, 311
Bonham, Jack, 246, 254
Booth, Ben, 302–3, 312
Booth, Willis, 82
Bradley, James, 188, 190–6, 201–3
Bradshaw, Ford, 279, 326
Brady, Bob (Big Boy), 321, 323, 326
Brandon, Ruby Dobson, 290
Brown, D. C., 105
Brown, Roy, *see* Bradley, James
Brown, Vivian, 204, 257, 274–8
Burks, Curtis, 213–4
Burns, C. A., 266, 275, 281
Burns, Clayton, 183
Burns Detective Agency, 122, 132
Burns, Robert, 237
Burns, William J., 132–3, 350

Bureau of Investigation, *see* F.B.I.

Caffrey, Raymond J., 314–5
Callahan, John, 102–6, 123
Cannon, V. S., 252, 257, 295–6
Capone, Al (Scarface), 165–7, 198, 224, 237, 250, 313
Carollo, Charley, 172
Carpenter, O. P., 247
Carroll, John, 187
Carter, Jr., George, 192
Cash, Wilber Joseph, 113
Casteel, Marvin, 303
Castner, Ralph (Zibe), 208–9, 211–2
Caulfield, Henry, 230
Chaney, Harry B., 319
Cheek, George, 224, 274, 349
Cherokee Bill, *see* Goldsby, Crawford
Chambers, Annie, 187–8
Chandler, Glenn, 191–2
Cheatham, George, 294
Chuculate, Clyde, 245–6
Chuculate, Perry, 179–80, 245
Clark, Bernard, 125
Clark, Jim, 323
Clark, Lucy, 303
Clark, Tom, *see* Bradley, James
Cobb, Ty, 48
Conkle, Ellen, *xi–xii,* 336–7, 341–2
Conley, Patrick, 194
Cook, Fred J., 322
Cooper, A. B., 253
Costello, Dr. Roy, 343
Cotton, Bert, 94, 143–4, 274
Counts, William, 252–4
Cox, James M., 95
Cramer, Charles, 202
Crowe, Billy, 128
Cummings, Homer, 323–4
Curry, Paul, 115–6

Dail, Hubert, 270
Dalton, Emmett, 115–6, 123, 227–9, 263
Danielak, Joe, 203
Daugherty, Emmet R., 150
Daugherty, Harry M., 132–3
Daugherty, Walter, 144
Davidson, Charles L., 103
Davis, Ed, 323, 326
Davis, Russell, 293–4
Dawson, Frank A., 340–1, 343, 346–7
Delora, Frank, 196
Dempsey, Jack, 49, 91, 158, 313
Denning, Homer & Maurice, 321, 323
Denny, Nellie, *see* Maxwell, Marie
Denton, Bill, 193, 202–3
Diamond, Jack (Legs), 224
Diamond, Jr., A. D., 279
Dillinger, John Herbert, 197–9, 326–7, 334, 345
Draper, W. R., 144
Dunn, Myrtle, 237
Durrell, Grover, 125
Dyke, Stewart & Florence, *xi–xii,* 337–8, 341–2

Echols, E. W., 264
Echols, Emma, 28–9, 33
Edgar, Charles B., *see* Nash, Frank
Edwards, Andy (Cowbell), 93
Egan, Jellyroll, 162
Elliot, Lon, 243

Elliott, Aussie, 268–9, 271–9, 326
Erwin, William, 331–2

Farmer, Aud, 76, 86
Fascone, Gus, 172
F.B.I., 90, 132, 231, 288, 312, 316, 320–4, 325, 327, 334, 344
Flegenheimer, Arthur (Dutch Schultz), 224
Fintelman, Billy, 105
Fitzsimmons, Bob, 272
Five Points Gang, 198
Fleagle, Jake, 189
Floyd family: first car, 73; genealogy, 6–8, 10–3, 22–3, 32; move to Akins, Oklahoma, 70; move to Hanson, Oklahoma, 28–9; photo, 27, 83–4
Floyd, Bayne, 95, 135, 174, 178, 183, 212, 225–6, 234
Floyd, Bessie Watson, 83–5, 131, 133–4, 145, 174–5, 178, 212, 217, 225, 259, 327, 348; birth: Bayne & Wayne, 95; Cleatus, 174; Glendon, 136; Charles, 259
Floyd, Beulah Wickett, 260
Floyd, Carl Bradley, 6, 25, 29, 69, 130, 133–4, 136, 140, 174–5, 178, 212, 216, 225, 257, 293, 301, 317, 327, 348–9, 353; Bonus Army, 264; marriage: Bessie Watson, 85; military service, 82–4; move to Earlsboro, 173; working oil fields, 174
Floyd, Charles, 259
Floyd, Charles Arthur (Pretty Boy)
    alias: Frank Mitchell, 195–6; Jack Hamilton, 219, 240; George Sanders, 326
    and Beulah Baird Ash (Juanita), 186–8, 206, 208–12, 219, 226, 239, 259, 279, 282, 304, 311, 318–92, 325–6
    and John Callahan: meets, 102; employment with, 106
    and Aussie Elliott, 268–9, 271–9
    and Ruby Hardgraves, 141, 144–5, 163–5, 179, 217–21, 226–7, 239–41, 243, 245–7, 252–3, 255–6, 259, 265, 328, 341; divorce, 163; courtship, 119, 130–1, 133–4; marriage, 134–5
    and the press, 248–9, 255–7, 260–1, 263, 270, 274–8, 291–3, 324–9, 337, 342–3, 346, 350–1
    arrests:
        Akron, Ohio, 195–6
        Kansas City, Kansas, 181
        Kansas City, Missouri, 173, 181–2
        Pueblo, Colorado, 181
        Sallisaw, 144–5, 146
    baking pies, 296, 319, 326, 329
    bootlegging, 181–2, 185, 213–4
    bravado, 238, 259, 261, 273
    burglary, Akins Post Office, 117–8
    childhood:
        birth, 3; defends teacher, 75; dog, 76–7; education, 32, 49, 70–1, 74; fighting, 75–6; friends, 76; heroes, 41, 45–59; Georgia, 24–6, 29; illness, 24, 260; Oklahoma, 32, 36, 47, 76; pranks: baby swap, 86–7
    death, xii, 338–41, 343–6; autopsy, 340–1, 343; controversy, 343–4; funeral, 346, 349–52; memento mori, 341–2, 346, 352; picks grave site, 296; public reaction, 347–51
    in Earlsboro, Oklahoma, 174–5, 178, 180, 214–17, 225
    escapes:
        after Maud bank robbery, 224
        attempted, 204
        Echols farm, 264–5
        Elizabeth Hill, 332–3
        liquor warehouse raid, 213–4
        train to prison, 204
        Tulsa shootout, 242–4

Floyd, Charles Arthur (cont.)
    gambling, 117, 187
    generosity, 226, 234, 241, 260, 262, 264, 269–70, 274, 278, 292–3, 296
    gun battles: Bennett farm, 252–8; Bowling Green, 208–9; Elizabeth Hill, 331–2; Echols farm, 264–5; Liquor warehouse, 213–4; Maud bank robbery, 224; Tulsa, 242–4; Union Station, Kansas City, 288; Haycock ambush, 190
    impersonators & lookalikes, 227, 323–4
    influence of Emmett Dalton, 227–8
    interview with Vivian Brown, 271–8
    in Kansas City, Missouri, 102, 106, 167–8, 173, 181, 184–90
    kidnapping Sheriff Jack Killingsworth, 306–11
    killings:
        Ash brothers, 207–8
        Curtis Burks, 214
        O. P. Carpenter, 247
        Ralph Castner, 208–9, 211–12
        Erv A. Kelley, 252–8, 317, 343
    moonshiner, 134, 141, 159
    myths & unproven allegations:
        association with Fred Barker, 246–7
        at Birdwell's funeral, 286
        avenging father's death, 184
        kidnapping of Frank Phillips, 264
        kidnapping of H. W. Nave, 270–1
        killing Booth & Wilson, 302–3, 312
        robberies falsely attributed to, 227, 233–5, 266, 279, 291, 297, 302–3
        shooting Harland Manes, 201
        Union Station Massacre, 316–7, 319–25, 328, 338, 343, 353
        Young brothers massacre, 229–32
    nicknames: Choc, 68–9; Pretty Boy, 186–8, 211; Sagebrush Robin Hood, 269
    on the road: arrives in Wichita, 101–2; bumming, 142; kicked out of Kansas City, 173; leaves home, 88, 96, 142; vagrancy, 181
    on the run, 212–5, 258–9, 264–6, 268, 289, 293–6, 329, 330–2; air search, 258; Buffalo, 218–9, 325–6, 328–9; Conkle farm, 336–9; Fort Smith, 219–20, 226–7, 239; man hunt, 238, 252–9, 262–3, 325, 329, 333–8; Muskogee, 267, 276; rewards offered, 238, 249, 252, 257, 262, 281; Tulsa, 239–44
    partnership with: Bob Amos, 190–6; Jack Atkins, 190–3; George Birdwell, 221–5, 232–4, 243–5, 251, 254, 257–9, 261–2, 264–5, 268, 271–4, 276, 279, 281–2, 286; James Bradley, 190–6, 201, 203; Fred Hildebrand, 142, 149–51; Marie Maxwell, 190–5; Willis Miller, 205–11; Adam Richetti, 289–91, 301, 304–12, 316, 318–9, 323, 325–6, 328–34, 338
    prison:
        State Penitentiary, Jefferson City, 151–64; disciplinary actions: drugs, 158–9; striking guard, 159; parole, 164
        Toledo Jail, 196–7; escape attempt, 203
    relationship with father, 35, 67, 87, 107–8, 118, 134, 163, 178
    relationship with son, 139–40, 219–21, 226, 278
    robberies:
        banks:
            Bowling Green, 208–11
            Castle State, 232–4
            Citizens Bank of Shamrock, 224
            Conowa First National, 224
            Dover State, 238–9
            Earlsboro, 223, 4
            Farmers & Merchants, Sylvania, 196
            Marlow State, 278–9
            Maud First National, 224
            Meeker, 251–2

Floyd, Charles Arthur (*cont.*)
    Morris State, 224–5
    Mount Zion Deposit, 208, 212
    Ohio, 190–3, 196
    Sallisaw State, 268, 271–4
    Stonewall State, 258
    Whitehouse, Ohio, 208
    cab drivers, 213
    cookie theft, 34–5
    Kroger payroll, 143–4, 149–50, 187
    method, 225
    Wewoka Dance Hall, 291
  surrender attempt, 239, 342
  swaps for first gun, 141
  working oil fields, 180
  wounded, 257
Floyd, Charles Dempsey (Jackie), 137–40, 145, 163, 217–21, 224, 226, 239–41, 243, 245–8, 252–3, 259, 265, 274, 292, 296, 301–2, 317, 328, 348–9, 351, 353
Floyd, Charles Murphy, 22–3, 117, 272, 274
Floyd, Chester Lee, 140, 296
Floyd, Cleatus, 225
Floyd, E. W., 25, 29, 179, 260, 327, 349, 353
Floyd, Emma Lucille, 25, 136, 259–60, 317; birth: Bernie, 260; Lawton, 136; marriage to Clarence Lessley, 135–6
Floyd, Glendon, 136, 174, 180, 184, 212, 226, 233–4
Floyd, General John Buchanan, 11
Floyd, Mamie Helena Echols, 6, 23–9, 31, 33, 108, 133–4, 136, 140, 163, 178, 184, 260–1, 296, 302, 346, 348, 350–1, 353–4; birth: Charles Arthur, 3; birth: Chester Lee, 140
Floyd, Mary Delta, 32–3, 136, 179, 317, 348–9, 351; marriage: Perry Lattimore, 260
Floyd, Patience, 10–3, 15, 18, 20, 22–3
Floyd, Ruby Hardgraves, 119–20, 130–1, 133–5, 141, 144–5, 163–5, 179, 217–21, 226–7, 239–41, 243, 252–3, 255–6, 259, 265, 274, 279, 282–3, 286, 296, 317, 348–9, 351, 353; on stage, 301–2, 328; arrest, 245–7; birth: Charles Dempsey, 137–9; divorce, 163; marriage: Charles Floyd, 134–5; Leroy Leonard, 218
Floyd, Ruby Mae, 6, 73–4, 135, 259; marriage: Silas Spear, 94–5
Floyd, Ruth, 6, 74, 95, 108, 259–60; birth: Frances, 95; marriage: Tom Wofford, 85
Floyd, Walter Lee, 6, 22–5, 27–8, 31, 33, 35, 134, 136, 140, 178, 296; gives Charles alibi, 118; Masons, 71, 118; merchant, 136, 183; moonshiner, 63, 67, 73, 93; road worker, 73; shot to death, *see* Mills, John; standoff with sheriff, 94; trucking business, 85
Floyd, Wayne, 95, 135, 174, 225
Floyd, William, 7–8
Flynn, William J., 90–1, 132
Foster, Frank, 105
Fraley, Arthur, 234
Franklin, L. E., 264
Franks, Orphus, 76, 86–7
Fritch, E. D., 202
Fryman, Joseph, 330–1
Fultz, John H., 331–4

Galatas, Richard, 314–5
Galliher, Carl (Shorty), 208–11, 231
Gandee, J. Sherman, 193–5
Gannon, Bertha, 193–4
Gannon, Bill, 193, 201
Gardner, Earl, 243
Gaston, L. U., 128
Gay, Hugh & Lydia, 119
Gibson, Furman, 258
Gillis, Lester M., 198, 342

Glass, Charles (Pete), 283–4
Goldsby, Crawford, 123
Goodall, Luther, 234
Gore, Senator Thomas P., 79, 96
Green, Frank (Tickey), 76, 86–7
Green, Fred, 274
Grooms, W. J., 314–5
Gum, Eugene, 233, 248, 281–2, 285

Haines, Thomas E., 262
Hall, Dave, 336
Hammer, Frank, 327
Hammer, Fred, 251
Hardgraves, Albert, 120, 240–1
Hardgraves, Ben F., 119–20, 255
  first wife Sarah (Deller), 119
  second wife Maggie, 120, 217, 348
Hardgraves, J. B., 120
Hardgraves, Jess, 120, 217–8
Hardgraves, Pauline, 120
Hardgraves, Ruby, *see* Floyd, Ruby Hardgraves
Hargreaves, George, 201
Hargus, Charles, 157, 159
Harreld, John W., 96
Harrison, Walter M., 248
Havens, Glenn, 213–4
Haycock, Burt, 189, 190
Hayes, George E., 333
Hell's Half-Acre, 329
Henry, O., 114
Henson, Estel, 258–9, 264
Herman, Hollis, 344
Higgins, Thomas J., 189, 319
Hildebrand, Fred (The Sheik), 142, 149–51
Hill, C. L., 301
Holden, Thomas, 299–300, 312
Holland, Dick, 289–90
Hoover, J. Edgar, 5, 90–2, 132–3, 203, 231, 288, 303, 316, 322–8, 334, 340, 342–5
Hopton, W. E. (Bud), 336, 344–5
Hotchkiss, H. G., 292
Houston, Robert, 258
Hovey, John, 196
Howard, Ed, 192–3
Howell, Joe, 325
Huber, John, 124

Iffland, John C., 191–3, 196
Iffland, Martha, 191–2, 196
Isely, Bliss, 105
Israel, Lon, 331–2

Jacobs, E. G., 191
James, Frank, 50–9
James, Jesse, 50–9, 107, 113, 115, 122, 127, 142, 145, 179, 190, 325–6
Jameson, J. D., 321
Jefferson City State Penitentiary, 151–62
Jenkins, Bud, 125
Jennings, Al, 114–6, 263
Jennings, T. W., 221–2
Johnson, Jack, 48
Johnston, Henry S., 179
Jones, R. B. (Blackie), 243

Karpis, Alvin, 342–3
Keating, Francis, 299–300, 312
Keesee, Troy, 301
Kelley, Erv A., 252–8, 267, 295, 317
Kelley, Howard, 347
Kelly, Curtis, 125
Kelly, Machine Gun, 299, 324
Kennedy, R. G., 244
Killingsworth, Jack, 306–12, 322
Kimes, George & Matthew, 179–80, 245, 249, 349

King of the Osage, *see* Spencer, Al
Knights of Liberty, 81, 111
Kovach, Sergent, 193–4
Ku Klux Klan, 88, 109–11, 113, 128–9, 135, 165, 170, 179

LaCapra, James, 328
Lackey, F. Joseph, 313–5, 321–2
Ladner, Judge John, 163
Lairmore, Milton L., 243, 253, 263
Lattimore, Pat, 260
Lattimore, Perry Floyd, 260, 348
Lattimore, Perry Lee, 260
Lazia, John, 172, 181, 189, 298, 300, 321, 325, 327–8
Leonard, Leroy, 218
Lessley, Charlene, 260
Lessley, Dorthene, 260
Lessley, James Lea, 317
Lessley, Lawton, 136, 260, 282, 329
Lessley, (Samuel) Clarence, 135–6, 259–60
Lessley, Samuel & Sarotha, 136
Licavoli mob, 212
Lindsay, S. F., 262
Link, Samuel, 320
Little Dixie, 80, 84, 88
Long, Alice Nash, 124–5
Long, Crockett, 253–4, 264, 266–7
Long, John, 124
Love, Phil, 302
Lovett, Red, 188
Lyle, W. O., 107
Lynn, Wiley, 176, 266–7
Lyons, Robert, 302

Maddi, Victor, 247
Majors brothers, 104–5
Maledon, George, 39–40
Malone, William J., 196
Manes, Harland, 194–6, 201
Masterson, James (Soap), 76, 86–7
Mathews, E. M., 210
Maxwell, Nellie, *see* Maxwell, Marie
Maxwell, Marie, 190–5, 202
McAlester State Penitentiary, 123–5, 180
McAnally, W. J., 180
McBee, William D., 129
McClung, D. C., 155–6
McCormack, Robert R., 92
McCormick, Langston, 284
McCormick, H. C., 284–5
McDermott, Hugh J., 336, 342, 346
McDonald, Alva, 126–7, 130
McDonnell, Edward J., 194, 203
McElroy, Mary, kidnapping of, 297–8, 321
McElroy, Judge H. F., 297–8
McGee, Walter, 297
McKee, Sam, 336, 344–5
McMullin, George, 332–3
McWilliams, Sam, 123
Means, Gaston Bullock, 132–3
Meramec, Hlavaty, 149–51
Merrifield, C. F., 302
Michaels, Herbert, 194
Miles, Clyde & Nellie, 104
Miller, Willis (Billy the Killer), 205–11, 223, 233, 239, 341
Miller, Joseph (Alabama Joe), 205
Miller, Verne, 299, 316, 320–1, 323, 325, 328
Mills, Jim, 183–4
Miskall, Dr. Ed, 343
Mitchell, Frank, *see* Floyd, Pretty Boy
Montgomery, Glen (Curly), 336, 340
Montgomery, Tom, 246
Moran, George (Bugs), 166–7

Moran, Ray, 242
Morgan, Frank, 197
Morgan, Ruth Ring, 295–6, 302, 349
Morgan, W. H., 246
Munroe, Thomas I., 244
Murray, William Henry (Alfalfa Bill), 235–7, 280–1, 285
Myers, Homer, 242

Nash, Francis Luce, 312, 314, 316
Nash, Frank (Jelly), 104, 123–5, 127, 130, 189, 299–300, 312–15, 320, 322, 325, 328
Nash, Jay Robert, 324
Nathan, R. G., 247
Nave, H. W., 270–1
Nelson, Baby Face, *see* Gillis, Lester
Nelson, E. L., 213–4
Nelson, William Rockhill, 169
Nichols, Jesse Clyde, 169
Northrup, Naomi, 345

Ogg, Ike, 125
O'Hanlon, David, 330–1
O'Hare, Kate Richards, 152
Ohio State penitentiary, 196–7, 203
Oklahoma Banker's Association, 122, 233, 235–6, 238, 248, 251, 280, 285
Oklahoma State Crime Bureau, 234, 252–3, 264, 266, 275, 284–5

Packo, Joe, 203
Parker, Bonnie, 199–200, 327
Parker, Isaac Charles, 38–41, 176, 267
Palmer, Alexander Mitchell, 90–2
Patterson, C. C. (Champ), 283–4
Patterson, George, 333
Patterson, Pat, 126
Pendergast, Thomas Joseph, 169–72, 189, 297–8
Peterson, Theodore, 332
Phantom Terror, *see* Spencer, Al
Philpott, Walter, 125
Pierpont, Harry, 198
Pinkerton, Allan, 55
Pinson, Thomas, 240–1
Pittman, Charles, 191–2, 196
Popp, Bob, 343
Possehl, Arthur, 194
Post, Wiley, 258
Potts, Homer, 331–2
Pratty, Bruce C., 212
Proffenberger, Major & Minor, 104
Purple Gang, 162
Purvis, Jr., Melvin H., 327, 334–7, 340, 342–6

Randall, Bob, *see* Bradley, James
Rascoe, Burton, 128
Ray, O. P., 234, 264, 285
Reber, C. M., 237, 264
Reed, Otto, 313, 315
Richards, Margaret, 315
Richetti, Adam, 251, 289–91, 295, 304–12, 316, 318–9, 323, 325–6, 329–34, 338, 347, 352–3
Richetti, Joseph, 289, 305–6
Riggs, Bob, 273
Riley, W. W., 284
Ring, Jess Lee, 138, 259, 275–6, 278, 295
Ring, Lavona, 296
Ring, Tempie Laura Edwards, 137–8, 275
Ries, Harry, 192–3
Robertson, Governor James B., 89, 96
Robinson, Robert, 336
Rockett, Rev. W. E., 351
Rose, Wonetta, *see* Ash, Beulah Baird
Ross, Will, 179–80

Roth, Herman, 336
Rumpf, Jr., Chris, 192
Rumpf, Sr., Chris, 192

Salee, Ed, 258
Schultz, Dutch, *see* Flegenheimer, Arthur
Scolla, Sam, 172
Scott, Lon, 229
Self, Tony, 234
Shelton Gang, 162
Shipman, Oris, 272
Shull, Jeannette, 191
Simmons, Bernice, 192
Singleton, Ed, 197
Smalley, Blackie, 286, 301
Smalley, L. C., 251
Smalley, Marie, 301
Smalley, W. A., 251
Smith, Chester C., *xii,* 336, 338, 340–1,
    343–5
Smith, Frank C., 313–5, 321
Smith, J. A., 253
Snyder, Stanley, 125
Social Banditry, 113, 115, 122, 128, 237
Spencer, Al, 104, 107, 122–3, 125–30, 179, 249,
    299
Starr, Douglas, 150
Starr, Henry (Bearcat), 34, 36, 107, 114–6, 122–3,
    150, 179, 190, 249
Steckmesser, Kent Ladd, 316
Steele, Elmer, 94, 269–70, 316
Sterling, William W., 230
Stewart, George, 243
Stone, Harlan Fiske, 133
Stormont, Jim, 253
Sturgis, E. G., 340
Sturgis, Ernie, 340, 343, 347
Sullivan, Diamond Joe, 104
Sustic, Henry & Minnie, 329

Taft, William H., 103
Terrill, Ray, 125, 179–80
Thayer, Earl (Dad), 125, 189, 299
Thompson, D. L., 152
Tilghman, Bill, 176, 267
Toledo jail, 196–7
Torrio, John, 165
Tower, Byron, 127
Trapp, Martin E., 129, 139
Trotter, Tom, 272–3

Turner, D. J., 283–6
Turner, Margaret, 320–1

Underhill, Wilbur, 298–9, 315, 320–3, 325

Vail, Tommy, 209
Van Glahn, Ralph, 192–3
Van Meter, Homer, 198
Verdigris Kid, *see* McWilliams, Sam
Vetterli, Reed E., 314–5, 321

Waddle, Ed, 231
Wagman, Carl, 154
Walker, Bert, *see* Bradley, James
Wall Street Crash, 182
Walton, Governor John C. (Jack), 127–9, 135
Watson, Sam & Ellen, 83, 95, 174
Weisberger, George, 105
Weissman, Solly, 172
Weissman, William, 321, 323
Wellman, Paul, 106, 123
Wells, Henry, 125
West, Lottie, 320–3
White, James, 85
White, Thomas, 300
Whitney, Lonnie, 144
Whittmore, Vol & Thelma Kennedy, 135
Wild Rider of Oklahoma, *see* Spencer, Al
Willard, Jess, 48–9, 91
Wilson, Earl, 193
Wilson, Mabel, 336
Wilson, Roger, 302–3, 312
Wilson, W. E., 242, 245, 247
Wofford, Bud & Fanny, 85–6
Wofford, Frances, 95
Wofford, Thomas B., 85
Woll, James, 94
Woll, J. C., 143–4, 179–80
Wolsey, John, 252
Woods, Bill, 243–4
Woods, E. W., 266
Woodward, Welborn, 9

Young brothers massacre, 229–31
Young, Harry, 229
Young, Jennings, 229
Young, Vinita, 231
Younger, Cole, 127

Zickefoose, S. W., 105

ABOUT THE AUTHOR

Michael Wallis, a writer since 1968, has won a reputation as a biographer and historian of American West subjects. Perhaps best known for his highly acclaimed *Route 66: The Mother Road,* published by St. Martin's Press in 1990, he is also the author of *Oil Man: The Story of Frank Phillips and the Birth of Phillips Petroleum,* a best-selling biography published by Doubleday in 1988.

An award-winning reporter, his work has been published in more than one hundred national and international magazines and newspapers, including *Time, Life, People, Smithsonian,* and *Texas Monthly.*

Wallis was born in Missouri in 1945 and has lived throughout the Southwest and Mexico. He and his wife, Suzanne Fitzgerald Wallis, currently reside in Tulsa, Oklahoma.